T0321970

Design Solutions for User–Centric Information Systems

Saqib Saeed
University of Dammam, Saudi Arabia

Yasser A. Bamarouf
University of Dammam, Saudi Arabia

T. Ramayah
University Sains Malaysia, Malaysia

Sardar Zafar Iqbal
University of Dammam, Saudi Arabia

A volume in the Advances in Human and Social
Aspects of Technology (AHSAT) Book Series

www.igi-global.com

Published in the United States of America by
    IGI Global
    Information Science Reference (an imprint of IGI Global)
    701 E. Chocolate Avenue
    Hershey PA, USA 17033
    Tel: 717-533-8845
    Fax: 717-533-8661
    E-mail: cust@igi-global.com
    Web site: http://www.igi-global.com

Library of Congress Cataloging-in-Publication Data

Names: Saeed, Saqib, 1970- editor.
Title: Design solutions for user-centric information systems / Saqib Saeed,
   Yasser A. Bamarouf, T. Ramayah, and Zafar Iqbal, editors.
Description: Hershey, PA : Information Science Reference, 2017.
Identifiers: LCCN 2016048908| ISBN 9781522519447 (hardcover) | ISBN
   9781522519454 (ebook)
Subjects: LCSH: Human-computer interaction.
Classification: LCC QA76.9.H85 D468 2017 | DDC 004.01/9--dc23 LC record available at https://lccn.loc.gov/2016048908

This book is published in the IGI Global book series Advances in Human and Social Aspects of Technology (AHSAT) (ISSN: 2328-1316; eISSN: 2328-1324)

British Cataloguing in Publication Data
A Cataloguing in Publication record for this book is available from the British Library.

All work contributed to this book is new, previously-unpublished material. The views expressed in this book are those of the authors, but not necessarily of the publisher.

For electronic access to this publication, please contact: eresources@igi-global.com.

Advances in Human and Social Aspects of Technology (AHSAT) Book Series

Ashish Dwivedi
The University of Hull, UK

ISSN:2328-1316
EISSN:2328-1324

MISSION

In recent years, the societal impact of technology has been noted as we become increasingly more connected and are presented with more digital tools and devices. With the popularity of digital devices such as cell phones and tablets, it is crucial to consider the implications of our digital dependence and the presence of technology in our everyday lives.

The **Advances in Human and Social Aspects of Technology (AHSAT) Book Series** seeks to explore the ways in which society and human beings have been affected by technology and how the technological revolution has changed the way we conduct our lives as well as our behavior. The AHSAT book series aims to publish the most cutting-edge research on human behavior and interaction with technology and the ways in which the digital age is changing society.

COVERAGE

- Computer-Mediated Communication
- Human Rights and Digitization
- End-User Computing
- Technology and Freedom of Speech
- Cultural Influence of ICTs
- Public Access to ICTs
- Information ethics
- Gender and Technology
- Activism and ICTs
- Technology Adoption

IGI Global is currently accepting manuscripts for publication within this series. To submit a proposal for a volume in this series, please contact our Acquisition Editors at Acquisitions@igi-global.com or visit: http://www.igi-global.com/publish/.

Titles in this Series

For a list of additional titles in this series, please visit: www.igi-global.com

Enriching Urban Spaces with Ambient Computing, the Internet of Things, and Smart City Design
Shin'ichi Konomi (University of Tokyo, Japan) and George Roussos (University of London, UK)
Engineering Science Reference • copyright 2017 • 323pp • H/C (ISBN: 9781522508274) • US $210.00 (our price)

Handbook of Research on Individualism and Identity in the Globalized Digital Age
F. Sigmund Topor (Keio University, Japan)
Information Science Reference • copyright 2017 • 645pp • H/C (ISBN: 9781522505228) • US $295.00 (our price)

Information Technology Integration for Socio-Economic Development
Titus Tossy (Mzumbe University, Tanzania)
Information Science Reference • copyright 2017 • 385pp • H/C (ISBN: 9781522505396) • US $200.00 (our price)

Handbook of Research on Human-Computer Interfaces, Developments, and Applications
João Rodrigues (University of Algarve, Portugal) Pedro Cardoso (University of Algarve, Portugal) Jânio Monteiro
(University of Algarve, Portugal) and Mauro Figueiredo (University of Algarve, Portugal)
Information Science Reference • copyright 2016 • 663pp • H/C (ISBN: 9781522504351) • US $330.00 (our price)

Human Development and Interaction in the Age of Ubiquitous Technology
Hakikur Rahman (BRAC University, Bangladesh)
Information Science Reference • copyright 2016 • 384pp • H/C (ISBN: 9781522505563) • US $185.00 (our price)

Examining the Evolution of Gaming and Its Impact on Social, Cultural, and Political Perspectives
Keri Duncan Valentine (West Virginia University, USA) and Lucas John Jensen (Georgia Southern University, USA)
Information Science Reference • copyright 2016 • 456pp • H/C (ISBN: 9781522502616) • US $190.00 (our price)

Handbook of Research on Human Social Interaction in the Age of Mobile Devices
Xiaoge Xu (Botswana International University of Science and Technology, Botswana)
Information Science Reference • copyright 2016 • 548pp • H/C (ISBN: 9781522504696) • US $325.00 (our price)

Defining Identity and the Changing Scope of Culture in the Digital Age
Alison Novak (Rowan University, USA) and Imaani Jamillah El-Burki (Lehigh University, USA)
Information Science Reference • copyright 2016 • 316pp • H/C (ISBN: 9781522502128) • US $185.00 (our price)

Gender Considerations in Online Consumption Behavior and Internet Use
Rebecca English (Queensland University of Technology, Australia) and Raechel Johns (University of Canberra,
Australia)
Information Science Reference • copyright 2016 • 297pp • H/C (ISBN: 9781522500100) • US $165.00 (our price)

www.igi-global.com

701 E. Chocolate Ave., Hershey, PA 17033
Order online at www.igi-global.com or call 717-533-8845 x100
To place a standing order for titles released in this series, contact: cust@igi-global.com
Mon-Fri 8:00 am - 5:00 pm (est) or fax 24 hours a day 717-533-8661

To
My Sweet Kids
Rameen Saqib, Eshaal Saqib and Huzaifa Saqib

.

Editorial Advisory Board

Table of Contents

Section 3
Usability Engineering

Detailed Table of Contents

Section 1
Introduction

This chapter explains the digital disruption that has occurred and is still happening in the retail industry. It explains the relative positions of the world's leading retailers Wal-Mart, Amazon and Alibaba and the business models of the two top online competitors. It focuses on the impact of SMAC (Social, Mobile, Analytics and Cloud) technologies and new retail trends enabled or boosted by technology such as omnichannel, customer experience, internet of things (IoT) and analytics, fulfillment and delivery. It deepens into IT and business model customer-centric design, the role of the customer and the store in the new digital retail and finishes with an assessment of ROI in retail digitization. The chapter concludes the fundamental IT-enabled changes of digital disruption are critical for all players, traditional brick-and-mortar retailers, pure online players and those with both an online and an offline presence.

Accurate and consistent death certification facilitates evidence-informed health policies, morbidity and mortality surveillance on the national level, and consequently serves increasingly demanding medical and statistical needs. This paper initially explores the current situation concerning the death certification in Slovenia, and identifies related deficiencies and systemic problems. Based on the research findings, the paper outlines a construction of ICT-based model of death certification and provides applicable guidelines for its implementation at the national level. The research is based on focus group methodology. Structured discussions were conducted with 29 experts from cross-sectional areas related to death certification. Research results imply that effective ICT-based transformation of the existing death certification model should involve a redefinition of functions and relationships between the main actors, as well as a reconfiguration of the technological, organizational, and regulatory elements in line with the long-term public health objectives.

E-government is an emerging field of research that has generated considerable interest recently. This research examines contributions from e-government as a means of providing solutions to developmental challenges that have been linked to corruption and a lack of transparency. Although the government has embarked upon a number of e-government initiatives, Nigeria ranks low in the area of e-government provision to its citizens. Initial findings show that the focus of existing studies have been on the supply side with little research focusing on the demand side. Initial findings also indicate that the e-government initiatives that have been implemented have little to no effect on increasing transparency and decreasing corruption. A framework for the evaluation of current e-government provision with a view to combating corruption is proposed. This will incorporate the users' perspectives into further development of e-government initiatives. The resulting framework will be applied to verify the contributions of e-government towards resolving some of the challenges facing the populace.

Chapter 4

Freight transportation and logistics decisions such as modal choice decisions are strategically important for effective supply chain operation and economic benefits. The freight selection logistic is a multi-criteria multi-objective (MCMO) process, crucial for smooth sourcing of materials, cost-effective delivery of products to customers in the right time, at the right quantity. The study discusses the major transport logistics attributes and the order preference by similarity ideal solution (TOPSIS) algorithm as the preferred MCMO model to support comparative ranking among the alternative freights. The entropy weight coefficient method minimizes the subjectivity in the selection of weight of the attribute. This study integrates the entropy technique on TOPSIS platform to improve the freight selection decision. A numerical example illustrates the procedure of the proposed algorithm and ranks the choices among truck, rail, and several intermodal transport combinations (rail/truck and air/truck) in a transportation selection model.

Chapter 5

Technology for learning is increasingly about enhancing users' interactions with the technology to improve learning outcomes. Of particular importance however to improving educational outcomes is the need to complement the technological advancements with advances in the educational practices of teachers to broaden the uptake of new technologies for learning. Recommender Systems are personalised services that aim to predict a learner's interest in some services or items such as courses, grades, references, links, etc. available in e-learning applications and to provide appropriate recommendations. Such systems can potentially enhance student learning by providing students with a more hands on, interactive and tailored learning experience.

Chapter 6

Hadeel Alharbi, University of New England, Australia
Kamaljeet Sandhu, University of New England, Australia

There is still a gap of knowledge on the usage of recommender systems in Saudi universities and the wider issue of technological change in the universities of developing countries. Relatively, this lack of knowledge is an issue to universities seeking to meet students/instructors' expectations and requirements by offering consistently high perceived service standards of e-learning services in a rapidly changing technological environment. To address this issue, this paper seeks to explore the impact of the acceptance and adoption of recommender systems in e-leaning for Saudi universities and this will help to investigate the students/ instructors experience according to the e-learning service quality. Thus, a proposed e-framework has been presented. Such framework describes the factors of acceptance (such as service quality, student/instructor experience, and Human Computer Interaction guidelines) should be considered in the e-learning system because it is viewed as a determinant of student/instructor/university satisfaction.

Chapter 7

Athary Alwasel, King Saud University, Saudi Arabia
Ben Clegg, Aston University, UK
Andreas Schroeder, Aston University, UK

In recent years Saudi Arabia has made great strides in higher education. This paper looks at the higher education sector in Saudi Arabia with special emphasis on outsourcing to Software as a Service based email systems as a positive enabler of higher education. Outsourcing can be defined as the process of contracting services to a third party with financial and contractual terms to govern that provision. There are many advantages and disadvantages of outsourcing and many reasons why an organization might decide to outsource specific services. This chapter describes the information systems outsourcing trend towards cloud based solutions (particularly email) in the Saudi Arabian higher education sector over the last few years and discusses the implications of this trend.

Section 2
User Centered Design

Chapter 8

Mariam Ahmed Elhussein, University of Dammam, Saudi Arabia

Tagging systems design is often neglected despite the fact that most system designers agree on the importance of tagging. They are viewed as part of a larger system which receives most of the attention. There is no agreed method when it comes to either analyzing existing tagging systems or designing new ones. There is a need to establish a well-structured design process that can be followed to create tagging systems with a purpose. This chapter uses practical inquiry methodology to generate a general framework that can be applied to analyze tagging systems and proceeds to suggest a design process that can be followed to create new tagging systems. Existing user behavior while tagging is the main guide for the methodology.

Community engagement is necessary for the success and sustainability of Information and Communication Technologies for Development (ICT4D) projects. To ensure active participation of community, researchers need to understand and adhere to the local cultural norms and adapt in the lifestyle of people. These cultural norms are mainly unwritten and implicit in nature. Hence the researchers spend maximum time of their field visits in observing and developing understanding of the community's life. In our long-term partnership with the indigenous Penan community of Long Lamai in Malaysian Borneo, we co-developed written guidelines for researchers and visitors. The researchers demonstrated their interest in aligning research process to the community's cultural values, however norm internalisation and development of associated behaviour is still a challenging. The written guidelines are yet only one of the attempts to the practices of community researchers' engagement and we are refining our methodology to enhance the researchers' learning process.

The success of any software application heavily depends on the success of its User Interface (UI) design. This is since users communicate with those applications through their UIs and they will build good or bad impressions based on how such UIs help them using the software. UI design evolves through the years to be more platform and even code independent. In addition, the design of an application user interface consumes a significant amount of time and resources. It is expected that not only the same UI design should be relatively easy to transfer from one platform to another, but even from one programming language release to another or even from one programming language to another. In this chapter, we conducted a thorough investigation to describe how UI design evolved through the years to be independent from the code, or any other environment element (e.g. operating system, browser, database, etc.).

It is generally observed throughout the world that in the last two decades, while the average speed of computers has almost doubled in a span of around eighteen months, the average speed of the network has doubled merely in a span of just eight months! In order to improve the performance, more and more researchers are focusing their research in the field of computers and its related technologies. World Wide Web (WWW) is one of the services provided by the Internet medium for sharing of information. As a result, millions of applications run on the Internet and cause increased network traffic and put a great demand on the available network infrastructure. With the increase in the number of Internet users, it is necessary to enhance the speed. This paper addresses the above issues and proposes a novel integrated approach by reviewing the works related to Web caching and Web pre-fetching.

A growing area of research in Human Computer Interaction (HCI) and Human Robotic Interaction (HRI) is the development of haptic-based user performance testing. User performance testing Usability forms a vital part of these test objectives. As a result, diverse usability methods/strategies and test features are being employed. Apparently, with the robustness of haptic-based user performance testing features, user performance still has challenges. With this regard, it is vital to identify the direction and effectiveness of these methods/strategies and test features, and improvements required in the test objectives and evaluation. This chapter seeks to investigate the challenges of user performance and the user performance indicators in some HCI and HRI researches involving haptic-based test, as well as presents a User Performance Indicator Tool (UPIT) as a test validation tool to aid designers/testers in enhancing their user performance test and test evaluation outcomes.

Chapter 13

Background: the involvement of the potential end users in the development processes is a relevant issue for the acceptance of Ambient Assisted Living (AAL) products and services. Objective: this study aimed to use the conceptual framework of the International Classification of Functioning, Disability and Health (ICF) to conceptualize instruments for the different phases of the AAL development processes. Methods: personas and scenarios were modified, considering the fundamental concepts of the ICF in order to highlight end user's functioning and health conditions, and an ICF based instrument for usability assessment was defined and validated. Results: the results of several observational studies suggest the adequacy of the ICF based instruments (personas and scenarios and usability assessment instrument). Conclusion: the present study indicates that the ICF based instruments can be useful tools for the development of Ambient Assisted Living products or services.

This study examined the impact of security champion and security training on protection behaviour in the context of IT service oriented SMEs in Bangladesh. Drawing upon protection motivation theory, this study examined the influence of security training on threat appraisal and influence of security training on coping appraisal which leads to protection behaviour via protection motivation. Data was collected from six different IT service oriented organizations with a sample size of 147 by survey questionnaire. Data was analysed using partial least squares (PLS) technique and result shows that perceived value of data, security training and threat appraisal are strong predictors of threat appraisal, protection motivation and protection behaviour. Theoretical contribution and practical implications of this research are also discussed.

Section 3
Usability Engineering

Chapter 15

Renuka Nagpal, Amity University - Uttar Pradesh, India
Deepti Mehrotra, Amity University - Uttar Pradesh, India
Pradeep Kumar Bhatia, Guru Jambeshwar University of Science and Technology, India

Measuring the usability of the website is a key metrics which all designers always tries to maximize. Compared to other software it is very difficult to estimate the website usability as each website has many objective and wide range of visitor with different learnability. The objective of this study is summarizing different approaches used to measure the usability of website. The current study includes the different approaches proposed in literature in last two decades. Approaches are classified in six broad categories and a comparison between them is done. Trends in web usability of evaluation approaches are understood in light of changing needs of website.

Chapter 16

Hina Gull, University of Dammam, Saudi Arabia
Sardar Zafar Iqbal, University of Dammam, Saudi Arabia

Government websites are the easy sources of getting access to the services offered by governmental organizations. These websites provide manifold benefits to their users i.e. efficiency of use, cost decline, effective communication between citizens and government, delivery of different service, transparency and time saving. However, users cannot get full benefit out of these services if the e-government websites are not interactive and user friendly. Keeping this view into consideration, study investigated the usability concerns of the e-government websites in Saudi Arabia. Cognitive walk-through is selected as the implication method to figure out usability related traits by the real users of the interfaces. Findings from the study showed that these websites are partially usable for the users, as they lack some of the major concerns of the usability. Evaluation results showed the clear picture of the usability features of the selected websites of Saudi Arabia both in positive and negative ways. Furthermore, recommendations are given to improve overall quality of these websites.

Many Small Micro-Medium Enterprises (SMMEs) fail within their first year of operation in South Africa mainly because of the lack of proper financial management skills. To address this, a number of software applications have been developed. However, they fail to cater for the needs of SMME owners. In this Chapter, we intend to design and implement a software application to address some of these financial management challenges faced by SMMEs. To achieve this, a through literature review was conducted. Then we designed and implemented a new system with additional features missing from the existing applications. The main objectives of this new system, is to help SMME owners manage their finances from anywhere, have access to real time data and be easy to use. To implement the system, PHP and MySQL database was used. Usability testing was done to evaluate the effectiveness of the system. The system performed 20% better in keeping records as compared to the manual accounting system.

Chapter 18

Urban growth adversely affects accesses to public spaces and to their physical and functional structures. Simple tasks become a challenge for visually impaired individuals either because of the difficulty getting reliable non-visual information from the surrounding space or the lack of information. In Smart Cities scenarios, important investments will be directed to urban accessibility, but nowadays people with sensory disabilities still have to face mobility problems in those spaces. Therefore, designing suitable solutions to provide more information about urban spaces is extremely important and requires user participation. This context motivated the development of the Electronic Long Cane project. The project enhances the features of traditional long canes to detect obstacles located above the waist. Nowadays, the electronic cane was redesigned including new functions based on the Internet of Things. As a result, evidences of User-Centric Design have emerged, increasing the probability of success of this technology in Smart Cities context.

Preface

OVERVIEW

In order to foster successful usage of information systems, it is important that systems design should focus on user work practices. As a result, traditional requirement gathering and evaluation methodologies fall short as they mainly rely on "official" viewpoint rather than actual practices. As a result, notions of "Participatory Design" and "User Centric Design" have emerged in information system domain. These concepts focus on empowering the user in design process as well so that users have more control on design processes which will lead to more successful usage of information systems. Technology appropriation is a complex task and in order to design appropriate technological systems there is a strong emphasis on involving users in system design process. As a result, the information systems and work practices of users are aligned together which increases the probability of technology adoption by end users. The goal of this book is to provide state of the art research and best practices.

This book, *Design Solutions for User-Centric Information Systems*, is a reference text. It is a collection of 18 chapters, authored by 36 academics and practitioners from around the world. The contributions in this book aim to enrich the information system discipline by providing latest research and case studies from around the world.

OBJECTIVE

The aim of *Design Solutions for User-Centric Information Systems*, is to publish high quality original research contributions on the specialized theme of user centric information system design processes. The content reports theoretical foundations and empirical studies to highlight the good practices for user centric information system development.

TARGET AUDIENCE

The contents of this volume contribute to Information system, Human computer interaction and Computer supported cooperative work disciplines. So this can serve as a reference text for the following audiences:

- Practitioners interested in user centric information processes
- Project managers interested in user involvement in the information system design processes

- Students and researchers interested in furthering their understanding of the subject.

BOOK ORGANIZATION

There are 18 chapters in this text. These are organised in three Sections as follows:

- **Introduction:** This section consists of seven chapters. The first chapter highlights how the user centric technologies are having an impact on the digital retailing, whereas the second chapter discusses the experiences of digitalizing the death certification process in Slovenia. The third contribution in this section is about the role of e-government in combating corruption in Nigeria and the next chapter advocates for employing entropy techniques to optimize logistics. The last three chapters of this section focus on the Saudi Arabian higher education sector to explore the application of recommender systems and technological outsourcing.
- **User-Centred Design:** This section comprises 7 chapters. The first chapter, which is chapter 8 in the book, discusses practical inquiry approach to model user behaviour, while the next chapter focuses on the ethical guidelines for ICT development in indigenous communities. The next contribution advocates for user interface isolation from underlying application while the chapter 11 proposed to use web caching to enhance the performance of information retrieval systems. The fifth contribution in this section discusses user performance testing indicator to measure the user performance whereas the sixth chapter discusses the development of ambient assisted living products and services. The last chapter in this section discusses the experience of Bangladesh in modelling cybercrime protection behaviour among computer users.
- **Usability Engineering:** This part of the book has four contributions. The first chapter provides a review of the methods for web usability evaluation and the next chapter focuses on usability evaluation of Saudi Arabian e-government websites. The next chapter presents a case study of designing a mobile system for managing personal finances. The final contribution of this section, which is the last chapter in the book, presents a study of providing autonomy to visually impaired citizens in the context of smart cities.

BRIEF DESCRIPTIONS OF THE CHAPTERS

Chapter 1 is titled 'Digital Retail: How Customer-Centric Technology is Reshaping the Industry – IT-Enabled Digital Disruption' and is authored by Pablo Penas Franco. This chapter explains the digital disruption that has occurred in the retail industry. It explains the relative positions of the world's leading retailers and the business models of the two top online competitors. It focuses on the impact of SMAC (Social, Mobile, Analytics and Cloud) technologies and new retail trends enabled or boosted by technology fulfillment and delivery. It deepens into IT and business model customer-centric design, the role of the customer and the store in the new digital retail and finishes with an assessment of return on investment in retail digitization.

Chapter 2 is 'Digitalization of Death Certification Model: Transformation Issues and Implementation Concerns'. Authored by Dalibor Stanimirovic, this chapter explores the current situation concerning the death certification in Slovenia. Based on the findings, the chapter outlines a construction of

ICT-based model of death certification and provides applicable guidelines for its implementation at the national level.

Chapter 3, 'E-Government Adoption in Nigeria: The Journey So Far', is authored by Sola Oni. This chapter examines contributions from e-government as a means of providing solutions to developmental challenges that have been linked to corruption and a lack of transparency. A framework for the evaluation of current e-government provision with a view to combating corruption is proposed.

Chapter 4 authored by Mohammad Anwar Rahman titled 'Freight Transport and Logistics Evaluation Using Entropy Technique Integrated to TOPSIS Algorithm' integrates the entropy technique on TOPSIS platform to improve the freight selection decision.

Chapter 5 titled 'A Multifactorial Analysis of the Acceptance of Recommender System for Saudi Universities the Literature Revisited' by Hadeel Alharbi and Kamaljeet Sandhu provides a critical review of current literature on recommender systems adoption in Saudi universities. They identify and discuss the basic determinants influencing the acceptance, and the continued usage intention, of Recommender Systems as an e-learning personalization tool.

Chapter 6 titled 'A Proposed Framework: Factors of the Acceptance of Recommender Systems in E-Leaning for Saudi Universities' is also authored by Hadeel Alharbi and Kamaljeet Sandhu. In this chapter based on the findings of previous chapter they propose a framework for the acceptance and adoption of recommender systems in e-leaning for Saudi universities.

Chapter 7 titled 'Outsourcing to Cloud-Based Computing Services in Higher Education in Saudi Arabia' by Athary Alwasel, Ben Clegg and Andreas Schroeder describes the information systems outsourcing trend towards cloud based solutions in the Saudi Arabian higher education sector and discusses the implications of this trend.

Chapter 8 authored by Mariam Ahmed Elhussein is titled 'Design Solutions Guided by User Behavior: A Practical Inquiry Approach'. This chapter uses practical inquiry methodology to generate a general framework that can be applied to analyze tagging systems. It proceeds to suggest a design process that can be followed to create new tagging systems.

Chapter 9 titled 'Mitigating Ethno-Cultural Differences: Ethical Guidelines for ICT Development in an Indigenous Community' by Hasnain Falak and Tariq Zaman presents guidelines for ICT Development in an Indigenous Community. The guidelines are based on their empirical work on indigenous Penan community of Long Lamai in Malaysian Borneo. This is important because community engagement is necessary for the success and sustainability of Information and Communication Technologies for Development (ICT4D) projects.

Chapter 10 titled 'User Interface Design in Isolation from Underlying Code and Environment' by Izzat Alsmadi discusses the isolation of user interface design from the underlying code.

Chapter 11 authored by Sathiyamoorthi titled 'Web Caching System: Improving the Performance of Web-Based Information Retrieval System' advocates for employing web caching approach to improve the performance of Web based information.

Chapter 12 'User Performance Testing Indicator: User Performance Indicator Tool' by Imuetinyan Bernadette Iyawe, investigates the challenges of user performance and the user performance indicators in haptic-based tests. The chapter proposes a User Performance Indicator Tool (UPIT) as test validation tool to aid designers/testers in enhancing their user performance test and test evaluation outcomes.

Chapter 13 titled 'Development of Ambient Assisted Living Products and Services: The Role of International Classification of Functioning, Disability and Health' by Ana Isabel Martins, Alexandra Queirós and Nelson Pacheco Rocha, discusses the use the conceptual framework of the International

Classification of Functioning, Disability and Health (ICF) to conceptualize instruments for the different phases of the Ambient Assisted Living (AAL) development processes.

Chapter 14 titled 'Modelling Cyber-Crime Protection Behavior among Computer Users in the Context of Bangladesh' is authored by Imran Mahmud, T. Ramayah, Md. Mahedi Hasan Nayeem, S.M. Muzahidul Islam and Pei Leng Gan. This chapter highlights the impact of security champion and security training on protection behavior in the context of IT service oriented SMEs in Bangladesh. It examines the influence of security training on threat and coping appraisal which leads to protection behavior via protection motivation.

Chapter 15 titled 'The State of Art in Website Usability Evaluation Methods' by Renuka Nagpal, Deepti Mehrotra and Pradeep Kumar Bhatia summarizes different approaches used to measure the usability of websites. Approaches are classified in six board category and a comparison between them is also discussed.

Chapter 16 authored by Hina Gull and Sardar Zafar Iqbal titled 'Usability Evaluation of E-Government Websites in Saudi Arabia by Cognitive Walkthrough" discusses their findings of usability evaluation of e-government websites in Saudi Arabia.

Chapter 17 titled 'A Mobile System for Managing Personal Finances Synchronously' by Jabulani Sifiso Dlamini and Paul Okuthe Kogeda discusses the experience of designing and implementing a software application to address financial management challenges faced by many Small Micro-Medium Enterprises (SMMEs) in South Africa.

Chapter 18 titled 'Towards Visually Impaired Autonomy in Smart Cities: The Electronic Long Cane Project' is authored by Alejandro Rafael Garcia Ramirez, Israel Gonzalez-Carrasco, Gustavo Henrique Jasper, Amarilys Lima Lopez, Renato Fonseca Livramento da Silva and Angel Garcia Crespo. The chapter describes electronic long cane project, that was designed to include new features based on the Internet of Things. As a result, new evidences of User-Centric Design have emerged, increasing the probability of success of this technology in Smart Cities.

Section 1
Introduction

Chapter 1

Digital Retail and How Customer–Centric Technology is Reshaping the Industry:
IT–Enabled Digital Disruption

Pablo Penas Franco
Syracuse University, USA

ABSTRACT

This chapter explains the digital disruption that has occurred and is still happening in the retail industry. It explains the relative positions of the world's leading retailers Wal-Mart, Amazon and Alibaba and the business models of the two top online competitors. It focuses on the impact of SMAC (Social, Mobile, Analytics and Cloud) technologies and new retail trends enabled or boosted by technology such as omni-channel, customer experience, internet of things (IoT) and analytics, fulfillment and delivery. It deepens into IT and business model customer-centric design, the role of the customer and the store in the new digital retail and finishes with an assessment of ROI in retail digitization. The chapter concludes the fundamental IT-enabled changes of digital disruption are critical for all players, traditional brick-and-mortar retailers, pure online players and those with both an online and an offline presence.

INTRODUCTION

Digital Disruption

Digital disruption is a mindset that ultimately leads to a way of behaving; a mindset that bypasses traditional analog barriers, eliminating the gaps and boundaries that prevent people and companies from giving customers what they want in the moment that they want it. (McQuivey, 2013)

DOI: 10.4018/978-1-5225-1944-7.ch001

In order to analyze how technology is reshaping the retail business, we must first understand digital disruption. Digital business is a reality, whether companies are ready or not to compete in a new, fast-pacing, and more competitive environment.

Let's provide a few examples of digital disruption. Goodwin (2015) states:

Uber, the world's largest taxi company, owns no vehicles. Facebook, the world's most popular media owner, creates no content. Alibaba, the most valuable retailer, has no inventory, and Airbnb, the world's largest accommodation provider, owns no real estate.

We could add additional examples such as:

- **Amazon:** The world's largest book retailer, has no bookshops or, more accurately, didn't have any till November 2015. The company has more than 3 million books available and sold around $7.5 billion in books in 2015[1].
- **Apple:** The largest music retailer in the world from 2010, sold 35 billion songs online till 2014 through its online iTunes service. With a minor role of its physical Apple stores, its online iTunes store made Apple become the new leader in the music industry.
- **Google:** A search engine or arguably the already biggest media company in the world generated $67.4 billion in online advertising revenues in 2015. No other company in the world generates that much only from advertising activities.
- **YouTube:** Acquired by Google, is the most populated video service in the world with more than a billion viewers and 6 billion hours of video watched every month, relying mostly in user-generated content.

These examples should lead all companies to reflect on how digital business is reshaping their industries. New digital disruptors menace the status quo relegating former industry leaders to lower rank positions, even leading those unable to adapt into bankruptcy (i.e. Blockbuster). And there is no room for self-complacency. Digital disruptors are subject to be attacked by a new breed of competitors whose business models could make them obsolete or even redundant. For instance, Apple now faces new competition from free streaming and cheap monthly subscription services like Spotify.

The survival of the fittest is neither new nor exclusive to business. A Darwinian view of business evolution explains different periods such as the industrial revolution powered by the steam engine. But this time there is a fundamental and more profound impact: its speed and global reach. According to Bradley, Loucks, Macaulay, Noronha and Wade, (2015), "digital disruption has the potential to overturn incumbents and reshape markets faster than perhaps any force in history." Let's include the impact of globalization. Most digital disruptors were born as global players in an enlarged economic world. Now companies are able to reach not only western traditional markets but also those coming from communist regimes and other traditionally off-limits countries. In this context, the impact of digitization will be remarkable. The digital world is only starting and some disruptors already enjoy more than a billion users a few years after their creation.

The impact of digital disruption undermines the way business are conducted around the world and the very essence of different activities is being challenged. Industries will not change due to digitization.

They probably already did and further changes are in process. Digital technologies have transformed and keep transforming several industries such as music, film, media, passenger transportation, accommodation, and retail!

Digital Retail

According to international rankings, such as Deloitte's Global 250 Powers of Retailing 2016, which includes information for fiscal years up to June 2015, Wal-Mart, a traditional US brick-and-mortar hypermarkets retailer is, by far, the biggest retailer in the world, roughly multiplying by 4.3 its more direct follower. It is the Moby-Dick of retail, the gigantic white whale created by Herman Melville in his renowned 1851 fiction book.

Amazon, which ranked 12th with $70.1 billion in revenues coming from www.amazon.com, is considered the biggest online retailer. If growth rates continue - it climbed to $79.3 billion in 2015 - it may reach a position in the global podium in a few years.

However, considering Wal-Mart for a gold medal may be arguable. The biggest player may not even be ranked, as most rankings only consider revenues from retail activities. Disruption is here, don't underestimate its impact. New business models come with new revenue generating activities and the very idea of traditional sectors/ industries may have limited value (don't forget that Google is, after all, a media company).

Many voices claim the Chinese e-commerce giant Alibaba, owner of www.alibaba.com (B2B), www.taobao.com (C2C) and www.tmall.com (B2C) websites, is bigger than Amazon. The boldest even claim it has overturn Wal-Mart as the biggest retailer in the world.

There are good reasons to support Alibaba's place in the world podium. The first and most obvious: Alibaba manages roughly the same gross merchandise value as Wal-Mart. According to both companies:

- Wal-Mart total revenue was $482.1 billion in fiscal 2016, $13.7 billion from e commerce (Wal-Mart, 2016a).
- Alibaba sold Gross Merchandise Value of 3.09 trillion Yuan in the 12 months to March 31, 2016 (Alibaba, 2016). This translates to 479.5 or 486.5 billion USD[2] depending on whether we take the exchange rate at the end of the period or an average during it. Roughly Alibaba sells the same as Wal-Mart!

Wal-Mart is by far the biggest retailer in the world in terms of revenues, but switching the focus to the GMV (gross merchandise value) managed by retailers, an online and relatively unknown player in most western markets, has already topped the world rank and will, most likely, consolidate the first position soon, regardless of the current relative decline due to exchange rate fluctuations. This is due to substantial differences in growth rates. While Alibaba has sustained a 2-digits growth rate during the last years, Wal-Mart's has been modest. If we take a look at the last available quarter, in the three months to June 2016, Alibaba (2016b) grew 24% compared to the same period in 2015, while Wal-Mart (2016b) grew only 0.5% from May till July 2016.

Alibaba also managed transactions on a single day worth $14.3 billion, more than Wal-Mart's yearly online sales ($13.7 billion), and way more than Amazon's $1.1 billion sales on a single day[3] . It exceeded $1 billion in the first 8 minutes. So considering Alibaba bigger than Amazon sounds plausible.

Can Alibaba be compared to Wal-Mart? In terms of revenue recognition, Alibaba is not even a retailer. According to The Economist (2013), Alibaba is "a platform for retail, rather than a retailer itself." It sells marketing services to companies and people selling through its websites, rather than charging a commission on merchandise sold. So, technically, the major part of its business does not generate a penny from retail activities. This explains why it is not even ranked by Deloitte and others: it does not sell by itself. It is a new kind of intermediary that facilitates trade and a strategic substitute for retailers. As it enables direct sales between the owner of the merchandise and the end customer, it menaces wholesalers and other intermediaries as well. It covers a number of functions in the retail value chain, regardless of the fact that it does not own the merchandise. From a customers' perspective, Alibaba is a competitor. They simply care about the offer, price, and delivery options, not about how companies organize internally to deliver the merchandise.

What about Amazon? Amazon does not disclose GMV but there are some estimations. It has both first party (1p) and third party (3p) sales, which understate their sales. 1p sales book the full price as revenue, while 3p sales generate a commission which is the only recognized revenue. Amazon's global GMV was estimated to be around $180 billion in 2014 (Chalaban, 2015). Bearing in mind its 1P and 3P sales in 2015, we could estimate this figure to have increased to around $240 billion[4].

GMV allows for a better comparison than revenues. Understanding retail size as the value of merchandise sold and profit as a percentage on that we can compare the three top retailers. Alibaba's amazing 42% profit on revenues is generated thanks to facilitating the sale of almost half a trillion dollars of GMV. Its profitability is above any curve or standard in the low-margin retail industry. But, in fact, comparing it to GMV puts its feet in the ground, as it would show a rather standard 1.4% profit, half than Wal-Mart's 3%. Both Alibaba and Amazon have relatively low profitability, something we can expect from fast-growing companies, who sacrifice relative margins to build a bigger volume of sales. We conclude there are two pure online players in the podium of a traditionally brick-and-mortar dominated sector and a traditional incumbent (see Table 1).

Relative profitability should not be a great concern as long as growth continues. Gordon Orr suggests (Alibaba) could become one of the world's most valuable companies five years from now, with potentially more than $1 trillion of sales passing through its platforms each year (as cited in The Economist, 2013). GMV may not be the only criteria to measure retailers' size. But regardless of Wal-Mart still being the biggest player or not, online sharks and crocodiles are successfully challenging the gigantic Moby-Dick and differences between them show great potential for new disruptors.

Table 1. Top three retailers by GMV in million USD (Note: Fiscal years ending January 31, 2016 (Wal-Mart), March 31, 2016, (Alibaba) and December 31, 2015 (Amazon). Exchange rate for Alibaba at March 31, 2016. Depending on the exchange rate used for comparison, Alibaba would be ahead or behind Wal-Mart in terms of GMV)

	GMV	Revenues	Profit	In % of GMV
Wal-Mart	482,130	482,130	14,694	3.0%
Alibaba	479,454	15,677	6,637	1.4%
Amazon	240,520	79,268	596	0.2%

A GAME OF SHARKS AND CROCODILES

eBay may be a shark in the ocean, but I am a crocodile in the Yangtze River. If we fight in the ocean, we lose—but if we fight in the river, we win. (Jack Ma – Alibaba)

Disruption may adopt different shapes. The well-known and commonly quoted sentence from Jack Ma, comparing eBay with a shark, which perfectly applies to Amazon, and Alibaba with a Crocodile, is a brilliant example. Amazon is strong in western countries, while Alibaba dominates in China. Moving to new markets has proven difficult for both as the online world is not as standard as we could think.

The way they sell merchandise online is almost antagonistic, but both are customer-centric in their own way. Amazon has a western style approach with strong focus on showing the product. Look for instance for a wedding dress and the product will be the center of the site. Alibaba has an apparently childish, even naive, look and feel for western standards. It focuses on trust and relationship. Look for a wedding dress and the main image may be a smiling woman who shows illusion on her face because she is getting married. The dress may not even be completely seen on the initial page.

This approach responds to different buying attitudes in China. Building trust and relationships helps Alibaba in a country where businesses are not always trustworthy. According to Erisman (2015) some people even meet and marry thanks to Alibaba. Would you imagine customers from America, Europe, and most other countries in the world telling they met their lifetime partners through Amazon.com? Probably not.

Another key difference is that Alibaba only facilitates commerce, without actually owning, warehousing or delivering the merchandise, being more similar to a software company than to a retailer. In contrast, Amazon's model strongly relies on 1p sales, selling directly to customers and excelling in logistics.

But success of both Amazon and Alibaba, among other new retailers, has strong underlying grounds that go relatively unnoticed: its customer-centric IT design. Technology enabled business models are reshaping the industry. While technology is a means to an end, not an end by itself, it is a fundamental factor which explains both the rise and success of new digital disruptors, and the digital transformation of traditional brick-and-mortar retailers.

While traditional competitors are soon credited with cutting-edge innovations when they make improvements on their existing business models, many pure online players are born digital with a user-centric focus that is taken for granted. Most of them were born with features that may not necessarily be noticeable. For instance, customers don't need to understand the analytics engine that enables personalized recommendations at Amazon.com. We simply see the result, usually with delight.

The new breed of retailers led by Amazon and Alibaba are changing the game because they are born digital. They use technological developments to unleash customer value. They are born SMAC!

SMAC RETAIL

In the new technological retail landscape, SMAC technologies are winning momentum. SMAC, an acronym which stands for Social, Mobility, Analytics and Cloud, is a term that helps explaining how customer-centric technologies are reshaping the industry, the emergence of digital competitors and business models, and the fundamental shift towards the customer. These technologies play a key role in retail digital transformation. According to Parikh (2014), retailers use:

- Social Media to engage with customers and convert.
- Mobile Platforms to stay connected 'on the go'.
- Analytics to personalize and derive insights.
- Cloud Business Models to quickly design customized solutions over the Internet.

Are retailers becoming SMAC? Let's briefly analyze its four components.

Social

We may intuitively believe online purchases are based solely on price. While price is still an important element in any digital offering, this is no longer true, if it ever was. As retailers enable new social shopping features, purchasing any product online may resemble the in-store shopping experience to a great extent. Thanks to technology we can involve our friends in the purchasing process, asking for opinions and recommendations. This means technology allows replicating online the social interactions that occur offline. The social customer has changed, rather than spending a day walking around a mall, many people now spend hours on visually pleasing product sites that make wish-listing easy and rewarding (Kamenec, 2014). So e-commerce sites also adapt, and are developed ad hoc to cater the taste of an increasingly demanding shopper.

Customer interactions on social networks, forums, etc. strongly determine purchasing decisions. Our friends' opinions are key in order to decide between two similar products. We even trust on unknown customers who write their reviews and tell about their experiences. Why? Because customers are saturated of traditional marketing messages and look for real users' opinions. If there are enough reviews of a product, the social feedback will probably be fair and accurate. Companies react with more targeted, and usually intrusive, marketing messages as they leverage social friends to endorse their products. Overall, 67% of shoppers say that either reading (45%) or writing (22%) social media reviews and comments influences their online shopping behavior (PWC, 2016).

Social commerce is on the rise. According to Smith (2015a) social media increased its share of e-commerce referrals nearly 200% between the first quarters of 2014 and 2015. The growing importance of social aspects encourages top tier competitors, such as Alibaba and Amazon, to add social features:

- Alibaba mixes social-networking functions into its platforms, trying to engage customers and to increase the time they spend on their websites.
- Amazon's 'Wish List' tries to encourage shopping by enabling the creation and sharing of lists of products people want as gifts.

Other pure players are born social, like Polyvore. Launched in 2007 and acquired by Yahoo in 2015 for around $200 million, it has become a visual search engine for clothing and outfits. Polyvore changes the purchasing experience as customers can create 'sets' (several products combined to create an outfit), share them in social networks, like and share the product, and see details of specific products in the set. It heavily relies on customer generated content - around 3 million sets/ month -, it enjoys 20 million users, mostly female, its conversion rate and average order value are among the highest in the industry, and its share of the social shopping market is second, only after Facebook and ahead of Twitter and Pinterest.

Social media is key to capture bigger shares in the retail market. The growth in social-driven retail sales and referral traffic is undeniable and social media has converted into the *great influencer* to make product decisions (PWC, 2016).

Mobility

As a tool for communication, socialization, leisure, and work, smartphones are becoming an extension of our own bodies. They are widespread devices, not only in rich countries, but also in some of the poorest, where smartphones allow rendering services to previously unreachable rural populations. More than 2 billion people already use them.

From a retailers' perspective, cell phones are used to compare prices (36% of customers), research products (36%), access coupons/ promotional codes (31%), and check reviews about the product/ retailer (25%), among others. Overall, 76% of customers are using it in the purchasing cycle (PWC, 2016).

These devices enable new mobility services ranging from providing information to managing transactions. Most retailers (88%) state their purpose with mobile strategies is to drive shoppers to the store (Rosenblum & Rowen, 2015). Customers can receive personalized marketing messages on their phones when they stand in front of a specific shelf, search for product information and customer reviews while navigating the store, etc.

However, one of the best-known success stories is based on getting the opposite: moving the stores closer to customers. If the mountain will not come to Mohammed, then Mohammed must go to the mountain. Homeplus virtual stores, which belong to Tesco, one of the world's biggest retailers, let the stores come to the people in South Korean subway stations. Customers are able to shop on their smartphones by scanning QR codes. As a result, online sales increased by 130% in 3 months and Homeplus soon became the first online retailer in the country and a close second offline[5].

Homeplus is only an example, but the shift towards mobile is global. Mobile commerce already represents 30% of total US online commerce (Brohan, 2015), but in this case, the US is lagging behind other countries. Many people in other nations increasingly rely on mobile devices to make their purchases, i.e. 69% of all transactions on Chinese Singles' day were made on mobile devices (PWC, 2016). The growing importance of mobility is a world-scale phenomenon.

Mobile devices' role has changed from a relatively simple communication device to an open gate to the digital world. As they enable socializing and purchasing functions, they became purchasing tools, which generates new challenges.

Analytics

What gets measured gets managed. (Peter Drucker)

20th century leaders could be successful relying on their intuition to make decisions. Not anymore. The current competitive landscape force business leaders to base their decisions on an increasing amount of previously captured, digitally stored, properly cured, and (hopefully) analyzed data. This is more obvious in the marketing function where traditional creative professionals ('mad men') are being substituted by more analytical profiles ('math men')[6].

The amount of collected data grows exponentially. Eric Schmidt told there were 5 exabytes of information created between the dawn of civilization through 2003, but that much information is now created every 2 days (as cited in Siegles, 2010). And figures kept growing since then. Internet traffic alone may reach 1.3 Zettabytes in 2016, with an increase from 2015 to 2016 almost equal to all IP traffic generated in 2011 (Cisco, 2012).

But, how is this data managed? Can retailers really derive insights or do they only collect information? Maybe the most famous example of the use of data analytics is Forbes article *How Target Figured Out A Teen Girl Was Pregnant Before Her Father Did* (Hill, 2012). The teenage girl with an upset father is only the tip of the iceberg. Back in 2012, through the analysis of customer purchases, Target could accurately predict the probability of pregnancy for their customers and due dates within very narrow windows. Having retailers managing sensitive information is controversial, as many customers may feel upset if they discover Target (or any other retailer) know about their pregnancies. So Target changed their ad hoc coupons to make them look random, including products a pregnant woman is not likely to buy such as a lawn mower close to those specifically intended for her: diapers, rattles, strollers… Hill makes an important reflection. If they are able to reach and measure your womb, what else they might be able to do?

The shocking part is that, as customers, we don't need to provide much information. Use your loyalty card or a credit card when you pay and the rest will be done in the backstage. Your profile will be enriched with a history of previous purchases and, in cases like Target, the information may be put into the right context to develop useful knowledge about your habits.

Data-driven decision making is a reality only for some companies. While many international retailers invest heavily on big data and analytics, most are still developing their capabilities. Most major players already have a loyalty program, but do not necessarily have the ability to use the information they store. They may even have a number of not interconnected databases lacking an integrated CRM with a 360 degrees view of their customers.

Regardless of their current situation, in order to be competitive retailers must develop their analytical skills. It is critical that they measure the right metrics, analyze their performance on these metrics and adapt accordingly to ensure they survive and thrive (Deloitte, 2015). If not, they risk collecting interesting data without deriving insights. Imagine a married couple buys Coca-Cola on a regular basis, and, occasionally, some Pepsi. It may be interesting to discover a Pepsi lover is visiting them from time to time, but it does not seem useful. Useful data is actionable; it can be leveraged to lead customers into additional purchases, such as predicting pregnancies. If the same customers stop buying meat and suddenly increase the purchase of vegan associated products, then retailers may be able to use this information to target them with a customized vegan offering to increase sales.

Integrating context aware data and information from social networks is another key challenge to improve marketing efficiency. Data generated during the purchasing cycle and the information customers freely share should enrich their profiles. Armed with this information, retailers can reach their customers in new business moments in order to boost their sales.

And customers are only one side of the coin. On the other side of marketing analytics, retailers must optimize their publicity. There are many intermediaries between the marketer or the retailer and the publisher. A typical chain includes an agency, a trading desk, a demand-side platform (DSP), third party data, a supply-side platform (SSP), and an ad server before finally reaching the publisher. The complexity of managing data give rise to data management platforms (DMPs), and allows disintermediating some of these actors (O'Hara, 2016). DMPs allow working with several DSPs simultaneously, integrating both 1p, 2p, and 3p data to get a better understanding of audiences, to do better segmentation and targeting, and increasing the efficiency of publicity budgets.

Cloud

It is difficult to find any computer or smartphone user who does not rely on some cloud computing services, even being unaware of this fact. As individuals, we are likely to use WhatsApp, whose services are rendered on IBM's Softlayer – an IaaS solution –, or e-mail. Gmail, Hotmail, Yahoo, and others deliver e-mail hosted services over the Internet.

Companies in general, and retailers are no exception, are moving to the cloud. Think about the main software categories such as ERPs or CRMs. Most, if not all, major software vendors are offering cloud-based solutions that are substituting on-site implementations. Corporate clients are embracing the cloud in search of greater efficiencies because it is cheaper and easier to implement, it reduces maintenance cost, it improves internal efficiency, and it is easily scalable. The cloud business value includes faster deployment of new technologies and services, create innovative business models that help customization and are based on services, and connect and interact with stakeholders (Parikh, 2014). This trend also reflects the evolution of corporate software. Standard solutions would probably not suffice 15 years ago. Nowadays, their higher quality, continuous upgrades, and sectorial adaptations make standard solutions fit retailers' business and improve value for money.

In order to understand the cloud effect, let's think about music. With Apple's iTunes on the Cloud - included in the iCloud service - customers can store their music, among other files, access, stream, or download it from different devices. It works as a backup not tied to any hardware that can be stolen, lost, or broken. The physical store is a customer touchpoint rather than a music store. From 2016, Spotify offers its streaming services on Google's cloud, without any physical store. Both business models completely differ from that of traditional brick-and mortar music retailers.

As the role of the store is expected to evolve into a showroom providing experiences, insights, and information, but not storing physical products (Gaudin, 2016), cloud computing may have an even greater role to play. Kilcourse (as cited in Gaudin, 2016) states that "by using cloud computing services, retailers won't need to buy new technology, learn how to use it, set it up and manage it." Its simplicity removes barriers and will speed-up adoption.

RETAIL TRENDS ENABLED OR BOOSTED BY TECHNOLOGY

SMAC and other technologies are enabling or boosting fundamental changes that are transforming the way retailers deal and relate with their customers.

Omni-Channel

Omni-channel is about offering continuous purchasing experiences. Customers start a purchase on any channel (i.e. web), continue on another (i.e. store) and place the order on a third one (i.e. smartphone app). Omni-channel implies integration, with all channels serving the customer indistinctly. It differs from multi-channel, in which several channels are in place but not closely intertwined. Though we usually see omni-channel and multi-channel used interchangeably, as omni-channel is the final objective of multi-channel retailers in different stages of maturity.

Retailers are transforming. Omni-channel competitors already dominate the e-commerce sphere, with 39 out of 50 top e-retailers being omni-channel brick and mortar retailers, and 11 out of 50 being pure online players (Deloitte, 2016). This does not necessarily mean that the experience in all their channels is identical, but at least they are working on improving it. Those unable to adapt to omni-channel may struggle to survive as customers' expectations and competing offerings keep raising the bar of customer service.

Customers are not loyal to a specific channel, "they expect online integration between social networks, mobile and physical stores" (Capgemini, 2012). This explains why retailers are accelerating their omni-channel approach, creating a more innovative retail environment where online and in-store shopping are a seamless experience for customers, and why they are including physical stores as part of their omni-channel strategies (Deloitte, 2016). Even pure online players like Amazon are currently opening some physical stores.

While many retailers still keep focus on individual channels, the seamless shopping experience, which includes the ability to shop across channels will improve if customers can check product availability prior to going to the store (Accenture, 2016).

Customer Experience

I've learned that people will forget what you said, people will forget what you did, but people will never forget how you made them feel. (Maya Angelou)

As customers become increasingly demanding, retailers face the challenge of offering better and better shopping experiences, both online and offline. Customer journeys are strongly linked to omni-channel capabilities, as they must be integrated across all channels. Shoppers used to look for social referrals and/or interactions online before shopping. Now they even do it while navigating the aisles in-store.

According to Kilcourse & Rowen research (2015), 95% of industry professionals believe the store and the digital experience must be brought together for a continuous, seamless experience. They identify the top three consumer-facing opportunities: bringing a digital/ online experience to stores, getting a deeper customer engagement to drive sales through personalized offers, and more personalized attention/ service from retailers' employees.

Customers motivations, behaviors, and actions substantially differ. Leading companies concentrate on the critical impact of understanding their customers and rendering a service that maximizes their experience. Retail winners, those with above average performance, "have been investing in understanding consumer behavior since the initial rise of omni-channel… they feel the imperative to understand what consumers want (thus their concern about falling behind in the consumer-retailer technology arms race)" (Baird & Rowen, 2015). Companies must also develop deep empathy to design a compelling and distinctive customer journey (Lhuer, Olanrewaju & Yeon, 2015).

But, why should customers go to the stores if they can check the price and inventory levels online? A technologically augmented in-store shopping experience may provide the answer from a customers' perspective and may enable cross-sell and up-sell opportunities from a retailers'. But retailers are still on their way to switch from product-focused organizations to customer-focused merchandise suppliers. 93% of industry professionals agree retailers have to do a better job to accommodate a younger, more tech-savvy consumer (Kilcourse & Rowen, 2015).

IoT and Analytics

The Internet of Things (IoT) refers to a world with billions (potentially trillions) of connected devices. Thanks to sensors such as RFID, wireless, QR codes, and Beacons, most daily products can be brought to life in the digital world.

The sensors monitor a wide variety of data that will be analyzed as the basis for decision making. Knowing customers is key to customize marketing messages and increase sales. Online tools for analytics - i.e. Google Analytics, Omniture - provide information on visited pages, number of views, time spent in each site, conversion of visits into sales with breakdown by operating system, device… These analytics are being replicated in-store thanks to IoT, combining sensors and analytical platforms.

Beacons, small low-cost devices that transmit information on Bluetooth Low Energy up to a 50-meter distance, are probably the quickest growing devices, especially in the US. They can be used to monitor location within stores and to submit customized marketing messages, among others. Smith (2015b) estimates 85% of the top 100 US retailers will use these devices in 2016 (up from 8% in 2014) and in-store sales influenced by beacons in these companies will multiply 10-fold in a year, from $4.1 billion in 2015 to $44.4 billion in 2016. Even Facebook is already offering its own beacons to leverage the use of its social network at retailers stores.

IoT is not about sensors or platforms, but about improving services. Customers can now be accompanied and advised through the entire purchasing cycle, with more accurate and targeted information even when the staff is busy. IT systems fed by IoT sensors allow delivering automated customized information without any action from sales staff, for instance in-store navigation to items in customers' wish lists when we enter a physical store.

Collected data also allows companies to reach their customers in different moments during their purchasing cycle that were not available before. For instance, retailers can offer proximity services in-store to digitally identified customers, offering them useful information when they are simply near a digital sign. Or they can accompany customers in different moments of their purchasing cycles such as providing product information when customers are searching from home, allowing them checking if the product is in stock when they are moving to the store, or improving the sales service with staff who is aware of the products they are looking for, who help customers finding them, and suggest related items[7].

IoT will have a profound impact in retail and we will see it soon. 80% of industry professionals believe the IoT will drastically change the way companies do business in the next three years (Baird & Rowen, 2015).

Efficient Fulfillment and Convenient Delivery

Cutting-edge fulfillment capabilities become a competitive advantage available in some leading retailers. For instance, fulfillment from several stores may speed-up delivery. There is a special difficulty with food products, as delivery may imply working with both refrigerated and non-refrigerated perishable merchandise simultaneously. The last mile of home delivery is an unresolved problem from the perspective that online orders are still complex and expensive to manage.

The market evolves to improve speed, narrowing delivery windows to increase convenience for customers. But not all retailers are keeping pace: 56% have next-day delivery capabilities, while just 11% can deliver on the same day (Accenture, 2016). Other alternatives such as click & collect are not yet widespread and reduce customer value by forcing them to collect the merchandise in-store when they substitute more efficient home delivery.

Amazon, acclaimed as a world-class competitor in terms of logistics and delivery, is getting ahead of competition. Its new service Amazon Prime Now was launched in December 2014, and first expanded abroad to London in June 2015 (Lomas, 2015). The service is already available for premium members in selected postal codes in 28 US cities, and selected locations in other 8 countries. Customers can choose a two-hour delivery window in the same day for free, or 1-hour delivery for a fee for all their orders above a minimum around 15USD/ 20€ /20 GBP depending on the country. The company also plans to reduce delivery time to 30 minutes using drones (unmanned aerial vehicles), though regulatory barriers must be overcome first.

"Delivery offers an incredibly effective means to differentiate from other competitors in the e-commerce landscape, a tool for boosting conversion rates and a powerful mechanism for building customer loyalty" (MetaPack, 2015: 2). It is so important than half of all customers would not buy online due to unsatisfactory delivery options and 96% would be encouraged to purchase again after a positive delivery experience (MetaPack, 2015).

OTHER TRENDS

- **Digital Payments:** As mobile establishes itself as the cornerstone of digital strategies, most innovative payment solutions focus on mobile apps. New solutions target both retailers and shoppers. New digital payments include: financed payments (Klarna, Affirm), NFC (Apple Pay, Google Pay, bank Wallets), Beacons (PayPal, Apple), credit card solutions (Square, iZettle), apps to access bank accounts (Trustly) or even banks via apps (Simple, Gobank).
- **Digital Fitting Rooms:** Popular in fashion. They are useful to try on digital clothes and increase conversion rates. As customers are willing to see how clothes fit their bodies, these fitting rooms remove a key adoption barrier. They can't actually try the garments on, but seeing themselves 'dressed' with them substantially encourages purchasing.
- **Dynamic Pricing:** Still to become widespread, dynamic pricing is supposed to be one of the future trends. According to Kilroy, MacKenzie & Manacek (2015), online pure players react to competitor prices in one hour, reprice top-selling items 3 or 4 times per day (up to 12), and sophisticated multichannel leaders change the price on 10 to 20 percent of their online assortment daily. Some retailers are also able to deliver personalized offers based on past shopping history. Whether or not personalizing pricing, product prices will differ in different moments and channels. Price changes must be carefully managed to avoid public relations problems.
- **Wearables:** New devices are being born and worn, providing new opportunities for retailers regarding in-store shopping experience, personalization and real-time marketing. For instance, an employee with a smart watch wired into the Internet of Things can effectively service new business moments via glanceable information. Bob O'Donnell argues that smart watches are the next kings of wearables in 2016 and head-worn devices, including virtual reality glasses, will be in 2020 (as cited in Anders, 2015).

DESIGNING DIGITAL RETAIL

A lot of people in our industry haven't had very diverse experiences. So they don't have enough dots to connect, and they end up with very linear solutions without a broad perspective on the problem. The broader one's understanding of the human experience; the better design we will have. (Steve Jobs)

Retailers must design solutions that may disrupt their existing business in order to satisfy customers who decide on when, how and who to interact with. They need a systemic view. Originated in the field of engineering by Forrester (1961) and adapted to business by management guru Peter Senge (1990), systemic thinking is the cornerstone to develop innovative business models and new services. Everything is interconnected: social shopping, mobile solutions, omni-channel capabilities, online and in-store analytics, etc. All these ideas merge from the value perspective to offer integrated solutions and IT departments should keep a systemic view in mind to digitize and transform organizations.

Former Apple CEO, Steve Jobs, is considered the father of the one-button smartphone, simplifying the use of an increasingly complex device with a bigger screen and users' fingers for any potential future use. Digital design must manage complexity through simplicity in a very similar fashion. As in the case of the smartphone, retail customers expect a new breed of apps, functionalities and services. But regardless of their being technologically savvy or not, retailers must keep simplicity in the front, i.e. an app that works with a simple button. While customer interaction is easy and intuitive, there may well be many processes, operations, and technologies working in the back, which is completely transparent for the unaware final user.

The Internet of Things is a good example of managing complexity through simplicity. For instance, customers enter stores and receive personalized marketing messages with special offers for the products they are more likely to buy. They are completely unaware of the backstage, where probably, the retailer's IT department has developed a platform to manage beacons, worked with marketing on the design and delivery of promotional messages and developed an app with an SDK (software development kit) embedded to make personalized communication possible. They simply downloaded an app at some point. All the rest just happens, like magic.

Personalization is another cornerstone. Hodkin (2014) explained how the Internet we experience as customers (The Internet of Me) is as unique as our fingerprints. Companies such as Facebook, Google or Netflix show us the information based on a 'relevance' algorithm, which means we receive only the information we want to see to the virtual exclusion of everything else. Customized content is "the new way of exposing users to the whole Internet through their own experiences, habits, and interests, using information that users are often not conscious of" (Hodkin, 2014). This Internet of Me "is changing the way people around the world interact through technology, placing the end user at the center of every digital experience" (Accenture, 2015).

This individualized customization is most obvious in e-commerce. Digital recommendations may rely in our specific tastes and purchasing histories to offer each of us the best of a myriad of alternatives leveraging *the long tail* (Anderson, 2006), or products with an individually low demand that collectively may generate more revenues than blockbusters, to boost sales.

The combination of a systemic view, simplicity and personalization is a winning value proposition for customers. Retailers should become more customer- centric. This has profound implications on how they think of their business in terms of assortment optimization, tailored advertising, marketing and promotions, improving service on loyalty programs, improving the shopping experience of target consumers, and removing organizational, operational and technical barriers to enable multichannel shopper-centric ways of working (Mercier, Jacobsen, & Veitch, 2012). Changes go beyond IT, affecting the supply chain and the entire organization.

We should make an important distinction between traditional brick and mortar retailers, who, in general, still struggle to integrate the online channel with their stores networks, and more agile, digitally born, pure online players. The former, like the Titanic, need a considerable amount of time and money to change their practices, as they are slaves of their current systems.

Legacy IT systems and practices may be too heavy to get rid of, but there is no need to substitute everything. Gartner's bimodal IT framework suggests using a second team focusing on agility, working in short cycles and centered on the business instead of IT (Gartner, 2016). By developing bimodal IT capabilities, traditional retailers may keep their business as usual running while they set specific teams up to manage new digital projects.

New technological developments also rely heavily on the cloud in its three main alternatives: SaaS (Software as a Service), PaaS (Platform as a Service) and IaaS (Infrastructure as a Service).

SaaS is the most obvious as some of the most important software solutions are directly hired as a Service from top vendors. Instead of traditional implementations, retailers rely on cloud-based solutions managed by third parties. While they may lose the feeling of uniqueness, as this software does not allow much customization to the specifics of their business models, most of them discovered they were not as unique as they used to believe in the first place. Market solutions fit, in general, most competitors' needs, and offer substantial advantages in terms of ease and cost of implementation, maintenance, upgrading, and scalability. The time in which all software had to be developed ad hoc is gone.

PaaS and IaaS are useful for retailers who wish to develop their own apps. For instance, apps developed for social interaction and mobile phones/ tablets are very popular. PaaS is a middleware that offers a framework to develop, customize, manage and execute apps, usually through a self-service portal. IaaS ensures the required underlying infrastructure (hardware) is in place. With these cloud services retailers can focus on faster development and deployment, without worrying about scalability or existing infrastructure capabilities.

Outsourced to third parties, cloud services are typically rendered on the basis of SLAs (service level agreements) and have developed a variety of pay-per-use revenue models that allow optimizing computing power. Nowadays, an American, a European and an Asian retailer may share some servers as new models make no longer attractive to own the needed computing power. When peak demand exceeds by far average utilization, having dedicated computer power round-the-clock implies wasting resources. Cloud services make economic sense allowing to share this power among several companies that work on different time zones or simply have peaks in different moments.

Acknowledging the cloud global importance and its increasing presence in retail, some capabilities may still be developed in-house. Analytics is a good example, as it may imply major customization needs where market solutions may be insufficient. Kilcourse & Rosenblum (2015) state that "if retailers are serious about getting deep into customer data, a purpose-built data warehouse with analytics both built in and discoverable is a must." Retailers have an agreement on wanting to know the customer but many are still unable to make proper use of their business intelligence and analytics tools.

Regardless of developing ad-hoc solutions or buying from top software vendors, the best design takes place in the digital realm, where several functions merge to offer customer-centered solutions developed over an IT backbone. The CDO (Chief Digital Officer) should not be a senior project/ programme manager, buy a member of the executive committee, who helps defining the strategy and coordinating marketing,

IT, and other functions. Putting all functions to work together is a must for successful implementation and a prerequisite to digitize both retailer's front and back ends, leveraging SMAC technologies.

Digitization also requires new methodologies and a portfolio approach. The traditional role of hierarchies is being challenged and new project management methodologies are losing ground to agile ones in which the focus switches from the product to quick delivery and adaptability to changes. Constant interaction between functions with digital professionals leading technical decisions over more senior but technologically outdated managers may become commonplace. Minimum viable products may be preferred to fully developed ones, favoring speed over perfection and improving through a test-and-learn approach. And agile IT methodologies are just the tip of the iceberg: the whole organization should become agile, like a start-up. (Lhuer, Olanrewaju & Yeon, 2015). The new retail is quick, adaptive, and digital.

Digital design must be a strategic priority and must be appropriately managed. According to Bonnet (2016), "success (in digital transformation) comes from consciously managing your digital transformation as a strategic portfolio over time." Design must bear in mind the differences among projects in terms of impact, time horizon, and risk levels. Managing digital transformation as a portfolio implies addressing the why, the what and the how. That is to say, understanding the changes in the industry and new sources of value creation - the why -, designing a portfolio of initiatives that balance short-term improvements with longer term strategic and business model evolution - the what -, and the ability to execute at the right time - the how - (Bonnet, 2016).

THE NEW DIGITAL CUSTOMER

The customer is at the very center of retail. Digital is the cornerstone of a new purchasing experience of an increasingly commanding target customer. However, there is still a huge gap between retailers' reality and customers' growing expectations. This gap between consumers' digital behaviors and expectations and retailers' ability to deliver the desired experiences has been defined as *The New Digital Divide* (Deloitte, 2015).

Shoppers purchasing habits are evolving. An increasing number of shoppers start purchases online even if they finally buy at traditional stores, the so-called ROPO (research online, purchase offline). According to Deloitte (2015), 80% interact with brands or products through digital before arriving at the physical store. Others buy online and collect the merchandise in the store (BOPUS - buying online, picking up in-store). ROPO and BOPUS illustrate changing shopping trends that retailers should be able to forecast and adapt to.

Keeping pace with expectations proves challenging. Without trying to be exhaustive, retail customers are looking for (Accenture 2015 & 2016, PWC 2016):

- Ordering out-of-stocks via mobile devices while they are in the store
- Accessing free Wi-Fi, scanning products and having them shipped home
- Using their mobile devices to locate items in the store
- Receiving real-time promotions and earn loyalty points/ member-only discounts
- Navigating websites optimized by device
- Doing one-click checkouts
- Improved delivery (one-hour delivery, delivery by drone…) and free shipping

- Receiving recommendations based upon social media activity
- Reading feedback from friends for items they are considering
- And, maybe the most important, personalized shopping experiences

So, what is the role of the customer in the new retail digital landscape? We cannot unbind social shopping from customer experience, mobile from omni-channel or analytics from IoT. Everything is deeply intertwined. Retail is digital, omni-channel and SMAC. Social, mobile, analytics and cloud reinforce each other. "While each of the technology elements has the capability of delivering business value individually, however, in combination with each other they become a potent strategic tool for the enterprise to deliver higher value to its customers" (Parikh, 2014).

Customers are, to some extent, at the center of all technological developments. Some of them may be unnoticed. For instance, as customers, we don't really care if our retailers' e-commerce web sites are powered by ATG (Oracle), Hybris (SAP), WebSphere (IBM), Demandware (Salesforce), or any other solution. We really want them to work properly, a user friendly design, and, hopefully, some extra features: social interaction and recommendations. Platforms may evolve in different ways such as providing new cloud services, enhancing analytical capabilities, enabling mobile functionalities, or adding social features.

After retailers upgrade their services, it takes time for customers to realize and get used to the new possibilities. Top tier retailers are competing to develop new solutions that help us interact with our friends - i.e. product recommendations -, manage our wish or gift lists and facilitate transactions. The easiest for consumers, the better for retailers, as they will increase loyalty and repeat orders. Whenever possible, we will avoid downloading apps or logging in to online services. It is about managing complexity in the backstage while offering simplicity in the front.

Technology also enables new business moments in which companies can support the purchasing process providing information and help at virtually any moment: when we research from home, when we enter a store, or while we are in the store waiting for the sales staff. These actions require customer-focused developments, so clients are part of the design objectives and their needs become key before even starting to develop anything.

Finally, the customer-centric approach is also changing the role of the store to "storefronts to choose and order products" (Capgemini, 2012). Worth mentioning some online retailers are also developing their stores networks. In an omni-channel retail world in which customers expect the best personalized experience across channels, having both a digitally enhanced physical presence and a virtual store seems a winning value proposition.

CONCLUSION: WILL DIGITAL RETAIL PAY-OFF?

No doubt SMAC technologies offer great value. Offering social interactions, mobile functionalities, deriving customer insights and improving efficiency are some of the most valued assets. But, as any new investment with uncertain returns, is SMAC, and digital in general, only a way to remain competitive or does it have a real impact in the bottom line? Will retailers monetize their digital investments? Overall, not only it has become a need to remain in business because disruptors are already in the industry, whether incumbents adapt or not, but also the return is clearly positive from a financial standpoint.

The digital influence is surprisingly high. It is not limited to digital, but it already affects most in-store sales. In 2014, only 6.5% of sales were online ($305 billion) but the influence of digital and mobile on store sales is much greater and quickly growing. 49% of total in-store sales ($1.7 trillion) were influenced by digital devices, up from 14% two years earlier. This figure is expected to have grown to almost two thirds (64%) in 2015. 28% of total in-store sales ($0.97 billion) were influenced by mobile devices up from 5% two years earlier (Deloitte, 2015). We also know consistent omni-channel offerings and improved customer experiences increase retention and boost sales.

The social impact is clear in customer behavior. Social shoppers are 29% more likely to make a purchase on the same day when they use social media, 4x times more likely to spend more on purchases as a result of a digital shopping experience in general and up to 6x times for those very influenced by social media (Deloitte, 2015).

Maximizing mobile or making it easier to purchase from smartphones and tablets, may be one of the most profitable steps retailers can take as there is still a huge gap between ease of purchase on physical stores - 92% of customers believe it is easy or very easy versus online and mobile - 65% and 42% respectively- (Accenture, 2015). Mobile is also reshaping the in-store purchasing experience for the better.

The new priority in terms of business intelligence and analytics is gaining a better understanding of customers. The focus changed from a reactive approach - providing customers with contextual information under demand - to a proactive one - using information about them to react more quickly to changes in demand - (Kilcourse & Rosenblum, 2015). Trying to establish the ROI at this stage may be misleading as the different initiatives are not easily comparable.

Let's remember the profit (Π) of any company is a function of the price (P) minus the variable cost (VC), multiplied by the number of units sold (Q), minus fixed costs (FC): $\Pi = (P - VC) \times Q - FC$. Social, mobile and analytics focus more on generating additional revenues by increasing sales, mostly selling more units. Prices can also be raised in the long run if additional value is created (dynamic pricing would have an additional impact, when it eventually becomes a widespread reality). Retailers can also substantially profit from cloud solutions in terms of reducing costs and time-to-market, which leads to quicker sales. SMAC technologies directly affect profit components and retailers' bottom lines. But all conversion and ROI numbers must be taken as simple references. Even the best international research shows no consistent figures as methodologies, target participants, and geographies substantially vary.

One thing is for sure. Retail has been and continues to be disrupted by SMAC and other digital technologies. Digital Disruption is a fundamental change boosted by technology that alters the status quo by generating new business models, and innovative products and services that make existing competition obsolete, or even redundant. In order to compete, retailers must digitize, whether they keep a brick-and-mortar stores network, an online presence or both, they must be prepared to leverage technology on their respective offerings and to manage digital transformation strategically. And don't forget:

The future is already here – it's just not evenly distributed. (William Gibson)

REFERENCES

Accenture. (2015). Seamless Retail Research Report 2015: Maximizing mobile to increase revenue.

Accenture. (2016). Retail customers are shouting – are you adapting?

Alibaba. (2016). Financial information extracted from http://www.alibabagroup.com/en/ir/financial

Alibaba. (2016b). Group Announces June Quarter 2016 Results (Press release). Retrieved from www.alibabagroup.com

Amazon. (2016). Amazon.com Announces Fourth Quarter Sales up 22% to $35.7 Billion. Press release. Retrieved from http://phx.corporate-ir.net/phoenix.zhtml?c=97664&p=irol-newsArticle&ID=2133281

Anders, G. (2015, May 7). Wearable Computing's Next Kings: Watches In 2016; Glasses In 2020. *Forbes*. Retrieved from www.forbes.com

Anderson, C. (2006). *The Long Tail. How endless choice is creating unlimited demand*. London: Random House.

Baird, N. & Rowen, S. (2015). *The Internet of Things in Retail: Great Expectations*. RSR (Retail Systems Research). August 2015.

Bonnet, D. (2016, August 3). *A Portfolio Strategy to Execute Your Digital Transformation*. Capgemini Consulting. Retrieved from www.capgemini-consulting.com

Bradley, Loucks, Macaulay, Noronha & Wade (2015, June). *Digital Vortex: How Digital Disruption Is Redefining Industries*. Global Center for Digital Business Transformation, initiative by IMD & Cisco. Retrieved from www.imd.org

Brohan, M. (2015, August 18). Mobile commerce is now 30% of all US e-commerce. Retrieved from www.internetretailer.com

Capgemini. (2012, July 11). Internet domina el proceso de compra online, pero redes sociales y aplicaciones móviles crecen con rapidez (Press note).

Chalaban, B. (2015). Why Amazon's Recent Sales Deceleration is Not the Full Story. *Treetisblog*. Retrieved from http://treetisblog.tumblr.com/post/112513225688/why-amazons-recent-sales-deceleration-is-not-the

Cisco. (2012). Cisco's VNI Forecast Projects the Internet Will Be Four Times as Large in Four Years. Retrieved from https://newsroom.cisco.com

Deloitte. (2015). *Navigating the New Digital Divide. Capitalizing on digital influence in retail*. Retrieved March 16, 2016 from www.deloitte.com

Deloitte. (2016). *Global 250 Powers of Retailing 2016*. Retrieved from www.deloitte.com

Erisman, P. (2015, December). El efecto Alibaba: cómo una compañía de Internet iniciada por un profesor está reconfigurando el comercio electrónico a nivel mundial (Keynote presentation). *Proceedings of FICOD '15*.

Forrester, J. W. (1961). *Industrial Dynamics*. Cambridge, Massachusetts, USA: The M.I.T. Press.

Gartner. (2016). IT Glossary: Bimodal IT. Retrieved from http://www.gartner.com/it-glossary/bimodal

Gaudin, S. (2016, January 18). IBM predicts that by 2025 many stores will be showrooms with merchandise shipped to customers. *Computerworld*. Retrieved from www.computerworld.com

Goodwin, T. (2015, March 3). The battle is for The Customer Interface. Retrieved from https://techcrunch.com

Hill, K. (2012). How Target Figured Out a Teen Girl Was Pregnant Before Her Father Did. *Forbes*. Retrieved from www.forbes.com

Hodkin, S. (2014). The Internet of Me: Creating a Personalized Web Experience. *Wired*. Retrieved from www.wired.com

Kamenec, K. (2014, November 26). 10 Best Social Shopping Sites Right Now. Retrieved from www.pcmag.com

Kilcourse, B. & Rosenblum, P. (2015, March). *Advanced Analytics: Retailers Fixate On The Customer*. RSR (Retail Systems Research).

Kilcourse, B. & Rowen, S. (2015, June). *Commerce convergence: Closing the Gap Between Online and In-Store*. RSR (Retail Systems Research).

Kilroy, T., MacKenzie, I., & Manacek, A. (2015). Pricing in retail: Setting strategy. Retrieved from www.mckinsey.com

Lhuer, X., Olanrewaju, T., & Yeon, H. (2015). What it takes to deliver breakthrough customer experiences. *McKinsey*. Retrieved from www.mckinsey.com

Lomas, N. (2015, June 30). Amazon takes prime now outside U.S., opens one-hour delivery in London. Retrieved from www.techcrunch.com

McQuivey, J. (2013). *Digital Disruption: Unleashing the Next Wave of Innovation*. Amazon publishing.

Mercier, P., Jacobsen, R., & Veitch, A. (2012). 'The New, Customer-Centric Retail Model. Retail 2020'. Boston Consulting Group. Retrieved from www.bcg.com

MetaPack. (2015). *Delivering Consumer Choice: 2015 State of eCommerce Delivery*. Retrieved from www.metapack.com

O'Hara, C. (2016, June). The Role of the Agency in Data Management. *eConsultancy*.

Parikh, K. (2014). *Revolutionizing Customer Experience Through SMAC: The New Technology Foundation*. Avasant.

Price Waterhouse Coopers. (2016, February). Total Retail 2016. They say they want a revolution.

Rosenblum, P. & Rowen, S. (2015, January). *Mobile Retail Finds New Purpose*. RSR (Retail Systems Research).

Senge, P. (1990). *The fifth discipline: The art and practice of the learning organization*. New York: Doubleday/Currency.

Siegles, M. G. (2010, August 4). Eric Schmidt: Every 2 days we create as much information as we did up to 2003., 2010. Retrieved from www.techcrunch.com

Smith, C. (2015a, June 30). It's time for retailers to start paying close attention to social media. Retrieved from www.businessinsider.com

Smith, C. (2015b, January). The Beacons Report: Sales-influence forecast, retail applications and adoption drivers. *Business Insider.*

The Economist. (2013, March 23). Alibaba. The world's greatest bazaar. Retrieved from www.economist.com

Wal-Mart. (2016a). Walmart reports Q4 adjusted EPS of $1.49, Fiscal year 2016 adjusted EPS of $4.59. Retrieved from www.news.walmart.com

Wal-Mart. (2016b). Walmart reports Q2 FY17 EPS of $1.21, adjusted EPS of $1.07'. Earnings release. Retrieved from www.stock.walmart.com

Youderian, A. (2014). Alibaba vs. Amazon: An In-Depth Comparison of Two eCommerce Giants. Retrieved from http://www.ecommercefuel.com/alibaba-vs-amazon/

KEY TERMS AND DEFINITIONS

Analytics: The search for meaningful patterns in data to derive insights.

App: Acronym for application. Small and specialized computer program.

Cloud Computing: Term that refers to the delivery of hosted services over the Internet. It is broken down in three main services: SaaS (Software as a Service), PaaS (Platform as a Service) and IaaS (Infrastructure as a Service).

Digital Disruption: A fundamental change boosted by technology that alters the status quo by generating new business models, innovative products and services that make existing competition obsolete or even redundant.

E-Commerce: Buying and selling of goods and services through electronic networks, normally through the Internet. The most popular types of e-commerce are: B2C (Business to Consumer), B2B (Business to Business) and C2C (Consumer to Consumer).

Internet of Things (IoT): It refers to the idea of connecting any device, including daily life products, and even machine components to the Internet, where they will enjoy a digital presence.

Omni-Channel: Delivery of services through different channels indistinctly, looking to offer a seamless shopping experience.

Retail: The sale of goods or services directly to consumers.

SMAC: Acronym which stands for Social, Mobility, Analytics and Cloud.

Social Shopping: A kind of commerce in which technology allows involving friends and/or other customers replicating online the social interactions that occur offline.

ENDNOTES

[1] Amazon does not disclose this figure. A 2014 Forbes articles estimated $5.25 billion in 2013 or 7% of its total revenue. Extrapolating this figure to 2015 revenues we get an estimation of $7.5 billion.

[2]   USD 479.5 billion translating the final figure at March 31, 2016 with a 6.449 Yuan/ USD exchange rate. USD 486.5 billion considering an average 6.356 Yuan/ USD exchange rate over the period April 2015 to March 2016. The evolution of the exchange rate would place Wal-Mart ahead of Alibaba in terms of GMV when this chapter was submitted. Alibaba was previously ahead. Its relative decline responds to a Yuan depreciation against the dollar. Growth in local currency keeps strong for Alibaba (+27% year on year).

[3]   Estimated by the author. In order to estimate how much is Amazon able to sell in one day, the author took Adobe's Digital Index total online sales on Cyber Monday – the major online shopping day in the US ($3.07 billion) and Slice Intelligence estimation that Amazon generated 36.1% of the total online sales on that day. The result is $1.1 billion. Cyber Monday online sales are above those of Black Friday ($2.72 billion) and Thanksgiving Day ($1.73 billion). Alibaba's number are for Chinese 'Singles' day', the major shopping day in China.

[4]   In 2014, Amazon's 3p sales represented $18.9 billion. $180 billion GMV implies around $109.9 billion from 3p sales or a 5.81 'multiplier' from recorded 3p sales to 3p GMV. Using this multiplier with 2015 data, we can estimate Amazon's 3p GMV at around 161.3 billion and total GMV at around 240.5 billion.

[5]   You can see how it works in YouTube: https://www.youtube.com/watch?v=nJVoYsBym88.

[6]   'Mad men' refer to stereotypical marketing professionals in the 20th century, which were hired for their creativity. 'Math men' represent 21st century new professionals, who derive insights from data. This is also related to the dominance of the right hemisphere in the brain, associated with creativity or the left one, with logical thinking. Another way of referring to these skills is the debate on the 'art or science of marketing'. New marketing professionals should be able to combine both approaches, but they are 'math' men because their job has an increasingly reliance upon data.

[7]   The author would like to thank fellow colleague Craig Templin, Director at Neoris US and head of the Neoris Global iBeacon Driven Initiative for his work on Beacons, that has been a key input to write the IoT section.

Chapter 2
Digitalization of Death Certification Model:
Transformation Issues and Implementation Concerns

Dalibor Stanimirovic
University of Ljubljana, Slovenia

ABSTRACT

Accurate and consistent death certification facilitates evidence-informed health policies, morbidity and mortality surveillance on the national level, and consequently serves increasingly demanding medical and statistical needs. This paper initially explores the current situation concerning the death certification in Slovenia, and identifies related deficiencies and systemic problems. Based on the research findings, the paper outlines a construction of ICT-based model of death certification and provides applicable guidelines for its implementation at the national level. The research is based on focus group methodology. Structured discussions were conducted with 29 experts from cross-sectional areas related to death certification. Research results imply that effective ICT-based transformation of the existing death certification model should involve a redefinition of functions and relationships between the main actors, as well as a reconfiguration of the technological, organizational, and regulatory elements in line with the long-term public health objectives.

INTRODUCTION

Death certification, in various forms and with different purposes, has been one of the essential measures for the monitoring of personal and legal existence since the medieval history (Glasser, 1981; Sim & McKee, 2011). As such, it is still one of the most typical instruments, which allows the analysis of different aspects, patterns and causes of death in the modern public health era. Certification of death has been recurrently highlighted as a foundation for monitoring mortality patterns and documenting the leading causes of death, with the results being used to inform health policies and improve prevention strategies (Sibai, 2004; Burger et al., 2015). Mortality statistics including the causes of death are essential data to

DOI: 10.4018/978-1-5225-1944-7.ch002

monitor population health, undertake epidemiological studies, and international comparisons (Lefeuvre et al., 2014). Research to date underline that comprehensive approach to death certification provides a valuable platform for the multi-stakeholder dialogues, as well as allocation of resources and prioritization of health programs and initiatives.

Mortality statistics are widely used and often provide a major and only source of data for comparing health characteristics between different countries. Because causes-of-death statistics relate to all deaths, the problems of biases and representation due to sampling are avoided (European Commission, 2001). Results of these comparisons have been used as a starting point to investigate the causes of differences in the level of mortality, health prevention policies and quality of health care. The ability to access and use complete records of deaths in a population has been noted as vital to the compilation of public health statistics (Flanders, 1992; Hill & Rosenwaike, 2001; Ali & Hamadeh, 2013). Clearly in order for anyone to make use of this kind of information, the cause of death must be determined by a qualified person, and reported to a central agency in a systematic, accurate and consistent way (D'Amico et al., 1999; Cohen et al., 2007). The only way to obtain good-quality mortality statistics is to have deaths certified by a medically trained and experienced doctor. How well a doctor manages to diagnose the diseases and conditions that led to a person's death depends upon a number of factors and circumstances (Lu, 2003). To ensure that doctors are able to competently certify deaths in accordance with World Health Organization (WHO) guidelines and standards (International Statistical Classification of Diseases and Related Health Problems – ICD, WHO, 1992), they must receive basic training in death certification and must understand the importance of good cause-of-death information.

Apart from considerable functions in the field of public health, death certificate has an important role for individuals as well. It is a significant document involving permanent legal and administrative implications for the deceased's family. It reveals underlying cause of death, provides a legal basis for cremation or burial services and is essential for arrangement of the property issues and civil status (insurance, pensions and other benefits). Because of such complex and profound implications, it is important that death certificates are filled out completely, accurately, and promptly (Brooks & Reed, 2015).

The death certification system itself is rather complex, in part because several organizations, professional groups and departments are involved in the process of certification and registration of death (Rahimi et al., 2015). These agencies include doctors and/or coroners, government bodies (who employ the registrar of births and deaths), the police, the local authorities (responsible for appointing coroners), and the national statistics agencies (Crowcroft & Majeed, 2001). Quality death certification process contains four elements of particular concern (Figure 1): the certifier, the certificate, the deceased and the cause of death, however in order to provide a consistent sequence of activities throughout the whole death certification process, appropriate organizational and legal infrastructure must be in place (Maudsley & Williams, 1994; Sibai, 2004).

Throughout the European Union (EU), as in most other parts of the world, the completion of a death certificate is a mandatory requirement of the doctor or other qualified individual reporting the death, however the accuracy of the recorded cause of death has often been called into question (Myers & Farquhar, 1998; Swift & West, 2002; Dash et al., 2014). In order to facilitate high quality death certification and to standardize reporting and coding practices among various countries, the United Nations (UN) and WHO periodically develop protocols and guidelines for the management, operation and maintenance of civil registration and death certification (UN, 2001; Nojilana et al., 2013). Moreover, WHO and other organizations produce rules and guidelines for mortality and morbidity coding (WHO, 2013). Notwithstanding the significant efforts made by the several international organizations, in order to standardize

Figure 1. Framework for factors affecting the death certification process and mortality data (Sibai et al., 2002)

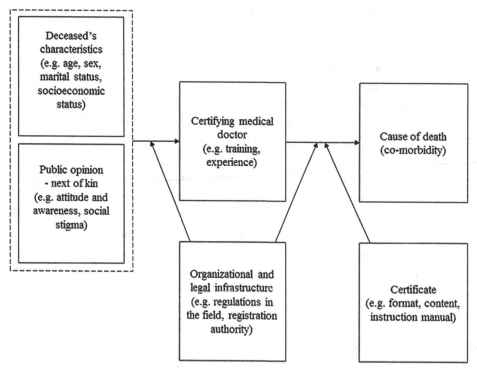

reporting and coding practices concerning the cause of death, death registration remains inadequate and fragmented in several countries, whereas mortality patterns are based on vague estimates and provisional assessments (Setel et al., 2007; Jain et al., 2015). In some developing countries, despite the effort and support of international organizations, death registration may have a number of flaws, including not only miss-diagnosis of causes of death (Lu et al., 2000; Sibai, 2004), but also a lack of reporting of the event altogether (Huyet et al., 2003; Cohen et al., 2007). Even the most developed countries face many obstacles in death reporting system that lead to inaccurate mortality reporting (D'Amico et al., 1999; Swift & West, 2002). For example, EU member states are generally thought to have more accurate and complete data than developing nations (Mahapatra et al., 2007), however there are still indications that there may be some shortcomings in the standards of completion of up to half of all death certificates written in some of the most developed countries in EU (Swift and West, 2002). It has been noted that the quality of data regarding specific causes of death may vary, owing to the nature of the recording and reporting procedures, which may vary considerably between the countries (Jougla et al., 1998; Joubert et al., 2014). However, the European region is noted by the WHO as having the most complete and up to date records of all regions (Mathers et al., 2005).

Factors contributing to deficient registration of death and direct sources of fault have been generally identified. They typically include, but are not necessarily limited to: diagnostic errors, late registration, missing information, coding errors, unavailability of medical records, misinterpretations of the certification process, and difficulties in ascertaining causal sequence of events leading to death, which considerably hinder the reliable classification of the causes of death (Sibai et al., 2002; Wall et al., 2005;

Rodriguez et al., 2006). In order to overcome these deficiencies, European Commission has repeatedly expressed the importance of high-quality mortality data and methods that improve the international comparability of cause of death statistics (Jougla et al., 2001; Rose et al., 2013). In the last years, electronic certification of death is becoming an issue of great interest in public health surveillance in all EU member states, since this issue is discussed extensively in recent EU public health policies and reports (European Commission, 2013).

Due to objective problems referred to above and other circumstances related to the access to the deceased's medical record, speed of data transmission, the confidentiality of personal data, faster execution of business processes, data archiving and standardization of death certification practices, there are a number of national initiatives in the field, which support the establishment of ICT-based solutions for the certification of death (Brooks & Reed, 2015).

Although the basic digitalization of the healthcare system was established relatively early, Slovenia still does not have an interoperable and comprehensive health information system (HIS) including the electronic death certification solutions (eDeath certification). The current death certification practice in Slovenia is not optimally organized, including paper-based manual data entries during the process, inadequate legal regulation, unresolved issues concerning the licensing, status and jurisdiction of the coroners, and information flows between the main stakeholders. The present situation prevents the cross-functional integration of processes and considerably inhibits the substantial utilization of the stakeholders' organizational capabilities. Moreover, available ICT solutions have remained largely ignored, while the existing and obsolete death certification model in Slovenia continues to operate significantly limited and unadapted to the increasing and ubiquitous penetration of ICTs into the area of public health surveillance. Ongoing national project for the digitalization of the healthcare system, named eHealth, is supposed to result in a wide-ranging HIS, which should be able to integrate all fragmented ISs into a functional mechanism and offer complete electronic services benefitting all interested parties (Stanimirovic, 2015). Unfortunately, otherwise very extensive eHealth project, does not include a sub-specialized IS for eDeath certification.

The aim of this paper is to examine the existing situation concerning the death certification model in Slovenia, and explore the possibilities regarding its transformation through innovative and comprehensive digitalization. Therefore, this paper primarily focuses on the following interrelated research objectives:

- An overview and analysis of the death certification practice in Slovenia and identification of related deficiencies and systemic problems.
- Conceptualization of ICT-based model of death certification and provision of applicable guidelines for its implementation at the national level.

Background

Generally, systems for certification of death are part of wider civil registration and vital statistics systems (CRVS). The ideal in properly functioning CRVS systems is complete civil registration presuming all births and deaths in the population are recorded including the adequate cause-of-death statistics. Each case of death should be attributed underlying cause of death assigned by a medically qualified doctor (CDC, 2007), and coded by someone trained in the ICD rules and principles (WHO, 2004). Data quality, access and use are critical determinants of any statistical system; however, these aspects are often being neglected. Some authors even claim, that disregard of civil registration systems is "the single most critical failure of development over the past 30 years" (Horton, 2007). Consequently, the information on births and deaths collected at great expense is not used optimally, and those collecting the data are not fully rewarded for their efforts (WHO, 2010). In order to be valuable for public health policy-making procedures, the acquired datasets have to be tested for relevance, and subsequently aggregated and standardized in the manner, which enables their maximum applicability. When charting data collection and data flow in CRVS systems, it is imperative to identify and distinct two related functions of CRVS systems; namely the registration of vital events through the civil registration process in order to permit the issuing of the relevant legal documentation, and the subsequent incorporation of vital event data into the vital statistics system, as illustrated in Figure 2 (WHO, 2013).

In order to standardize the presentation of "underlying cause of death" and uniform the death certification and operative reporting process, the international form of medical certificate of cause of death can be applied. This form ensures transparency and simplifies the death certification (including the determination of underlying cause of death) and reporting process even in more complex cases.

Although at first glance the above-mentioned death certification concept may seem rather straightforward, experience and existing international practice reveal just the opposite. As noted in several WHO documents (2010 and 2012, 2013), the percentage of all deaths registered through the existing CRVS systems varies widely between different countries, while the quality of death certification varies even more. Assessments most frequently disclose significant global discrepancies in the death certification practice, quality of cause-of-death data based on the estimated timeliness, completeness and coverage of death registration, and on the proportion of deaths assigned to ill-defined causes (WHO, 2013). Only about 70 WHO member countries (as of 2015, the WHO has 194 member countries) conduct adequate death certification including cause-of-death data of acceptable quality from their CRVS systems (Mathers et al., 2005). In the other 50 or so countries, death certification includes some cause-of-death data; however, the quality of the information is poor due to low competencies and coding practices. Currently, millions of people in Africa, Asia and South America are born and die without leaving any trace in legal records or official statistics – because these systems have stagnated over the past 30 years (WHO, 2013). Most deaths in these countries that occur outside hospitals are not medically certified, and a high proportion of these deaths are assigned to non-specific or "ill-defined causes" (WHO, 2010). Such imprecise diagnoses ultimately cannot provide evidence based platform for public health surveillance and policy-making. Despite the paucity of research in this area and based on limited information, Sibai

Figure 2. Two functions of CRVS systems and their components (WHO, 2013)

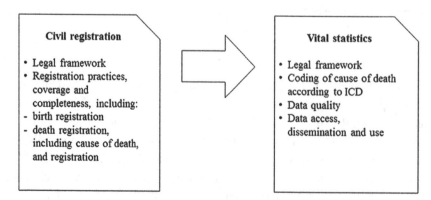

(2004) maps the most likely causes for inadequate death certification in developing countries. She argues that inaccuracies in the data are mostly derived from characteristics of the certifier (e.g. no training), the certificate (e.g. not aligned with ICD practice), the deceased person (e.g. older age groups) and the cause of death (e.g. sudden death).

Notwithstanding the broader systemic issues (political, economic, organizational, infrastructural, cultural etc.), the following main challenges have been identified in establishing the comprehensive death certification systems on the global scale (WHO, 2014):

- Inadequate CRVS (insufficient coverage and completeness of birth and death registration)
- Poor quality of causes-of-death data (structural and organizational problems of health care systems, inappropriate ICD coding of causes of death, due to several reasons including inadequate training of coders, insufficient number of medically certified deaths using the International Medical Certificate of Cause of Death, poor supplementation of data from other sources – electronic health record, police, etc.)
- Lack of trained manpower in the field of ICT and inadequate ICT infrastructure and equipment
- Costs of death certification services
- Need for better coordination and collaboration among key stakeholder (health care and government sector)
- Lack of regular multilateral audits to improve data quality, analysis procedures, and compilation/aggregation of vital statistics from existing data

Despite often narrow definitions, CRVS systems are not only a source of legal documentation and empowerment for individuals, whereas they generate crucial evidence for economic, social and health decision-making and development (WHO, 2013). Such systems represent solid grounds for planning of different local/national public policies (public health, social security, education, economic development, etc.), and promote social equity by providing a wider range of public services to disadvantaged and vulnerable groups of citizens. Reliable information on mortality and causes of death facilitates identification of public health threats and emergencies (magnitude and distribution of major diseases), definition of necessary measures and actions, better targeting of vulnerable social groups using specialized programs and allocation of resources. There is increasing evidence that long-term improvements to civil registration systems will provide a more cost-effective way to accurately measure reductions in mortality than relying on separate disease-focused approaches, in which data are collected on specific areas of interest (AbouZahr et al., 2007).

Unfortunately, international collection and comparison of health data (including vital statistics) is less available and much more limited than the comparison of often trivial economic indicators. This unfavorable situation is extremely detrimental for all developing countries that are trying to implement health care reforms, while they cannot get trustworthy, well-timed and relevant data in order to conduct the planned measures and implement systemic changes (AbouZahr et al., 2012). Nevertheless, global health organizations and public health community should encourage countries to develop robust CRVS systems, eliminate corrupted, fragmented and obsolete data, and enhance death certification practice in every aspect. On the other hand, national authorities must recognize the opportunity and approach to the development of comprehensive CRVS systems (especially death certification segments) with utmost responsibility.

METHODS

Research Design

This paper employs a focus group methodology to investigate the research questions. The focus group sessions on the current death certification practice in Slovenia, potential construction of ICT-based solution in the field, and provision of applicable guidelines for its implementation at the national level were conducted in 2014 and 2015. A selection of the research method was adapted to the particularities of the research problem (Patton, 1990; Yin, 2009), given the fact that quantitative empirical research could not yield a satisfactory and credible picture, since the complex field of research is still in an early development stage, and it would be difficult to ensure the representativeness of the research sample. Controlled and structured focus groups were used as the main data collection technique during the entire research process.

Sample

Selection of the focus groups participants was based primarily on their expertise and experience. Participants' good knowledge of structural, organizational, and contextual characteristics of the healthcare system, public health and especially the area of mortality and causes of death was supposed to ensure credibility of their views and facilitate constructive participation in the study. In order to obtain the dependable results, the participants had to meet very high professional standards. A non-random stratified sampling approach was used to ensure a representative sample of the healthcare experts that satisfy the required conditions. The final sample size comprised 29 experts from cross-sectional areas strongly related to public health, different aspects of mortality, determination of causes of death, death certification and health care informatics. Participants, which have been already engaged in the similar undertakings over the past years, were affiliated with different institutions: Institute of Forensic Medicine (2 participants), National Institute of Public Health (7 participants), Ministry of Health (1 participant), Ministry of the Interior (5 participants), coroners form different health care providers (12 participants) and ICT companies (2 participants). The participants were qualified health care professionals (general practitioners and specialists), ICT experts from the health care and private sector (consultants and analysts), health care managers (managers of public health care institutions), experts in public health (analysts and statisticians), and senior government officials.

The number of potential participants has not been previously specified. Quotas of experts in each area were determined after reaching saturation point. The sample was relatively equally distributed in terms of gender, as 45% of the sample was male (13 participants), and 55% was female (16 participants). The participants were aged between 40–60 years. The experts involved in the focus groups are currently occupying the top positions on different levels of the healthcare system and government administration.

Data Collection

Before the actual start of the focus group sessions, some preparatory work in the form of summoning, coordination of appointments and provision of suitable premises was required. The final goals of the focus group sessions were revised with the participants in line with their comments and suggestions, which helped to resolve some conceptual weaknesses and ambiguities. Focus group sessions were conducted in the period from January 2014 to December 2015. The response rate was 100%, namely all invited experts responded to the invitation and ultimately participated in the focus group sessions. Focus group sessions, which lasted approximately 90 to 120 minutes, were held at the premises of National Institute of Public Health. All participants were explained the purpose and objectives of the study in order to clarify the last details and potential uncertainties pertaining to their assignments. All focus group participants were provided anonymity and assured confidentiality of the information obtained. Given the active role of participants in the later stages of the research, special authorization of their responses was not required. Several open-ended and in-depth compound questions were focused on the existing death certification practice in Slovenia and related problems, potential construction of ICT-based solution for death certification, and provision of applicable guidelines for its implementation at the national level. Discussions and responses of the focus group participants were recorded in writing.

Data Analysis

The data obtained through the theoretical and empirical qualitative research, have been analyzed in accordance with the guidelines proposed by the focus group methodological framework. Analysis of the data obtained and their interpretations were carried out using the conventional content analysis, while the platform for ICT-based solution and guidelines for its implementation were derived directly from the focus group discussions and argumentations. Following the execution of the data analysis procedural phases, conceptualization of the ICT-based death certification model was conducted in collaboration with the participating experts, who took a constructive part throughout all phases of the study. After an extensive review of the literature and investigation of primary and secondary online resources, papers, strategies, project reports, and other materials containing death certification-related content, the existing death certification practice was systematically analyzed. In this phase, the research was especially focused on the potential effects of digitalization on the death certification procedures, versatile implications of ICT-based death certification practice on different stakeholders, and organizational performance of the healthcare and administrative organizations. Unresolved issues, existing limitations and potentials, as well as future directions were further analytically discussed within the focus groups. Namely, the role of the participating experts within the proposed research was twofold. First, they had to participate in the analysis of the existing death certification practice, and second, drawing from their own experience and knowledge in the field, they had to provide their vision of the transformation, and propose a conceptual design of the ICT-based death certification model.

SOLUTIONS AND RECOMMENDATIONS

The occurrence of death, although phenomenologically common event in everyday life, generates a very complicated course of action that triggers activities in different governmental and institutional subsystems. Accordingly, death certification and notification concept can be observed and thus analyzed from different legal/administrative, education and training, organizational and informational perspectives, which are often complex and intertwined with each other.

Legal and Administrative Perspective

Legislation that defines procedures in connection with the notification and certification of person's death can be divided into three sets:

- Legislation dealing with the deceased from medical perspective.
- Legislation which refers to administrative procedures.
- Other legislation.
  Education and Training Perspective

Coronary service in Slovenia is exclusively performed by medical doctors. During formal education on medical faculties, the medicine students get familiar with the basics of forensic medicine as a part of a general education and training program. Afterwards, in the course of compulsory residency, the doctors get acquainted with the data collecting procedures concerning the deceased and essentials of death certification, including the coding of causes of death.

Organizational Perspective

All organizational aspects of the post mortem examination service are elaborated and defined in the Rules on the conditions and method for the performance of post mortem examination service (Government of the Republic of Slovenia, 2008). These Rules regulate the responsibilities, organizational structure and functions, duties of coroners, necessary documentation, autopsy and burial, and other technical issues relating to the post mortem examination service. Post mortem examination service performs the following tasks: notification on death and determination of causes of death, investigation on the manner of death, and classification of death (natural death, unnatural or violent death). The municipal health authority keeps a record of all coroners within a designated area, organizes post mortem examination service, and is responsible for its appropriate operation.

Informational Perspective

Existing database on deceased includes verified demographic data of the deceased person and data on all circumstances and causes of death, both physiological and external. Moreover, a special anonymous yearly database is created for the needs of various analyses of data on deceased. It generally provides aggregated or less specific variables. These variables are available to authorized users for the preparation of various statistical data analyses. The collecting of data is a manual process, which has not changed a lot over the years.

Causes of Death Registry (CODR) is additionally supplemented using secondary sources from the Statistical Office of the Republic of Slovenia (SORS). These secondary sources provide mainly socio-economic data (education, profession, working status – active/inactive, retired, etc.). Mortality data is collected from Administrative units, which regularly send in "Notifications on death" including annexed form "Medical death certificate and report on the cause of death". This form is completed in the field by the coroner and used for determining the underlying cause of death. Death certification consists of rather complex and branched sequence of events and is carried out by using paper based forms.

Insight into the current death certification practice including the analysis from various perspectives uncovered significant inconsistencies and shortcomings in different areas:

Legal and Administrative Area

- Non-compliance with the existing legislation in the field (especially the Rules on the conditions and method for the performance of post mortem examination service (Government of the Republic of Slovenia, 2008)
    ◦ Designated forms (Medical report on deceased and Notification on death) are not used in practice.
- Weak political commitment; Ministry of Health has not issued specific authorizations and licenses to the coroners, so any doctor registered in Slovenia can perform post mortem examination service
- Divergence between legislation and practice can be frequently detected
- The existing normative acts do not foresee the possibilities for introduction of the electronic death certification
- Evaluation of the doctors' work in connection with the post mortem examination service is not comprehensively defined

Education and Training Area

- Most doctors perform death certification infrequently, whereas their medical school training may have been forgotten or is out of date.
- Contents of education and training programs for post mortem examination service have not been defined.
- Education and training of the doctors (future coroners) has not been implemented.

Organizational Area

- A network of post mortem examination services has not been established.
- Inconsistent practices (between municipalities, and between municipalities and large medical centers).
- Post mortem examination services outside bigger cities are mainly carried out by family doctors.
- Official post mortem examination services are available only in large medical centers.

Informational Area

- The slow data and information flow between the stakeholders and the absence of fast and effective control of the data entered (paper-based forms)
- Rights of access to information are vaguely defined (unauthorized access, no traceability of logs and views).
- Certain amount of data collected is doubled (different forms – the same data)
- Inaccessibility of data from the medical records of the deceased at the time of death
- Existing death certification practice does not facilitate the systematic management of the related documentation.

The issues revealed are manifested in several limitations of the current death certification practice and have a significant impact on the business model in the field. Death certification system is consequently not optimally organized and structured; including paper-based manual data entries during the process, inadequate legal regulation and non-compliance, unresolved issues concerning the licensing, status and jurisdiction of the coroners, and unsecured and untimely information flows between the main stakeholders.

Conceptualization of ICT-based Model of Death Certification and Applicable Guidelines for Its Implementation at the National Level

Deriving from the research findings, we have been striving for the conceptualization of an ICT-based death certification model. The proposed conceptual solution addresses the identified issues directly through the ICT-based solution for eDeath certification, and indirectly through the promotion of guidelines for the national implementation of eDeath certification, including the regulatory amendments, organizational and educational changes, and business process reengineering. Hence, conceptual proposal for eDeath certification exceeds the current incapacities concerning the data/informational aspect and ensures better speed of data flows, protection of personal data, access to deceased's medical documentation, higher quality and control of data, adequate documentation and archiving of data, unification of national data-bases and registries. The conceptual solution for eDeath certification is based on more transparent data flow; foreseen sequence of events is presented below:

1. Occurrence of death
2. Post mortem examination—certified coroner with professional card/authorization
3. Online notification on death to Central Population Registry (CPR - administrative part of death certification)
4. Access/insight to all medical documentation (electronic health record), consultations with treating/ personal doctor, etc.
5. Decision—autopsy YES/autopsy NO
6. Autopsy NO—recording all necessary diagnoses for "Medical death certificate and report on the cause of death" form
7. "Medical death certificate and report on the cause of death" form "waits" for the confirmation of final identification of the deceased by CPR.
8. After confirmation "Medical death certificate and report on the cause of death" form is handled by the National Institute of Public Health.
9. Autopsy YES—"Medical death certificate and report on the cause of death" form waits for the confirmation of final identification of the deceased by CPR and for autopsy diagnoses.
10. After obtaining autopsy report, the coroner finalizes filling in "Medical death certificate and report on the cause of death" form.
11. Finalized "Medical death certificate and report on the cause of death" form is sent to National Institute of Public Health.

The graphical sketch of the conceptual solution displays the main actions within the eDeath certification process and the main actors including their inherent health care / administrative functions (Figure 3).

Figure 3. Conceptual design of ICT-based model of death certification

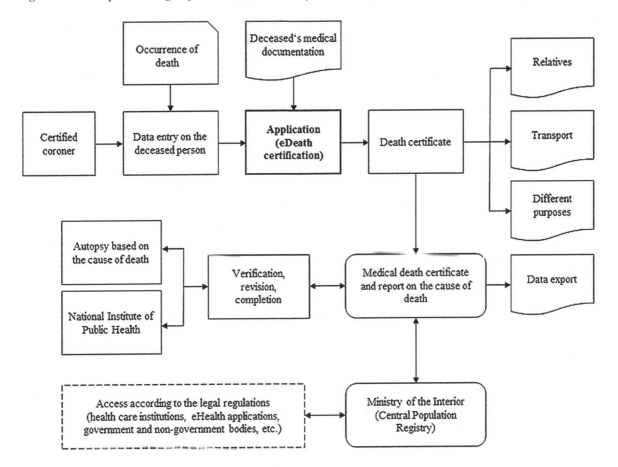

Conceptual solution assumes the redefinition of the functions and relationships of and between the main actors of within the death certification field, and the reconfiguration of the technological, organizational, and regulatory elements according to affirmed public health objectives.

At the same time, the conceptual solution includes and promotes reengineered, optimized and streamlined business processes and considerable organizational changes (certification of coroners, education and training, network of coronary services, etc.), dependent on the preliminary amendments of the regulatory and administrative provisions. The proposed solution assumes the complete transformation of the existing business model, including the translation of existing paper based forms into the web-based application. Use of the web-based application for electronic death certification presumes that all transactions of the certified coroners will be signed with a qualified digital certificate, thus providing a higher level of data protection throughout the entire process of data transmission. In the first phase, while establishing the identification of the deceased, the process of data transmission will be unified, in the later phases the process of data transmission will bifurcate into two distinctive parts, namely health care part and administrative part. This functionality will prevent unauthorized access of administrative workers to personal health data and provide opportunities to health professionals to complement the data on the deceased based on the final conclusions and lab results.

The presented ICT-based solution for eDeath certification has already been developed, whereas the referred systemic measures and institutional actions are still in the initial stage. Currently, talks are under way with major decision-makers and other stakeholders to support the preparation of the national guidelines in the field, and promote gradual introduction of eDeath certification. The final solution for eDeath certification presumes the unification of death certification practice outside and inside the health care institutions.

The entire process, from concept to product, was based on user-centered design principles, including active involvement of participating experts at each stage of the system analysis, planning, conceptual design and testing, which were conducted in iterative manner. This collaborative approach facilitated the initial identification and later consideration of actual user needs, requirements and expectations at all levels; namely data, operational, security and ergonomic level. Despite certain system limitations and implementation concerns, particularly related to regulation, funding, organization and human resources, the solution for eDeath certification has proven to be of significant benefit for all involved parties, offering a well-designed and practical solution to all end users regardless of their tasks, roles or working environment. Accordingly, in the future, optimized and preferably personalized solutions should provide more control, necessary operational flexibility, better access to the required data, and faster data transfers to all stakeholders in the system.

Obviously, prior to potential national implementation of eDeath certification political and professional consensus on the national level would have to be reached regarding the several open issues stressed in the text above, especially amendments of regulatory and administrative provisions, professionalization and certification of coronary service and related expenses.

It is evident that successful development and implementation of eDeath certification depends on various factors, which were clearly revealed throughout this study. In order to provide a starting platform for further efforts concerning the establishment of quality and efficient eDeath certification systems, we present a set of applicable guidelines, which would expectantly alleviate the problems revealed by this research. The guidelines are mainly based on the synthesis of the research results, derived deductions from the focus group discussions, and general recommendations of the WHO (WHO, 2013):

- Ensure political support from the highest level
  - Bring together stakeholders from the health care and public administrative system, and the vendor from the private sector
  - Ensure the necessary funds, human and other resources
  - Prepare credible and viable strategy documents, feasibility studies and action plans (define all parameters of the eDeath certification project and set measurable objectives, align project objectives with healthcare and administrative system objectives, analyze the different informational needs of the stakeholders, define appropriate medical, administrative and financial indicators for management needs, check the financial parameters and financial projections related to the eDeath certification budget in the medium and long term, examine potential obstacles for the realization of the project, assess risks and conduct a sensitivity analysis, etc.)
  - Promote international collaboration and provide evidence-based projections for the development of eDeath certification in future

- Mobilize all stakeholders to ensure commitment, material and moral support, encourage their active participation and constructive criticism
  - Promote collaboration between policymakers, healthcare professionals, government officials, ICT professionals
  - Provide an inclusive plan for communication within the project team and between the project team and all stakeholders
- Promote legislative amendments and adopt necessary regulations concerning the implementation of eDeath certification (personal data protection, authorization and licensing of coroners, training and education, liability and risk issues, data storage and security, professional ethics, terms of use, electronic signature, record keeping, transfer of data and lab results for medical purposes, maintenance of the system and recovery of data, responsibilities and financing, etc.)
  - Establish collaborative mechanisms between the Ministry of Health, national statistics office and local registrars to ensure the collection of better-quality data, harmonize national legislation with international standards, recommendations and resolutions (international cooperation, bilateral and multilateral agreements, healthcare and Administrative service and health insurance issues, transfer of medical data to other countries, etc.)
- Provide a review of medical records and death certificates, and assess the current quality of death certification
  - Examine the current and projected health care issues, incorporate country specificities, define nature and coverage of services and projected results, and provide an action plan clearly specifying how eDeath certification will contribute to the addressing of national healthcare priorities, as well as enabling the desired reorganization, business process reengineering and restructuring of the healthcare system itself
- Establish a robust evaluation framework for eDeath certification, including the motivations and objectives of evaluation, benchmark and evaluation metrics, qualitative and quantitative data, define and specify strategic and operative measures
- Select a top manager and a quality project team with experience in complex ICT projects, form a steering committee including diverse experts
  - Assess risk and define change management issues, clearly structure the project plan, project phases, budgets and deliverables for each phase, determine the objectives and timeline of the project by reaching mutual consensus with all stakeholders, distribute assignments and strictly monitor and inspect work on the project
- Ensure adequate resources before the start of each phase of the project and make realistic plans in both temporal and financial terms, define milestones, analyze capital and operating costs
- Perform constant supervision and strict control of already executed project tasks with respect to substantive and temporal objectives, and ensure close monitoring of tasks, which are in the execution phase
- Improve or build a comprehensive ICT infrastructure (assess the current ICT infrastructure, departmental IS, legacy IS, interoperability issues, broadband connections, operating system, technical solutions, interoperability platform, network protocols, data standards)
  - Provide the blueprint for future enterprise architecture (business, application and technology layers), encourage the transfer of good practice (case studies, international experience, consultancy, etc.), specify and adopt standard technical and medical protocols, deploy intended eDeath certification components and technical solutions

      ○   Ensure testing, optimization and technology watch, ensure quality maintenance of the system and focus on innovations and development
- Test the applicability of eDeath certification components in pilot projects and gradually implement individual ICT solutions in healthcare institutions
  - Promote the application of eDeath certification (assure contingency plan)
  - Organize education and training and consequent authorization and licensing of coroners, issue standard practice guidelines on death certification to the coroners, (including the training in death certification according to the rules and procedures of the ICD, the training in ICD mortality coding according to the rules and regulations of ICD-10, the training in verbal autopsy techniques)
  - Facilitate internal and external communication and collaboration, provide service standardization and align business processes with medical protocols, organize a new business model and ensure openness for user opinions, ideas and criticism, provide a reasonable transition period, arrange for early detection and problem-solving
- Inform stakeholders promptly and report about all developments
  - Promote project achievements so far in order to improve and expedite acceptance of eDeath certification between the stakeholders, facilitate comprehensive methodological explanations, user manual and helpdesk, gain support from the media, experts and citizens

The listed guidelines depend on several success factors and cannot be easily transferred into practice. They basically provide a multitude of necessary activities, some of which can be carried out simultaneously, while others have to be performed in chronological order. All these cooperative activities must be combined into functional and well-coordinated action, which is essentially the most challenging task of the project management team.

FUTURE RESEARCH DIRECTIONS

Not surprisingly, increasing the proportion of medically certified deaths and raising the share of digitally certified deaths based on the causes of death are one of the most important challenges for health information systems worldwide. Many national evaluations of health information systems have found significant flaws in the generation of mortality statistics. Accordingly, the analysis of the strengths and weaknesses of the national health information systems in individual countries recognized the consolidation of death certification systems and cause-of-death statistics as a priority government action (Tangcharoensathien et al., 2006). Generally, initiatives are directed towards accelerated development of ICT solutions to assure more effective death certification procedures and facilitate more reliable, timely and complete cause-of-death data. Discussions in the field are therefore often focused on the scope of national capacity building and the use of innovative ICT. Several initiatives have been underway to harness the potential of ICT, and though the success has varied, there is a wealth of lessons learned and significant body of knowledge to lead the establishment of effective and well-functioning death certification systems. The construction of infrastructure, reengineering of business processes, adoption of data standards, integration of registers and databases, sourcing and budgeting, and interoperability in every aspect, should be prioritized. The introduction of ICT solutions should be supported and promoted by the simultaneous structural and organizational changes needed for integration of eDeath certification systems and data sharing across state administration bodies and existing health ICT solutions.

Reduction in prices of ICT equipment in recent years has accelerated the introduction of ICT solutions for CRVS systems in many countries. Recent advances in ICT, including mobile phones and other hand-held devices capable of data collection such as laptop computers, tablets and personal digital assistants are revolutionizing the way in which data are collected, especially in remote areas (WHO, 2013). Besides expediting the compilation and enhancing availability of health care data and consequently vital statistics, ICT facilitates collection, storage, transfer, manipulation, and analysis of the data using specialized software. Obviously, the use of electronic records will not entail changes in the data quality as such; however, it could streamline the control processes and help detecting irregularities in large datasets (Becker et al., 2006). Such advancement has been made in countries, which have been investing substantially in the health care ICT in the recent period. Yet, some developing countries are still facing the difficulties with the infrastructure and the lack of computers at the local level, where events initially occur, which significantly complicates the transfer of data to the designated point. One important advantage of electronic records is that they permit cross-matching and linking, (CDC, 2008; WHO, 2013), thus preventing time-consuming and strenuous manual work. However, all ICT initiatives in such a sensitive area should be regulated by clear policies and procedures, and particularly record linkage has to be very carefully managed, especially in terms of optimizing its use, and defining roles and responsibilities in areas such as managing access, ensuring confidentiality and data application (Australian Government, 2010). On the other hand, some concerns regarding safety and confidentiality of data have been highlighted, as well as the potential ambiguities related to long-term archiving and data retrieval due to rapid development of new computer hardware and software.

The use of ICT solutions has manifestly provided considerable benefits in data transfer, with internet and wireless technologies significantly shortening the time needed to transfer the data and conduct a required analysis, which was successfully confirmed in several international projects. One high-profile project, which has recently attracted a lot of international attention in the field is the IRIS project. IRIS is an automatic system for coding multiple causes of death and for the selection of the underlying causes of death. The aim of IRIS is twofold (German institute of medical documentation and information, 2016):

1. To provide a system in which the language-dependent aspects are separated from the software itself. Moreover, the language-dependent parts are stored in database tables and can easily be modified.
2. To improve international comparability. IRIS is based on the international death certificate form provided by WHO and the causes of death are coded according to the ICD-10 rules. Updates to ICD-10 are included according to the WHO-timelines.

The system can be used in two modes, namely in the code entry mode and in the text entry mode. Following the interactive actions, when the user enters ICD-10 codes corresponding to the conditions reported on the death certificates, or when the user enters the causes of death in free text, as they are reported on the death certificate, the IRIS tool selects the underlying cause of death. IRIS has been designed and developed as a collaborative project of several countries including France, Germany, Hungary, Italy, Spain, Sweden and USA. A joint initiative of these countries, which represents a good example of international cooperation in the field, has probably set the general example and could demarcate the future development of this kind of web-based solutions for certification of death including the qualified determination of the causes of death.

In order to provide the well-organized and efficient death certification practice in the country, the normative framework as well as commitment and collaboration of all stakeholders is evidently crucial. Appropriate legal framework, qualified health care professionals, technological infrastructure, stable health care environment, public administration and judiciary system, are obviously necessary, but not sufficient conditions for the establishment of comprehensive, effective and reliable national death certification scheme.

CONCLUSION

The pervasive penetration of ICT solutions into clinical and business processes in the last years has raised a number of questions about the adequacy of existing practices in the health care environment. The death certification system in Slovenia has remained somewhat unchanged over the last decades. Analysis of the current arrangements revealed a number of organizational, process and regulatory deficiencies and indicated risks related to the quality and protection of personal data. Research evidence uncovered that digitalization of the current death certification model in Slovenia could have a positive effect on the integration of processes, coordination between the main actors and overall performance of data exchange between the main actors. The actual success of ICTs as being a facilitator of innovation and development in the death certification field largely depends on the quality of ICT management at the national level and the effective integration of ICTs with business processes in the health care ecosystem.

The research presented does not seek to impose a 'one-size-fits-all' solution for the myriad of problems related to development, implementation and utilization of eDeath certification model. However, it could provide a valuable platform for the analysis of the existing death certification practice: in particular, the identification of critical success factors. The findings obtained could help pin-point necessary modifications and indicate appropriate measures for the transformation of existing death certification model, which is materially and technologically outdated and does not meet the needs of the health care system, or general public.

Results and guidelines from this study could be used as starting points for gradual integration and digitalization of the death certification model and more effective leveraging of ICT in the associated health care and administrative processes. Although reasonably susceptible to different interpretations, the presented study provides valuable insight into the existing death certification practice in Slovenia and may provide the groundwork for further developments in this area. Successful transformation of the death certification model evidently requires government impetus, the mobilization of all stakeholders, and their maximum consensus on the various and often conflicting issues within the death certification field. Notwithstanding these difficulties, transformation of the death certification model in Slovenia, and possibly elsewhere, certainly represents a developmental opportunity which can, subject to proficient coordination with other ecosystem factors and pending structural reforms, ensure better utilization of public health resources and provide tangible public health benefits.

The project e-Certification of Causes of Death was funded by the European Commission - Eurostat, under the Grant Agreement Number 07154.2013.002-2013.629.

REFERENCES

AbouZahr, C., Cleland, J., Coullare, F., Macfarlane, S. B., Notzon, F. C., Setel, P., & Zhang, S. et al. (2007). The way forward. *Lancet, 370*(9601), 1791–1799. doi:10.1016/S0140-6736(07)61310-5 PMID:18029003

AbouZahr, C., Mikkelsen, L., Rampatige, R., & Lopez, A. (2012). Mortality statistics: A tool to enhance understanding and improve quality. *Pacific Health Dialog, 18*(1), 247–270. PMID:23240364

Ali, N. M. A., & Hamadeh, R. R. (2013). Improving the Accuracy of Death Certification among Secondary Care Physicians. *Bahrain Medical Bulletin, 35*(2), 1–6.

Australian Government. (2010). High Level Principles for Data Integration Involving Commonwealth Data for Statistical and Research Purposes. Canberra, AUS: Australian Government.

Becker, R., Silvi, J., Ma Fat, D., L'Hours, A., & Laurenti, R. (2006). A method for deriving leading causes of death. *Bulletin of the World Health Organization, 84*(4), 297–304. PMID:16628303

Brooks, E. G., & Reed, K. D. (2015). Principles and Pitfalls: A Guide to Death Certification. *Clinical Medicine & Research, 13*(2), 74–82. doi:10.3121/cmr.2015.1276 PMID:26185270

Burger, E. H., Groenewald, P., Rossouw, A., & Bradshaw, D. (2015). Medical certification of death in South Africa-moving forward. *SAMJ: South African Medical Journal, 105*(1), 27–30. doi:10.7196/SAMJ.8578 PMID:26046158

Centers for Disease Control and Prevention – CDC. (2007). *Core curriculum for certifiers of underlying cause of death*. Atlanta, GA: Centers for Disease Control and Prevention.

Centers for Disease Control and Prevention – CDC. (2008). Electronic Record Linkage to Identify Deaths among Persons with AIDS - District of Columbia, 2000–2005. *Morbidity and Mortality Weekly Report, 57*(23), 631–634. PMID:18551099

Cohen, J., Bilsen, J., Miccinesi, G., Löfmark, R., Addington-Hall, J., Kaasa, S., & Deliens, L. et al. (2007). Using death certificate data to study place of death in 9 European countries: Opportunities and weaknesses. *BMC Public Health, 7*(1), 283–283. doi:10.1186/1471-2458-7-283 PMID:17922894

Crowcroft, N., & Majeed, A. (2001). Improving the certification of death and the usefulness of routine mortality statistics. *Clinical Medicine, 1*(2), 122–125. doi:10.7861/clinmedicine.1-2-122 PMID:11333456

DAmico, M., Agozzino, E., Biagino, A., Simonetti, A., & Marinelli, P. (1999). Ill -defined and multiple causes on death certificates – A study of misclassification in mortality statistics. *European Journal of Epidemiology, 15*(2), 141–148. doi:10.1023/A:1007570405888 PMID:10204643

Dash, S. K., Behera, B. K., & Patro, S. (2014). Accuracy in certification of cause of death in a tertiary care hospital – A retrospective analysis. *Journal of Forensic and Legal Medicine, 24*, 33–36. doi:10.1016/j.jflm.2014.03.006 PMID:24794848

European Commission – EC. (2001). *Quality and comparability improvement of European causes of death statistics.*

European Commission – EC. (2013). Report of the Task Force on Satellite Lists for Causes of Deaths (COD). Eurostat.

Flanders, W. D. (1992). Inaccuracies of Death Certificate Information. *Epidemiology (Cambridge, Mass.)*, *3*(1), 3–5. doi:10.1097/00001648-199201000-00002 PMID:1554807

German institute of medical documentation and information (2016). *About IRIS*. Retrieved from https://www.dimdi.de/static/en/klassi/irisinstitute/

Glasser, J. H. (1981). The quality and utility of death certificate data. *American Journal of Public Health*, *71*(3), 231–233. doi:10.2105/AJPH.71.3.231 PMID:7468853

Government of the Republic of Slovenia. (2008). *Rules on the conditions and method for the performance of post mortem examination service (OG RS 56/93 and 15/2008)*. Ljubljana, SI: Ministry of Health.

Hill, M. E., & Rosenwaike, I. (2001). Social Security Administration's Death Master File: The Completeness of Death Reporting at Older Ages. *Social Security Bulletin*, *64*(1), 45–62. PMID:12428517

Horton, R. (2007). Counting for health. *Lancet*, *370*(9598), 1526–1526. doi:10.1016/S0140-6736(07)61418-4 PMID:17992726

Huy, T. Q., Long, N. H., Hoa, D. P., Byass, P., & Eriksson, B. (2003). Validity and completeness of death reporting and registration in a rural district of Vietnam. *Scandinavian Journal of Public Health*, *31*(6), 12–18. doi:10.1080/14034950310015059 PMID:14640146

Jain, K., Bala, D. V., Trivedi, K., & Chandwani, H. (2015). Situational analysis of Medical Certification of Cause of Death (MCCD) scheme in Municipal Corporation of Ahmedabad. *Indian Journal of Forensic and Community Medicine*, *2*(2), 95–99.

Joubert, J., Bradshaw, D., Kabudula, C., Rao, C., Kahn, K., Mee, P., & Vos, T. et al. (2014). Record-linkage comparison of verbal autopsy and routine civil registration death certification in rural north-east South Africa: 2006–09. *International Journal of Epidemiology*, *43*(6), 1945–1958. doi:10.1093/ije/dyu156 PMID:25146564

Jougla, E., Pavillon, G., Rossollin, F., De Smedt, M., & Bonte, J. (1998). Improvement of the quality and comparability of causes-of-death statistics inside the European Community. *Revue d'Epidemiologie et de Sante Publique*, *46*(6), 447–456. PMID:9950045

Jougla, E., Rossolin, F., Niyosenga, A., Chappert, J., Johansson, L., & Pavillon, G. (2001). Comparability and quality improvement in European causes of death statistics. Eurostat.

Lefeuvre, D., Pavillon, G., Aouba, A., Lamarche-Vadel, A., Fouillet, A., Jougla, E., & Rey, G. (2014). Quality comparison of electronic versus paper death certificates in France, 2010. *Population Health Metrics*, *12*(1), 1–9. doi:10.1186/1478-7954-12-3 PMID:24533639

Lu, T. H. (2003). Using ACME (Automatic Classification of Medical Entry) software to monitor and improve the quality of cause of death statistics. *Journal of Epidemiology and Community Health*, *5*(6), 470–471. doi:10.1136/jech.57.6.470 PMID:12775799

Lu, T. H., Lee, M. C., & Chou, M. C. (2000). Accuracy of cause-of-death coding in Taiwan: Types of miscoding and effects on mortality statistics. *International Journal of Epidemiology, 29*(2), 336–343. doi:10.1093/ije/29.2.336 PMID:10817134

Mahapatra, P., Shibuya, K., Lopez, A. D., Coullare, F., Notzon, F. C., Rao, C., & Szreter, S. (2007). Civil registration systems and vital statistics: Successes and missed opportunities. *Lancet, 370*(9599), 1653–1663. doi:10.1016/S0140-6736(07)61308-7 PMID:18029006

Mathers, C. D., Ma Fat, D., Inoue, M., Rao, C., & Lopez, A. D. (2005). Counting the dead and what they died from: An assessment of the global status of cause of death data. *Bulletin of the World Health Organization, 83*(3), 171–177. PMID:15798840

Maudsley, G., & Williams, L. (1994). Death certification—a sad state of affairs. *Journal of Public Health, 16*(3), 370–371. PMID:7999397

Myers, K. A., & Farquhar, D. R. (1998). Improving the accuracy of death certification. *Canadian Medical Association Journal, 158*(10), 1317–1323. PMID:9614825

Nojilana, B., Brewer, L., Bradshaw, D., Groenewald, P., Burger, E. H., & Levitt, N. S. (2013). Certification of diabetes-related mortality: The need for an international guideline. *Journal of Clinical Epidemiology, 66*(2), 236–237. doi:10.1016/j.jclinepi.2012.07.017 PMID:23159105

Patton, M. (1990). *Qualitative evaluation and research methods.* Thousand Oaks, CA: Sage Publications.

Rahimi, K., Duncan, M., Pitcher, A., Emdin, C. A., & Goldacre, M. J. (2015). Mortality from heart failure, acute myocardial infarction and other ischaemic heart disease in England and Oxford: A trend study of multiple-cause-coded death certification. *Journal of Epidemiology and Community Health, 69*(10), 1000–1005. doi:10.1136/jech-2015-205689 PMID:26136081

Rodriguez, S. R., Mallonee, S., Archer, P., & Gofton, J. (2006). Evaluation of death certificate based surveillance for traumatic brain injury – Oklahoma 2002. *Public Health Reports, 121*(3), 282–289. PMID:16640151

Rose, R. F., Boon, A., Forman, D., Merchant, W., Bishop, R., & Newton-Bishop, J. A. (2013). An exploration of reported mortality from cutaneous squamous cell carcinoma using death certification and cancer registry data. *The British Journal of Dermatology, 169*(3), 682–686. doi:10.1111/bjd.12388 PMID:23600487

Setel, P. W., Macfarlane, S. B., Szreter, S., Mikkelsen, L., Jha, P., Stout, S., & Anderson, R. N. et al. (2007). A scandal of invisibility: Making everyone count by counting everyone. *Lancet, 370*(9598), 1569–1577. doi:10.1016/S0140-6736(07)61307-5 PMID:17992727

Sibai, A. M. (2004). Mortality certification and cause-of-death reporting in developing countries. *Bulletin of the World Health Organization, 82*(2), 83–83. PMID:15042227

Sibai, A. M., Nuwayhid, I., Beydoun, M., & Chaaya, M. (2002). Inadequacies of death certification in Beirut, Lebanon: Who is responsible? *Bulletin of the World Health Organization, 80*(7), 555–561. PMID:12163919

Sim, F., & McKee, M. (2011). *Issues in Public Health* (2nd ed.). Oxford, GB: Open University Press.

Stanimirovic, D. (2015). A Framework for Information and Communication Technology Induced Transformation of the Healthcare Business Model in Slovenia. *Journal of Global Information Technology Management, 18*(1), 29–47. doi:10.1080/1097198X.2015.1015826

Swift, B., & West, K. (2002). Death certification: An audit of practice entering the 21st century. *Journal of Clinical Pathology, 55*(4), 275–279. doi:10.1136/jcp.55.4.275 PMID:11919211

Tangcharoensathien, V., Faramnuayphol, P., Teokul, W., Bundhamcharoen, K., & Wibulpholprasert, S. (2006). A critical assessment of mortality statistics in Thailand: Potential for improvements. *Bulletin of the World Health Organization, 84*(3), 233–238. doi:10.2471/BLT.05.026310 PMID:16583083

United Nations – UN. (2001). *Principles and Recommendations for a Vital Statistics System (Revision 2). Department of Economic and Social Affairs Statistics Division.* New York, NY: United Nations.

Wall, M., Huang, J., Oswald, J., & McCullen, D. (2005). Factors associated with reporting multiple causes of Death. *BMC Medical Research Methodology, 5*(1), 1–4. doi:10.1186/1471-2288-5-4 PMID:15655070

World Health Organization – WHO. (1992). *International Statistical Classification of Diseases and Related Health Problems – ICD, 10th Revision.* Geneva, CH: World Health Organization.

World Health Organization – WHO. (2004). *International Classification of Diseases (ICD).* Geneva, CH: World Health Organization.

World Health Organization – WHO. (2010). *Improving the quality and use of birth, death and cause-of-death information: guidance for a standards-based review of country practices.* Geneva, CH: World Health Organization.

World Health Organization – WHO. (2012). *Strengthening civil registration and vital statistics for births, deaths and causes of death. Resource Kit.* Geneva, CH: World Health Organization.

World Health Organization – WHO. (2013). *Strengthening civil registration and vital statistics for births, deaths and causes of death. Resource Kit.* Geneva, CH: World Health Organization.

World Health Organization – WHO. (2014, June 16–17). Covering every birth and death: Improving civil registration and vital statistics (CRVS). Report of the technical discussions. Geneva, CH: World Health Organization.

Yin, R. (2009). *Case study research: design and methods (4thed.).* Thousand Oaks, CA: Sage Publications.

KEY TERMS AND DEFINITIONS

Cause of Death: An established term for the officially determined conditions and circumstances resulting in a human's death.

Coroner: Qualified person who certifies and confirms the occurrence of death. A coroner fills out the medical death certificate and report on the cause of death.

eHealth: A comprehensive mechanism based on the internet and other related ICTs, expected to facilitate integration of all stakeholders and evidence-based decision making at all levels, in order to improve quality of health care, administrative and managerial processes as well as related outcomes in the health care system.

ICD: International Statistical Classification of Diseases and Related Health Problems (ICD) is a list developed by the WHO. It contains codes for diseases, signs and symptoms, abnormal findings, complaints, social circumstances, and external causes of injury or diseases.

Medical Death Certificate and Report on The Cause of Death: Form, which is filled out by the coroner (doctor). It constitutes a source for the determination of the underlying causes of death and pertinent circumstances (external causes and mechanisms of death).

Mortality: Also referred to as "death rate", is a measure for the number of deaths in a certain population. It is normally measured in the number of deaths per 1,000 individuals per year.

Vital Statistics: Basic statistics on births, deaths, marriages and divorces in the country, usually collected through civil registration.

Chapter 3
E–Government adoption in Nigeria and the Journey So Far:
The End of Corruption?

Sola Oni
Pan Atlantic University, Nigeria

ABSTRACT

E-government is an emerging field of research that has generated considerable interest recently. This research examines contributions from e-government as a means of providing solutions to developmental challenges that have been linked to corruption and a lack of transparency. Although the government has embarked upon a number of e-government initiatives, Nigeria ranks low in the area of e-government provision to its citizens. Initial findings show that the focus of existing studies have been on the supply side with little research focusing on the demand side. Initial findings also indicate that the e-government initiatives that have been implemented have little to no effect on increasing transparency and decreasing corruption. A framework for the evaluation of current e-government provision with a view to combating corruption is proposed. This will incorporate the users' perspectives into further development of e-government initiatives. The resulting framework will be applied to verify the contributions of e-government towards resolving some of the challenges facing the populace.

INTRODUCTION

Nigeria is currently faced with a number of challenges. Falling oil prices, high rates of inflation, a weakening currency and attacks from extremist groups in the north-eastern and southern regions of the country are just a few of the challenges plaguing the current regime and the citizens. More than at any point in the country's history, there is a need for reassurance that the government is quite capable of handling these challenges and coming out on the other side. One way of achieving this is by ensuring that better services are provided to citizens and businesses through electronic government. This also ensures that the government is close to its citizens and may as a result inspire confidence.

DOI: 10.4018/978-1-5225-1944-7.ch003

Electronic government and electronic governance are terms that have been used interchangeably in existing literature and are arguably close in meaning. For the purpose of this research however, the terms are defined as follows. Electronic Government has been described as the use of ICT by Government agencies in order to better manage relationships with citizens, business and other arms of Government (Silcock, 2001), while Electronic Governance is the application of technology by government to transform itself and its interactions with customers, in order to create an impact on the society (Estevez & Janowski, 2013). The benefits of e-government for citizens have been widely published. They include, saving time and money (Gilbert, Balestrini & Littleboy, 2004), bringing government closer to people (Veljković, Bogdanović-Dinić & Stoimenov, 2012). It has also been used to improve transparency in the government sector and to combat corruption (Kim, Kim & Lee, 2009). Furthermore, it can be used to simplify bureaucratic procedures or even eliminate them altogether (Silvia & Adela, 2014). Although several countries have been enjoying the benefits of e-government, the phenomenon can be said to be in its infancy in Nigeria. Admittedly, there are barriers to its adoption including, trust, financial security, information quality (Gilbert, Balestrini & Littleboy, 2004). However, on balance, the benefits so far, outweigh the risks for countries that have fully adopted the phenomenon.

Nigeria is a country of approximately 182,202,000 million people (World Bank, 2015) who speak over 500 languages (Gordon, 2005). Over the years, factions have developed, corruption has been rife and there is a deep distrust of government (Friedman, 2006; Obadare, 2005) indicating even more of a need to bring government closer to the populace. E-government is an avenue that makes this possible. The government can have a chance of regaining the people's trust by providing services electronically and a platform for information exchange between citizens and the government agencies.

Although the subject matter of e-government has appeared as an area of concern in a number of government initiatives, Nigeria ranks low in the area of e-government provision to its citizens. This is in spite of the fact that the country has the fastest growing and most lucrative telecommunications, and Information and Communications Technology (ICT) market in Africa (Adeyemo, 2011). In terms of e-government provision, Nigeria is currently ranked in the 141st position, out of 193 member states (United Nations, 2014). Furthermore, data that could be useful in ensuring the success of e-governance is not widely available within this area. For example, the north-eastern region of Nigeria has been plagued by violence in the wake of attacks from terrorists, which has led to millions being displaced from their homes. However, there is scant data from this region regarding casualties and displaced people. This is a general problem within the country and the continent. In 2014 more than 50 per cent of the countries in the world regions, except for Africa, provided some data pertaining to disadvantaged and vulnerable groups (United Nations, 2014) indicating limited transparency.

The success of e-government deployment among developed countries has been well detailed in existing literature. Themes of e-government research in developed countries are more specific and focused. This is indicated by several focused themes such as trust, information quality, data privacy, personal identity, and intelligent information (Wahid, 2013). There is however limited research as far as the phenomenon is concerned among developing countries. Wahid (2013) mapped the themes of e-e-government research in developing countries published between 2005 and 2010 and listed the following themes as the main focus of research on e-government in developing countries. These include design/implementation, adoption, impact, evaluation and context. In Africa, there is scant documentation of how effective e-government initiatives have been (Rorissa & Demissie, 2010). In addition, there is little or no evidence to suggest that a clear framework for the adoption of e-government is being followed in Nigeria (Mundy &Musa,

2010; Olatokun & Adebayo, 2012). Furthermore, there is scant research on the user experience of e-government in the country (Okunola, 2015).

This research therefore aims to propose a framework that may help to evaluate the adoption of e-government in the country and to examine its possible contribution to the resolution of some of the worst problems facing the citizens. This paper is structured as follows. Section 2 provides a background to this study and reviews studies of e-government, particularly examining issues of transparency, trust and corruption. Section 3 provides an overview of the theoretical underpinning, while Section 4 discusses the proposed framework and finally, section 5 provides a conclusion, limitations and further research directions.

BACKGROUND

Although Beynon-Davies (2005) stated that it is difficult to establish the specific benefits derived from e-government, there are many benefits of e-government that have been discussed in existing literature. These include saving time and money, bringing government closer to the people and improving transparency and trust. E-government can help to collect of information that will enable decision makers to serve citizens more effectively. It can allow government agencies to centralize decision making and purchasing to reduce costs (Evans & Yen, 2006). For developing countries however, the possible benefits of e-government cannot be overstated. They include quick access to government services, lower costs for administrative services, increased public access to budgets and documents and consequently, increase in the transparency and accountability of government activities (Basu, 2004).

Despite these benefits, there are barriers. Lack of awareness is one of such barriers, which makes it a necessity for governments to market online services that they offer to citizens (Reddick, 2005). Barriers to e-government in Nigeria as identified by Ifinedo (2006) include institutional problems, human capital problems and infrastructural problems. The term institutional problem is explained to include organisational problems, attitudinal problems and cultural problems. Human capital problems cover poverty, low literacy levels and poor information technology skills. Finally, infrastructural problems cover poor internet access, high cost of ICT services, and poor power generation. The author goes on to highlight some positive plans and developments in Nigeria to aid the development e-government such as the development of a national IT policy, liberalisation of telecommunications sector, and IT awareness campaigns indicating a roadmap towards the improvement of e-government services in the country (Ifinedo, 2006; Ifinedo, 2007).More recently, threats to the implementation of e-government services in Nigeria have been identified to include fraud, lack of IT experts, lack of policy regulating IT, illiteracy, poor power supply, cost of IT equipment, the lack of a maintenance culture, poor remuneration of IT staff and an organisational culture that resists change (Azeez et al, 2012).

Admittedly, some of the concerns raised remain valid, but there are also some noticeable improvements particularly in the provision of internet access. This is an area which is still developing, albeit slowly. The country has a current plan for deploying broadband for a number of reasons, one of which is to leverage broadband infrastructure for good governance. The objectives of e-government as listed in the Nigerian national broadband plan of the (Federal Ministry of communication, 2013) include:

- Streamlining and standardizing of institutional processes;
- Reducing the hassle for citizens to access government services;

- Optimizing content and speed of service delivery chain by all tiers of government;
- Encouraging wholesome recording and dissemination of information and knowledge.

The government has commendable plans for broadband and its use for good governance. However, there is a gap between those plans and the reality so far. Firstly, according to Tayo, Thompson and Thompson (2016), although Nigeria has made huge strides during the past decade with the adoption of mobile communication using smart phones and other smart mobile devices, broadband Internet penetration has grown at a slower pace particularly in the rural areas. The authors also emphasise the fact that the cost of accessing the internet is out of the reach of many Nigerians. In addition, as reported by Omiere and Omeire (2014), many government ministries and departments now have websites which are simply used as information boards which are rarely updated, public figures now use social media platforms such as Facebook and twitter to communicate with citizens. Further e-government applications include Police dairy, which is a public radiophone in program where citizens can communicate with and make complaints to the police. Others include the provision of e-passport, Voters registration, tax payment, land registration and e-payment. Even though these possibilities exist, the question remains, are the users experiencing these benefits that the government has planned with the infrastructure behind and the provision of e-governance? Unfortunately, there cannot be a positive response to that question with the current situation. This is because low bandwidth and internet penetration, inadequate ICT infrastructure and technicians, incessant power outages and technological obsolescence remain obstacles between users and access to e-government (Asogwa, 2013). At the moment, majority of the citizens may have access to internet able devices, but access to the internet remains out of the reach of many Nigerians as a result of high connectivity costs (Tayo, Thompson & Thompson, 2016).

Generally, the provision of e-government services on the supply-side is increasing but improvements are needed on the demand-side. Mundy and Musa (2010) argue that governments are proceeding with the implementation of e-government initiatives without getting the views of the citizens. They also argue that not responding to citizens needs in the adoption and provision of e-government services is common to both developed and developing countries alike. The focus of e-government research so far has been on the provision of the service with a particular emphasis on the supply side. However, to maximise the impact of investments in e-government by various governments, it would be necessary to increase the uptake of the phenomenon (UN, 2014).Considering the fact that an estimated 15% of e-government projects in developing and transitional countries are adjudged to be successful with the remaining 85% being either total failures or considered as partial failures (Heeks, 2002), this research argues that the demand side matters and will focus on the user experience in terms of the issues identified in the previous section such as transparency, corruption and an improvement to the lives of citizens.

Corruption and Transparency

Corruption means the misuse of public office for private gain (Treisman, 2000). Corruption favours a particular class of people and creates inequality in opportunities (Mo, 2001) and has been blamed for the failures of some particular developing countries to develop (Treisman, 2000). While transparency means knowing the reasons, facts, logics and basis of the decision taken by the public administrations (Casalino, Buonocore, Rossignoli, & Ricciardi, 2013).

It has been well reported that corruption is a huge problem in many developing countries that are rich in natural resources (Kaufman & Bellver, 2005). Additionally, it is worth bearing in mind that a lack of transparency in the functioning of the government agencies can make it easy for perpetrators of corruption to cover their tracks and unearthing corruption becomes very difficult (Bhatnagar, 2003). Corruption can also stifle competition while transparency can stimulate it (Boehm & Olaya, 2006). Furthermore, transparency has been viewed as a key factor in reducing corruption and other dysfunctions in natural resource-rich countries (Kolstaad and Wiig, 2009).

While corruption levels may vary around the different countries in the world, transparency remains a core concern and some countries have tried to address the issue with adequate provision of transparency as part of e-government projects. However, other countries have implemented e-government services without necessarily providing more transparency. It may be argued that e-government does not have to involve transparency but it is worth bearing in mind that extant studies agree that e-government is supposed to bring government closer to the people by providing transparency and accountability (Basu, 2004). Additionally, transparency lends legitimacy to governmental actions (International Telecommunications Union (ITU), 2002) and when a higher level of transparency is involved in decision making, it increases the probability that corruption or wrongdoing will be uncovered (Bac, 2001). Furthermore, In democratic societies, access to information and transparency can also be considered as a human right (Kauffman & Bellver, 2005).

Similarly, even some non-democratic countries recognise the pertinence of transparency. In Singapore for example, at some point the government was going through challenging economic times which meant that some tough, unpopular decisions had to be taken. Transparency in this instance was of particular importance because it helped to keep the public informed about the tough actions that the government had to take along with the rationale behind the decision making process. Transparency in this instance also helped to promote confidence among foreign investors (ITU, 2002). On a more general note, transparency does appear to have an effect on foreign investment. According to Zhao, Kim and Du (2003) the presence of corruption and a lack of transparency are often perceived to damage the investment environment of a country. The authors found that in 40 countries examined, low levels of transparency and high levels of corruption resulted in a significantly reduced flow of foreign direct investment. Similarly, Ellis and Fender (2003) argue that there are significant links between corruption, fiscal transparency, investment, and economic growth. Countries that are corrupt tend to be less transparent, have less investment and slow economic growth. Furthermore Habib and Zurawicki (2003) also argue that corruption is a serious obstacle for investment.

According to Ndou (2004), e-government helps to increase the transparency of decision-making processes. The author further argued that government websites can be tools for transparency particularly when they are designed effectively. Many current models of e-Government have an unstated assumption that a desire to fulfil democratic functions motivates the creation of e-Government initiatives and that the ultimate goal of e-Government initiatives is increased transparency and accountability (Johnson & Kolko, 2010). The diversity of publications covering the administrative, economic and legislative activities of governments that could also be made available can also prove to be useful in ensuring transparency (Ndou, 2004). However, according to Armstrong (2011) online transparency may be a more complex concept than just putting information online.

In the past, governments may have been reluctant to allow for transparency (Reylea, 2009) but increasingly, there have been reforms to ensure that it is entrenched in the fabric of government. One of the ways in which governments have managed to increase transparency is with the use of e-government. There are several examples of countries that have experienced an increase in transparency as a result of adopting e-government. Consequently, increases in the use of e-government have led to reductions in corruption over the decade 1996–2006 in non-OECD countries (Andersen, 2009).

Internationally, the internet has made transparency easier for governments to accomplish in practical ways, but it has also added new complications to ensuring equal access to and preservation of digital-born government information (Jaeger and Bertot, 2010). Halachmi and Greiling, 2014 also agree with this view and argue that greater use of information and communications technology and e-government can increase governmental transparency. This, in turn, may invite citizen participation, foster e-governance, and facilitate e-democracy. However, beyond a certain point, more government openness may be dysfunctional if it reduces operational capacity. This implies that although transparency is important, it stands to reason that maximal, complete and absolute transparency may not necessarily be the best approach. If a public sector spends so much time keeping the public informed of every single detail of activities, that division will not be very effective in carrying out their daily duties (Kolstad & Wiig, 2009).

Admittedly there might be instances of too much information which would not be beneficial to any government department. Nevertheless, it is expedient that every effort is made to ensure that such departments make every effort to be transparent because according to Kolstad and Wiig (2009).

- A lack of transparency makes corruption less risky and more attractive
- A lack of transparency makes it harder to use incentives to make public officials act cleanly
- A lack of transparency makes it hard to select the most honest and efficient people for public sector positions or as contract partners. Informational advantages give access to rents, making reform difficult
- A lack of transparency makes cooperation more difficult to sustain, and opportunistic rent-seeking more likely
- A lack of transparency may undermine social norms and reduce trust

On the one hand, although several researchers agree that there is a link between transparency and corruption, Kolstad and Wiig (2009) argue that however much and whichever way transparency may affect corruption, it is insufficient in itself, and needs to be complemented by other types of reforms. In other words, transparency on its own may not end corruption. They further argue that in certain cases, transparency can also increase corruption. On the other hand, Jaeger and Bertot (2010) highlighted the importance of transparency and argued that transparency is key to democracy. It can be a powerful tool to build trust in institutions among citizens. It also plays a key role in the relation between corruption, trust, and citizen satisfaction (Park and Blenkinsopp, 2011). In other words, the more transparent a government is, the better the citizen satisfaction and the greater the likelihood of citizens trusting the government.

Corruption and Transparency in Nigeria

According to Svensson (2007), a common definition of public corruption is the misuse of public office for private gain. This captures the sale of government property by government officials, kickbacks in public procurement, bribery and embezzlement of government funds. Corruption has been said to be endemic in Nigeria and can be linked to the economic woes of the populace. Ogbeidi (2012) notes that in spite of the natural resources available in the country, Nigeria has more than 70 percent of its population living below the poverty line as a result of corruption and economic mismanagement.

Indeed, corruption comes with quite a high price, which is continually paid by the country and its citizens. Salisu (2000) asserts that corruption has an adverse effect on the growth rate of GDP in Nigeria, while Mohammed (2013) lists the various ways that corruption has threatened sustainable development in the country. Some of which include: a high incidence of conflict, violence, crime, insecurity and instability; erosion of values of hard work and integrity; lack of access to productive opportunities; low foreign investment; a high dependence on foreign sources for goods and services; leakages of national assets to foreign countries through money laundering; misallocation of resources towards programmes and projects amenable to corrupt practices; high cost of doing business and low investment in productive sectors; political ethno-religious and communal conflicts usually resulting in violence; poor social welfare conditions and the loss of public trust and legitimacy by the government. Similarly, Agbiboa (2012) established a link between corruption and underdevelopment and that corruption is responsible for the shortcomings and poor performance of the Nigerian political economy. In addition, as noted by Fagbadebo (2007), Nigeria's economic and political landscape is pervaded by corruption and abuse of office.

Awofeso and Oduyemi (2007) argue that corruption has been the biggest impediment to Nigeria's socio-economic development and the wellbeing of citizens and blame Nigeria's underdevelopment and corruption on the country's leadership. Successive Nigerian military and civilian governments have all succeeded in mismanaging the national economy to a point of collapse (Kebonang & Kebonang, 2013). State control of the limited resources in the country has encouraged a system for government officials to manipulate government spending to advance their personal fortunes. This system has led to weak legitimacy, as the citizens lack faith in their political leaders, and, by extension, the political system (Fagbadebo, 2007).

The lack of faith may also be as a result of a lack of transparency and accountability stemming from years of bad governance from the military and civilian governments (Oluwatobi & Ogunrinola, 2011). Until the auctioning of GSM lines in 2000, where information on the progress of the auction was made available to as wide an audience as possible after the conclusion of each round, such a high level of transparency was almost unheard of in Nigeria (Doyle & McShane, 2003).

Shadrach and Ekeanyanwu (2003) argued that the public's respect for government is increasingly eroded owing to a lack of transparency and as such, there is a need for governments to interface with citizens through innovative ways and means. The current provision of e-government in the country can be seen as a response to this need. However, it remains to be seen if the e-government initiatives that have commenced so far, have made any impact on corruption.

E-Government as a Tool for Transparency and Trust

Mistry and Jalal (2012) argued that IT enabled e-government could improve the transparency of the bureaucratic process and therefore, promote accountability. They also postulated that providing easy access to information for all citizens through the use of e-government initiatives can tackle corruption and that as the use of ICT or e-government increases corruption decreases in both developed and developing countries but with developing countries benefiting the most from increased use of ICT. Several texts mention transparency as a means of tackling corruption. However, according to Lindstedt and Naurin (2010), transparency in itself is not sufficient. They argue that just making information available will not prevent corruption if there are no strong conditions for publicity and accountability in place. Transparency can also come with unexpected consequences. According to Bannister and Connolly (2011), it is sometimes best avoided. They argue that expectations about e-transparency tend to be based on assumptions about the nature of transparency that may not be practical or even beneficial to citizens (Bannister & Connolly, 2011).

To ensure that transparency does indeed tackle corruption, the information made available through transparency reforms must also be available to and be absorbed by the public (Lindstedt & Naurin, 2010). Another necessity in the fight against corruption is education. While Kolstad and Wiig (2009) also agree that transparency might be a necessary though insufficient constituent in the war against corruption, they argue that education is a precondition in order for a population to have the ability to process the information, and a capability to act on the processed information. Similarly, Grimmel (2013) argue that public officials and political leaders should expect no wonders from transparency as it is no magic and universal cure for trust in government. Bannister and Connolly (2011) assert that the nature of transparency needs to be carefully managed because it may not always be in the best interest of either the citizens or the government. For society an actual risk is that in a world of instant, real-time information, citizens tend to expect a type of e-transparency from their government and their public servants that may not necessarily be in the best interests of government. For governments, a real risk is that transparency will not only hamper their operations, it may possibly damage their reputation (Bannister & Connolly, 2011).

Although transparency on its own may not be sufficient for tackling corruption, it can be argued that e-government can enhance transparency and possibly lead to less corruption since e-government not only provides transparency but also the ability to process information. Admittedly, there might be dissenting voices. Nevertheless, Andersen (2009) established that an increase in the use of e-government has led to reductions in corruption over a decade (1996–2006) in non-OECD countries. Similarly, Asogwa (2013) also argued that e-government would provide faster access to government information, lower administrative costs, increase transparency in government ministries, and reduce bribery and corruption in Nigeria.

E-government is seen as a route to better governance as it is open and transparent, and an enabler for participatory democracy; it is service-oriented, and it provides personalised and inclusive services to every citizen (Ayo, Adebiyi & Afolabi, 2008). It is clear what the expectations are on the surface. However, there is scant evidence of studies that have evaluated the contribution of e-government to providing the openness and transparency that is desired when considering how far Nigeria has come with the adoption of e-government. ICT helps to prevent public employees' corrupt behaviour by transparently providing information about governmental policy-making and service delivery processes to the public (Shim & Eom, 2009). The authors also revealed that both ICT and social capital have significant and independent roles in reducing a country's corruption. Both e-government effectiveness and Internet penetration exhibited a negative relationship with the corruption index, even after controlling for traditional anti-corruption approaches. They also noted that e-government and Internet penetration was more powerful in terms of being able to explain the variations of corruption among countries than were bureaucratic quality and law enforcement, which have been traditionally regarded as principal agents for anti-corruption. The Nigerian policy makers appear to believe accountability and transparency in governance can be enhanced through e-government (Ifinedo, 2006). It is therefore a worthwhile effort to investigate whether the populace believe that they can trust the government more as a result of the introduction and implementation of e-government initiatives.

Lupu and Lazar (2015) in their investigation of the practical influence of e-government on the level of corruption in some EU and none EU states found that increasing the use of e-government will reduce corruption. Specifically, the models suggest that a 1% increase in the index of e-government can result in a decrease in corruption by 6.7% for countries entering the EU, and 6.3 for non-EU member.

Considering the fact that corruption and a lack of transparency are core issues plaguing governance and development in Nigeria, it is reasonable to explore how certain phenomena such as e-government have helped to prevent or resolve the same issues in other countries.

Bertot, Jaeger and Grimes (2010) list short-term actions that are possible which can lead to long-term success in terms of transparent and open government that reduces corruption. They are as follows:

1. Developing measures of transparency with clear evaluation criteria, measures, or methods for determining the extensiveness and success of transparency efforts
2. Developing transparency readiness criteria. Since not all nations or states within nations are able to engage in e-government initiatives, it is important to develop readiness criteria for transparency initiatives and to provide metrics against which to gauge different areas along those criteria
3. Evaluate existing systems for portability and expansion. Successful ICT-enabled transparency systems exist and can be further studied
4. Re-using instead of reinventing
5. Creating and investing in collaborative pilot initiatives

Kim, Kim and Lee (2009) also provide an analysis of criteria, which have made the OPEN anti- corruption e-government system in South Korea, which is a successful one that is being emulated within the country and acclaimed internationally. The system combined three institutionalization mechanisms, four strategies to fight corruption and strong leadership to achieve the level of success it has accomplished. The three institutionalized mechanisms that are at the centre of institutional theory are regulatory/coercive, cognitive/mimetic, and normative. While the four strategies include access to information and empowerment, prevention, enforcement and capacity building.

A FRAMEWORK FOR EVALUATING E-GOVERNMENT IN NIGERIA AND ITS CONTRIBUTION TO TACKLING CORRUPTION

Considering the success levels that have been achieved in South Korea and the criteria which have proven to be tried, tested and trusted for the purpose of reducing corruption with the aid of e-government initiatives applied in the OPEN system, the same criteria will form the basis of the framework to be applied in this study following Kim, Kim and Lee (2009).In the authors' view, e-government initiatives are institutions that are multifaceted, durable social structures, made up of symbolic elements, social activities, and material resources.

Institutionalization Theory

As applied in their study, institutionalization is the process by which those structures are maintained and reproduced. Following Scott (2001), central to institutional theory are three mechanisms that produce consistencies within or across organizations over time. These include regulatory/coercive, cognitive/ mimetic, and normative.

A regulatory or coercive mechanism is based on political and legislative practices. The regulatory factors are affected by politics and legislative measures and are influenced an organisation's decisions to adopt a specific organisational tradition. A mimetic mechanism refers to copying other organisation's practices. This is applicable when uncertainty is prevalent, when organisations become likely to model themselves on other organisations. A normative mechanism is motivated by norms that are prevalent and observed in the domain to which the organisations belong (Kim, Kim & Lee, 2009). According to the authors, when applied in the context of e-government, institutional theory can help to uncover challenges that may be experienced when attempting to implement e-government systems. By examining the three mechanisms of institutionalization, the theory elucidates how an innovation or new system developed in an organization is diffused, adopted, or copied by others (ibid). This makes it apt as a lens through which e-government provision in Nigeria may be examined to ensure that not only are the initiatives adequate, they are also able to combat corruption within government agencies in the country.

In addition to the theory of institutionalization, the stages of e-government transformation according to West (2004) provides an outline of how to measure the extent of change. As previously stated in section 1, there is little or no evidence to suggest that a clear framework for the adoption of e-government is being followed in Nigeria. This study therefore hopes to provide a means of evaluating e-government provision from the users' perspective according to tested stages as well as providing a view to what impact, if any, such initiatives have made towards the fight against corruption. To this aim, the stages of e-government transformation will be applied as a way of verifying how far the government has come with the provision of e-government.

Stages of E-Government Transformation

The four general stages of e-government development (West, 2004) that distinguish where different government agencies are on the road to transformation include:

1. The billboard stage
2. The partial-service-delivery stage
3. The portal stage, with fully executable and integrated service delivery
4. Interactive democracy with public outreach and accountability enhancing features

At the first stage of development, government web sites are more or less like billboards that only display information without any input from citizens. Publications and reports are regularly posted and databases are available to be viewed by users. This is purely communication that is in no way interactive in that although the information may be available, the citizens can only access it but have no means of providing their own input.

The second stage is one of partial service delivery. At this stage, citizens can begin to order and execute a few services online and may also have access to databases that can be manipulated. Citizens can also search for what they would rather view instead of the previous stage where they could only view what government officials provided. This stage also means that services may be irregular and limited to specific areas. Privacy and security statements would not be posted and there are no allowances for speakers of other languages (apart from English) and disabled citizens.

At the third stage, a fully integrated and executable one-stop government portal is provided. Various agency sites would be integrated and various services are offered to citizens and businesses. Attention is paid to privacy and security and policies covering those areas are posted online. There are translation services for citizens who do not speak English as well as services for the disabled.

At the fourth stage, interactivity is optimised. Accountability measures are provided to citizens and there is a move from a mere service delivery model to a complete political transformation. Personalisation is an option at this stage where services and information can be tailored to an individual citizen's needs. Citizens can also provide feedback and make comments that could boost democratic participation and leadership accountability.

The stages have already been applied to evaluate the supply side of e-government provision. This research however argues that views from the demand side also matter and will therefore form the basis of the application of the framework derived in this study. This research intends to follow a pattern of social constructionist e-government studies, which according to Heeks and Bailur (2007), assumes that what matters about any variable is the particular meaning given to that variable by each individual. With a social constructionist view, the nature of technology and what it can do are perceived as a product of human interpretation. Therefore, the conceptual framework will incorporate the four strategies for preventing corruption, which include access to information and empowerment, prevention, enforcement and capacity building; with the institutional theory and stages of e-government transformation. The result of which will be applied not only to the supply side, but the demand side as well. The conceptual framework is presented below in Figure 1.

DISCUSSION

From existing literature, one can surmise that at best, many of the e-government initiatives in Nigeria where they exist, are at the second stage which is the partial service delivery stage as outlined by West (2004). According to Omiere and Omeire (2014), many government ministries have websites, which are simply used as information boards, which are rarely updated, public figures use social media platforms such as facebook and twitter to communicate with citizens and citizens are able to make e-payments. At this stage however, it will be useful to examine any effect such provisions have had on corruption. That way, departments may start to include best practices at the lower stages of e-government even before the services become optimised. This could then provide a chance to rebuild trust from the side of the citizens.

Heeks and Bailur (2007) note the dominance of positivist research approaches in e-government research. In contrast, this research adopts an interpretivist approach which according to Klein and Myers (1999) can help IS researchers to understand human thought and action in social and organisational contexts. It has been applied in areas of information systems research such as organisational intervention and management of IS and social implications of IS (Walsham, 1995). Interpretive research does not predefine dependent and independent variables, but focuses on the complexity of human sense making as the situation emerges (Kaplan & Maxwell 1994). The interpretive research approach in IS research is "aimed at producing an understanding of the context of the information system, and the process whereby an information system influences and is influenced by the context" (Walsham 1993, pp4-5). This implies that our knowledge of reality is a social construction by human actors (Walsham, 1995).

Considering the field of study, it stands to reason that the same view is unlikely to be held by both the supply and demand side. The framework proposed in this study may therefore be useful for unearthing what the views are on each side of the coin. What the populace may expect in terms of transparency and accountability may not match the government's view of what they entail. Grimmel (2013) notes that national cultures play a significant role in how people perceive and appreciate government transparency. This implies that in designing e-government initiatives with the aim of providing transparency and ren-

Figure 1. A conceptual framework for the evaluation of e-government provision

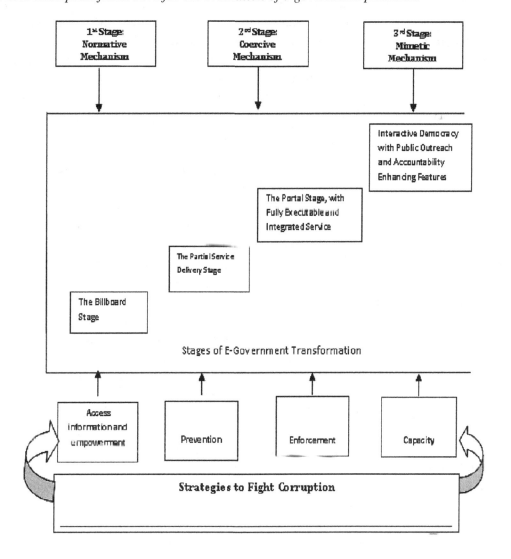

dering higher levels of citizen trust, the culture within Nigeria must be taken into account. Unfortunately, however, from the outset of independence attainment, successive sets of the nation's political leaders and decision makers at various levels of public life have institutionalised corrupt acts and abusive behaviour in Nigeria (Awofeso & Odeyemi, 2014). This suggests that corruption may be deeply entrenched in the culture and it may be difficult to expect that e-government services will change this overnight.

Nevertheless, the intention is to apply the model to verify the contributions of e-government towards resolving some of the most difficult problems facing the populace. As previously discussed, extant studies agree that corruption is the source of many difficulties facing the country and its citizens. E-government is an initiative, which aims to break down barriers and bring government closer to citizens. It is therefore hoped that e-government provision in Nigeria can also increase transparency and encourage more discourse between citizens and government agencies. In addition to transparency, education and accountability can also be encouraged using e-government, which taken together, should help to combat corruption.

Asogwa (2013) recommended that the Nigerian government should carry out a SWOT analysis of the e-government project in the country, strengthen the e-government infrastructure and ensure steady power supply before embarking on the e-government project again. This study takes a similar view but also emphasises the need to carry the users along now, while development is still at the early stages since e-government initiatives are for the benefit of users or citizens after all. If the citizens are able to see how beneficial e-government can be to alleviating their challenges, they might be more inclined to engage with the services provided.

CONCLUSION LIMITATIONS AND FUTURE RESEARCH DIRECTIONS

E-government as a research area has been vibrant in a number of countries, Nigeria inclusive. However, the focus of majority of the studies revolves around the provision and availability of the service, with a limited focus on the demand side. The previous sections have considered corruption and how it can be impacted by e-government and the framework generated will hopefully provide a lens through which initiatives in Nigeria can both be introduced and evaluated not only by the institutions themselves but also by the citizens, which the systems are designed to serve.

There are obvious limitations with this study, which provides an avenue for future research. No primary data has been collected or analysed so far. Consequently, a further exploratory study is in view, which will encompass a variety of methods for data collection. A major source of data collection will be with the use of multiple case studies considering specific government organisations that already provide e-government services. Additionally, interviews and questionnaires will be applied to citizens to provide a version of their own reality as far as e-government services are concerned. Document reviews will also be a useful data source as a few agencies collect hand written feedback from users at the end of various processes such as obtaining driving licenses for example. All in all, it is hoped that after data has been collected and analysed, a richer picture will emerge of the citizen's perspective of e-government provision in Nigeria, particularly with a view to aiding in the battle against corruption. This will provide an opportunity for better development and the resolution of resulting challenges.

On the one hand, this research is aimed at examining e-government from the user's perspective. On the other hand, however, it is hoped that results from the research will inform policy and practice in the maintenance and further development of e-government initiatives and hopefully will increase citizen engagement.

REFERENCES

Adeyemo, A. B. (2011). E-government implementation in Nigeria: An assessment of Nigeria's global e-gov ranking. *Journal of Internet and Information System, 2*(1), 11–19.

Agbiboa, D. E. (2012). Between corruption and development: The political economy of state robbery in Nigeria. *Journal of Business Ethics, 108*(3), 325–345. doi:10.1007/s10551-011-1093-5

Andersen, T. B. (2009). E-Government as an anti-corruption strategy. *Information Economics and Policy, 21*(3), 201–210. doi:10.1016/j.infoecopol.2008.11.003

Armstrong, C. L. (2011). Providing a clearer view: An examination of transparency on local government websites. *Government Information Quarterly, 28*(1), 11–16. doi:10.1016/j.giq.2010.07.006

Asogwa, B. E. (2013). Electronic government as a paradigm shift for efficient public services: Opportunities and challenges for Nigerian government. *Library Hi Tech, 31*(1), 141–159. doi:10.1108/07378831311303985

Awofeso, O., & Odeyemi, T. I. (2014). The Impact of Political Leadership and Corruption on Nigerias Development since Independence. *Journal of Sustainable Development, 7*(5), 240. doi:10.5539/jsd.v7n5p240

Ayo, C. K., Adebiyi, A. A., & Afolabi, I. T. (2008). E-Democracy: A requirement for a successful E-Voting and E-Government implementation in Nigeria. *International Journal of Natural and Applied Sciences, 4*(3), 310–318.

Azeez, N. A., Abidoye, A. P., Adesina, A. O., Agbele, K. K., Venter, L. M., & Oyewole, A. S. (2012). Threats to E-Government Implementation in the Civil Service: Nigeria as a Case Study. *The Pacific Journal of Science and Technology, 13*(1), 398–402.

Bac, M. (2001). Corruption, connections and transparency: Does a better screen imply a better scene? *Public Choice, 107*(1-2), 87–96. doi:10.1023/A:1010349907813

Bannister, F., & Connolly, R. (2011). The Trouble with Transparency: A Critical Review of Openness in e-Government. *Policy & Internet, 3*(1), 1–30. doi:10.2202/1944-2866.1076

Basu, S. (2004). E-government and developing countries: An overview. *International Review of Law Computers & Technology, 18*(1), 109–132. doi:10.1080/13600860410001674779

Bertot, J. C., Jaeger, P. T., & Grimes, J. M. (2010). Using ICTs to create a culture of transparency: E-government and social media as openness and anti-corruption tools for societies. *Government Information Quarterly, 27*(3), 264–271. doi:10.1016/j.giq.2010.03.001

Beynon-Davies, P. (2005). Constructing Electronic Government: The case of the UK Inland Revenue. *International Journal of Information Management, 25*(1), 3–20. doi:10.1016/j.ijinfomgt.2004.08.002

Bhatnagar, S. (2003). *Transparency and corruption: Does E-government help? Draft paper for the compilation of CHRI 2003 Report OPEN SESAME: looking for the Right to Information in the Commonwealth.* Commonwealth Human Rights Initiative.

Boehm, F., & Olaya, J. (2006). Corruption in public contracting auctions: The role of transparency in bidding processes. *Annals of Public and Cooperative Economics, 77*(4), 431–452. doi:10.1111/j.1467-8292.2006.00314.x

Casalino, N., Buonocore, F., Rossignoli, C., & Ricciardi, F. (2013). Transparency, openness and knowledge sharing for rebuilding and strengthening government institutions. Proceedings of WBE '13 conference (Vol. 10). Zurich, Innsbruck, Austria: IASTED-ACTA Press. doi:10.2316/P.2013.792-044

Doyle, C., & McShane, P. (2003). On the design and implementation of the GSM auction in Nigeria—the worlds first ascending clock spectrum auction. *Telecommunications Policy, 27*(5), 383–405. doi:10.1016/S0308-5961(03)00011-9

Ellis, C. J., & Fender, J. (2006). Corruption and transparency in a growth model. *International Tax and Public Finance*, *13*(2-3), 115–149. doi:10.1007/s10797-006-1664-z

Evans, D., & Yen, D. C. (2006). E-Government: Evolving relationship of citizens and government, domestic, and international development. *Government Information Quarterly*, *23*(2), 207–235. doi:10.1016/j.giq.2005.11.004

Fagbadebo, O. (2007). Corruption, governance and political instability in Nigeria. *African Journal of Political Science and International Relations*, *1*(2), 28–37.

Federal Ministry of Communication Technology. (2013). *Nigeria's National Broadband Plan 2013-2018*. Abuja, Nigeria: Federal Ministry Of Communication Technology.

Friedman, T. L. (2006). The first law of petropolitics. *Foreign Policy*, *154*(3), 28–36.

Gordon, R. G. Jr., (Ed.). (2005). *Ethnologue: Languages of the World* (15th ed.). Dallas, Tex.: SIL International.

Grimmelikhuijsen, S. G., Porumbescu, G., Hong, B., & Im, T. (2013). The effect of transparency in trust in government: A cross-national comparative experiment. *Public Administration Review*, *73*(4), 575–586. doi:10.1111/puar.12047

Habib, M., & Zurawicki, L. (2002). Corruption and foreign direct investment. *Journal of International Business Studies*, *33*(2), 291–307. doi:10.1057/palgrave.jibs.8491017

Halachmi, A., & Greiling, D. (2013). Transparency, e-government, and accountability: Some issues and considerations. *Public Performance & Management Review*, *36*(4), 562–584. doi:10.2753/PMR1530-9576360404

Heeks, R. (2003). *Most E-Government-for-Development Projects Fail: How Can Risks be Reduced?* iGovernment Working Paper Series, Institute for Development Policy and Management, University of Manchester, UK.

Heeks, R., & Bailur, S. (2007). Analyzing e-government research: Perspectives, philosophies, theories, methods, and practice. *Government Information Quarterly*, *24*(2), 243–265. doi:10.1016/j.giq.2006.06.005

Ifinedo, P. (2006). Towards e-government in a Sub-Saharan African country: Impediments and initiatives in Nigeria. *Journal of E-Government*, *3*(1), 3–28. doi:10.1300/J399v03n01_02

Ifinedo, P. (2007). Moving towards E-Government in a developing society: Glimpses of the Problems, Progress, and Prospects in Nigeria. In *Al-Hakim, L., Global E-Government: Theory, Applications and Benchmarking* (p. 383). Hershey: Idea Group Publishing. doi:10.4018/978-1-59904-027-1.ch009

International Telecommunication Union (ITU). (2002). *Trends in Telecommunication Reform*. Geneva: International Telecommunication Union.

Jaeger, P. T., & Bertot, J. C. (2010). Transparency and technological change: Ensuring equal and sustained public access to government information. *Government Information Quarterly*, *27*(4), 371–376. doi:10.1016/j.giq.2010.05.003

Johnson, E., & Kolko, B. (2010). e-Government and transparency in authoritarian regimes: comparison of national-and city-level e-government web sites in Central Asia. *Digital Icons: Studies in Russian. Eurasian and Central European New Media, 3,* 15–48.

Kaplan, B., & Maxwell, J. A. (1994). Qualitative Research Methods for Evaluating Computer Information Systems. In J. G. Anderson, C. E. Aydin, & S. J. Jay (Eds.), *Evaluating Health Care Information Systems: Methods and Applications* (pp. 45–68). Thousand Oaks, CA: Sage publications.

Kaufmann, D., & Bellver, A. (2005, July 6–7). Transparenting transparency—initial empirics and policy applications. *Presentation at the Pre-Conference on Institutional Change for Growth and Poverty Reduction in Low Income Countries at the International Monetary Fund,* Washington DC.

Kebonang, Z. & Kebonang, S. (2013). Does leadership matter to development: The case of Botswana, Zimbabwe, Nigeria and Indonesia. *International Journal of Politics and Good Governance, 4*(4.4), 1-24.

Kim, S., Kim, H. J., & Lee, H. (2009). An institutional analysis of an e-government system for anti-corruption: The case of OPEN. *Government Information Quarterly, 26*(1), 42–50. doi:10.1016/j.giq.2008.09.002

Klein, K. K., & Myers, M. D. (1999). A Set of Principles for Conducting and evaluating Interpretive Field Studies in Information Systems. *Management Information Systems Quarterly, 23*(1), 67–94. doi:10.2307/249410

Kolstad, I., & Wiig, A. (2009). Is transparency the key to reducing corruption in resource-rich countries? *World Development, 37*(3), 521–532. doi:10.1016/j.worlddev.2008.07.002

Lindstedt, C., & Naurin, D. (2010). Transparency is not enough: Making transparency effective in reducing corruption. *International Political Science Review, 31*(3), 301–322. doi:10.1177/0192512110377602

Lupu, D., & Lazăr, C. G. (2015). Influence of e-government on the Level of Corruption in some EU and Non-EU States. *Procedia Economics and Finance, 20,* 365–371. doi:10.1016/S2212-5671(15)00085-4

Mistry, J. J., & Jalal, A. (2012). An empirical analysis of the relationship between e-government and corruption. *The International Journal Of Digital Accounting Research, 12*(18), 145–176.

Mo, P. H. (2001). Corruption and economic growth. *Journal of Comparative Economics, 29*(1), 66–79. doi:10.1006/jcec.2000.1703

Mohammed, U. (2013). Corruption in Nigeria: A Challenge to Sustainable Development. *European Scientific Journal, 9*(4), 118–137.

Mundy, D., & Musa, B. (2010). Towards a framework for egovernment development in Nigeria. *Electronic. Journal of E-Government, 8*(2), 148–161.

Ndou, V. (2004). E-government for developing countries: Opportunities and challenges. *The Electronic Journal of Information Systems in Developing Countries, 18*(1), 1–24.

Obadare, E. (2005). A crisis of trust: History, politics, religion and the polio controversy in Northern Nigeria. *Patterns of Prejudice, 39*(3), 265–284. doi:10.1080/00313220500198185

Ogbeidi, M. M. (2012). Political Leadership and Corruption in Nigeria Since 1960: A Socioeconomic Analysis. *Journal of Nigeria Studies, 1*(2), 1–25.

Okunola, O. M. (2015). *Users' experience of e-government services: a case study based on the Nigeria immigration service* [Unpublished doctoral thesis]. Manchester Metropolitan University, Manchester, England.

Olatokun, W. M., & Adebayo, B. M. (2012). Assessing E-Government Implementation in Ekiti State, Nigeria. *Journal of Emerging Trends in Computing and Information Sciences, 3*(4), 499–505.

Oluwatobi, S. O., & Ogunrinola, I. O. (2011). Government expenditure on human capital development: Implications for economic growth in Nigeria. *Journal of Sustainable Development, 4*(3), 72–80. doi:10.5539/jsd.v4n3p72

Omeire, E., & Omeire, C. (2014). New Wine in Old Wine Skin: An Exploration of Major Constraints to E-Government Implementation in Nigeria. *European Scientific Journal, 10*(14), 481–487.

Park, H., & Blenkinsopp, J. (2011). The roles of transparency and trust in the relationship between corruption and citizen satisfaction. *International Review of Administrative Sciences, 77*(2), 254–274. doi:10.1177/0020852311399230

Reddick, C. G. (2005). Citizen interaction with e-government: From the streets to servers? *Government Information Quarterly, 22*(1), 38–57. doi:10.1016/j.giq.2004.10.003

Relyea, H. C. (2009). Federal freedom of information policy: Highlights of recent developments. *Government Information Quarterly, 26*(2), 314–320. doi:10.1016/j.giq.2008.12.001

Rorissa, A., & Demissie, D. (2010). An analysis of African e-Government service websites. *Government Information Quarterly, 27*(2), 161–169. doi:10.1016/j.giq.2009.12.003

Salisu, M. (2000). Corruption in Nigeria, Lancaster University Management School, Working Paper 2000/006, Department of Economics, Lancaster.

Scott, W. R. (2001). *Institutions and organizations*. London: Sage Publications.

Shadrach, B., & Ekeanyanwu, L. (2003, May 25-28). Improving the transparency, quality and effectiveness of pro-poor public services using the ICTs: An attempt by Transparency International. *Proceedings of the11th International Anti-Corruption Conference*, Seoul, Korea.

Shim, D.C. & Eom, T.H. (2009) Anticorruption effects of information communication and technology (ICT) and social capital. *International review of administrative sciences, 75*(1), 99-116.

Silcock, R. (2001). What is e government. *Hansard Society for Parliamentary Government. Parliamentary Affairs, 54*, 88–101. doi:10.1093/pa/54.1.88

Silvia, N. C., & Adela, D. (2014). Romanian Public Sector Transparency Approached by E-governance. *Procedia Economics and Finance, 15*, 414–420. doi:10.1016/S2212-5671(14)00470-5

Svensson, J. (2005). Eight questions about corruption. *The Journal of Economic Perspectives, 19*(3), 19–42. doi:10.1257/089533005774357860

Tayo, O., Thompson, R., & Thompson, E. (2015). Impact of the Digital Divide on Computer Use and Internet Access on the Poor in Nigeria. *Journal of Education and Learning, 5*(1), 1. doi:10.5539/jel.v5n1p1

The World Bank. (2015). World Development Indicators. Retrieved from http://data.worldbank.org/country/nigeria

Treisman, D. (2000). The causes of corruption: A cross-national study. *Journal of Public Economics, 76*(3), 399–457. doi:10.1016/S0047-2727(99)00092-4

vanVelsen, L.; van der Geest, T., terHedde, M., & Derks, W. (2009). Requirements engineering for e-Government services: A citizen-centric approach and case study. *Government Information Quarterly, 26*(3), 477–486. doi:10.1016/j.giq.2009.02.007

Veljković, N., Bogdanović-Dinić, S., & Stoimenov, L. (2012) Building E-Government 2.0 – A Step Forward in Bringing Government Closer to Citizens. *Journal of e-Government Studies and Best Practices.* Retrieved from http://www.ibimapublishing

Verdegem, P., & Verleye, G. (2009). User-centered E-Government in practice: A comprehensive model for measuring user satisfaction. *Government Information Quarterly, 26*(3), 487–497. doi:10.1016/j.giq.2009.03.005

Wahid, F. (2013) Themes of research on eGovernment in developing countries: Current map and future roadmap.*Proceedings of the 46th Hawaii International Conference on System Sciences (HICSS 2013)* doi:10.1109/HICSS.2013.547

Walsham, G. (1993). *Interpreting Information Systems in Organizations.* Chichester, UK: Wiley.

Walsham, G. (1995). The Emergence of Interpretivism in IS Research. *Information Systems Research, 6*(4), 376–394. doi:10.1287/isre.6.4.376

West, D. M. (2004). E-government and the transformation of service delivery and citizen attitudes. *Public Administration Review, 64*(1), 15–27. doi:10.1111/j.1540-6210.2004.00343.x

Zhao, J. H., Kim, S. H., & Du, J. (2003). The impact of corruption and transparency on foreign direct investment: An empirical analysis. *Management International Review, 2003*, 41–62.

KEY TERMS AND DEFINITIONS

Citizens: People who legally belong to a country and have the rights and protection of that country.
Corruption: The misuse of public office for private gain.
Developing Country: A country with little industrial and economic activity and where people generally have low incomes.
Electronic Government: The use of ICT by Government agencies in order to better manage relationships with citizens, business and other arms of Government.
Institutionalization: This is the process by which those structures are maintained and reproduced.
Transformation: A major change in someone's or something's appearance, form. A major change in e-government.

Transparency: Transparency means knowing the reasons, facts, logics and basis of the decision taken by the public administrations.

Trust: The belief that someone or something is reliable, good, honest, effective.

Users: An entity that has authority to use an application, equipment, facility, process, or system, or one who consumes or employs a good or service to obtain a benefit or to solve a problem.

Chapter 4
Freight Transport and Logistics Evaluation Using Entropy Technique Integrated to TOPSIS Algorithm

Mohammad Anwar Rahman
Central Connecticut State University, USA

Vivian A. Pereda
Central Connecticut State University, USA

ABSTRACT

Freight transportation and logistics decisions such as modal choice decisions are strategically important for effective supply chain operation and economic benefits. The freight selection logistic is a multi-criteria multi-objective (MCMO) process, crucial for smooth sourcing of materials, cost-effective delivery of products to customers in the right time, at the right quantity. The study discusses the major transport logistics attributes and the order preference by similarity ideal solution (TOPSIS) algorithm as the preferred MCMO model to support comparative ranking among the alternative freights. The entropy weight coefficient method minimizes the subjectivity in the selection of weight of the attribute. This study integrates the entropy technique on TOPSIS platform to improve the freight selection decision. A numerical example illustrates the procedure of the proposed algorithm and ranks the choices among truck, rail, and several intermodal transport combinations (rail/truck and air/truck) in a transportation selection model.

INTRODUCTION

In today's economy, buyers and suppliers are closely linked in domestic and international supply chain for constant sourcing of materials and economic benefits. The buyer company's major decision regarding mode of transportation has a direct effect towards competitive analysis and increasing efficiencies and profits. In supply chain, the business application that connects a range of activities, starting with the

DOI: 10.4018/978-1-5225-1944-7.ch004

procurement of materials from suppliers, followed by delivery of semi-finished or finished products to distributors or retailers and then to the consumers, requires freight transportation. Intermodal transportation has become a driving force in the current economy, in large part due to capacity and cost benefits. With advances in information technology and logistics innovations, the freight transportation process has improved extensively. Companies are now able to respond to customer demands swiftly, and deploy policies to adopt market changes efficiently in a short period of time. The freight carrier maintains the flow of products between facilities and marketplaces on a global scale in a safe, reliable and cost-effective way to meet any new challenges. Technological advances enable companies to implement cutting-edge logistics technologies, such as a cloud-based transportation management system, to obtain real-time data for quick analyzing and decision making, tracking and moving freights in many different locations. The freight transport costs, shipment characteristics, transportation mode, availability, route, and compliance to the buyer company policy and objective influence the choice of mode of transportation.

High-tech products, such as computer chips, are designed in one facility at a certain location. Meanwhile, pre-processing raw materials, intermediate production, final assembly, quality control and packaging are each completed in many locations, often at a distance, in a coordinated fashion. Likewise, daily consumable and functional products such as food, beverages, apparel, pharmaceutical products, sports items, packaged letters and goods continuously flow through a supply chain with increased collaboration to deliver products in the right quantity, at the right time and place. The freight selection is a complex and dynamic process that decision makers must solve with a multiple criteria decision problem (MCDP) using real-time market data, transport, and business attributes in order to find the best option of all feasible alternatives. Business sectors can use the MCDM analysis, as several new methods have been developed, and the methods are becoming considerably easier for the users.

A global supply chain is made up of a global network of suppliers, manufacturers, warehouses, distribution centers, and retailers through which raw materials are procured, transformed and delivered to customers (OECD, 2002). A transport chain focuses on a consignment and extends over movement, physical handling, and other activities directly related to transport such as dispatch, reception, planning, and control. As more customers enter the market, competition increases and prices inevitably fall. This results in higher product availability and the need to continuously improving transportation systems to keep up with the pace of growing customer demand (Coyle et al., 2006). There is tremendous growth on commercial implication of freight transport due to the globalization of the market. It is almost a requirement for success for companies entering today's market to take part in global sourcing (Zeng, 2005). Across the globe, hundreds of millions of shipping containers are moving through seaports, carrying product in different stages of production (raw material, sub-assembly, and finished goods). These goods contribute almost $5.8 billion per year to the world economy. In the current economic system, the growing role of freight is a fundamental component that enables companies to meet the need for goods to circulate at the global, regional and local scales. Freight transportation costs in the United States amount to approximately 6% of the GDP. This indicates that a significant portion of a company's supply chain costs come from transportation (Robinson, 2015). Freight volumes are expected to increase in the foreign trade oriented countries. The value of freight shipments, imports and export, for the U.S. only has increased from $16.651 trillion dollars in 2007 to $17.983 in 2013 and is expected to reach almost $40 trillion in 2040 (Federal et al., 2015).

The most critical activities in supply chain management are freight selection and understanding of the attributes related to the movement and delivery of products, as well as support services such as storing product and receiving customer orders. Supply chain's impact on facilities depends on seamless material flow from suppliers through manufacturing facilities, and into retail stores. Many manufacturers and retailers realize that appropriate selection of freight carriers with the right policy attributes reduces transportation costs, inventory quantity, and warehousing costs while speeding up delivery to the end customer. Transportation provides additional value to the product by enabling it to be delivered to the customers as demand is needed. The customer may refer to the end user, the warehouse center, or the next step in the product's process. Figure 1 demonstrates the impact of transportation links in a supply chain system.

Every company creates its own logistics policy and supply chain preferences to coordinate procurement and distribution of materials and finished products, in the right quantities, to and from the right places. On the verge of the losing competitive advantage, Wal-Mart spent $4 billion on its supply chain system. This investment resulted in Wal-Mart's suppliers investing a collective and additional $40 billion to match their supply chain operations. This effort led Wal-Mart to increased performance, resulting in a per square foot sale of $446, compared to Kmart's $227 (Leeman, 2010). Typically, transportation is the second highest cost component in a supply chain, accounting for approximately 25% of the overall operating expenses (Lancioni et. al., 2000). A vast majority of retail chains and companies have moved toward adopting some form of transportation management system, in an effort to determine the best way to get their product into the hands of customers. Often, third party logistics (3PL) companies provide such services on a larger scale, including transportation, packing, warehousing, cross-docking, delivery and portfolio management. Companies continuously extend the supply chain by managing transportation fleets that support the extensive market and growing customer demand. Buyer firms need to develop strategies to aid in supplier selection, and must use the resources at their disposal to find qualified suppliers (Wathne & Heide, 2004).

This study implements a multi criteria decision model (MCDM) to identify the best freight transport option for a selected supply chain. Selection of the right freights in supply chain significantly reduces costs, improves competitiveness in the market, and enhances end user satisfaction. The selection process involves MCDM analysis to evaluate freight attributes related to the business policies and needs. This study will benefit companies that are increasing their market capability as well as engaging in day-to-day strategic decision-making processes regarding which transportation modes and carriers to select to meet customer demands. The primary benefit of this model during the decision making process is the multi criteria data on relevant factors of different transportation alternatives and the ability to use the importance of an attribute (i.e., assign weights) to select the transport carrier that will have the most significant effect on overall business performance. The priority of transporting goods in a supply chain system urges decision makers to choose the best freight carrier.

Figure 1. Transportation links in a supply chain system

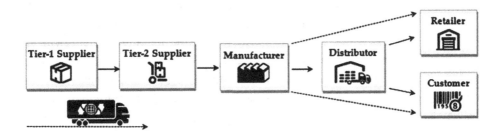

The rest of the chapter is organized as follows: Section 2 presents a description of multi criteria decision making models on transportation selection. The relationship between global commerce and transportation is presented in Section 3. Transportation logistics and intermodal transport cost function has been presented in Section 4. Subsequently, theoretical background of the TOPSIS algorithm integrated with entropy technique is proposed in Section 5. The numerical exercise of this proposed method is illustrated in Section 6. Finally, Section 7, the conclusion, includes a discussion of future research directions and concluding remarks.

MULTICRITERIA MODELS TO SELECT TRANSPORT CARRIER

The success of a business relies on the skills of efficient decision making and coordinated distribution between the supply chain connections, via the selection of the transport carrier that best satisfies the needs of the business. The facility location, proximity, infrastructure, risks, and government regulation all influence the transport carrier selection decision. Multi criteria decision making (MCDM) methods are used to rank the alternatives. Application of multi criteria decision models has grown considerably over the past last decades due to the easy and user-friendly solution approaches, as well as the ability to integrate subjective expert choices in the decision-making process. Steps for the Technique for Order Preference by Similarity to an Ideal Solution (TOPSIS) is a widely accepted fact-based decision model that sets priority among the feasible alternatives. Several recent studies provide in-depth analyses of multi-criteria decision models integrating fuzzy analysis and Bayesian analysis to improve the selection process and satisfy customer needs. Often, the selection is made based on a small number of carefully selected criteria, instead of gathering standardized information from a large, statistically significant sample, which utilizes design of experiment techniques and applications. Fuzzy numbers are a set of discrete values assigned to linguistic variables when it is too difficult or impossible to assign a numerical value to the criteria (Zavadskas, 2011). The TOPSIS method is applicable for a combination of qualitative and quantitative data. The quantitative data in the model may consist of any criteria that is ascending in order of preference and descending.

Two types of transport modeling exist: passenger transport modeling and freight transport modeling. In freight transport modeling, a high degree of specialization and established tools and methodologies have evolved since the past. Tuzkaya and Onut (2008) used a fuzzy analysis network process (FANP) to select a transportation mode between two countries. Often, the FANP is utilized to avoid the ambiguity of qualitative selection. Zhao et. al. (2010) implemented the Markov Decision Process (MDP) for ordering and delivering, including the different modes of available transportation options. The MDP algorithm analyzes the transportation cost, carrier, and inventory. The author used MDP to transport materials in a JIT (just-in-time) based production system. Awasthi et. al. (2011) implemented fuzzy TOPSIS method to obtain a sustainable solution for a transportation system. Abo-signal and Amer (2005) extend the concept of TOPSIS to solve multi-objective nonlinear programming problems. Jahanshahloo et. al. (2005) utilized TOPSIS approach for solving multi-criteria decision-making problems with interval data. They considered a transportation system that is environment-friendly and sustainable. Jahanshahloo et. al. (2006) implemented TOPSIS method by expressing the rating of each alternative and the weight of each criterion in triangular fuzzy numbers. Singh and Ben Yousef (2011) presented entropy method to enumerate the weights of various attributes without directly involving decision makers' subjective choice for weight selection. The model demonstrated a multi-attribute methodology for solving the sealed bid, reverse auction problem of e-sourcing using a fuzzy TOPSIS based approach along with the entropy method of automatic weight selection.

Demand uncertainty, competitive intensity, and technological turbulence are the three fundamental forms of market uncertainty. They represent the influences of customers, competition, and technology in the market (Zhou, Yim, & Tse, 2005). Companies want reduced uncertainty in supplier performance, a major motivation factor in selecting potential suppliers. Utility theory of multi criteria decision making upholds the preference of the decision maker. That model is applied when it is believed there is significance in the correlation in the way people process information and make decision based on problems from that information. It is known that while people are rational and capable of personal emotional independence a complete separation and unbiased judgement has not been achieved (Zavadskas, 2011). Uncertainty equates to risk and variability; both of which have ideal states of zero in the marketplace. Risk management is an important variable for company to grow strategically. Addressing vulnerabilities is as important as creating an ideal state. "Certainty renders existence meaningful and confers confidence in how to behave and what to expect from the physical and social environment" (Hogg & Mullin, 1999: 253). Pomerol and Romero (2000) present entropy method to determine weight using quantitative information to rate each alternative on criteria in the data matrix. The entropy method indicates that the weight factor is a direct function of the intrinsic value presented in the data. Business managers inquire about how to identify an appropriate transport carrier for quick and efficient flow of products. However, it can be difficult to make decisions based on subjective facts and complex information. It is even harder to choose from many options without the assistance of purpose-built software or an artificial intelligence method. This study assists with the decision approach without the use of expensive software or complex mathematical models, instead using simple information on carrier performance and transportation costs. Managers can create a simple criteria-based matrix using the available information on transportation mode for a particular route. The rank of the transport mode relies on the performance criteria and sample data. Each business has different options for transportation based on advantages and disadvantages, service commitment, costs, and customer benefits. Managers must review the available transportation mode, along with relevant facts and quantifiable data, to compare and rank the options in a supply chain within a short period of time. After forming the matrix, the performance status can be obtained for each transport mode using the multi criteria based TOPSIS method. The evaluation of weights is necessary for the TOPSIS method. To avoid subjectivity in choosing the weight factor for the selected criteria, an entropy method is used to determine the weight using the quantitative information conveyed. Each alternative is rated with respect to the criteria presented in the data matrix. The advantages of using TOPSIS integrated entropy methods include straightforward computational process and avoiding uncertain human judgment on choosing the weight. The TOPSIS method aids decision makers in choosing the best option among multiple alternatives, the solution closest to the ideal state when considering all the criteria and their importance.

Global Commerce and Transportation

A variety of trade agreements between companies located in different countries incentivize the global trade. The increasing trend of reducing cost through vertical integration creates additional movement of product. Through specific activities, industries develop supply chain partnerships to procure materials, transform those materials into finished products, and deliver them to the customer. Transportation has been the central focus for the production of increasingly complex products such as microprocessor chips, sophisticated nozzles, aerospace components and engines, and reactor components. Manufacturing companies engage in global commerce, utilizing MCDM to identify carriers that ensure shipment and transport of materials, components, and sub-assemblies to partner industries, at a minimum cost, in compliance with local and federal laws, to complete the production processes and marketing. Design of products, sources of raw materials, fabrications, testing, and assembly operations are spread over multiple locations around the globe. For example, Intel Corporation, the world's largest and highest valued manufacturer of microprocessor chips, holds 80% of the global market, powering personal computers, servers, and iPhones. The production of Intel's integrated circuits (IC) chip involves a complex global collaboration that includes, among others, Taiwan Semiconductor Manufacturing Corporation (TSMC), United Microelectronics Corporation (UMC), Global Foundry (GF) and Semiconductor Manufacturing International Corporation (SMIC). Intel chip production begins via the formation of single crystal, which grows into large ingots of silicon at Toshiba Ceramics in Japan. At Toshiba, the sliced ingots transform into thin wafers, which then transport across the Pacific Ocean to one of Intel's semiconductor fabricating plants, in either Arizona or Oregon. At the fabricating facility, hundreds of IC chips are etched and layered on each wafer. Ashable hard masks (AHMs) are films used in semiconductor processing. The finished wafers are then packed and transported back across the Pacific Ocean to Intel's assembly and test operations plant in Malaysia. In Malaysia, chips are tested and the end products are set into sealed ceramic packaging. Packaged chips are shipped across the Pacific, again, to Intel's warehouses in Arizona. Finally, chips are distributed to computer manufacturers around the globe.

Outside of globalization, industries also engage in innovation to achieve higher profit margins. With improvements, companies connect to a steady stream of sourcing. The modern transport carrier, advanced communication technology, and the remarkable achievement in logistic solutions all lead to global supply chain. However, finding efficient transport carriers to manage the flow between facilities in the supply chain is far more challenging and complex. The decision makers should first focus on identifying intermodal services, and then turn their attention to deciding on individual transport carriers and service providers within the mode. The modal choice and carrier selection are based on shipment conditions, transport capacity, transit time, reliability, availability, geographic coverage, product protection, and freight rates (Coyle et. al., 2008). Table 1 illustrates a comparative performance rating of the carrier capabilities.

Another specialized form of transportation available combines multiple means of transport. For example, a truck-rail combination known as the Container on Flatcar (COCF) transports using a trailer

Table 1. Performance rating of transportation carrier

Criteria	Mode of Transportation				
	Truck	Air	Rail	Water	Pipelines
Accessibility*	1	3	2	4	5
Transit time*	2	1	3	4	5
Reliability*	2	3	4	5	1
Security*	3	2	4	5	1
Cost**	4	5	3	2	1

*Benefit Criteria 1 = Best to 5 = Worst
**Cost Criteria 1 = Lowest cost to 5 = Highest cost

first moved by truck, and then, by rail transport from an intermodal port near to the origin for a long distance to the next intermodal port near to the destination. Many companies are looking at supply chains for determining the affordability of goods and services. Performance rating in regards to environmental responsibility has become an important issue in the carrier selection process. There are several other logistics costs categories such as inventory holding, customs charges, risk and damage, packaging, shipping and handling, and administration. As an example, a total logistics cost elements adapted from Zeng and Rossetti (2003) is shown in Table 11, Appendix A.

TRANSPORTATION LOGISTICS

Planning and control of transportation is a key component for every manufacturing and business organization. A short-and-long range transportation plan and improvement strategies would address those needs. Therefore, freight selection and the cost of transportation and attributes associated with the freights and policies should be optimized. This is in the interest of reducing customer price sharing on products and capturing increased market. The selection of correct freight ensures the ability to deliver goods with the right quantities, at the right place and time with appropriate price levels. Appendix B (Table 12) presents the management review for transportation policy. It includes comprehensive business strategies, goals and objectives, attributes and the evaluation process.

Regarding management review, first, review the existing transporting policy, focusing on sustainability in the current state and the requirements of creating additional capability. If there is a need to increase capacity or change existing service, it is essential to identify the best transportation decision given the policy, which may include making a lease or buy decision. Return on Investment is a key criterion for determining this decision. If the decision is to lease the transport service, the next important step is to collaborate with the 3PLs or relevant transport agencies. Following the management review, the next crucial step is to define what strategies and attributes are necessary for freight operations. Offer proposals to particular 3PLs, transport agencies electronically, auction or reverse auction style of contracts based of management review findings. Finally, current and projected future transportation alternatives should be evaluated through mathematical models. The shipping cost in the supply chain is always a factor in the final product price. These logistics decisions are made with the overall objective of minimizing total logistics costs.

According to Ben-Akiva & de Jong (2013) the freight logistics decisions depend on:

- Frequency/shipment size (including inventory decisions)
- Choice of loading unit (e.g., containerized)
- Use of distribution centers, terminals, and the related consolidation and distribution of shipments
- Mode/vehicle type used for each leg of the transport chain

Among the freight transport modes, road transportation is a dominant mode for domestic transportation. Road transportation is primarily via trucks and lorry, which are moderately fast, reliable, and available to nearly every point in a location. The fixed costs are low, but variable costs are high. The inherent advantages and convenience of trucking are door-to-door services that include loading and unloading between origin and destination (Ballou, 1999). Disadvantages include low capacity, safety concerns due to accidents, and slower speed in busy city areas.

Railway transportation is a slower mode of transportation and less flexible than trucking. However, it is exceptionally useful for low value, bulky, and high volume product. Fixed costs are high because of the infrastructure, installation, and maintenance costs, while the variable costs are low. Railway transport has advantages of high carrying capacity, lower influence by weather conditions, and lower energy consumption. Disadvantages include high cost of essential facilities, difficult and expensive maintenance, lack of elasticity of urgent demands, and time consumption in organizing railway carriages (Tseng et al., 2005). Rail service is available in limited scale and less frequent in terms of trip frequency. However, railroads offer a diversity of special services to the shipper, ranging from movement of bulk commodities such as coal and grain, to refrigerated products and automobiles, which require special equipment. Other services include expedited service to guarantee arrival within a certain number of hours, stop-off privileges that permit partial loading and unloading between origin and destination points, pickup and delivery, and diversion and re-consignment, which allows circuitous routing and changes in the final destination of a shipment (Ballou, 1999).

The primary unique features of water transport are the capability of moving vast quantities of cargo in one ship, on one voyage that is continuously moving, and the relatively low cost. It is the most dominant transport mode when moving goods worldwide. Water transportation accounted for 71.6% of U.S. freights in weight and 44.2% in cost (Federal et al., 2015). The primary drawbacks are the slow speed (360 nautical miles per day) and the inherent need for additional transportation modes and their corresponding load and unload time.

The most physically dynamic mode of freight transport is air. At its core, transportation via air is unlimited in direction and unaffected by congestion. Air is a more expensive mode of transportation and volume is a limiting criterion. Customers demanding faster deliveries have this option as it is also the shortest transportation time per distance than any other mode.

There are several transport modes available for shipping and freight movement. Freight transport cost model can be used as a tool for estimating the expected transport cost. For long distance logistic chains, a transport chain can involve a sequence of modes and terminals where containerization and an intermodal strategy, explained later in this chapter, help improve the efficiency of transport chains and consequently of supply chains (Rodrigue et. al., 2013). Intermodal freight is critical in international trade, import/export, high-value-added product supply chain, and military supply. The number of containers moving though ports has doubled over the last few decades and continues to grow rapidly.

In unimodal transportation, the transfer between the vehicles occurs within the same mode of transportation. For example, transporting a trailer load from one truck to another for consolidation or distribution. In most cases, road transportation is the unimodal transport; however, it can also be via water, rail, or air transportation. Unimodal transportation mode is most commonly found in domestic business transactions and shorter transportation distances. Unimodal transfers are easy to manage, from a logistics standpoint, and accomplish faster delivery, since the vehicles are similar and operate in the same medium (Mahoney, 1985). For instance, one train can transfer a truckload to another by simply switching the railcar.

The terms intermodal and multimodal are often used interchangeably, although there are perceived differences. The movements of passengers or freights from one mode of transport to another commonly take place at a terminal specifically designed for such a purpose (Rodrigue et. al., 2013). "Intermodalism" is a coordinated and sequential shipment or passenger movement involving two or more modes: rail/truck, barge/ship, plane/truck, bus/rail, rail/auto, etc. Intermodal is defined as the movement of cargo from origin to destination by several modes of transport where each of these modes have a different transport carrier responsible, each with its own independent contract. The objective of intermodalism is to make optimal use of the different modes and improve the connections among them. Multiple carriers during a single journey collaborate per the terms and conditions of their customer's contract. Each leg of the shipment is handled by a separate transport carrier. The shipper will have several contracts, one with each transport carrier to handle the specific leg of the shipment each is responsible for. The U.S. has 5,941 recognized private and public ports for intermodal connections and handoffs. Conversely, multimodal transport is defined as the movement of cargo from origin to destination by several modes of transport, where each of these modes has a different transport carrier responsible, but all carriers operate under a single contract or bill of lading. A single contract is used to facilitate part movement during a single journey. The same transport carrier is responsible for moving the shipment in all legs, in all modes. In simple terms, multimodal uses various modes of transport, but with one transport bill of lading (Logistics blog, 2015).

The piggyback is the specialized form of Trailer-on-Flat-Car (TOFC) transportation (i.e., road trailers ride in special rail cars). Piggybacking became common in the 1950s, and later moved towards stacking and double-stacking of containers in the 1980s (Container on Flat Car; COFC). Because of the height clearance for bridges and tunnels (5.5 meters), double-stacking is not always possible on some older rail routes. In North America, double-stacking in truck-rail intermodal transportation has become a high priority, reliable, moderately fast, and economical mode of transportation. The transportation combination between air and truck, Air-Truck, has also become popular for smaller, expensive items and documents that require faster transportation. However, Air-Truck is limited and is an expensive mode of transportation. Among the common freights, the truck is moderately fast and reliable, while rail is slower and less reliable than trucking. Trucking offers more flexibility than any other mode of transportation. It is a necessity for pre- and post-haulage and businesses need to determine what amount of trade-offs should be made in order to make decisions based on truck and other mode of transportation combinations.

The freight transport cost is an important selection criterion. Transport cost function primarily depends on transport network, volume and the transport modes. Several authors have proposed a series of studies that analyze the economic cost structure of unimodal and intermodal transport. The mode selection has been based on their methodologies. In one study, Boardman, et. al. (1999) compares total transportation cost among shippers: truck/rail, truck/barge, and rail/barge combinations for container transport. The study points out that the mode choice is strongly influenced by the distance covered and shipment characteristics. The authors conclude that road transport is the best option for short distances. Boardman, et. al. (1999) defines the total transportation costs (TC) as follows:

$$TC = T_m + D_m + T_{sm} + CC_m$$

Where:

T_m Transportation cost (in dollars) for mode m
D_m Dray cost (transporting goods a short distance via ground freight, in $) for mode m
T_{sm} Transfer cost (in dollars) at terminal for mode m
CC_m Carrying cost (in dollars) for mode m

Among other necessary shipment inputs, Ben-Akiva & de Jong (2013) noted that number of shipments, tons, ton-miles, and vehicle/containers per year are important factors. Following the model, the total annual freight transport costs *TC* of commodity *k* transported between zone *r* (e.g., port location *m*) to zone *s* (e.g., warehouse location *n*) of shipment size *q* with transport chain *l* (including number of legs, modes, vehicle types, loading units, transshipment locations) can be derived as:

$$TC = D_k + I_{KQ} + K_{kq} + Q_{kq} + T_{(r \to s)kl} + Y_{(r \to s)kl} + Z_{(r \to s)kq}$$

where

TC Total logistics costs
D Cost of deterioration and damage during transit
k Commodity type
l Transport chain type (number of legs, mode and vehicle/container type used for each leg, terminals used, loading unit used)
m Sending location (e.g., port, zone r)
n Receiving location (e.g., warehouse, zone s)
q Shipment size
I Inventory costs (storage costs)
K Capital costs of inventory
Q Order costs
t Transport, consolidation and distribution costs
Y Capital costs of goods during transit
Z Stock out costs

In freight transportation, pre-haulage is the process of gathering all the individual shipments, also known as "the first mile". Trucking is the most common mode of transport for completing this step. The choice of truck is common due to facility locations typically being at a distance from ports and rails. Additionally, it is not uncommon for business to utilize their own trucks to perform the pre and post haulage. The major concern is the selection of the long-haul transportation. It may be conducted via road, rail, air, and/or water. The post-haulage transportation, also known as the "last mile", is primarily conducted via trucks, similar to the first mile. This is largely due to the fact that various retail stores, distribution centers, and warehouses typically make up the last mile destinations. Tavasszy (2013) points out that intermodal container transport is an alternative to road container transport when the internal costs of the intermodal trip are competitive in comparison to the internal costs of trucking. Freight transportation modeling requires information such as fixed and variable costs related to transport modes, vehicle types and product group, origin-destination data, route networks, and terminals information for transferring containers between transport modes.

Transportation Cost Model Implementation

A cost analysis is provided to compare the cost of four modal transports: (i) a unimodal transport chain by truck, two multimodal transport chains by (ii) rail/truck and (iii) air/truck and an intermodal (iv) container on flat car (COFC)/Truck for container transport. A detailed description of transportation cost implementation process, using different types of transportation modes between the points of origin (O) to the destination (D), is shown in Figure 2.

Time sensitivity is another major criteria that effects the freight selection decision. Constraints that directly affect the transportation time include road infrastructure, types of products, and availability of the transports. To compare the total cost of a transport, several cost items need to be taken into account: transport cost (major transport + pre-post haulage transport), tariff, and transshipment cost. The freight transport cost model, adapted from Ben-Akiva & de Jong (2014), illustrates the cost to transport a container from a point of origin to a destination. The total cost (TC) of transportation is the following.

$$TC_m = Z_m \times \left(\frac{\beta_m}{h_m} + \tau_m \right) + a_m \times \left(\frac{\beta_m}{h_m} + g_1 \right) + b_m \times \left(\frac{\beta_m}{h_m} + g_2 \right) + w_m + \beta(r)$$

Where

TC_m Total cost for modal transportation

$Z_m \times \left(\dfrac{\beta_m}{h_m} + \tau_m \right)$ Main modal transport cost ($)

$a_m \times \left(\dfrac{\beta_m}{h_m} + g_1 \right)$ Pre-haulage transport cost ($)

$b_m \times \left(\dfrac{\beta_m}{h_m} + g_2 \right)$ Post-haulage transport cost ($)

w_m Transshipment cost for modal transport ($/Container)

$\beta(r)$ Time to transfer container at the intermodal terminal

a_m Pre-haulage distances (road transport) (miles)

Figure 2. Intermodal transport modes between points of origin (O) to the destination (D)

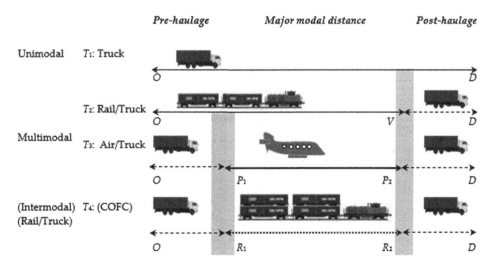

b_m Post-haulage distances (road transport) (miles)

h_m Transport speed (transport mode) (mile/hour)

τ_m: Main transport tariff, ($/Container mile)

r Transshipment time at intermodal terminal (hours)

β_m Value of time (transport mode) ($/Container/hour)

g_1 Pre-haulage tariff ($/Container mile)

g_2 Post-haulage tariff ($/Container mile)

Numerical Example

Assume the distance between the point of origin and destination, z, is 2,000 miles. Distance travelled by a major transport mode is described as $z = a - b$, where a is pre-haulage distance and b is post haulage distance. Road transport is only used for pre- and post-haulage. Table 2 provides the comparative intermodal cost elements.

It is assumed that the selected modes carry the same commodity groups (product) and have the same transport distance. Total transport cost comparison of selected freight transport mode is shown in Table 3.

For example, (Rail/Truck), there is no pre-haulage distance; it only includes rail transport as the main mode of transport and truck for the post-haulage transport.

Sample Calculation 1

$$TC_{R/T} = Z_R \times \left(\frac{\beta_R}{h_R} + \tau_R \right) + b_T \times \left(\frac{\beta_T}{h_T} + g_2 \right) + w_m + \beta(r)$$

$$= [2000 \times ((1/40)+0.9)] + [30 \times ((1/50)+5)] + 25 + [(1) \times (2)] = \$1151.85$$

Table 2. Comparative intermodel cost elements

Variables	Road	Rail/Truck	Air/Truck	COFC
z: Distance, (mile)	2000	1970	1950	1960
a: Pre-haul distance, (mile)	n/a	n/a	25	n/a
b: Post-haul distance, (mile)	n/a	30	25	40
r: Transshipment time (hours)	n/a	2	3	1
w: Transshipment costs, ($/container)	n/a	25	50	15
τ: Transport tariff, ($/Container mile)	1.1	0.5	1.1	0.7
h: Transshipment speed (mile/hour)	40	50	300	50
g: Post-haul tariff, ($/Container mile)	0.0	3	3	3
β: Value of time ($/Container/hour)	1	1	1	1

Table 3. Transport cost comparison of selected freight transport modes

Mode	Total cost
TC (Road)	$1,840.00
TC (Rail/Truck)	$1,151.85
TC (Air/Truck)	$2,280.00
TC (COFC)	$1,361.80

The freight cost analysis is useful when a complete and precise freight cost comparison is needed. The preliminary result shows, among the different transport modes, the rail/truck is relatively cheaper than the other modes of transportation. Although freight transport cost is a key role, further analysis with several other variables such as the shipment characteristics, route availability, compliance to the buyer's policy, and goals are needed to determine the freight transport mode.

FREIGHT SELECTION MODEL

This section highlights the theoretical background of the TOPSIS method integrating the entropy weight coefficient method to determine the weights for the criteria proposed in this study. The TOPSIS method is applied to find the best alternative satisfying the decision maker's requirements and constraints. In a supply chain, the carrier selection decision is based on discrete information of performance rate regarding the chosen criteria. The carrier performance rates are also based on discrete information, some of which are straightforward, collected from past data. While performance rates for other measures may be difficult to obtain due to incomplete and non-obtainable sources. TOPSIS method is a preferable choice to find the best option using this multi-attributed data matrix. The method allows the uncertainty of human judgment to be introduced into the model; weights can be precisely assigned to each attribute. An entropy weight coefficient method is implemented to determine the weight factor for each selected criteria given the performance rate information of the carrier alternatives. The advantage of entropy method over the conventional methods is the ability to identify weights without associating decision makers' subjective judgment about the significance of criteria. The entropy method is useful in the cases when policy makers conflict on the values of weights (Singh & Ben Youcef, 2011). The best transport carrier decision is to not only reduce cost, but also attain supply chain gain by the quick and efficient flow of the freights at the right time for the right purpose. The procedure to identify the ranks among the alternative carriers using TOPSIS based method integrated with entropy weight coefficient method can be expressed in a series of steps and their equations.

Step 1: Identify Evaluation Criteria to Construct Decision Matrix

This step includes identification of the evaluation criteria, generating alternatives, evaluating alternatives in terms of criteria and identifying the weights of criteria. Assume the decision maker identify n selections criteria C_j ($j = 1, 2, ..., n$) through which m alternative transportation modes A_i ($i = 1, 2,..., m$) are evaluated. In this step, the data is expressed in a ($m \times n$) matrix, and represents the discrete choices between the criteria and alternatives. The matrix format is shown below:

Table 4. Performance rating of criteria C_j for each A_i

	C_1	C_2	...	C_n
A_1	$\tilde{x}_{11}$	$\tilde{x}_{12}$	...	$\tilde{x}_{1n}$
A_2	$\tilde{x}_{21}$	$\tilde{x}_{22}$	...	$\tilde{x}_{2n}$
A_3	$\tilde{x}_{13}$	$\tilde{x}_{32}$	...	$\tilde{x}_{3n}$
☐	☐	☐	☐	☐
A_m	$\tilde{x}_{m1}$	$\tilde{x}_{m2}$	...	$\tilde{x}_{mn}$

Matrix element, $\tilde{x}_{ij}$ is the performance rating of criteria C_j for each transportation mode alternative A_i. The squared normalization of the data eliminates the differences of measurement units and inconsistent scale. The normalized value Q_{ij} is calculated as

$$Q_{ij} = x_{ij} / \sqrt{\sum_{i=1}^{m} x_{ij}^2} \, , \ i\epsilon\left(1,2...,m\right) \ j\epsilon\left(1,2...,n\right) \tag{1}$$

where x_{ij} represents the numerical evaluation of alternative A_i for criterion C_j.

Step 2: Evaluate the Weight Factor for Each Criteria using Entropy Method

Entropy weight coefficient method determines weight $\tilde{w}_j$ for each criteria, C_j ($j = 1, 2, ..., n$). Using the general normalized decision matrix, p_{ij}, entropy weight coefficient E_j is calculated as follows:

$$E_j = -k\sum_{j=1}^{n} p_{ij} \ln\left(p_{ij}\right) \tag{2}$$

where $p_{ij} = x_{ij} / \sum_{i=1}^{m} x_{ij}$, k (constant) $= 1 /\ln (m)$. The principle of entropy method states a criterion tends to be more important, if a greater dispersion is observed in the evaluations of the alternatives. The larger the entropy within the criteria the more like it is to be an important criterion. The higher D_j value indicates the importance of the criterion in the decision matrix. The measurement of dispersion D_j for a criterion is calculated as the following:

$$D_j = 1 - E_j \tag{3}$$

The weight w_j for each attribute C_j is calculated by using the following formula:

$$w_j = \frac{D_j}{\sum_{k=1}^{n} D_k} \qquad (4)$$

$w_j = \tilde{w}_1, \tilde{w}_2, \ldots, \tilde{w}_n$, where $\tilde{w}_j$ is the weight of jth criterion C_j.

Step 3: Construct Weighted Normalized Decision Matrix

The elements in decision matrix are updated by multiplying the weights obtained in Step 2 implementing entropy method with the normalized value Q_{ij} (obtained in Step 1) as follows:

$$\widetilde{V_{ij}} = \left(\widetilde{Q_{ij}} \times \widetilde{w_j} \right) \qquad (5)$$

where $\widetilde{w_j}$ is the weight factor. $\widetilde{V_{ij}}$ is the element in decision matrix, $i \epsilon \left(1,2\ldots,m \right)$ $j \epsilon \left(1,2\ldots,n \right)$.

Step 4: Positive Ideal Solution and Negative Ideal Solution

This step is to identify the positive ideal reference point, (*PIRP*, V^+) and the negative ideal reference point (*NIRP*, V). The set of benefit criteria, J_b ($J \in J_b$); the set of cost criteria J_c ($J \in J_c$) are the following.

$$V^+ = \left\{ \left(max_i V_{ij} | J \in J_b \right), \left(min_i V_{ij} | J \in J_c \right) \right\} = \left\{ V_1^+, V_2^+, \ldots, V_n^+ \right\} \qquad (6a)$$

$$V^- = \left\{ \left(min_i V_{ij} | J \in J_c \right), \left(max_i V_{ij} | J \in J_c \right) \right\} = \left\{ V_1^-, V_2^-, \ldots, V_n^- \right\} \qquad (6b)$$

Step 5: Separation of Measures

The distance of each alternative from the positive ideal reference point (S_i^+ from *PIRP*) and negative ideal reference point, (S_i^- from *NIRP*) obtained as follows:

Positive Ideal Separation: $S_i^+ = \sqrt{\sum_{j=1}^{n} d \left(V_{ij} - V_j^+ \right)^2}$ $\quad i = 1,2,\ldots,m$ $\qquad (7a)$

Negative Ideal Separation: $S_i^- = \sqrt{\sum_{j=1}^{n} d \left(V_{ij} - V_j^- \right)^2}$ $\quad i = 1,2,\ldots,m$ $\qquad (7b)$

where $d\left(V_{ij} - V_j^+\right)$ is the distance between an element and the maximum value. S_i^+ represents the distance of alternative from *PIRP* and S_i^- represents the distance of alternative from *NIRP*.

Step 6: Obtain the Closeness Co-Efficient and Rank the Alternatives

The relative closeness index C_i is calculated using the values obtained in Step 5, S_i^+ for *PIS* and Si- for *NIS*. The number C_i determines the priority range of the selected transport carriers with respect to the given criteria. The C_i value is obtained as follows:

$$C_i = \frac{S_i^-}{S_i^+ + S_i^-} \quad i = 1,2,\ldots,m; 0 \leq C_i \leq 1 \tag{8}$$

Closeness index C_i approaching 1 denotes a carrier is in high priority (i.e., close to the positive ideal reference point and away from negative ideal reference point). Using TOPSIS model ensures the best solution found is, not only, the shortest distance to $C_{i=1}$ but, also the furthest distance from $C_{i=0}$.

NUMERICAL ILLUSTRATION

The transport carriers welcome the procurement activities and freight distribution between locations. This numerical example explores the process and critical elements necessary to distinguish the transportation alternatives given a supply chain relation and company policy. Studies in supply chain transportation have shown some variables and criterion to be important in the decision-making process to select carriers given a known supply chain and company policy. The performance carrier rate is easier to obtain for of these criteria while the performance information of some other criteria is not clearly attainable. Decision makers often use realism for this purpose depending on their experience.

In intercontinental freight carrier selection, the capacity of high volume cargo is often considered to be a dominant criterion. Gibson et al. (2002) studied shippers' and carriers' rank among different criteria measures. The shippers ranked cost as the most important factor, followed by the effectiveness of services, trust, flexibility, and channel perspectives. For the carriers, reliability is the most important factor, followed by efficiency, flexibility, cost, and planning. Kent et. al. (2001) surveyed five different freight transport industry segments: dry van, intermodal, temperature control transport, tank transport and flatbed. They found the following service criteria to be of considerable attribution: reputation, quality, integrity, knowledge, problem-solving skills of contact personnel, quality of drivers, competitive pricing, action and follow up service complaints, billing accuracy, equipment availability, consistency, and dependable transit times. Garcia-Mendez, et. al. (2004) indicated price and transit time of a shipment for both land and sea transportation are the key determinants. Other freight shippers concluded that transit time, reliability, accessibility, capability, and security are essential transportation service criteria (Coyle, et al., 2008). Based on information collected from road and rail freight forwarders, Grue and Ludvigsen (2006) concluded that reliability and price of the service are important factors to consider in the carrier selection process. The time and distance, e.g., how fast are the freights required to go in order to reach its destination at the right time is the critical part of freight transportation planning process.

Consider the example to demonstrate the TOPSIS method carrier selection integrated with entropy weight coefficient method. A typical inbound supply chain to the United States ships a (brand name) carry-on luggage. A company located in California designs a new line of carry-on luggage model, which primarily gets manufactured overseas. After the production reaches completion, the luggage passes through some warehouses, ports, and modes of transportation in the shipping container along the way to the destinations. The finished product arrives at a seaport on the west coast, U.S. The carry-on luggage producer distributes a significant portion of the product to its company-owned warehouses on the east coast. The product needs to transport from the west coast port to a store location on the east coast. The objective is to find an appropriate carrier to ship the carry-on luggage from the west coast seaport to a store located on the east coast in the U.S. The rating of each transport alternative and the weights of criterion collected from a survey by a panel of professionals who enrolled in the supply chain and logistics graduate program. These responders are full-time students while others are working professionals involved in the transport industry.

Suppose there are four alternative carriers, T_1, T_2, T_3, and T_4 representing all truck, rail/truck, air/truck, and COFC intermodal carriers are available. Decision makers identify the suitable freight alternative based on the three benefit criteria (reliability, time sensitivity and capability) and cost criteria (price), denoted by A_1, A_2, A_3, and A_4, respectively. The average freight transportation price (cent/ton-mile) by mode: railway (2.50), truck /motorway (25.08), water/seaway (0.73) and airway (58.75) (Ballou, 1999). The alternative freight modes and selected criteria is shown in Figure 3.

The performance rates are graded on a 1 through 9 scale (1 = least; 9 = best) in terms of the criteria for each transport carrier mode. The following is the numerical guide. The data matrix discussed in Step 1 evaluates the performance rate of each carrier alternative and the corresponding criteria, presented in

Figure 3. Alternative freight modes and selected criteria

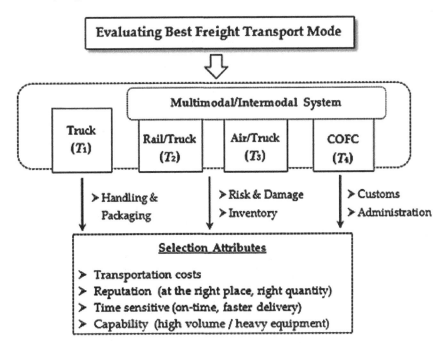

Table 5. The freight carrier alternatives T_j ($j = 1, 2\ldots 4$), evaluated against the selected attributes A_i ($i = 1, 2\ldots, 4$), the data is expressed in a (4×4) matrix represents the discrete choice between the attributes and alternatives.

Squared normalization value of in Q_{ij} is calculated as $Q_{ij} = x_{ij} / \sqrt{\sum_{i=1}^{m} x_{ij}^2}$., presented in Table 6.

Sample Calculation 2

From Equation 1: $Q_{ij} = x_{ij} / \sqrt{\sum_{i=1}^{m} x_{ij}^2}$. In Table 6, $Q_{11} = 6 / (\sqrt{6^2 + 8^2 + 9^2 + 7^2}) = 0.3956$

For weight calculation using entropy method, we used normalized method such that $p_{ij} = x_{ij} / \sum_{i=1}^{m} x_{ij}$. Following is the calculation of entropy weight coefficient discussed in Step 2, presented in the Table 7.

Sample Calculation 3

In Table 7, Row 1: The E_j value is obtained using Equation 2: $E_j = -k\sum_{j=1}^{n} p_{ij} \ln(p_{ij})$.

Therefore, P_i values correspond to $T_{j=1}$ with respect to attributes A_1, A_2, A_3 and A_4 are 0.30, 0.25, 0.25 and 0.20.

$$E_{j=1} = \left[-\left(0.30 \times \ln 0.30\right) + \left(0.25 \times \ln 0.25\right) + \left(0.25 \times \ln 0.25\right) + 0.20 \times \ln 0.20\right] / \left[\ln(4)\right] = 0.9927.$$

Table 5. Data matrix to evaluate transportation mode in regards to criteria

Transport Mode	A_1	A_2	A_3	A_4	Sum
T_1: Truck	8	5	5	4	20
T_2: Rail/Truck	6	6	8	6	28
T_3: Air/Truck	9	9	6	9	33
T_4: COFC*	7	6	8	5	26

COFC* = Container on Flat Car, (Rail-Truck)

Table 6. Normalized value in decision matrix

Transport Mode	A_1	A_2	A_3	A_4
T_1	0.3956	0.3748	0.3637	0.3182
T_2	0.5275	0.4497	0.5819	0.4773
T_3	0.5934	0.6746	0.4364	0.7160
T_4	0.4616	0.4497	0.5819	0.3978

Table 7. The weight for m=4 is determined

Entropy Weight Method	A_1	A_2	A_3	A_4
$E_j = -k \sum_{j=1}^{n} p_{ij} \ln(p_{ij})$	0.9927	0.9926	0.9904	0.9892
$D_j = 1 - E_j$	0.0073	0.0074	0.0096	0.0108
$w_j = D_j / \sum_{j=1}^{n} D_j$	0.2075	0.2111	0.2740	0.3074

Table 7, Row 2: From Equation 3: $D_j = \left(1 - E_j\right) = \left(1 - 0.9927\right) = 0.0073$.

Table 7, Row 3: The weight, w_j value is obtained using Equation 4: $w_j = \dfrac{D_j}{\sum_{j=1}^{n} D_j}$ where

$$\sum_{j=1}^{n} D_j = 0.0073 + 0.0074 + 0.0096 + 0.0108 = 0.2308.$$

Therefore, $w_j = D_j / \sum_{j=1}^{n} D_j = 0.0073 / 0.2308 = 0.2075$.

To construct weighted normalized decision matrix described in Step 3, the weight factors (obtained in Step 2 and found in the last row of Table 7) multiplied with the normalized value P_{ij} (obtained in Step 1 and found in Table 6) is presented in Table 8.

Sample Calculation 4

From Equation 5: $\widetilde{V}_{ij} = \left(\widetilde{Q}_{ij} \times \widetilde{w}_j\right)$. Using values in Table 6 and Table 7,

$V_{11} = 0.3956 \times 0.2075 = 0.0821$ (Railroad)

Table 8. Weighted normalized decision matrix

Transport Mode	A_1	A_2	A_3	A_4
T_1	0.0821	0.0791	0.0996	0.0978
T_2	0.1095	0.0949	0.1594	0.1468
T_3	0.1232	0.1424	0.1196	0.2201
T_4	0.0958	0.0949	0.1594	0.1223

$$V_{14} = 0.4616 \times 0.2075 = 0.0958 \text{ (COFC)}$$

The reference points discussed in Step 4 (Equation 6a and Equation 6b) are the Positive Ideal Reference Point (*PIRP*) and Negative Ideal Reference Point (*NIRP*). From Table 8, the (v^+) in *PIRP* and (v^-) in *NIRP* are the maximum and minimum values correspond to each criterion, presented in Table 9.

Attributes 1-3 are benefit criteria meaning the highest value is the most preferred. Attribute 4 is a cost criteria meaning the lowest value is preferred. Calculation in Step 5 represents is the distance from the ideal reference points. The S_i^+ and S_i^- follows the Eq. (7a) and 7(b).

$$S_i^+ = \sqrt{\sum_{j=1}^{n} \left(v_{ij} - v_j^+ \right)^2}$$

(v_{ij} from Table 5, and v_j^+ from Table 6)

$$S_i^- = \sqrt{\sum_{j=1}^{n} \left(v_{ij} - v_j^- \right)^2}$$

(v_{ij} from Table 5, and v_j^- from Table 6)

Sample Calculation 5

From Equation 7a:

$$S_1^+ = \sqrt{\left(0.082 - 0.123\right)^2 + \left(0.079 - 0.142\right)^2 + \left(0.099 - 0.159\right)^2 + \left(0.098 - 0.098\right)^2} = 0.0962$$

From Equation 7b:

$$S_1^- = \sqrt{\left(0.082 - 0.082\right)^2 + \left(0.079 - 0.08\right)^2 + \left(0.099 - 0.0996\right)^2 + \left(0.098 - 0.22\right)^2} = 0.1223$$

The relative closeness of the alternate transport with respect to S$^+$ and S$^-$ has defined in Equation 8 as:

$$C_i = \frac{S_i^-}{S_i^+ + S_i^-} \text{ for } i = 1,2,\ldots,m; 0 \leq C_i \leq 1.$$

Table 9. Ideal reference points (PIRP, v$^+$ and NIRP, v$^-$)

v^+	0.1232	0.1424	0.1594	0.0978
v^-	0.0821	0.0791	0.0996	0.2201

Since $S^+ > 0$ and $S^- > 0$, the relative closeness index, $C_i \in [0,1]$. The S_i^+ and S_i^- and closeness index C_i in Step 6 for each alternate carrier mode ranking is presented in Table 10.

Sample Calculation 6

$$C_i = \frac{S_i^-}{S_i^+ + S_i^-}; i = 1,2,\ldots,m; 0 \leq C_i \leq 1. \text{ Therefore, } C_i = \frac{0.1815}{0.1791 + 0.1815} = 0.5032$$

The choice of freight must ensure the delivery time, cost, and capability to transport intended products are maximized. The reliability to ensure that delivery is available and the products reach the right place, at the right time without any damage is crucial. Inadequate capability, service commitment and uncertain transit times may cause a company to pay extra for the penalty due to longer in-transit inventory holding, missing deadlines, spoiled goods, and service interruption. As illustrated in Table 8, the COCF transportation mode has ranked number 1, considered to be the most economical, commonly used, reliable, on time service, and flexible. In the numerical study, the truck mode has ranked 2, which indicates a feasible alternative to COCF carrier mode. As companies grow larger in their respective supply chain industries, they are beginning to realize the benefit of managing the transportation process rely on leveraging the contract terms and negotiation with carriers regarding issues such as costs, reliability, time sensitivity and capability.

CONCLUSION

The global trade, supply chain coordination, and increased opportunity to procurement and marketing established the extensive links between companies and new markets regardless of location. To ensure value creation along the supply chain occurs, a seamless flow of goods and services have become vital, which rapidly influence the increase of high volume cargo demand. The criteria based TOPSIS method integrated with the entropy weight coefficient method discussed in this study determine the best carrier option to transport goods in freights and rank all the available options. This approach is simple to understand, permits the pursuit of the best alternative along a network of facilities and distribution options, and benchmarks a simple mathematical calculation. Besides business corporations and manufacturing companies, support agencies such as supply chain transporters and logistics providers benefit from the carrier selection aspect of decision making. Transporting goods across the continent or interstate may

Table 10. S_i^+ and S_i^- for each transport carrier (distance from v_j^+ and v_j^-)

Transport Mode	Si+	Si-	C_i	Rank
T_1: Truck	0.0962	0.1223	0.5596	3
T_2: Rail/Truck	0.0695	0.0998	0.5894	2
T_3: Air/Truck	0.1286	0.0780	0.3775	4
T_4: COFC	0.0600	0.1165	0.6602	1

use any major mode of transportation, i.e., trucks, rail, air, or COCF, options, depends on geographical location and customer service levels. Certain modes will be more advantageous than others will depending on routes and climates. The air carrier is often fast, reliable, good for shipping lightweight goods in small quantities, which requires maintaining secondary safety stocks, but expensive. Meanwhile, freight by rail/truck or COCF may be much cheaper, but takes a longer time, which necessitates companies to hold relatively large amounts of inventory in WIP to buffer against the resulting longer lead times and the inherent uncertainty associated with the carrier. Companies may use this to their advantage by strategically placing longer transportation times in front of bottlenecks effectively load leveling the chain. In the illustrative example, the COCF option is the most preferable in moving the freight. Cleary, the solution is to get the advantage of the motor flexibility and rail's long haul economic benefit. The acquired algorithm can be applied other cargo selection strategies such as routing and scheduling.

With the increase of computer usage and computation power, the application of MCDM methods has become easier for the users. With ability to obtain the best option regarding price, reliability, time, and flexibility businesses benefit, not only from a cost savings standpoint but, also enjoy the high reputation and service values gained from reliable delivery to the customers. Businesses also have the flexibility to change the criteria compared and measured to reflect and align with corporate policies, changing marketplace, customer demands, quality standards, and competitive advantages. The rapid adjustment capabilities computers offer allow businesses to turn analysis into a tool for counter-offers, maximizing cost saving potential. The decision maker should examine the service capabilities of the carrier in the same mode as services can vary widely between carriers. The final rank depends on the interpretation of the criteria on the alternatives and their perspective weights. Keep in mind the alternatives vary on the market in the bid is placed in. Transportation modes are obtained through reverse bidding, auctions, e-sourcing, and other means (Engerlbrecht et al., 2006). A business manager must ensure that the preference rating of the criteria is based on the company values, historical data, and unbiased subjective assessment while developing the framework of the decision matrix. Other selection criteria and variables can be used such as trip distances, the maximum legal capacity of transportation modes, infrastructures, cargo weight, operational cost, the total number of available vehicle, demand, and ability to accommodate product size or particular product to obtain more precise results using the TOPSIS.

An interesting future exercise will be to perform a sensitivity analysis replacing new values of the variables and adding new variables such as energy usage and fuel consumption (ton-miles per gallon of fuel), environmental impacts (air pollution), infrastructure, availability and accessibility of the transport in the freight selection process. It is perceived that the priority of the freight selection in regards to general conditions will remain similar.

REFERENCES

Abo-Sinna, M. A., & Amer, A. H. (2005). Extensions of TOPSIS for multi-objective large-scale non-linear programming problems. *Applied Mathematics and Computation*, *162*(1), 243–256. doi:10.1016/j.amc.2003.12.087

Awasthi, A., Chauhan, S. S., Omrani, H., & Panahi, A. (2011). A hybrid approach based on SERVQUAL and fuzzy TOPSIS for evaluating transportation service quality. *Journal of Computers and Industrial Engineering*, *61*(3), 637–646. doi:10.1016/j.cie.2011.04.019

Ballou, R. H. (2003). Business Logistics: Supply Chain Management (5th ed.). Prentice Hall.

Ben-Akiva, M., & de Jong, G. (2013). The Aggregate-Disaggregate-Aggregate (ADA) Freight Model System. In M. Ben-Akiva, E. van de Voorde, & H. Meersman (Eds.), *Freight Transport Modelling* (1st ed., pp. 69–90). Bingley, United Kingdom: Emerald. doi:10.1108/9781781902868-004

Boardman, B., Trusty, K., & Malstrom, E. (1999). *Intermodal Transportation Cost Analysis tables.* Department of Industrial Engineering, University of Arkansas.

Coyle, Bardi, Novack (2006). *Transportation* (Vol. 6). Mason: Thomson South-Western.

Coyle, J.J., Langley, C.J., Brian Gibson, B., Novack, R.A. and Bardi, E.J. (2008). *Supply Chain Management A Logistics Perspective.* South-Western College Pub; 8 ed.

Engelbrecht-Wiggans, R., & Katok, E. (2006). E-sourcing in procurement: Theory and behavior in reverse auctions with non-competitive contracts. *Management Science, 52*(4), 581–596. doi:10.1287/mnsc.1050.0474

Federal Highway Administrator Office of Freight Management and Operations. Statistics. (2015). *Freight Facts and Figures 2013* (Report No. FHWA-HOP-14-004). Washington, D.C.: Bureau of Transportation.

García-Menéndez, L., Martinez-Zarzoso, I., & Pinero De Miguel, D. (2004). Determinants of Mode Choice between Road and Shipping for Freight Transport: Evidence for Four Spanish Exporting Sectors. *Journal of Transport Economics and Policy, 38*(3), 447–466.

Grue, B., & Ludvigsen, J. (2006). Decision factors underlying transport mode choice in European freight transport. Institute of Transport Economics, Oslo, Norway. Association for European Transport and contributors.

Hogg, M. A., & Mullin, B. A. (1999). Joining groups to reduce uncertainty: Subjective uncertainty reduction and group identification. In D. Abrams & M. A. Hogg (Eds.). Social identity and social contagion (pp. 249–279). Oxford: Blackwell.

Hwang, C. L., & Yoon, K. (1981). *Multiple Attribute Decision Making Methods and Applications.* Berlin, Heidelberg: Springer. doi:10.1007/978-3-642-48318-9

ITRS. (2012). *International Roadmap for Semiconductor (ITRS).* Korea: Factory Integration Report. ITRS.

Jahanshahloo, G. R., Lotfi, F. H., & Izadikhah, M. (2006). An algorithmic method to extend TOPSIS for decision-making problems with interval data. *Applied Mathematics and Computation, 175*(2), 1375–1384. doi:10.1016/j.amc.2005.08.048

Jahanshahloo, G. R., Lotfi, F. H., & Izadikhah, M. (2006). Extension of the TOPSIS method for decision-making problems with fuzzy data. *Applied Mathematics and Computation, 181*(2), 1544–1551. doi:10.1016/j.amc.2006.02.057

Lancioni, R. A., Smith, M. F., & Oliva, T. A. (2000). The Role of the Internet in Supply Chain Management. *Industrial Marketing Management, 29*(1), 45–56. doi:10.1016/S0019-8501(99)00111-X

Leeman, J. A. (2010). *Supply Chain Management: Fast, flexible Supply Chains in Manufacturing and Retailing* (1st ed.). Books on Demand.

Logistics Blog. (2015). *Difference between Intermodal shipping and Multimodal shipping*. Retrieved from http://logisticsportal.org/community/blogs/-/blogs/difference-between-intermodal-shipping-and-multimodal-shipping

Logistics Blog (2015). Difference between Intermodal shipping and Multimodal shipping.

Mahoney, J. H. (1985). Intermodal Freight Transportation. Westport, Connecticut: Eno Foundation for transportation.

OECD. (2002). *Supply Chains and the OECD Guidelines for Multinational Enterprises*, 2002. Retrieved from http://www.oecd.org/investment/mne/45534720.pdf

Özceylan, E. (2010). A Decision Support System to Compare the Transportation Modes in Logistics. *International Journal of Lean Thinking*, *1*(1), 58–83.

Pomerol, J. C., & Romero, S. B. (2000). *Multicriteria Decision in Management: Principle and Practice*. Kluwer Academic Publishers. doi:10.1007/978-1-4615-4459-3

Robinson, A. (2015). The Transportation Supply Chain: Transportation's Role in Supply Chain Management to Lower Total Costs. *Supply Chain Transportation Management*. Retrieved from http://cerasis.com/2015/05/21/transportation-supply-chain/

Rodrigue, J.-P., Comtois, C., & Slack, B. (2013). *The Geography of Transport Systems. 3 edition*. Routledge.

Singh, R. K., & Benyouce, L. (2011). A fuzzy TOPSIS based approach for e-sourcing. *Engineering Applications of Artificial Intelligence*, *24*(3), 437–448. doi:10.1016/j.engappai.2010.09.006

Skjott-Larsen, T., Schary, P. B., & Mikkola, J. H. (2007). *Managing the Global Supply Chain* (3rd ed.). Copenhagen Business School Press.

Tavasszy, L. (2013). *Modelling Freight Transport* (1st ed.). Elsevier.

Tuzkaya, G., Ozgen, A., Ozgen, D., & Tuzkaya, U. R. (2009). Environmental performance evaluation of suppliers: A hybrid fuzzy multi-criteria decision approach. *International Journal of Environmental Science and Technology*, *6*(3), 477–490. doi:10.1007/BF03326087

Wathne, K. H., & Heide, J. B. (2004). Relationship governance in a supply chain network. *Journal of Marketing*, *68*(1), 73–89. doi:10.1509/jmkg.68.1.73.24037

Zavadskas, E. K., & Turskis, Z. (2011). Multiple criteria decision making (MCDM) methods in economics: An overview. *Technological and Economic Development of Economy*, *17*(2), 397–427. doi:10.3846/20294913.2011.593291

Zeng, A. Z., & Rossetti, C. (2003). Developing a framework for evaluating the logistics costs in global sourcing processes An implementation and insights. *International Journal of Physical Distribution & Logistics Management*, *33*(9), 785–803. doi:10.1108/09600030310503334

Zhao, Q. H., Chen, S., Leung, S., & Lai, K. K. (2010). Transportation Research Part E, Logistics and Transportation Review. *Transportation Research Part E, Logistics and Transportation Review, 46,* 913–925. doi:10.1016/j.tre.2010.03.001

Zhou, K. Z., Yim, C. K., & Tse, D. K. (2005). The effects of strategic orientations on technology- and market-based breakthrough innovations. *Journal of Marketing, 69*(2), 42–60. doi:10.1509/jmkg.69.2.42.60756

APPENDIX A

Table 11. A logistics cost category adapted from Zeng and Rossetti (2003)

Logistics Cost Category		Brief Definition
(2) Transportation	Freight charge Consolidation Transfer fee Pickup and delivery	Cost incurred during delivery using various transportation modes (rate depends on shipment size, product and destination) The fee for combining small shipments to form larger shipments Cost incurred during the transfer of goods between different modes of transportation Transportation charges incurred between shipper's warehouse and consolidator terminals
(2) Inventory holding	Pipeline holding Safety stock	Holding cost during the transfer Holding cost of safety stock
(3) Administration	Order processing Communication Overhead	Salaries of employees responsible for purchasing and order management Telephone, fax and information transfer related costs associated with international logistics Rent paid by international logistics group
(4) Customs	Customs clearance Brokerage fee Allocation fee	Fee imposed by local customs to clear goods Charge levied by an agent acting on behalf of the shipper or the receiver depending on the delivery terms Per house-bill
(4) Risk and damage	Damage/loss/delay Insurance	Percentage of the value of each unit shipped that will be lost, damaged or delayed Min $25 or $0.50 per $100.00 insured value
(4) Handling and packing	Terminal handling Material handling In/out handling Disposal charge Packaging/supplies Storage	Material handling fee charged by the transportation company Cost of labor and equipment used to move goods within shipper's or receiver's warehouse Material handling charge levied by the freight forwarder for use of its facilities Fee for taking away an empty container from the receiver's warehouse Cost of preparing goods for shipment Rental fee of the warehouse space

APPENDIX B

Table 12. The management review for transportation policy

Item 1. Review the current policy	Review of the transportation policy: ■ Review the existing conditions ■ Is there a need for changes to new freight, carrier, or route? ■ Forecast future population and employment growth
Item 2. Internal review and corrective action notices	Status of the internal review and transporter corrective action. Three corrective actions: ■ Are there any instances of a no show transporter? ■ Missing the deadline in delivering the product. ■ Are there any incorrect shipments, deliveries or incorrect processes?

Item 3.
Internal review results after a transport failure
	The status report includes:
	■ Are there any new suggestions, changes or transporter training requests?
	■ If trained, warning should be issued for the first time incidence.
	   o If changes are needed, look for new bidding of the freight
	      o If no findings, keep the same transport carrier and route.

Item 4. Review of resources	Review of resources needed to maintain and improve the efficiency. ■ Is there any new product delivery predicted? ■ Is any new route available? ■ Are there any new customers available?
Item 5. Review of effectiveness	Review of effectiveness of continuous improvement ■ Are positive trends realized throughout the supply chain? ■ Arrange training/ setup to teach transportation rules ■ Include visual boards for reminders on product delivery, customer location, route, delivery, due date, etc.
Item 6. Review of critical route	Review of critical route: ■ Transport route regarding critical product, such as hazmat. ■ Any trend of specific misuse activity of a transporter. ■ Is there new technology needed to identify secured and synchronized a more efficient route?
Item 7. Review or renew contract	Review or renew contract with transporter: ■ Discuss issues regarding existing contracts and costs. ■ Are necessary amendments needed for an existing or new service? ■ (If yes), discuss the need for the new contract.
Item 8. Review of service quality	Review of service quality objectives, data, and goals: ■ Review transporter service performance or delivery issues. ■ Review the service quality issues directed from customer. ■ Develop a survey card, service manual and methodology service.

Chapter 5

A Multifactorial Analysis of the Acceptance of Recommender System for Saudi Universities the Literature Revisited

Hadeel Alharbi
University of New England, Australia

Kamaljeet Sandhu
University of New England, Australia

ABSTRACT

Technology for learning is increasingly about enhancing users' interactions with the technology to improve learning outcomes. Of particular importance however to improving educational outcomes is the need to complement the technological advancements with advances in the educational practices of teachers to broaden the uptake of new technologies for learning. Recommender Systems are personalised services that aim to predict a learner's interest in some services or items such as courses, grades, references, links, etc. available in e-learning applications and to provide appropriate recommendations. Such systems can potentially enhance student learning by providing students with a more hands on, interactive and tailored learning experience.

INTRODUCTION

Over the last few years, there has been a great deal of attention in examining users' decisions to continue or discontinue using information technology (IT) and information systems (IS) (Dağhan, and Akkoyunlu, 2016; Mou et al., 2016; Al-Debei et al., 2013; Deng et al., 2010; Bhattacherjee, 2001; Flavian et al., 2006; Thong et al., 2006). This attention highlights the critical role of continuous adoption of IT/IS (i.e. post-adoption) for the long-term viability and eventual success of IT/IS systems (Dağhan, and Akkoyunlu, 2016; Deng et al., 2010; Bhattacherjee, 2001; Thong et al., 2006). The main purpose of this paper is to develop and test a research model on the basis of the Technology Acceptance Model (TAM) that

DOI: 10.4018/978-1-5225-1944-7.ch005

investigates the effects of user experience and service quality on students' acceptance and continuance usage intention of e-learning recommender systems. Given that more and more students are now using e-learning systems, and because some of them discontinue using such systems especially in developing countries such as Saudi Arabia, there is an emerging need to understand students' continuance interaction and participation at a deeper level.

Electronic learning (E-learning), also known as web-based learning system, is a new innovation in the educational technology environment which has received a great deal of attention over the last few years. E-learning has become progressively more vital for academia and corporate professional training. The worldwide growth of this technology is due to the increased competition amongst higher educational institutions to attract learners and meet their educational aims and needs (Clark and Mayer, 2011) either face-to-face or remotely without the constraints of time and distance. In conventional adaptive e-learning applications, the release process of learning material is personalized based on the model of the learner and user. The materials inside the application are a priori established by the application's designer. In contrast, with open e-learning applications, learning materials already exist on the Internet and are integrated into the application based on learners' connections with the application. Thus, learners participate in indirect communication with the open Internet, and updated learning materials in the open Internet could enhance their learning experiences through custom-made recommendations (Maâtallah and Seridi, 2012a, 2012b; Tang and McCalla, 2005; Tang and McCalla, 2009). To meet this need, software technologies and solutions known as recommender systems can offer recommendations for items of interest to users. The existing class of recommender approaches and methods are normally categorized into the following: collaborative, content-based, and hybrid recommendation approaches. Recommender systems such as collaborative filtering systems are personalized services that aim to predict learners' interests in some services/items (such as courses, grade, references, links, etc.) available in e-learning applications. However, adopting personalized recommendations in e-learning is more complicated than simply using existing systems (Basu et al., 1998; Melville et al., 2002; Schein et al., 2002).

The motive to conduct this study in Saudi Arabia is that Saudi Arabia represents an ideal market for ICT activities among those countries in the Middle East region (Eid, 2011). It has the largest and fastest growing ICT sector with a strong anticipation for considerable growth in the future (Al-Gahtani, 2011). It also enjoys high financial resources with GDP per Capita of $52,800 (CIA, 2015). In fact, Saudi Arabia is considered as one of the largest twenty economies in the world (Al-Somali et al., 2015). The Saudi Arabia economy is largely dependent on oil with about 16% of the confirmed petroleum reserve worldwide. About 45% of Saudi Arabia GDP, 80% budget revenues, and 90% of export earnings comes from the petroleum industry (CIA, 2015). Recently Saudi Arabia developed several ICT national strategies, plans and initiatives with the objective of transforming the country into a knowledge-based society and a digital economy (Al-Gahtani, 2011). In 1997, Internet services were officially made available in the Saudi Arabia for business and individuals. Since then the Internet has become a fundamental part of the Saudi Society and economy. According to the Saudi Communications and Information Technology Commission (CITC), the internet penetration rate in Saudi Arabia is rapidly growing and has significantly increased from 5% in 2001, 20% in 2006, 41% in 2010 and to 55% in 2013 (CITC, 2013). In educational institutions, Internet penetration is relatively high, as 75% of them are being connected to the internet (CITC, 2012).

However, despite the rapid growth in the Saudi ICT market the adoption of ICT applications such as e-learning solutions is still limited (Alenezi et al., 2012; Al-Gahtani, 2016; Asiri et al., 2012). As such Saudi Arabia is still considered as a late adopter in the e-learning field. Therefore, explanation of the decision behaviour of individuals toward the acceptance and continual usage of e-learning in academic settings in Saudi Arabia is the second motivation for conducting this research. In addition, although the careful review of the literature indicated that there are some empirical studies on the e-learning recommender systems adoption conducted in the developed countries; there is very little empirical research which focuses on e-learning recommender systems adoption and post-adoption in the Arab countries in the Middle East including Saudi Arabia. Filling this gap in the literature is another motivation for conducting this research. The aim of this chapter is to critically review the current literature in order to establish a clear understanding of the complexities of e-learning Recommender Systems adoption. It also seeks to identify basic determinants that may influence the acceptance and the continuance usage intention of Recommender Systems as an e-learning personalisation tool. This chapter initially provides an overview of e-learning and recommender system definitions, concepts, characteristics, advantages and disadvantages. This is followed by a critical review of the existing literature on determinants of e-learning Recommender Systems adoption in Saudi Arabia. Finally, the chapter presents a proposed conceptual model built to illustrate e-learning recommender system acceptance.

BACKGROUND AND LITERATURE REVIEW

E-Learning Recommender Systems

Recommender Systems primarily help students who lack adequate personal experience or competence to evaluate and make better choices from the potentially overwhelming number of alternative items (Kepeghom et al., 2015). In conventional adaptive e-learning applications, the process of releasing learning material is personalised, based on the model of the learner and user. The materials inside the application are a priori established by the application's designer. In contrast, with open e-learning applications, learning materials already exist on the Internet and are integrated into the application based on learners' connections with the application. Thus, learners participate in indirect communication with the open Internet, and updated learning materials in the open Internet could enhance their learning experiences through custom-made recommendations (Maâtallah & Seridi, 2012a, 2012b; Tang & McCalla, 2005; Tang & McCalla, 2009).

In order to meet this need, software technologies known as Recommender Systems offer recommendations for items of interest to the user. The existing class of recommender approaches and methods are normally categorised as: collaborative, content-based, and hybrid. Recommender Systems such as collaborative filtering systems are personalised services that aim to predict a learner's interest in some services/items (such as courses, grade, references, links, etc.) available in e-learning applications. However, adopting personalised recommendations in e-learning is more complicated than simply using existing systems (Basu et al., 1998; Herlockeret al., 1999; Melville et al., 2002; Schein et al., 2002). One of the main challenges for an e-learning Recommender System is that the items/services liked by learners may not be suitable for them. For instance, a learner without extensive knowledge of the methods of web mining could be interested only in descriptions of the up-to-date web mining methods in e-commerce.

Another challenge is that Saudi universities are not able to accept and adopt the good practices of Western universities such as those located in the United Kingdom (UK) to solve the problems they face (Elfaki et al., 2014). Regarding the problems specifically: first, the two countries have different cultures and university environments in terms of technology use, educational regulations, and technical support.

Second, service quality levels proposed by Saudi universities do not depend on British standards and criteria, and they have different local technical issues. Moreover, e-learning and information technology regulations are not used and may not even exist. Finally, the social Recommender Systems enabled in UK universities through use of the e-learning systems have been limitedly adopted or may not even exist in Saudi universities (Elfaki et al., 2014). Furthermore, user experience research is increasingly attracting researchers' attention in the Recommender System community.

In the context of IT usage, user experience of IT is considered to be of paramount importance for technology adoption and success. Users draw on their direct experiences with IT to develop their future behavioural intentions. However, despite the important role of user experience in technology usage, few studies have investigated the implication of this construct for continued IT usage (Deng et al., 2010) in general and e-learning tools in particular. To address these issues, this research explores the factors influencing the acceptance and the continuance usage intention of e-learning Recommender Systems in Saudi universities. The study investigates the experiences of students and instructors according to service quality and their user experience of e-learning Recommender Systems. Thus, the factors of acceptance such as service quality and user experience are considered in the e-learning system because they are viewed as a determinant of student/instructor/university satisfaction. Consequently, a number of dimensions have been taken into account for the way they facilitate the relationship between the student and instructor, and the university via electronic means such as electronic services.

E-Learning Adoption in Saudi Arabia

Although earlier there was a slow rate at which the Saudi Arabia universities was adopting e-learning technology, nowadays it is being more and more rapidly adopted because of the benefits it offers to students and teachers as well as education systems administrators (Hussein, 2011). Recently, Saudi Arabian student population in higher institutions is rapidly increasing. At the same time, these institutions suffer from a shortage of local faculty members. Therefore, e-learning technology could offer a valuable option that helps to decrease the dependency on local faculty staff (Alzamil, 2006). In addition, due to the dominant culture in Saudi Arabia, the higher education institutions have to separate students and teaching staff based on gender. For this reason, these institutions provide isolated buildings and distinct faculty members for their female and male students. This issue raises the challenge of wasting the financial and the academic resources especially with the noted shortage of female faculty staff in Saudi Arabia (Asiri et al., 2012). E-learning and its various tools are regarded as a fruitful solution to overcome this issue. Accordingly, higher education institutions are highly encouraged to introduce e-learning technology as a cost effective and culturally accepted solution wherein male faculty are able to teach female students remotely (Al-Sarrani, 2010). Although there is a well-established research on e-learning adoption worldwide (e.g. Abdullah and Ward, 2016; Chu and Chen, 2016; King and Boyatt, 2015; Tarhini et al., 2015; Tarhini et al., 2014; Cheung and Vogel, 2013; Lee, 2010), As shown in Table 1, it is evident in the related literature that only a paucity of research into e-learning adoption in Saudi Arabia can be found.

Alenezi (2012) explored the e-learning adoption in Saudi Arabia from faculty members' perspective. The results of his research showed that there was an overall positive outlook toward e-learning by faculty members. The results also revealed that there is a difference between the levels of e-learning based on gender, age, level of education and teaching experience. Similarly, Hussein (2011) investigated faculty members' attitude toward e-learning systems in Saudi Arabia. This study also reached the same conclusions in terms the positive attitude of faulty members toward e-learning management systems.

Table 1. Previous studies on e-learning/m-learning adoption in Saudi Arabia

Authors/ domain	Theoretical Background	Factors	Methods/ sample population
Alenezi (2012) E-learning	Have developed their own model	Demographic variables: age, gender, education level and teaching experience. Perceived self-efficacy, perceived enjoyment, perceived usefulness, perceived system satisfaction, multimedia instructions and behavioral intention to use e-learning	Survey Faculty members
Al-Harbi (2011) E-learning	Theory of Planned Behavior (TPB) and TAM	Perceived usefulness, perceived ease of use, attitude, intention to use, self-efficacy, university support, perceived e-learning accessibility, perceived e-learning flexibility, perceived e-learning interactivity, Internet experience, subjective norm, and demographics	Survey Students
Al-Gahtani (2016) E-learning	TAM3	Behavioral intention, computer anxiety, job relevance, computer playfulness, computer self-efficacy, enjoyment, image, perception of external control, result demonstrability, subjective norm, usefulness, objective usability, output quality, experience, and voluntariness	Survey Students
Al-Hujran et al. (2014) M-learning	Unified Theory of Acceptance and Use of Technology (UTAUT)	Performance expectancy, effort expectancy, social influences, facilitating conditions, and behavioural intention	Survey Students
Hussein (2011) E-learning	No model, only descriptive analysis	Attitude, gender, colleges classification and scientific ranking	Survey Faculty members
Nassuora (2012) M-learning	UTAUT	Performance expectancy, effort expectancy, social influences, facilitating conditions, attitude, and behavioural intention	Survey Students

However, the research found that there is no difference in attitudes towards using the e-learning system among the faculty members based on their gender or the college's classification. In a recent study, Al-Gahtani (2016) developed and empirically tested an e-learning model that is based on the third version of the Technology Acceptance Model (i.e., TAM3). Findings of this study indicated that TAM3 holds well in the Arabian culture such as Saudi Arabia. The results also demonstrated that most of TAM3 variables such computer anxiety, job relevance, computer self-efficacy, enjoyment, image, perception of external control, subjective norm, usefulness, objective usability, output quality, experience, and voluntariness are key determents of students' adoption of e-learning systems. Further and built on TAM and TPB theories, Al-Harbi (2011) developed a combined model to examine factors affecting Saudi university students' adoption intention of e-learning systems. The results showed that attitudes toward e-learning, perceived behavioral control, subjective norms and e-learning system attributes have critical impact on students' behavioral intention to use such systems.

Advanced technologies which is known as m-learning has also gained popularity and positive attitude among educators and students in Saudi Arabia for carrying out their educational activities in more flexible and comfortable style (Al-Gahtani, 2016). Few studies have explored students' intentions to use such technologies in their education. For example, Al-Hujran et al. (2014) adopted the UTAUT framework to investigate students' intentions to use m-learning in Saudi Arabia. The results of this study demonstrated that performance expectancy, effort expectancy and social influences were the main factors affecting students' adoption intention to use m-learning. Nonetheless, the results also showed that facilitating conditions has no significant effect on the intention to use m-learning. Nassuora (2012) also adopted the same framework (i.e., UTAUT) to identify the the factors influencing students' acceptance of m-learning in Saudi higher education institutions concluding that performance expectancy, effort expectancy, social influences, facilitating conditions and students' attitudes were significant determinants of the behavioral intention to use m-learning.

RESEARCH MODEL AND HYPOTHESES DEVELOPMENT

Technology Acceptance Theories

Previous research has utilised and employed a number of theories to predict and explain the underlying factors that motivate users to accept and adopt information technologies. These include Theory of Reasoned Action (TRA) (Fishbein and Ajzen, 1975), Theory of Planned Behavior (TPB) (Ajzen, 1985), Technology Acceptance Model (TAM) (Davis, 1989), Innovation Diffusion Theory (IDT) (Rogers, 1995), (UTAUT) (Venkatesh et al., 2003).

According to Venkatesh et al. (2003), the existing Information Technology (IT) adoption research can be classified into two broad streams. The first stream mainly focuses on the individual acceptance of IT, in which a potential user's behavioral intentions or/and actual usage are explored, while the second is more focused on IT implementation success at the organisational level. This thesis is from the first type and focusing on the individual adoption of e-learning Recommended Systems.

In this research, the researcher will study the usage factors of acceptance and continue use of e-learning recommender systems via e-learning on student–instructor relationships in Saudi universities. Figure 1 presents a proposed framework that is conceptually based on the integration of the technology acceptance model (TAM) with two external variables: user experience and service quality. The constructs – perceived ease of use and perceived usefulness – were adopted from TAM. In the proposed framework, the first external construct is the user experience variable. This variable includes elements that assist us to measure the user experience which is critical for the success of e-learning recommender systems in Saudi universities. The process of using e-learning recommended system as an innovative technology requires user experience in interacting with this system. Users need to have enough skills such as using toolbars, navigation, searching for information, and switching between different functions. The second external construct is service quality which is associated with the information quality that the electronic university information system delivers to its users, and is measured in relation to currency, accuracy, format, and completeness. Service quality determines the success of a website design (Wixom and Todd, 2005).

Figure 1. A proposed conceptual model of e-learning recommender system acceptance

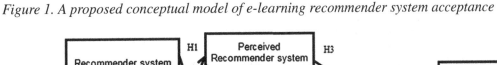
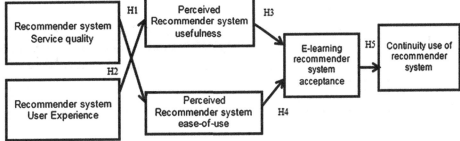

Overview of Technology Acceptance Model (TAM)

The technology acceptance model (TAM) (Davis, 1989) is one of the various models that IT/IS researchers have used to predict and explain why and how individuals make a decision about the adoption and use of information technologies. TAM shown in Figure 2 below was adopted from the Theory of Reasoned Action (TRA) (Ajzen and Fishbein 1980). TAM has been extensively used to explain and predict users' acceptance or use of IT by assuming that the constructs: perceived ease of use (PEOU) and perceived usefulness (PU) are the key determinants of users' positive or negative attitudes towards using the technology. TAM also postulates that attitude towards using the technology affects behavioural intention to use the technology. Behavioural intention to use technology then determines actual use.

Davis (1989, p. 320) defined PU as "the degree to which a person believes that using a particular system would enhance his or her job performance", and PEOU as "the degree to which a person believes that using a particular system would be free of effort". Fishbein and Ajzen (1975, p. 216) defined attitude as "an individual's positive or negative feelings (evaluative affect) about performing the target behaviour", and defined behavioural intention as "the strength of one's intention to perform a specified behaviour".

The existing literature on IS/IT adoption indicated that TAM has been applied to understand users' behaviour in different contexts such as cloud computing (e.g. Alharbi, 2012; Gangwar et al., 2015), e-commerce (e.g. Gefen et al., 2003; Fuller et al., 2010); e-government (e.g. Al-Hujran et al., 2015; Carter and Bélanger, 2005); internet banking (e.g. Boateng et al., 2016; Yen et al., 2016), mobile services (e.g. Bhatti, 2015; Park and Kim, 2014), social networking (e.g. Rauniar et al., 2014; Liao et al., 2015) and e-learning (e.g. Mohammadi, 2015; Tarhini et al., 2015; Tarhini et al., 2014; Cheung and Vogel, 2013).

TAM is adopted for this research as a ground theory to develop an Extended Technology Acceptance Model for el-learning recommender systems acceptance for several reasons. First, it has been extensively tested and validated across different settings and has been found to be predictive and robust model (Abdullah and Ward, 2016; Al-Harbi, 2011). Second, the TAM has reliable instruments and is empirically sound (Fan and Farn, 2007). Third, it could be extended and integrated with various external variables to improve its predictive power (Abdullah and Ward, 2016; Taylor and Todd, 1995a). Finally, TAM was the most commonly used theory in e-learning acceptance studies based on systematic review of the existing literature conducted by Sumak et al (2011), with 86% of the studies using TAM as a ground theory. In light of the above discussion and based on the assumptions of the original TAM, the following hypotheses are proposed:

Figure 2. TAM (Davis et al, 1989)

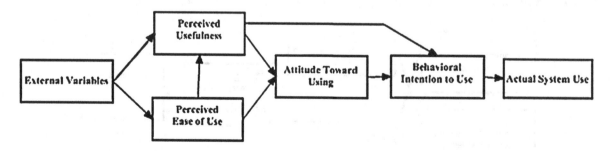

H1: The Perceived recommender system usefulness affects E-learning recommender system acceptance.

H2: The perceived recommender system ease of use affects E-learning recommender system acceptance.

Initial Acceptance vs. Post-Adoption of E-Learning Recommended Systems

Initial acceptance reflects the likelihood that a potential user will use an IS/IT system for a one-time or infrequent manner (Davis, 1989). Initial acceptance is usually explored by different theories and models such TPB, TRA or TAM. The IS/IT adoption literature showed that many researchers have further developed these theories through the integration of new factors or by combining previous theories in order to explain more efficiently the users' behavioural intention (Terzis et al., 2013). On the other hand, post-adoption or continuance acceptance takes into consideration user's expectations and the evolvement of user's perceptions over time (Dağhan, and Akkoyunlu, 2016; Karahanna et al., 1999). Indeed, repeated users (i.e. post-adopters) are better at evaluating the information and attributes of an IS/IT system as they have developed their experience with the system (Chiu et al., 2014).

In the last decade, various theoretical models have emerged which offer new insights into continuance intention. For example, Bhattacherjee (2001) developed the Expectation–Confirmation model (ECM) by combining TAM (Davis, 1989) with Expectation-Confirmation Theory (ECT) (Oliver, 1980). ECT is a widely used theory to understand continued usage by employing three variables, namely user satisfaction, confirmation, and post-adoption expectations (Lee, 2010).

However, although a number of IS/IT adoption studies have examined user acceptance of e-learning systems (e.g. Abdullah and Ward, 2016; Chu and Chen, 2016; King and Boyatt, 2015; Lee, 2010; Sanchez and Hueros, 2010; Karaali et al., 2011; Cheung and Vogel, 2013; Mohammadi, 2015), a limited number of studies have paid special attention to user retention and continued use of such systems (e.g. Dağhan, and Akkoyunlu, 2016; Lee, 2010; Terzis et al., 2013). While the initial acceptance of an e-learning system is a significant first step toward achieving e-learning success, long-term success still requires continued usage (Dağhan, and Akkoyunlu, 2016; Lee, 2010; Lin 2011). In other words, the success of an e-learning service depends on both its initial acceptance and its continued usage. Hence, understanding the factors affecting users' intention to continue using e-learning is very noteworthy for a successful implementation of e-learning recommender systems as it will assist vendors and developers to provide better services for learners and teachers. This study, therefore, employed both initial acceptance and continued usage in the research model and the following hypothesis is posited:

H3: The e-learning recommender system acceptance affects the continuity use of recommender system

Service Quality

The concept service quality has been widely studied in many fields of study, including marketing, commerce, management, and IT/IS. Parasuraman et al. (1998) defined *service quality* as the total evaluation or the overall experience of services. Service quality explains the difference between users' expectations and their perception of the service delivered by service firms (Wang and Chich-Jen, 2006). The results of Parasuraman et al.'s (1998) study illustrated that service quality has a number of dimensions (factors) including: reliability, responsiveness, competence, access, communication, security and understanding the user. Later, Sureshchandar et al. (2002) reduced the above dimensions of service quality to five: tangibility, reliability, responsiveness, assurance, and empathy. In their study, Cronin and Taylor (1992) determined four different models to measure service quality, namely SERVQUAL, SERVPERF, Weighted SERVQUAL, and Weighted SERVPERF. Service quality was introduced and further developed in many different ways. For example, Web quality, system quality and information quality were introduced to predict users' acceptance and usage of Web-based systems (Fang et al., 2016; Al-Debei et al., 2015; Zheng et al., 2013; Lin and Lee, 2006). Providing information with a satisfactory performance is the basic goal of an e-learning recommender system. Therefore, in this study, service quality is associated with the quality of information that the e-learning recommender system delivers to its users as well as the system quality. Information quality refers to the quality of outputs the information system produces (DeLone and McLean, 1992) and is measured in terms of accuracy, currency and completeness (Huh et al., 1990). Similarly, information quality captures the e-learning recommender system content issues such as information timeliness (i.e. up-to-date) and information accuracy (i.e. free from errors). System quality concerns about the quality of the e-learning recommender system itself and measures its performance and functionality issues (i.e. the system works correctly and performs necessary tasks) (Chatfield and AlAnazi, 2013). Previous research suggested that information quality and system quality are a key determinant of the success of an information system (Rana et al., 2015; Gorla et al., 2010; DeLone and McLean, 1992). Accordingly, in the context of e-learning recommender system, it could be argued that deciding what content to be recommended to potential users is extremely important to the success of this state-of-the-art system.

Many studies have investigated the relationship between service quality and perceived ease of use. Previous studies (Rana et al., 2015; Ahn et al., 2007; Cheong and Park, 2005; Liaw and Huang 2003) found service quality had a positive effect on individual perceived ease of use of information systems. Therefore, this research proposes the following hypothesis:

H4: The recommender system service quality affects perceived recommender system ease of use.

User Experience

User experience research is increasingly attracting IS/IT researchers' attention in the field of human-computer interaction (HCI) and interaction design. User experience focuses and addresses all issues related to how users use an interactive technology (Zaharias and Pappas, 2016). The User Experience contributes IS/IT research by providing guidelines for designing successful IS/IT systems and strengthen the design and development process for user-centric systems (Djamasb et al., 2016). Users usually develop their experience with an IT systems by repeatedly interacting and using them. Indeed, researchers started to investigative issues related to users' subjective opinions. In recent years, user experience issues with information technology systems such as design guidelines, usability, trust, quality and many more have been explored (Zaharias and Pappas, 2016; Deng et al., 2010; Knijnenburg et al., 2012). Researchers have also recognized the importance of user experience for the continuous usage as a determinant of IT success (Deng et al., 2010). Marketing literature empathized the significance role of consumption experience with product/services for evaluating the performance of such product/service (Oliver, 1993). Similarly, in the IT context, users depend on their direct experience with IT systems in order to evaluate them and develop their future behavioral intentions toward such systems (Deng et al., 2010). Previous studies have shown a significant relationship between experience and user acceptance and post-adoption IT usage (Davis et al., 1989, Taylor and Todd, 1995a; Karahanna et al., 1999; Agarwal and Karahanna, 2000; Hsu and Lu, 2004; Castaneda et al., 2007; Deng et al., 2010). As users' experiences develop over time, their familiarity with IT systems would increase and one would expect them to experience less frustrating practice (Karapanos, 2013). In addition, effort saved due to the improved experience with an IT system may enable a user to accomplish more tasks with the same effort and thus improve her/his performance (i.e. perceived usefulness). Hence, this chapter suggests the following hypothesis:

H5: The recommender system user experience affects perceived recommender system usefulness.

CONCLUSION

Two main findings emerged from the review of the literature providing in this chapter. The adaptability and practicability of the recommender system is critical to acceptance of the system by the user as well as its continued use. Also of significant importance to user acceptance is service quality and user experience. It turns, understanding the relationship between technology acceptance variables and Recommender System adoption has important implications for education service delivery improvement in Saudi Arabian universities. This chapter argued the TAM provides insights into how policy-makers can better integrate technology-based teaching in Saudi Universities. Such integration will provide a more progressive cultural orientation towards technology use for learning in Saudi Arabia. Moreover, if well-implemented, it will help to close the gap that exits between male and female students. E-learning fits in well with the objective to enhance the progressiveness of the tertiary education sector and TAM can be applied as a framework to guide a much needed revolution in Saudi tertiary education.

REFERENCES

Abdullah, F., & Ward, R. (2016). Developing a General Extended Technology Acceptance Model for E-Learning (GETAMEL) by analysing commonly used external factors. *Computers in Human Behavior*, *56*, 238–256. doi:10.1016/j.chb.2015.11.036

Ahn, T., Ryu, S., & Han, I. (2007). The impact of Web quality and playfulness on user acceptance of online retailing. *Information & Management*, *44*(3), 263–275. doi:10.1016/j.im.2006.12.008

Ajzen, I., & Fishbein, M. (1980). *Understanding attitudes and predicting social behavior*. Englewood Cliffs, NJ: Prentice-Hall.

Al-Debei, M. M., Akroush, M. N., & Ashouri, M. I. (2015). Consumer attitudes towards online shopping: The effects of trust, perceived benefits, and perceived web quality. *Internet Research*, *25*(5), 707–733. doi:10.1108/IntR-05-2014-0146

Al-Debei, M. M., Al-Lozi, E., & Papazafeiropoulou, A. (2013). Why people keep coming back to Facebook: Explaining and predicting continuance participation from an extended theory of planned behaviour perspective. *Decision Support Systems*, *55*(1), 43–54. doi:10.1016/j.dss.2012.12.032

Al-Gahtani, S. S. (2011). Modeling the electronic transactions acceptance using an extended technology acceptance model. *Applied Computing and Informatics*, *9*(1), 47–77. doi:10.1016/j.aci.2009.04.001

Al-Gahtani, S. S. (2016). Empirical investigation of e-learning acceptance and assimilation: a structural equation model. *Applied Computing and Informatics*, 12(1), 27e50.

Al-Harbi, K. A. S. (2011). E-Learning in the Saudi tertiary education: Potential and challenges. *Applied Computing and Informatics*, 9(1), 31–46. doi:10.1016/j.aci.2010.03.002

Al-Hujran, O., Al-Debei, M. M., Chatfield, A., & Migdadi, M. (2015). The imperative of influencing citizen attitude toward e-government adoption and use. *Computers in Human Behavior*, 53, 189–203. doi:10.1016/j.chb.2015.06.025

Al-Hujran, O., Al-Lozi, E., & Al-Debei, M. M. (2014). "Get Ready to Mobile Learning": Examining Factors Affecting College Students' Behavioral Intentions to Use M-Learning in Saudi Arabia. *Jordan Journal of Business Administration*, 10(1).

Al-Sarrani, N. (2010). Concerns and professional development needs of science faculty at Taibah University in adopting blended learning [Doctoral dissertation]. Kansas State University. Retrieved from http://krex.kstate.edu/dspace/bitstream/2097/3887/1/NauafAl-Sarrani2010

Al-Somali, S. A., Gholami, R., & Clegg, B. (2015). A stage-oriented model (SOM) for e-commerce adoption: A study of Saudi Arabian organisations. *Journal of Manufacturing Technology Management*, 26(1), 2–35. doi:10.1108/JMTM-03-2013-0019

Alben, L. (1996). Quality of experience: Defining the criteria for effective interaction design. *Interaction*, 3(3), 11–15. doi:10.1145/235008.235010

Alenezi, A. M. (2012). Faculty members' perception of e-learning in higher education in the Kingdom of Saudi Arabia (KSA) [Doctoral dissertation]. Texas Tech University.

Altimeter, T. (2011). Contextual mobile learning system for Saudi Arabian universities. *International Journal of Computers and Applications*, 21(4), 21–26. doi:10.5120/2499-3377

Alzamil, Z. A. (2006). Students' perception towards the e-Learning at the GOTEVOT and the Arab Open University in Riyadh. Journal of King Saud University. *Educational Sciences and Islamic Studies*, 18(2), 655–698.

Asiri, M. J. S., Mahmud, R. B., Abu Bakar, K., & Mohd Ayub, A. F. B. (2012). Factors influencing the use of learning management system in Saudi Arabian Higher Education: A theoretical framework. *Higher Education Studies*, 2(2), 125. doi:10.5539/hes.v2n2p125

Basu, C., Hirsh, H., & Cohen, W. W. (1998). Recommendation as classification: Using social and content-based information in recommendation. *Proceedings of the Fifteenth National Conference on Artificial Intelligence* (pp. 714–720). AAAI/IAAI.

Bhattacherjee, A. (2001). Understanding information systems continuance: An expectation confirmation model. *Management Information Systems Quarterly*, 25(3), 351–370. doi:10.2307/3250921

Bhatti, T. (2015). Exploring factors influencing the adoption of mobile commerce. *The Journal of Internet Banking and Commerce*.

Boateng, H., Adam, D. R., Okoe, A. F., & Anning-Dorson, T. (2016). Assessing the determinants of internet banking adoption intentions: A social cognitive theory perspective. *Computers in Human Behavior*, *65*, 468–478. doi:10.1016/j.chb.2016.09.017

Carter, L., & Bélanger, F. (2005). The utilization of e-government services: Citizen trust, innovation and acceptance factors. *Information Systems Journal*, *15*(1), 5–25. doi:10.1111/j.1365-2575.2005.00183.x

Central Intelligence Agency (CIA). (2015). The world factbook. Retrieved from https://www.cia.gov/library/publications/resources/the-world-factbook/index.html

Chatfield, A., & Alanazi, J. (2013). Service quality, citizen satisfaction, and loyalty with self-service delivery options: a strategic imperative for transforming e-government services. *Proceedings of the24th Australasian Conference on Information Systems (ACIS)* (pp. 1-12). RMIT University.

Cheung, R., & Vogel, D. (2013). Predicting user acceptance of collaborative technologies: An extension of the technology acceptance model for e-learning. *Computers & Education*, *63*, 160–175. doi:10.1016/j.compedu.2012.12.003

Chu, T. H., & Chen, Y. Y. (2016). With Good We Become Good: Understanding e-learning adoption by theory of planned behavior and group influences. *Computers & Education*, *92*, 37–52. doi:10.1016/j.compedu.2015.09.013

Clark, R. C., & Mayer, R. E. (2011). *E-learning and the science of instruction: proven guidelines for consumers and designers of multimedia learning*. New York: Pfeiffer. doi:10.1002/9781118255971

Communications and Information Technology Commission (CITC). (2012). Internet Usage Study in Saudi Arabia. Retrieved from http://www.internet.sa/en/internet-usage-study/#more-120

Cronin, J., & Taylor, S. (1992). Measuring service quality: A reexamination and extension. *Journal of Marketing*, *56*(3), 55–68. doi:10.2307/1252296

Dağhan, G., & Akkoyunlu, B. (2016). Modeling the continuance usage intention of online learning environments. *Computers in Human Behavior*, *60*, 198–211. doi:10.1016/j.chb.2016.02.066

Davis, F. D. (1989). Perceived Usefulness, Perceived Ease of Use, and User Acceptance of Information Technology. *Management Information Systems Quarterly*, *13*(3), 319–340. doi:10.2307/249008

DeLone, W. H., & McLean, E. R. (1992). Information systems success: The quest for the dependent variable. *Information Systems Research*, *3*(1), 60–95. doi:10.1287/isre.3.1.60

Deng, L., Turner, D. E., Gehling, R., & Prince, B. (2010). User experience, satisfaction, and continual usage intention of IT. *European Journal of Information Systems*, *19*(1), 60–75. doi:10.1057/ejis.2009.50

Djamasbi, S., Strong, D., Wilson, E. V., & Ruiz, C. (2016). Designing and Testing User-Centric Systems with both User Experience and Design Science Research Principles.

Eid, M. I. (2011). Determinants of e-commerce customer satisfaction, trust, and loyalty in Saudi Arabia. *Journal of Electronic Commerce Research*, *12*(1), 78.

Elfaki, A. O., Alhawiti, K. M., AlMurtadha, Y. M., Abdalla, O. A., & Elshiekh, A. A. (2014). *Rule-based recommendation for supporting student learning-pathway selection* (pp. 155–160). Recent Advances in Electrical Engineering and Educational Technologies.

Fan, Y. W., & Farn, C. K. (2007). Investigating factors affecting the adoption of electronic toll collection: A transaction cost economics perspective. *Proceedings of the 40th Annual Hawaii International Conference on System Sciences HICSS '07* (pp. 107-107). IEEE.

Fishbein, M., & Ajzen, I. (1975). *Belief, attitude, intention and behavior: An introduction to theory and research*. Reading, MA: Addison-Wesley.

Flavián, C., Guinalíu, M., & Gurrea, R. (2006). The role played by perceived usability, satisfaction and consumer trust on website loyalty. *Information & Management, 43*(1), 1–14. doi:10.1016/j.im.2005.01.002

Fuller, M. A., Serva, M. A., & Baroudi, J. (2010). Clarifying the integration of trust and TAM in e-commerce environments: Implications for systems design and management. *IEEE Transactions on Engineering Management, 57*(3), 380–393. doi:10.1109/TEM.2009.2023111

Gangwar, H., Date, H., & Ramaswamy, R. (2015). Understanding determinants of cloud computing adoption using an integrated TAM-TOE model. *Journal of Enterprise Information Management, 28*(1), 107–130. doi:10.1108/JEIM-08-2013-0065

Gefen, D., Karahanna, E., & Straub, D. W. (2003). Inexperience and experience with online stores: The importance of TAM and trust. *IEEE Transactions on Engineering Management, 50*(3), 307–321. doi:10.1109/TEM.2003.817277

Gorla, N., Somers, T. M., & Wong, B. (2010). Organizational impact of system quality, information quality, and service quality. *The Journal of Strategic Information Systems, 19*(3), 207–228. doi:10.1016/j.jsis.2010.05.001

Hu, P. J.-H., Clark, T. H. K., & Ma, W. W. (2003). Examining technology acceptance by school teachers: A longitudinal study. *Information & Management, 41*(2), 227–241. doi:10.1016/S0378-7206(03)00050-8

Huh, Y. U., Keller, F. R., Redman, T. C., & Watkins, A. R. (1990). Data quality. *Information and Software Technology, 32*(8), 559–565. doi:10.1016/0950-5849(90)90146-I

Hussein, H. B. (2011). Attitudes of Saudi universities faculty members towards using learning management system (JUSUR). *TOJET: The Turkish Online Journal of Educational Technology, 10*(2).

Karaali, D., Gumussoy, C. A., & Calisir, F. (2011). Factors affecting the intention to use a web-based learning system among blue-collar workers in the automotive industry. *Computers in Human Behavior, 27*(1), 343–354. doi:10.1016/j.chb.2010.08.012

Karahanna, E., Straub, D. W., & Chervany, N. L. (1999). Information technology adoption across time: A cross-sectional comparison of pre-adoption and post-adoption beliefs. *Management Information Systems Quarterly, 23*(2), 183–213. doi:10.2307/249751

Karapanos, E. (2013). User experience over time. In Modeling Users' Experiences with Interactive Systems (pp. 57-83). Springer Berlin Heidelberg. doi:10.1007/978-3-642-31000-3_4

Karapanos, E., Zimmerman, J., Forlizzi, J., & Martens, J.-B. (2009). User experience over time: An initial framework.*Proceedings of the 27th International Conference on Human Factors in Computing Systems (CHI '09)*, Boston, MA (pp. 729–738). doi:10.1145/1518701.1518814

King, E., & Boyatt, R. (2015). Exploring factors that influence adoption of e-learning within higher education. *British Journal of Educational Technology*, *46*(6), 1272–1280. doi:10.1111/bjet.12195

Knijnenburg, B. P., Willemsen, M. C., Gantner, Z., Soncu, H., & Newell, C. (2012). Explaining the user experience of recommender systems. *User Modeling and User-Adapted Interaction*, *22*(4-5), 441–504. doi:10.1007/s11257-011-9118-4

Lee, K., Palsetia, D., Narayanan, R., Patwary, M. D., Agrawal, A., & Choudhary, A. N. (2011). Twitter trending topic classification. *Proceedings of the11th IEEE International Conference on Data Mining Workshops* (pp. 251–258).

Lee, M., Cheung, C., & Chen, Z. (2005). Acceptance of Internet-based learning medium: The role of extrinsic and intrinsic motivation. *Information & Management*, *42*(8), 1095–1104. doi:10.1016/j.im.2003.10.007

Liao, Y. W., Huang, Y. M., Chen, H. C., & Huang, S. H. (2015). Exploring the antecedents of collaborative learning performance over social networking sites in a ubiquitous learning context. *Computers in Human Behavior*, *43*, 313–323. doi:10.1016/j.chb.2014.10.028

Liaw, S. S., & Huang, H. M. (2003). An investigation of user attitudes toward search engines as an information retrieval tool. *Computers in Human Behavior*, *19*(6), 751–765. doi:10.1016/S0747-5632(03)00009-8

Lin, H. F., & Lee, G. C. (2006). Determinants of success for online communities: An empirical study. *Behaviour & Information Technology*, *25*(6), 479–488. doi:10.1080/01449290500330422

Maâtallah, M., & Seridi, H. (2012a). Enhanced collaborative filtering to recommender systems of technology enhanced learning.*Proceedings of ICWIT'12* (pp. 129–138).

Maâtallah, M., & Seridi, H. (2012b). Multi-context recommendation in technology enhanced learning. *Proceedings of ITS'12* (pp. 720–721).

Martensen, A., & Gronholdt, L. (2003). Improving library users perceived quality, satisfaction and locality: An integrated measurement and management system. *Journal of Academic Librarianship*, *19*(3), 140–147. doi:10.1016/S0099-1333(03)00020-X

Melville, P., Mooney, R. J., & Nagarajan, R. (2002). Content-boosted collaborative filtering for improved recommendations. *Proceedings of theEighteenth National Conference on Artificial Intelligence*.

Mohammadi, H. (2015). Investigating users perspectives on e-learning: An integration of TAM and IS success model. *Computers in Human Behavior*, *45*, 359–374. doi:10.1016/j.chb.2014.07.044

Mou, J., Shin, D. H., & Cohen, J. (2016). Understanding trust and perceived usefulness in the consumer acceptance of an e-service: A longitudinal investigation. *Behaviour & Information Technology*, 1–15. doi:10.1080/0144929X.2016.1203024

Nassuora, A. B. (2012). Students acceptance of mobile learning for higher education in Saudi Arabia. *American Academic & Scholarly Research Journal, 4*(2), 1.

Oliver, R. L. (1980). A Cognitive Model for the Antece- dents and Consequences of Satisfaction. *Journal of Marketing Research*, 17, 460-469.

Parasuraman, A., Zeithamal, V., & Berry, L. (1988). SERVQUAL: A multiple-item scale for measuring consumer perceptions of service quality. *Journal of Retailing, 64*(1), 12–40.

Park, E., & Kim, K. J. (2014). An integrated adoption model of mobile cloud services: Exploration of key determinants and extension of technology acceptance model. *Telematics and Informatics, 31*(3), 376–385. doi:10.1016/j.tele.2013.11.008

Rana, N. P., Dwivedi, Y. K., Williams, M. D., & Weerakkody, V. (2015). Investigating success of an e-government initiative: Validation of an integrated IS success model. *Information Systems Frontiers, 17*(1), 127–142. doi:10.1007/s10796-014-9504-7

Rauniar, R., Rawski, G., Yang, J., & Johnson, B. (2014). Technology acceptance model (TAM) and social media usage: An empirical study on Facebook. *Journal of Enterprise Information Management, 27*(1), 6–30. doi:10.1108/JEIM-04-2012-0011

Sanchez, R. A., & Hueros, A. D. (2010). Motivational factors that influence the acceptance of Moodle using TAM. *Computers in Human Behavior, 26*(6), 1632–1640. doi:10.1016/j.chb.2010.06.011

Schein, A. I., Popescul, A., Ungar, L. H., & Pennock, D. M. (2002). Methods and metrics for cold-start recommendations.*Proceedings of the 25th Annual International ACM SIGIR Conference on Research and Development in Information Retrieval SIGIR '02* (pp. 253–260). New York, NY, USA: ACM. doi:10.1145/564376.564421

Sumak, B., Hericko, M., Pusnik, M., & Polancic, G. (2011). Factors affecting acceptance and use of Moodle: An empirical study based on TAM. *Informatica, 35*, 91–100.

Sureshchandar, G. S., Rajendran, C., & Anantharaman, R. N. (2002). The relationship between service quality and customer satisfaction: A factor specific approach. *Journal of Services Marketing, 16*(4), 363–379. doi:10.1108/08876040210433248

Tang, T., & McCalla, G. (2005). Smart recommendation for an evolving e-Learning system: Architecture and experiment. *International Journal on e-Learning, 4*(1), 105–129.

Tang, T. Y., & McCalla, G. (2009). A multidimensional paper recommender: Experiments and evaluations. *IEEE Internet Computing, 13*(4), 34–41. doi:10.1109/MIC.2009.73

Tarhini, A., Hone, K., & Liu, X. (2014). The effects of individual differences on e-learning users behaviour in developing countries: A structural equation model. *Computers in Human Behavior, 41*, 153–163. doi:10.1016/j.chb.2014.09.020

Tarhini, A., Hone, K., & Liu, X. (2015). A cross-cultural examination of the impact of social, organisational and individual factors on educational technology acceptance between British and Lebanese university students. *British Journal of Educational Technology, 46*(4), 739–755. doi:10.1111/bjet.12169

Taylor, S., & Todd, P. A. (1995). Understanding information technology usage: A test of competing models. *Information Systems Research*, *6*(2), 144–176. doi:10.1287/isre.6.2.144

Teng, C., Lin, C., Cheng, S., & Heh, J. (2004). Analyzing user behavior distribution on e-learning platform with techniques of clustering.*Proceedings of Society for Information Technology and Teacher Education International Conference* (pp. 3052–3058).

Terzis, V., Moridis, C. N., & Economides, A. A. (2013). Continuance acceptance of computer based assessment through the integration of users expectations and perceptions. *Computers & Education*, *62*, 50–61. doi:10.1016/j.compedu.2012.10.018

Terzis, V., Moridis, C. N., & Economides, A. A. (2013). Continuance acceptance of computer based assessment through the integration of users expectations and perceptions. *Computers & Education*, *62*, 50 61. doi:10.1016/j.compedu.2012.10.018

Thong, J. Y., Hong, S. J., & Tam, K. Y. (2006). The effects of post-adoption beliefs on the expectation-confirmation model for information technology continuance. *International Journal of Human-Computer Studies*, *64*(9), 799–810. doi:10.1016/j.ijhcs.2006.05.001

Venkatesh, V., Morris, M. G., Davis, G. B., & Davis, F. D. (2003). User acceptance of information technology: Toward a unified view. *Management Information Systems Quarterly*, 2003, 425–478.

Wang, M., & Chich-Jen, S. (2006). The relationship between service quality and customer satisfaction: The example of CJCU Library. *Journal of Information & Optimization Sciences*, *27*(1), 193–209. doi: 10.1080/02522667.2006.10699686

Wixom, B. H., & Todd, P. A. (2005). A theoretical integration of user satisfaction and technology acceptance. *Information Systems Research*, 16, 85-103.

Yen, L. H., Malarvizhi, C. A., & Mamun, A. A. (2016). Customer switching resistance towards internet banking in Malaysia.*International Journal of Business Information Systems*, *21*(2), 162–177. doi:10.1504/IJBIS.2016.074256

Zaharias, P., & Pappas, C. (2016). Quality Management of Learning Management Systems: A User Experience Perspective. *Current Issues in Emerging eLearning, 3*(1), 5.

Chapter 6
A Proposed Framework Factors of the Acceptance of Recommender Systems in E Learning for Saudi Universities

Hadeel Alharbi
University of New England, Australia

Kamaljeet Sandhu
University of New England, Australia

ABSTRACT

There is still a gap of knowledge on the usage of recommender systems in Saudi universities and the wider issue of technological change in the universities of developing countries. Relatively, this lack of knowledge is an issue to universities seeking to meet students/instructors' expectations and requirements by offering consistently high perceived service standards of e-learning services in a rapidly changing technological environment. To address this issue, this paper seeks to explore the impact of the acceptance and adoption of recommender systems in e-leaning for Saudi universities and this will help to investigate the students/instructors experience according to the e-learning service quality. Thus, a proposed e-framework has been presented. Such framework describes the factors of acceptance (such as service quality, student/instructor experience, and Human Computer Interaction guidelines) should be considered in the e-learning system because it is viewed as a determinant of student/instructor/university satisfaction.

INTRODUCTION

Traditionally, a personalised model of learner is used to drive adaptive e-learning applications and the way in which learning material is provided to the learner. As such, the learning materials available in the system are a priori according to the application designer. Open e-learning applications however rely only learning materials that are already available online. The user's interaction with the application then determines the materials that become integrated into the system. In this way, users are conceptualised

DOI: 10.4018/978-1-5225-1944-7.ch006

to be communicating (indirectly) with the open online application and would therefore benefit greatly from the provision of updated learning materials in the form of tailored recommendations (Maâtallah & Seridi, 2012a; Maâtallah & Seridi, 2012b; Tang & Mc Calla, 2005; Tang & McCalla, 2009).

Currently, software applications can offer recommended items of interest (e.g. movies, websites etc.) to uses which are related to particular search fields. These Recommender Systems are typically categorised as collaborative, content-based, or hybrid recommendation filters. Collaborative filtering systems for example are part of a personalised Recommendation System that first predicts and then responds to a user learner's particular area of interest (e.g. courses, grades, links etc.). Personalised recommendation systems have one short-coming however in that the recommendations being made may not in fact to the most suitable outcomes for the users (Basu, Hirsh, & Cohen, 1998; Herlocker, Konstan, Borchers, & Riedl, 1999; Melville, Mooney, & Nagarajan, 2002; Schein, Popescul, Ungar, & Pennock, 2002). For instance, a learner with only basic knowledge of a particular topic (e.g., data mining) may only be interested in accessing simple and descriptive information of the topic related to a particular learning field.

USER EVALUATIONS OF SERVICE QUALITY AND LEVELS OF SATISFACTION

Service quality and user satisfaction are vital concepts to academia and industry in order to study the user evaluations and experience, and to practitioners as means of building competitive benefits and user loyalty (Iacobucci et al, 1995). Iacobucci et al. (1995) presented two reports to determine whether or not service quality and user satisfactions have special antecedent reasons, consequential effects or both. As a result, the two reports introduced fairly robust user concepts of service quality and satisfaction. It should be noted that sometimes the service quality and user satisfaction are used interchangeably in both industry and academia.

In another study, DeRuyter et al. (DeRuyter et al, 1997) performed an empirical test to the health care service using SERVQUA[1] in attempt to indicate the relationship between service quality and user satisfaction. The results showed that the service quality can be treated as an antecedent of user satisfaction. Further study, the authors (Brady et al., 2001) used statistical analysis to study clients of fast-food restaurants in USA and South America. The results illustrated that there was a special relationship between service quality and user satisfaction with consideration to different cultural background. In addition, Sureshchandar and others (2002) pointed out the relationship and interaction between service quality and user satisfaction. Therefore, most of academic surveys and studies stated that the terms quality and satisfaction are appeared highly similar.

However, some researchers in quality pointed out that there is a difference between both terms in that the satisfaction is more specific, short-range evaluation and quality is more general and is long-range evaluation (Parasuraman at el, 1998).

Figure 1 shows the relationship and intersection between the service quality and user satisfaction. When applying this model in Figure 1 to any randomly data set, the result gives identical fit statistics whether quality was hypothesised (MacCallum, 1993).

Several research studies have pointed out that web service quality is an antecedent of user satisfaction (MacCallum, 1993; Parasuraman at el, 1998; Udo, 2010). E-learning systems model provides tool for assessing and comparing the level of e-service maturity. So the objective of this dissertation study is to build an e-user satisfaction strategy and measuring service quality by relating it to the e-learning service quality via adopting recommender systems.

Figure 1. Consumer evaluation model (service quality and customer satisfaction) (MacCallum, 1993)

According to Parasuraman et al. (Parasuraman & others, 1998) study, the results illustrated that the service quality had a number of dimensions (factors) including:

- **Reliability**: The consistency of a measure
- **Responsiveness**: The specific ability of a system or functional unit to complete assigned tasks within a given time
- **Competence**: The ability of an individual to do a job properly
- **Access**: The ability of accessing to perform a job properly
- **Communication**: How to communicate between services and other elements
- **Security**: The ability of making a service secure
- **Understanding:** The user

By understanding the relational benefits students/instructors obtain, universities can better understand how they can achieve the relationship results they want from their different student/instructor groups. Organisations need to understand, for example, whether:

1. Customers are likely to stay with the organisation
2. The relational benefits a company offers are a point of differentiation against their competitors
3. The company's internal processes work for or against delivering these benefits.

Positive personal and customer relationships involve understanding and effort from both parties. But, customer relationships need to be considered from a business perspective. Organisations should be very clear about the benefits they and their different customer groups receive from the relationship – and how this assists them achieve their business objectives (BOLLEN & EMES, 2008).

Furthermore, Sureshchandar et al. (Sureshchandar et al, 2002) reduced the above ten dimensions of service quality to five ones: tangibility, reliability, responsiveness, assurance and empathy. Note that the empathy is the capacity to recognise feelings that are being experienced by another person. In this study (Cronin & Taylor 1992), the authors determined four different models to measure the service quality such as SERVQUAL[1], SERVPERF, Weighted SERVQUAL and Weighted SERVPERF, which are explained below.

Moreover, Martensen and Gronholdt (2003) surveyed groups of people to indicate the key determinants for library service quality were: electronic resources, collection of printed publication, technical facilities and human side of user service.

EMPIRICAL RESEARCH OF SOCIAL NETWORK PLATFORMS FOR E-LEARNING

Ongoing advances in Internet enabled mobile devices such as smartphones and tablets continue to drive growth in the use of social networking platforms as evidenced by the growing popularity of Facebook, LinkedIn, Twitter, Instagram, Flicker, and YouTube.

Social networking sites are fundamentally designed to support social connections among users, be they individuals, groups or organisations). Moreover, the sites are designed to provide access to a range of services and to facilitate content sharing and social interaction (Correa & Ma, 2011). As such, social networking sites can be regarded as a social structure comprised of many and varied social networking actors who are linked together in various types of relationships (Wasserman & Faust, 1994).

Indeed, the purposes for which social networking actors access social networking sites can include employment reasons, general social interactions, a way to keep connected with friends and family as well as for academic pursuits (Pollara & Zhu, 2011). With regard to academic pursuits specifically, Gundecha and Liu (2012) suggest that students of all ages are key actors who use social networking sites to support the learning process. This has clear implications for learning institutions at all levels of education (i.e. primary school, high school and university) and their capacity to provide relevant and effective technology based learning tools to support student learning outcomes. Indeed, compelling research evidence continues to mount showing the advantages to students that can be gained from the use social networking sites for learning. For example, DiMicco et al. (2008), and Pollara and Zhu, 2011) present research findings to show that the use of social networking sites not only supports student interactions, but also can improve their results and create a sense of belonging and adapt to campus customs.

The emergence of social networking sites also enables learners to combine face-to-face learning methods with web-based social learning processes to develop their knowledge and skills (Teng, Lin, Cheng, & Heh, 2004). Moreover, wireless connectivity, mobile smart devices and ever more sophisticated social networking sites has made it possible for students to engage in learning in virtually any location and at any time as an individual or as a member of a learning group (Liccardi et al., 2007). Lastly, it is also the case that increasing prevalence in the use of social networking sites for learning in universities or schools created ever-increasing amounts of user-generated data that can be mined for use as e-learning material.

Because e-learning platforms continue to be adopted by learners instead of traditional learning pathways, and blended (face-to-face and online) learning approaches become more commonplace in universities and schools, it is crucial for educators to recognise that learner now represent diverse technological demographics. Furthermore, educators must acknowledge that learners present with different learning needs and preferences (e.g. visual learners, kinaesthetic learners, auditory learners etc.) and that this must be reflected in the way lessons and learning materials are designed and implemented. In turn, this points to the importance of personalised approaches to learning and the incorporation of blended learning methods to ensure that knowledge is something that is both consumed and created by learners (Kim, 2010).

The combination social networking platforms and e-learning approaches now provides educational institutions with the opportunity to utilise technological space to support the learning process.

RECOMMENDER SYSTEMS

Recommender systems (also called recommendation systems/engines) assist users to select items they can locate relevant to their interest (Almeida, 2013). Thus, recommender systems have been designed to cover the gap between information collection and analysis by filtering all available data, and presenting the most appropriate items to the user. Such systems improve the capacity and efficiency of this process. In the meanwhile, the major issue with recommender systems is obtaining the ideal match between those recommending and those receiving the recommendation; that is, indicating and discovering the relation between users' interests. Nowadays, recommender systems are widely adopted in various fields for the recommendation of research papers, articles, music, objects, videos, movies, and even people. Professional databases and portals such as Facebook, LinkedIn, IBM, Cisco, and Amazon use recommender systems to suggest items (e.g. products, contacts, and others) to their users (Cleomar & Oliveira, 2011).

To provide such suggestions, the most-used approaches employed in recommender systems are collaborative filtering and content-based systems. Collaborative filtering does not take into consideration the kinds of items or their attributes, but bases its recommendations solely on the expressed opinions/posts for other items. On the other hand, content-based filtering uses the information it has about the items and their attributes to make recommendations (Adomavicius & Tuzhilin, 2005; Balabanovic & Shoham, 1997; Cleomar & Oliveira, 2011).

One of the common algorithms used in recommender systems is k-NN. In a social network, finding neighbours of a certain user with the same preference and/or interests may be taken into account. To accomplish this, the Pearson Correlation coefficient should be computed by selecting the preferred data of the top N neighbours of a certain user (weighted similarity) and then using particular methods to compute whether the preference of the user can be predicted (Cleomar & Oliveira, 2011). Further details about the recommender systems are discussed in (Alharbi at el., 2014).

CURRENT PRACTICES IN SOCIAL NETWORK
AND E-LEARNING PLATFORM MINING

This sub section examines the recent existing approaches that attempt to address the lack of social mining and e-learning issues. The existing approaches and systems include filtering recommendation systems, a model of student-centred learning, the approach of sentiment analysis and opinion mining, a toolbox for analysing interactions between the leaders and peripheral students, an approach for generating trending topics in Twitter, and a framework of friendship relations by characterising emotional interactions in social networks (Alharbi at el., 2014).

Data mining tools and techniques can be utilised to extract knowledge from social networks. This knowledge is used to enhance the way students are using e-learning systems. Data mining techniques can be used to analyse the data that exist in the form of data formulated by students in terms of posts or comments when they use social networks such as Facebook. This section analyses the current research and trends of using data mining techniques and tools to mine social networks in order to personalise e-learning services.

Figure 2 illustrates a framework that depicts the process of learning analytics (Siemens, 2010). Learning analytics is associated with similar developments in other fields including big data, e-science, web analytics, and educational data mining, all of which depend on large data collections. To help make sense

Figure 2. Analytics framework components

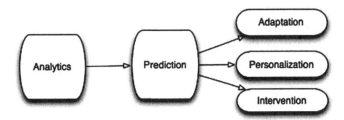

of the data, users can use a tool called a dashboard or in this case a "learner dashboard.". As shown in Figure 2, the process of learning prediction produces three features: adaptation, personalisation, and intervention.

In Hanna (2004) and Teng et al. (2004), the authors described how data mining approaches and methods can be integrated to e-learning platforms and how they can be used to develop the learning activities. The authors showed how data clustering was used as a tool to support group-based collaborative learning and to supply incremental student diagnosis, which can be conducted through analysing students' groups in social networks.

Tang and McCalla (2005) introduced the student-centred learning (SCL) model, which is implemented through a learning experience that straightforwardly extracts students' interests using Web 2.0 technologies. The model permitted students to work together and participate in the process of creating and building their camera-friendly knowledge in social networking sites through communications about their images. The model also activated normal and immediate feedback between learners and instructors.

Tang and McCalla (2005; 2009) designed a tutorial system to offer a highly developed course on data mining and web mining. Their system includes fourteen units, containing the basics of data mining operations, web mining and their applications in e-commerce, intelligent tutoring, bioinformatics, and recommender systems. In their system, learners are allowed to study no matter what they need, which is dissimilar from the popular conventional web-based learning applications. Under the Tang and McCalla (2005; 2009) system, every recommended article is tagged based on its technical factors and content. Students are involved in providing feedback (scorings) about the articles suggested to them. Thus, in response to both the usage and scorings (ratings) of an article, the application alters an article's tags and states whether or not the article must be kept, removed, or put into a repository.

Gundecha and Liu (2012) described the use of sentiment analysis and opinion mining. The purpose of this is to obtain opinions expressed in the user-generated content in social networks. Sentiment analysis and opinion mining methods permit businesses to realise product sentiments, the reputation of the organisation, brand awareness, and new product perception. As such, this tool can be used to analyse students' interactions in a social network in order to understand the students' perceptions of their e-learning.

Rabbany, Takaffoli, and Zaïane (2011) explained the importance of using social network analysis to mine structural information and its applicability in the educational field. They developed a software program for analysing interactions between the leaders and peripheral students as well as collaborative student groups. They also summarised the discussed topics, which gave the teacher an immediate vision of what students discussed online, but this tool was based only on the evaluation of students' participation in online courses.

Pollara and Zhu (2011) described Facebook usage in a high school. They indicated that the use of Facebook optimistically influenced the relationships between students and teachers. The authors noted that the students and mentors interacted regularly through a Facebook group by posting questions and receiving feedback through the page. Furthermore, students assumed that using Facebook improved their education, and they expressed interest in adopting Facebook for other learning aims.

Xu (2011) presented a study on students at the United Institute of Technology – New Zealand who were using Facebook, which is the most fashionable social networking site for e-learning to reach their study goals. The study illustrated that students agree or strongly agree that the use of social networking tools in e-learning will become part of their learning at a tertiary level in the near future. In addition, the study concluded that integrating an e-learning system into social networks would be another method to assist instructors and students in attaining their educational purposes. In Malaysian universities, Tasir et al. (2011) investigated students' perceptions of the current e-learning system and the idea of adopting social networking as a main platform of the university e-learning. The study concluded that students would prefer an interactive e-learning environment with the features of social networking.

Zaidieh (2012) presented a review of the benefits and obstacles of using social networking as an educational tool. The study described the key issues facing education through social networking: real friendship, confidentiality, time out, and miscommunication. In addition, the authors described a set of features such as repeatable content and convenience, flexibility, and accessibility as having a major impact on using social networking sites in education.

Veletsianos and Navarrete (2012) presented a case study based on the experiences of students in an online course that used the online social network Elgg. The report concluded that students enjoyed and valued the experience of the social learning afforded by the social networking site and supported one another in their learning, improving their processes and other experiences of students.

Lee et al. (2011) presented an approach for generating trending topics (a catalogue of the topics most tweeted about) on Twitter. The approach presented was based on classifying Twitter trending topics into 18 common categories such as technology, sports, and politics for topic classification. Then they used the Bag-of-Words approach for text classification and network-based classification. The classification of tweets was based on word vectors with a definition of trending topic and tweets, and the regularly used tf-idf weights were used to sort the topics by a naive Bayes multinomial classifier. Lee et al. (2011) used the network-based approach to perform the prediction of the topic category and recognise related topics. Related topics were recognised based on a user-similarity metric, which was defined as the cardinality of the junction of leading users between two topics. Their experiments were conducted using the C5.0 classifier.

Human-Computer Interaction

The field of Human-Computer Interaction (HCI) focuses on five main technology service domains: supply, accessibility, security, usability, and HCI theory guidelines (Bosch, 2004). Across these five domains is the examination of how users interact with technology systems in a functional, safe and efficient way. As such, the focus is on how to develop or improve technology systems in terms of their utility, safety, effectiveness and efficiency for human users. Furthermore, the emphasis in the field of HCI is on the extent to which the technology systems and programs are both easy to learn and to use (Jenny & others, 1994; Folmer & Bosch, 2004; Winter, 2008).

Therefore, the following should be considered when designing computers systems and programs: what the user will be doing; what the user will require; and what is the most efficient order for information delivery (Dix, 2004).

System Usability

Four elements determine technology system usability: flexibility, user friendliness, user satisfaction and user ability (Bosch, 2004; Allwood, 1994). Prior to developing a computer system, the designer will endeavour to understand the types of tasks the user will undertake with the assistance of the computer and how the computers should fit and support the users' needs (Jenny & others, 1994). In terms of e-learning, the tasks undertaken by the student educator users include course selection; adding, storing and retrieving learning material; participating in collaborative learning groups etc. Hence, the e-learning systems and programs at universities should be designed according to these criteria in order to optimise usability.

It is also important to take into account the heterogeneity of the student and educator users. Differences in cognitive abilities, motivation, user experience etc. are all important factors which need to be considered when designing a computer system for use. Thus, learning programs must offer flexibility in the way they are used if they are to cater to heterogeneous user groups (Jenny & others, 1994).

System Accessibility

Service accessibility is important in the interaction process since users should be able to access help whenever using the targeted system. If there is no effective accessibility, the system will fail when interacting with the users. All components of the systems must be supported because the designer cannot know where and when users will need a help (Abascal, 2004). For example, if students/instructors use their e-learning system at any time then they should be able to do so without any complications. Help system should be flexible so it can help different students/instructors to solve their problems such as disabilities. Help system should also not prevent users from doing their normal work (Abascal, 2004; Charif, 2006).

System Security

To measure the online system's level of security attention will be given to the authorisation, authentication and file access functions (AC Nielsen, 2005; Aljawarneh et al., 2013). According to Aljawarneh et al. (2013), the majority of Arab small- and medium-sized businesses still rely on face-to-face interactions with customers rather than the utilisation of online platforms due to concerns about information security. Because these businesses were insufficiently prepared for the ICT revolution only a small number are able to conduct online transaction and credit card payments. Of most concern for education institutions is data not validated or not properly validated leading to security vulnerabilities in their online learning platforms.

Human Computer Interaction theory

HCI deals with the concepts and rules that need to be taken into consideration when universities are developing programs and designing their e-learning interfaces. These guidelines support the overall interaction and provided e-learning services (Sutcliffe, 1991).

The increasing demand for interaction and communication between countries, it is important to understand the necessity of national culture in human communication on the Web. In addition, a culture has become an important human-computer interaction (HCI) issue, because it impacts both the substance and the vehicle of communication via communication technologies. Organisations will depend more on the Internet as an integral component of their communication infrastructure. What must be addressed are the cultural factors surrounding Web site design. Specifically argued is that culture such as Saudi Arabia is a discernible variable in international Web site design, and as such, should better accommodate Saudi students who seek to access online information or products (Faiola, 2006).

User Experience

The most significant challenge that universities must overcome when implementing a university website is to ensure that the student and educator users are able to properly navigate the site to meet their needs and to encourage continued use (Faiola, 2006).

Interviews will be conducted with high ranking educators at the universities. In addition, the reliability of the participants' interview responses will be tested by comparing their comments with the online information available and based on our own use of the services.

Technology Acceptance Model

In this article, we reveal a number of models including the Theory of Reasoned Action (TRA) and Technology Acceptance Model (TAM) (Davis, 1985; Davis, 1989; Venkatesh & Davis, 2000).

Most of the current frameworks conceptually are based on the Theory of Reasoned Action (TRA), Technology Acceptance Model (TAM), Theory of Planned Behaviour (TPB) and HCI theory with five independent variables including service accessibility, service security, service usability, and HCI theory guidelines. Note that according to Wixom and Todd (Wixom & Todd, 2005), TAM provides limited guidance about how to influence usage through design and implementation. TRA is a model for the prediction of behavioral intention, spanning predictions of attitude and predictions of behavior. TPB is a theory about the link between attitudes and behavior. TRA and TPB will assist our framework to perform the suitable validation method (Davis, 1985; Davis, 1989; Venkatesh & Davis, 2000).

Thus, it is recommender to adopt the theoretical and empirical support from TRA and TPB, which service quality positively effects on Perceived usefulness (PU), Perceived ease-of-use (PEOU), and user (student/instructor) acceptance of e-learning in Saudi Arabia.

The TAM explains that individuals' perceptions are based on perceived usefulness (PU) and perceived ease of use (PEOU) which, in turn, influence users' intention and usage behaviour towards a particular Information System (IS) (Venkatesh & Davis, 2000).

PU is referred as "the degree to which person believes that using a particular system would enhance his or her job performance" (Jenny, 1994; Davis, 1985). PEOU is defined as "the degree to which a person believes that using a particular system would be free from efforts" (Jenny, 1994). The TAM proposes that PU and PEOU beliefs affect users' attitude towards using information systems. Their attitude directly relates to behavioural intention (BI) to use, which, in turn, will determine usage of the system. PU and PEOU both have an effect on BI. PEOU also affects PU. BI is also indirectly influenced by external variables through PU and PEOU (Davis, 1985; Davis, 1989). Therefore, in accordance with the TAM, they will be hypothesised that PU, PEOU or BI would have a significant positive influence on user acceptance of e-learning via using recommender systems for Saudi universities.

In general, service quality is associated with to the quality of information that the electronic university information system delivers to its customers, and is measured in terms of accuracy, currency, completeness, and format. Service quality determines the success of a website design (Venkatesh & Davis, 2000). Today's online learning web-based systems provide users the means to access information systems directly by performing transactions. Therefore, universities' web sites can be viewed as information systems.

Research Design

In this chapter, we study the impact of the use of social recommender systems via e-learning on student/ instructor relationships in the Saudi universities and this assist in the investigation of the user experience according to the e-learning service quality in Saudi Arabia. The design for of this study uses a quantitative and qualitative methodology. Quantitative and qualitative data provides very strong evidence to support the hypothesis of this study.

In this Section, we describe the research design in this paper and provide the conceptual framework for this study. In addition, the proposed approach and the data sampling that will be used in the proposed surveys have been described.

Conceptual Framework

A review of the literature reveals the availability of a range of useful frameworks such as the the Theory of Reasoned Action (TRA) and Technology Acceptance Model (TAM) for an investigation of user adoption and continued use of e-learning Recommender Systems in Saudi Universities of e-learning services on customer relationships in Saudi universities, the literature review reveals a number of models including. It should be noted that demographics such as age, education level, socio-economic status etc.) are not required in the framework because there is no need to classify users of online learning services.

As shown in Figure 3, we have proposed framework that is conceptually based on extended the Theory of Reasoned Action (TRA), Technology Acceptance Model (TAM), Theory of Planned Behaviour (TPB) and HCI theory with five independent variables including service accessibility, service security, service usability, and HCI theory guidelines. TRA and TPB will assist our framework to perform the suitable validation method.

Before going through with the data analysis process, several validation tests were performed in order to ensure the reliability and discriminated validity of the instruments. Thus we will perform Cronbach alpha test on the items of each construct to ensure the validity of the questionnaire and its internal consistency (Davis, 1985).

Based on theoretical and empirical support from TRA and TPB, we will assume that the factors for acceptance of recommender systems via e-learning positively effects on Perceived usefulness (PU), Perceived ease-of-use (PEOU), and customer acceptance of online learning in Saudi Arabia.

Figure 3 illustrates the relationship and intersection between the service quality and user satisfaction. When applying this framework to any random data set, the result might give identical fit statistics whether quality was hypothesised. This means, we will use the *T*-test, which is the best statistical method for the collected data we have, to test the hypothesis of this study. Our Framework model consists of five variables that should be integrated to improve the e-learning service quality and customer satisfaction.

Figure 3. A proposed conceptual framework of online learning framework acceptance

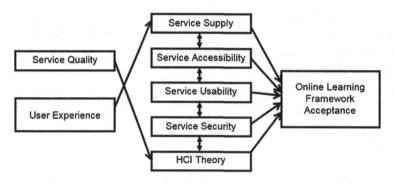

1. In the proposed framework, the user experience variable includes four elements that assist us to measure the customer experience and the factors for acceptance of recommender systems in Saudi universities (as shown in Figure 4):
   a. **Flexibility**: Means that the functions of the system are designed in a way which follows the structures of the task the user is trying to solve. Universities must have designed programs for E-learning that is developed after the organisation's culture and after what users require.
   b. **Usability**: Includes a number of aspects which all have influence on the Human-Computer Interaction.
   c. **User Satisfaction**: Means how users feel about using the program, how well motivated they are.
   d. **Users' Abilities**: Means that the users have enough knowledge and skills to have a basic interaction with the computer.
2. The second variable is a service accessibility which is important in the interaction process since users should be able to access help whenever using the targeted system. In case that there is no

Figure 4. The four elements of service usability in the proposed framework model

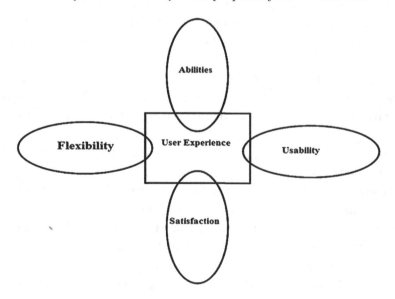

effective accessibility, the system will fail when the users attempt to interact. All components of the systems must be supported because the designer cannot know where and when users will need help.

3. The third variable is a service security. It should be noticed that it is difficult to measure this variable because there is no specific standard that can be followed. When measuring the online systems quality, customers are facing several security issues such authorisation, authentication and file access.

4. The fourth variable is HCI theory guidelines. HCI deals with the concepts and rules that need to be taken into consideration when universities are developing programs and designing their Internet universities interfaces. These guidelines support the overall interaction and provided e-learning services.

5. Finally, the fifth variable is the service supply. Customers must overcome one important challenge when using a university web site, how to navigate a web site that will meet customers' need and provide good service in order to create customer loyalty.

RESEARCH SITES AND DATA COLLECTION PROCESSES

Three proposed Saudi universities will be selected for the study, specifically the universities, which they provide electronic learning, services to their students/instructors, but also dominate the Saudi universities industry. Furthermore, some universities are chosen since they operate at a national level. Note that the survey questionnaires in this study are translated into Arabic language because some students/instructors have difficulties in understanding the surveys in English language.

Due to these factors the three universities are deemed to be appropriate for the study the university industry's perspective. Interviews will be conducted with each university, where the universities will be given closed questions about their electronic learning services before and after adopting the social recommender systems. The interviews will be selected with the basis of quantitative and qualitative interviews in order to study e-learning from the universities' perspective and students/instructors' perspective. The quantitative method may be allowed the interviewees to express themselves and their opinions with their own words.

The universities will be approached by telephone where our study will be introduced and times for meetings agreed upon. The students/instructors will be approached via email or face-face interaction. The universities will be received the questions in advance in order to gain a better understanding of our study and disposition of the interview.

The following user experience evaluations have been carried out:

1. Questionnaire survey for three universities' students/instructors.
2. Focus group experience evaluation by conducting questionnaire survey for three universities' representatives.
3. The semi-structured evaluation technique needed extra time to obtain more accurate data about the factors for the acceptance of social e-learning recommender systems in Saudi universities.

Note that the first and second evaluations will be used to find the individuals (both employees and students) who could supply us with the accurate data and ensure that this will reflect the acceptance of social e-learning recommender systems in Saudi universities.

The third proposed evaluation technique in this work that will be analysed and designed is called semi-structured interview. In this way, we have to take screen shots of some interfaces of e-learning services that are provided by the university and so it explains ask them 'what can you do on this screen', 'how does it work' etc. This is because in HCI generally there is a trend away from quantitative evaluation, where the validity of the results (and the commitment of the participants) might be hard to assure, towards more qualitative, holistic approaches intended to enhance the designer's understanding of the interaction design challenge.

Generally, the questionnaires are also used very frequently in evaluation work to keep track of data about users such as their age, experience, and what their expectations are about the system that will be evaluated.

It is important to remember that these three items (effectiveness, efficiency, and satisfaction) do not always give the same answers: the social e-learning recommender systems via e-learning may be effective and efficient to use, but students/instructors may still find it unsatisfactory.

Prior to distributing the questionnaire to the sample, a pilot study is conducted to identify or discover any ambiguities, errors, inadequate answers and highlight any confusing questions. The original questionnaire will be developed in English; however, it will also be translated in the native language of users. The researcher will use statistical software packages to analyse the collected data.

The SPSS for Windows package version 21 could be utilised for the data analysis that collected from the survey. The researcher used the frequencies, cross tabulations, means, and variables, in addition to independent-sample T-test to test for statistical significance of the problem statement. Smart PLS will be obtain for structural equation modelling.

CONCLUSION AND FUTURE WORK

According to the literature review, our investigation reveals insufficiency of research in the field of HCI and factor for acceptance of E-learning in Saudi universities. In addition, a dramatic change in Saudi Arabia economy is happened and that there is little information about the development and use of recommender systems in Saudi universities. Saudi education industry has been identified as an industry that plays a crucial role in the social and economic development of the Saudi Arabia as well as providing valuable e-learning services to both indigenous people and huge expatriates residing and working in Saudi Arabia. Furthermore, there is no specific strategy or approach for exploiting the opportunities offered by Internet. The implication of this study will be vital in assisting learning practitioners and academies to re-consider the types of recommender services they provide and identify methods of enhancing and encouraging students/instructors to utilise service offered.

Indeed, there is still a gap of knowledge on the usage of recommender systems in Saudi universities and the wider issue of technological change in the universities of developing counties. Relatively, this lack of knowledge is an issue to universities seeking to meet students/instructor's expectations and requirements by offering consistently high perceived service standards of e-learning services in a rapidly changing technological environment.

As part of a larger research project, the chapter proposed conceptual framework for e-learning recommender acceptance. As a future work, an extensive empirical survey research will be carried out in Saudi Arabia, involving the administration of the survey both to a large random sample of university students and instructors to test the research model hypotheses. In addition, other qualitative research methods such as focus groups and semi-structured interviews will be employed to validate the obtained quantitative results from the survey.

The implication of this study will be vital in assisting learning practitioners and academies to reconsider the types of recommender services they provide and identify methods of enhancing and encouraging students/instructors to utilize service offered. In general, it will be expected that perceptions of e-learning technology would impact on the Saudi universities – student/instructor relationship. This perception of the relationship could lead respondents to develop a perception of e-learning technology.

REFERENCES

Adomavicius, G., & Tuzhilin, A. (2005). Toward the next generation of recommender systems: A survey of the state-of-the-art and possible extensions. *Knowledge and Data Engineering. IEEE Transactions on*, *17*(6), 734–749.

Alharbi, H., Jayawardena, A., & Kwan, P. (2014). Social Recommender System for Predicting the Needs of Students/Instructors: Review and Proposed Framework. *Proc. of the First IEEE International Workshop on Social Networks Analysis, Management and Security SNAMS '14*, Spain.

Aljawarneh, S., Al-Rousan, T., Maatuk, A.M., & Akour, M. (2013). Usage of data validation techniques in online banking: A perspective and case study. *Security Journal*.

Allwood, C. M. (1998). *Människa-Datorinteraktion – ett psykologiskt perspektiv*. Lund: Studentlitteratur.

Almeida, F. A. D. C. (2013). Hybrid approach to content recommendation. Retrieved from <http://repositorio-aberto.up.pt/bitstream/10216/67427/1/000154009.pdf>

Balabanovic, M., & Shoham, Y. (1997). Combining content-based and collaborative recommendation. *Communications of the ACM*, *40*(3), 66–72. doi:10.1145/245108.245124

Basu, C., Hirsh, H., & Cohen, W. W. (1998). Recommendation as classification: Using social and content-based information in recommendation.*Proceedings of the Fifteenth National Conference on Artificial Intelligence (AAAI/IAAI)* (pp. 714–720).

Bollen, A., & Emes, C. (2008). Understanding Customer Relationships – how important is the personal touch. *Ipsos MORI*. Retrieved from www.ipsos-mori.com/_assets/reports/understanding-customer-relationships.pdf

Brady, M., & Robertson, C. (2001). Searching for consensus on the antecedent role of service quality and satisfaction: An exploratory cross-national study. *Journal of Business Research*, *51*(1), 53–60. doi:10.1016/S0148-2963(99)00041-7

Charif, L., Aronsohn, M., & Charif, H. (2006), E-banking and Service Quality Online [Master dissertation]. Lunds University, Sweden.

Cleomar, B., Jr., & Oliveira, M. (2011). Recommender systems in social networks. *JISTEM - Journal of Information Systems and Technology Management, 8*(3), 681–716.

Correa, C. D., & Ma, K.-L. (2011). Visualizing social networks. In C. C. Aggarwal (Ed.), *Social network data analytics* (pp. 307–326). Boston, MA, USA: Springer US. doi:10.1007/978-1-4419-8462-3_11

Cronin, J., & Taylor, S. (1992). Measuring service quality: A reexamination and extension. *Journal of Marketing, 56*(3), 55–68. doi:10.2307/1252296

Davis, F.D. (1985). A technology acceptance model for empirically testing new end-user information systems: theory and results. *DSpace@MIT: Massachusetts Institute of Technology*. Retrieved from http://www.temoa.info/node/257608

Davis, F. D. (1989). Perceived Usfulness, Perceived Ease of Use, and User Acceptance of Information Technology. *Management Information Systems Quarterly, 13*(3), 319–340. doi:10.2307/249008

DeRuyter, K., Bloemer, J., & Pascal, P. (1997). Merging service quality and service satisfaction: An empirical test of an integrative model. *Journal of Economic Psychology, 8*(4), 187–406.

DiMicco, J., Millen, D. R., Geyer, W., Dugan, C., Brownholtz, B., & Muller, M. (2008). Motivations for social networking at work. *Proceedings of the 2008 ACM Conference on Computer Supported Cooperative Work, CSCW '08* (pp. 711–720). New York, NY, USA: ACM. doi:10.1145/1460563.1460674

Dix, A., Finlay, J., Abowd, G. D., & Beale, R. (2004). *Human-Computer Interaction* (3rd ed.). Essex: Pearson Prentice Hall.

Faiola, A. (2006). Toward an HCI Theory of Cultural Cognition. In Encyclopedia of Human Computer Interaction (pp. 609-614). Hershey, PA, USA: IGI Global. doi:10.4018/978-1-59140-562-7.ch090

Folmer, E., & Bosch, J. (2004). Architecting for Usability: A Survey. *Journal of Systems and Software, 70*(1-2), 61–78. doi:10.1016/S0164-1212(02)00159-0

Gronroos, C. (1984). A service quality model and its marketing implications. *European Journal of Marketing, 18*(4), 36–44. doi:10.1108/EUM0000000004784

Gundecha, P., & Liu, H. (2012). *Mining social media: A brief introduction*. The Institute for Operations Research and the Management Sciences (INFORMS) TutORials in Operations Research.

Hanna, M. (2004). Data mining in the e-Learning domain. *Campus-Wide Information Systems, 21*(1), 29–34. doi:10.1108/10650740410512301

Herlocker, J. L., Konstan, J. A., Borchers, A., & Riedl, J. (1999). An algorithmic framework for performing collaborative filtering. *Proceedings of the 22nd Annual International ACM SIGIR Conference on Research and Development in Information Retrieval SIGIR '99* (pp. 230–237). New York, NY, USA: ACM. doi:10.1145/312624.312682

Iacobucci, D., Ostrom, A., & Grayson, K. (1995). Distinguishing Service Quality and Customer Satisfaction: The Voice of the Consumer. *Journal of Consumer Psychology, 4*(3), 277–303. doi:10.1207/s15327663jcp0403_04

Jenny, P., Yvonne, Y., Sharp, X., Helen, A., Benyon, W., David, M., & Carey, A. et al. (1994). *Human-Computer Interaction*. Essex: Addison-Wesley.

Kim, T. (2010). A self-directed dynamic web-based learning environment: Proposal for personalized learning framework. *Journal of Security Engineering, 9*(2), 177–187.

Learning objects, content management, and e-learning. (n.d.). InFerrer, N., & Alfonso, J. (Eds.), *Content management for e-learning* (pp. 43–54). New York, NY: Springer New York.

Lee, K., Palsetia, D., Narayanan, R., Patwary, M. D., Agrawal, A., & Choudhary, A. N. (2011). Twitter trending topic classification. *Proceedings of the 11th IEEE International Conference on Data Mining Workshops* (pp. 251–258).

Liccardi, I., Ounnas, A., Pau, R., Massey, E., Kinnunen, P., Lewthwaite, S., & Sarkar, C. et al. (2007). The role of social networks in students' learning experiences. In *ITiCSE-WGR '07: Working Group Reports on ITiCSE on Innovation and Technology in Computer Science Education* (pp. 224–237). New York, NY, USA: ACM. doi:10.1145/1345443.1345442

Maâtallah, M., & Seridi, H. (2012a). Enhanced collaborative filtering to recommender systems of technology enhanced learning. *Proceedings of ICWIT, 2012*, 129–138.

Maâtallah, M., & Seridi, H. (2012b). Multi-context recommendation in technology enhanced learning. *Proceedings of ITS, 2012*, 720–721.

MacCallum, R. C., Wegener, D. T., Uchino, B. N., & Fabrigar, L. R. (1993). The problem of equivalent models in applications of covariance structure analysis. *Journal of Psychological Bulletin, 114*(1), 185–199. doi:10.1037/0033-2909.114.1.185 PMID:8346326

Martensen, A., & Gronholdt, L. (2003). Improving library users perceived quality, satisfaction and locality: An integrated measurement and management system. *Journal of Academic Librarianship, 19*(3), 140–147. doi:10.1016/S0099-1333(03)00020-X

Melville, P., Mooney, R. J., & Nagarajan, R. (2002). Content-boosted collaborative filtering for improved recommendations. *Proceedings of the Eighteenth National Conference on Artificial Intelligence* (pp. 187–192). Menlo Park, CA, USA: American Association for Artificial Intelligence.

Nielsen, A. C. (2005). Online banking continues despite security concerns. *ACNielsen*. Retrieved from http://www.acnielsen.com.au/news.asp?newsID=301

Parasuraman, A., Zeithamal, V., & Berry, L. (1988). SERVQUAL: A multiple-item scale for measuring consumer perceptions of service quality. *Journal of Retailing, 64*(1), 12–40.

Pollara, P., & Zhu, J. (2011). Social networking and education: Using Facebook as an edusocial space. *Proceedings of Society for Information Technology & Teacher Education International Conference, 2011*, 3330–3338.

Rabbany, R., Takaffoli, M., & Zaïane, O. R. (2011). Social network analysis and mining to support the assessment of on-line student participation. *SIGKDD Explorations, 13*(2), 20–29. doi:10.1145/2207243.2207247

Schein, A. I., Popescul, A., Ungar, L. H., & Pennock, D. M. (2002). Methods and metrics for cold-start recommendations.*Proceedings of the 25th Annual International ACM SIGIR Conference on Research and Development in Information Retrieval SIGIR '02* (pp. 253–260). New York, NY, USA: ACM. doi:10.1145/564376.564421

Siemens, G. (2010). What are learning analytics? *eLearnspace.* Retrieved from <http://www.elearnspace. org/blog/2010/08/25/what-are-learning-analytics/>

Sureshchandar G. S., Rajendran C., and Anantharaman R N. (2002), The Relationship Between Service Quality and Customer Satisfaction: A Factor Specific Approach, Journal of Services Marketing (16:4), pp. 363-379.

Sutcliffe, A., Carroll, J., Young, R., & Long, J. (1991), HCI theory on trial. In S.P. Robertson, G.M. Olson, & J.S. Olson (Eds.), *Proceedings of the SIGCHI conference on Human factors in computing systems: Reaching through technology (CHI '91)* (pp. 399-401). ACM, New York, NY, USA, DOI: http:// doi.acm.org/10.1145/108844.10897410.1145/108844.108974 Retrieved from

Tan, H., & Ye, H. (2009). A collaborative filtering recommendation algorithm based on item classification.*Proceedings of the 2009 Pacific-Asia Conference on Circuits, Communications and Systems (PACCS '09)* (pp. 694–697). Washington, DC, USA: IEEE. doi:10.1109/PACCS.2009.68

Tan, P.-N., Steinbach, M., & Kumar, V. (2005). *Introduction to data mining* (1st ed.). Addison Wesley.

Tang, T., & McCalla, G. (2005). Smart recommendation for an evolving e-Learning system: Architecture and experiment. *International Journal on E-Learning*, *4*(1), 105–129.

Tang, T. Y., & McCalla, G. (2009). A multidimensional paper recommender: Experiments and evaluations. *IEEE Internet Computing*, *13*(4), 34–41. doi:10.1109/MIC.2009.73

Tasir, Z., Al-Dheleai, Y., Harun, J., & Shukor, A. N. (2011). Students perception towards the use of social networking as an e-learning platform. *Proceeding of the 10th WSEAS International Conference on Education and Educational Technology'11*, China.

Teng, C., Lin, C., Cheng, S., & Heh, J. (2004). Analyzing user behavior distribution on e-learning platform with techniques of clustering.*Proceedings of Society for Information Technology and Teacher Education International Conference* (pp. 3052–3058).

Udo, G. J., Bagachi, K. K., & Kris, P. J. (2010). An assessment of customers eservice quality perception, satisfaction and intention. *International Journal of Information Management*, *30*(6), 481–492. doi:10.1016/j.ijinfomgt.2010.03.005

Veletsianos, G., & Navarrete, C. (2012). Online social networks as formal learning environments: Learner experiences and activities. *International Review of Research in Open and Distance Learning*, *13*(1), 144–166.

Venkatesh, V., & Davis, F. D. (2000). A Theoretical Extension of the Technology Acceptance Model: Four Longitudinal Field Studies.*Management Science,46*(2), 186–204. doi:10.1287/mnsc.46.2.186.11926

Wasserman, S., & Faust, K. (1994). *Social network analysis in the social and behavioral sciences. Social network analysis: Methods and applications* (pp. 1–27). Cambridge University Press.

Winter, S., Wagner, S., & Deissenboeck, F. (2008). A Comprehensive Model of Usability. In E. I. Systems, J. Gulliksen, M. B. Harning, P. Palanque, G. C. Veer, & J. Wesson (Eds.), Engineering Interactive Systems, LNCS (Vol. 4940, pp. 106–122). Berlin, Heidelberg: Springer-Verlag. Doi:10.1007/978-3-540-92698-6_7

Wixom B.H., Todd P.A. (2005), A theoretical integration of user satisfaction and technology acceptance. *Information Systems Research*, 16, 85-103.

Xu, G. (2011). *Social networking sites, Web 2.0 technologies and e-learning* [Master thesis]. New Zealand. Retrieved from http://hdl.handle.net/10652/1864

Zaidieh, A. J. (2012). The use of social networking in education: Challenges and opportunities. *World of Computer Science and Information Technology Journal*, 2(1), 18–21.

ENDNOTES

[1]   A service quality framework. SERVQUAL was developed in the mid-eighties by Zeithaml, Parasuraman & Berry. SERVQUAL means to measure the scale of Quality in the service sectors. It was originally measured on 10 elements of service quality: reliability, responsiveness, competence, access, courtesy, communication, credibility, security, understanding the customer and tangibles.

Chapter 7

Outsourcing to Cloud-based Computing Services in Higher Education in Saudi Arabia

Athary Alwasel
King Saud University, Saudi Arabia

Ben Clegg
Aston University, UK

Andreas Schroeder
Aston University, UK

ABSTRACT

In recent years Saudi Arabia has made great strides in higher education. This paper looks at the higher education sector in Saudi Arabia with special emphasis on outsourcing to Software as a Service based email systems as a positive enabler of higher education. Outsourcing can be defined as the process of contracting services to a third party with financial and contractual terms to govern that provision. There are many advantages and disadvantages of outsourcing and many reasons why an organization might decide to outsource specific services. This chapter describes the information systems outsourcing trend towards cloud based solutions (particularly email) in the Saudi Arabian higher education sector over the last few years and discusses the implications of this trend.

INTRODUCTION

Outsourcing can be simply defined as the process of contracting to a third-party or "the purchase of a good or service that was previously provided internally" (Lacity & Hirschheim, 1993). Outsourcing is often viewed as the contracting out of a service to an external provider in exchange of payments. It involves two organizations signing a mutual agreement that defines services to be performed and financial terms that govern them. There are many advantages and disadvantages of outsourcing (Ketler & Walstrom, 1993). Moreover, there are different reasons why an organization might decide to outsource specific services

DOI: 10.4018/978-1-5225-1944-7.ch007

or the production of certain goods. This chapter looks at outsourcing on information based technology services in higher education in Saudi Arabia, particularly the use of e-mail.

Outsourcing has taken on a new meaning in the last two decades for many industries. Many major companies have outsourced parts of their operations or selected projects and functions for many years (Quinn & Hilmer, 1994) and the growth in outsourcing has been exceptionally high as organizations and businesses have looked for cheap labor, cost saving measures, and greater work efficiency (Ketler & Walstrom, 1993). As a result, outsourcing is becoming more and more popular in today's global business era as most organisations nowadays outsource some of their operational services (Kakabadse & Kakabadse, 2005). Without outsourcing, these services would be otherwise carried out in-house, as it had been previously done. Generally speaking, companies usually outsource services and functions that are not core to their business (Arnold, 2000). So many organizations outsource at least some of their non-core functions or activities (Tastle et al., 2008). Large and small firms, particularly small businesses, can benefit greatly from outsourcing non-essential activities to better focus on high value core business. However, some companies are outsourcing highly critical applications. For most businesses, reducing costs might be realized with outsourcing business functions through lower-cost labor, proximity to major markets, and by eliminating overhead costs associated with operations. Also, outsourcing offers flexibility, with a clear focus on the outsourcing business and on developing its core business (Lankford & Parsa, 1999). With an increased focus in business direction, an improvement in quality might also be achieved. For some businesses, outsourcing can even bring new expertise and a competitive edge to its services, functions and products (Quélin & Duhamel, 2003).

With global business taking a lead in the twenty-first century, companies have sought to implement outsourcing as a cost-saving measure for tasks that a company requires but does not constitute to be a core business activity. Therefore, outsourcing allows a company to focus on its core competency by outsourcing non-core activities that generally consume a substantial amount of organizational time and budget and requires specialized skills and knowledge (Power et al., 2004).

IT Outsourcing

In the information technology side of businesses, outsourcing has become commonplace (Lacity & Willcocks, 1998; Lee, Huynh et al., 2003). For example, the cost of information systems development is significantly cheaper in India than in the United States, so many American companies have outsourced some coding / application development to India (Bardhan & Kroll, 2003; Dossania & Kenney, 2007).

Another commonly outsourced IT function is customer service and support. Many Indian companies and universities have focused on training employees for the United States call center function, including accent negation, taking on American names, and keeping their employees familiar with American events such as sports (Poster, 2007). However some companies like Dell have actually brought some call center support functions back to the United States to cut the number of complaints they have received due to difficulty in language and cultural understanding.

Technical support has also been a major IT outsourcing trend from the US where call center support tends to be low-level support like resetting a password and giving users first level support. High level trouble shooting of technology and networks requires individuals with a high competency level and needs to be treated differently by outsourcing such functions to regions on high education. For instance the

Indian Institutes of Technology has done an excellent job of training students with this higher level of support background. Other areas of IT outsourcing include training, systems planning and development, and data centers (Behara, Gundersen, & Capozzoli, 1995).

IT OPPORTUNITIES AND CHALLENGES

There are key opportunities that can be realized from outsourcing, regardless of industry or type of organization. Mainly, we identify the following advantages:

- **Cost Savings:** Insufficient financial resources have made many organizations unable to offer better IT products and services. With outsourcing, more organizations have been able to afford IT solutions and to offer better services and products, without allocating huge investment in infrastructure.
- **Availability of Specialized Skills:** IT projects require a high level of technical expertise, which is difficult to find and attract. Difficulty of hiring and retaining skilled IT human resources provides an opportunity for organizations to outsource their IT services or certain functions and free their internal IT departments to better deal with high demand services.
- **Better Focus on Core Business:** Outsourcing gives organizations an advantage in terms of freeing up their internal resources and focusing more on the core business processes. By focusing more on core business, organizations can realize competitive advantage in their industry.
- **Quick Availability on Demand:** Some IT projects and services require a lot of time to construct and develop internally. With outsourcing, organizations can gain access to important IT tools and services when they need it. This can be advantageous, especially when there is uncertain or unpredictable demand changes.

Based on a literature review of outsourcing theories, Gottschalk and Solli-Sæther (2005) identified 11 critical success factors in IT sourcing, which are:

1. **Core Competence Management:** IT needs are to be identified by the organization in order to manage IT services.
2. **Transaction Cost Reduction:** The idea behind outsourcing is to introduce cost saving measures, and the organization has to implement certain measures to minimize transaction costs.
3. **Contract Completeness:** Outsourcing needs a complete contract with a layout of responsibilities and power to minimize conflict and confusion.
4. **Relationship Exploitation:** Common ground had to be developed and secured.
5. **Stakeholder Management:** Effective communications are to be established with and between stakeholders to make the IT outsourcing work for the benefits of all stakeholders.
6. **Vendor Resource Exploitation:** Integration of IT resources within the organization, along with IT resources from the vendor, is to be performed to increase competitiveness.
7. **Production Cost Reduction:** Integration of IT services from the vendor in a cost-effective way can be achieved to reduce costs.
8. **Alliance Exploitation:** The organization ought to have an experience in alliances and alliance management, and how to choose vendors.

9. **Social Exchange Exploitation:** The exchange between the organization and the vendor has to produce better social and economic outcomes.
10. **Vendor Behavior Control:** The organization has to make sure that it can control vendors' behavior in an economic way.
11. **Demarcation of Labor:** A clear boundary of labor between the organization and the vendor has to be established by the organization.

However, outsourcing has its own disadvantages as it may expose organizations to potential quality risks and legal issues. With services being transferred to an outside partner, staff redundancies may be due to the outsourcing might be necessary. With outsourcing involving two or more partners, miscommunications may lead to unexpected results. It must be noted that outsourcing is not an easy process, and organizations should be mindful of some challenges that may come with outsourcing certain IT functions and services. One of the biggest challenges is data security and privacy and handling control over your data to another party. Legal challenges may make organizations hesitant in outsourcing IT services as it may involve data privacy and liabilities. Subsequently, organizations need to make sure that limitation of liability is negotiated within its contract with the outsourcing agency (Davis, et al., 2006). A clear contract that lays out deliverables and responsibilities should be put in place to avoid pitfalls from outsourcing.

Furthermore, outsourcing implies a lack of control as some control and support can be transferred to the other party. Organizations need to make sure that a set of measures and procedures and a support system are put in place to continuously monitor outsourced services.

OUTSOURCING IN HIGHER EDUCATION

Outsourcing might prove to be successful, if done correctly. Otherwise, organizations may not realize its benefits, and the outcome may even lead to complications and prove that outsourcing was not the right decision in the first place. Overall, outsourcing can be a cost-effective method of providing IT functions that have to be otherwise provided internally, by reaching out to needed expertise, and allowing an organization to concentrate its valuable resources to support its strategic mission, objectives and goals.

Although outsourcing has been applied primarily in the commercial market to save cost and concentrate on its core business, more recently, higher education institutes are looking into outsourcing certain services that benefit their students, faculty, and staff. Colleges and universities are under pressure to compete in the evolving and expanding sector of higher education, with higher and rising education costs. For example, in the US, public colleges and universities have seen a decreasing trend in support from state and federal government, and have increasingly started to cut costs and diversify their income to supplement the loss of state and federal funding (Lee & Clery, 2004). It is worth mentioning that the concept of outsourcing is not new to higher education institutes, as the list of outsourcing activites within colleges and universities is growing, from support functions such as online bookstores and food services to financial servcies (Collis, 2004), human resource functions, payment systems and accomodation reservation. Educational based systems are also being outsoured mor and more as on line virtual learning environments, managed learning environments, examination and test systems have been the norm in the UK for decades (e.g. Blackboard). Research shows that higher education institutes are now widely embracing outsourcing to save costs, improve quality of services, reach out to expertise, and compete more effectively with other peer institutions (Gupta et al., 2005).

CLOUD COMPUTING IN HIGHER EDUCATION

Cloud computing can be classified as a new type of IT outsourcing. Certain IT functions and services can be performed on the cloud, such as e-mail service, data storage, applications, and hardware. Organizations that need quick availability of certain applications without investing heavily in hardware installation and software licenses can consider cloud computing as a form of IT outsourcing. Startup organizations in particular may find cloud computing a fast and reliable way to run their IT services. Cloud computing is generally divided into three functions: SaaS (Software as a Service), IaaS (Infrastructure as a Service), and PaaS (Platform as a Service).

Software as a Service (SaaS) can be one of the easiest to implement. Many companies have outsourced their e-mail functions to the cloud (Dikaiakos et al., 2009; Lin et al., 2009). For instance when an employee or a student uses Gmail (the email service from Google) they are using software running on servers located away from the user organization (a.k.a. "in the cloud") – as a SaaS cloud function. SaaS in particular makes complete applications available over the Internet and users can access them from anywhere at anytime (Bhadauria, Borgohain, Biswas, & Sanyal, 2014).

Infrastructure as a Service (IaaS) is when hardware and resources other than just software are provided remotely. When a company outsources infrastructure, the host company has the hardware, personal and associated resources to support the technology – and can use these to support multiple enterprises simultaneously (in multi-tenancy agreements). For example, a university in Riyadh, Saudi Arabia needs four networking staff, but if they outsource some of their infrastructure to a cloud company, that company may support five or more universities with the same telecommunications and virtual infrastructure support – thus creating significant potential savings for a university.

Platform as a Service (PaaS) occurs when an institution uses cloud based infrastructure and a development environment to develop and maintain new information systems applications which can then be hosted, along with its associated data, on the cloud. It can be similar to IaaS in that the host company may support multiple companies, and thus the development and hosting costs to any one company is smaller.

Several studies have looked at the trend of outsourcing educational services and the effective use of cloud computing in higher education institutes. Universities and colleges, especially those under budget constraints, now have the option to outsource computing services and operate their much-needed computer applications on the cloud, without allocating a lot of investment for buying and maintaining hardware and software applications. This will enable university users to perform academic tasks more effectively, and to improve their educational experiences. Ercan (2002) analyzed the advantages of cloud computing in higher educational services, and suggested that universities should begin by outsourcing e-mail service (SaaS), and then gradually move on to outsource software licenses, hardware, and maintenance. Wyld and Juban (2010) observed that the adaptation of cloud-based applications in higher education will bring lots of potential benefits and capabilities to make communication and collaboration more effective; especially as policies to overcome security and privacy issues improve.

HIGHER EDUCATION IN SAUDI ARABIA

Higher Education in Saudi Arabia has mostly been under the supervision of the Ministry of Higher Education (except vocational colleges), with public universities now established all over the country: in the central area, on the east coast, on the west coast, the north area, and the south area of the country. In 2015, the Ministry of Higher Education and the Ministry of Education were merged into one Ministry.

In recent years, permission was given for private colleges and universities to be established, with the support of loans and students' scholarships from the government. Most public universities have two campuses: men's campus and women's campus under a central management and with one IT department. Most public universities offer a variety of majors: arts, science, engineering, IT, computer science, and health sciences. One particular public university is specialized in engineering and petroleum and minerals. One of the public universities in the capital city is a women-only university, with 15 colleges and a capacity of accommodating 40,000 students. The Government has taken a massive project to overhaul higher education, and has awarded huge contracts to build many campuses and college buildings all over the country to accommodate the increase in higher education enrollments.

As a result of Government initiatives, higher education in Saudi Arabia has undergone a tremendous growth over the last fifteen years, due to rapid increase in population and a massive government initiative to increase its capacity (Higher Education in Saudi Arabia in numbers, 2014). In the 2000-2014 period, the college-age population (18-24 years) in Saudi Arabia has seen a growth of about 30%. The Government since then has allocated a record budget to expand higher education services. In 2014, budget allocation for higher education reached budget record of more than $22bn, which represented 2.9% of the country GDP. Within the same period, the number of public universities has grown from 8 to 25 universities, over 212% growth (Figure 1), whereas the number of colleges has seen a growth of 123% (Figure 2).

Figure 1. The number of private and public universities in Saudi Arabia in 2000 and 2014

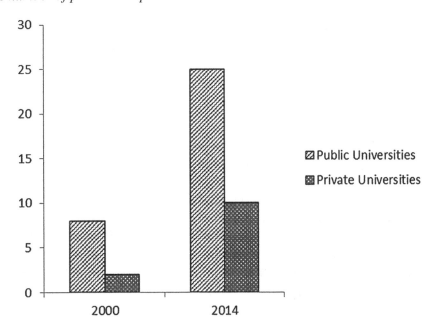

Figure 2. A big jump in the number of private and public colleges from 2000 to 2014

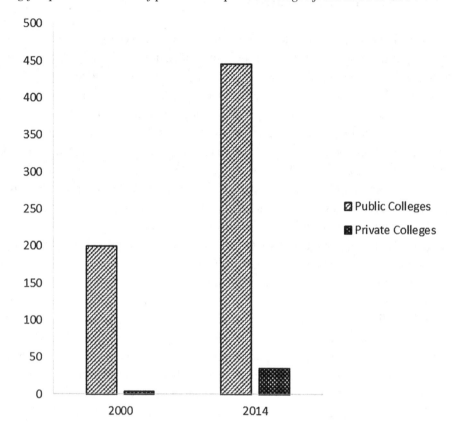

Public universities are made up of a number of colleges, including two-year community and four-year teachers colleges. Furthermore, private colleges and universities are on the rise to satisfy high demand for higher education and the rapid increase in high school graduates. As a result, in the same period, the number of private universities has grown from 2 to 10 universities, (400% growth) (Figure 1), whereas the number of private four-year colleges has increased by 775% (Figure 2).

Moreover, a number of health colleges and institutes as well as technical colleges under the supervision of other governmental agencies have been established to absorb the high demand for two-year and four-year college degrees.

Universities and colleges have seen a record of enrollment, with an increase of 200% in freshmen students in the last fifteen years (Figure 3). Among that, the number of female freshmen students has increased by 117%.

The number of students graduating with a bachelor degree, including male and female students, has increased by 110%. At the graduate level, the number of first-year students at the master's degree level has increased by 800%, whereas the number of first-year PhD students has increased by 215% (Figure 4).

In response to the rapid increase in student enrollment and in the same period, the total number of faculty members has seen a rapid increase (200%). Among them, the number of female faculty members has particularly increased by 285% (Figure 5).

Figure 3. The number of total enrolled undergrad students (male and female) in 2000 and 2014

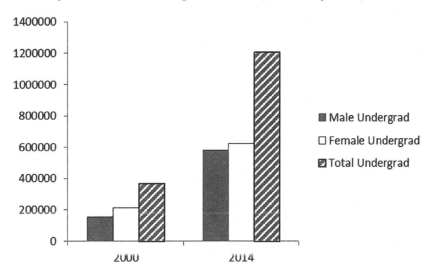

Figure 4. The number of total enrolled graduate students (male and female) in 2000 and 2014

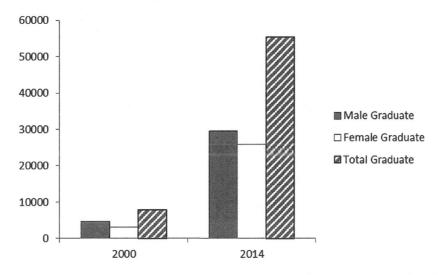

Most faculty members hold PhD degrees and are either citizens of the country, mostly educated in the USA or the UK, or come from neighboring Arab countries. A small percentage of faculty members come from Pakistan, India, and Western countries.

CLOUD COMPUTING IN HIGHER EDUCATION AND USER-CENTRIC APPROACH

Cloud computing services are making huge leaps in the market of Saudi Arabia. In a report published by international market research and advisory company IDC in 2013, the Saudi Arabia market was in its

Figure 5. Increase in the number of faculty members (male and female) from 2000 to 2014

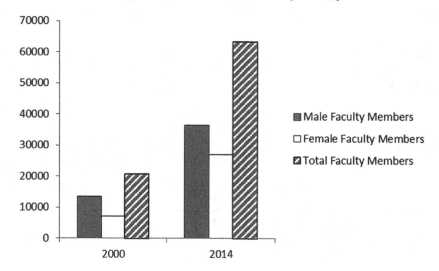

early stages of showing interest in adopting cloud computing services. The report saw a growing demand in cloud services and wisely projected that spending would expand at a compound annual growth rate of almost 50 percent between 2012 and 2016 (Ministry of Communications and Information Technology, 2016).

Alshwaier, Youssef, and Emam (2012) represented educational cloud computing as a new trend for e-learning in Saudi Arabia and showed how universities and higher education institutions can benefit from the cloud in terms of portability, flexibility, and efficiency. Alhazzani (2014) surveyed faculty members at King Saud University, one of the largest public universities in Saudi Arabia, to determine their view of cloud computing and its use in the education sector. The survey indicated that most faculty are familiar with the concept, rate highly its ease of use and accessibility, and perceived cloud based services as a huge step towards furthering the development of higher education. However, the majority of faculty were also concerned about its security and privacy threats. Therefore, an appropriately designed user-centric system is needed for cloud services to ensure that they have flexibility and reliability, and address users' security concerns (Takabi, et al., 2010).

Alamri and Qureshi (2015) conducted a survey to evaluate utilizing cloud computing to support learning and teaching and improve higher education in Saudi Arabia. Their survey showed that the majority of IT professionals and faculty are in support of including cloud computing with the traditional methods of teaching and learning.

Although usability may present a challenge in cloud computing services, it is also believed that relevant services can be achieved based on user-centric approaches that emphasis user requirements in early planning and ongoing evaluation of user satisfaction (Joshi, et al., 2010).

In order to enhance student experience and allow for better education, students get to use e-mail services provided by their university to communicate and interact with faculty and their peers. However, e-mail and computing services consume university resources and put a lot of pressure on the internal servers and IT maintenance staff, which otherwise could be used more efficiently for other internal needs. And so more universities observe that the majority of their students are setting up their university e-mail account to forward their e-mails to third party providers. For instance, in the case of the University of Westminster in the UK, a survey has shown that 96% of students are receiving their university e-mail by forwarding mail to their external e-mail service providers (Sultan, 2010).

With the high enrollment of students in higher education institutes in Saudi Arabia, and the expanding of computing services to faculty and students, there is an urgent need to outsource certain computing services and free up internal resources for more secure and internal transactions. In addition, a high number of public and private universities in Saudi Arabia are less than ten years old (Figure 1), which constitutes a relatively high cost of IT hardware, software and IT staff bills for maintenance and support.

One option that may be considered is using Google Apps for Higher Education as a Software as a Service (SaaS). The platform provides free e-mail and other tool services (such as calendar, document, audio and video sharing, websites and group wikis) for student and staff, with high-capacity disk storage capability. More importantly, the e-mail system does not require users to shift addresses and let users retain their domain names in their e-mail address, for example, student@university.edu.sa.

Furthermore, Google Apps has the ability to be localized in more than 40 languages. As a result, colleges and universities can save cost and free up their IT storage and maintenance resources for IT needs which are more core and need to be more secure. There is no need to install hardware or buy software licenses for web e-mail and management as associated with traditional information systems. Moreover Google Apps are designed to enhance educational experience for students and staff by promoting tools for communications, collaboration and document sharing (e.g. Google Documents, WebEx). So not only will higher education institutes gain economic advantages but students will also gain educational advantages through a more user-centric service.

Several years ago, Yanbu Industrial College in the eastern part of Saudi Arabia announced offering e-mail service for its students and staff via Google Apps. Furthermore, two private colleges in the Central and Western areas are outsourcing e-mail services to Google Apps. In neighboring countries, three higher education institutes are also using Google Apps for their students and staff. In Egypt, the Ministry of Higher Education announced that it is offering three million university students Google Apps with two gigabytes of e-mail storage per student. The Faculty of Science at Cairo University made the switch to Google Apps, as prior to switching the Faculty of Science did not have an efficient way for communication between its faculty members and students. Furthermore, the American University in Cairo has made an alliance with Google to offer Google Apps to its students, faculty and staff.

Another example is in the United Arab Emirates (UAE), where the UAE University was facing high costs related to managing growing lifelong e-mail accounts for its alumni. The University replaced its in-house e-mail service with the Microsoft live@edu cloud service for its alumni account to save costs and reduce workload for IT support staff (Microsoft Case Studies, 2011).

Universities and colleges in the UK are also shifting to Google Apps to take advantage of the user-centric services on offer, such as demonstrated by the University of Westminster (Sultan, 2010).

Several top universities in the US, such as the Ivy League school Brown University, the University of Minnesota, and the University of Norte Dame, have also made the switch to Google Apps to offer better services and connect faculty with students in an enhanced way. Yale University began its switch to Google Apps from the academic year 2011-2012 to free up its internal IT resources (Yale Daily Bulletin, 2011).

E-mail services are often a first step towards further IT outsourcing which fits into the Software as a Service (SaaS) cloud computing category. Besides e-mail services, other IT services in higher education, such as learning management systems and high-processing computing for research, can also be considered. However, security and privacy issues need to be addressed adequately before moving in to full blown outsourcing. Furthermore, outsourcing requires skilled staff with expertise to manage contracts and maintain a strategic overview the outsourcing process.

CONCLUSION

This chapter has looked at outsourcing of higher education IT services in Saudi Arabia with a particular focus on the provision of e-mail services. IT staff are expensive, and the infrastructure costs of e-mail servers and storage can add up. With the very rapid growth of university and college enrollment in Saudi Arabia, some Saudi institutions have opted to outsourced e-mail functions and learning management systems (LMS). This move towards the cloud for e-mail and LMS is a first step into cloud computing outsourcing in the Software as a Service (SaaS) area. This seems to be a cost driven solution which meets the needs of students, faculty and support staff and their institutions to a great extent. It is anticipated that as HE's technology requirements continue to grow in Saudi Arabia, and elsewhere, that additional information and technology outsourcing will take place to meet this demand.

Future research should focus on which information systems servies are best to outsource to:

1. Maximize efficiency for the higher education organisaiton
2. Increase perceive user-centricity by users
3. Stimulate growth for the higher education sector
4. Better design requirements for information systems providers

REFERENCES

Alamri, B., & Qureshi, M. (2015). Usability of Cloud Computing to Improve Higher Education. *I.J. Information Technology and Computer Science*, 9, 59-65.

Alhazzani, N. (2014). A proposed plan to use cloud computing in higher education at the Kingdom of Saudi Arabia. Proceedings of ICERI '14 (p. 2895).

Alshwaier, A., Youssef, A., & Emam, A. (2012). A new trend for e-learning in KSA using educational clouds. *Advanced Computing: An International Journal*, 3(1), 81-96.

Arnold, U. (2000). New dimensions of outsourcing: a combination of transaction cost economics and the core competencies concept. *European Journal of Purchasing & Supply Management*, 6(1), 23-29.

Bardhan, A., & Kroll, C. (2003). *The New Wave of Outsourcing*. Berkeley: Fisher Center for Real Estate and Urban Economics, University of California.

Behara, R. S., Gundersen, D. E., & Capozzoli, E. A. (1995). Trends in Information Systems Outsourcing. *Journal of Supply Chain Management*, 31(1), 45-51.

Bhadauria, R., Borgohain, R., Biswas, A., & Sanyal, S. (2014). Secure authentication of Cloud data mining API. *Acta Technica Corviniensis-Bulletin of Engineering*, 183.

Collis, D. (2004). The paradox of scope: A challenge to the governance of higher education. In W. G. Tierney, Competing Conceptions of Academic Governance: Navigating the Perfect Storm (pp. 33-76). Batlimore: Johns Hopkins University Press.

Davis, G. B., Ein-Dor, P., King, W. R., & Torkzadeh, R. (2006). IT Offshoring: History, Prospects and Challenges. *Journal of the Association for Information Systems.*

Dikaiakos, M., Katsaros, D., Mehra, P., Pallis, G., & Vakali, A. (2009). Cloud Computing: Distributed Internet Computing for IT and Scientific Research. *IEEE Internet Computing, 13*(5), 10–13. doi:10.1109/MIC.2009.103

Dossania, R., & Kenney, M. (2007). The Next Wave of Globalization: Relocating Service Provision to India. *World Development, 35*(5), 772–791. doi:10.1016/j.worlddev.2006.09.014

Ercan, T. (2002). Effective use of cloud computing in educational institutions. *Procedia: Social and Behavioral Sciences, 2*(2), 938–942.

Gottschalk, P., & Solli-Sæther, H. (2005). Critical success factors from IT outsourcing theories: An empirical study. *Industrial Management & Data Systems, 105*(6), 685–702. doi:10.1108/02635570510606941

Gupta, A., Herath, S. K., & Mikouiza, N. C. (2005). Outsourcing in higher education: An empirical examination. *International Journal of Educational Management, 19*(5), 396–412. doi:10.1108/09513540510607734

Joshi, K. P., Yesha, Y., Ozok, A. A., Yesha, Y., Lahane, A., Kalva, H., & Furht, B. (2010). User-centric smart services in the cloud. In M. Chignell, J. Cordy, J. Ng, & Y. Yesha (Eds.), *The smart internet* (pp. 234–249). Berlin, Heidelberg: Springer-Verlag. doi:10.1007/978-3-642-16599-3_16

Kakabadse, A., & Kakabadse, N. (2005). Outsourcing: Current and future trends. *Thunderbird International Business Review, 47*(2), 183–204. doi:10.1002/tie.20048

Ketler, K., & Walstrom, J. (1993). The outsourcing decision. *International Journal of Information Management, 13*(6), 449–459. doi:10.1016/0268-4012(93)90061-8

Lacity, M. C., & Hirschheim, R. (1993). The information systems outsourcing bandwagon. *Sloan Management Review*, Fall, 74–86.

Lacity, M. C., & Willcocks, L. P. (1998). An Empirical Investigation of Information Technology Sourcing Practices: Lessons from Experience. *Management Information Systems Quarterly, 22*(3), 363–408. doi:10.2307/249670

Lankford, W., & Parsa, F. (1999). Outsourcing: A primer. *Management Decision, 37*(4), 310–316. doi:10.1108/00251749910269357

Lee, J., & Clery, S. (2004). Key Trend in Higher Education. *Academic Journal.*

Lee, J.-N., Huynh, M. Q., Kwok, R. C.-W., & Pi, S.-M. (2003). IT outsourcing evolution---: Past, present, and future. *Communications of the ACM, 46*(5), 84–89. doi:10.1145/769800.769807

Lin, G., Fu, D., Zhu, J., & Dasmalchi, G. (2009). Cloud Computing: IT as a Service. *IT Professional, 11*(2), 10–13.

Microsoft. (2011, May 17). Microsoft Case Studies. Retrieved from http://www.microsoft.com/casestudies/Microsoft-Exchange-Server-2007-Enterprise-Edition/United-Arab-Emirates-University/University-Enhances-Messaging-While-Saving-IT-Time-and-Cutting-Storage-Costs/4000009662

Ministry of Communications and Information Technology (Saudi Arabia). (2016, February 28). Saudi firms explore cloud computing to reduce costs: IDC. Retrieved from http://www.mcit.gov.sa/En/InformationTechnology/Pages/SubjectsandInformation/Tech-Subject-10032013_169.aspx

Ministry of Higher Education. (2014). *Higher Education in Saudi Arabia in numbers*. Riyadh: Ministry of Higher Education.

Poster, W. (2007). Whos On the Line? Indian Call Center Agents Pose as Americans for U.S.-Outsourced Firms. *Industrial Relations*, *46*(2), 271–304. doi:10.1111/j.1468-232X.2007.00468.x

Power, M., Bonifazi, C., & Desouza, K. C. (2004). The ten outsourcing traps to avoid. *The Journal of Business Strategy*, *25*(2), 37–42. doi:10.1108/02756660410525399

Quélin, B., & Duhamel, F. (2003). Bringing Together Strategic Outsourcing and Corporate Strategy: Outsourcing Motives and Risks. *European Management Journal*, *21*(5), 647–661. doi:10.1016/S0263-2373(03)00113-0

Quinn, J. B., & Hilmer, F. G. (1994). Strategic Outsourcing. *Sloan Management Review*, Summer, 43–55.

Sultan, N. (2010). Cloud computing for education: A new dawn? *International Journal of Information Management*, *30*(2), 109–116. doi:10.1016/j.ijinfomgt.2009.09.004

Takabi, H., Joshi, J. B., & Ahn, G.-j. (2010). SecureCloud: Towards a Comprehensive Security Framework for Cloud Computing Environments. *Proceedings of theFirst IEEE International Workshop on Emerging Applications for Cloud Computing*, Seoul. doi:10.1109/COMPSACW.2010.74

Tastle, W., White, B., Valfells, Á., & Shackleton, P. (2008). Information Systems, Offshore Outsourcing, and Relevancy in the Business School Curriculum. *Journal of Information Technology Research*, *1*(2), 61–77. doi:10.4018/jitr.2008040105

Wyld, D. C., & Juban, R. L. (2010). Education in the Clouds: How Colleges and Universities are Leveraging Cloud Computing. *Technological Developments in Networking, Education and Automation*.

Yale Daily Bulletin. (2011, August 12). Coming to a computer near you: Google Apps for Education. Retrieved from http://dailybulletin.yale.edu/article.aspx?id=8460

Section 2
User Centered Design

Chapter 8
Design Solutions Guided by User Behavior:
A Practical Inquiry Approach

Mariam Ahmed Elhussein
University of Dammam, Saudi Arabia

ABSTRACT

Tagging systems design is often neglected despite the fact that most system designers agree on the importance of tagging. They are viewed as part of a larger system which receives most of the attention. There is no agreed method when it comes to either analyzing existing tagging systems or designing new ones. There is a need to establish a well-structured design process that can be followed to create tagging systems with a purpose. This chapter uses practical inquiry methodology to generate a general framework that can be applied to analyze tagging systems and proceeds to suggest a design process that can be followed to create new tagging systems. Existing user behavior while tagging is the main guide for the methodology.

INTRODUCTION

User-centric approach in information systems tries to discover how users' behavior is affected by the design of the system. With users in mind, user-centric design tailors how the information system is constructed according to the user group that is expected to interact with the system. This chapter introduces the concept with social tagging by following a methodology that is focused on providing solutions to specific problems. After a solution is found, the methodology suggests ways to expand it to similar problems within the domain.

Social tagging has been linked to Web 2.0 technologies. Most of the current online systems employ tagging to support retrieval, categorization or ranking of shared content. Tagging is also provided as means for self-organization and future reference. For such diverse functions, social tagging has been studied extensively. Researchers explored tagging starting from answering the question of "why do users tag?" to modeling tagging behavior.

DOI: 10.4018/978-1-5225-1944-7.ch008

Tagging is a low-cost attachment of metadata since it is done voluntarily by non-expert users. It is also considered to be a democratization of the classification process where people have their say on the different aspects of the content (G. Smith, 2007). The return value of tagging has two dimensions; one dimension concerns the user and the other concerns the designers of the system.

From the system designer's point of view, tagging is favored over expert indexing since the latter is expensive and time consuming. Tagging is done by far more users who will do it for free most of the time. Quality might be questioned in this case, but research conducted by Heymann and Garcia-Molina (2009) showed that 50% of the keywords used by expert indexers were also used by free-lance taggers.

Although tags are considered useful to the support of the system in many ways, it is sometimes problematic. One problem that can be associated with this freedom is that users can be unpredictable as to which type of tags they may provide (or provide tags at all). Existing online systems that allow tagging are bound to continue to support freedom of tagging and deal with the problems that arise from that such as tags used for self-reference. The designers of these systems usually state the reasons behind adding tagging in their help sections, but they do not enforce users to tag accordingly. The main issue here is to preserve users' freedom while tagging and benefit from their tags to support the web content. Attempts to solve this problem have previously all focused on working around the outcome of tagging. An immediate concern of allowing users to tag freely is that tags can be exploited in spamming. They can be used to promote products and services that are not of direct benefit to the tagged resource. Other problems were linked to tagging that was directly influenced by taggers motivations. Researchers propose three possible ways to overcome the problems that were identified with tagging; identification-based (detection), rank-based, and interface-based (prevention) (Heymann, Koutrika, & Garcia-Molina, 2007). This chapter presents a method based on interface-based (prevention) solution.

According to Liu (2000) there is always a need to incorporate methodologies that depend on the social aspects of information systems rather than the technical aspects. This need drove research into incorporating theories and methods that enable the consideration of people within the system of information. Organizational semiotics (OS) and activity theory (AT) are examples of theories that have been used in research to accommodate people as an integral part of the information system.

The questions that this chapter is based on call for changing the existing behavior of users in a certain context by understanding how they interact together. The research aims at contributing to the practice of a problem that has been developed and used. Existing tagging systems are studied in order to verify the problem and propose a solution by following practical inquiry methodology.

Background

A 'tag' is defined as a user-generated keyword and "A lightweight way to enhance the description of online resources to improve their access through broader indexing." (Trant, 2009, p. 1). When tagging is conducted in a shared context, it is called 'Collaborative Tagging'. According to Golder and Huberman (2006, p. 1), "Collaborative Tagging describes the process by which many users add metadata in the form of keywords to shared content". Systems with tagging capabilities enable users to add terms that classify or describe certain content. In that way, users add different tags to the same content depending on the way they see it, which provides diverse views for the same content. One image can be tagged many times which allows it to be grouped in many categories depending on these tags. An image of a flower can be tagged as 'flower', 'spring' or 'yellow' and can be found using any of these terms. Tags can also take the form of content evaluation. Reddit.com allow their users to rank content using 'up' and 'down' tags which reduces or increases its ranking and reflects how popular it is (Morrison, 2008). A visual display of tags is provided using tag-clouds, where tags that are shown in larger bolder fonts are the most popular tags.

The collection of all tags produced is called, folksonomy (Trant, 2009). The term folksonomy was derived from the words 'folks' and 'taxonomy'[1]. The 'folk' was added to reflect on the fact that the conceptual structures created were by non-professional indexers as opposed to taxonomies that are created by professional indexers (Hotho, Jäschke, Schmitz, & Stumme, 2006). There are other terms in the literature that refer to the same concept, including 'democratic indexing' (M. Smith, 2006), 'communal categorization' (Sturtz, 2004), 'collaborative tagging' (Golder & Huberman, 2006) and 'user-generated metadata' (Dye, 2006).

The main focus of research is to identify the reasons that motivate users to provide tags. This is also known as studying user tagging behavior or tagging models (Peters & Becker, 2009). The significance of these studies comes from the fact that taggers' freedom, while tagging, is supposed to be maintained. Tagging motivations are explored in order to provide systematic solutions to encourage users to provide more tags while their autonomy is preserved. In general, tags are objective depending on the purpose behind tagging which is referred to as 'tagging motivation'. Gupta, Li, Yin and Han (2010) provided a classification of users' tagging motivations as follows:

- **Future Retrieval**: This can be aimed at personal retrieval or for others to retrieve content.
- **Contribution and Sharing**: Tags are used as a way of categorizing content and group it with other similar content.
- **Attract attention**: Using popular tags, users can attract other users to view resources.
- **Play and Competition**: Some systems use incentives and competition to encourage users to tag.
- **Self-Referential Tags**: Tags are used as a mark or an identity on the content. A good example for this can be tags that start with 'my'.
- **Opinion Expression**: They can be used as a way to express opinion such as 'like'.
- **Task Organization**: Tags such as 'to read' or 'view later' are used for self-organization. The user can use tags to organize content according to tasks.
- **Social Signaling**: This is how tags are used in Facebook where users use tags to identify people in an image or signal users to view certain content.
- **Money**: Users can tag in order to receive money, sites such as Amazon pay users for tags.
- **Technological Ease**: Users sometimes tag because it is easy. Some systems make it very easy for users to add tags such as allowing tag suggestion.

Tagging takes place within tagging systems. They are the context where tagging takes place. The basic structure model of social tagging system consists of: the user, the resource, and tag(s); Figure 1 shows this structure. According to the figure users can tag each other (dotted lines between users) such as on Facebook and Twitter. Resources can also be linked to each other. The resource is the content to be tagged which can be an anything, a video, a blog or an image. The user is the tagger who will perform the tagging and the tag is the keyword that will be attached to the resource.

There are many ways to classify tagging systems. One of these is dependent on the type of content it allows its users to publish. This includes many content types such as: social bookmarking services (e.g. Delicious), e-commerce (e.g. Amazon), libraries 2.0 (e.g. PennTags), photosharing services (e.g.

Figure 1. A model of tagging systems (Marlow, Naaman, Boyd, & Davis, 2006)

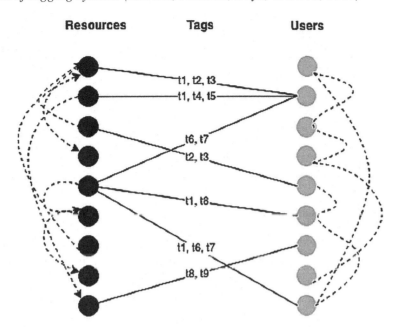

Flickr), videosharing services (e.g. YouTube), social networks (e.g. Facebook), blog search engines (e.g. Technochrati), and games with purpose (GWAP) (Bateman, Brooks, McCalla, & Brusilovsky, 2007).

Tagging Systems Design

Farooq et al. (2007) suggested some guidelines to be followed when designing a tagging system. They suggested three heuristics to be followed when constructing a tagging system:

1. Tagging interface is supposed to induce tag reuse
2. Recommend tags that are considered powerful from an informational point of view
3. Enhancement of tagging by showing relevant resources i.e. supporting the categorization function of tagging

Another attempt was presented by Marlow et al. (2006), who identified two areas that would affect tagging outcome. This includes:

- Tagging systems' design attributes
- User incentives to provide tagging

They defined seven attributes that affect design decisions when designing tagging systems. Table 1 provides a summary of these design attributes, the tagging systems types they identify and the expected impact of each of these. Despite the contribution, there is no guide on how these attributes are to be used in an arranged step-by-step process that can be followed. It might also be difficult to predict how tagging

Table 1. Summary of tagging systems design attributes adopted from Marlow et al. (2006)

Attribute	Tagging system types	Potential impact
Tagging Rights	Self-tagging, permission based, free-for-all	Nature and type of tags, role of tags in system
Tagging Support	Blind, suggested, viewable	Convergence on folksonomy or overweighting of tags
Aggregation Model	Bag, set	Availability of aggregation statistics
Object Type	Textual, non-textual	Nature and type of tags
Source of Material	User-contributed, system, global	Different incentives, nature and type of tags
Resource Connectivity	Links, groups, none	Convergence on similar tags for links/grouped resources
Social Connection	Links, groups, none	Convergence on the localized folksonomy

behavior would be influenced when different combinations of the attributes are applied. On another note, the design process did not explain the dynamic and interrelations that governs attributes together.

There is a need to establish concrete theoretical grounds to base the understanding of the different components of a tagging system and hence identify how they affect tag quality. The theoretical analysis of tagging systems points out the way each of its components affects the users while tagging which leads to supporting the system by enhancing those components. The framework can also be the basis for identifying a design process that can be followed to create new tagging systems.

PRACTICAL INQUIRY METHODOLOGY

The purpose of practical inquiry methodology is to apply "empirical study on practical matters in local practices, to contribute to general practical knowledge. This practical knowledge will be part of the scientific body of knowledge and it aims to be useful for practical affairs" (Goldkuhl, 2008, p. 1).

According to Figure 2, the methodology starts by identifying problems that are faced by practitioners in a local practice. The problem is investigated through empirical data that is researched extensively to formulate a solution. Once a solution is reached and applied to the local practice, it is generalized and becomes part of the scientific body of knowledge. The generalization of the problem is often done by the introduction of a theory. Despite the fact that the major outcome of IS research is tools and artefacts, introduction of theory in IS was inevitable since researchers are expected to produce knowledge out of their works (Gregor, 2002). Gregor (2006) believes that theory is required to understand what constitutes IS, linking the natural world, the social world and the artificial world of human constructions.

Theories are used to explain or predict human or organizational behavior in order to assess existing tools or develop new ones (Hevner, March, Park, & Ram, 2004). They are used to inform researchers about the interaction between people, tools and the organization they all operate within.

In this chapter, semiotics theory and activity theory are used in order to study tagging systems as local practice, Figure 3 explains the role of theories within the methodology. Both theories were applied to different types of problems. In this chapter these are applied for specifically discover particular matter in order to discover the factors that influence tagging behavior. An empirical analysis of data from existing tagging systems is done which resulted in an understanding of the components of the tagging

Figure 2. Practical inquiry (A research approach aiming at knowledge as a general practice contribution) Source: Goldkuhl (2008a)

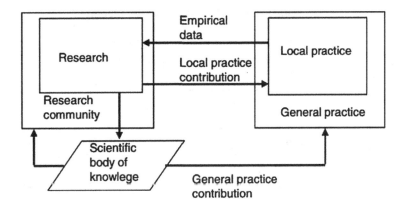

Figure 3. The role of practical theories (semiotics and activity theory) in practical inquiry methodology to solve the social tagging design problem. Source: Goldkuhl (2008a)

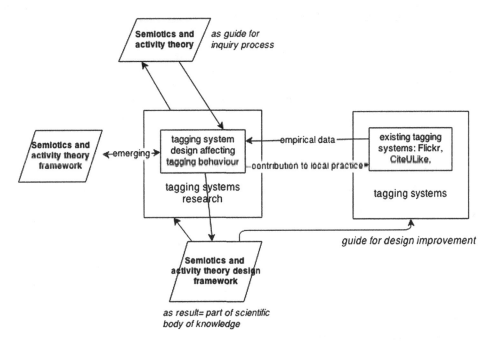

system. The methodology goes on to suggest a design process for tagging systems based on a framework identified using organizational semiotics and activity theory. Figure 4 shows the research process based on practical inquiry. Practical inquiry methodology consists of two stages, practice theorizing and situational inquiry (Goldkuhl, 2011).

1. The first step is practice theorizing, at this stage, practical theories are identified as guide for the inquiry process. Semiotics analysis and activity theory are shown as bases for analysis of existing

Figure 4. The research process based on practical inquiry. Source: Goldkuhl (2011)

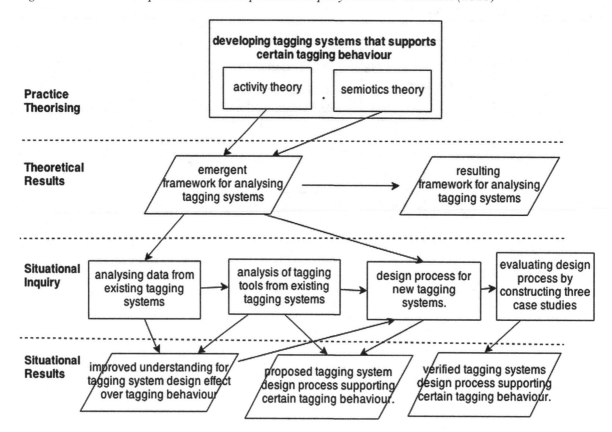

tagging systems. As the process of inquiry evolves, the need for an emergent practical theory arises where a new framework based on both theories is identified. This analysis framework is considered as theoretical result of practice theorizing.

2. The second stage is the situational inquiry, where the analysis framework is used in order to analyze existing tagging systems and to identify a design process for new tagging systems. This process is considered an outcome of the first stage of practice theorizing and the framework identified from the emergent practical theory. Situational inquiry calls for empirical analysis to verify the design process. Data was collected based on the situational model (the design process) and finally the situational results are achieved. Data collection of the situational model was done by retrieving data from existing tagging systems.

The following sections explain each step of the methodology.

Practice Theorizing

Using semiotics theory, organizations are understood to have messages communicated and acted upon. A simple definition of Semiotics might be 'the study of sign' (Chandler, 2002). Semiotics theory has been linked to many disciplines including linguistics, communication, computer science, human-computer interaction, and advertising. Semiotics originated in the first works of the Swiss linguist Ferdinand de

Saussure (1857-1913) (cited in Chandler 2002) who called it 'semiology' and linked it to social sciences (Eco, 1979). The work was formalized by the American philosopher Charles Sanders Peirce, who provided an early definition of semiotics as being the: "quasi-necessary, or formal doctrine of signs" (cited in Hartshorne et al. 1967, p.139). Pierce's definition of sign to cover its meaning/interpretant. In this definition, the representation is: the form which the sign takes, an interpretant is the sense made of the sign and an object is to which the sign refers. The Peircian model shows the relation between the three components. The interaction between the three is called 'semiosis' which was described as 'the process of signification' (Peirce, 1960). From this definition many branches of semiotics emerged. One branch of semiotics is 'organizational semiotics' which was started by Ronald Stamper in 1973 (Chandler, 2000). According to Liu (2000, p.19): "Organizational semiotics is the study of organizations using the concept and methods of semiotics". This means that for the organization to function, it is important to study the communication that takes place between the people and groups within it. In order to analyze a sign to its components, the semiotics ladder was introduced. Originally it was called the sign's three dimensions which include the syntactic, semantic and pragmatic layers. These were extended later by Roland Stamper to include the physical world, the social world and empirics (Liu, 2000). The semiotic ladder is divided into two groups, the 'human-information function' and the 'IT-platform'. The human-information layers include the social world, pragmatics and semantics while the IT-platform includes the syntactic, empiric, and physical world.

According to Huang and Chuang (2009) a tag fits into Peirce's definition of a sign. It can be described using the triadic model comprising representamen, object, and interpretant. The representamen is the form the sign takes, which is the tag itself. The object is the entity to which the sign points to, which is the content to be tagged; it can be an image, a video, a book or a URL. The interpretant of the tag is the assignment of meaning the representamen is giving to the object.

Within the tagging system, the semantic layer is about the meaning of adding tagging capabilities to a system. This means that the system allows for its users to add tags to content. The pragmatic layer is about the system designers' intentions behind allowing users to tag. This means the reasons for allowing users to tag from the system designer's point of view. The social world is the user's understanding of the purpose behind adding tagging capabilities within the tagging system. Figure 5 shows the SL-based analysis of the tags tagging system while Table 2 summarizes the previous analysis of tags and tagging systems according to the semantic, pragmatic and social layers of SL.

According to the semiotics analysis of tags and tagging systems these are viewed as messages that are conveyed from a sender to a receiver. A tag itself is a message communicated between the tagger who provided the tag and the reader who would view, interpret and act according to that tag. The tagging system is also considered to be a sign with semantic, pragmatic and social implications. When a certain

Table 2. Tag and tagging system analysis according to SL human information functions

Layer	Tag level	Tagging System Level
Semantics	The direct meaning of the tag-content association	The direct meaning of adding tagging capabilities to the system.
Pragmatics	Intention of the user (description, categorization, self-reference, organization...)	Intention of the system designer (allowing users to categorize, facilitate retrieval, encourage imitation...)
Social	Social effect the tag has over taggers (imitation, forming an opinion, CLIR...)	Social effect of adding tagging capabilities to the system (forming groups of interest)

Figure 5. Semiotics ladder for tags and tagging systems

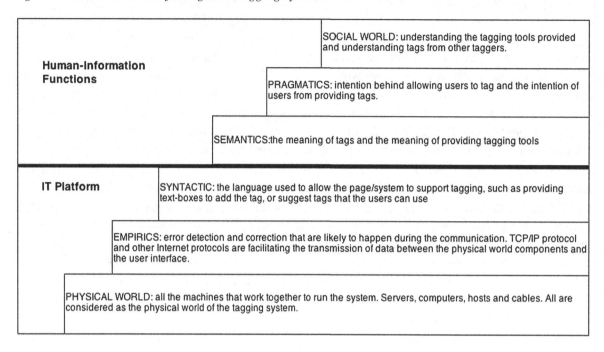

system is supported by a tagging system, the system designer sends a message to the users of the system. These messages will accordingly act within the system towards the tagging facilities provided. Semiotic analysis of tags and tagging systems have allowed for an in depth view of the messages sent and their possible effects. It has also provided different dimensions of signs. However, while this analysis was useful in understanding the different layers of tags and tagging systems; it does not capture the tagging process as actions that are performed by individuals or groups. The semiotics ladder does not allow for a description of the tagging activity that takes place within the tagging system; hence activity theory (AT) is introduced here to depict tagging as an activity performed.

Activity theory (AT) is used to analyze the issues that comprise an activity, including cultural and social ones. It provides a language that describes people's behavior in certain context (Mwanza, 2001). AT has established presence in HCI research and has been used to analyze and improve existing systems, and constructing new ones. It became a tool for designing and analyzing in many disciplines including education, human computer interaction (HCI) and professional training (Westberry, 2009). The new development of AT by Engestrom was aimed at expanding the activity triangle defined by Vygotsky to include other components including community, rules, and division of labor. Figure 6 shows the model as realized by Engestrom. In a tagging system context, AT has not been utilized to describe tagging activity, yet it has been used to analyze social systems of a similar nature.

Kuutti (2005, p. 3) defines AT as "a school of thought on the relation and interaction between humans and the material and social environment- a kind of theory practices". The influence of activity theory on HCI research is notable in the attention it receives within the research community. AT is preserved as a tool that is used for both the design and redesign of computer tools used in systems such as BUILT-IT, a user-monitoring environment for activity systems and SupportTracker for Hewlett-Packard (Lazarou, 2011). As a theoretical framework, AT is used to analyze human practices in a form of a development

Figure 6. The expanded Activity Triangle Model
Source: (Engestrom 1987, p. 78)

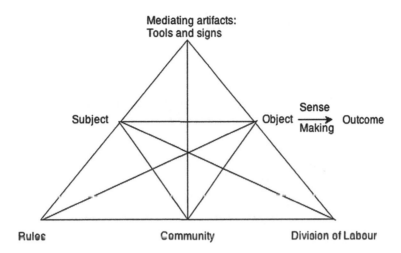

process by describing both individual and social levels at the same time (Kuutti, 1995). In this context, AT is utilized to analyze tagging activity that takes place within a tagging system.

Activity theory is not a methodology, nor a predicative theory, but it provides researchers with a descriptive tool that clarifies how a goal of an activity is achieved (Westberry, 2009). The theory was built around five principles identified by Blanton et al. (2001) to include:

1. Human behaviour is social.
2. Human activity is mediated through tools.
3. Centrality of communication during the activity
4. Normative expectations and rules
5. Learning and development are incorporated in the activities of the community.

Activity theory-based analysis is built around the object of the activity. The object of the activity separates one activity from the other, that is why it is said that activities are object-oriented (Kuutti, 2010).

The tagging activity which takes place within tagging systems is identified by its object. The unit of analysis is the activity directed at an object (goal). This includes the cultural (community, rule, role effects) and technical mediation (tool effect). This object is supported by the actions of the tagger who is considered to be the subject of the activity. The activity consists of goal-directed actions performed by the subject towards the object of the activity. The act of tagging performed by the subject is medicated through tools which are considered to be enabling and limiting, they enable the subject to perform the activity yet they limit what they can do (Kuutti, 1995). Tagging is considered a human behavior that is mediated through tools and conducted through communication within the tagging system. The tagger is found within a community consisting of taggers, tag consumers and the system designer. They all represent the community where the tagging activity takes place. Figure 7 shows the activity structure of a tagging activity.

The subject of the activity is affected by all other components of the activity while performing the actions towards the goal. The subject represents the internalization of the activity when taggers try potential

Figure 7. Tagging activity

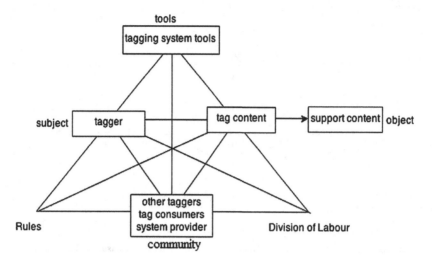

interactions in reality without performing actual actions. This includes mental stimulations, imaginings, considering alternative ways (Kuutti, 1995). In a tagging system, tools refer to the user interface components used to facilitate tagging, such as textboxes and buttons that allow users to provide tagging of contents. The rules of the activity are those set by the system designer and may take two forms, either the general terms of service of the system or other rules that govern how users of the system interact together. The latter can be rules that regulate who can tag or whether someone can tag someone else's content etc. As for the roles of taggers in a tagging system, following are the possible roles they may take on: taggers, tag consumers and the system designers. The object of the activity is the goal that the subject is works towards achieving. The community of the tagging activity includes taggers, content publishers and moderators. In the tagging activity, the community is governed by rules. In all the publicly servicing tagging systems, there are is a set of terms that a user agrees to when s/he signs up for a username.

The outcome of the tagging activity is the goal of providing tagging support to the content (Maier, 2007). All of the abovementioned components of the activity work together to achieve this outcome. Echarte et al. (2007) found that tags can define the content, its type and/or the author among many other things. Each tag typically contributes to one or more function of tagging, which can be considered as the outcome of the tagging activity.

A Framework for Analyzing Tagging Systems

The suggested framework combines activity theory and semiotics ladder from semiotics theory.

It consists of the top three levels of the semiotics ladder interlacing with activity theory components (see Figure 8). AT components represent human functions within the semiotics ladder. By viewing the tagging system as a sign, the system is decomposed into three levels of sign Semantic, Pragmatic and Social world. When decomposing the tagging system into activity components, they are reflected in the three levels of the ladder. This produces three types of activity components, Social components (rules, community and roles), Pragmatic components (subject and object) and the Semantic component (tools). The social components of the tagging system represent the social effects the system has on its users

Figure 8. A framework for analyzing tagging systems (FATS)

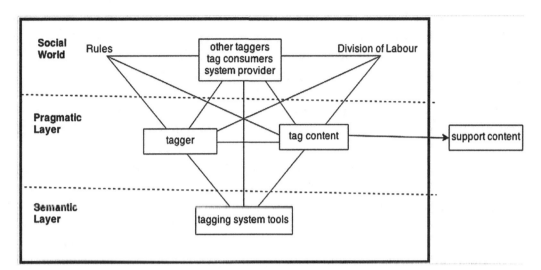

including identifying who they are (community), how the work is divided between them (roles) and what governs their behavior (rules). The community of the system describes the members who are part of the tagging system and affect or affected by it. The roles of the system represent how the community members are expected to contribute towards the system. While the rules are devised to govern how the tagging system ought to perform. The pragmatic components of the system represent the intention of the doers of the activity (subject) or taggers and the intention behind creating the tagging system (object). The subject is the tagger's intention towards the tagging system i.e. using tagging for retrieval purposes, categorization, self-organizing, or even vandalism by spamming the system. The object represents the intention that stands behind allowing tagging of content within the system. It can be understood as the main purpose of the tagging system which is expected to be the motive for taggers. According to the concept of mediation from AT, the relation between pragmatic components and semantic components can be described as follows:

- Object directs the subject of the activity.
- The subject is mediated through the tools.
- Tools shape how the subject interacts with the object.

As a semantic component of the tagging system, tools reflect the direct meaning of the system. They mediate the subject towards the object i.e. reflect the intention of the taggers towards the system by allowing them to tag. Tools are also affected by the object of the system i.e. the intention of the system designers affects the types of tools used for tagging.

The social components of the tagging systems include rules, community and division of labor (roles). The community includes the group of people who are part of the system. This includes taggers, consumers of tags and system providers. The subject may affect the community of the system either in a positive or negative manner. The tagger's intention maybe encouraged if for example they receive positive feedback from the community or may be discouraged if no feedback was provided. Community members divide how tasks are performed amongst them. This division of labor identifies what each member is supposed to do within the system. Roles are set based on the object and they affect the subject of the system. They also shape the relationship between the subject and the community. The third social component here is the rules, which are influenced by the object of the tagging system. In other words, they are shaped based on the object. "Rules shape the interactions of subject and tools with the object" (Russell 2003, p. 11). Rules are also created to influence the subject within the community and to resolve conflicts that may take place within the community that is related to roles.

From the previous discussion, FATS was shown to provide a new way of looking into tagging system components using semiotics and activity theory. The next section will identify the steps that can be followed based on the framework in order to analyze existing tagging systems.

The analysis process aims at measuring performance and identifying problems in existing tagging systems if there are any. By following the proposed FATS, the analysis process starts by identifying the object of the tagging system based on the other components of the system. To provide a starting point, tools represent the direct meaning of the tagging system. If the system contains a textbox with a tag label for tagging tools, this means that it is a system that allows tagging i.e. attaching keywords to content. Starting from this point, the analysis process will be based on the tools used within the tagging system as follows:

1. Identify the tools that are used in the tagging system. This includes all visible tools in the tagging interface where users can attach tags to specific content.
2. Using the tools identified, the social components of the tagging system are described:
    a. Rules are inferred by reviewing what is allowed and what is not allowed. This can be shown from the tools.
    b. The Community component is revealed by identifying how the subject of the system is affected by the community.
    c. Division of labor (roles) are described by showing what possible roles the community members can play.
3. At the end of this analysis, the object of the system is determined.

To relate this phase of work to the practical inquiry methodology, the semiotics and activity theory framework Delicious has been selected as a practical theory that will be used in the analysis phase of inquiry. Tagging systems can be analyzed using FATS as described. The following section uses the FATS to analyze Delicious tagging system CiteULike and Flickr. The purpose of the analysis is to reveal the object of each system based on their tagging interface. The analysis is used later to show the effect of the design over the tagging behavior of the users of the system. Another advantage of the analysis is to show the different types of tagging tools used. This allows for a more comprehensive understanding of which tools to use in new tagging systems.

SAMPLE ANALYSIS

The main purpose behind the analysis of well-set up tagging systems is to identify their object according to the way they were designed. By analyzing tagging systems that are already functioning, there is an opportunity to retrieve data and examine tagging behavior from the actual users of the systems. The analysis is conducted for the system based on FATS, and then data is explored to investigate some of the users' tagging behaviors. The sample analysis is done over Delicious tagging system, one of the most extensively researched systems.

Delicious is an online bookmarking system that was created with the purpose of providing an online list of bookmarks that can be accessed from anywhere. It allows users to add URLs and provide textual descriptions and titles for them. It also allows users to optionally add tags to each URL they add. When researching social tagging, Delicious provides a rich database of bookmarks with tags. Delicious was used in the highly cited study by Golder and Huberman (2006) which described one of the earliest tagging models explaining stable patterns in tagging.

Using FATS, the analysis starts by defining each component of the Delicious tagging system.

1. The semantic component of Delicious which is represented by the tools used for tagging consists of:
    a. **Tool1**: A toolbox where tags can be typed into and it is marked optional.
    b. **Tool2**: A list of suggested tags that can be used instead of creating new tags. The list was extracted from the added URL. It can be an extract from meta HTML tags of the website, or a keyword extraction of its content.
    c. **Tool3**: Title and description textboxes
    d. **Tool4**: A checkbox that says 'Make private link' i.e. the link is by default public and can be made private.
    e. **Tool5**: 'No Image' checkbox, which means that the system will provide an image from the link but the user can choose not to use an image by checking this checkbox.
2. The pragmatic components of the tagging system include the subject and the object of the tagging system. The subject of Delicious is the users' intention towards the tagging system. Every user with an account is able to sign in, add a link and tag it. Delicious has over two million users since it was launched in 2003 (Chu, Rathi, & Du, 2010). There is no special profile for users in Delicious; they can be students or lawyers whose intentions are to benefit from the tagging system by saving their bookmarks. The users can have any intention for assigning tags to a bookmark including the list of tag intentions that were listed above (categorizing, providing opinion, retrieval, personal reference, and grouping). They can also be surfers with malicious intentions that aim at abusing the system.

The object of the tagging system is the reason why was it created by the system providers of Delicious. That is, the object of the tagging system represents their intention. According to the Delicious help page, the reason for allowing tagging is to for users to categorize their links and facilitateretrieval[2]. Nonetheless, this analysis is concerned with revealing the intention through the components of tagging system, so what is written in the help section will be overlooked. The social components of Delicious include the community, rules and roles within the system. The rules of Delicious are set by the system provider:

-   When a user adds a new link, they do not have to add tags to it; it is entirely optional. This means a user can add links without providing tags to the newly added link. This rule was understood from the first tool which had the 'optional' label attached to it.
-   Users are encouraged to provide tags through tag suggestions. These suggestions are related to the link and extracted from it. They have no link to a user's previous tags or community tags. This rule was deduced from the tag suggestion list.

- In Delicious, links are by default public and seen by all users along with all their attached meta-data. Users are allowed to search other users' link collections. Users can choose to make a certain link private. This rule is understood according to the fourth tool that gave the option for private links.

The Community of Delicious consists of taggers, tag consumers and system providers. The community has an effect on the subject since users in Delicious can view each other's content unless it is private. This affects their intention in the sense it prevents socially unacceptable tagging behavior.

The roles the users can play in a tagging system in general is to tag their own content and/or consume tags of others. According to the tagging interface of Delicious, public tagging allows for consumers to view how others tagged. The subject is influenced by consumers as they will be using the tags provided by taggers.

To identify the object of the tagging system, we summarize the analysis as follows:

- The user is allowed to tag freely, or not tag.
- Tagging is encouraged by providing tag suggestions that are extracted from the link.
- The subject is affected by the fact the links are public until made private. This leads to the assumption that the role of tag consumers has an effect on the subject.
- One additional influence of the object is the fact that there is a separate space for title and description. This may affect the subject to employ tags in other ways, such as categorization.

The analysis of Delicious was conducted by applying the analysis process based on activity theory and semiotics. The analysis showed the object of the tagging system as shown by the tools, rules, role and community components of the system. These components were revealed by interpreting the tagging system as a sign with semantic, pragmatic and social components. The structure of activity theory allowed for interpreting how each component was represented in the tagging system interface.

The tools used in tagging systems are limited to a small set of graphical user interface components such as textboxes and drop-down lists. In general, there are two tools used with tagging systems, tools that are used to insert tags and others that are used to provide tagging assistance. Free tagging is usually allowed using textboxes with labels that ask users to provide tags. When it comes to tagging assistance, it is in the form of suggested tags. Tag suggestion is provided is Delicious in the form of clickable buttons, each button represents a tag that can be attached to the URL.

In CiteULike tag suggestion is provided by clicking on a button that shows tags as links. When the links are clicked, tags are attached to the article being posted. In Flickr, tag suggestion is provided as a drop-down list that appears within the tagging textbox when the user types a tag. In some tagging systems, such as a system called nationbuilder[3], tag suggestion is provided in a form of checkboxes where users can check multiple tags to attach to content. In some cases, tags are provided in the form of specified list of choices from which users are supposed to select such as in the case of the priority tag list in CiteULike. Tag lists can also be optional such as in the case of Flickr's 'people tag' list, 'set' list and 'group' list. Table 3 summarizes the general guidelines to be followed when selecting tagging tools based on the analysis above.

Table 3 shows how tagging tools are selected according to the system's specification. The main issue here is the method to be followed in order to determine what the suitable type of tagging system is accord-

Table 3. Tagging tools selection guidelines

Type of Tagging	Description	Suggested Tools
Free and optional tagging	**Used when users are free to provide any number of tags or no tags at all.**	**Textboxes that state that tagging is optional.**
Restricted tagging list	When users are supposed to select tags from a restricted list of tags where choice must be made	A drop-down list that has a default value and no empty option is allowed
Optional tagging list	Users are provided with a tagging list to choose from with the ability to choose no tags	A drop-down list with an empty option or 'no tag' option.
Tag suggestions	Tag suggestions are provided from users previous tagging experience, the community tagging preferences or through automatic suggestion based on the content being tagged	Suggested tags can be in the form of links that can be clicked, checkboxes to choose from or can be incorporated with the free tagging textbox appearing when users attempt to type tags as a drop-down list

ing to system's needs. The following sections propose a step by step process to design tagging systems. The process leads to a set of system rules that are translated into tools that form the tagging system.

Situational Inquiry

Data analysis is conducted in the photo-sharing system, Flickr, in order to explain tagging behavior using the results from the previous discussion. This will be done by comparing two version of Flickr tagging system.

Flickr introduced its new design sometime between 2007-2008. Before that time, the online photo-sharing system was using an older design. No reference was found to when the changes of the photo upload page were enforced (the interface where tagging takes place). These dates were tracked from the previous studies that discussed Flickr's tagging system (Marlow et al., 2006; Nov & Ye, 2008; Specia & Motta, 2007). The main difference between the two designs is about the metadata that are applied to the photo when uploaded. Their earlier design did not incorporate user groups as part of the uploading interface of Flickr. The older uploader systerm of Flickr is still accessible.

The following is an analysis of the older design using the analysis process supported by activity theory and semiotics analysis. The tools of the tagging system consist of:

- 'Add tags' textbox, where tags can be added optionally.
- 'Add to a Set' textbox, where a set acts like a folder that combines similar resources. There is an option to create a new set.
- 'Title' textbox, which represents the image title and is automatically extracted from the name of the file.
- 'Description' text-area, where users can write lengthy descriptions about the photo being uploaded.
- 'Privacy Settings', where content is by default public and can be made private or visible to family and/or friends.

The next step was to identify the rules of the old tagging system of Flickr:

- When content is added all values are optional and the user can proceed to upload the content without add any of the data.
- Tags are optional, users get suggestions from previously applied tags when typing a new tag.
- Users can create new sets or use existing sets to add content to.
- Content is by default public and can be set to private or viewed by family and/or friends.

The system allows for the identification of two community members, family and friends. These groups of users can be allowed to view private content and add tags to it. The roles of users are no different from those identified in the new Flickr tagging system.

From the analysis, the object of the tagging system in Flickr can be summarized as follows:

- Users can add content to sets as a way of organizing content. This influences the subject to provide tags that support the content in other ways i.e. descriptive tags which facilitate the retrieval of content.
- No tag suggestion is provided, which means that the subject is influenced to provide new tags instead of reusing existing ones.

The main difference between the two interfaces is that the new Flickr supports user groups, people tagging and sets for categorization. The system provides tag suggestions based on user's existing tags which also reduces the introduction of new tags. The old system gives more emphasis on the part tags can play in supporting the system; it provides categorization support in the form of sets which allow tags to support other types of categorization. This analysis may suggest that there will be a decrease in tags per user when comparing data from the two systems. To verify this assumption, data from Flickr was downloaded covering the tagging activity from January 2004 to September 2005 and another batch covering data from January 2010 to September 2011. The reason for the selection of these dates is to make sure that the right tagging system is being used since there is no exact date to refer to. Data retrieved contains user records consisting of, userID, contentID, date of upload, title and tags. The comparison here is based on the overall tagging behavior of users where the average number of tags per user is calculated. Table 4 provides a description of the data retrieved.

According to the analysis, the first thing to notice is the average number of tags per user has decreased with the new Flickr tagging system. The average user in the old system applied 6.3 tags while in the new

Table 4. Breakdown of tagging data from old Flick and new Flickr tagging systems

	Old Flickr	New Flickr
Number of Users	6197	9829
Number of Tags	1464542	1956568
Number of Items	230312	134906
Avg. Number of Tags/User	236	199
Avg. Number of Tags/Item (per user)	6.3	14.5
Number Untagged Items	21264	10268
Percentage of Untagged Items	9%	7%

Flickr system they applied 14.5 tags. This decrease can be explained by the fact that the new system introduced multiple ways for users to tag images while the old system gave the option of free textual tagging. It is also worth noting that the percentage of untagged items decreased with the new system. The reason for that can be linked to the fact that the new tagging system provided tag suggestion, allowing users to choose from their previous list of tags.

Another analysis was conducted to extract a list of users who have records in both batches. The main reason for that was to compare tagging behavior of the same user using the two tagging systems. From the data retrieved, a total of 161 users were found to have posted images to the system within the two identified time frames i.e. having used both versions of Flickr's tagging system. The average number of tags applied by users who used the old Flickr was 18.7 tags per content. The same users applied an average of 12.4 tags per content using the new Flickr tagging system. This means that using the new Flickr tagging system, users reduced the number of tags applied by six tags on average. Again this can be attributed to the fact that the new design provided other options for users to annotate their images rather than textual tags.

FATS that was introduced in this was used as an analytical tool to understand current tagging systems dynamics. Semiotics analysis and activity theory allowed for a new approach to comprehend tagging systems' components and the relationship between each of them. The principles of mediation and object-orientedness coming from activity theory showed how components of the tagging activity are influenced, while the view of tagging systems as a sign identified how components of the tagging system are contributing to the dynamic of delivering the message of the system. Tools represent meaning to the tagging system that was conceptualized as intentions from users and system providers. Meanings and intentions have social effects that are reflected in how the rules are set, the community is formed and the roles are divided. The analysis process is the basis of a suggested design process that can be followed to design new tagging systems. The following section will introduce design processes that were based on activity theory. This will show how the theory can be implemented as a design tool.

SITUATIONAL RESULTS: PROPOSED DESIGN PROCESS FOR DESIGNING TAGGING SYSTEMS (DPTS)

The design process that is described here is based on the principle of object-orientedness. This means that the activity is directed towards transforming the object into its outcome, hence it is described by its object. The object of the tagging system activity is identified by the intention behind creating the system which motivates the tagging system while tagging. Tagging tools are designed based on the interaction of the other components of the system would result in what the possible tools are to be used to support the tagging system towards its object. In order to identify the tagging tools, we need to identify the object, community, roles and will then be followed by identifying the rules. The reason rules are identified at the end is because they represent the other three components of the system. There are object rules, community rules and role rules. Rules represent the constraints that need to be enforced to ensure the object is transformed into the desired outcome. In the design process, rules are to be expressed following the norm representation of business rules and regulations for clarity. These rules will "determine the conditions of events and actions" (Stamper & Liu, 2000, p. 16). The description consists of a condition, state, agent, deontic operator and action. The state of the rule is optional and determines a special circumstance or situation within the condition. The agent represents the person/concept that will be affected by the condition. Deontic operator specifies how the agent is expected to behave. There are three passives values "obliged", "permitted" and "prohibited" (Stamper & Liu, 2000). The action describes the expected result from the condition. The general structure of the rules is as follows:

- whenever <condition>
- if <state>
- then <agent>
- is <deontic operator>
- to do <action>

The following is an example of a rule expressed using the previous form, the rule states that taggers are supposed to provide three tags per content. (Note that the state part was not included since it is optional):

- whenever tagging for categorization
- if content is tagged
- then tagger
- is obliged
- to provide three tags per content

According to Stamper & Liu (2000), norm specifications can be translated into low-level language or a programming language. DPTS can be summarized by the following points and Figure 9:

1. Explicitly identify the object of the activity by stating the designer's intention behind allowing users to tag. This can be categorization/classification, retrieval facilitation, encourage giving opinion or feedback or description of content.
2. Setting the desired outcome: System contains few new tags and tag reuse, system provides, more new tags, etc.
3. Define the community members of the system.
4. Identify roles that the community members are playing within the system.

Figure 9. Design process for creating tagging systems (DPTS)

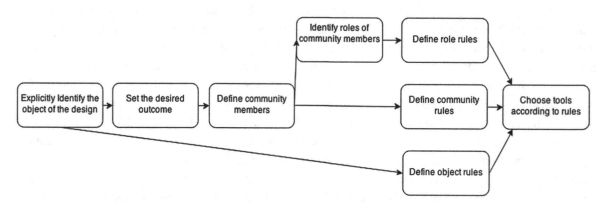

5. Define the rules of the system by identifying: object rules, community rules and role rules. Rules are to be expressed using norms format.

6. Choose proper tools to make sure that all rules are satisfied.

By following DPTS, a new design for tagging system can be generated based on the object i.e. the intention behind tagging. In terms of practical inquiry methodology, this is considered as a situational result that can be added to the body of knowledge. It can also be generalized and applied to similar problems as discussed in the following section.

FUTURE RESEARCH DIRECTIONS

This section discusses the wider implications of this research that can expand its findings to cover other parts of knowledge. An area that is being considered is the application of FATS and the DPTS into other types of systems that may exhibit similar attributes to tagging systems. Such systems that are based on user collaboration can be analyzed using the analytical framework (FATS) for possible improvements and new systems can be designed by following the design process. This can be achieved since these systems are built to satisfy a goal by making the most out of user collaboration. Analysis of similar systems can be done using FATS in order to gain understanding of what influences user collaboration. The design process can be applied by setting the community component effect the roles users can play in the system. Rules and tools will emerge from the identification of the other components as applied in tagging systems within this chapter.

The future work gives the opportunity to identify other areas of strengths and weaknesses of the research. Some of the future research that can be conducted include the following:

- Design tagging systems based on DPTS and explore how the design affects the tagging behavior of the users.
- Applying DPTS by setting multiple objects for the tagging system. In some cases, the tagging system is provided to support the system in more than one way. This can be achieved by either doing this in one iteration of the design process or apply DPTS for each object at a time. When setting the first object, design rules and tools are produced. These will be built upon when the design rules and tools of the second object are identified and so forth.

CONCLUSION

Through this study, tagging systems were analyzed using an analytical framework that provided an understanding of their different components. This allowed for capturing tagging systems as interacting elements that affect each other. By applying the analytical framework, existing tagging systems could be studied to identify problems and evaluate what tagging behavior is expected from users. The research followed the practical inquiry methodology which attempts to solve problems while contributing to general knowledge. The design process that was identified can be followed to create new tagging systems based on desired tagging behavior. The design process can aid system designers in deciding about how user tagging is employed to support the entire system.

The following conclusions can be drawn from this chapter:

1. The semiotic analysis incorporated in FATS enables specification of norms for tagging system design, focusing on pragmatic components.
2. Better understanding of the effect tagging components have over tagging behavior was achieved through FATS. Although this is useful, it is sometimes hard to explain tagging behavior coming from multiple tagging interfaces e.g. Flickr taggers provide tags from the web-based system and/ or the mobile based system.
3. By following DPTS, tagging systems that supports certain types of tagging behavior can be created.
4. DPTS supports single tagging behavior which leads to directing users to this behavior. This can obstruct users from providing other types of tags that can support the system. This appears in the case of designing a system for organization, it limits the number of descriptive tags that the user can apply per content.

The overall conclusion of this chapter is that design can be guided by exploring user behavior. Following practical inquiry methodology, the design process emerged from investigating existing systems along with the support of organizational semiotics and activity theory.

REFERENCES

Bateman, S., Brooks, C., McCalla, G., & Brusilovsky, P. (2007). Applying collaborative tagging to e-learning. *Proceedings of theWorkshop on Tagging and Metadata for Social Information Organization, held in conjuction with the 16th International World Wide Web Conference*. Banff, Canada.

Blanton, W., Simmons, E., & Warner, M. (2001). The Fifth Dimension: Application of cultural-historical activity theory, inquiry-based learning, computers, and telecommunications to change prospective teachers. *Journal of Educational Computing Research, 24*(4), 435–463. doi:10.2190/YGJ0-WXUW-D0TR-9BGU

Chandler, D. (2000). *Semiotics for beginners*. Daniel Chandler.

Chandler, D. (2002). *Semiotics for beginners: glossary of key terms*. Aberystwyth University. doi:10.4324/9780203166277

Chu, S., Rathi, D., & Du, H. (2010). Users' Behaviour in Collaborative Tagging Systems. *Proceedings of theAnnual Conference of the Canadian Association for Information Science (CAIS)*.

Dye, J. (2006). Folksonomy: A game of high-tech (and high-stakes) tag. *EContent*.

Echarte, F., Astrain, J. J., Córdoba, A., Villadangos, J., & Navarra, P. (2007). Ontology of Folksonomy: A New Modeling Method. Proceedings of Semantic Authoring, Annotation and Knowledge Markup (SAAKM).

Eco, U. (1979). *A theory of semiotics*. Indiana University Press.

Engestrom, Y. (1987). *Learning by Expanding: An Activity-theoratical Approach to Developmental Research*. Helsinki: Orienta-Konsultit.

Farooq, U., Kannampallil, T. G., Song, Y., Ganoe, C. H., Carroll, J. M., & Giles, L. (2007). Evaluating tagging behavior in social bookmarking systems: metrics and design heuristics. In *Human-Computer Interaction* (Vol. 1, pp. 351–360). ACM; doi:10.1145/1316624.1316677

Golder, S., & Huberman, B. (2006). Usage patterns of collaborative tagging systems. *Journal of Information Science, 32*(2), 198–208. doi:10.1177/0165551506062337

Goldkuhl, G. (2008). Practical inquiry as action research and beyond. *Proceedings of theEuropean Conference on Information Systems '08.*

Goldkuhl, G. (2011). Generic regulation model: the evolution of a practical theory for e-government. *Transforming Government: People. Process and Policy, 5*(3), 249–267.

Gregor, S. (2002). A theory of theories in information systems. *Management Information Systems Quarterly, 30*(3), 611–642.

Gregor, S. (2006). The nature of theory in information systems. *Management Information Systems Quarterly, 30*(3), 611–642.

Gupta, M., Li, R., Yin, Z., & Han, J. (2010). Survey on social tagging techniques. *SIGKDD Explor. Newsl., 12*(1), 58–72. doi:10.1145/1882471.1882480

Hevner, A., March, S., Park, J., & Ram, S. (2004). Design science in information systems research. *Management Information Systems Quarterly, 28*(1), 75–105.

Heymann, P., & Garcia-Molina, H. (2009). Contrasting Controlled Vocabulary and Tagging: Do Experts Choose the Right Names to Label the Wrong Things? *Proceedings of theSecond ACM International Conference on Web Search and Data Mining (WSDM 2009), Late Breaking Results Session* (pp. 1–4). Stanford InfoLab.

Heymann, P., Koutrika, G., & Garcia-Molina, H. (2007). Fighting Spam on Social Web Sites: A Survey of Approaches and Future Challenges. *IEEE Internet Computing, 11*(6), 36–45. doi:10.1109/MIC.2007.125

Hotho, A., Jäschke, R., Schmitz, C., & Stumme, G. (2006). Information retrieval in folksonomies: Search and ranking. *Proceedings of the European Semantic Web conference* (pp. 411–426).

Kuutti, K. (1995). Activity theory as a potential framework for human-computer interaction research. In *Context and consciousness* (pp. 17–44). Cambridge, MA, USA: Massachusetts Institute of Technology.

Kuutti, K. (2010). Defining an object of design by the means of the Cultural-Historical Activity Theory. *Proceedings of the European Academy of Design Conference.*

Lazarou, D. (2011). Using Cultural-Historical Activity Theory to design and evaluate an educational game in science education. *Journal of Computer Assisted Learning, 27*(5), 424–439. doi:10.1111/j.1365-2729.2011.00410.x

Liu, K. (2000). *Semiotics in information systems engineering.* Cambridge UP. doi:10.1017/CBO9780511543364

Maier, R. (2007). *Knowledge Management Systems: Information and Communication Technologies: Information and Communication Technologies for Knowledge Management.* Springer.

Marlow, C., Naaman, M., Boyd, D., & Davis, M. (2006). HT06, tagging paper, taxonomy, Flickr, academic article, to read. In *Hypertext and Hypermedia* (pp. 31–40).

Morrison, P. J. (2008). Tagging and searching: Search retrieval effectiveness of folksonomies on the World Wide Web. *Information Processing & Management, 44*(4), 1562–1579. doi:10.1016/j.ipm.2007.12.010

Mwanza, D. (2001). Where theory meets practice: A case for an Activity Theory based methodology to guide computer system design.*Proceedings of INTERACT' 2001: Eighth IFIP TC 13 Conference on Human-Computer Interaction*, Tokyo, Japan.

Nov, O., & Ye, C. (2008). What Drives Content Tagging : The Case of Photos on Flickr.*Proceeding of the twenty-sixth annual SIGCHI conference on Human factors in computing systems,*Florence (pp. 1–4). . doi:10.1145/1357054.1357225

Peirce, C. D. (1960). *Collected Papers of Charles Sanders Peirce* (C. Hartshorne, P. Weiss, & A. W. Burks, Eds.). Harvard University Press.

Peters, I., & Becker, P. (2009). *Folksonomies: Indexing and Retrieval in Web 2.0.* De Gruyter/Saur. doi:10.1515/9783598441851

Russell, D. (2002). Looking beyond the interface: Activity theory and distributed learning. In *Distributed learning: social and cultural approaches to practice*. Routledge Falme.

Smith, G. (2007). *Tagging: People-powered Metadata for the Social Web, Safari.* New Riders.

Smith, M. (2006). *Viewer tagging in art museums: comparisons to concepts and vocabularies of art museum visitors. In 17th Annual ASIS* (pp. 1–19). Austin, Texas, USA: T SIG/CR Classification Research Workshop.

Specia, L., & Motta, E. (2007). Integrating Folksonomies with the Semantic Web. *The Semantic Web Research and Applications, 4519*(September), 624–639. doi:10.1007/978-3-540-72667-8_44

Stamper, R., Liu, K., Hafkamp, M., & Ades, Y. (2000). Understanding the roles of signs and norms in organizations-a semiotic approach to information systems design. *Behaviour & Information Technology, 19*(1), 15–27. doi:10.1080/014492900118768

Sturtz, D. (2004, December). Communal categorization: the folksonomy. *INFO622: Content Representation*. Retrieved from http://www.davidsturtz.com/drexel/622/sturtz-folksonomy.pdf

Trant, J. (2009). Studying social tagging and folksonomy: A review and framework. *Journal of Digital Information, 10*(1), 1–44.

Westberry, N. (2009). *An activity theory analysis of social epistemologies within tertiary-level eLearning environments*. The University of Waikato.

KEY TERMS AND DEFINITIONS

Activity Theory: A theory that focuses on human activities from a social perspective. It has been applied in many disciplines specifically in Human-computer interaction.

Delicious: An online bookmarking system that allows users to store, tag and share their favorite bookmarks.

DPTS: Stands for Design Process for Tagging Systems. A step-by-step process that can be following to create tagging systems that directs tagging behavior.

FATS: Stands for Framework for Analyzing Tagging Systems. A framework based on Semiotics and Activity theory used for analyzing tagging systems.

Flickr: An online system for posting, tagging and sharing pictures and videos.

Organizational Semiotics: The study of the organization based on Semiotics theory.

Semiotics: A theory that studies signs.

Practical Methodology: A research methodology that investigate the problem with a system and finds solutions that can be generalized to other similar systems. It employs theories to understand the problem and generate the solution.

Tagging: Annotating objects using words that relevant to it. They are used to organize and facilitate retrieval.

Tagging System: The interface where tagging takes place.

ENDNOTES

[1] http://vanderwal.net/folksonomy.html

[2] http://Del.icio.us.com/help

[3] http://nationbuilder.com/jerimee/visitors_can_choose_multiple_tags_checkboxes_on_signup_form

Chapter 9
Mitigating Ethno–Cultural Differences:
Ethical Guidelines for ICT Development in an Indigenous Community

Hasnain Falak
Institute of Social Informatics and Technological Innovations (ISITI), Malaysia

Tariq Zaman
University Malaysia Sarawak, Malaysia

ABSTRACT

Community engagement is necessary for the success and sustainability of Information and Communication Technologies for Development (ICT4D) projects. To ensure active participation of community, researchers need to understand and adhere to the local cultural norms and adapt in the lifestyle of people. These cultural norms are mainly unwritten and implicit in nature. Hence the researchers spend maximum time of their field visits in observing and developing understanding of the community's life. In our long-term partnership with the indigenous Penan community of Long Lamai in Malaysian Borneo, we co-developed written guidelines for researchers and visitors. The researchers demonstrated their interest in aligning research process to the community's cultural values, however norm internalisation and development of associated behaviour is still a challenging. The written guidelines are yet only one of the attempts to the practices of community researchers' engagement and we are refining our methodology to enhance the researchers' learning process.

INTRODUCTION

Community engagement is an essential requirement for the success of ICT4D projects (Gumbo et al., 2012). The "engagement" becomes vital when the interaction is between indigenous and rural community and researchers from a different cultural background. The community is the center of ICT4D project so the researchers need to develop a holistic understanding of the community's daily lives and

DOI: 10.4018/978-1-5225-1944-7.ch009

role of designed products and services (Winschiers-Theophilus & Bidwell, 2013). The researcher needs to attain "sufficient input" from the end-users to provide sustainable solution and it will also ensure to avoid the problematic translation of researchers' desires into community's needs. Recent empirical verification of relationship between community engagement and research shows an increase in success of ICTD projects (Balestrini et al., 2014; Chamberlain et al., 2013).

This interaction between researchers and community can be considered a multifaceted process of negotiations and participation (Winschiers-Theophilus et al., 2010). Indigenous communities have diverse procedures, rules and regulations that regulate their interactions within community, with outsiders and with the territory and environment upon which they depend. However, these norms are mainly in unwritten (tacit and implicit) forms the researchers often do not understand and in result sometimes fail to respect. The failure to respect these norms, whether intentional or not, results in conflict and deterioration of relationships that leads to failures of the projects (Balestrini et al., 2014).

The authors of this chapter have been engaged in long term partnership and joint endeavour of developing/using technologies for socio-economic development of the Penan community of Long Lamai, Sarawak Malaysia. The community is receptive to new technologies; however, the process of researchers-community engagement has been equally challenging due to the social, cultural and language barriers. The situation became more complex in recent years due to the influx of less experienced and short term researchers. Therefore, the authors and community elders engaged in the process of answering the simple question, how can we inform and educate researchers about the local culture and norms of the community?

In this chapter, we introduce the guidelines designed for researchers and visitors of Long Lamai community. The aim of the guidelines is to educate novice researchers working with the Penan community of Long Lamai. The chapter is organized as follows. Section 2 presents the research background and related work. Section 3, discusses the methodology applied in research. Section 4 presents designed framework and guidelines for researchers and Section 5 provides discussion. Section 6 concludes the chapter.

Background

The literature on ICT4D is replete with empirical evidence showing that ICT interventions often fail since they are often externally initiated, with very limited involvement from the affected (Heeks, 2002). The Digital Collectives in Indigenous Cultures and Communities meeting held in Hawaii brought together cultural leaders, researchers, community representatives, and development project to discuss the way digital technology might be used so that the cultures of indigenous communities could be preserved and public perception of these communities improved. The recommendations from the meeting included respect of community's cultural values and their right to decide the degree of their participation in information technology plans related to digital collectives (Holland, 2002). The recent approaches such as Participatory Design and Community-based Co-design consider local community's insight in design processes as a strong component (Holland, 2002). These approaches highlight the importance of creating and accommodating people's insight in the process of design, evaluation and implementation of a system which they will be using (Winschiers-Theophilus, Bidwell, & Blake, 2012). The end-users are treated as experts – and the goal is "mutual learning" (Kapuire, 2015). Ranjay K. Singh et al. (2013) conducted a study to highlight the ethical prospects for researchers while engaging Indigenous tribes. A framework for devising a Prior Informed Consent (PIC) agreement is developed stating the detail process and terms of research. Many researchers highlighted the important factors such as appropriate solution, cost, time, infrastructure provision, local context, community perception and perspective for facilitating sustained community participation in ICT4D projects (Balestrini et al., 2014; Chamberlain et al., 2013; Blake, 2014; Singh, 2013; Saeed & Rohde, 2010; Saeed, Reichling, & Wulf, 2008; Van Zyl, 2014).

Community participation is important for the success of any ICT4D project, but there are some caveats. A wide range of issues can hinder and constrain the promotion of participation, including those arising from institutional, socio-cultural, technical, and logistical factors. Botes and Van Rensburg (2000) identify nine obstacles and impediments, or plagues, prohibiting the promotion of participation processes within ICT4D projects. These plagues are introduced to guide our discussion and are same important in context to our project.

Balestrini et al. (2014) investigates the factors that are important for developing sustainable community ICT interventions. Based on experiences of developing and deploying CrowdMemo, a project for preserving local heritage in rural Argentina, the authors provided five recommendations for facilitating sustained community engagement in ICT4D projects. The recommendation includes facilitation of valued ownership of community, use of off-the-shelf technologies in novel ways, face-to-face social encounters, design for appropriation and broad media coverage of the project that leads to community pride and engagement.

THE PROBLEM

Penans have diverse procedures, rules and regulations that regulate their interactions within community, with outsiders and with the territory and environment upon which they depend. The importance of these rules becomes more significant when they engage with external factors such as government agencies, researchers, companies, and non-governmental organizations (NGOs). However, outsiders often do not understand these cultural protocols as they are mainly unwritten and customary practices. The failure to respect these cultural protocols, whether intentional or not, can lead to conflict, deterioration of otherwise constructive relations, and negative impacts on the environment. To address this issue, one of the effective ways is the documentation of these cultural protocols in explicit form which can also understand by the researchers and external actors. The process of documentation is used to foster the engagement process, development of mutual understanding and respect for customary laws, values and decision-making processes, particularly those concerning stewardship of resources and territories.

OUR CURRENT COLLABORATION CONTEXT

ISITI-CRI is one of the active implementers of ICT4D projects in Malaysia (Zaman et al., 2015). By applying a people-centered/ participatory approach, ISITI-CRI, project aim to empower and train the communities through the application of ICTs in improving their livelihood. In last 15 years, ISITI-CRI, has developed a strong relationship with indigenous communities, where all its sites' population comprise different indigenous groups of different social and cultural settings. One of the project sites is Long Lamai, a Penan village in Upper Baram East Malaysia.

Long Lamai is located in Sarawak near the border of Kalimantan, Indonesia. Travelling to the settlement from Miri takes eight hours on rough logging roads and an hour of hiking through the dense rainforest. Alternately, it is reachable by flying from Miri to Long Banga by an hour's flight via a 19-seater Twin Otter and then taking a one-and-half hour boat ride to Long Lamai. There are approximately 598 Penans living in Long Lamai. Most of the local people (92%) are farmers (Falak et al., 2016). With exception of Irau Ajaú (harvesting festival), the community does not presently celebrate other cultural festivals. Penans are shy and gentle people, with a strong community bonding. They are egalitarian and do not follow any hierarchal structure of community leadership however, major community decisions are made by a consensus of the community elders supported by the village headman. The village is a true picture of "remote" and "rural" community with no road access, health clinic and piped water though having limited power supply and telecommunication services. The available infrastructures at Long Lamai consist of a Penan school, a church and a Telecentre. The telecentre is equipped with three networked PCs, three laptops, a printer and a scanner and a number of community members also have their own devices such as laptops, tablets and smartphones. The community has appointed a local champion as a liaison for ISITI-CRI projects. The local champion is a fluent speaker of English and local languages and has a vast experience of working with government organizations. His tasks as a local champion include facilitating researchers' and their field activities during their visits to the community. After the telecentre project, the Long Lamai community opened their doors for more development activities, such as, using ICT for documentation of traditional botanical knowledge, indigenous language, e-health and tourism projects. The development sprang up along new challenges such as significant increase in number of tourists and guest researchers.

Methodology

We conducted an interpretive case study to understand the local context of and to observe the interactions between researchers and community members, as well as to examine these factors' around 10 interviews were conducted in two villages. Interviews ranged from 20 to 60 minutes and focused on understanding the state of the community's development and how the community members' interaction leads to the formation and extension of community social capital bonding, bridging, and linking. For this reason, we queried different social groups and institutions in the studied villages. The data were transcribed, coded, and categorized. Based on the finding, we developed the guidelines with 17 fundamental themes. The guidelines have been drafted in English language which was later on translated into local Penan language. The guidelines have been presented and approved in the community council of elders and endorsed by the village head. The community made a consensus on providing the guidelines to researchers for endorsement during their visit to Long Lamai. As a public announcement, the English and Penan versions of the guidelines have been put on the telecentre wall too. The researchers and local champion presented the guidelines in Ba'Lai (another Penan village) and to academicians and experts for their opinions (Figure 1 & Figure 2).

Results

With active participation of community members, in the first stage, we developed a generalized framework for community-researcher engagement (Figure 3) and guidelines for researchers. The framework explains step-by-step processes of engagement, access and coordination of research partnership between the local community of Long Lamai, ISITI-CRI and guest researchers. Guest researchers are the first time visitors and partners of ISITI-CRI.

The process described in Figure 3 is explained as follows:

Figure 1. Focus group discussion and community meetings

Figure 2. Community representative sharing the guidelines with academicians and researchers

- The guest researcher/visitor submit a formal expression of interest to ISITI-CRI
- ISITI-CRI consults the local community representative and discuss about the visit plan and the expression of interest as submitted by the guest researcher
- If the community representative agrees, then the guidelines developed for researchers will be provided to the guest researcher and the guest researchers are invited for the first visit to community. In first visit, the guest researcher meets with the community elders to obtain their consent and to explore the relatedness of his/her research in local community context.
- If elders of the community agree with the research idea the guest researcher gets a green signal to prepare for larger community meeting and he/she will be invited for a second visit.
- During the second visit of the researcher a larger community meeting will be called by the community elders and researcher gets an opportunity to present his/her idea to the larger community. Every one as community member has a right to express his opinion in this meeting and this meeting can take few hours or few sessions to reach to conclusion.

Figure 3. Framework for community-researcher engagement

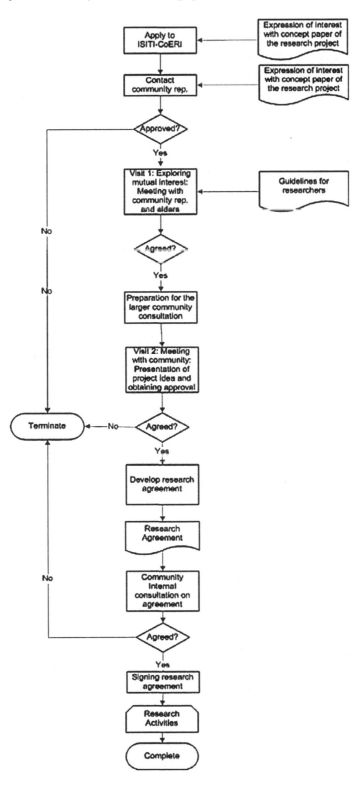

- The conclusion is either "go ahead" or "wait and see". The "wait and see" response is in the case where community is not sure or has a consensus on agreement.
- If community agree then researcher need to develop detail research plan and share it with the community representative who takes some time for internal consultation about the terms and condition of the agreement.
- After the principal agreement, the community representative sign the agreement on behalf of the community and researcher can start research activities.

THE GUIDELINES FOR RESEARCHERS

The guidelines comprise 17 fundamental themes, which are as follows:

1. **Respect Penan Customs and Belief:** The researcher should understand and respect the Penan's customs and belief, including responsibilities to the community, land, culture and environment. The research process and agenda should not be in conflict with the community way of life. The first principle of these guidelines is premised on a need for researchers to understand and respect indigenous world views, particularly when engaging in the sphere of sacred knowledge, and the corresponding responsibility that possession of such knowledge entails. Researchers should understand the broader senses of accountability in order to understand the responsibility they have when entering into a research relationship with the community.

2. **Jurisdiction Over Research Process:** The community should have an equal jurisdiction over the research process and design. The researcher should comply with the rules and procedures adopted by the community in any other existing project. The researcher should comply with any by-laws, policies, rules or procedures adopted by the community. It is not necessary to be in the same domain but there could be possibilities where the communities are engaged in other research areas.

3. **Participatory Research:** The research should be conducted on participatory-research approach and should be beneficial to the whole community. The community expects that the research will enhance mutual trust and cooperation within community and between community and researchers. Genuine research collaboration is developed between researchers and the community when it promotes partnership within a framework of mutual trust and cooperation. Participatory research enables a range of levels and types of community participation while ensuring shared power and decision-making. Such partnerships will help to ensure that research proceeds in a manner that is culturally sensitive, relevant, respectful, responsive, equitable and reciprocal, with regard to the understandings and benefits shared between the partners (the researchers and the community).

4. **Free Consent (Collective and Individual):** The researcher should consult local champion and village head to conduct his/her research activities. It is important to obtain their consent before approaching local community members. The obtained consent should be free, prior and informed at both levels; community elders as well as individual participant. A process to obtain the free, prior and informed consents from both the community affected and its individual participants should be undertaken sufficiently in advance of the proposed start of research activities and should take into account the community's own legitimate decision-making processes, regarding all the phases of planning, implementation, monitoring, assessment, evaluation and wind-up of a research project. The requirement for community consent is distinct from the obligation of researchers to obtain

individual consent from research participants. For Free, Prior and Informed Consent agreement please see (Zaman & Yeo, 2014).

5. **Privacy and Confidentiality:** The researcher should address the concern regarding privacy and confidentiality of individuals and community. The research agreement should address the matters arises from the usage of community's indigenous knowledge. The use and dissemination indigenous knowledge should be subject to the permission of community. The researcher, the individual participants and the community should have a clear prior understanding as to their expectations with regard to the extent to which research data and results will remain confidential to the researcher. If confidentiality is not possible, or if there are necessary limitations, these should be clearly communicated.

6. **Support Mechanism for Sacredness of Indigenous Knowledge:** The community retains their inherent rights to indigenous knowledge. The researcher should also respect and address the issues relating to protection of such knowledge. Any research involving Indigenous people will involve the sharing of some cultural knowledge, practices and/or traditions even when these are not the subjects of the study, as they provide necessary context. The recording of knowledge, practices and traditions in any form (written notes, audio, video, or otherwise) should only be done with explicit permission and under mutually-agreed terms that are set out in advance of the research with the guidance of appropriate elders and knowledge holders. All uses and wider dissemination of cultural knowledge, practices and traditions should also be by permission.

7. **Intellectual Property Rights:** The collective and individual intellectual property rights should be discussed and addressed before initiating research activities. Community and individual concerns over, and claims to, intellectual property should be explicitly acknowledged and addressed in the negotiation with the community prior to starting the research. Expectations regarding intellectual property rights of all parties involved in the research should be stated in the research agreement. To respect the intellectual property rights of each party is the joint responsibility of the researcher and the community involved. Research with explicit commercial objectives and/or direct or indirect links to the commercial sector should be clearly communicated to all research partners.

8. **Mutual Benefits:** The research process and outcomes should be of benefit to the community and research institution. The collective benefits should prevail over individual benefits. Benefit sharing vis-à-vis a community should be interpreted from the community's perspective. This may include tangible and intangible benefits, including those arising from altruism.

9. **Capacity Building for Active Participation:** The researcher should educate and train community members in all relevant research methods. In reciprocal exchange, the community members should facilitate the researchers to understanding indigenous lifestyle.

10. **"Peer Review":** The research findings, analysis and final research report should be shared with the community or community representatives for their final approval. It is the responsibility of researcher to get community / community representatives' consent before submitting the reports for publishing.

11. **Cross-Cultural Communication:** The researcher should have the skills of cross-cultural communication and should understand the way how the local community interacts. He/she should have close coordination and communication with the community. Indigenous communities often have cultural protocols involving interactions within the community. It is important that researchers learn about these and respect them. When providing a research project report to the community, the researcher should provide it in the language of the community unless the community has expressly

waived this. The reports or other communications of results should use language and terminology that are readily understood by the community.

12. **Rights Generated from Data:** The researcher should respect the rights of the community and individuals on data and information gathered or generated during the course of research.

13. **Transfer of Data:** Any transfer of data and information to a third party should be subject to the approval of community and researcher.

14. **Secondary Use of Data:** Secondary use of data and information gathered should be subject to the consent of community and researcher.

15. **The Other Party's Product "On Loan":** The product of each party activities should be considered "on loan" to the other party unless otherwise specified in the research agreement.

16. **Interpretation of Data:** Researcher should engage community in interpretation and analysis of data. The process will ensure authenticity and cultural sensitivity of produced results. Research involving Indigenous people is susceptible to misinterpretation or misrepresentation when information about the group is analyzed without sufficient consideration of other cultural characteristics that make the group distinct. The opportunity for review of research results by the Indigenous community should be provided before the submission of research findings for publication, to ensure that sensitive information is not inappropriately divulged to the public and that errors are corrected prior to wider dissemination. This should not be construed as the right to block the publication of legitimate findings; rather, it refers to the community's opportunity to contextualize the findings and correct any cultural inaccuracies.

17. **Explicit Way of Acknowledgement for Community's Contribution in Research:** The researcher should respect the way how community wants to be acknowledged for their contribution to the research. The community should, at its discretion, be able to decide how its contributions to the research project should be acknowledged. Community members are entitled to due credit and to participate in the dissemination of results. Publications should recognize the contribution of the community and its members as appropriate, and in conformity with confidentiality agreements.

Discussion

The guidelines were developed and grounded on the community's concerns and experiences with researchers during the time period of three years. There are some good results of sharing the written guidelines with researchers. The community found researchers more open for discussion and providing space to community in designing their instruments and technologies. However, to deal with the gaps between research and community's timeframes is still a challenge. To address the issue of "best" timings for research in Long Lamai community we have developed a yearly-based community activity calendar (Table 1).

The researchers have adopted the practice of sharing research findings with community prior to publication. A small hindrance is the project's deadline that restrains the researchers providing insufficient amount of time to develop community's understandings of the researched data. We found that the role of local champion is very important and the institutions can leverage on him/her for grooming their young researcher in community's context.

The community members are part of the research design process, they help in data collection and analysis of results so few of the members have expressed their interest to be mentioned as co-authors in the research publications. However, the community found that researchers are reluctant due to the institutional setups and copyright regulations which designate authorship based on written contributions.

Another challenge and limitation of the research process is "internalization" of the principles provided in guidelines. Our experiences lead us to the conclusion that mere providing written guidelines is not enough so we are designing for academic workshop for researchers and using the guidelines as reference material to practically accept the message in the workshop.

We also found that community is more concerned about the issues related to privacy, protection, collection, disclosure, use and transfer of data. The details of safeguards protecting the privacy and confidentiality of data should be negotiated as part of the research process and specified in a research agreement. Subject to the community's views on sacred knowledge, co-ownership of data between researchers and communities is recommended because the community and the researcher are both integral to the production of data. If there is a transfer of research data to a third party, this should be done only with the consent of the researcher, the individual participants and the community. If the third party is to engage in secondary use of the transferred data, then a further consent to that use must be obtained. The consent should address how confidentiality and privacy will be respected. In any case, secondary use of data and esp. sacred knowledge requires a new consent unless such use is specifically agreed to in the research agreement. Notwithstanding the above, individuals retain the right to access data about themselves.

Table 1. Long Lamai activity calendar

Moth	Week	Seasons	School Holidays	Toro Gaharu	Tourists Attractions	Farm	Festivals
January	1st week	Rainy					
	2nd week	Rainy					
	3rd week	Rainy					
	4th week	Rainy			Frogs		
February	1st week	Rainy				Harvesting	
	2nd week	Rainy				Harvesting	
	3rd week	Rainy				Harvesting	
	4th week	Rainy			Fruit	Harvesting	
March	1st week	Rainy			Fruit	Harvesting	
	2nd week	Rainy			Fruit	Harvesting	
	3rd week	Rainy			Fruit	Harvesting	
	4th week	Rainy	Holidays		Frogs	Harvesting	Irau Ajau
April	1st week	Dry			Birds		
	2nd week	Dry		Busy			
	3rd week	Dry		Busy			
	4th week	Dry		Busy	Birds and Frogs		
May	1st week	Rainy		Busy		Cleaning fields	
	2nd week	Dry		Busy		Cleaning fields	
	3rd week	Dry		Busy		Cleaning fields	Irau Penan
	4th week	Dry	Holidays	Busy	Frogs	Cleaning fields	

continued on following page

Table 1. Continued

Moth	Week	Seasons	School Holidays	Toro Gaharu	Tourists Attractions	Farm	Festivals
June	1st week	Dry	Holidays	Busy	Fishing	Cleaning fields	
	2nd week	Dry		Busy		Cleaning fields	
	3rd week	Dry		Busy		Cleaning fields	
	4th week	Rainy		Busy	Fishing and Frogs	Cleaning fields	
July	1st week	Rainy		Busy		Cleaning fields	
	2nd week	Rainy		Busy		Cleaning fields	
	3rd week	Dry		Busy			
	4th week	Dry		Busy	Fishing and Frogs		
August	1st week	Dry	Holidays	Busy			
	2nd week	Dry	Holidays			Sowing	
	3rd week	Dry				Sowing	
	4th week	Dry			Frogs	Sowing	
September	1st week	Dry				Sowing	
	2nd week	Dry				Sowing	
	3rd week	Dry		Busy			
	4th week	Dry		Busy	Frogs		
October	1st week	Rainy				Weeding out	
	2nd week	Rainy				Weeding out	
	3rd week	Rainy				Weeding out	
	4th week	Rainy			Frogs	Weeding out	
November	1st week	Rainy		Busy			
	2nd week	Rainy		Busy			
	3rd week	Rainy	Holidays	Busy			
	4th week	Rainy	Holidays	Busy	Frogs		
December	1st week	Rainy	Holidays	Busy			
	2nd week	Rainy	Holidays	Busy			
	3rd week	Rainy	Holidays				
	4th week	Rainy	Holidays		Frogs		Christmas

CONCLUSION

After exercising this practice for a year, we reflected on the outcomes and lessons learned and found that still community and ISITI-CRI are facing challenges to educate researchers on the local and cultural norms. We also found that due to the different cultural backgrounds the community and researchers should be in close coordination which will help to minimize communication gap between both parties.

The observation for further development in this research is still in progress and in-depth analysis and reflections is part of our future research.

ACKNOWLEDGMENT

The research was carried out with the aid of a grant from University Malaysia Sarawak. We also thank all the community members who participated in the one or other of our research activities.

REFERENCES

Balestrini, M., Bird, J., Marshall, P., Zaro, A., & Rogers, Y. (2014). Understanding Sustained Community Engagement: A Case Study in Heritage Preservation in Rural Argentina. *Proc. CHI '14*(pp. 2675-2684). doi:10.1145/2556288.2557323

Blake, E., Tucker, W., & And Glaser, M. (2014). Towards communication and information access for Deaf people. *South African Computer Journal, 54*(2), 10–11.

Botes, L., & Van Rensburg, D. (2000). Community Participation in Development: Nine Plagues and Twelve Commandments. *Community Development Journal: An International Forum, 35*(1), 41–58. doi:10.1093/cdj/35.1.41

Chamberlain, A., Crabtree, A., & Davies, M. (2013). Community engagement for research: Contextual design in rural CSCW system development. *Proc. Int. Conf. on C&T '13* (pp. 131-139). ACM Press. doi:10.1145/2482991.2483001

Falak, S., Chiun, L. M., & Wee, A. Y. (2016). Sustainable rural tourism: An indigenous community perspective on positioning rural tourism. *Turizam: znanstveno-stručni časopis, 64*(3), 311-327.

Gumbo, S., Thinyane, H., Thinyane, M., & Terzoli, A. And Hansen, S. (2012). Living lab methodology as an approach to innovation in ICT4D: The Siyakhula Living Lab experience. Pro. of the IST Africa 2012 Conference.

Heeks, R. (2002). Information Systems and Developing Countries: Failure, Success and Local Improvisations. *The Information Society, 18*(2), 101–112. doi:10.1080/01972240290075039

Holland, M. P. (2002). Digital Collectives in Indigenous Cultures and Communities Meeting: *Meeting Report (S. O. Information, Trans.)*. Michigan: University of Michigan.

Kapuire, G. K., Winschiers-Theophilus, H., & Blake, E. (2015). An insider perspective on community gains: A subjective account of a Namibian rural communities perception of a long-term participatory design project. *International Journal of Human-Computer Studies, 74*, 124–143. doi:10.1016/j.ijhcs.2014.10.004

Saeed, S., Reichling, T., & Wulf, V. (2008). Applying Knowledge Management to Support Networking among NGOs and Donors. *Paper presented at theIADIS international conference on E-Society*.

Saeed, S., & Rohde, M. (2010). Computer enabled social movements? Usage of a collaborative web platform within the European social forum.*Proc. COOP '10*. doi:10.1007/978-1-84996-211-7_14

Singh, R. K. (2013). Singh, & Turner, N. J. (2013). A special note on Prior Informed Consent (PIC) Why are you asking our gyan (knowledge) and padhati (practice)?: Ethics and prior informed consent for research on traditional knowledge systems. *Indian Journal of Traditional Knowledge, 12*(3), 547–562.

Van Zyl, I. (2014). Indigenous Logics: Anthropological reflections on Participatory Design in Community Informatics.*Proc. of PDC*. ACM Press.

Winschiers-Theophilus, H., ... (2010) Being participated: a community approach. *Proc. of the 11th PDC '10*. ACM.

Winschiers-Theophilus, H., & And Bidwell, N. J. (2013). Toward an Afro-Centric Indigenous HCI Paradigm. *International Journal of Human-Computer Interaction*, 29(4), 243–255. doi:10.1080/1044 7318.2013.765763

Winschiers-Theophilus, H., Bidwell, N., & Blake, E. (2012). Community Consensus: Design Beyond Participation. *Design Issues*, 28(3), 89–100. doi:10.1162/DESI_a_00164

Zaman, T., & Winschiers-Theophilus, H. (2015). *Penan's Oroo'Short Message Signs (PO-SMS): Co-design of a Digital Jungle Sign Language Application. In Human-Computer Interaction – INTERACT 2015* (pp. 489–504). Springer.

Zaman, T., & Yeo, A. W. (2014). Ensuring Participatory Design Through Free, Prior and Informed Consent: A Tale of Indigenous Knowledge Management System. In S. Saeed (Ed.), *User-Centric Technology Design for Nonprofit and Civic Engagements* (pp. 41–54). Springer. doi:10.1007/978-3-319-05963-1_4

Chapter 10
User Interface Design in Isolation from Underlying Code and Environment

Izzat Alsmadi
University of Texas A&M, USA

ABSTRACT

The success of any software application heavily depends on the success of its User Interface (UI) design. This is since users communicate with those applications through their UIs and they will build good or bad impressions based on how such UIs help them using the software. UI design evolves through the years to be more platform and even code independent. In addition, the design of an application user interface consumes a significant amount of time and resources. It is expected that not only the same UI design should be relatively easy to transfer from one platform to another, but even from one programming language release to another or even from one programming language to another. In this chapter, we conducted a thorough investigation to describe how UI design evolved through the years to be independent from the code, or any other environment element (e.g. operating system, browser, database, etc.).

INTRODUCTION

Graphical User Interface (GUI) is a recent term for an area that is used to be called Human Computer Interaction (HCI). While both terms are not identical or synonymous, they refer to the same area or subject on how to design the interfaces of software applications through which users interact with those underlying software. On the other side, Application Peripheral Interfaces (APIs) indicate low level interfaces between software applications and other applications, operating systems, databases, hardware components, etc. The commonality between GUI and API (in addition to the last word; Interface) is that both include how the subject software is going to interact with its environment (users; GUI, other applications; API).

The design of the GUI is considered very important and critical to any software. A very successful software, from the inside, may fail by large if its GUI fails to attract users to use and understand features

DOI: 10.4018/978-1-5225-1944-7.ch010

that exist in this software. Alternatively, a very attractive GUI may boost, a shallow software, from the inside to be more successful. You may see many applications or websites in the market that offer the same features or services. Why certain ones are more popular?! Their GUI can be the first thing to think of.

The evaluation of GUIs is also unconventional and we should usually combine some formal verification or testing techniques with some informal techniques. In other words, while the automatic testing of user interfaces is important and continuously growing (Alsmadi & Magel 2007), there are some important parts of the user interface that they should manually be validated by users or testers. In this context validation is the term usually used to indicate those parts of the requirements, unlike verification, that need to be evaluated and tested through the users and not by formal methods, mathematical proofs or test automation tools.

Test automation for user interfaces is very popular and convenient. Testing application interfaces usually consumes a significant amount of project time and resources. The percentage of automating testing activities can vary from one software product to another and from one software module/component to another. In general, it is desirable to achieve 100% or high percentage coverage in user interface testing (Alsmadi, 2014). However, there are many obstacles toward achieving such 100% coverage. There are some user interface aspects that need human or manual validation for approvals. For example, the possible appropriateness of GUI components' layouts or coloring can be very hard for tools to automatically verify without human visual eyes assistance. In addition, the continuous evolution of graphical user interface components creates a challenge on test automation tools. In particular, the majority of those tools use some reverse engineering methods or libraries (e.g. Reflection in Java) to read all GUI components at run time and be able to interact with those components (Amalfitano et al., 2012; Banerjee et al., 2013). Those reverse engineering libraries may not have methods that can extract information from new GUI components that they are not developed to normally handle or serialize.

In this chapter, we will focus on evaluating how the design of user interfaces evolve to be more independent. We will focus on two aspects of this independency: Platform independent, and UI design patterns and principles.

PLATFORM-INDEPENDENT UI DESIGN

The term "platform-independent" or "cross-platforms" have been very important marketing or selling themes for many software applications to show signs of robustness and flexibility. For example, Java, in comparison with C# considers its main distinguished different is being platform-independent where C# can only run within Windows environments whereas Java can run on Windows and many other environments (e.g. MAC, Unix, etc.). User Interface design contributes significantly to making one software application platform-independent or not. In some cases, UI can be platform-independent while optimized to work on one specific platform.

UI interfaces exist in different platform versions or forms. The same application can have a web browser version, Desktop version, console or terminal version and mobile version. There are two main important factors that justify the need to have a unified UI for the same software application on the different platforms:

1. For users, it will be easier to deal with the different versions or forms of the same application on the different platforms if those forms are unified. Their learning curve can be faster and they can

remember or memorize the same features or services from the different forms. Having a unified form does not mean necessary to have identical copies because this is impossible. For example, a button in a Desktop application will look somewhat different from a button in a web browser or a mobile platform. Nonetheless, with this shift from one platform to platform in mind, the different versions should be symmetric or consistent and easy to correlate with each other.

2. For UI designers, testers, technical support, etc. having a unified UI for the different platform can help them accelerate their design, testing or maintenance tasks. This does not eliminate the fact that many errors can be unique to certain platforms and not the others. In fact, for websites, there are many cases where some errors will show in a website using a particular browser (e.g. Microsoft Internet Explorer) and not the other browsers (e.g. Google Chrome, or Firefox) or even the same browser but different release versions. There are many technologies that are used across the different browsers. However, some recent features and technologies are developed to work or be optimized with a particular browser and may not work well for other browsers.

Here are some recent technology information targeting the issue of UI cross browsers support:

- Microsoft introduced recently (Coded UI Tests) for cross browsers testing to enable writing tests on one browser and be able to run or execute those test cases on different Internet browsers. On the other hand, Selenium web test automation tool or framework provides different drivers or libraries to be able to support testing the different Internet browsers.

- Java recently added Java FX libraries to replace previous GUI: Swing, AWT, or SWT. Java FX is fully object oriented where not only GUI nodes or components are objects but even their attributes and actions are objects that can be instantiated and declared with different instance properties. In addition, Java FX includes Scene Builder tool which seems to be similar to the toolbox module in Visual Studio .NET releases. The Scene Builder allows users to create GUI components on the fly. Those GUI components are in a CSS scripting file isolated from Java source code files. The model file that this GUI is preserved through can be imported to different other applications.

- There are several XML-based existing scripting languages or standards (e.g. Extensible Style Sheet Language: XSL, XSL Beans, Extensible User Interface Language: XUL, User Interface Markup Language UIML, Microsoft Extensible Application Markup Language XAML (Moonlight), WPF, QML) that are used to document the user interfaces (Tubishat et al., 2009). Saving and reusing this mobile-form of the UIs may not only be important for making the UI platform-independent, but it can also help in storing or preserving those UI and an easy to move, transfer or store format. This can further facilitate testing, evolution and maintenance activities. Those UIs that can be saved in static file formats, can be regenerated into a new UI for possibly a complete or different application. In Tubishat et al. (2009), we proposed a method to automatically evaluate if an application GUI structure is changed. This may then trigger several other activities (e.g. regression testing). Most of similar approaches use a form of XML structure to ensure that GUI hierarchical structure is preserved through XML representation or tree.

- There are some applications or middle-wares that are used to render interfaces of applications that are described or developed in the previously mentioned UI markup languages. For example, jXUL is a Java-based rendering middle to recreate user interfaces in Java Swing libraries based on XUL input files.

- Object serialization in programming refers to storing (e.g. in memory or a file) an object with all its attributes values, state, etc. as one entity. In GUI, serialization, for persistence storage, can be extended to enable storing the whole GUI and all its objects, attributes, events and relations as one entity or object.
- In their Office products, and starting from MS Office 2010, Microsoft allowed users to make "theme" changes across all UI components. Giving the users the ability to customize their UIs is another recent trend in the design of UIs. Users may not like the standard theme (i.e. colors, styles, fonts, sizes, etc.) of a particular application UI. In those models, they are given the opportunity to either create their own customized UI theme or for the least choose one from several available themes.
- Console or terminal based applications are usually platform independent due to the simplicity of their UI design. Unlike all other UI platforms (e.g. Desktop, mobile, tablet and Web) console-based UI uses only the keyboard and does not allow the users to interact with the application through the mouse at all. This makes the design and interaction of those UIs very simple and easy to transfer from one platform or environment to another.

Many low-level software applications (e.g. embedded systems, hardware controls, robots, etc.) prefer to use console or terminal-based UIs as simplicity is more important than UI richness or flexibility. In addition, users in those domains are considered as technically experts and are able to understand and communicate with command-based applications or environments. On the other hand, web and desktop applications tend to rely heavily on new and very rich UI components. On one hand, this will make those UIs more attractive and allow the users of those UIs or applications to have more flexible options and interactive environments. On the other hand, this continuous update of UI components and evolution can cause a lot of compatibility, testing and maintenance issues. UIs of mobile applications are somewhat in between lightweight terminal-based UIs and desktop or web rich UIs. Mobile platforms allow users to use the touch screen (which acts more like a mouse in the classical no-touch screen environments). In addition, some mobiles include physical keyboards that can be used or alternatively mobile platform provides emulated keyboards.

UI DESIGN PATTERNS AND PRINCIPLES

Software design principles and patterns show experienced well-designed or evaluated software design approaches or templates. They can be used as decent practices to follow when trying to design a new software. For UI design, and since UI software is unique and different from code written in the main program, those principles are patterns may not be applicable to UI design (Cerny & Donahoo 2015). This does not eliminate the idea that many software design principles are still applicable to UI design in the general sense. For example, the principle of "separation of concerns" or "separate what varies from what does not vary and encapsulate what varies" is a general software design principle related to Abstraction and Encapsulation. Those two high level design concepts are considered cores in current software design architectures. In abstraction, we design software as a solution to a problem. Hence it's important for software designers to first understand the problem and the problem domain and then design a solution that fits or solves that problem. In this scope, abstraction is related to what should and should not be included as requirements and features in the solution program. Later on abstraction is related to what methods and attributes should and should not be included in each class of our designed classes. Some attributes in some classes should not be included because they are irrelevant and does not serve any specific feature related to our program. In coordination with abstraction, encapsulation is related to include in interfaces only what should be used by service consumers. At the class level, method should or should not be public based on whether they are serving other classes or methods in their own class. At the user interface level, encapsulation is related to "shielding the users from irrelevant and unnecessary details". They need to know from the program services only what they are using. Excessive, redundant, or unnecessary information can be as misleading and confusing to users just as the lack of information.

User interfaces of software applications contribute significantly to the success of those applications. There are many factors in which the user interface of an application can be evaluated. For example, a software user interface should be multi-model and adaptive, (Peissner et al., 2012). From an environment perspective, most applications expect to be deployed in the current main three platforms:

1. Web
2. Desktop
3. Mobile

While the underlying features can be the same, however, the user interface between those different platforms can be significantly different. Even in one environment of those the UI can vary based on one instance of that specific environment to another. For example, web browsers (e.g. Microsoft Internet Explorer, Google Chrome, Firefox, etc.) can have support for a wide variety of technologies or features. This make some services of the application only workable, or at least optimized for one of those browsers. In fact, this can vary from one version of one browser type to another. Developing an application that can work perfectly normal in all those different platforms may not be possible or may result in a developing a large or complex application. This is especially true as technologies, add-ons, etc., on those environments keep changing rapidly.

Encapsulation in UI design has also several other dimensions. Recent user interfaces are context-sensitive from several different dimensions. In one part, user interfaces should show/hide different components based on what users are currently doing or which services they are interacting with. Anything from the application or its user interface that is not relevant to the current user context or activities should not be displayed. Help is also context-sensitive in most current applications. Unlike previous historical help formats where users can call them explicitly and they will basically read text from the manual, recent help services pop up to the users to respond to queries that users may not explicitly issued. The user interface should be able to "see" if the user is having some difficulties using a feature or a service and provide relevant help information.

As users communicate with the application only through its interface, it's important that the UI provides informative and interactive help messages and feedback to users. All golden rules of UI design are related to how effectively the application UI interacts with the users. For example, error messages cause the most significant complains of users from software applications. In some cases, error messages are very generic and do not provide any helpful information for the users to understand what mistakes they made and why the service from the software application they are trying to request or interact with is not functions as it should be. A robust UI design is the one which has the ability to predict or know the types of mistakes users may be exposed to and hence provide them with very informative helpful feedback. Further, the UI may propose hints or offer solutions for users in order to fix or bypass those errors. From a code perspective, this may require the design and development of a very effective exception handling that is designed to consider and evaluate all or most possible errors that users may be exposed to.

From a security perspective, the design of user interface should use a robust user input validation system to make sure that many of the intentionally or unintentional incorrect/invalid user inputs are caught and handled at the user interface level. It is important to validate those user inputs and the user interface level or as early as possible before further processing those inputs or allow them to reach the back-end databases and data. Security threats or attacks such as SQL injection or Cross-Site Scripting (CSS) can be significantly prevented based on a robust user-input validation system or roles.

In the principles of UI design also is to offer users alternatives to access the same software services. The standard two inputs that users classically interact with software applications, through their UIs, include the mouse and the keyboard. Accordingly, most of the alternative access to features are based on giving the options to use either the keyboard or the mouse. New touch screen options can fall within the category of mouse options and work in the same way. Flexibility and accessibility have been important UI design goals. In accessibility also, there are many UI design recommendations to allow users with special needs or senses' impairments to interact properly with those software applications. For example, web accessibility metrics include many standards, metrics and tools to evaluate the ability of a web site or application to provide users with special needs different or alternative options. (Alsmadi et al., 2010; Kamal et al., 2016).

User interfaces should help users interact with the software but not control their actions. Users should always feel that they are in control of what they want to do, select, modify, etc. The user interface should not make assumptions on behalf of the users. For example, many "auto-complete" options were designed to help users write or select quickly through remembering their previous selections. Those "auto-complete" options can be either collected or saved from users' previous selections or can be selected based on general public selections. However, in some cases this "auto-complete" option can be annoying (e.g. in Microsoft Word) where the application will reject user modifications of some of the auto-complete selections or decisions. This is an example of where UI should help but not control users or their decisions and selections.

User interfaces should be designed to forgive users and their mistakes. They should not "punish" users for their mistakes or should not "take revenge". Even if users are intentionally trying to force the user interface to crash by entering incorrect or invalid inputs intentionally. The UI should be robust enough to handle all different or strange inputs, while at the same time it should forgive users and communicate with them effectively.

One testing activity that is used in UI testing is what is called "random or monkey testing". In this activity random and very strange inputs and sequence of inputs are generated. Those inputs are then used to generate test cases, and execute them on the user interface. The goal is to make sure that the user interface is robust and will not crash even under abnormal conditions where users can, intentionally or unintentionally input very strange and invalid inputs or sequence of inputs.

In this context, there is a significant quality or design goal contradiction between UI and security designs. For example, from a good UI design perspective, UI should provide information feedback to users when they do mistakes. Users should know why they are seeing errors or why the software is not functioning as they thought it should. This informative feedback should help them understand their mistakes and how they can fix it to be able to correctly deal with the software and use its services. However, from security design goals and perspectives, the software and its UI should not be revealing and should not initiate or volunteer to provide "extra" information that may help users expose information that they are not authorized to see or interact with. This is of course with the assumption that those are illegal users who do not have enough privileges to access the services that they are trying to access or use. A balance is always required between the different design goals or requirements. In addition, the nature of the software or the domain where it is used in can judge which design goals should be given more precedence when conflicts occur.

A unique aspect in UI design is that it combines structured with unstructured approaches, engineering with art, following UI design standards while developing an intuitive, creative, new, different or likeable user interfaces. While we can tell that is UI can be a complete failure or will not be successful, on the other hand, it will be really hard to predict whether a UI will be successful and likeable by users or not. Some software companies try always to develop all their applications or their future releases of those applications based on their standard convention. It will be then easier for users to memorize or predict how to interact or use application services. Some other companies try to follow an intuitive, creative approach with the hope that users will like and will be willing to learn this new UI.

Studying user or usage sessions from application logs (Alsmadi & Magel 2008) can help us understand how users often use the different features and design the layout of the UI to consider this usage. For example, features that are more frequently used by users should be more visible and should have alternative accessibility options. In addition, history or memory based options, where the UI can remember user last time selections for those services is also plausible.

In websites' design, there are some other UI design principles that should be mentioned. For example, the principle "Late or lazy registration" refers to the idea that websites should not push users to register as soon as they visit the website. Many users tend to avoid visiting such websites for two main reasons: First those websites expect users to trust them and register with several attributes or information to the users' private details while those websites are not trusting the users to allow them to browse some information without the need to be registered users. Some website designers may not visualize this users' viewpoint and may have some other reasons why they want users to register from early stages. Nonetheless, in user-centric designs, users and their viewpoints should be considered first. The second reasons that users may not be tempted to register and be able to go further in those websites is that users these days are knowledgeable. They know that they have or can have many options and hence they are not pressured to spend time and register in those websites before knowing important details about those websites and their services.

CONCLUSION AND FUTURE DIRECTIONS

User interfaces will continue to evolve in future. They represent the most volatile component of software applications. They have a major factor in the success or the failure of the software product. They also consume a significant amount of project resources. Companies want to expand their applications to be used in a wide spectrum of environments or platforms. The design of a flexible UI can play a major role in making their software application platform-independent or cross-platform. A decision by users or stake-holders that a software is obsolete or is about to be can be highly related to its user-interface and how users are dealing with or accepting this user interface or how can this interface accommodate the evolution of its surrounding environments. For example, a game that was very popular under Windows 95, 98, etc. may not be popular once a new Windows version is released with many new GUI related features and enhancements. Not only has the software (e.g. Operating systems) continuously evolved, but also the hardware. Memory is continuously increasing with new computers; graphic cards include more memory and support more bits of colors related to the quality of pictures or graphics. The developed applications and their UI in particular should be able to utilize those hardware evolutions to develop richer and more interactive UI-components.

The standard UI model of Mouse-Keyboard users-applications interaction is also evolving. In the same personal computer environments, users can now use touch screens. While touch screen may look, from a UI design perspective, as a mouse, however, they give users more flexibility and options when compared to the mouse features or options. Future software applications should consider using those new options.

Finally, many applications, especially games, utilize virtual reality environments. In virtual reality environment, the model of mouse-keyboard is replaced by a completely different model where in this new model, software applications are brought to users in their own environments. Users in this environment can use their own sensing (e.g. hearing, speaking, touching) members as well as their own actuators (e.g. hands and legs).

REFERENCES

Kamal, I.W., Alsmadi, I.M., Wahsheh, H.A., & Al-Kabi, M.N. (2016). Evaluating Web Accessibility Metrics for Jordanian Universities. *International Journal of Advanced Computer Science and Applications*, 7(7).

Abrams, M., Phanouriou, C., Batongbacal, A. L., Williams, S. M., & Shuster, J. E. (1999). UIML: an appliance-independent xml user interface language. In *Computer Networks (Vol. 31)*. Elsevier Science. doi:10.1016/S1389-1286(99)00044-4

Alsmadi, I., & Magel, K. (2007). GUI path oriented test generation algorithms. *Proceeding of IASTED Human-Computer Interaction '07*.

Alsmadi, I. (2010). *Ahmad T. Al-Taani, and Nahed Abu Zaid. "Web Structural Metrics Evaluation", Developments in E-systems Engineering* (pp. 225–230). DESE.

Alsmadi, I. (2011). Activities and Trends in Testing Graphical User Interfaces Automatically. *Journal of Software Engineering*, 5(1), 1–19. doi:10.3923/jse.2011.1.19

Alsmadi, I. (2014). How much automation can be done in testing? In I. Alsmadi (Ed.), Advanced automated software testing. Hershey, PA, USA: IGI Global.

Alsmadi, I., & Alda, S. (2012). Test cases reduction and selection optimization in testing web services. *International Journal of Information Engineering and Electronic Business*, 4(5), 1–8. doi:10.5815/ijieeb.2012.05.01

Alsmadi, I., & Magel, K. (2007). *An object oriented framework for user interface test automation. Proceedings of MICS '07*. Citeseer.

Alsmadi, I., & Magel, K. (2008). The Utilization of User Sessions in Testing. *Proceedings of the Seventh IEEE/ACIS International Conference on Computer and Information Science ICIS '08*, Portland, OR, USA.

Amalfitano, D., Fasolino, A. R., Tramontana, P., De Carmine, S., & Memon, A. M. (2012, September). Using GUI ripping for automated testing of Android applications. *Proceedings of the 27th IEEE/ACM International Conference on Automated Software Engineering* (pp. 258-261). ACM. doi:10.1145/2351676.2351717

Banerjee, I., Nguyen, B., Garousi, V., & Memon, A. (2013). Graphical user interface (GUI) testing: Systematic mapping and repository. *Information and Software Technology, 55*(10), 1679–1694. doi:10.1016/j.infsof.2013.03.004

Cerny, T., & Donahoo, M. (2015). On separation of platform-independent particles in user-interfaces, survey on separation of concerns in user interface design. *Cluster Computing, 18*(3), 1215–1228. doi:10.1007/s10586-015-0471-7

Limbourg, Q., Vanderdonckt, J., Michotte, B., Bouillon, L., & Lopez-Jaquero, V. UsiXML: a language Supporting Multi-Path Development of User Interfaces. *Proc. EHCI-DSVIS '04*. doi:10.1007/11431879_12

Mejía-Figueroa, A., de los Ángeles Quezada Cisnero, M., Reyes Juárez-Ramírez, J. (2016). Developing Usable Software Applications for Users with Autism: User Analysis, User Interface Design Patterns and Interface Components. *Proceedings of the 2016 4th International Conference in Software Engineering Research and Innovation (CONISOFT)*. IEEE.

Peissner, M. et al. MyUI: generating accessible user interfaces from multimodal design patterns. *Proceedings of the 4th ACM SIGCHI symposium on Engineering interactive computing systems*. ACM. doi:10.1145/2305484.2305500

Schmidt, V. A. (2010). *User interface design patterns*. Air Force Research Lab Wright-Patterson AFB OH Human Effectiveness Directorate.

Tubishat, M., Alsmadi, I., & Al-Kabi, M. (2009, March). Using XML files to document the user interfaces of applications. *Proceedings of the '09 5th IEEE GCC Conference & Exhibition* (pp. 1-4). IEEE. doi:10.1109/IEEEGCC.2009.5734242

Chapter 11
Web Caching System:
Improving the Performance of Web-based Information Retrieval System

Sathiyamoorthi V.
Sona College of Technology, India

ABSTRACT

It is generally observed throughout the world that in the last two decades, while the average speed of computers has almost doubled in a span of around eighteen months, the average speed of the network has doubled merely in a span of just eight months! In order to improve the performance, more and more researchers are focusing their research in the field of computers and its related technologies. World Wide Web (WWW) is one of the services provided by the Internet medium for sharing of information. As a result, millions of applications run on the Internet and cause increased network traffic and put a great demand on the available network infrastructure. With the increase in the number of Internet users, it is necessary to enhance the speed. This paper addresses the above issues and proposes a novel integrated approach by reviewing the works related to Web caching and Web pre-fetching.

INTRODUCTION

Web caching is an intermediate storage between client and server and used to store the Web objects that are likely to be accessed in the near future.

Web pre-fetching is used to load webpages into the cache before the actual request arrives. When combined, these can complement each other where Web caching technique makes use of temporal locality, whereas Web pre-fetching technique use spatial locality of Web objects (Teng et al., 2005).

Web caching plays a predominant role in improving the performance of the Web today, due to the following reasons (Sathiyamoorthi, 2016):

- More and more Web users
- High cost of bandwidth
- Broken bandwidth and latencies

DOI: 10.4018/978-1-5225-1944-7.ch011

- Ever-increasing network distances
- Bandwidth demands continue to amplify

Therefore, Web caching reduces the bandwidth utilization as well as the server load by temporarily storing the Web objects nearer to the *client*. This provides the benefits such as reducing the cost of connection to the Internet, the latency of WWW and server workload and network traffic (Kumar & Norris, 2008).

There are many aspects which affect the performance of Web today, including discrepancies in network connectivity, real-world distances and overcrowding in networks or servers due to unforeseen demand (Sathiyamoorthi & Murali Baskaran, 2010b).

Some of the methodologies addressed here that help to increase the performance are Web caching, Web pre-fetching and integration of Web caching and Web pre-fetching.

Web caching can be positioned at different locations that are client side, server side and proxy side (Chen et al., 2003). In these, proxy-based Web caching is widely used to reduce the latency problem of today's Webpages as it resides in between client and server. It plays a major role in dropping the response time and saves the bandwidth. The main element of Web caching is its page replacement policy (Chen et al., 2007). When a new document arrives and if the cache is full, then the replacement policy has to make critical decision in replacing an existing Webpage from the cache. The subsequent sections examine some of the existing Web caching policies and Web pre-fetching techniques. It also summarizes the various Web pre-fetching approaches with its pros and cons.

RESARCH PROGRESS IN WEB CACHING

The traditional cache policies are not appropriate for Web atmosphere since they concentrate on any one parameter (age, frequency, cost recentness and so on) and ignore other factors that have an impact on the Web caching (Koskela et al., 2003; Cobb & ElAarag, 2008; Ayani et al., 2003). Moreover, traditional policies are best suited for memory caching since it involves fixed page size whereas, Web caching involve pages of varying sizes. Also the authors have discussed that the popular objects will have innumerable requests from the users, while other objects which are present in the cache, are never accessed again. It is observed that many researchers have proposed various methods for improving the performance of Web caching (Kumar & Norris, 2008; Chiang et al., 2007).

However, infinite sized cache can only improve the hit rate from 40% to 50% (Lee et al., 2009; Jianhui et al., 2008; Abhari et al., 2006). Since most of the users will discover information by just browsing and searching it to find new information (Abhari et al., 2006).

Further to improve the performance of Web cache, Web pre-fetching is used. Web pre-fetching is one of the intensifying areas of research in Web mining. The pre-fetching preloads some Webpages before the users' actual requests arrive in. Thus it helps in reducing the delay encountered by the users while accessing Webpages. Many research works have shown that when these techniques are pooled together it would double the performance than simple caching (Huang & Hsu, 2008; Pallis et al., 2008). Further, this will improve Web latency up to 60%, whereas simple Web caching improves the latency up to 26% only (Kroeger et al., 1997; Acharjee et al., 2006).

The main issue associated with pre-fetching is that the users may not request some of these pre-fetched objects. In this case, it increases the network traffic; Web server load and inefficient use of cache space

(Huang & Hsu, 2008). Hence, the Web pre-fetching and Web caching should be incorporated efficiently in order to prevail over the above said limitations (Pallis et al., 2008; Feng et al., 2009).

One key factor for civilizing the performance of Web-based applications is Web caching (Sathiyamoorthi & Murali Baskaran, 2010a). Caching anticipates the popular objects that are likely to be accessed in the near future and hence they should be kept in a location nearer to the client. Thus, it helps in reducing the network traffic over the Internet and apart from that, the server load ultimately improves the scalability of the Web-based system (Sathiyamoorthi & Murali Bhaskaran, 2013).

Wong (2006) and Wang (1999) have reviewed and discussed about various Web cache replacement algorithms that were carried out in the past. Venketesh (2009) have proposed an intelligent Web caching approach which is based on neural network and evolutionary techniques.

Web caching provides the following paybacks to users such as clients, network administrators and content providers (Acharjee et al., 2006):

- The user delay in accessing a Webpage is reduced i.e., Latency Reduction
- Efficiency in using network bandwidth
- Reduction in the loads on the Web server
- Network traffics reduction

Types of Web Caching

Web caching is a means that keeps the Web objects in a location nearer to the end users. On the basis of location, Web caching system is classified into browser cache, proxy cache, and server cache as in Figure 1:

1. **Browser Cache:** This type of cache is located at the client side helping the users to access the pages that have been accessed recently or visited already. Some of the modern browsers that support Web caching are Internet Explorer, Mozilla and Google chrome. This is useful when user presses the

Figure 1. Web caching locations

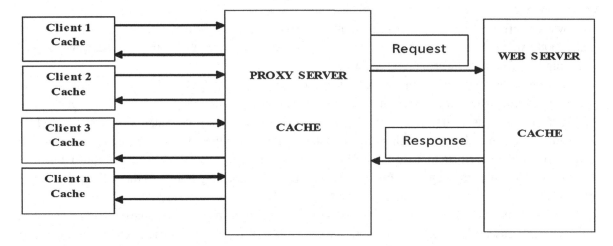

'Back' button to view the previous page or clicks a link that was accessed already in the current Website or session. It focuses on one single user only (Chen, 2007; Krishnamurthy, 2001).

2. **Proxy Cache:** It is located at the proxy server which acts as an intermediate storage of Web objects between the clients and the servers. Its major role is to reduce the latency in accessing a Web page and serves the need of the user groups. It differs from browser cache and deals with single user. When a client request arrives, the proxy intercepts it and checks it in local cache. If the requested object is found then it sends the object back to the client. If the requested object is not found, then proxy will fetch it from origin server, store it in the cache and sends back to the client (Chen, 2007; Krishnamurthy, 2001).

3. **Server Cache:** In this category, a server side cache is employed eventually for storing the pages which will reduce the server work load. Thus, the redundant computation at the server side can be reduced. This is also known as Reverse Proxy Cache. (Chen, 2007; Krishnamurthy, 2001).

Among the above three approaches, a proxy-based Web caching is widely used by the computer network administrators, content providers, and business firms to reduce user delays and network traffic (Kaya et al., 2009; Kumar 2009; Kumar & Norris, 2008).

The basic steps involved in processing a user request include:

*   Client makes a request for an object which is passed through proxy server
*   Proxy checks its local cache for the requested object
*   If the requested object is found, then it revalidates it to make sure that it is fresh and sends it to the client
*   If the requested object is not found then the proxy fetches it from the origin server, stores it in a local cache and then sends it back to the client.

Working Principles of Proxy-based Web Caching

Basic proxy-based Web caching algorithm is shown in Figure 2. In this system, an object might be cached based on information present in the HTTP response header. Web server can also control objects caching by using Cache-Control directories. They are:

*   **No-Store:** An object cannot be cached.
*   **Private:** It means that, this is private and it can only be accessed by the person who originally requested it.

Some heuristics methods are applied in order to identify dynamic Web objects. There are file names ending with .cgi, .asp, or .jsp or path names containing cgi-bin or servlet categorized as dynamic Web objects. Hence caching them is not useful.

The problem with Web caching is staleness of objects present in the cache. If the cache size is too large to store Webpages then they often stale. Such objects need to be refreshed or revalidated before sending it to client. This is accomplished using If-Modified-Since (IMS) query.

Web pre-fetching can resolve staleness issue. By predicting which object will be requested next and revalidate it if it is already in cache else adds them into the cache. Pre-fetching can further reduce latency in retrieving Web objects. Figure 3 shows the initial Web object request.

Figure 2. Basic proxy cache algorithm

```
If (Page is in the Cache)
If (Page is expired or stale)
            Validate it //if-modified-since (IMS Query)
            If (Page is not modified)//IMS Query Response
                    Serve from cache
            Else
                    Get from server and serve
    Else
            Serve from cache
    Else
    Get from server and serve
```

Figure 3. Initial web object retrieval

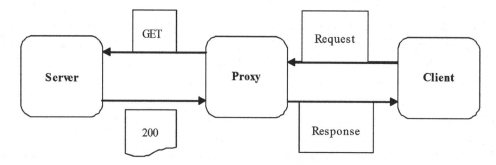

If a requested object is present in the cache then it must be revalidated to make sure that it is fresh copy. This is achieved by sending IMS query along with the timestamp of the cached objects in the request. If the object has changed then the server response might contain the status code 200 (OK) and an updated version of the object is sent as the message body in response header which is shown in Figure 4.

If the object has not changed then the server's response contains the status code 304 (Not Modified) and no body part which is shown in Figure 5. If response header contains Expires information, it shows that the object will not change before the specified timestamp. Then no validation is necessary before this time period. Figure 6 shows the validation using Expire information present in the cached Web objects.

Figure 4. Validation of web object if it has changed

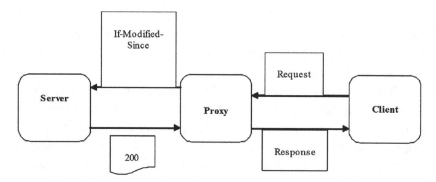

Figure 5. Validation of web object if it has not changed

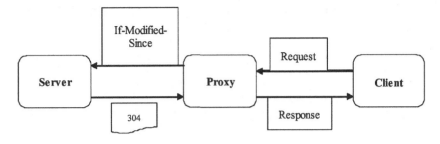

Figure 6. Web object validation using expire information

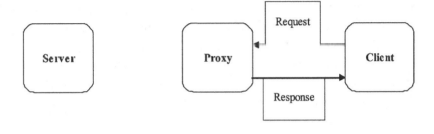

Web Caching Policies

Cache replacement policy, being the heart of Web caching makes critical decision when cache is full on arrival of new documents. This is because cache has limited space and hence efficient cache replacement policy must be adapted to manage the cached objects. Web caching and traditional memory caching is different since the former deals with the variable sized objects whereas the later deals with fixed sized page (Koskela et al., 2003). Hence there is a need for an intelligent algorithm which will consider the various factors such as network distance, size and so on (Cobb & Elaarag, 2008).

The traditional cache replacement algorithms used are FIFO, LRU and LFU. FIFO expels an object based on arrival time. The object which has entered first will be removed first regardless of its accessibility (Sathiyamoorthi & Murali Baskaran, 2011b). LRU will evict the least recently used Web objects when cache is full. It is easy to implement but efficient only for uniform sized objects; it is not suitable for Web caching as it does not consider the object size or the download latency of Web objects and object access frequency in removal policy (Koskela et al., 2003).

The LFU policy throws out an object with the least number of user accesses. LFU stores the often-accessed Web objects and evicts the rarely-accessed ones. The problem with LFU is that the objects with large reference count are never replaced, even if they are not re-accessed again. It fails to consider the recentness and size of a Web object in making decision.

SIZE is another Web caching policy that replaces the largest object from a fully filled cache when new object arrives. Thus, the cache contains large number of small-sized objects that are never requested again. To overcome the above problem, Pei and Irani (1997) have put-forward a new algorithm called GDS. GDS considers several factors such as cost, recency and size in decision making process and assigns priority value for each of the Web object present in the cache. Thus the object with least priority value is evicted first.

Mathematically, it is represented as in Equations 1 and 2 below. When the user requests a Web object 'o_i', GDS algorithm assigns priority value P(oi) to Web object 'oi' as shown in Equations 1 and 2 below:

$$P(\text{oi}) = L + \frac{Cost\left(oi\right)}{Size\left(oi\right)} \tag{1}$$

Where

$$Cost(\text{oi}) = 2 + Size(\text{oi})/536 \tag{2}$$

Here, Cost(oi) is the cost of fetching an object 'oi' from server that is calculated from Equation 2; Size(oi) is the size of an object 'oi'; L is an aging factor. L is initialized to 0 and is updated to the priority value of the recently replaced object. Thus, larger priority value is assigned to the recently visited object. The problem with GDS is that it fails to consider the object frequency in decision making process.

Therefore, in order to overcome the above situation, Cherkasova (1998) has proposed an enhanced GDS algorithm called Greedy Dual-Size-Frequency (GDSF) by considering the object access frequency and the priority value assigned P(oi) as in Equation 3.

$$P\left(\text{oi}\right) = L + F\left(oi\right) * \frac{Cost\left(oi\right)}{Size\left(oi\right)} \tag{3}$$

Here F(oi) is access frequency of an object 'oi'. When object is accessed for the first time then F(oi) is initialized to 1. If object is in the cache, its current frequency is updated by incrementing it by one. The problem with GDSF is that it fails to consider the objects popularity. Also, cost factor considered here is dynamic which changes on available network traffic and server load. Table 1 gives an outline of various replacement algorithms (Waleed et al., 2011; Koskela et al., 2003).

Following are some of the important features of Web objects that must be considered while making decisions (Chen et al., 2003; Podlipnig & Boszormenyi, 2003; Vakali, 2002).

- **Recency:** Last access time, on accessing a Web object;
- **Frequency:** Number of times an object is accessed since it is in the cache;
- **Size:** Size of an object in bytes;
- **Cost:** Cost to fetch an object from server into the cache.

Depending on these factors, the replacement policies can be further classified into five classes (Waleed et al 2011) which are given in Table 2.

Ali and Shamsuddin (2009) have proposed an intelligent Web Caching called Intelligent Client Side Web Caching Scheme (ICWCS). The Web objects have been classified into either cacheable or un-cacheable objects. They have used neuro-fuzzy system to predict Web objects that are likely to be accessed in the near future. A trained neuro-fuzzy system with LRU has been employed. The simulation results show that ICWCS would provide better Hit Rate (HR) but it provides low Byte Hit Rate (BHR)

Table 1. Replacement policies merits and demerits (Waleed et al., 2011)

Policy	Brief description	Merits	Demerits
LRU	The least recently used object is evicted first	Simple and efficient	It does not consider download latency, frequency and size of objects in removal policy
LFU	The least frequently used object is evicted first	Simple to implement	It does not consider download latency and size of objects in removal policy and might have stale Web objects indefinitely
SIZE	Largest object is evicted first	It provides high cache hit rate	Low byte hit rate. Also cache is polluted with smaller sized Web objects
GDS	It assigns a priority value based on Equation 3. Object with the lowest priority is evicted first	It provides high byte hit rate	It does not consider the object access frequency in removal policy
GDSF	It assigns a priority value as per Equation 3 and object with low priority value is evicted first	It overcomes the problems of GDS policy	It does not consider the popularity of an object in decision making process

Table 2. Classes of page replacement policies (Waleed et al 2011)

Classes	Description	Example Policies	Demerits
Recency	It uses the recency or aging factor to remove objects from the cache	LRU, LRU-threshold, LRU-hot	It does not consider access frequency, size and downloads latency of Web objects
Frequency	These policies use object access frequency to remove Web object	LFU, LFU-Aging, LFU-DA	It does not consider recency, size and download latency of Web objects
Size	These policies use object size for removing Web object	SIZE, LRU min, partitioned caching	It does not consider recency, frequency and downloads latency of objects
Function	These policies assign a priority value to each cached object which is calculated based on some functions	GDS, GDSF, GD*	Assigning weight factors is a difficult task and the cost of fetching Web object is dynamic and it differs time to time
Randomized	These policies use randomized decisions for object removal policy	RAND, HARMONIC, LRU-C, LRU-S	It is inaccurate and difficult to evaluate

since it ignored the factors such as cost and size of the objects in the cache replacement process. This client side implementation poses other issues like the training process which requires longer time and higher computational cost.

The Authors Cobb and ElAarag (2008), Elaarag and Romano (2009) have used an Artificial Neural Network (ANN) in making cache replacement decision which classifies Web objects into different classes. However, objects that belong to the same classes are removed without any precedence between them. Moreover they have considered only conventional algorithm. Tian et al. (2002) have proposed an adaptive Web cache access predictor using neural network. They have presented an intelligent predictor design that uses back propagation neural network algorithm to improve the performance of Web catching by predicting the most likely re-accessed objects and then keeping these objects in the cache for future access.

However, they have ignored recency factor in Web objects removal policy. Even though the above methods are better than traditional algorithms, practically it is difficult as it is time consuming and moreover it does not consider the objects cost and size in the cache replacement process.

RESARCH PROGRESS IN WEB PRE-FETCHING

Pre-fetching or Pre-loading is a technique adopted in order to reduce the latency problem and also to boost up the Web caching system performance. It uses intelligent algorithms to predict the Webpages expected to be accessed in the near future before the actual user request. Then, the predicted objects are fetched from the server and stored in a location close to the client. Thus, it helps in increasing the cache hit rate and reduces the latency in accessing Webpages.

Types of Web Pre-Fetching

Similar to Web caching, Web pre-fetching can also be implemented on server side, proxy side and client side. Table 3 summarizes the merits and demerits of pre-fetching based on its location.

It is inferred from Table 3(Zhijie et al., 2009) that the client-based pre-fetching only deals with access behavior of a single user while sever-based pre-fetching deals with access behavior of all the users to a single Website. The proxy-based pre-fetching deals with access behavior of user group segments which reflect a common interest for user's community. Hence, proxy-based pre-fetching is the most widely used method as it is more and more useful and accurate to predict the pages of many Websites (Pallis et al., 2008; Domenech et al., 2010).

Web Pre-Fetching Approaches

Web pre-fetching techniques can be categorized into two main classes:

1. Content-based approach
2. History-based approach

Table 3. Types of Pre-Fetching based on Location (Waleed et al 2011)

Pre-Fetching Location	Data Sources	Merits	Demerits
Client Side	User historical request	It is easy to partition user sessions and useful in personalized pre-fetching	It does not share pre-fetching content among users and it needs a lot of network bandwidth
Proxy Side	Proxy Log	It reflects common interests for a group of users. It shares pre-fetching content from different servers among users	It does not reflect common user interests for a single Website from all users. Privacy information is ignored
Server Side	Server Log	It records single Website access information from all users and reflects their common interests	It does not reflect the users actual browsing behavior and so difficult to identify user session. It needs additional communications cost between clients and servers for deciding pre-fetching content

The content-based pre-fetching analyses the current Webpage contents and identifies hyperlinks that are likely to be visited. The prediction is carried out using ANN mechanism depending on keywords in URL (Ibrahim & Xu, 2000). It is suitable for client side pre-fetching technique. At the server side, it negatively affects the server performance due to high overhead involved in parsing every Webpage by affecting the server service time with an increase in the server load (Domenech et al., 2010).

According to Zhijie et al. (2009), in history-based pre-fetching, prediction is done based on the historical page access recorded in the Web log file. It is mainly used in server side pre-fetching techniques where user's history of accesses is recorded in the form of server log. Pre-fetching can be done using any one of the approaches given below:

- Graph based approach
- Markov model approach
- Cost based approach
- Data mining approach

Dependency Graph Based Pre-Fetching Approach

According to Padmanabhan and Mogul (1996), pre-fetching technique can be based on Dependency Graph (DG). The DG consists of nodes representing Webpages, and links representing access sequence from one page to other. Weight associated with each of the links represents the probability of accessing the target node from the current node. Domenech et al. (2010) have presented a pre-fetching approach based on Double Dependency Graph (DDG). DDG is used to predict inter and intra Webpage access. The main drawbacks of DG are that it is controlled by the threshold value and it will predict only one page at a time which will increase the server load and the network traffic when multiple users are accessing the server (Nanopoulos et al., 2003).

Markov Model Based Pre-Fetching Approach

Pre-fetching approach based on Markov model is more appropriate to predict user's next request by comparing the user's current access with the user's past access sequences that are recorded in Web log file (Pitkow and Pirolli, 1999).

This approach follows different order that is either the first order Markov model or the higher order Markov model which are discussed below. A user access sequence consists of sequence of pages of the form:

$x_1 \rightarrow x_2 \rightarrow .... x_{k-1}$ where $k \geq 2$ (Palpanas & Mendelzon, 1999)

In the first-order Markov model, also known as low-order Markov model, the next page access x_k depends only on current page x_{k-1}. If the access of x_k depends on consecutive two access of the form $x_{k-2} \rightarrow x_{k-1}$, then it is called a second-order Markov model. In general, if next page access depends on set of K previously accessed Webpages then it is called a Kth higher-order Markov model (Palpanas & Mendelzon, 1999; Pitkow & Pirolli, 1999).

In the low-order Markov model, the prediction accuracy is very low, since it considers only the current Web page access. Therefore, Pitkow and Pirolli (1999) have proposed higher-order Markov model to improve the prediction accuracy. In this, predictions are carried out first using the higher- order Markov model. If there is no match then predictions is done by using lower-order Markov model. The order of Markov is decreased until the state is covered. The problem with higher-order Markov model is that it involves higher complexity in constructing probability matrix.

Palpanas and Mendelzon (1999) have proposed pre-fetching based on Prediction-by-Partial-Match which depends on higher-order Markov model where prediction is done based on Markov decision tree that is constructed from the past access sequence of the users. The main drawback is, the tree size is increased based on number of past requests of user. The researchers Pitkow and Pirolli 1999, Chen et al. (2002) have proposed different methods to control the tree size. The PPM based pre-fetching approach is not suitable for proxy side because proxy server can receive requests for pages on different server instead of a single Web server (Liu, 2009).

Cost based Pre-Fetching Approach

This approach uses a function to pre-fetch the Web objects into the cache based on some factors including page popularity and its lifetime. According to Markatos and Chronaki (1998), 'pre-fetch by popularity' predicts and keeps top ten popular Webpages in cache. It is also known as Top-10 approach. The other work presented by (Jiang et al., 2002) is called 'pre-fetch by lifetime' where the 'n' objects are selected based on their lifetime minimizing the bandwidth consumption.

Data Mining based Pre-Fetching Approach

The data mining based pre-fetching approach is classified based on the two data mining techniques namely, Association Rules and Clustering (Sathiyamoorthi & Murali Baskaran, 2012).

Association Rules based Pre-Fetching Approach

In association rule, the prediction is done using the set of rules revealed from different user sessions which is segregated using Web log file. These sessions describe the sequence of Webpages accessed by a single user during some period of time. In association rules, support measure is used to identify frequent pages whereas confidence measure is used to discover rules from these frequent pages (Yang et al., 2004). Yang et al. (2001) have proposed an N-gram based pre-fetching approach which is based on association rule.

The problem in this approach is that too many useless rules are produced from the user's session which makes incorrect predictions, especially when the dataset is large. Hence, the predictions become inaccurate (Khalil et al., 2009; Xiao et al., 2001). The research progress in association rule mining is given below.

Jianhan (2002) have used the Markov model to predict the user's next access. In their work, they have applied a transition matrix to predict Webpages based on past visitor behavior which makes the user find information more efficiently and accurately.

An improved Apriori algorithm proposed by Wang and Pi-lian (2005) consumes less time and space complexity than the original algorithm. It adds an attribute called 'userid' during each and every step of producing the candidate set. It can decide whether an item in the candidate set should be added into the large set which will be used to produce the next candidate set or not. This makes the algorithm widely and aptly useful in Web mining.

Two common data mining approaches such as FP Growth and PrefixSpan in sequential data mining have been presented by Hengshan et al. (2006). It helps in Web content personalization and user navigation through pre-fetching and caching. It also uses the Maximum Forward Path (MFP) in Web usage mining model.

Sandeep (2010) has proposed a custom-built Apriori algorithm based on the traditional Apriori algorithm, to find the effective pattern. They have tested the proposed work in educational log file. This algorithm helps the Website developer in making effective decisions to improve the efficiency of the Website.

Navin et al. (2011) have proposed a recommendation methodology based on correlation rules where Association rules are generated from log data using FP Growth algorithm. Further the cosine measure is used for generating correlation rules.

Clustering based Pre-Fetching Approach

All the methodologies employed in previous section covers only a single object pre-fetching which will increase network traffic and server load when multiple users are accessing the server. In order to overcome these problems clustering-based pre-fetching techniques have been proposed (Sathiyamoorthi & Murali Baskaran, 2011a).

Clustering is the process of grouping the users based on similarity present in the user session. The objects present in the same clusters are highly similar whereas objects present in different clusters are highly dissimilar. An effective clustering algorithm should minimize the intra-cluster distance and maximize inter-cluster distance. Many research works have been carried out related to clustering (Papadakis et al., 2005; Cadez et al., 2003; Adami et al., 2003).

Clustering can be either Webpage clustering or user session clustering (Khalil et al., 2009). The Webpage clustering is achieved by grouping the pages into different clusters based on the content similarity (Tang & Vemuri, 2005; Xu et al., 2006). In session-based clustering technique, users are grouped based on the similarity between different user sessions. Clustering-based approach is widely used in fields like Webpage prediction, personalization and Web pre-fetching. Pallis et al. (2008) have proposed an algorithm called ClustWeb for clustering inter-site Webpages in proxy servers based on DG and association rule. The problem with this approach is that the high complexity involved in construction of DG and moreover it is pruned by support and confidence measures.

As per Paola (2007), Self Organized Maps (SOM) is a kind of artificial neural network, in the process of WUM to detect user patterns. The authors have stated that, in order to identify the common patterns in Websites, SOM is better than K-means.

Mehrdad (2008) have proposed an approach that was based on the graph partitioning for modeling user navigation patterns. In order to perform mining on user navigation patterns, they have established an undirected graph based on connectivity between each pair of the Webpages. They have also proposed novel formula for assigning weights to edges of the graph.

Another clustering-based pre-fetching approach has been proposed by Rangarajan et al. (2004), based on ART1 neural network. It includes grouping the users' access patterns and pre-fetch the prototype vector of each group. In their experiment they have focused only on the pre-fetching and did not address the issues related to interaction between Web caching and pre-fetching. In recent years, data mining approaches have been widely used in Web pre-fetching area (Huang & Hsu, 2008; Pallis et al., 2008).

Sujatha and Iyakutty (2010) have proposed a new framework to improve the cluster quality from k-means clustering using Genetic Algorithm.

The above discussed works were found to be inefficient because they use association rules for pre-fetching Web objects which ultimately leads to inaccuracy due to the prediction of a particular page depending on the patterns observed from all the user's preferences (Khalil et al., 2009; Xiao et al., 2001). Furthermore, these approaches employed traditional replacement algorithms that are not suitable for clustering-based pre-fetching environment.

PERFORMANCE MEASURES

The most commonly used metrics to measure the performance of Web caching and Web pre-fetching systems are given below (Koskela et al., 2003; Cobb & ElAarag, 2008; Wong, 2006):

- Hit Ratio (HR) also known as Hit Rate
- Byte Hit Ratio (BHR) also known as Byte Hit Rate

HR is the percentage of user requests that are served from the cache. That is HR is the ratio of total number of cache hit to the total number of user requests while BHR is the ratio of total bytes served from the cache to the total bytes requested by user.

The mathematical representation is as follows:

Let N be the total number of user requests (objects) and $\delta_i = 1$, if the requested object 'i' is in the cache (Cache Hit), and $\delta_i = 0$ otherwise (Cache Miss). Equation 4 mathematically represents HR while Equation 5 mathematically represents BHR:

$$HR = \frac{\sum_{i=1}^{N} \delta i}{N} \tag{4}$$

whereas BHR is as follows

$$BHR = \frac{\sum_{i=1}^{N} bi \delta i}{\sum_{i=1}^{N} bi} \tag{5}$$

Here b_i = size of the ith requested object.

The most commonly used metrics to measure the performance of Web pre-fetching (Huang & Hsu, 2008; Domenech et al., 2010) are given in Equations 6 and 7 below.

- Precision (Pc): The ratio of pre-fetch hits to the total number of objects pre-fetched.

$$Pc = \frac{No. \ of \ Prefetch \ Hits}{No. \ of \ Objects \ Prefetched} \tag{6}$$

- Recall (Rc): The ratio of pre-fetch hits to the total number of objects requested by users.

$$Rc = \frac{No. \ of \ prefetch \ Hits}{No. \ of \ User \ Requests} \tag{7}$$

SUMMARY AND PROBLEM FORMULATION

The vast amount of literature studied and reported so far in this paper has yielded the proposal of new Web caching and pre-fetching approach to improve the scalability of the Web-based system. The literature also points out the importance of Web caching and pre-fetching using Web mining techniques as important findings which stood as the base for the formulation of research problem, which are tabulated and presented in Table 4.

Table 4. Literature support for formulation of research problem

S. No.	Base papers	Authors	Issue and Inference
1	Web user clustering and its application to pre-fetching using ART neural networks	Rangarajan et al (2004)	It presents a pre-fetching approach based on ART1 neural network. It does not address the issues while integrating Web caching and Web pre-fetching
2	Integrating Web caching and Web pre-fetching in Client-Side Proxies	Teng et al (2005)	Have proposed pre-fetching approach based on association rule. They have proposed an innovative cache replacement policy called (Integration of Web Caching and Pre-fetching (IWCP). They have categorized Web objects into implied and non-implied objects.
3	A clustering-based pre-fetching scheme on a Web cache environment	Pallis et al (2008)	Proposed a graph-based pre-fetching technique. Have used DG for pre-fetching. It is based on association rule and it is controlled by support and confidence. Moreover they have used traditional policies in Web cache environment and didn't address issues while integrating these two.
4	Intelligent Client-side Web Caching Scheme Based on Least Recently Used Algorithm and Neuro-Fuzzy System	Ali & Shamsuddin (2009)	It uses the neuro-fuzzy system to classify a Web object into cacheable or un-cacheable objects. It has LRU algorithm in cache to predict Web objects that may be re-accessed later. Training process requires long time and extra computational cost. It ignored the factors such as cost and size of the objects in the cache replacement policy
5	A survey of Web cache replacement strategies	Podlipnig & Böszörmenyi (2003)	The authors have reviewed and presented an overview of various page replacement policies. It is observed that GDSF perform better in Web cache environment. They also have presented merits and demerits of various page replacement policies.
6	A Keyword-Based Semantic Pre-fetching Approach in Internet News Services	Ibrahim & Xu (2004)	It predicts users' future access based on semantic preferences of past retrieved Web documents. It is implemented on Internet news services. The semantic preferences are identified by analyzing keywords present in the URL of previously accessed Web. It employs a neural network model over the keyword set to predict user future requests.
7	A Survey of Web Caching and Pre-fetching	Waleed et al (2011)	The authors have discussed and reviewed various Web caching and Web pre-fetching techniques. It is observed that most of the pre-fetching techniques discussed here were focusing on single user which will ultimately reduce server performance if number of users increase. Moreover, in recent year's data mining plays a major role in Web pre-fetching areas and most of the data mining-based approach uses association rule mining.

From this, it is also observed that both the techniques would improve the performance by reducing server load and latency in accessing Webpages. However, if the Web caching and pre-fetching approaches are integrated inefficiently then this might cause huge network traffic; increase in Web server load in addition to the inefficient use of cache space (Waleed et al., 2011). Hence, the pre-fetching approach should be designed carefully in order to overcome the above said limitations. Therefore, the importance of Web usage mining to optimize the existing Web cache performance has been realized in Figure 7.

Traditional cache replacement policies are not suitable for clustering-based pre-fetching technique since it increases the number of objects pre-fetched and hence poor bandwidth utilization. Hence, the Web caching policy should be designed carefully in order to overcome the above said limitations. It would provide better performance in terms of hit rate and it also reduces the number of objects pre-fetched and thereby saving the bandwidth.

CONCLUSION

From this literature study, it is understood that Web caching and pre-fetching are two different techniques used for improving the performance of a Web based application. Then, the integration of these two would complement each other. The literature also points out the importance of Web caching and pre-fetching using Web mining techniques as important findings which stood as the base for the formulation of research problem. The survey also reviews and summarizes the work related to Web caching and pre-fetching techniques. From this, it is observed that both the techniques would improve the performance

Figure 7. Architecture of the proposed system

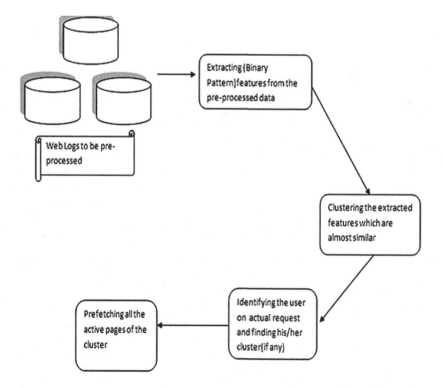

by reducing server load and latency in accessing Webpages. As the user datasets containing the privacy information should not be exposed to the outside world, privacy preserving data mining techniques can be applied in order to hide personal information about the users. Evolutionary optimization techniques can be applied in order to optimize the system further. A session-based approach can also be adopted to improve bandwidth utilization. A hybrid approach out of the existing algorithms can be tried out for cache replacement process. This system can also be implemented to extend the performance of Content Distribution Network (CDN) server and Enterprise Resource Planning (ERP) system for effective content distribution and decision making process. This system can also be used in the application areas where Web search, access and retrieval are involved, such as Predicting user purchase pattern of commodities in E-Commerce Website, Redesigning of a site according to user interest.

REFERENCES

Acharjee, U. (2006). *Personalized and Artificial Intelligence Web Caching and Pre-fetching* (Master thesis). University of Ottawa, Canada.

Ali, W., & Shamsuddin, S. M. (2009). Intelligent Client-Side Web Caching Scheme Based on Least Recently Used Algorithm and Neuro-Fuzzy System. *The sixth International Symposium on Neural Networks (ISNN 2009)*. Springer-Verlag Berlin Heidelberg.

Balamash, A., & Krunz, M. (2004). An Overview of Web Caching Replacement Algorithms. *IEEE Communications Surveys and Tutorials*, *6*(2), 44–56. doi:10.1109/COMST.2004.5342239

Bamshad, M. (2007). *Data Mining for Web Personalization*. Heidelberg, Germany: Springer-Verleg Berlin.

Brin, S., & Pange, L. (1998). The Anatomy of a Large-scale Hyper Textual Web Search Engine. *Computer Networks and ISDN Systems*, *30*(1-7), 107–117. doi:10.1016/S0169-7552(98)00110-X

Chen, T. (2007). Obtaining the Optimal Cache Document Replacement Policy for the Caching System of an EC Website. *European Journal of Operational Research*, *181*(2), 828–841. doi:10.1016/j.ejor.2006.05.034

Chen, X., & Zhang, X. (2002). Popularity-based PPM: An effective Web pre-fetching technique for high accuracy and low storage. In *Proceedings of the International Conference on Parallel Processing*, (pp. 296-304). doi:10.1109/ICPP.2002.1040885

Cobb, J., & ElAarag, H. (2008). Web Proxy Cache Replacement Scheme based on Back-Propagation Neural Network. *Journal of Systems and Software*, *81*(9), 1539–1558. doi:10.1016/j.jss.2007.10.024

Cyrus, S., Zarkessh, A. M., Jafar, A., & Vishal, S. (1997). Knowledge discovery from Users Web Page Navigation. In *Workshop on Research Issues in Data Engineering*.

Domenech, J., Pont-Sanju, A., Sahuquillo, J., & Gil, J. A. (2010). *Evaluation, Analysis and Adaptation of Web Pre-fetching Techniques in Current Web. In Web-based Support Systems* (pp. 239–271). London: Springer.

Dunham, M. H. (2006). *Data Mining Introductory and Advanced Topics* (1st ed.). Pearson Education.

ElAarag, H., & Romano, S. (2009). Improvement of the neural network proxy cache replacement strategy. *Proceedings of the 2009 Spring Simulation Multiconference*, (SSM'09).

Fan, L., Cao, P., & Jacobson, Q. (1999). Web Pre-fetching between Low-Bandwidth Clients and Proxies: Potential and Performance. In *Proceedings of the Joint International Conference on Measurement and Modeling of Computer Systems (SIGMETRICS'99)*.

Feng, W., Man, S., & Hu, G. (2009). *Markov Tree Prediction on Web Cache Pre-fetching. In Software Engineering, Artificial Intelligence (SCI)* (Vol. 209, pp. 105–120). Berlin: Springer-Verlag.

Hengshan, W., Cheng, Y., & Hua, Z. (2006). Design and Implementation of a Web Usage Mining Model Based on FPgrowth and Prefixspan. Communications of the IIMA, 6(2).

Huang, Y. F., & Hsu, J. M. (2008). Mining Web Logs to Improve Hit Ratios of Pre-fetching and Caching. *Knowledge-Based Systems*, *21*(1), 62–69. doi:10.1016/j.knosys.2006.11.004

Ibrahim, T. I., & Xu, C. Z. (2000). Neural Nets based Predictive Pre-fetching to Tolerate WWW Latency. In *Proceedings of the 20th International Conference on Distributed Computing Systems*. IEEE.

Ibrahim, T. I., & Xu, C. Z. (2004). A Keyword-Based Semantic Pre-fetching Approach in Internet News Services. *IEEE Transactions on Knowledge and Data Engineering*, *16*(5), 601–611. doi:10.1109/TKDE.2004.1277820

Jianhan, Z. (2002). Using Markov Chains for Link Prediction in Adaptive Web Sites. *LNCS*, *2311*, 60–73.

Jiawei, H., Micheline, K., & Jian, P. (2006). *Data Mining Concepts and Techniques*. Pearson Education.

Kaya, C. C., Zhang, G., Tan, Y., & Mookerjee, V. S. (2009). An Admission-Control Technique for Delay Reduction in Proxy Caching. *Decision Support Systems*, *46*(2), 594–603. doi:10.1016/j.dss.2008.10.004

Khalil, F., Li, A. J., & Wang, H. (2009). Integrated Model for Next Page Access Prediction. Int. *J. Knowledge and Web Intelligence*, *1*(2), 48–80. doi:10.1504/IJKWI.2009.027925

Koskela, T.J., Heikkonen, & Kaski, K. (2003). Web cache optimization with nonlinear model using object feature. *Computer Networks Journal, 43*(6), 805-817.

Krishnamurthy, B., & Rexforrd, J. (2001). *Web Protocols and Practice: HTTP/1.1, Networking Protocols, Caching and Traffic Measurement*. Addison-Wesley.

Kroeger, T. M., Long, D. D. E., & Mogul, J. C. (1997). Exploring the Bounds of Web Latency Reduction from Caching and Pre-fetching. *Proceedings of the USENDC Symposium on Internet Technology and Systems*, (pp. 13-22).

Kumar, C., & Norris, J. B. (2008). A New Approach for a Proxy-level Web Caching Mechanism. *Decision Support Systems, Elsevier*, *46*(1), 52–60. doi:10.1016/j.dss.2008.05.001

Lan, B., Bressan, S., Ooi, B. C., & Tan, K. L. (2000). Rule-Assisted Pre-fetching in Web-Server Caching. In *Proceedings of the 9th International Conference on Information and Knowledge Management*.

Lee, H. K., An, B. S., & Kim, E. J. (2009). Adaptive Pre-fetching Scheme Using Web Log Mining in Cluster-Based Web Systems.*IEEE International Conference on Web Services (ICWS)*, (pp. 903-910).

Liu, Q. (2009). *Web Latency Reduction with Pre-fetching* (Ph.D Thesis). University of Western Ontario, London, Canada.

Loon, T. S., & Bharghavan, V. (1997). Alleviating the Latency and Bandwidth Problems in WWW Browsing. In *Proceedings of the USENIX Symposium on Internet Technologies and Systems (USITS).*

Markatos, E. P., & Chronaki, C. E. (1998). A Top-10 Approach to Pre-fetching on the Web. In *Proceedings of INET.*

Mehrdad, J. (2008). Web User Navigation Pattern Mining Approach Based on Graph Partitioning Algorithm. *Journal of Theoretical and Applied Information Technology.*

Mobasher, B., Cooley, R., & Srivastava, J. (2000). Automatic Personalization Based on Web Usage Mining. *Communications of the ACM*, *43*(8), 142–151. doi:10.1145/345124.345169

Mobasher, B., Dai, H., Luo, T., & Nakagawa, M. (2002). Discovery and Evaluation of Aggregate Usage Profiles for Web Personalization. *Data Mining and Knowledge Discovery*, *6*(1), 61–82. doi:10.1023/A:1013232803866

Nanopoulos, A., Katsaros, D., & Manolopoulos, Y. (2003). A Data Mining Algorithm for Generalized Web Pre-fetching. *IEEE Transactions on Knowledge and Data Engineering*, *15*(5), 1155–1169. doi:10.1109/TKDE.2003.1232270

Navin, K., Tyagi, & Solanki, A.K. (2011). Analysis of Server Log by Web Usage Mining for Website Improvement. *International Journal of Computer Science Issues*, *7*(4).

Padmanabhan, V. N., & Mogul, J. C. (1996). Using Predictive Pre-fetching to Improve World Wide Web Latency. *ACM Computer Communication Review*, *26*(3), 23–36. doi:10.1145/235160.235164

Pallis, G., Vakali, A., & Pokorny, J. (2008). A Clustering-Based Pre-Fetching Scheme on A Web Cache Environment. ACM Journal Computers and Electrical Engineering, 34(4).

Palpanas, T., & Mendelzon, A. (1999). Web Pre-fetching using Partial Match Prediction. In *Proceedings of the 4th International Web Caching Workshop.*

Paola, B. (2007). Web Usage Mining Using Self Organized Maps. *International Journal of Computer Science and Network Security*, *7*(6).

Pei, C., & Irani, S. (1997). Cost-Aware WWW Proxy Caching Algorithms. In *Proceedings of the USENIX Symposium on Internet Technologies and Systems*, (pp. 193-206).

Pitkow, J., & Pirolli, P. (1999). Mining Longest Repeating Subsequences to Predict World Wide Web Surfing.*Proceedings USENIX Symposium on Internet Technologies and Systems* (USITS).

Podlipnig, S., & Boszormenyi, L. (2003). A Survey of Web Cache Replacement Strategies. *ACM Computing Surveys*, *35*(4), 374–398. doi:10.1145/954339.954341

Rangarajan, S. K., Phoha, V. V., Balagani, K., Selmic, R. R., & Iyengar, S. S. (2004). *Web User Clustering and its Application to Pre-fetching using ART Neural Networks*. IEEE Computer.

Sandeep, S. (2010). Discovering Potential User Browsing Behaviors Using Custom-Built Apriori Algorithm. *International Journal of Computer Science & Information Technology, 2*(4).

Sathiyamoorthi, V. (2016). A Novel Cache Replacement Policy for Web Proxy Caching System Using Web Usage Mining. *International Journal of Information Technology and Web Engineering, 11*(2), 1–12. doi:10.4018/IJITWE.2016040101

Sathiyamoorthi, V., & Murali Bhaskaran, V. (2010a). Data Preparation Techniques for Mining World Wide Web through Web Usage Mining-An Approach. *International Journal of Recent Trends in Engineering, 2*(4), 1–4.

Sathiyamoorthi, V., & Murali Bhaskaran, V. (2010b). Data mining for intelligent enterprise resource planning system. *International Journal of Recent Trends in Engineering, 2*(3), 1–4.

Sathiyamoorthi, V., & Murali Bhaskaran, V. (2011a). Improving the Performance of Web Page Retrieval through Pre-Fetching and Caching. *European Journal of Scientific Research, 66*(2), 207–217.

Sathiyamoorthi, V., & Murali Bhaskaran, V. (2011b). Data Pre-Processing Techniques for Pre-Fetching and Caching of Web Data through Proxy Server. *International Journal of Computer Science and Network Security, 11*(11), 92-98.

Sathiyamoorthi, V., & Murali Bhaskaran, V. (2012). Optimizing the Web Cache performance by Clustering Based Pre-Fetching Technique Using Modified ART1. *International Journal of Computers and Applications, 44*(1), 51–60.

Sathiyamoorthi, V., & Murali Bhaskaran, V. (2013). Novel Approaches for Integrating MART1 Clustering Based Pre-Fetching Technique with Web Caching. *International Journal of Information Technology and Web Engineering, 8*(2), 18–32. doi:10.4018/jitwe.2013040102

Srivastava, J., Cooley, R., Deshpande, M., & Tan, P. N. (2000). Web Usage Mining: Discovery and Applications of Usage Patterns from Web Data. *SIGKDD Explorations, 1*(2), 12–23. doi:10.1145/846183.846188

Sujatha, N., & Iyakutty, K. (2010). Refinement of Web usage Data Clustering from K-means with Genetic Algorithm. *European Journal of Scientific Research, 42*(3), 464-476.

Teng, W., Chang, C., & Chen, M. (2005). Integrating Web Caching and Web Pre-fetching in Client-Side Proxies. *IEEE Transactions on Parallel and Distributed Systems, 16*(5), 444–455. doi:10.1109/TPDS.2005.56

Tian, W., Choi, B., & Phoha, V. V. (2002). An Adaptive Web Cache Access Predictor Using Neural Network. *Proceedings of the 15th international conference on Industrial and engineering applications of artificial intelligence and expert systems: developments in applied artificial intelligence.* Springer-Verlag. doi:10.1007/3-540-48035-8_44

Venketesh, P., & Venkatesan, R. (2009). A Survey on Applications of Neural Networks and Evolutionary Techniques in Web Caching. *IETE Technical Review, 26*(3), 171–180. doi:10.4103/0256-4602.50701

Waleed, A., Siti, M. S., & Abdul, S. I. (2011). A Survey of Web Caching and Prefetching. *Int. J. Advance. Soft Comput. Appl., 3*(1).

Wang, G. T., & Pi-lian, H. E. (2005). *Web Log Mining by an Improved AprioriAll Algorithm* (Vol. 4). World Academy of Science, Engineering and Technology.

Wang, J. (1999). A Survey of Web Caching Schemes for the Internet. *ACM Comp. Commun. Review*, *29*(5), 36–46. doi:10.1145/505696.505701

Wessels & Duane. (2001). Web Caching. O'Reilly Publication.

Wong, A. K. Y. (2006). Web Cache Replacement Policies: A Pragmatic Approach. *IEEE Network*, *20*(1), 28–34. doi:10.1109/MNET.2006.1580916

Xiao, J., Zhang, Y., Jia, X., & Li, T. (2001). Measuring Similarity of Interests for Clustering Web-users.*12th Australasian Database Conference (ADC)*, (pp. 107-114).

Xu, L., Mo, H., Wang, K., & Tang, N. (2006). Document Clustering Based on Modified Artificial Immune Network. Rough Sets and Knowledge Technology, 4062, 516-521.

Yang, Q., Li, T., & Wang, K. (2004). Building Association-Rule Based Sequential Classifiers for Web-Document Prediction. *Journal of Data Mining and Knowledge Discovery*, *8*(3), 253–273. doi:10.1023/B:DAMI.0000023675.04946.f1

Yang, Q., Zhang, H., & Li, T. (2001). Mining Web Logs for Prediction Models in WWW Caching and Pre-Fetching. *Proceedings of the 7th ACM International Conference on Knowledge Discovery and Data Mining*, (pp. 473-478).

Zaiane, O. (2000). Web Mining: Concepts, Practices and Research. In *Proc. SDBD, Conference Tutorial Notes*.

Zhijie, B., Zhimin, G., & Yu, J. (2009). A Survey of Web Pre-fetching. *Journal of Computer Research and Development*, *46*(2), 202–210.

KEY TERMS DEFINITIONS

Association Rule: In association rule, the prediction is done using the set of rules revealed from different user sessions which is segregated using Web log file. These sessions describe the sequence of webpages accessed by a single user during some period of time. In association rules, support measure is used to identify frequent pages whereas confidence measure is used to discover rules from these frequent pages.

Cache Replacement Policy: Cache replacement policy, being the heart of Web caching makes critical decision when cache is full on arrival of new documents. When a new document arrives and if the cache is full, then the replacement policy has to make critical decision in replacing an existing Webpage from the cache.

Clustering: Clustering is the process of grouping users based on their similarity present in the user sessions. The objects present in the same clusters are highly similar whereas objects present in different clusters are highly dissimilar.

Data Mining: It is also known as knowledge discovery in database. It is process or extracting implicit and previously unknown information from database.

Web Caching: Web caching is an intermediate storage between client and server and used to store the Web objects that are likely to be accessed in the near future.

Web Mining: Applications of data mining techniques over a web based application is known as Web mining.

Web Pre-Fetching: Web pre-fetching is used to load webpages into the cache before the actual request arrives.

Web Usage Mining: It is also known as web log mining. It is the process of extracting implicit and potentially useful information present in the web log file through data mining techniques.

Chapter 12
User Performance Testing Indicator:
User Performance Indicator Tool (UPIT)

Bernadette Imuetinyan Iyawe
University of Benin, Nigeria

ABSTRACT

A growing area of research in Human Computer Interaction (HCI) and Human Robotic Interaction (HRI) is the development of haptic-based user performance testing. User performance testing Usability forms a vital part of these test objectives. As a result, diverse usability methods/strategies and test features are being employed. Apparently, with the robustness of haptic-based user performance testing features, user performance still has challenges. With this regard, it is vital to identify the direction and effectiveness of these methods/strategies and test features, and improvements required in the test objectives and evaluation. This chapter seeks to investigate the challenges of user performance and the user performance indicators in some HCI and HRI researches involving haptic-based test, as well as presents a User Performance Indicator Tool (UPIT) as a test validation tool to aid designers/testers in enhancing their user performance test and test evaluation outcomes.

INTRODUCTION

The field of Human Computer Interaction (HCI) and Human Robot Interaction (HRI) is growing with usability studies. Testing usability and user performance are two dimensions that have received major attention. Usability strategies can either be user-centred or usage-centred and are widely employed in haptic-based user performance testing, yet usability and user performance still remains a challenge. Knowingly or unknowingly, the amount of user-centred and usage-centred strategies employed in a haptic-based user performance testing tends to have a great impact on user performance and overall usability. Regardless of the robustness of the interface features and user pre-trial/pre-test/training/background test strategy employed, user performance challenges and interface usability shortcomings in several haptic-

DOI: 10.4018/978-1-5225-1944-7.ch012

based user performance testing outcomes have been identified. This may be as a result of the diverse usability strategies being employed in such tests, which in most cases have contextual objectives.

The Quality in Use Integrated Measurement (QUIM) (Seffah et al, 2006) presents a consolidated model with ten usability factors for software usage, including efficiency, effectiveness, productivity, satisfaction, learnability, safety, trustfulness, accessibility, universality and usefulness. QUIM (Seffah et al, 2006) includes feedback as one of its usability criteria and describes it as the responsiveness of the software products to user inputs or events in a meaningful way. Feedback in haptic-based user performance testing is more virtual presence-context unlike general software, websites and general touch display devices. The System Usability Scale (SUS) reveals that increase in user 's product experience results in higher SUS (McLellan et al., 2012). The MUSiC performance measurement method (Macleod, 1997) focuses on task performance usability for prototyping and iterative improvement in development processes. This method presents effectiveness and efficiency as key performance measures, and relative user efficiency, productivity, and snag, search and help action times as optional performance measures. The User Centred Design Process aims to improve user experience in website developments (Usability.gov, 2015). The Logical User-Centered Interaction Design (LUCID) framework (Kreitzberg, 1998) defines a context in which to conduct product, user interface design and usability activities, as well as provides background and tools required to manage those activities. The Haptic-Audio-Visual (HAV) system architecture (Jia et al, 2013) presents a user capability evaluation method for virtual training systems. While these efforts show prospects for aiding haptic-based user performance testing processes the unique feedback feature of haptic-based user performance testing requires a more universal usability strategy for better haptic interface design, implementation and user performance outcomes.

A growing amount of researches in the area of Computer Science and Engineering has been done utilizing haptic-based user performance testing regardless of the challenges in user performance or usability that exist. While some researchers or testers reflect on the interface feedback impact on the user for the sake of doing research and increasing research databases, the user performance challenges may begin to be overshadowed. Where is the position and direction of haptic-based user performance testing and choice of user performance indicators in usability? Observing and participating in haptic-based test, haptic device and other HCI and HRI technologies from field experience building, literature and interview with user performance test designers/researchers/testers, has contributed to the identification of test design and user performance challenges in haptic-based user performance testing. How can this be effectively addressed to provide better solutions or proffer a better quality approach to address these challenges for haptic-based test researches, and its designers, testers or researchers? How do we identify improvements required besides from utilizing previous study findings and online forum strategy? The objectives of this chapter is to proffer a more universal, quality and generic user performance indicator tool that can aid designers/testers in enhancing their user performance test pre, present and post design usability, and also their user performance evaluation outcomes.

BACKGROUND

We can say research advancement and release of product versions owe its objectives to ongoing user demands and quest for better product evaluation outcomes. Stakeholders, manufacturers, researchers and designers of product/research ideas continue to seek solid standing in their various competitive environments by investing in a wide range of product testing. Products are tested for several purposes such as product performance, user performance, design pot-holes/faults, product durability, user satisfaction, product deliverables, and amongst others. Performance testing forms a vital part of almost every HCI/HRI research and product development lifecycle. In the research environment, the objective of performance testing either focuses on the test participant/end users, the product/technology or both. Performance testing can be hardware or software based. Performance testing can simply be considered as:

testing hardware or software products by engaging human participants directly or indirectly in activities that involve the hardware or software product under various testing criteria or standards to achieve a set of pre-defined or unforeseen objectives or answer a set of research questions.

This chapter section will consider performance testing with regards to user performance testing, user engagement and user experience in some Haptic Based Test (HBT), as well as investigate the user performance indicators employed in them.

Interface designers are expected to think of themselves as custodians to users (Henderson and Harris, 2012) part of which is achieved by developing user or usability testing platforms. Usability testing reveals the problems real users experience with the product under the actual usage settings (User Focus, 2015) such as haptic-based testing. A very vital aspect of haptic-based user performance testing is the availability of unique feedback features. Haptic interface researchers employ various methods and usability strategies in their user performance testing, as well as define user performance indicators. Haptic interface designers utilize performance indicators as a useful and systematic tool to foster continuous improvement (Fortuin, 1988) in the interface design and usability. User performance indicators also aid testers in retrieving qualitative data. The question now is: how quality is this qualitative data? However, the quality and effectiveness of the user performance indicator applied or utilized in the haptic interface matters and should be given key enhanced focus to eradicate assumptions in test evaluations and possibly improve user performance in the haptic-based test.

User Performance Testing

The objective of user performance testing varies in every test design. A simple definition of User Performance Testing is

the assessment of user's participation or engagement in a single test activity or a test comprising of several tasks/activities in line with defined test objectives, research questions and user performance indicators.

User Performance Testing can be more software focused or hardware focused. Regardless, both software and hardware focused user performance test are designed to address the defined objectives and research questions of the software or hardware technology involved. User performance in Haptic-Based Test (HBT), being the focus of this chapter, is a user utilizes haptic technology. A simplified typical User Performance Test process is shown in Figure 1.

Some user performance test objectives are subject-based, aimed at testing the user's performance in certain skills. Examples include testing users for cognition skills (Yamagata et al, 2013), Hand Writing skills (Bayousuf et al, 2013), advanced mathematical skills (Van Scoy et al, 2005), amongst others. These user performance test objectives mentioned may indicate categorized user learning abilities at different

Figure 1. Simplified User Performance Test process

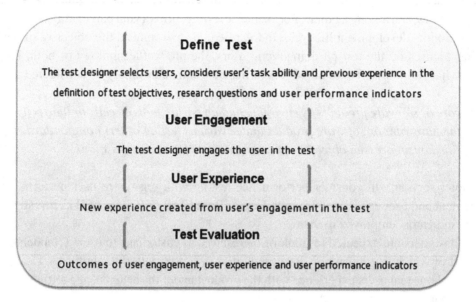

levels and can be viewed as being assistive-based, aimed at contributing to the user's Quality of Life (QOL) or Activities of Daily Living (ADL).

Haptic-Based Test (HBT) Environment

The haptic study domain has broadened over the years and still has great potentials, even with some challenges identified with using some haptic devices. This can be linked to the growing demand for more human feedbacks and information processing in all user types. Haptic and vision integration enables users make sense of the world (Ernst & Banks, 2002). Haptic relates to kinaesthetic i.e. users movement of muscles, tendons and articulations, and cutaneous i.e. users skin sensory of temperature, pressure or pain (Johnsor & Semwel, 2014). The concept of haptic (touch) is able to provide effective processing of measurable subject and object features (Lederman & Klatzky 2009). Haptic interfaces serve as a user testing platform for various HCI studies involving different categories of users. Findings have shown that Haptic promotes three-dimensional understanding, which is crucial for learning and design of instructional materials (Jones et al, 2005) and representation of meaningful aspects of real environments (Sanchez-Vives & Slater, 2005). While a major section of real haptic object recognition studies vary user performance parameters utilizing object type such as deformable, 3D-Printed, geometrical shape, size, mapping and information processing.

Haptic-based test interfaces can provide real experiences in a virtual scene via the designated interface and processing of haptic information in the form of feedbacks, which can be processed with the user's hands, feet, toes, fingers, ears, eyes or whole body. For instance, the electric motors called actuators in a PHANToM Omni haptic device utilized in a haptic-based test can exert force on the user (Laycock & Day, 2003). As a result, a force feedback is exerted on the user serving as clues of the virtual or haptic space (Lahav et al, 2015). Most haptic-based device design features deliver portability and ease of use for the user. Most of them have Degree of Freedom (DOF) feature, which is the quantity that describes how many 'translations' and 'rotations' are used by the haptic device (Laycock & Day, 2003). However, a three-Dimensional object interaction is enhanced using 6-DOF haptic feedback device (Laycock & Day, 2007).

In haptic-based test activity, virtual objects including virtual space can have haptic properties (Kassuba et al, 2013). Force feedback devices and supporting software can allow users to haptically feel and manipulate haptic objects along with their haptic properties (McLaughlin et al, 2002). Exploring more HBT enabled user performance test and feedback concepts, a Virtual Nine Peg in a Hole Test (VNPHT) engaging three (3) sighted and three (3) non-sighted users applying sound and force feedbacks with PHANToM Omni haptic device revealed test completion time was higher performance by non- sighted than sighted participants (Bowers et al, 2013). A Shape Game comprising of three separate user performance test -Single Shape Training, Single Shape and Multiple Shape - with test design features containing three solid and draggable shapes (sphere, cube and pyramid) and three corresponding shape containers (cylinder, box and prism) engaged four sighted and blindfolded, and one legally blind participants using the PHANToM Omni haptic device. This research which incorporated sound, haptic and visual feedbacks revealed a higher performance in shape perception/identification and shape-container matching by the legally blind test participant in the Training Test (Johnsor & Semwal, 2014). An Audiopolis Videogame utilizing the Novint Falcon haptic device engaging twelve vision challenged school users in three training task and orientation and mapping test. This research also utilized audio, haptic, combined audio-haptic and force feedbacks and results revealed high performance by the test participants in the training task, as well as in the orientation and mapping test (Sánchez et al, 2014).

Furthermore, a set of haptic-based test carried out with blind users revealed that haptic interface has great potentials in aiding blind users through navigation, object overview, physical interaction, menus and widgets (Sjostrom, 2001). A Unknown Object Exploration test engaging forty five (45) sighted and four (4) blind student users split into three feedback groups - haptic (only blind group), visual and visual-haptic groups – utilizing the PHANToM Desktop device revealed accuracy of perception, exploration time, object description, shape recall; more accuracy in the users identifying smoothly curved shapes and slower exploration of sharp-edged shapes in the Exploration Test by the haptic group than the visual and visual-haptic groups (Jones et al, 2005). An Unknown Space Exploration Task with seven objects in a room with walls engaging thirty-one (31) congenitally blind and late blind users split into control and experimental groups utilizing the Force Feedback Joystick with haptic and audio feedbacks revealed varied exploration results by the users (Lahav & Mioduser, 2004). We will now explore more specific user haptic experience in haptic-based testing.

User Haptic Experience

Here, we would draw on user experience with regards to haptic technology or haptic-based test. User haptic experience is created from the user's engagement in the user performance haptic-based test. The quality or efficiency of a user haptic experience can be determined by the haptic interaction usability present in the haptic enabled environment. Generally, in a haptic-based test, there is combination of software and hardware interfaces designed to enable user haptic interaction functionalities. However, the provision of more feedback options attributes and boost user haptic experience (Cook et al, 2005), allowing the user to feel and manipulate haptic three-dimensional object properties, even vision challenged users (McLaughlin et al, 2002).

User haptic experience is unique to the interaction purpose, targeted user(s) and interface functionality. The quality of user haptic experience can be derived from the combined utilization of real and virtual touch. It has been shown that engaging users who have reduced vision abilities in haptic-based test can result in their increased reliability on force feedback and processing of haptic information (Ernst & Banks, 2002), such as haptic object identification. Hence, this creates an interesting user haptic experience for such users as their superior sensory abilities in their alternative senses (Gori et al, 2012; Jacobson, 1993) enable them perform fast and accurate haptic abilities (Klatzky et al, 1985). User experience can be transferable also owing to flexibility considered by the designer/tester in the user performance test. Furthermore, the engagement of vision challenged users in a haptic and audio feedback enabled test involving the orientation task of identifying shapes in an unknown space revealed that the test flexibility allowed participants transfer exploration strategies commonly used in real environment into the virtual unknown space and in return robust performance in real space (Lahav & Mioduser, 2004).

Applications of Haptic-Based Test

The growing practice of engaging users in haptic-based test could be attributed to its exceptional application and importance, not only in HCI and HRI researches, but also its applications in other various fields. We shall explore this in this section. The purpose of user engagement in haptic-based research is mostly to identify factors or measure outcomes centred on user performance. User engagement is also referred to as user participation. Generally, user selection or test participant recruitment is mostly based on the research or product design aim, objectives, research questions and/or user/stakeholder requirements. With regards to this chapter's focus, User Engagement can be referred to as:

The selection and deployment of users (random, specific or focus group) for research/product/user performance evaluation or improvement. Users' engagement with test strategies utilized and defined by the test designer/tester can positively or negatively affect user performance and evaluation outcomes.

In HCI and HRI researches, users are varied and mostly categorized in context of 'abled or non-disability' users and 'disability' users. In haptic-based researches that utilize assistive technology, users with single or multiple disabilities are engaged in its assistive-based user performance test such as investigating Orientation and Mobility capabilities of vision challenged users (Sánchez et al, 2014; Kawai & Tomita, 1996). In addition, the selection of more test participants or more user performance test most likely considers different user personas and background. This strategic consideration may broaden the user performance test evaluation. However, the quality of the user performance test evaluation should be given more focus than the number of test evaluations.

HBTs can be applied in teaching and learning, high level training and research, amongst others. In its application in teaching and learning, we can find a typical HBT in a haptic-based game called Audiopolis designed for blind users. This haptic-based game, Audiopolis, served as a learning system and revealed an increase in the user's virtual navigation, orienting and mapping skills. This also indicates that the predisposition to learning haptic information can be favoured (Sánchez et al, 2014), which in turn benefits learners' performance if the over-all HBT is presented in a format that captures the users or test participants interest at the same time meets test objectives. Users can participate in haptic interface interaction by drawing on their varied touch skills (Bowers et al, 2013). Also vision challenged users also benefit from haptic-based learning even users who have never experienced vision input are able to perform several tasks and navigate in an HBT environment (Struiksma et al, 2009). Educators and instructors always seek better ways of delivering teaching and learning content to users, in this case learners, especially users who require additional or special education needs (Jones, 2005). Effective learning of various subjects by learners can be achieved incorporated into haptic-based enabled learning and teaching. Haptic learning can be achieved when the user is able to control directly or indirectly the manipulation/dispensation of haptic-based test or process the haptic information (real objects, abstract objects or text properties). For instance, the feedback features incorporated in a HBT can easily enable geometric shape learning for extremely vision challenged learners. The field of Medicine and Air Navigation also utilizes haptic-based test environment/interfaces for training purposes, employing multiple haptic devices (SenseAble, 2015). This advancement in haptic enabled interfaces is brought about by the simulation of real objects or scenarios for such training purposes (Jones et al, 2005).

Another aspect of HBT inspired learning environment is its application in enabling more user object perception. Generally, in haptic information processing, virtual object perception features include size, shape form/pattern (deformable, texture, temperature, and weight, curves, static, dynamic or geometric), space navigation and others. The benefit of virtual object perception is an intriguing area of haptic-based testing and provides an additional capability to user's real object perception. User familiarity in static and dynamic object forms reveals significant effects in learning activities (Bulthoff & Newell, 2006). Two experiments carried out to examine the effects of varied object size on real familiar haptic object recognition, revealed that haptic size information processing was usually through direct contact (Craddock & Lawson, 2009).

In addition to haptic object perception, there exists a performance demand emergence in HCI and HRI technology applications for varied users, especially users with disabilities to improve their Quality of Life. Haptic or feedback augmentation can aid more haptic information processing for both vision and non-vision users, in the form of haptic assistance. Depending on the type of user disability type, users can receive carefully designed haptic assistance to process haptic information. Such haptic assistance can be through the incorporation of audio-vision guidance such as directed and undirected path findings (Lim, et al, 2015), application of mental mapping of spaces for effective orientation (Lotery et al, 2007), utilization of interaction aid tools such as Tactons (Brewster and Brown, 2004) or combination of these tools such as Braille and Tactons (Brewster, 1998) or haptic Braille (Jayant et al, 2010). Another example is Flutter, a wearable assistive garment utilized haptic feedback augmentation to provide support to hearing disability users (Profita et al, 2015). These and more can aid disability users in participating in simple and extended HBT task that contribute to the user's Quality of Life (QOL) or Activities of Daily Living (ADL).

Furthermore, vision challenged users have been given a significant amount of recognition partly due to the uniqueness of their lifestyle. The user performance test design criteria can also influence the quality of user engagement. Exploring more contextual user performance test with this regard, outcomes have shown that regardless of the engagement of vision challenged and sighted participants either in same task (Johnsor & Semwal, 2014; Sánchez et al, 2014) or separate task (Bowers et al, 2013), both the participants faced some challenges in handling some educational subject-based task, while in some user performance test these two categories of test participants both perform equally well with task practice (Jones et al, 2005). Not discarding iterative testing, this chapter suggests that 'Quality' is better than 'Quantities' with regards to user performance test evaluations.

USER PERFORMANCE INDICATORS IN HAPTIC-BASED TEST

With regards to this chapter's focus, a User Performance Indicator can simply be defined as an aspect or feature of the user performance test and design, defined by the designer/tester that acts as a measure or criteria for assessing the user or test participant performance in the test.

An investigation into the user performance indicators utilized in some HBTs, shows that the test evaluation process, validation, findings and conclusion of user performance testing can be boosted through the utilization of a more universal and quality the user performance indicator approach. A Multi-Sensory Virtual Environment (MSVE) called 'Shape', Game (Johnsor & Semwal, 2014) involving Single Shape Training, Single Shape Test and Multiple Shape Test utilized haptic interface consisting of touch (haptic), scent and sound feedbacks, three solid draggable virtual objects (shapes),(sphere, cube and pyramid), three appropriate shape containers (cylinder, box and prism) in an empty constrained space, revealed higher performance in shape and shape-container matching by the legally blind participant in the training test. This task utilized two force feedback models: Contact model to build the shape containers and allow the user/player to place much force along the object to determine its shape; and Constraint Model to assist the user/player in finding the draggable shapes. A Tangible Model made from cardboard and a normal ink pen was employed to assist the user /player in finding objects in the virtual environment without any haptic or force assistance and provide real experience. This informed the haptic-based user performance testing features by the addition of two virtual walls. Accuracy of perception, exploration time, user object description and shape recall formed the user performance indicators. Results showed that sound cues and guides in the virtual environment helped players to identify object selected, dragged, placed in correct or incorrect container, when left wall and back wall touched and limited exploring of object surface (Johnsor & Semwel, 2014). In another dimension, the Virtual Nine Hole Peg Test (VNHPT) (Bowers et al, 2013) requiring non-sighted and sighted participants in pre-trial training, intervention/steering training and main test to place nine virtual cylinders into corresponding nine holes. The expected time for task completion formed the major user performance indicator in this study. Results showed that the Guided Discovery Method used evenly for both groups of participants in the steering training allowed unhindered information processing and space navigation by the participants during the iterative process (Bowers et al, 2013).

From observation, the test features in the VNHPT and MSVE haptic-based user performance test (mentioned earlier), although yielded good user outcomes, it is important to note that mix method integration can sometimes result in mixed focus and in turn missed objectives and unwanted overlooked user outcomes. Also in this case user performance outcomes can be mis-interpreted and test purpose/objectives misdirected. For instance, haptic guide or assistance which is intended to serve as an advantage challenged some aspects of the user performance in the VNHPT and MSVE haptic-based user performance testing. Findings in VNHPT haptic-based user performance testing revealed lower time completion performance by the sighted participants regardless of the paired haptic cue and pointer and the Guided Discovery Method employed for both user groups. Also in the MSVE haptic-based user performance testing, findings showed that most users gave more attention to listening to the sound guide than applying their perception. Sound guide applied here thereby acted as a distractor, diminished user performance and interface usability. Although the VNHPT and MSVE user tests considered most usability standards, these standards are designed for objective-based context and do not meet all the requirements for each unique haptic-based user performance testing. HAV (Jia et al, 2013) system architecture suggests several training modes for user capability evaluation in virtual training systems. VNHPT user test considered pre-trial training and intervention/steering training before the main test and also paired its haptic cues with a pointer which is expected to improve user performance, yet still some of the participants experienced longer time of completion than others, which was the key user performance indicator in the test. Also, findings in the MSVE user test showed that some participants faced frustration and longer time of completion in the Multiple Shape game regardless of the prior Single Shape Training and Single Shape tests considered.

The user performance indicator tool proposed in this chapter considers user capabilities as being very dynamic regardless of user categories or grouping. The users in VNHPT and MSVE user tests, though are of the same user group (blind/sight impaired and sighted), differ in their capabilities and in both haptic-based user performance testing. Time efficiency is one deficient usability factor in the VNHPT and MSVE haptic interface design and test processes. As quality-based as video coding is it is not a supporter of time efficiency, as used in VNHPT. Qualitative data collection time can be saved or utilized for other quality user test processes by using the intended performance indicator tool introduce in this research. Haptic interface usability factors should be applied with ease. Even though some challenges have been identified in using the PHANToM Omni haptic device such as the construction of the physical device, real time collision detection, simulation of complex mechanical system and force control (McLaughlin et al, 2002), more importantly how do we better validate pre-existing or present user performance test evaluation outcomes? This chapter seeks to develop a more generic, quality and easy to use user performance indicator tool for better haptic-based user performance testing, as well as test validation and evaluation. Other haptic-based test and their user performance indicators include the following in Table 1.

'CENTRED' CONCEPTS

'Centred' concepts majorly deal with identifying what drives the designer/tester, the user performance test design and the test objectives. The test features used to identify such drive are regarded as Test Variables. Test variables can be dependent (outcomes to be measured) or independent (alterable test conditions) (Oehlert, 2000). Regardless of the dependency and independency of the test variables, the definition of variables and test objectives are contextual. For instance, a particular haptic-based user performance test is contextual to the interface design purpose and the target users. The centred concepts of each test variable or the over-all test, can either be more or less user-centred focused, usage-centred focused or a combination of both. In view of the HBT user performance indicators explored in the section "User Performance Indicators in HBTs," we can identify, classify or allocate the HBT test variables and usability strategies under these three 'Centred' concepts - User-Centred, Usage-Centred and User-Usage-Centred. Also, the user performance indicator tool presented in this chapter adopts the 'Centred' Concepts as a more quality obtainable approach for user performance test validation and evaluation outcomes.

User-Centred (UrC) Concept

User-centred concepts focus on the user as the centre of attention. The user-centred design approach focuses on understanding the practical user (Sripathi & Sandru, 2013). In most user performance haptic-based testing variables under this concept would likely be:

Table 1. Other HBTs and their user performance indicators

Designers/ Testers	Users /Test Participants	Haptic Technology/ Feedback Strategy	User Performance Test	Key User Performance Indicators	Outcome
Sánchez et al, 2014	12 school-age People with Visual Impairment: 11 blind and 1 low vision	Novint Falcon device, Speakers/ Head phone & Computer System; audio, Haptic, combined audio-Haptic & force feedbacks	Audiopolis Videogame: 3 Training Task & O&M Test (12 Cognitive Tasks)- Physical objects in Training Task & Haptic spatial structures /environment in O&M Test; No calibration	Audio & Haptic Sensory Development (ASD & HSD), Tempo-Spatial Development (TSD), O&M Technique & O&M Global Indicator Dimensions	High performance of blind in Training Task & navigational skills in O&M Test
Jones et al, 2005	45 sighted, 4 blind students (split into three feedback groups)	PHANToM Desktop device; Haptic (only blind group), visual & visual-Haptic feedbacks	Unknown Object Exploration- Mirrored or rotated 4 connected cubes: 10 without texture, 10 with bump texture, 2 complex shapes; No calibration	Accuracy of perception,, exploration time, object description, shape recall	More accuracy in identifying smoothly curving shapes (aiding in science)& slower exploration of sharp-edged shapes of blind group than the visual or visual-Haptic groups in Exploration Test
Lahav & Mioduser, 2004	31 congenitally blind and late blind users split into control and experimental groups	Force Feedback Joystick (FFJ) in learning mode; haptic and audio feedback	Real and Virtual (MVE) Unknown Space Exploration Task - 7 objects (2 cubes, 2 poles, 1 prism cylinder, diagonal box, box) in a room with walls; No calibration	Exploration Strategies and Learning Process (use of information and storage aids during the exploration)	Varied exploration strategies by control and experimental groups (mapping and orientation skills) in real and virtual Exploration Task

- Test purpose
- User categories
- User profile/persona
- User capability
- User experience
- Knowledge of virtual object type/form (examples: visual, non-visual, familiar, unfamiliar, unknown, 3D, multi-object, morph)
- User motivation
- User perception
- Haptic assistance
- User engagement
- User-centred design model, and
- Others (as required by test objectives or designer/tester)

More typically, for example exploring the Multi-Sensory Virtual Environment (MSVE) 'Shape' Game (Johnsor & Semwal, 2014) HBT interface in section 3 using this Centred concept, the utilization of touch (haptic), scent and sound feedbacks; as well as the accuracy of object perception and shape recall as user performance indicators and the introduction of the Force Feedback Model called Constraint Model to assist the user/player in finding the draggable shapes can be classified as user-centred concept. In addition, in the Virtual Nine Hole Peg Test (VNHPT) (Bowers et al, 2013) HBT interface, the notion of pre-trial training and intervention/steering training before the main test can be classified as user-centred concept.

Usage-Centred (UgC) Concept

Usage-Centred concepts focus on usage rather than users and abstract rather than real models (Constantine, 2004). Usage concepts in usability can be software or hardware focused. In most user performance haptic-based testing variables under this concept would likely include:

- Test purpose
- Enhancement strategy
- Conditions
- Device/technology set up
- User performance indicator
- Haptic rendering
- Haptic assistance
- Parameters
- Feedback evaluation
- Context
- Object type recognition
- Parameters
- Conditions
- Technology matching methods and
- Others (as required by test objectives or designer/tester)

More typically, for example exploring the Multi-Sensory Virtual Environment (MSVE) 'Shape' Game (Johnsor & Semwal, 2014) HBT interface in section 3 using this Centred concept, the Single Shape Training, Single Shape Test and Multiple Shape Test; the three solid 'draggable' virtual solid shape objects (sphere, cube and pyramid shapes); the three appropriate shape containers (cylinder, box and prism) for the virtual solid shape objects in an empty constrained space; as well as the exploration time defined and employed as the user performance indicator can be classified as usage-centred concept. In addition, the tasks' expected completion time defined and employed as the user performance indicator in the Virtual Nine Hole Peg Test (VNHPT) (Bowers et al, 2013) HBT can be classified as usage-centred concept.

User-Usage-Centred (UrUgC) Concept

In haptic-based user performance testing, designers/testers employ various testing strategies and features intentionally or unintentionally. However, a particular test feature or variable can be regarded as having a measure or attribute of both user-centeredness and usage-centeredness simultaneously. For this reason, such haptic-based user performance testing feature can be ranked under the User-Usage-Centred concept, which connotes a variable is a both user-centred and usage-centred in nature. We can also somewhat relate this concept with the 'variableness of variables' discussed more under Sub-Variables and Sub-UPITs section.

More typically, for example exploring the Multi-Sensory Virtual Environment (MSVE) 'Shape' Game (Johnsor & Semwal, 2014) HBT interface in the "User Performance Indicators in HBTs" section using this Centred concept, the utilization of the Tangible Model to assist the user/ player in finding objects in the virtual environment without any haptic or force assistance and at same time to provide a real experience; the force feedback model: Contact Model to build the shape containers and allow the user/player to place much force along the object to determine its shape; the user's object description ability as user performance indicator; as well as the employment of sound cues and guides evidenced in the haptic/touch, audio and scent feedbacks and resulting in aiding users in object manipulation in the virtual environment can be classified as user-usage-centred. In addition, in the Virtual Nine Hole Peg Test (VNHPT) (Bowers et al, 2013) HBT in the Virtual Nine Hole Peg Test (VNHPT) (Bowers et al, 2013) HBT, the utilization of the Guided Discovery Method which involved the use of an iterative process known as haptic cues in the haptic interface to engage the non- sighted and sighted test participants in the pre-trial training, intervention/steering training and main test can be classified as user-usage-centered.

From observation, the VNHPT (Bowers et al, 2013) and MSVE (Johnsor & Semwal, 2014) user performance haptic-based test design features and user performance indicators here utilized an integration of and diverse degrees of user-centred, usage-centred and user-usage-centred concepts. However, the key concern is how do we better validate the test evaluation outcomes with regards to the user performance challenges still experienced in both test, and in turn achieve a better test evaluation outcome? We will now demonstrate the User Performance Indicator Tool (UPIT) presented in this chapter in a means of proffering an answer to this question.

USER PERFORMANCE INDICATOR TOOL (UPIT)

Having explored Centred Concepts, we now look at how these concepts are utilized in UPIT. UPIT is a more universal and generic user performance indicator tool that aims to enhance user performance testing design in HCI and HRI usability researches by better enabling and equipping the designer/tester with saved time, quality resource usage and better user performance test evaluation outcomes. UPIT applies the User-Centred, Usage-Centred and User-Usage-Centred concepts as a measure for 'quality' test evaluation and validation.

The objectives of UPIT are to:

- Comprehend the direction, objectives and features of user performance testing.
- Identify and understand the challenges that exist at each stage of the user interface test design.
- Investigate the user performance outcomes in user performance testing compared to test objectives.
- Identify the user performance indicators employed in the user performance testing.
- Proffer a solution for a more universal and generic user performance indicator and testing usability.

UPIT would aid HCI and HRI designers/testers in answering the following questions:

- What are the existing participant and tester challenges in user performance testing?
- What are the correlations of these challenges identified in user performance testing?

- What are the usability factors in the user-centred, usage-centred and user-usage-centred methods employed in existing user performance testing?
- How can a more universal and generic user performance tool be achieved and utilized to better validate and enhance user performance testing, as well as evaluation outcomes?

UPIT simply adopts both 'manual' and 'computerized' formats. Manual UPIT simply depicts a manual ticking structure as shown in Figure 2.

TVL = Total Tick Occurrences for UrC, UgC and UrUgC respectively.
UPIT Outcome (UPITO) = Highest TVL(s)
Highest TVL(s) = UrC, UgC, UrUgC or a combination of UrC, UgC or UrUgC

A total ticking summation approach, presented as the Total Variable Levels (TVL) in Figure 2 is used to identify and measure the User-Centeredness, Usage-Centeredness and User-Usage-Centeredness levels of the user performance testing and evaluation outcomes. This can better inform the designer/tester on proffering a better user performance test. In a case where the same TVL is obtained for UrC, UgC or UrUgC, that is two or more centred concept have the same TVL value, in a particular UPIT Outcome, this also informs the test design objectives by guiding the designer/tester on the user's performance evaluation. A unique feature of the Manual UPIT is the provision of designer-defined variables.

Computerized UPIT format is simply the web-based or software application version of the manual UPIT. See Figure 3. It serves the same purpose as the manual UPIT. In computerized UPIT the TVLs can be presented in percentages (%). Each UPIT or Sub-UPIT done, as well as test date and time, is automatically saved allowing its reusability and accessibility. Several UPITs can be carried out, which permits a large pool of UPITs and Sub-UPITs to be carried out by the designer/tester for validation or evaluation as required. Just like Manual UPIT, there is provision of designer-defined variables.

We have been elaborating on UPIT contributions in enhancing test evaluation. Now let us consider its test validation attributes.

Figure 2. Manual UPIT

UPIT (User Performance Indicator Tool)			
Label	User-Centred (UrC)	Usage-Centred (UgC)	User-Usage-Centred (UrUgC)
Variable(s) ☐ Sub-Variable(s) ☐	Tick (√) or Blank (-) below as many as apply		
e.g. User Persona	-	-	√
e.g. Technology Set Up	-	√	-
Total Variable Levels (TVL)			
UPIT Outcome (UPITO)	UPIT outcome indicates		

Figure 3. A test computerized UPIT

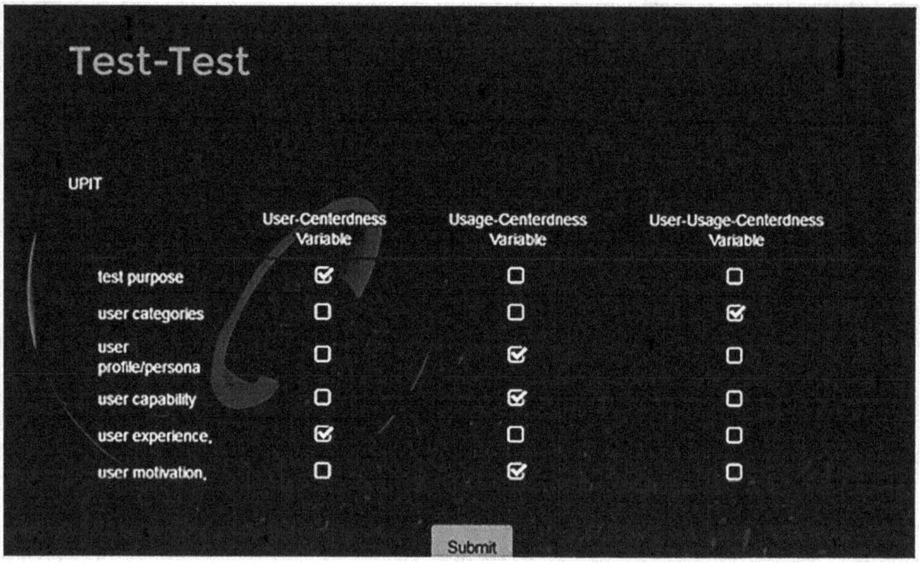

Test Validating with UPIT

Generally, and in addition to HBT requirements satisfaction, test validation is important in user performance testing to identify the truthfulness of the overall test outcomes, including evaluation outcomes. Test validating using UPIT is simply identifying the degree of user-centeredness, usage-centeredness and user-usage-centeredness of all aspects of the user performance test. This is achieved by applying the process of 'Identification' and 'Matching' at the pre, present and post stages of the user performance test design.

Identification

This is the process where UPIT as a validation tool can identify the aspects such as the test features of the over-all test that is more user-centred, more usage-centred or more user-usage-centred. For instance, a particular UPIT Outcome (UO) for a particular UPIT or Sub-UPIT carried out on a particular user performance haptic-based test reveals value 'usage-centredness'.

Matching

This is the process where UPIT as a validation tool can match the identified aspects or features of the over-all test that agrees with the test objectives and evaluation outcomes. For instance, the UPIT Outcome (UO) value matches a test objectives or evaluation outcomes.

'Identification' and 'Matching' can depict multiple forms depending on the test design, test outcome and validation purpose. For instance:

- **Null Matching:** This scenario may occur as a result of when a particular identified UO for a user performance test has no value. A high number of this occurrence may indicate a low level of test quality.
- **Mismatching:** A scenario may occur where a particular identified UO value for a user performance test does not match or is wrongly matched with the test objective or evaluation outcome.
- **Repetitive Matching or Multiple Identification:** A scenario may occur when a single test feature has more than one matching. This depicts the Sub-UPIT, which is further discussed in the Sub-Variables and Sub-UPITs section

Furthermore, UPIT can be applied at the pre, present and post stages of the user performance test process captioned in Figure 1.

Define Test Stage

In defining a user performance haptic-based test for instance, we may consider defining test features such as user selection, user background, user task, User performance indicators, test purpose, research questions and test objectives. However, applying UPIT as a validation tool at this stage of the user performance test process is a measurement of the degree of each three 'Centred' concepts – user-centeredness, usage-centeredness and user-usage-centeredness of each test feature defined.

User Engagement Stage

Applying UPIT as a validation tool in this user performance test process stage is a measurement of the degree of user-centeredness, usage-centeredness and user-usage-centeredness of the user requirements and test interface.

User Experience Stage

Applying UPIT as a validation tool in this user performance test process stage is a measurement of the degree of user-centeredness, usage-centeredness and user-usage-centeredness of the user haptic experience.

Test Evaluation Stage

Applying UPIT as a validation tool in this user performance test process stage is a measurement of the degree of user-centeredness, usage-centeredness and user-usage-centeredness of the over-all test outcomes.

Role of UPIT in Data Analysis

Haptic-based test has been used widely for more diverse user capabilities such as healthy, disabilities and impairments user performance over the decade. As a result, a high level of importance is placed on the analysis of such test outcomes and data. In quantitative data analysis method such as survey or questionnaire, a UPIT 'centred' concept ranking system such as that depicted in the Appendix can be used to collect such data. In Qualitative data analysis UPIT can play a role in retrieving quality data from methods such as interviews, observation and also in validating UO values from UPITs or Sub-UPITs by considering categorized questions like:

1. **Test Strategies:**
   a. What are the user–centred, usage–centred and user-usage-centred strategies?
   b. How were the user–centred, usage–centred and user-usage-centred strategies selected?
   c. Which of these user–centred, usage–centred and user-usage-centred strategies do you consider most effective for user performance?
   d. Which of these user–centred, usage–centred and user-usage-centred strategies do you consider less effective for user performance?
2. **User Performance Indicator(s):**
   a. What are the user performances indicator(s) defined and utilized in the HBT?
   b. How and why were the user performance indicator(s) in the HBT selected?
   c. Please state the reason for this selection:
3. **Impact of the User–Centred Strategies on test Participants**
4. **Impact of the Usage–Centred Strategies on test Participants**
5. **Impact of the User-Usage–Centred Strategies on test Participants**
6. **User Performance Challenges:**
   a. User performance indicator(s) selection strategy?
   b. User performance challenge(s) identified in the test?
   c. Solutions to handle existing user performance challenge(s)?

In overview, does the user performance haptic-based test meet user requirements or criteria, usage requirements and test objectives? Does the evaluation outcome of the user performance test provide a more quality outcome such that possible assumptions are avoided? With the feedback and haptic assistance already incorporated in HBTs, how do we better validate the test evaluation outcomes with regards to the user performance challenges still experienced in both test by some of the test participants, and in turn come up achieve a better user performance test evaluation? All these are questions UPIT usability can address.

UPIT USABILITY

Usability forms a vital part of user performance testing. All HBTs that engage humans are aimed at identifying, enhancing or evaluating user performance. Similarly, the methods utilized in HBTs can either have a positive or negative impact on the user, test outcomes, over all evaluation and the user's performance. However, more quality and standard user performance indicators in HBT strategies is required to enable undisputed test outcomes. The usability of UPIT is empowered by its unique contributions in Flexibility, Efficiency, Quality and Universality. Applying its functions in user performance haptic-based test designs and evaluations, we achieve the specific usability benefits depicted in Table 2.

Next we shall discuss these key usability attributes of the User Performance Indicator Tool (UPIT) that contributes to its acceptability.

Table 2. UPIT usability

Flexibility	Simplicity, ease of use and dynamism
Efficiency	Time and cost
Quality	Centred concepts, test data and test validation
Universality	Widely applicable and quality acceptability

Flexibility

UPIT's flexibility resides in its ease of use as depicted in its simplified manual and computerized format design. In addition, UPIT also owes its flexibility attribute to its application capabilities in the prior, present and post-test stages of the user performance test or haptic-based test. UPIT flexibility is experienced in the availability of designer defined variables, the concept of Sub-Variables and Sub-UPITs, as well as the ability for the designer/tester to carry out tracing or linking of multiple UPITs and Sub-UPITs via the concept of label tracking. These would be further explained in the following two sections.

Designer-Defined Variables

Mentioned earlier, is the fact that manual and computerized UPIT allows designer-defined variables. This customization of variables can also be referred to as the 'variableness of variables'. Each user performance test is unique with regards to test purpose, objectives and participants. In haptic test design the designer/tester may have several unique UPIT variables. Hence, this attributes the UPIT flexibility.

Figure 4 shows a typical manual UPIT that can be applied in a haptic-based test. Each variable is input manually by the designer/tester before user engagement, before or after the user performance test. The provision of designer-defined variables gives the designer/tester the privilege of customizing and modifying variables at any stage for both UPIT and Sub-UPITs (discussed in the next section) at any stage of the user performance test. The practice of variable customization and modification can arise due to the test dynamic nature exhibited by the over-all test itself, the users/test participants, technical capabilities or issues, or as the designer/testers wishes. However, unforeseen test objectives features can call for variable customization and modification in each UPIT or Sub-UPIT.

Sub-Variables and Sub-UPITs

It is important to note that some variables may have sub-variables or may reoccur inside other variables. In this case, a better test evaluation outcome would be obtained if Sub-UPITs in conjunction with the final UPIT are carried out by the designer/tester. The existence of Sub-Variables and Sub-UPITs as well as linking their individual TVLs and UOs can be better organised via labelling. Labelling allows easy linking, tracking or tracing through several UPITs and Sub-UPITs to arrive at the final UPIT. In such a tracking scenario, the final UPIT should serve as the final UO for the final or future test evaluation. Now let's expatiate on this extensional feature of the UPIT.

The designer/tester can have several Sub-Variables and Sub-UPITs depending on the defined or pre-defined or unforeseen test objectives as illustrated in Figure 5. As depicted in Figure 5: The Final UPIT has Variables 1, 2, 3, 4 and 5. Variable 1 has Sub-Variables 1a, 1b and 1c. Variable 2 has Sub-Variables

Figure 4. A typical manual UPIT for a haptic-based test

UPIT (User Performance Indicator Tool)			
Label [ ]	**User-Centred (UrC)**	**Usage-Centred (UgC)**	**User-Usage-Centred (UrUgC)**
Variable(s)☐Sub-Variable(s)☐	*Tick (√) or Blank (-) below as many as apply*		
Test Purpose			
User Categories			
User Persona			
User Capability			
Virtual Object Type			
User Perception			
User Haptic Assistance			
User Engagement			
Design Model			
Enhancement Strategy			
Test Conditions			
Device/Technology Set Up			
Haptic Rendering			
Haptic Assistance			
Parameters			
Feedback Strategy			
Object Type Recognition			
Total Variable Levels (TVL) (Click here for Summation)			
UPIT Outcome (UPITO)			

Figure 5. Illustration of Sub-Variables and Sub-UPITs

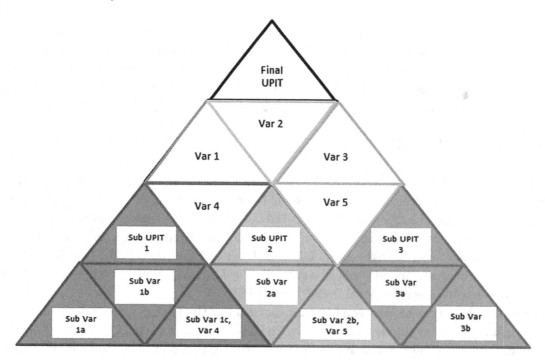

2a and 2b. Variable 3 has Sub-Variables 3a and 3b. Sub-UPITs are carried out for Variables 1, 2 and 3. Due to the fact that they each have Sub-Variables we have Sub-UPIT 1, Sub-UPIT 2 and Sub-UPIT 3. Variables 4 and 5 have no Sub-Variables but notice the reoccurrence of Variable 4 in Sub-Variable 1c and the reoccurrence of Variable 5 in Sub-Variable 2b. This agrees with the notion of 'shared variables' amongst the Variables of the Final UPIT and amongst the Variables of Sub-UPITs.

Figure 6 is a depiction of a Sub-UPIT labelled 'Feedback Strategy' (FS), a UPIT variable under a user performance haptic-based test, which contains Sub-Variables: 'Time of Completion', 'Force Feedback' and 'Audio Feedback'. The UPIT outcome (UO) of Sub-UPIT 'FS' should be represented as the 'FS' true value under the Final UPIT. Such that for a typical sample user performance haptic-based test we can have:

Final UPIT = UO (Variable 1, Variable 2, Variable 3, Variable 4, Variable 5, ... Variable n)
Where, for instance, Variable 3 = UO Value of Variable 3 Sub-UPIT

Sub-UPITs can be done for such test features or variables that are categorized as having sub-categories, just as Figure 5 depicts somewhat sub-tree systems in a tree. This concept of Sub-UPITs and Sub-Variables benefits all test types, including non-iterative and iterative testing scenarios. Regardless of the number of user performance testing being carried out the focus is on quality and improved test evaluation and test evaluation outcomes.

Efficiency

UPIT is efficient in terms of time and cost. Time saving in test design is a benefit for designers/testers especially in cases of meeting deadlines and achieving budgets. There is tremendous gain for the designer/tester with regards to cost. By deploying UPIT in the user performance test the designer/tester is able to achieve saved quality time spent on certain data collection processes such as time in in administering questionnaires and interviews.

Figure 6. A typical Sub-UPIT

UPIT (User Performance Indicator Tool)			
Label — Feedback Strategy (FS)	User-Centred (UrC)	Usage-Centred (UgC)	User-Usage-Centred (UrUgC)
Variable(s) ☐ Sub-Variable(s) ☑	Tick (√) or Blank (-) below as many as apply		
Time of Completion	√	-	√
Force Feedback	-	√	-
Audio Feedback	-	-	√
Total Variable Levels (TVL)	1	1	2
UPIT Outcome	UPIT outcome indicates User-Usage-Centredness		

Quality

Quality is the key attribute of UPIT in terms of not just test data but quality test data findings that better inform the test, test objectives and the designer/tester. The prospect of quality test outcomes is obviously achievable. How is this achieved? One way is through the utilization of the user-centeredness, usage-centeredness and user-usage-centeredness paradigms for validating test and test outcomes, as well as aiding the designer/tester to identify key features and areas of the user performance test that can better inform the test objectives and research questions. Another is the extended validation capabilities of UPIT. This means its consideration in breaking down of variables in Sub-UPITs or in other words the UPITing of Sub-Variables. With this capability, the designer/tester is able to validate and evaluate, in terms of quality and depth, the UPIT Outcome (UO) of the test final UPIT, which can be derived from a single UPIT or several Sub-UPITs. Hence, this is vital for quality test data retrieval. As earlier mentioned under UPIT Flexibility, the availability of designer-defined variables gives room for easy test modification or adjustability to meet unforeseen test objectives features. With this advantage, the designer/tester obtains improved outcomes in the user performance test evaluation and also in the overall research as a return on quality test data.

Universality

UPIT can be universally accepted as it is quality-oriented, which benefits all users (tester and test participants). Also, its centred concepts, user-centeredness, usage-centeredness and user-usage-centeredness, embraces all major facets of user performance testing usability - the user, the designer/tester and the test interface or technology. UPIT can be applied in a broad area of study and fields including haptic and non-haptic based testing, product development, all business and technology solutions, and small and large performance projects. UPIT universality also encompasses its usability in a way.

FUTURE RESEARCH DIRECTIONS

So far we have explored in this chapter the presented User Performance Indicator Tool (UPIT) with regards to user performance testing in haptic-based interfaces. Specifically, UPIT sustainability is sure due to its quality focus attribute. Broader exploration of UPIT can entail its effectiveness in software (code/programming) test validation. Hence, there are future research opportunities that can be explored. Nonetheless, at its present form, UPIT can still be universally applied to all HCI and HRI research involving user performance haptic-based test.

CONCLUSION

HCI researches influence both the user and the interface design (Lazar et al, 2010). Today, user performance forms key focus in user studies involving haptic-based user performance testing. The usability strategies employed in haptic-based user performance testing is diverse. The employment of test features and strategies such as user training test, haptic assistance methods, test conditions/parameters and design models, amongst others, in user performance haptic-based test could be more user-centred or more usage-centred focused or a balanced combination of both. The utilization of the user-centred, usage-centred and user-usage-centred concepts by UPIT produces a quality based paradigm to enhance user performance test outcomes, its validation and evaluation outcomes.

UPIT benefits HCI and HRI users, designers, researchers and testers. Its usability is more universal and beneficial to all the users (tester and test participant) involved in the user performance test, as well as the application of HCI and HRI technologies such as haptic technology. There is need for a more universal and quality standard usability strategy for effective haptic interface design process, user performance and testers. Haptic-based user performance testing is increasingly utilized in various aspects of HCI studies. A User's dynamic capabilities can either be unveiled or overlooked in the user-centred or usage-centred methods utilized in the haptic-based user performance testing. The indicators for user performance and interface methods may not always synergize with all user capabilities but can be enhanced. The UPIT approach draws on findings from literature, correlations between existing data sets, pilot study, feedbacks from participants and researchers/testers of existing haptic-based user performance testing. The incorporation of Sub UPITs further seeks to enhance user performance, improve haptic-based user interface usability, and reduce user performance evaluation discrepancies and designer/researcher/tester challenges.

REFERENCES

Bayousuf, A. S., Al-Khalifa, H. S., & Al-Salman, A. S. (2013). Towards the development of haptic-based interface for teaching visually impaired Arabic handwriting. In *Proceedings of the 15th International ACM SIGACCESS Conference on Computers and Accessibility* (p. 73). ACM. doi:10.1145/2513383.2513400

Bowers, L., Bowler, M., & Amirabdollahian, F. (2013). Haptic Cues for Vision Impaired Peoples: Seeing through Touch. In *Proceedings of the 2013 IEEE International Conference on Systems, Man, and Cybernetics* (pp. 547-552). IEEE Computer Society. doi:10.1109/SMC.2013.99

Brewster, S., & Brown, L. M. (2004). Tactons: structured tactile messages for non-visual information display. In *Proceedings of the fifth conference on Australasian user interface*, (vol. 28, pp. 15-23). Australian Computer Society, Inc.

Brewster, S. A. (1998). Using Nonspeech Sounds to Provide Navigation Cues. *ACM Transactions on Computer-Human Interaction*, *5*(3), 224–259. doi:10.1145/292834.292839

Bulthoff, I., & Newell, F. N. (2006). The role of familiarity in the recognition of static and dynamic objects. *Progress in Brain Research*, *154*, 315–325. doi:10.1016/S0079-6123(06)54017-8 PMID:17010720

Constantine, L. (2004). Beyond user-centered design and user experience: Designing for user performance. *Cutter IT Journal*, *17*(2), 16–25.

Cook, A. M., Bentz, B., Harbottle, N., Lynch, C., & Miller, B. (2005). School-based use of a robotic arm system by children with disabilities. *Neural Systems and Engineering. IEEE Transactions on*, *13*(4), 452–460.

Craddock, M., & Lawson, R. (2009). Size-sensitive perceptual representations underlie visual and haptic object recognition. *PLoS ONE*, *4*(11), e8009. doi:10.1371/journal.pone.0008009 PMID:19956685

Craddock, M., & Lawson, R. (2009). The effects of size changes on haptic object recognition. *Attention, Perception & Psychophysics, 71*(4), 910–923. doi:10.3758/APP.71.4.910 PMID:19429968

Drigas, A., Koukianakis, L., & Papagerasimou, Y. (2006). An E-Learning Environment for Nontraditional Students with Sight Disabilities. In *Frontiers in Education Conference, 36th Annual* (pp. 23-27). IEEE. doi:10.1109/FIE.2006.322633

Ernst, M. O., & Banks, M. S. (2002). Humans integrate visual and haptic information in a statistically optimal fashion. *Nature, 415*(6870), 429–433. doi:10.1038/415429a PMID:11807554

Fortuin, L. (1988). Performance indicators—why, where and how? *European Journal of Operational Research, 34*(1), 1–9. doi:10.1016/0377-2217(88)90449-3

Gori, M., Tinelli, F., Sandini, G., Cioni, G., & Burr, D. (2012). Impaired visual size-discrimination in children with movement disorders. *Neuropsychologia, 50*(8), 1838–1843. doi:10.1016/j.neuropsychologia.2012.04.009 PMID:22569216

Henderson, A., & Harris, J. (2012). Curating Evolution. *Journal of Usability Studies, 7*(2), 51–55.

Jacobson, W. H. (1993). *The art and science of teaching orientation and mobility to persons with visual impairments*. New York, NY: American Foundation for the Blind.

Jayant, C., Acuario, C., Johnson, W., Hollier, J., & Ladner, R. (2010,). V-braille: haptic braille perception using a touch-screen and vibration on mobile phones. In *Proceedings of the 12th international ACM SIGACCESS conference on Computers and accessibility* (pp. 295-296). ACM. doi:10.1145/1878803.1878878

Jia, D., Bhatti, A., Nahavandi, S., & Horan, B. (2013). Human performance measures for interactive haptic-audio-visual interfaces. *Haptics. IEEE Transactions on, 6*(1), 46–57. PMID:24808267

Johnsor, K. A., & Semwal, S. K. (2014). Shapes: A multi-sensory environment for the B/VI and hearing impaired community. In *Virtual and Augmented Assistive Technology (VAAT), 2014 2nd Workshop on* (pp. 1-6). IEEE.

Jones, M. G., Bokinsky, A., Tretter, T., & Negishi, A. (2005). A comparision of with haptic and visual modalities. *Haptics-e Electronic J. Haptics Res, 4*(0).

Kawai, Y., & Tomita, F. (1996). Interactive tactile display system: a support system for the visually disabled to recognize 3D objects. In *Proceedings of the second annual ACM conference on Assistive technologies* (pp. 45-50). ACM. doi:10.1145/228347.228356

Klatzky, R. L., Lederman, S. J., & Metzger, V. A. (1985). Identifying objects by touch: An expert system. *Perception & Psychophysics, 37*(4), 299–302. doi:10.3758/BF03211351 PMID:4034346

Kreitzberg, C. (1998). *The LUCID Design Framework (Logical User-Centered Interaction Design)*. Princeton, NJ: Cognetics Corporation.

Lahav, O., & Mioduser, D. (2004). Exploration of unknown spaces by people who are blind using a multi-sensory virtual environment. *Journal of Special Education Technology, 19*, 15–24.

Lahav, O., Schloerb, D. W., & Srinivasan, M. A. (2015). program integrating virtual environment to improve orientation and mobility skills for people who are blind. *Computers & Education*, *80*, 1–14. doi:10.1016/j.compedu.2014.08.003 PMID:25284952

Laycock, S. D., & Day, A. M. (2003). Recent developments and applications of haptic devices. *Computer Graphics Forum*, *22*(2), 117–132. doi:10.1111/1467-8659.00654

Laycock, S. D., & Day, A. M. (2007). A survey of haptic rendering techniques. *Computer Graphics Forum*, *26*(1), 50–65. doi:10.1111/j.1467-8659.2007.00945.x

Lazar, J., Feng, J. H., & Hochheiser, H. (2010). *Research methods in human-computer interaction*. John Wiley and Sons.

Lederman, S. J., & Klatzky, R. L. (2009). Haptic perception: A tutorial. *Attention, Perception & Psychophysics*, *71*(7), 1439–1459. doi:10.3758/APP.71.7.1439 PMID:19801605

Lim, K. L., Yeong, L. S., Seng, K. P., & Ang, L. (2015). Assistive Navigation Systems for the Visually Impaired. In M. Khosrow-Pour (Ed.), *Encyclopedia of Information Science and Technology* (3rd ed.; pp. 315–327). doi:10.4018/978-1-4666-5888-2.ch030

Lotery, A., Xu, X., Zlatava, G., & Loftus, J. (2007). Burden of illness, visual impairment and health resource utilisation of patients with neovascular age- related macular degeneration: Results from the UK cohort of a five-country cross-sectional study. *The British Journal of Ophthalmology*, *91*(10), 1303–1307. doi:10.1136/bjo.2007.116939 PMID:17504847

Macleod, M., Bowden, R., Bevan, N., & Curson, I. (1997). The MUSiC performance measurement method. *Behaviour & Information Technology*, *16*(4-5), 279–293. doi:10.1080/014492997119842

McLaughlin, M. L., Hespanha, J. P., & Sukhatme, G. S. (2002). *Touch in virtual environments*. Prentice Hall.

Mclellan, S., Muddimer, A., & Peres, S. C. (2012). The Effect of Experience on System Usability Scale Ratings. *Journal of Usability Studies*, *7*(2), 56–67.

Oehlert, G. (2000). *A First Course in Design and Analysis of Experiments*. New York: Freeman and Company.

Profita, H., Farrow, N., & Correll, N. (2015). Flutter: An Exploration of an Assistive Garment Using Distributed Sensing, Computation and Actuation. In *Proceedings of the Ninth International Conference on Tangible, Embedded, and Embodied Interaction* (pp. 359-362). ACM. doi:10.1145/2677199.2680586

Sánchez, J., de Borba Campos, M., Espinoza, M., & Merabet, L. B. (2014). Audio haptic videogaming for developing wayfinding skills in learners who are blind. In *Proceedings of the 19th international conference on Intelligent User Interfaces* (pp. 199-208). ACM. doi:10.1145/2557500.2557519

Seffah, A., Donyaee, M., Kline, R. B., & Padda, H. K. (2006). Usability measurement and metrics: A consolidated model. *Software Quality Journal*, *14*(2), 159–178. doi:10.1007/s11219-006-7600-8

SenseGraphics. (2014). *H3D API - Open Source Haptics*. Retrieved December 13, 2014 from http://www.h3dapi.org

Sjostrom, C. (2001). Designing haptic computer interfaces for blind people. In *Signal Processing and its Applications, Sixth International, Symposium on*. 2001 (Vol. 1, pp. 68-71). IEEE. doi:10.1109/IS-SPA.2001.949777

Sripathi, V., & Sandru, V. (2013). Effective Usability Testing–Knowledge of User Centered Design is a Key Requirement. *International Journal of Emerging Technology and Advanced Engineering*, *3*(1), 627–635.

Struiksma, M. E., Noordzij, M. L., & Postma, A. (2009). What is the link between language and spatial images? Behavioral and neural findings in blind and sighted individuals. *Acta Psychologica*, *132*(2), 145–156. doi:10.1016/j.actpsy.2009.04.002 PMID:19457462

User Focus. (2014). *User Focus*. Retrieved December 28, 2014 from http://www.userfocus.co.uk/consultancy/personas.html

Van Scoy, F., McLaughlin, D., & Fullmer, A. (2005). Auditory augmentation of haptic graphs: Developing a graphic tool for teaching precalculus skill to blind students. In *ICAD 05-Eleventh Meeting of the International Conference on Auditory Display*.

KEY TERMS AND DEFINITIONS

HBT: Haptic-Based Test.

HCI: Human Computer Interaction.

HRI: Human Robot Interaction.

Performance Testing: Testing hardware or software products by engaging human participants directly or indirectly in activities that involve the hardware or software product under various testing criteria or standards to achieve a set of pre-defined or unforeseen objectives or answer a set of research questions.

TVL: Total Variable Level.

UPIT: User Performance Indicator Tool.

UPITO: User Performance Indicator Tool Outcome.

User Haptic Experience: The experience created as a result of the user's engagement with or in the user performance haptic-based test.

User Performance Indicator: An aspect or feature of the user performance test and design, defined by the designer/tester that acts as a measure or criteria for assessing the user or test participant performance in the test.

User Performance Testing: The assessment of user's participation or engagement in a single test activity or a test comprising of several tasks/activities in line with defined test objectives, research questions and user performance indicators.

APPENDIX

Sample UPIT-Based Survey Questionnaires

Table 3. User-centered methods/ strategies

	Strongly Agree 5	Agree 4	Undecided 3	Disagree 2	Strongly Disagree 1	Comments
User capability-persona						
Test features and objectives						

Table 4. Usage-centered methods/ strategies

	Strongly Agree 5	Agree 4	Undecided 3	Disagree 2	Strongly Disagree 1	Comments
User capability-persona						
Test features and objectives						

Table 5. User-usage-centered methods/ strategies

	Strongly Agree 5	Agree 4	Undecided 3	Disagree 2	Strongly Disagree 1	Comments
User capability-persona						
Test features and objectives						

Chapter 13
Development of Ambient Assisted Living Products and Services:
The Role of International Classification of Functioning, Disability, and Health

Ana Isabel Martins
University of Aveiro, Portugal

Alexandra Queirós
University of Aveiro, Portugal

Nelson Pacheco Rocha
University of Aveiro, Portugal

ABSTRACT

Background: the involvement of the potential end users in the development processes is a relevant issue for the acceptance of Ambient Assisted Living (AAL) products and services. Objective: this study aimed to use the conceptual framework of the International Classification of Functioning, Disability and Health (ICF) to conceptualize instruments for the different phases of the AAL development processes. Methods: personas and scenarios were modified, considering the fundamental concepts of the ICF in order to highlight end user's functioning and health conditions, and an ICF based instrument for usability assessment was defined and validated. Results: the results of several observational studies suggest the adequacy of the ICF based instruments (personas and scenarios and usability assessment instrument). Conclusion: the present study indicates that the ICF based instruments can be useful tools for the development of Ambient Assisted Living products or services.

DOI: 10.4018/978-1-5225-1944-7.ch013

INTRODUCTION

The active ageing paradigm aims to contribute to the expectation of a healthy, autonomous and independent life with quality, as well as to a continuous participation in social, economic, cultural, civil or spiritual matters, as people get older, not forgetting those who are vulnerable, physically disabled or in need of care (World Health Organization, 1998; World Health Organization, 2002).

In this context, the technological solutions might have a key role in the promotion of human functioning and in the mitigation of disabilities, particularly those resulting from the natural ageing process. This perspective is evident in the development of Ambient Assisted Living (AAL) products and services (Calvaresi et al., 2016).

One obvious way to get knowledge about the potential end users of new AAL products and services is to involve them in the development process. Flynn and Jazi (1998) argue that the involvement of the end users is a complex approach and, in general, the level of communication between those that develop the technological solutions and those that might use them is very low, namely because developers and end users have different contexts and expectations. This is in opposition to the supposition that the end users' requirements can be fully understood at the beginning of any development process.

In fact, the end users may not even be aware of their needs or be able to express them. Additionally, the end users have difficulties to understand the solutions proposed by developers due to their unfamiliarity with development methods and other technical aspects (Flynn & Jazi, 1998). Another important issue is that the requirements and needs of the end users evolve over time as they acquire knowledge about what can be achieved with the technological solutions being proposed (Ståhlbröst, 2008).

AAL solutions, by their nature and complexity, require efficient development methods that should consider a broad range of aspects such as the personal characteristics of the end users, including their functioning capabilities.

There are several models to better represent and explain how human functioning and incapacity interact. In particular, the International Classification of Functioning, Disability and Health (ICF) is a key element because it presents a conceptual framework for functioning and disability with consolidated concepts and terminologies that allows a multidisciplinary approach centered on the individuals (World Health Organization, 2001).

Considering the current maturity of AAL products and services, many of the developments are still oriented to the technological perspective and not to the characteristics of end users, namely functioning capabilities (Queirós, Silva, Alvarelhão, Rocha, & Teixeira, 2015). The development processes of AAL products and services should have different phases, including the conceptual validation, prototype test and pilot test, which should be supported by adequate and consistent instruments (Teixeira et al., 2011). In addition, given that the AAL products and services aim to improve individual performance in carrying out daily activities as well as the participation in life situations, then AAL products and services are, according to the ICF perspective, environmental factors that influence the functioning of the individuals. Therefore, the authors argue that the ICF conceptual framework can be used to conceptualize instruments for the different phases of the AAL products and services development processes.

In this context, this chapter shows that ICF concepts can be used to support the definition of personas, scenarios, and usability assessment instruments intended to be used during the AAL products and services development processes. For that, several observational studies were conducted. In addition, this chapter also reports an observational study to show an integrated application of the proposed instruments at different phases of the development process of an AAL service supported in the TV Internet Protocol that aims to support remote monitoring of vital signs.

Background

AAL has emerged as an initiative of the European Union aimed at addressing the growing needs of the elderly population, which is one of the greatest concerns in terms of the sustainability of health and social care systems (AAL Association, 2010). The European Commission and several Member States have established, in July 2008, a joint program of research and development that aimed to promote AAL products and services as a possible answer to the challenges related to the population ageing (AAL Association, 2010).

AAL is related to digital environments with ubiquitous and no obstructive intelligence organized to support a wide range of products and aiming to extend the time that elderly people can remain active in their homes. Therefore, it represents a new generation of products and services that must meet several requirements, including (Avilés-López, Villanueva-Miranda, Garcia-Macias, & Palafox-Maestre, 2009):

- **Invisibility:** Embedded in clothing, appliances or furniture.
- **Mobility:** Ability to be transported by the end users.
- **Spontaneity:** Ability to establish communication between various nodes.
- **Heterogeneity:** Integration of different technologies.
- **Context Awareness:** Ability to interpret the actions of the end users and the conditions of the surrounding environment.
- **Proactivity:** Ability to infer actions according to the end users' behaviors.
- **Natural Interaction:** Multimodal interaction including, for instance, voice or gestures.
- **Adaptation:** Ability to react to unexpected situations that may occur.

The automation depends on intelligent mechanisms, the context awareness mechanisms, to adequately distinguish people, identify their needs and preferences, and recognize their surroundings. These mechanisms allow the prevention of specific situations, the location of people, the detection of activities or the monitoring of human behaviors and emotions (Queirós et al., 2015). Therefore, detecting, communicating and acting are crucial issues within the AAL paradigm, together with requirements related to ubiquity, transparency for the end users, reliability or scalability (van den Broek, Cavallo, & Wehrmann, 2010).

AAL products and services combine a wide range of sensors, including comfort sensors (e.g., sensors for measuring temperature, humidity, carbon dioxide or atmospheric pressure), safety sensors (e.g., sensors for detecting water flooding or fires), security sensors (e.g., anti-intrusion detectors or video surveillance devices), sensors that can provide information on the environment, human activity sensors (e.g., detecting presence of people), or vital signs sensors (e.g., alarms).

Based on the perception of the end users' activities and of the surrounding conditions, AAL products and services use actuators to change the environment (e.g., a smart bedroom in which the person lies down on the bed and the blinds close automatically). For the translation of the available sensory information on actions that benefit end users, AAL products and services present high-level reasoning and decision-making processes. Therefore, the technological AAL infrastructure, safeguarding the security and privacy of the end users, can help to decide which services should be provided and how they should be provided.

The document Ageing Well in the Information Society: An i2010 Initiative Action Plan on Information and Communication Technologies and Ageing (European Commission, 2007) identifies three areas where technological products and services can support elderly people, namely: ageing well at work, ageing well in the community and ageing well at home.

Ageing well at work or active ageing at work means staying active and productive as long as possible through accessible workplaces and technological services that compensate the deficits associated with ageing and allow flexibility in space and time. In turn, ageing well in the community means staying socially active and creative, using technological solutions to maintain social networks, to access to public and private services or, simply, to enjoy entertainment and leisure activities. Finally, ageing well at home means living with quality as long as possible and promotes the use of technological solutions to ensure autonomy (i.e., ability to control, cope with and make personal decisions on a day-to-day basis) and independence (i.e., the ability to perform functions related to daily living with no, any or little help from others) (World Health Organization, 2002).

In turn, the project Bridging Research in Ageing and ICT Development (BRAID) (BRAID, 2011), based on a comprehensive perspective of elderly people, proposed a slightly different model divided into four areas: independent living, health and care in life, occupation in life, and recreation in life (Camarinha-Matos, Rosas, Oliveira, & Ferrada, 2015).

According to this perspective, in addition to the contribution for ageing well at work, in the community and at home, the AAL products and services also have a great potential in terms of reorienting health systems (Botella Arbona, García Palacios, Baños Rivera, & Quero Castellano, 2009), currently organized around acute episodes of illness by enabling the development of a wide range of home care services to complement the services provided by formal and informal caregivers, including, for example, remote rehabilitation programs (Cruz et al., 2013) or provision of accurate and updated information to promote the efficiency and efficacy of care providing (e.g., monitoring or controlling vital signs). Concerning specific diseases, the literature reports several studies targeting neurological diseases, cardiovascular diseases, hypertension, stroke, diabetes, cancer, chronic obstructive pulmonary disease, musculoskeletal conditions, mental health conditions or blindness and visual impairment (Heath, 2008; Calvaresi et al., 2016).

AAL has several generic and specific challenges that difficult its implementation and generalization.

Nowadays, the use of AAL products and services by its end users (primary stakeholders) is limited. In fact, in terms of the potential end users, there are barriers that must be overcome, including general reluctance to use technology, lack of clear evidence about the real benefits of AAL products and services, or inability to select the appropriate technologies (Kleinberger, Becker, Ras, Holzinger, & Müller, 2007).

The main barriers related to the use of AAL technologies by elderly people are related to psychological factors, prejudices, habits and education. Often elderly people reject solutions which entail changes in their habits and lifestyle since they are not aware that these changes could represent an improvement of their quality of life (i.e., perception of their position in life within the context of the surrounding culture and value system) (World Health Organization, 2002). One way to overcome these problems is to promote awareness among the potential end users about the benefits that AAL products and services can provide.

AAL products and services must be in line with the organization of care providing, in order to promote adequate answers to the real needs of the end users and to optimize the available human resources (van den Broek et al., 2010). Thus, there are also challenges related to secondary AAL stakeholders (i.e., people or organizations in contact with end users, including caregivers, friends, neighbors, health care and social care organizations, or organizations that may benefit directly or indirectly from new services), such as incorrect perspective of the requirements and objectives of the products and services, lack of reference standards for technological developments, or low quality of communication networks in certain geographical regions (van den Broek et al., 2010).

The challenges related to AAL tertiary stakeholders (i.e., public and private institutions that contribute to the organization and payment of the services, such as social welfare systems or insurance companies) include the diversity of the existing health care and social care systems, the lack of visible value, the heterogeneity of the end users or the immaturity in terms of standards, certification and funding sources (van den Broek et al., 2010).

Finally, yet importantly, a transversal challenge is related to the development of appropriate methods and instruments to ensure the involvement of end users (Memon, Wagner, Pedersen, Beevi, & Hansen, 2014; Calvaresi et al., 2016). In fact, the specialists promoting new solutions are often responsible for the conceptualization, design and development of products and services, from a preliminary identification of end users' requirements, and are the ones that decide which features and services to integrate and how the end users will interact with them. Only at a later stage, when the prototypes are already developed, end users are involved in the evaluations, which means that the initial assumptions were not based on their needs, experiences or mental models (Martins, Queirós, Cerqueira, Rocha, & Teixeira, 2012).

The user-centered design (Bevan, Claridge, & Petrie, 2005) aims to overcome these difficulties and includes a set of structured procedures to be implemented from the early stages of the development processes and that focus on the characteristics, needs and requirements of the end users. This allows the potential end users to influence the development of the products and services, so that these can be used in an efficient way (e.g., optimization of the time required to perform a given task), do not require long learning effort (e.g., the operations may be learned by observation) or provide a high degree of satisfaction.

For the consolidation and communication of users' needs and requirements Cooper (2004) proposed the persona and scenario method. This method aims to facilitate the understanding of users' needs and requirements throughout the whole development process (Miaskiewicz & Kozar, 2011; Rönkkö, 2005).

Still in terms of the involvement of the end users, questionnaires and scales play an important role because they allow the collection of qualitative and quantitative data related to characteristics, thoughts, feelings, perceptions, behaviors or attitudes of the end users. Several questionnaires and scales have been used for the assessment of AAL products and services, because they allow the collection of large amounts of data with reduced costs. Examples include general purpose usability instruments such as the Post-Study System Usability Questionnaire (PSSUQ) (Lewis, 2002) and the System Usability Scale (SUS) (Bangor, Kortum, & Miller, 2008).

METHODS

In order to ensure the involvement of end users in the conceptualization, design and development of AAL products and services, there is the need for iterative development cycles, flexible enough to allow advances and retreats and that comprises various phases, including conceptual validation, prototype test and pilot test (Teixeira, et al., 2011). These phases are not isolated from each other, but complementary, and serve to guide the AAL products and services development processes.

AAL products and services aim to improve individual performance in carrying out activities and participating in daily life and society, which is in line with the ICF conceptual framework. Therefore, the authors argue that this framework can be used as an underlying conceptual model for the design, development and evaluation of AAL products and services (Queirós et al., 2014).

Thus, in methodological terms, several observational studies were implemented, namely to validate instruments consistent with the ICF conceptual framework and designed to the various phases of the iterative cycle of the AAL products and services development.

In particular, the personas and scenarios proposed by Cooper (2004) (the research baseline) were modified, considering the fundamental concepts of the ICF, in order to highlight end users' functioning and health conditions (Queirós et al, 2014).

In addition, the authors defined and validated the ICF based Usability Scale (ICF-US) that aims to provide the advantages of quantitative and qualitative methods of usability assessment in a single instrument and, simultaneously, to introduce a terminology that is coherent with the ICF conceptual framework.

The next sections present the instruments that were developed in accordance with the ICF conceptual framework (i.e., personas, scenarios and ICF-US), and show their application through an observational study that included the conceptual validation and the prototype test of an AAL service.

Although the data collected in the performed observational studies do not have a sensitive nature, the authors considered the principles of the Helsinki Declaration (World Medical Association, 2013). Therefore, all the necessary authorizations have been requested, all collected data were anonymized and all participants signed informed consents that were part of the experimental protocol.

INSTRUMENTS

A formal terminology able to characterize the human functioning is a major challenge, namely because there is still a conceptual ambiguity in the field, which is evident by the multiplicity of concepts and terms (Stucki, Reinhardt, Grimby, & Melvin, 2008).

The functioning decline is a common problem for elderly people and is associated with changes related to age, health status or social factors (Stucki et al., 2008). When the decline is very significant, there is a decrease in the functioning reserve, turning the elderly people more vulnerable to chronic diseases, which affect their autonomy and independence and, therefore, their quality of life (Stucki et al., 2008).

The ICF (World Health Organization, 2001), approved at the 54th World Health Assembly in 2001, attempts to provide a coherent view of health and health related status (Jette, 2006). The title reflects the priority given to functioning as a health component and less to the consequences of the diseases.

ICF does not classify people, but rather interprets their characteristics, namely, body structures and functions (including psychological functions), activities, participation, and contextual factors, both personal factors and environmental factors (i.e., the personal characteristics and the influences of the environment), which allows the description of the respective functioning capabilities. Thus, the ICF conceptual framework emphasizes less the individual as a disabled person, even if temporary, and more the factors that favor or hinder the execution of activities or the participation. On the other hand, the adopted nomenclature promotes a positive view of body functions, activities and participation (World Health Organization, 2001; Nordenfelt, 2003).

In this multidimensional view the personal and environmental factors (i.e., the physical or social world environment, including technological services such as those associated with AAL) are as important as the functions and structures of the body (Jette, 2006).

Additionally, different environments may have a different impact on people with the same health condition. An environment with or without barriers can limit or facilitate the individual performance (World Health Organization, 2001). Since the functioning of an individual is considered as a result of a dynamic interaction between health conditions and contextual factors (Federici, Meloni, & Presti, 2009), then the environment in which people live and conduct their lives can be enhanced by the existence of products and services that meet the individual characteristics. Consequently, since AAL products and services aim at changing the environment in a non-intrusive manner to improve individual performance, they may be considered environmental factors, according to the ICF conceptual framework.

Taking into account the importance of human functioning for the AAL products and services, the authors have been developing research efforts to take advantage of the conceptual richness of ICF for creating instruments able to support the AAL products and services development processes, including personas, scenarios and usability assessment instruments.

Personas and Scenarios

The data collected using techniques such as preliminary questionnaires, diary studies or brainstorming are the basis for the definition of personas and scenarios. Due to the complexity of AAL products and services, personas and scenarios are important tools to support the definition of the users' requirements as well as the functional requirements. To define personas and scenarios is crucial to consider sociodemographic data, health conditions, safety issues, basic and instrumental activities of daily living, recreational activities and hobbies, social participation, social activities, services being used, or types of access and attitudes related to the technology acceptance (Queirós et al., 2014).

According to the ICF, such information can be subdivided into different components, including tasks or actions being performed (i.e., activities), involvement in daily life and social situations (i.e., participation), personal characteristics (i.e., personal factors), physical, social and attitudinal environment (i.e., environmental factors), which have an impact on daily routines.

To illustrate the application of the ICF concepts in the definition of personas, Table 1 shows the persona Maria Kovács that was defined according to the principles proposed by the authors.

Thus, instead of a heterogeneous description of personal history, the authors propose a clear distinction between personal factors and daily routines, as this information is considered essential in the context of the development processes of AAL products and services. Furthermore, considering the importance of the health conditions (Queirós, Carvalho, Pavão, & Rocha, 2013; Queirós et al., 2014), it should be noted that, according the ICF conceptual framework, health conditions should not be understood as diseases, but as a set of characteristics that constrain or facilitate the use of a specific product or service.

On the other hand, the neutral perspective associated with ICF should be adopted for the description of the life story (the description should only include facts that determine functioning or performance). For example, instead of referring 'as she was not feeling complete with her job as a history professor, she decided to get a new job as a freelance editor/proofreader of history books' it is preferable to refer 'recently she started a part-time job as a freelance editor/proofreader of history books' (i.e., only neutral information). Following this perspective, the descriptions of the personas should not include references to frustrations, but only references to capabilities and personal factors.

Table 1. Example of a persona in accordance with the ICF conceptual framework

Persona: Primary Name: Mária Kovács **[Personal Factor]**. Age: 68 years **[Personal Factor]**. Mária lives in Győr, with her husband, Zoltán Kovács **[Personal factor]**. They have been married for 40 years and have two adult children (her daughter is a PhD student and his son works in Vienna). Mária is a history professor and has basic computers skills **[Personal factor]**. Her husband is an engineer and helps her with the computer. Recently she started a part-time job as a freelance editor/proofreader of history books. Her husband is about to retire. She speaks French and her husband speak German **[Personal factor]**. She has a visual impairment **[Health condition]**, as she wears glasses for reading and work **[Environmental factor]**. Usually she wakes up early and take care of the vegetables in the farm near her house **[Daily routine]**. Mária likes to cook for the whole family and recently discovered Italian food and loves to try new recipes. She regularly has dinner with her husband and together they search the internet for cultural programs around **[Type of activity]**. Occasionally, they participate in cultural events. She enjoys the theater and classical music, but her husband prefers jazz **[Type of participation]**. During the weekends they visit their daughter and grandchildren **[Daily routine]**. At least 2 or 3 times a year they travel to spas and visit their relatives in Vienna every 2 or 3 months **[Type of participation]**.

In turn, a scenario is a narrative of events or situations experienced by the personas. The emphasis should be given to activities and tasks that are performed at these events (Rosson & Carroll, 2009). Scenarios should identify the current situation, situations or events that influence the activities of the personas (i.e., problem identification), information units that the system needs to incorporate (i.e., data requirements), actions that the system must be able to perform (i.e., functional requirements), details of the interaction management mechanisms (i.e., interaction requirements) and other requirements (e.g., business, corporate, or customers' requirements).

Table 2 shows an example of a scenario for the persona Mária Kovács according to the perspective of the authors.

The identification of the scenario problems is an important issue, because it contextualizes the activity to be performed. For example, the persona Mária makes notes on paper to discuss with her husband and then transcribes them into a word sheet. If she had an easy-to-use device to introduce her notes that was also collaborative, she could share it with her husband and easily send it without having to transcribe the whole document. Another problem identified was the tiring trips. An intelligent and easy to use GPS device would help them to enjoy their travels without feeling lost and worried about the routes.

Table 2. Example of a scenario in accordance with the ICF conceptual framework

Scenario for the Persona Mária Kovács Mária usually receives the material to be reviewed by e-mail. During the review, she makes notes on paper and read them to discuss with Zoltán **[Problem identification]**. She makes revisions on her personal computer using a traditional word processor (Ofiice Word) and sends the revised copy back via e-mail **[Functional requirement]**. Since she discovered the Italian food she is always looking for new recipes on websites and online forums. Her favorite recipes include specific ingredients, including vegetables, and this is the main reason why she plants their own products. The grown vegetables are not typical of Hungary due to different climates. So to produce them, they must be protected from rain in some periods and in winter need a lot of light and must be protected from frost **[Problem identification]**. When she wakes up, Mária likes to be informed about the headlines of the day, and weather forecasts **[Data Requirement]**. Usually she hears it on the radio and sometimes sees on TV. The Kovács couple regularly visits the grandchildren in Vienna. This is a tiring journey for them, although the trip takes only 3 hours from their home to the destination. The main reason for the trip to be so tiring is because they use a paper map, and often have problems due to routes that are temporarily unavailable **[Problem identification]**. Mária read the map and gives directions to Zoltán **[Problem identification]**. As they only travel a few times a year, they do not have GPS and because they think that it can distract the drivers' attention when looking at the monitor and they feel that the voice information is not sufficient **[Requirement of interaction]**.

ICF Based Usability Scale

The ICF-US, developed by the authors, is a usability assessment instrument that is divided into two components:

- ICF-US I, a scale to conduct a generic usability assessment.
- ICF-US II, a questionnaire to classify the components of specific prototypes as barriers or facilitators, identifying their strengths and weaknesses in terms of usability.

The construction of the ICF-US I was based on a review of the literature and on the opinion of a group of usability experts. The resulting 10 item scale is presented in Table 3 (Martins, Rosa, Queirós, Silva, & Rocha, 2015).

The ICF qualifiers for environmental factors were used for the answer key. However, taking into account that the evaluation of each item should be positive or negative, the neutral qualifier was removed. The group of usability experts involved in the development of this scale agreed that a range from -3 (barrier) to 3 (facilitator) would be the most appropriate, making possible the identification of small, medium and large barriers or facilitators (see Table 4) instead of a range from -4 to 4 (i.e., the one proposed by ICF).

Thus, when using ICF-US I all items should be classified from -3 to 3, being the value 3 the most positive one and the value -3 the less positive. If a participant does not respond to an item or classify it as 'Not Applicable', then the average value of the remaining items is assigned to this item, rounded to the nearest unity. The final score of the ICF-US I is calculated by adding the scores of all the items and ranges between -30 and 30.

An observational study was set-up for the validation of the two components of the ICF-US. This study had a sample of 32 participants with an average age of 47 years (SD = 14.6), and aimed to evaluate the usability of a web application, especially developed for that experiment (Martins et al., 2015). Usability

Table 3. Items of the ICF-US I

How would you rate the application regarding:
1. The ease of use. 2. The satisfaction with its use. 3. The learning easiness. 4. The achievement of expected results. 5. The similarity in the operation mode in the different tasks. 6. The possibility to interact in various ways. 7. The understanding of the messages presented. 8. The application responses to your actions. 9. The knowledge of what was happening in the application during the utilization. 10. **Overall, I consider that the application was...**

Table 4. ICF-US answer key

Barrier			Facilitator		
Large	Medium	Small	Small	Medium	Large
-3	-2	-1	1	2	3

was evaluated with the ICF-US I, PSSUQ and SUS, along with a general usability question. Additionally, ICF-US II was applied, together with the registration of critical incidents, including the number of tasks successfully executed and the number of tasks executed with errors.

The value of the Intraclass Correlation Coefficient (ICC) of the ICF-US I was 0.46 indicating a satisfactory reliability between evaluators (ICC 95% - 0.10; 0.71). The correlation between the ICF-US I and PSSUQ and SUS was evaluated by the Spearman correlation coefficient indicating a high negative correlation between the ICF-US I and PSSUQ (r = -0.84) and a high positive correlation between the ICF-US I and the general usability question (r = 0.84). Additionally, the ICF-US I and SUS had a lower correlation (r = 0.68). The results suggest acceptable values of reliability and validity for the ICF-US I indicating that this scale can be a useful tool for the usability assessment.

The ICF-US I, as other generic usability scales, allows the assignment of a total score for a product or service, but does not favor the detection of its weakness (which should be corrected and improved) or its strengths (which should be recorded and replicated).

In turn, the ICF-US II was designed to complement the information gathered with the ICF US I and aims to collect suggestions for improvements in terms of usability, or suggestions for the overall improvement of the product or service.

The instantiation of the ICF-US II is made from items that identify the different components of a prototype (e.g., sound, image or tactile interface). Each item is then classified as a barrier or facilitator. Whenever an item is classified as a barrier, the participant must identify the feature that is causing this classification (i.e., open registration). For example, a specific sound can be classified as a barrier due to high volume, inaudibility, or any other reason.

This procedure should be performed for all identified components. Thus, it is possible to list the components of the prototype that should be improved. Figure 1 shows an example of an item from the ICF-US II that evaluates a component associated with the status of a remote session.

Figure 1. Items from an instantiation of the ICF-US II to evaluate a component associated with the status of a remote session

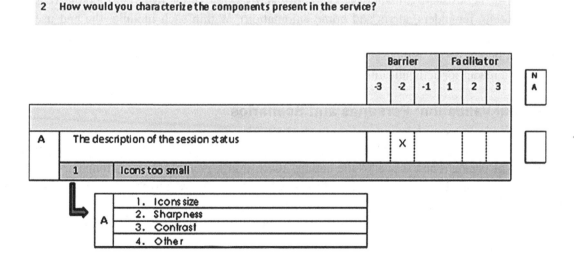

The cutoff point set to decide if ICF-US II should be applied is a score lower than 10 on the ICF-US I. That is, whenever a product or service is considered small facilitator or barrier, the ICF-US II should be applied in order to understand the impact of the various components in terms of usability and to identify the ones that act as barriers.

The adequacy of the ICF-US II was evaluated in the same observational study that was set-up to validate the ICF-US I. The results of the ICF-US II were compared with the critical incidents that were recorded, including the number of tasks successfully executed and the number of tasks executed with errors.

The concordance between ICF-US II and the critical incident records was 96.4%, which is a highly significant result. In fact, when there were critical incidents for a specific component, the results of the ICF-US II also considered it as a barrier. Furthermore, the ICF-US II showed a strong negative correlation with the tasks executed with errors (-0.78) and a positive correlation with the number of tasks performed with success (0.78).

The validations that were conducted for the two components of the ICF-US (ICF-US I and ICF-US II) seem to indicate that this instrument is a good measure to discriminate between facilitators and barriers, clearly identifying the aspects to improve during the prototype evaluation.

RESULTS

The instruments presented in the previous section were used to develop an AAL service supported on the TV Internet Protocol, the aal@meo.

The aal@meo service was developed considering the concept of interactive digital television, in which the end users have a TV set and the remote control as core components of the interaction. The aal@meo aims to support remote monitoring of vital signs (e.g., weight, blood pressure or heart rate). Furthermore, it also allows the scheduling of reminders (e.g., medication or appointments), the presentation of alerts (e.g., personal alert or about the house) and the controlling of home automation equipment via a TV set connected to a Set Top Box of a TV cable commercial service.

The aal@meo consists of a main dashboard with an overview of the different modules (e.g., vital signs monitoring, reminders, alerts and home automation). Within each module, the end users can navigate using the vertical and horizontal menus that can be activated by the navigation buttons and the confirmation button on the remote control. The end users also interact with other peripheral devices, such as a card reader for authentication purposes or measurement devices.

Conceptual Validation: Personas and Scenarios

Personas and scenarios were used for conceptual validation of the aal@meo service. To support the construction of personas and scenarios the authors used several preliminary questionnaires aiming to collect information about the overall profile of the target end users in order to characterize their expectations about the proposed service.

Table 5 presents a short version of one of the personas developed during the conceptual validation of aal@meo.

The scenario corresponding to the persona Diana Soares is presented in Table 6.

Table 5. Persona created for the aal@meo

Persona: Primary.
Name: Diana Soares [**Personal factor**].
Age: 66 years [**Personal factor**].
Diana Soares is a widow and lives alone in Aveiro [**Personal factor**]. She has two daughters and one son: the eldest daughter is a family doctor in Algarve and lives with her husband and three children; the youngest daughter finished her Communication Technologies degree and emigrated to London, where she lives with her husband; the other son owns a restaurant in Aveiro [**Personal factor**].
She lives in an apartment in the city center for more than 30 years, on the 2nd floor without elevator. She has a cat that is her joy and company called Pantufa [**Environmental factor**].
Diana was a seamstress. Her expertise in the use of technologies is very basic [**Personal factor**].
For her birthday her sons decided to give her a new phone. Whenever she needs help, she asks her son that visits her daily [**Personal factor**].
She has hypertension, which is controlled by regular medication. She also has celiac disease, which is controlled through a balanced gluten free diet [**Health condition**]. Her doctor recommended daily walks and regular swimming activities [**Type of activity**].
Usually she wakes up early and goes to the market to buy the meat and vegetables needed for her diet [**Daily routine**]. After lunch she goes out for a walk and normally stops in the pharmacy of Mr. Alves, her neighbour, to control the hypertension and, whenever necessary, take some advice related to celiac disease [**Daily routine**].
On Sundays, her son, daughter-in-law and two grandchildren have lunch at her house [**Daily routine**].

Table 6. Scenario created for the aal@meo

Scenario for the persona Diana Soares
While Diana was out for a walk, she fell and broke her arm [**Requirement of interaction**]. Since that day she doesn't cook anymore and have all meals in her sons' restaurant. This concerns the eldest daughter because Diana must have a disciplined diet: low salt and gluten free. In her brother restaurant it is not always possible to control all dishes and Diana doesn't always check all the food she eats [**Problem identification**].
Her sons are also concerned that since Diana fell, she no longer walks so often, because she has fear of falling again. Diana does not recognize this fact, and her sons just realized the situation because Mr. Alves alerted them that their mother no longer goes to the pharmacy to measure blood pressure [**Problem identification**].
Diana watches TV every day and does not miss an episode of her favourite TV show. As the commercial breaks take so long and Diana no longer monitors her blood pressure, her son installed a mobile application to enter the data resulting from the portable measurement device. But Diana did not get along with the application on the phone. The icons were very small [**Interaction requirement**] and had too much information to fill [**functional requirement**].
Lately Diana has felt angry and is thinner, she thinks that it may be due to the lack of gluten-free diet control. She misses the advices of her neighbour and pharmacist, Mr. Alves. She decided to call him to clarify some doubts [**Problem identification**]. She would like to find a way to get information without having to bother Mr. Alves. Her son taught her how to search for information on the phone, but the screen is too small [**Interaction requirement**]. Moreover, the way to get the results is very difficult. She would like to have the information she needs without having to search [**Data requirement**].

Prototype Test: ICF-US

In the prototype test, the authors were interested in verifying the general usability of the aal@meo. The aal@meo prototype had been submitted to small evaluations, particularly in terms of system performance. Therefore, in this context, the authors wanted to evaluate the prototype as a whole in a controlled environment and check if it was ready to be used in a real context or, in the opposite, if there were aspects that still needed to be improved.

Therefore, a test case based on the characteristics of the personas and scenarios defined during the conceptual validation was designed. In experimental terms, for each participant it was performed the registration of the success/failure and the number of errors on the executed tasks, and applied the ICF-US I and ICF-US II.

The sample consisted of 11 members of a charity institution with an average age of 60 years (SD = 3.8), and a maximum age of 68 years and a minimum of 56 years.

According to ICF-US I, the aal@meo was a facilitator for 4 participants and a barrier for 7 participants. The mean scores of all participants was -5, in a range from -30 to 30 (SD = 15.29), which indicates that in general the application was a small barrier. The participant with the highest score had the value 21, and the participant with the lowest score had the value -24.

Examining the ICF-US I items individually it was important to classify them as barriers or facilitators. The barriers, in order of severity, were:

- The similarity of the operation mode in the different tasks (-1.55).
- The achievement of expected results (-1.45).
- The ease of use (-1.45).
- Overall, I consider that the application was... (-1.18).
- The learning easiness (-1.09).
- The knowledge of what was happening in the application during the utilization (-0.73).

In turn, the facilitators were:

- The application responses to your actions (1.91).
- The satisfaction with its use (0.45).
- The understanding of the messages presented (0.37).

The item 'the possibility to interact in various ways' was considered not applicable since there was only one-way of interaction with the service (via remote control).

By analyzing the items identified as barriers, it is possible to verify that most participants had difficulty with tasks related to the interaction with the remote control. In turn, considering the items identified as facilitators, it is possible to verify that most of the participants easily understood the information included in the dashboard.

In what concerns to the application of ICF-US II, in a range from -3 to 3, it was found that:

- The mean value for the evaluation of the aal@meo components was -0.30 (SD = 1.46).
- The mean value of the detailed usability evaluation was 0.27 (SD = 1.11).
- The mean value for the overall usability of the application was -1.27 (SD = 2.05).

The barriers detected with the ICF-US II, in order of severity, were:

- The icons/symbols/graphics (-2.72).
- The confirmation of measurements (-1.90).
- The evolution charts related to vital signs (-1.73).
- The horizontal navigation menu (-1.55).
- The navigation using the remote control (-1.27).
- The progress of the session (-1.27).
- The interpretation of the functions of the service (-1.09).
- The navigation on the vertical menu (-0.27).

In turn, the facilitators were:

- The colors of the menus (2.64).
- The contrast between the background and the information (2.55).
- The size and type of the character font (2.36).
- The entry into the system with the ID card (1.91).
- The information related to the alert menu (0.64).
- The information related to the monitoring menu (0.55).

Considering the items identified as a barrier, most participants had difficulty in tasks related to the confirmation of the measurements, the understanding of the charts representing the vital signs, the navigation on vertical and horizontal menus, the interaction with the remote control and the interpretation of the service functions. In turn, regarding the items identified as facilitators, the participants easily understood the information on the alert and monitoring menus, were able to authenticate themselves, and have positive opinions in respect of the colors of the menus, the contrast between the background and the information, and the size and type of the character font.

In terms of performance, the most problematic tasks, with a larger number of participants with a high error rate, were the navigation tasks (i.e., horizontal and vertical menu and confirmation button) followed by other tasks where participants had difficulty understanding the session unfold. These results are correlate with the results of the ICF-US II.

Consequently, with the prototype test it was possible to identify a number of aspects, which had to be improved before aal@meo service could be used by a larger group of users.

Discussion

The inclusion of personal factors in the definition of personas can influence the way the interaction with products and services is perceived. For example, if a persona has basic computer skills it can be assumed that, presumably, the persona would be able to interact successfully with applications with some degree of complexity. The same is not true for a persona with no experience with electronic devices and, consequently, the interaction mechanisms should be simplified.

Daily routines are also important elements in the definition of personas as they may restrict the use of available products and services. For example, if a persona has the habit of talking on the phone with her family while preparing meals, this routine will necessarily influence the way she uses the phone, and there is the need to have a hands free device to be used while she is cooking.

The information related to health conditions is relevant since they affect the performance of activities and participation. For example, if a persona with hypertension and diabetes needs to maintain a balanced diet and regular physical exercises, then her daily routines and the execution of specific activities are influenced by her health conditions (e.g., trekking).

In terms of scenarios, the identification of problems is an important issue because it contextualizes the functions that the AAL product or service should provide. For example, a persona who likes to keep in touch with her relatives using the phone can change her own routine if she realizes that the use of facebook is more economical, although it may contain too much information. In this example, in association with the identification of problems it can also be identified interaction requirements, particularly in terms of usability. One possible solution would be to use a filter application to block ads, offers or games of the facebook, or configure its settings to select only the information that the specific end user would consider most relevant.

There are also other important requirements such as, for example, data requirements (e.g., the interest in receiving updated information about the weather conditions or about the side effects of a particular medication).

The advantage of the ICF based approach followed by the authors in the study reported by this chapter is related to the fact that it is possible to make a clear distinction between the different aspects that are essential in the development of AAL products and services, such as personal factors, types of activities, daily routines or participation. In particular, the concept participation emerges as an innovation in the development of personas since, according to an informational point of view, it is richer than the concept activity when used alone.

In addition, the proposed solution also allows the clarification of how health conditions and surrounding context interfere with the individuals' performance in carrying out daily routines and participation, by using terminology with a neutral perspective (i.e., as proposed in ICF) avoiding, the emphasis of negative connotations.

In turn, the ICF based instrument used for the aal@meo prototype test allowed to conduct a multifaceted usability assessment. The ICF-US I allows a generic usability evaluation because it assigns a total score that reflects the quality of the interaction mechanisms with the end users. In addition, the ICF-US II evaluates the strengths and weaknesses of the AAL product or service, classifying its components as barriers or facilitators. This is an important benefit in relation to general usability assessment scales, which assign a score but do not identify or classify the barriers that must be revised in order to improve the prototype. Therefore, ICF-US II can be a fundamental element of methodological approaches promoting cyclical evaluations for the continuous improvement of AAL products and services.

It should also be noted that the data collected to validate the ICF-US II, in terms of critical incident records, are in agreement with the barriers identified by the instrument itself. Also in the evaluation of the aal@meo prototype, the performance evaluation indicated similar problems to those identified by the ICF-US II, namely difficulties related to the navigation through menus, the interaction with the remote control and the interpretation of the aal@meo functions.

The fact that ICF-US II presented an agreement with the performance evaluation and critical incident records seems to indicate that ICF-US II enables a qualitative assessment, without any loss of information, when compared with the use of techniques such as performance evaluation or critical incident records.

Thus, the experimental results seem to indicate that the application of ICF-US I can be enriched if it is complemented with the ICF-US II. The ICF-US II allows the addition of qualitative information about the positive aspects (i.e., facilitators) and the negative aspects that have to be improved (i.e., barriers) to the quantitative information related to the ICF-US I.

SOLUTIONS AND RECOMMENDATIONS

As people age their quality of life is largely determined by their ability to maintain autonomy and independence (World Health Organization, 2002). The technology cannot completely supply all the needs of elderly people, but can mitigate their dependency by means of specialized solutions. This is in line with international public health directives, which highlight the need to empower the citizens on matters concerning their health conditions through the promotion of self-care (van den Broek et al., 2008).

AAL has a huge potential in terms of innovative solutions that might mitigate, in political, economic and social terms, the consequences of the contemporary demographic ageing (Queirós et al., 2015).

AAL aims to combine conventional services provision together with intelligent applications to increase the efficiency and productivity of the available resources and to extend the time people can live in their preferred environment by promoting their autonomy and independence, maintaining, or even increasing, their confidence in their domestic spaces and their general wellbeing (Calvaresi et al., 2016).

In order to guarantee that AAL products and services meet the expectations of potential users, usability should be considered as one of their major quality attributes, mainly because end users (i.e., including elderly people, patients and people with disabilities or specific health deficiencies) should not need to have technical expertise in handling the different products, services or supporting infrastructural components (Memon et al., 2014).

Elderly people have much to gain from bringing technology into their daily lives. The extent to which this is possible strongly depends on the careful design of accessible and easy-to-use products or services. This means that AAL products and services should be systematically designed based on the end users' needs and requirements, with user-centered and participatory development methods, including fast prototyping and interactive feedback, able to support iterative cycles of development and assessment (Memon et al., 2014).

However, the literature reports that most systems are tailored on specific solutions and their developers try to adapt or optimize existing technologies to what they perceive as the end users' needs and requirements, instead of looking at the users' needs and proposing ways to solve them (Queirós et al., 2015; Calvaresi et al., 2016). Moreover, although aiming at the wellbeing of elderly people, requirements analysis of AAL products and services should also consider a broad range of other users, including relatives, informal caregivers, social workers and health professionals.

Therefore, the technological developers must understand all the situations and the needs of the stakeholders of the AAL ecosystem (Calvaresi et al., 2016). First of all, they should take several viewpoints, from the end users and their relatives to formal caregivers. Secondly, they need to carefully consider different motivations and conflicting interests. Moreover, the design and development teams need to be able to fully communicate their knowledge and ideas, and consolidate the different team viewpoints towards the best possible outcome.

In this context, the authors argue that personas and scenarios are powerful tools that can contribute to evidence and to systematize the needs and requirements not only related to the end users but also related to the relatives and professionals that support them. Moreover, the use of personas and scenarios together with iterative short development cycles, encompassing the definition of the requirements, design, prototyping and respective assessment by the target users (e.g., using instruments such as the ICF-US) to provide feedback for further improvements in the subsequent development cycles, should be considered to promote the development of accessible and easy-to-use AAL products and services.

A significant percentage of AAL products and services intend to address the needs of elderly people considering their respective major diseases, such as neurological diseases, cardiovascular diseases, diabetes or musculoskeletal conditions (Heath, 2008; Calvaresi et al., 2016). Furthermore, the ageing process is inevitably associated with comorbidities, which mean there is the need to cope with more than one disease at a time.

In this respect, providing care services at the home of the individual, together with intelligent applications, requires a multifunctional network around the individual, including caregivers and care organizations. Therefore, the definition of what technological services should be implemented and how they should be integrated within the existing ecosystem for the care providing requires the participation of a broad range of non-technological professionals, including healthcare professionals. However, in a significant percentage of developed applications, care providers or care organizations were not involved in the design process nor in the assessment of the functions provided by the applications or the information that should be delivered (Rosser & Eccleston, 2011).

Therefore, ideas with a high potential fail to scale due to the adopted approach (i.e., technology centered approach), without considering the adequate clinical and organizational context or not finding a sustainable business approach for wider deployment (Camarinha-Matos et al., 2015).

To surpass these difficulties, the research teams should include not only technological professionals, but other professionals, such as health care or social care professionals able to actively involve all the stakeholders, including potential end users, in all the stages of the AAL products and services development processes. Moreover, conceptual models related to the application domains, such as the ICF conceptual framework, should be considered.

The state of the art of AAL products and services includes medical devices (Memon et al., 2014). These are required for chronic disease management applications, namely self-management (e.g., self-management of the chronic obstructive pulmonary disease) (Marshall, Medvedev, & Antonov, 2008), expert feedback to patients (e.g., helping diabetic patients by calculating the dose of insulin based on carbohydrate intake, pre-meal blood glucose, and anticipated physical activity reported) (Charpentier et al., 2011), support to rehabilitation programs (e.g., real-time remote monitoring of the heart rate during rehabilitation exercises), measurement of physical activity level (Bexelius et al., 2010), or integration of data from wearable health sensors (Boulos, Brewer, Karimkhani, Buller, & Dellavalle, 2014).

The obligation of an appliance or application being classified as a medical device depends on its functions and the corresponding level of patient risks. For instance, a device able to measure heart rate as a fitness tool is not a medical device, but it is definitely a medical device if the resulting information is sent to a health care professional (US Food and Drug Administration, 2013).

Worldwide, a wide range of organisms, including the United States Food and Drug Administration and the European Medicines Agency, have the mission to safeguard the interests of the citizens by establishing standards for the development, manufacture and marketing of medical devices. Medical devices are divided into risk classes catering to different criteria, namely, the intended purpose, potential risks arising either from its technical conception and in its manufacturing methods, duration of contact with the human body (i.e., temporary, short or long period), invasiveness of the human body (i.e., invasive, invasive of bodily orifices, surgically invasive, implantable and implantable absorbable) or the anatomy affected by the use of the device.

Despite all the regulations, it is perhaps surprising that the literature reports that relatively little research has been undertaken so far in order to clinically validate new health care devices (Mosa, Yoo, & Sheets, 2012; Rosser & Eccleston, 2011). A great number of applications are subject to very little or absolutely no regulatory oversight, with a small percentage of articles reporting evaluations or trials. However, AAL health solutions deal with sensitive health-related aspects of a persons' life and this should put strong demands in the development of these technologies. Consequently, it is necessary to consider the risks associated with AAL products and services, including the possibility of the individuals being misled. This is reinforced by the fact that, often, the potential end users are fragile and vulnerable individuals, or their families, desperately seeking solutions to acute problems. Thus, even for AAL products and services that appear to be extremely useful, there should be a concern for their efficacy and efficiency, or for possible adverse effects when being used.

These difficulties give strength to the already mentioned recommendation to complement the competencies of technological professionals with the competencies of health care or social care professionals and to complement technological models with conceptual models related to the application domains, such as the ICF conceptual framework.

Although the AAL products and services can optimize therapeutic treatments, or in some situations can be part of a therapeutic treatment (e.g., a specific system to provide remote physical rehabilitation), it is quite clear that they do not substitute any form of treatment that should be administered to treat or cure a disease, a physical disorder or an injury. Moreover, although AAL products and services can contribute to support caregivers, families and care organizations and can increase the efficiency and productivity of available resources in the ageing societies (Calvaresi et al., 2016), its main contribution is related to human functioning, namely by extending the time people can live in their preferred environment, increasing their autonomy and independence, promoting a better and healthier lifestyle for individuals at risk, enhancing security, preventing social isolation and maintaining multifunctional supporting networks.

Within the existing models to represent and explain the human functioning, the ICF presents a conceptual framework with consolidated concepts and terminologies that allows a multidisciplinary approach with multiple dimensions, namely structures and body functions, activities and participation and environmental factors, that include: the physical dimension that is related to motor performance (e.g., functional activities related to movement, such as running, walking, moving or using objects) or daily life activities; mental dimension that is related to sensory and cognitive performance (e.g., communication, understanding, learning and cognitive skills like orientation, attention, memory or concentration); the emotional dimension that is related to the psychosocial components and establishes an association between the psychological aspect and the experience of the individuals in their environment (e.g., emotional states, feelings, behaviors, identity or self-concept); the social dimension (e.g., social interactions, roles that the individuals play in their social contexts, cultural influences, lifestyles or social and economic resources); and the dimension related to the environment that surrounds the individuals.

ICF presents a comprehensive conceptual framework that helps to understand how to maintain health conditions and functioning capabilities of the individuals from simple actions required to daily life activities to less tangible values related to participation, such as social, religious, civic and political participation. Therefore, its concepts should be considered when evaluating the impact of AAL products and services.

Considering that the ICF conceptual framework is accepted within the healthcare domain, the use of its concepts and terminologies to promote multidisciplinary approaches for AAL products and services development processes can help to overcome difficulties of communication between users, careers and technological developers. The different stakeholders with different backgrounds need a common language in order to make the teamwork more efficient and effective. Therefore, the authors recommend that more studies should be designed to promote the suitability of the ICF as a conceptual framework for the AAL products and services development processes, as it was done in the study reported by this chapter.

FUTURE RESEARCH DIRECTIONS

Regarding the interaction of individuals with the AAL products and services, usability is just one of many aspects to take into account. In particular, we need to consider the user experience, which is a broader concept than usability itself, goes beyond efficiency, quality of tasks and user satisfaction, and considers the cognitive, affective, social and physical aspects of interaction. On the other hand, the usability is measured at the time of interaction, while the user experience is measured by anticipating usage and/or reflecting about the post-use (International Standards Organization, 2010).

In the study reported by this chapter, the research was addressed to usability; nevertheless, the ultimate goal is to develop a set of instruments to cover a range of aspects that are fundamental for a positive user experience.

Despite a high level of technological innovation and implementation, and promising early results, the AAL products and services must evolve from prototypes assessments (i.e., proof-of-concept) to large scale field trials. These are essential to collect robust evidence supported on statistical significance to show that the new developments are able to make a difference and are cost-effective.

Large scale field trials require multidisciplinary collaboration between developers and all the others AAL products and services stakeholders, and present several methodological challenges. The involvement of elderly and disabled people is not straightforward in a laboratory context, but to monitor and interact with elderly and disabled people in their home environments require to solve additional organizational challenges.

Furthermore, high-quality scientific evidence requires efficient instruments to determine the impact and to assess the significance of AAL products and services when they are introduced into the day-to-day routine of real end users. Therefore, to explore the ICF conceptual framework to develop assessment instruments for large field trials of AAL products is also a future research objective of the authors.

The contexts where AAL products and services can be used are very complex and can either require simple solutions or a combination of existing technologies. Therefore, it should be possible the interoperability of AAL products and services. This will not only provide a better answer to the existing needs, but will also save time and decrease costs, namely if new organizational and services models are adopted. In this respect, the authors will evaluate if the ICF can be used as a semantic structure to normalize and classify AAL products and services, which could promote the composition of complex services based on third party services development and provision, stimulating, therefore, the establishment of value chains that facilitate the business opportunities of AAL products and services.

CONCLUSION

The described persona and scenario models are being used to develop AAL products and services within several research and development projects (Teixeira, et al., 2013; Hämäläinen et al., 2015). The experimental evaluation seems to indicate that the ICF based personas and scenarios are suitable for this purpose.

On the other hand, the ICF-US validation results suggest appropriate values for its reliability and validity, which indicates that this instrument can be a useful tool for evaluating the usability of AAL products and services, because it adds quantitative (i.e., ICF-US I) with qualitative aspects (i.e., ICF-US II).

One of the main advantages of applying the described instruments is related with the fact that they are based on the ICF conceptual framework that includes concepts and terminologies established by the World Health Organization, which means that they have a universal diffusion. Additionally, the ICF conceptual framework may facilitate the understanding of what are barriers or facilitators, as well as consolidate knowledge, due to the existence of models, concepts and generalized terms, which is essential not only for the involvement of end users and careers in the AAL products and services development processes, but also for technological innovation and strategic planning.

REFERENCES

AAL Association. (2010). *The Ambient Assisted Living (AAL) Joint Programme*. Brussels: AAL Association.

Avilés-López, E., Villanueva-Miranda, I., Garcia-Macias, J. A., & Palafox-Maestre, L. E. (2009). Taking Care of Our Elders through Augmented Spaces. In *LA-WEB/CLIHC* (pp. 16–21). Merida: IEEE Computer Society. doi:10.1109/LA-WEB.2009.30

Bangor, A., Kortum, P. T., & Miller, J. T. (2008). An empirical evaluation of the system usability scale. *International Journal of Human-Computer Interaction, 24*(6), 574–594. doi:10.1080/10447310802205776

Bevan, N., Claridge, N., & Petrie, H. (2005). Tenuta: Simplified Guidance for Usability and Accessibility. In *Proceedings of HCI International*. Las Vegas, NV: Lawrence Erlbaum Associates.

Bexelius, C., Löf, M., Sandin, S., Lagerros, Y. T., Forsum, E., & Litton, J. E. (2010). Measures of physical activity using cell phones: Validation using criterion methods. *Journal of Medical Internet Research, 12*(1), e2. doi:10.2196/jmir.1298 PMID:20118036

Botella Arbona, C., García Palacios, A., Baños Rivera, R. M., & Quero Castellano, S. (2009). Cybertherapy: Advantages, limitations, and ethical issues. *PsychNology Journal, 7*(1), 77–110.

Boulos, M. N. K., Brewer, A. C., Karimkhani, C., Buller, D. B., & Dellavalle, R. P. (2014). Mobile medical and health apps: State of the art, concerns, regulatory control and certification. *Online Journal of Public Health Informatics, 5*(3). PMID:24683442

BRAID. (2011). Consolidated Vision of ICT and Ageing. Brussels: Bridging Research in Ageing and ICT Development (BRAID).

Calvaresi, D., Cesarini, D., Sernani, P., Marinoni, M., Dragoni, A. F., & Sturm, A. (2016). Exploring the ambient assisted living domain: a systematic review. *Journal of Ambient Intelligence and Humanized Computing*, 1-19.

Camarinha-Matos, L. M., Rosas, J., Oliveira, A. I., & Ferrada, F. (2015). Care services ecosystem for ambient assisted living. *Enterprise Information Systems, 9*(5-6), 607–633.

Charpentier, G., Benhamou, P. Y., Dardari, D., Clergeot, A., Franc, S., Schaepelynck-Belicar, P., & Bosson, J. L. et al. (2011). The diabeo software enabling individualized insulin dose adjustments combined with telemedicine support improves HbA1c in poorly controlled type 1 diabetic patients A 6-month, randomized, open-label, parallel-group, multicenter trial (TeleDiab 1 study). *Diabetes Care, 34*(3), 533–539. doi:10.2337/dc10-1259 PMID:21266648

Cooper, A. (2004). *The inmates are running the asylum*. Indianapolis, IN: Sams.

Cruz, V. T., Pais, J., Bento, V., Mateus, C., Colunas, M., Alves, I., ... Rocha, N. P. (2013). A rehabilitation tool designed for intensive web-based cognitive training: Description and usability study. *JMIR Research Protocols, 2*(2), e59.

European Commission. (2007). *Ageing well in the Information Society: An i2010 Initiative, Action Plan on Information and Communication Technologies and Ageing*. Brussels: European Commission.

Federici, S., Meloni, F., & Presti, A. L. (2009). International literature review on WHODAS II. *Life Span and Disability*, *12*(1), 83–110.

Flynn, D. J., & Jazi, M. D. (1998). Constructing user requirements: A social process for a social context. *Information Systems Journal*, *8*(1), 53–83. doi:10.1046/j.1365-2575.1998.00004.x

Hämäläinen, A., Teixeira, A., Almeida, N., Meinedo, H., Fegyó, T., & Dias, M. S. (2015). Multilingual speech recognition for the elderly: The AALFred personal life assistant. *Procedia Computer Science*, *67*, 283–292. doi:10.1016/j.procs.2015.09.272

Heath, I. (2008). Never had it so good? *BMJ (Clinical Research Ed.)*, *336*(7650), 950–951. doi:10.1136/bmj.39532.671319.94 PMID:18397944

International Standards Organization. (2010). *ISO9241 - Ergonomics of human-system interaction*. Geneva: International Standards Organization.

Jette, A. M. (2006). Toward a common language for function, disability, and health. *Physical Therapy*, *86*(5), 726–734. PMID:16649895

Kleinberger, T., Becker, M., Ras, E., Holzinger, A., & Müller, P. (2007). Ambient intelligence in assisted living: enable elderly people to handle future interfaces. In *International Conference on Universal Access in Human-Computer Interaction* (pp. 103-112). Berlin: Springer. doi:10.1007/978-3-540-73281-5_11

Lewis, J. R. (2002). Psychometric evaluation of the PSSUQ using data from five years of usability studies. *International Journal of Human-Computer Interaction*, *14*(3-4), 463–488. doi:10.1080/10447318.2002.9669130

Marshall, A., Medvedev, O., & Antonov, A. (2008). Use of a smartphone for improved self-management of pulmonary rehabilitation. *International Journal of Telemedicine and Applications*, *2008*, 2. doi:10.1155/2008/753064 PMID:18615186

Martins, A. I., Queirós, A., Cerqueira, M., Rocha, N., & Teixeira, A. (2012). The International Classification of Functioning, Disability and Health as a conceptual model for the evaluation of environmental factors. *Procedia Computer Science*, *14*, 293–300. doi:10.1016/j.procs.2012.10.033

Martins, A. I., Rosa, A. F., Queirós, A., Silva, A., & Rocha, N. P. (2015). Definition and Validation of the ICF-Usability Scale. *Procedia Computer Science*, *67*, 132–139. doi:10.1016/j.procs.2015.09.257

Memon, M., Wagner, S. R., Pedersen, C. F., Beevi, F. H. A., & Hansen, F. O. (2014). Ambient assisted living healthcare frameworks, platforms, standards, and quality attributes. *Sensors (Basel, Switzerland)*, *14*(3), 4312–4341. doi:10.3390/s140304312 PMID:24599192

Miaskiewicz, T., & Kozar, K. A. (2011). Personas and user-centered design: How can personas benefit product design processes? *Design Studies*, *32*(5), 417–430. doi:10.1016/j.destud.2011.03.003

Mosa, A. S. M., Yoo, I., & Sheets, L. (2012). A systematic review of healthcare applications for smartphones. *BMC Medical Informatics and Decision Making*, *12*(1), 1. doi:10.1186/1472-6947-12-67 PMID:22781312

Nordenfelt, L. (2003). Action theory, disability and ICF. *Disability and Rehabilitation, 25*(18), 1075–1079. doi:10.1080/0963828031000137748 PMID:12944163

Queirós, A., Carvalho, S., Pavão, J., & Rocha, N. (2013). AAL information based services and care integration. In *International Conference on Health Informatics - HealthInf 2013* (pp. 403-406). Barcelona: INSTICC.

Queirós, A., Cerqueira, M., Martins, A. I., Silva, A. G., Alvarelhão, J., & Rocha, N. P. (2014). Personas and Scenarios Based on Functioning and Health Conditions. In S. Saeed, I. S. Bajwa, & Z. Mahmood (Eds.), *Human Factors in Software Development and Design* (pp. 274–294). Hershey, PA: IGI Global.

Queirós, A., Silva, A., Alvarelhão, J., Rocha, N. P., & Teixeira, A. (2015). Usability, accessibility and ambient-assisted living: A systematic literature review. *Universal Access in the Information Society, 14*(1), 57–66. doi:10.1007/s10209-013-0328-x

Rönkkö, K. (2005). *Making methods work in software engineering: Method deployment as a social achievement.* Ronneby: School of Engineering, Blekinge Institute of Technology.

Rosser, B. A., & Eccleston, C. (2011). Smartphone applications for pain management. *Journal of Telemedicine and Telecare, 17*(6), 308–312. doi:10.1258/jtt.2011.101102 PMID:21844177

Rosson, M. B., & Carroll, J. M. (2009). Scenario based design. In J. Jacko & A. Sears (Eds.), *The Human-Computer Interaction Handbook: Fundamentals, Evolving Technologies and Emerging Applications* (pp. 1032–1050). Boca Raton, FL: Lawrence Erlbaum Associates. doi:10.1201/9781420088892.ch8

Ståhlbröst, A. (2008). *Forming future IT the living lab way of user involvement.* Luleå: University of Technology.

Stucki, G., Reinhardt, J. D., Grimby, G., & Melvin, J. (2008). Developing Human Functioning and Rehabilitation Research from the comprehensive perspective. *Journal of Rehabilitation Medicine, 39*(9), 665–671. doi:10.2340/16501977-0136 PMID:17999002

Teixeira, A., Pereira, C., Silva, M. O., Alvarelhão, J., Silva, A. G., Cerqueira, M., & Rocha, N. (2013). New telerehabilitation services for the elderly. In I. Miranda & M. Cruz-Cunha (Eds.), *Handbook of Research on ICTs for Healthcare and Social Services: Developments and Applications* (pp. 109–132). Hershey, PA: IGI Global.

Teixeira, A. J., Rocha, N. P., Dias, M. S., Braga, D., Queirós, A., Pacheco, O., . . . Pereira, C. (2011). A New Living Lab for Usability Evaluation of ICT and Next Generation Networks for Elderly@ Home. In *AAL 2011 - 1st Int. Living Usability Lab Workshop on AAL Latest Solutions, Trends and Applications* (pp. 85-97). Roma: INSTICC.

US Food and Drug Administration. (2013). *Mobile medical applications: guidance for industry and Food and Drug Administration staff.* Rockville: US Food and Drug Administration, Division of Dockets Management, Food and Drug Administration.

van den Broek, G., Cavallo, F., & Wehrmann, C. (2010). *AALIANCE ambient assisted living roadmap* (Vol. 6). Amsterdam: IOS press.

World Health Organization. (1998). *Growing older, staying well. Ageing and physical activity in everyday life*. Geneva: World Health Organization.

World Health Organization. (2001). *International Classification of Functioning, Disability and Health: ICF*. Geneva: World Health Organization.

World Health Organization. (2002). *Active ageing: a policy framework: a contribution of the World Health Organization to the Second United Nations World Assembly on Ageing*. Madrid: World Health Organization.

World Medical Association. (2013). World Medical Association Declaration of Helsinki: Ethical principles for medical research involving human subjects. *Journal of the American Medical Association, 310*(20), 2191. doi:10.1001/jama.2013.281053 PMID:24141714

KEY TERMS AND DEFINITIONS

Activities: The individual's perspective of the respective execution of tasks or actions.

Ambient Assisted Living: The heterogeneous field of technologies, products and services to enable elderly people with specific needs to live longer in their natural environment.

Bodys' Functions: The individuals' physiological functions.

Conceptual Validation: The set of structured procedures aiming to evaluate if a particular idea of a product or service has sustainability and should be further developed.

Contextual Factors: The environmental and personal factors which either enhance or limit the individual's functioning.

Participation: The individual's involvement in daily life and society.

Personas: The hypothetical representations of user groups that emphasize relevant characteristics for a better understanding of the requirements that need to be fulfill during the development process of a particular product or service.

Scenarios: The description of hypothetical events or situations experienced by the personas.

Usability: The efficiency of the interaction of products or service when used by specific users to achieve certain objectives.

Chapter 14
Modelling Cyber-Crime Protection Behaviour among Computer Users in the Context of Bangladesh

Imran Mahmud
University Sains Malaysia, Malaysia & Daffodil International University, Bangladesh

T. Ramayah
University Sains Malaysia, Malaysia & International Business School, Universiti Teknologi Malaysia

Md. Mahedi Hasan Nayeem
Daffodil International University, Bangladesh

S. M. Muzahidul Islam
Daffodil International University, Bangladesh

Pei Leng Gan
University Sains Malaysia, Malaysia

ABSTRACT

This study examined the impact of security champion and security training on protection behaviour in the context of IT service oriented SMEs in Bangladesh. Drawing upon protection motivation theory, this study examined the influence of security training on threat appraisal and influence of security training on coping appraisal which leads to protection behaviour via protection motivation. Data was collected from six different IT service oriented organizations with a sample size of 147 by survey questionnaire. Data was analysed using partial least squares (PLS) technique and result shows that perceived value of data, security training and threat appraisal are strong predictors of threat appraisal, protection motivation and protection behaviour. Theoretical contribution and practical implications of this research are also discussed.

INTRODUCTION

The advancement of the information and telecommunication technology (ICT) in Bangladesh in recent years has improved the infrastructure of information sharing through the Internet. According to the Ban-

DOI: 10.4018/978-1-5225-1944-7.ch014

gladesh Telecommunication Regulatory Commission (BTRC), the total number of Internet subscribers has reached 61.288 million in Bangladesh. Among the 61 million, mobile internet has the biggest subscribers with 58.045 users, followed by 0.131 million Wimax users and 3.112 million users from Internet service providers. Aligned with cyber infrastructure growth, the possibilities of computer users being vulnerable to various security threats via Internet are higher too (Anderson & Agarwal 2010). Despite being ranked 11th globally in cyber security preparedness (Bhuiyan et al. 2016), recently at a seminar in Bangladesh, experts and researchers observed that cybercrimes increased at an alarming rate along with the rapid rise of Internet users at both individual and institutional levels (Nashique, 2015). The recent case of cyber-attack on Bangladesh's central bank that let hackers steal over $80 million from the Federal Reserve bank account was reportedly caused by the Malware installed on the Bank's computer systems. Development of ICT changed the how organizations operate, data and information which were once stored and kept in cabinets and files and today they are paperless. Similar to other organizations in developing countries, the modern organizations in Bangladesh depend on information systems (IS) for their survival. The systems used in the organizations contained priceless organizational data and resources (Cavusoglu et al., 2004; Ifinedo, 2009, 2012). In order to safeguard the critical IS assets held in such systems from misuse, abuse and destruction; organizations often utilize a variety of tools and measures such as installing firewalls, updating anti-virus software, backing up their systems, maintaining and restricting access controls, using encryption keys, using surge protectors, and using comprehensive monitoring systems (Workman et al., 2008; Lee & Larsen, 2009, Ilfendo, 2011). Individual level digital crimes include cyber stalking, cyber harassment, morphing and obscene publication, email/profile hacking, spoofing, cyber pornography including revenge porn, internet voyeurism, cyber defamation, cyber bullying, email harassment, cyber blackmailing, threatening, emotional cheating by impersonation, intimate partner violence through internet and abetment of such offences. It was also acknowledged by the Central Bank that "Bangladesh remains vulnerable to cyber-attacks because traditional cyber defences such as anti-virus software and firewalls are ineffective against new threat vectors such as zero-day malware and Advanced Persistent Threats (APT)" (Zamir, 2016). This has led the Information and Communication Technology (ICT) Ministry of Bangladesh to take the importance of activities related to building awareness to prevent such cybercrimes (Zamir, 2016). Despite having technological measures such as antivirus software, regulations and security policy are also widely used as methods to reduce the chance of cyber-attacks. In a study conducted by Warkentin and Willison (2009) indicated that many users do not follow the policy to protect organizations or themselves from cybercrime. The major reason behind this is insufficient crime protection behaviour from the users (Anderson & Agarwal 2010).

The goal of this paper is to understand the phenomenon of protection motivation, its antecedents and protection behaviour of individual computer users of government banks. Recently Srisawang et al. (2015) and Ifinedo (2012) investigated the factors rooted in protection motivation theory and theory of planned behaviour to explain computer users' protection behaviour. Our study aims to extend the knowledge of this particular behaviour by identifying several other factors like communication between IT department and other users, security champion and IT security training (Soto-Acosta et al. 2013; Travica, 2007). In doing so, the research questions of our study are:

RQ1: What are the antecedents of protection motivation and its impact on protection behaviour?

Drawing on the protection motivation theory (PMT) of Rogers (1983), research models proposed by Srisawang et al. 2015, we proposed that users' protection behaviour which is affected by protection motivation is influenced by threat and coping appraisal. Threat and coping appraisal also affected by perceived value of data, security knowledge, safeguard cost and subjective norm which are rooted from PMT. We also investigate factors which influence the understanding of the importance of IT security: security champion and security training. We answer the research questions related to the antecedents of a user's protection motivation using survey data which will be collected from the computer users of a diverse set of small- medium IT service oriented organizations.

The chapter is organized as follows: The first section will present a brief review of the relevant literature and highlights the unique contributions of our work, while the second section will lay out the theoretical foundation of the research where we discuss the research model (Figure 1) and develop the hypotheses to be tested, followed by a summary of the research method, and description of the data analysis and presentation of the results. Finally, we will discuss the findings, their implications, and future research direction.

THEORETICAL BACKGROUND AND MODEL DEVELOPMENT

We began with the model of Srisawang et al (2015) because it was grounded in the IS literature (Rogers (1983) protection motivation theory) as the most comprehensive and current model focused on protection motivation and behaviour published recently. Model proposed by Srisawang et al (2015) explained that conscientiousness personality of users, their perceived value of data and prior experience have positive impact of threat appraisal of the users. Subjective norm has positive impact on both threat and coping appraisal. They also explored that, security knowledge has positive influence and safe guard cost has negative impact on coping appraisal. Finally, they conclude their research by identifying the impact on threat and coping appraisal on protection motivation which also influence positively the protection behaviour of general people who use personal computer.

In the context of Bangladesh, we have included information technology (IT) security training and IT security champion as key predictors of threat and coping appraisal.

Protection Motivation Theory (PMT)

Based on Witte (1992), fear is the negative emotion cause by threat and it comes together with high level of arousal. Fear can be expressed psychologically via body language or facial expressions. Witte (1992) also added fear is operationalized as anxiety, psychological arousal, responses to mood adjectives and ratings of concern or worry in fear appeal literature. On the other hand, threat is regarded as external stimulus variables that exist whether a person knows it or not. If a person perceived there is a threat thus it can be concluded that the person is aware of the threat (Johnston & Warkenton, 2010). In other words, when a person is aware of the threats, the person will establish beliefs as to the seriousness of the threat and probability of personally experiencing the threat.

Johnston and Warkentin (2010) stated in their study, PMT are based on fear appeals. Fear appeals motivates individual to comply with suggested response the changes through persuasion. Fear appeals related research has long history of over 50 years. Johnston and Warkentin (2010) also added, fear appeals related studies started as early as 1953 by Hovland, Janis and Kelly named fear-as-acquired model. The fear-as-acquired model later was modified by Janis in 1967 and McGuire uses the similar inverted U shaped relationship as Janis in 1968 in explaining fear arousal and attitude change. McGuire's model explains when fear is seen as driver it motivates people to accept suggestions in response towards the fear. Whereas when fear is seen as cue, it produces habitual responses which will affect the person's to accept the message. However, McGuire and Janis's model has been rejected due to similar reason after testing. There is no evidence available to support both model.

In 1970, another researcher, Leventhal suggested a model to differentiate emotional response to fear-inducing communication from a cognitive response and based on the parallel process model. Protective adaptive behaviour rooted from effort to control the threat instead of effort to control the fear. If the person thought about the threatening message and developed strategies to prevent the threat and it can be concluded that the person is engaging in danger control process. Leventhal (1970), made general statements on condition leading to fear or danger control processes. Unfortunately, Leventhal was not able to identify when one process should dominate over another or which factor causes the different processes. Leventhal's parallel response model provides useful distinction between cognitive and emotional reactions to fear appeal but it fails to provide proof for its veracity with single study.

PMT was introduced by Rogers in 1975 and later expanded in 1983. Based on PMT was designed to investigate the effects of fear appeals upon attitude change in health-related behaviour and the extended version focus on the general theory of persuasive communication emphasized on the cognitive process mediating behavioural change (Boer & Seydel, 1996). The earlier model has three components known as perceived susceptibility, perceived severity and response efficacy, while another component named self-efficacy was later added to the model in 1983. There are four messages that leads to corresponding cognitive mediation process:

1. Probability of occurrence depictions in a message lead to perceived susceptibility
2. Magnitude of noxiousness is the appeal produces perceived severity
3. Descriptions of the effectiveness of he recommended response result in perceived response efficacy
4. Characterization of individual's ability to perform the recommended response produce perceived self-efficacy

PMT are used in health-related behaviour research, such as reducing alcohol use, enhancing healthy lifestyles, enhancing diagnostics health behaviour and preventing diseases. However, Floyd and Prentice-Dunn (2000) in their research revealed that PMT also been applied in other areas including political issues, environmental concerns, injury prevention and protecting others. PMT are also widely used in information security related studies which focus on employees' compliance with information security compliance procedures (Ifinedo, 2012). Floyd and Prentice-Dunn (2000) concluded PMT is threat with recommended response can be carried out by individual.

PMT are based on two cognitive mediating processes named threat appraisal process and coping appraisal process. The cognitive process is believed to stimulate the protection motivation and also determine the response towards the threat. Witte (1992) added, the PMT model differentiate into maladaptive threat appraisal and adaptive coping appraisal. Both processes combine the intervening variable protection motivation. Threat appraisal is process of evaluating the threat and coping appraisal is the process of choosing the available alternatives to cope with the threats. The process starts with threat appraisal followed by the coping appraisal (Floyd & Prentice-Dunn, 2000).

Threat Appraisal (TA)

Johnston and Warkentin (2010) argued, threat is external stimulus perceived by individual and if the individual perceives the threat therefore it can be concluded that the individuals are aware of the threats. Based on the understanding of threat, Johnston and Warkentin (2010) also stated properly constructed fear appeal will serve to induce cognition that a threat existed and convey severity of the treat and its target population susceptibility to the threat. In other words, threat appraisal refers to individuals' assessment of the level of danger posed by threatening event. It assesses maladaptive behaviour (Floyd & Prentice-Dunn, 2000). Threat appraisal comprised of items perceived vulnerability and perceived severity. Perceived vulnerability took place when individual assesses the threatening events and, perceived severity is the severity of consequences of the event. Witte (1992) explained people may still engage in maladaptive behaviour if the rewards of performing the actions is greater than the perceived severity and perceived susceptibility to the danger. For example, probability of getting a disease (perceived vulnerability and susceptibility) and estimation of seriousness of a disease (perceived severity).

Coping Appraisal (CA)

Coping appraisal refers to individual's assessment of their ability to cope with and avert the potential loss or damage arising from the threat (Woon et al. 2015). Coping appraisal comprised of self-efficacy, response efficacy and response cost. Self-efficacy was added in the extended model in 1983. Self-efficacy is the individual's confidence in their own ability to perform the recommended behaviour. Whereas response efficacy is related to belief in the perceived benefits of the action ought to be carried out. On the other hand, response cost is the perceived opportunity cost such monetary, time and effort in adopting the recommended behaviour. Both self-efficacy and response efficacy increases the chances of choosing the adaptive response, and the response cost decreases if the chances of choosing the adaptive response (Floyd & Prentice-Dunn, 2000).

Coping appraisal process evaluates the components that are relevant for the evaluation of the coping responses.

Protection Motivation (PM)

According to Boer and Seydel (1996), protection motivation is the intention to perform the desired behaviour. It encompasses of threats with effective recommended response (coping appraisal) which can be perform by individual (Floyd and Prenrice-Dunn, 2000). Srisawang et al (2015) claims behaviour is affected by the individual's personality and environment evolving them. The researcher further explained that actual behaviour is predicted by motivation. In our case the higher the protection behaviour in the employees of the company, it is like higher the motivation to protect the information in the company.

As a result, the researcher hypothesized:

H1: Threat appraisal has positive impact on protection motivation
H2: Coping appraisal has positive impact on protection motivation
H3: Protection motivation has positive impact on protection behaviour (PB)

Perceived Value of Data (PV)

At first, Srisawang et al. 2015 suggested that perceived value of information is a factor inspiring users to execute the protection behaviour. Previously, Cheng et al. 2009 explained that users who deal with important data could measure the cyber threats and take necessary action to prevent those threats. According to Warkentin and Willison (2009), perceived value has positive impact on protection behaviour such as installation and use of antivirus software. Align with Srisawang et al. 2015, the researcher hypothesized:

H4: Perceived value of data has positive impact on threat appraisal.

IT Security Training (TR)

Training related IT security assists users to understand about threat related to IT. Evidence from Travica (2007) expressed that on the use of IT system, training plays an important role by making users strongly focused. Recently, the research of Bartnes et al. 2016 described how training was given low priority in various industries and faced well-known attacks, such as Stuxnet/Duqu/Flame (Perlroth, 2012), Night-Dragon (McAfee, 2011), and the cyber espionage campaign by Dragonfly (Lee and Reid, 2014), as well as statistics presented by ICS-CERT (2013), demonstrate that industrial control organizations are attractive targets for attacks. According to these statistics, 59% of the incidents reported to the Department of Homeland Security in 2013 occurred in the energy industry. Challenges for improving information security incident management practices should be concerned for the creation of cross-functional teams and learning to learn. As a result, training program could only be implemented successfully with the assistance from management and acceptance by the end users to become aware of security threats. Furthermore, Awawdeh and Tubaishat (2014) mentioned that the effective training programs could make employees accountable for their actions. So, IT security training will lead to higher level of threat appraisal. Thus, the researcher hypothesized:

H5: IT security training has positive impact on Threat appraisal.

Security Knowledge (SK)

As noted by Siponen et al. 2010, knowledge of security has positive influence on user's learning which leads to protection motivation. Organizations can use various electronic mediums like email, videos, social network group to promote security knowledge to the users. In case of home users, security awareness ascends after a crisis when the user faces security threats like virus (Srisawang et al. 2015). It is obvious that higher level of security knowledge will lead to higher level of individual's assessment of his or her ability to cope with and avert the potential loss or damage arising from the threat. Thus the researcher hypothesized:

H6: Security knowledge has positive impact on coping appraisal.

Safeguard Cost (SFC)

Safeguard costs are defined as the perceived costs incurred by a user in performing a recommended coping behavior (i.e., installing and configuring antispyware software). About the safeguard cost Chenoweth et al. 2009 suggested about the effort related to protecting the data or IT, not the amount of money spent for anti-virus or other kinds of security software. Prior studies of Srisawang et al. 2015 and Ifenido (2012) found safeguard cost has negative impact on coping appraisal of computer users. Thus the researcher hypothesized:

H7: Safeguard cost has a negative impact on coping appraisal.

Security Champion (SC)

According to Soto-Acosta et al. 2013, IT project champion plays an important role in IT project management. Falkowski et al. 1998 suggested a project champion sets goals and legitimize change for projects throughout the organization. Drawing on this literature, we identify "Security Champion" as a key predictor of user's coping appraisal. Previously, research conducted by Ahmad and Maynard (2014) observed, the security champion can boost the motivating force for learning was the competitive spirit amongst learning teams. So the researcher hypothesized:

H8: Security Champion has positive impact on coping appraisal of users

Figure 1. Research model

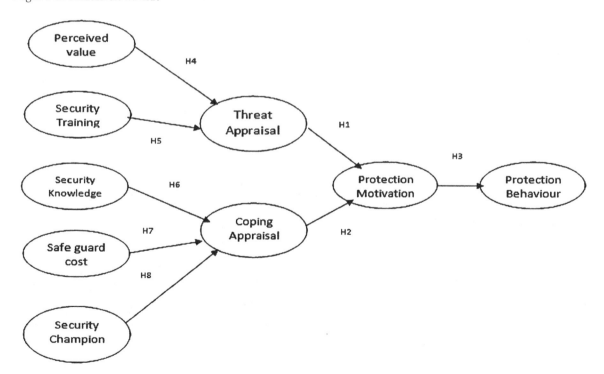

RESEARCH METHOD

Participants

A survey questionnaire was administrated to participants to explore protection motivation and behaviour. The survey was administrated to participants in six renowned, well established IT service oriented organizations in Bangladesh. Our sample was 130 IT professionals (81.54% male, 18.46% female), all of whom operate on a daily basis on programming, networking or IT support and therefore have a significant experience of IT systems. Among the IT professionals, 24.62% have experienced below 1 year, 56.92% have experience between 1-3 years, 8.46% have experience between 3-5 years and the rest have more than 5 years of IT experience. The demographic information provided in Table 1.

Instruments

The survey questionnaire items were adapted from validated instruments from previous research. All items were measured using a 5 – point likert scale (1- Strongly Disagree to 5- Strongly Agree). Items to measure construct PV, SK, SFC, PM and PB were adapted from recent research of Srisawang et al. 2015. Items for SC and TR were adapted from the research of Soto-Acosta et al. 2013. List of items and sources are given in Appendix 1.

DATA ANALYSIS AND RESULT

Data Analysis Technique

Common method variance needs to be examined when data are collected via self-reported questionnaires and, in particular, both the predictor and criterion variables are obtained from the same person (Podsakoff, MacKenzie, Lee, & Podsakoff, 2003). Podsakoff and Todor (1985) also noted that: "Invariably, when self-reported measures obtained from the same sample are utilized in research, concern over same-source bias or general method variance arise" (p. 65). There are several remedies to this issue suggested in the

Table 1. Demographic information

	Frequency	Percentage
Gender		
Male	106	81.54
Female	24	18.46
Experience		
Below 1 year	32	24.62
1-3	74	56.92
3-5	11	8.46
More than 5	13	10.00

literature. One of the common method used to detect this issue is the Harman's single factor test. This is done by entering all the principal constructs into a principal component factor analysis (Podsakoff & Organ, 1986). Evidence method bias exists when a single factor emerges from the factor analysis, or one general factor accounts for the majority of the covariance among the measures (Podsakoff et al., 2003). Look at the principal constructs inter-correlations using the correlation matrix and if any of the correlations are substantially large r > 0.90 (Bagozzi et al., 1991) then there is evidence of a common method bias.

Our test result shows that the restricted extraction of a single factor only explains 15.39% of the variance that means data did not have CMV problem.

Structural equation modelling (SEM) is a procedure to assess a research model which contains linear relationship among the observed variables (Roberts and Grover, 2009). To test our model, we shifted it to structural equation modelling using the partial least squares technique (Hair et al. 2014) and used SmartPLS3 software (Ringle et al. 2014) to calculate data. Every construct of our model was measured with reflective indicators.

Measurement Model

Hair et al. 2014 suggested after the research model was formed, researchers must test the outer model. For evaluation of outer model, we measured average variance extracted (AVE) and composite reliability (CR) and discriminant validity. See Table 2 and Table 3

From Table 2, by focusing on the quality criteria, where AVE must be greater than 0.5 which will reflect at least 50% of items explains the construct and composite reliability must be greater than 0.7 (Hair et al. 2014), we can state that both criteria are fulfilled for our variables. Table 3 shows that the square root of AVE is greater than the corresponding construct correlation which indicates that our construct is truly distinct from other constructs (Hair et al. 2011).

Table 2. AVE and CR

	Composite Reliability	**Average Variance Extracted (AVE)**
CA	0.769	0.528
PB	0.709	0.562
PM	0.796	0.567
PV	0.749	0.507
SC	0.740	0.593
SFC	0.829	0.714
SK	0.747	0.500
TA	0.804	0.579
TR	0.836	0.562

PV1, SK1, SC1, SFC2, CA3, PM1 and PB2 removed for better AVE and CR.

Table 3. Discriminant validity

	CA	PB	PM	PV	SC	SFC	SK	TA	TR
CA	**0.718**								
PB	-0.138	**0.749**							
PM	-0.095	0.586	**0.752**						
PV	-0.126	0.171	0.266	**0.712**					
SC	0.339	0.008	0.001	-0.202	**0.779**				
SFC	-0.174	0.204	0.128	-0.002	-0.097	**0.847**			
SK	0.379	0.147	0.282	0.035	0.346	0.039	**0.821**		
TA	-0.136	0.337	0.549	0.410	0.117	0.210	0.125	**0.76**	
TR	0.100	0.454	0.418	0.254	0.122	0.178	0.276	0.366	**0.749**

Note: Diagonal represents the square root of Average Variance Extracted (AVE) while the other entries represent squared correlations

Structural Model

Focusing on their significance level of their path coefficients, our result indicates, antecedents of threat appraisal: PV and TR explain 24% variance on TA and antecedents of coping appraisal: security champion, security knowledge and safeguard cost explain 21.9% variance on CA. Both TA and CA explain 30.2% variance on user protection motivation (PM). Finally, PM explains 34.4% variance on user's PB.

After analysis the AVE, reliability and validity of our data, we moved to analyze the structural model by using the evaluation coefficient of determination and the significance level of each path coefficient. Next, the hypotheses developed for this study were tested by running a bootstrapping procedure with a resample of 5,000, as suggested by Hair et al. (2014).

The result is presented in Table 4:

Result indicates within the protection motivation theory CA has negative impact on PM but not supported (β= -0.021, p > 0.05) and TA strongly influence PM (β= 0.546, p< 0.05). . PM is very strong significant predictor of PB (β= 0.586, p< 0.05). In case of threat appraisal (TA), PV (β= 0.339, p< 0.05) and TR (β= 0.280, p< 0.05) both have positive significant impact whereas among the predictors of TA;

Table 4. Hypothesis testing result and path coefficient

Hypothesis	Relationship	Path Coefficient	T-Statistics	Result
H1	TA -> PM	0.546	5.967	Supported
H2	CA -> PM	-0.021	0.231	Not supported
H3	PM -> PB	0.586	6.804	Supported
H4	PV -> TA	0.339	3.350	Supported
H5	TR -> TA	0.280	3.020	Supported
H6	SFC -> CA	-0.165	1.498	Not supported
H7	SK -> CA	0.310	2.974	Supported
H8	SC -> CA	0.216	2.071	Supported

Figure 2. Final research model
P< 0.001**, p < 0.05*, p > 0.05ⁿˢ

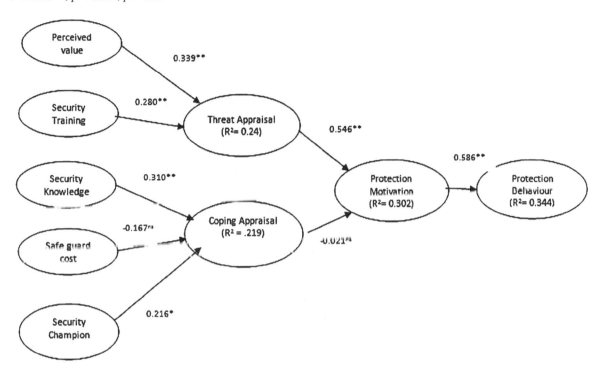

SK (β= 0.310, p< 0.05) and SC (β= 0.216, p< 0.05) both have positive significant influence but, SFC (β= -0.165, p > 0.05) has negative impact but surprisingly not significant.

To assess the structural model Hair et al. (2014) suggested looking at the R^2, beta and the corresponding t-values via a bootstrapping procedure with a resample of 5,000. They also suggested that in addition to these basic measures researchers should also report the predictive relevance (Q^2) and the effect sizes (f^2).

Further to that we also assessed the predictive relevance of the model by using the blindfolding procedure. Blindfolding is a sample reuse technique that omits every dth data point in the endogenous construct's indicators and estimates the parameters with the remaining data points (Chin, 1998; Henseler et al., 2009; Tenenhaus et al., 2005). Hair et al. (2014) further suggested that the blindfolding procedure should only be applied to endogenous constructs that have a reflective measurement (multiple items or single item).

If the Q^2 value is larger than 0 the model has predictive relevance for a certain endogenous construct and otherwise if the value is less than 0 (Hair et al. 2014; Fornell & Cha, 1994). All the four Q^2 values

Table 5. Predictive relevance

Constructs	Q^2
CA	0.095
TA	0.111
PM	0.163
PB	0.153

Table 6. Variance explained

Endogenous Variables	R Square
CA	0.241
PB	0.342
PM	0.302
TA	0.242

for coping appraisal ($Q^2 = 0.0.095$), threat appraisal ($Q^2 = 0.111$), protection motivation ($Q^2 = 0.163$) and protection behaviour ($Q^2 = 0.153$) are more than 0 suggesting that the model (Figure 2) has sufficient predictive relevance (See Table 5).

Next we also assessed effect sizes (f^2). As asserted by Sullivan and Fein (2012), "While a *P* value can inform the reader whether an effect exists, the *P* value will not reveal the size of the effect. In reporting and interpreting studies, both the *substantive significance* (effect size) and *statistical significance* (*P* value) are essential results to be reported".

As posited by Hair et al. (2014) who suggested that the change in the R^2 value should also be examined. The method suggested is to examine the R^2 change when a specified exogenous construct is omitted from the model can be used to evaluate whether the omitted construct has a substantive impact on the endogenous constructs (See Table 6).

Results from Table 7 indicated that the predictors of CA explained 24% variance on CA and the predictors of TA explained 24.2% variance on TA. Both TA and CA explained 30.2% variance on PM. Finally PM explained 34.2% variance on PB.

To measure the effect size we used Cohen (1988) guideline which are 0.02, 0.15, and 0.35, respectively, represent small, medium, and large effects (Cohen, 1988).

DISCUSSION

The result indicates among eight hypotheses, six of our hypotheses are strongly significant. From the first and second hypothesis test result, we can conclude that threat appraisal increases protection moti-

Table 7. Effect size

Relationships	f square	Effect Size
CA-> PM	0.000	No Effect
PM->PB	0.520	Large
PV-> TA	0.142	Small
SC->CA	0.055	Small
SFC->CA	0.023	Small
SK->CA	0.138	Small
TA->PM	0.423	Large
TR-> TA	0.097	Small

vation of IT users that leads to protection behaviour which is similar to the findings of the research of Srisawang et al. 2015 and Ifenido (2012). It is obvious that IT employee who are motivated will show awareness and better action in case of IT security protection.

Second hypothesis (H2) about the impact of coping appraisal on protection motivation is not significant which is inconsistent with previous research of Srisawang et al. 2015 and Ifenido (2012). We assume that IT professionals are too much focused on their software development or IT services, but they pay little attention to their own computers' protection. According to Eminagaoglu et al. 2009, companies need effective compliance of security policies and proper integration of people, process and technology for successful information security management.

The significant relationship between perceived value of data and threat appraisal (H4) shows that a person who deals with important information will display better awareness of data protection. In case of II5, our result is consistent with previous research as Ashenden (2008) explains the need for security training for information security management which will make the users understand about rules, importance, threats and control of IT security management.

Our finding indicates that security knowledge has positive impact on coping appraisal (H6). Moreover, the result is aligned with the findings of Srisawang et al. 2015. In case of H7, our study fails to confirm the negative influence of safeguard cost on coping appraisal. We assume that sometimes it is up to IT manager to take necessary steps for coping with IT threat within the organization, so our respondents did not consider it as an important construct of coping appraisal.

Just like project champion, a security champion is necessary for an organization to motivate top management to purchase security related software and hardware as well as to communicate efficiently with all level of IT staff to support the IT security. Our result shows that security champion influences coping appraisal positively (H8).

THEORETICAL CONTRIBUTION

This paper contributes to the body of work dedicated to helping us better understand protection motivation and behaviour. It complements the primarily macro-level examinations of IT security perception and protection behaviour of individuals. Protection motivation theory is the underpinning theory to support present study. Specifically, this paper examined IT security motivation in which SMEs want invest for the purpose of helping their users to protect the data and the system.

This work identifies opportunities and threat of security protection motivation in terms of providing right information at the right time and the right context. Further this paper takes the first step to identifying how protection motivation can be improved and leads to protection behaviour of computer users. This work complements the extant IS research that has discussed the role of protection motivation theory in the context of IT security.

Theoretically, we are extending this theory by integrating IT security champion and IT security training as constructs. In this research, these two constructs have been considered as central in the explanation of protection motivation of IT users of IT service oriented SMEs. Our combined theory will enrich the literature related IT security.

PRACTICAL IMPLICATIONS

Beyond the theoretical advances that this work presents, it has implications for practitioners. If organizations could control the naturally occurring computer user's security knowledge, security training and recruit security champion, they could potentially maximize the likelihood of IT security protection behaviour.

This study will reveal the linkage to IT staff of software companies or various IT service-oriented industries. Stakeholders of those organizations will get a clear picture of the root problem of employee negligence of IT protection. This research will assist decision makers in IT oriented service settings to improve the factors which will increase protection motivation behaviour of employees.

CONCLUSION

IT security protection is a key area in the field of IT and Management. Anderson and Agarwal (2010 p.613) state for example: "there is limited understanding of what drives home computer users to behave in a secure manner online, and even less insight into how to influence their behaviour". As a result, these issues influenced us to conduct this research in the context of Bangladesh; as Bangladesh recently faced various IT security threats. The question arises what are the factors influences protection motivation which will lead the general IT user to protection behaviour. To answer this question, we proposed that the protection motivation theory is a suitable theory to take as a starting point for further study. We extended this model with the integration of security champion and security training. Both of those factors have positive influence on threat and coping appraisal. Overall, our result model explains 34% variance of protection behaviour.

REFERENCES

Ahmad, A., & Maynard, S. (2014). Teaching information security management: Reflections and experiences. *Information Management & Computer Security*, *22*(5), 513–536. doi:10.1108/IMCS-08-2013-0058

Anderson, C. L., & Agarwal, R. (2010). Practicing safe computing: A multimedia empirical examination of home computer user security behavioral intentions. *Management Information Systems Quarterly*, *34*(3), 613–643.

Ashenden, D. (2008). Information Security Management: A human challenge? *Information Security Technical Report*, *13*(4), 195–201. doi:10.1016/j.istr.2008.10.006

Awawdeh, S., & Tubaishat, A. (2014). An Information Security Awareness Program to Address Common Security Concerns in IT Unit. *Information Technology: New Generations (ITNG), 2014 11th International Conference on* (pp. 273-278). IEEE.

Bartnes, M., Moe, N. B., & Heegaard, P. E. (2016). The future of information security incident management training: A case study of electrical power companies. *Computers & Security, 61*, 32–45. doi:10.1016/j.cose.2016.05.004

Baumgartner, H., & Homburg, C. (1996). Applications of structural equation modeling in marketing and consumer research: A review. *International Journal of Research in Marketing, 13*(2), 139–161. doi:10.1016/0167-8116(95)00038-0

Bhuiyan, T., Alam, D., & Farah, T. (2016). Evaluating the Readiness of Cyber Resilient Bangladesh. *Journal of Internet Technology and Secured Transactions, 4*(3), 405–415. doi:10.20533/jitst.2046.3723.2015.0051

Boer, H., & Seydel, E. R. (1996). *Protection motivation theory*. Retrieved July 16, 2015 from http://doc.utwente.nl/34896/1/K465____.PDF

Brown, J., Cohen, P., Johnson, J. G., & Smailes, E. M. (1999). Childhood abuse and neglect: Specificity of effects on adolescent and young adult depression and suicidality. *Journal of the American Academy of Child and Adolescent Psychiatry, 38*(12), 1490–1496. doi:10.1097/00004583-199912000-00009 PMID:10596248

Cavusoglu, H., Mishra, B., & Raghunathan, S. (2004). A model for evaluating IT security investments. *Communications of the ACM, 47*(7), 87–92. doi:10.1145/1005817.1005828

Cheng, A. L., Kang, Y. K., Chen, Z., Tsao, C. J., Qin, S., Kim, J. S., & Xu, J. et al. (2009). Efficacy and safety of sorafenib in patients in the Asia-Pacific region with advanced hepatocellular carcinoma: A phase III randomised, double-blind, placebo-controlled trial. *The Lancet Oncology, 10*(1), 25–34. doi:10.1016/S1470-2045(08)70285-7 PMID:19095497

Chenoweth, T., Minch, R., & Gattiker, T. (2009). Application of protection motivation theory to adoption of protective technologies. In *Proceedings of the 42nd Hawaii international conference on system sciences*. IEEE

Falkowski, G., Pedigo, P., Smith, B., & Swanson, D. (1998). A recipe for ERP success. *Beyond Computing, 6*(3), 44-45.

Floyd, D. L., Prentice-Dunn, S., & Rogers, R. W. (2000). A meta-analysis of research on protection motivation theory. *Journal of Applied Social Psychology, 30*(2), 407–429. doi:10.1111/j.1559-1816.2000.tb02323.x

Fornell, C., & Cha, J. (1994). Partial least squares. *Advanced Methods of Marketing Research, 407*(3), 52-78.

Goodro, M., Sameti, M., Patenaude, B., & Fein, G. (2012). Age effect on subcortical structures in healthy adults. *Psychiatry Research: Neuroimaging, 203*(1), 38–45. doi:10.1016/j.pscychresns.2011.09.014 PMID:22863654

Hair, J. F., Ringle, C. M., & Sarstedt, M. (2011). PLS-SEM: Indeed a silver bullet. *Journal of Marketing Theory and Practice, 19*(2), 139–152. doi:10.2753/MTP1069-6679190202

Hair, J.F., Sarstedt, M., Hopkins, L., & Kuppelwieser, , V. (. (2014). Partial least squares structural equation modeling (PLS-SEM) An emerging tool in business research. *European Business Review*, *26*(2), 106–112. doi:10.1108/EBR-10-2013-0128

Hassan, A. R., & Bhuiyan, M. I. H. (2016). Computer-aided sleep staging using complete ensemble empirical mode decomposition with adaptive noise and bootstrap aggregating. *Biomedical Signal Processing and Control*, *24*, 1–10. doi:10.1016/j.bspc.2015.09.002

Henseler, J., Ringle, C. M., & Sinkovics, R. R. (2009). The use of partial least squares path modeling in international marketing. *Advances in International Marketing, 20*(1), 277-319.

ICS-CERT. (2013). *ICS-CERT Monitor*. Retrieved Aug 9, 2015, from https://ics-cert.us-cert.gov/sites/default/files/Monitors/ICSCERT_Monitor_Oct-Dec2013.pdf

Ifinedo, P. (2009). Information technology security management concerns in global financial services institutions: Is national culture a differentiator? *Information Management & Computer Security*, *17*(5), 372–387. doi:10.1108/09685220911006678

Ifinedo, P. (2012). Understanding information systems security policy compliance: An integration of the theory of planned behaviour and the protection motivation theory. *Computers & Security*, *31*(1), 83–95. doi:10.1016/j.cose.2011.10.007

Janis, I. L. (1967). Effects of fear arousal on attitude change: Recent developments in theory and experimental research. *Advances in Experimental Social Psychology*, *3*, 166–224. doi:10.1016/S0065-2601(08)60344-5

Johnston, A. C., & Warkentin, M. (2010). Fear appeals and information security behaviours: An empirical study. *Management Information Systems Quarterly*, *34*(3), 549–566.

Lee, R. M., & Rid, T. (2014). OMG Cyber! Thirteen Reasons Why Hype Makes for Bad Policy. *The RUSI Journal*, *159*(5), 4–12. doi:10.1080/03071847.2014.969932

Lee, Y., & Larsen, K. R. (2009). Threat or coping appraisal: Determinants of SMB executives decision to adopt anti-malware software. *European Journal of Information Systems*, *18*(2), 177–187. doi:10.1057/ejis.2009.11

Leventhal, H. (1970). Findings and theory in the study of fear communications. *Advances in Experimental Social Psychology*, *5*, 119–186. doi:10.1016/S0065-2601(08)60091-X

Line, M. B., Zand, A., Stringhini, G., & Kemmerer, R. (2014). Targeted attacks against industrial control systems: Is the power industry prepared? In *Proceedings of the 2nd Workshop on Smart Energy Grid Security* (pp. 13-22). ACM. doi:10.1145/2667190.2667192

McAfee. (2011). *Global Energy Cyberattacks: "Night Dragon", McAfee Found stone Professional Services and McAfee Labs, Feb. 10, 2011*. Retrieved July 25, 2015 from, http://www.mcafee.com/in/resources/white-papers/wp-global-energy-cyberattacks-night-dragon.pdf

Nashique, N. (2015). *Cyber Crime Bangladesh*. Retrieved September 16, from http://www.thefinancialexpress-bd.com/2015/02/17/81536/print

Perlroth, N. (2012, October 23). In Cyberattack on Saudi Firm, US sees Iran firing back. *New York Times*.

Podsakoff, P. M., MacKenzie, S. B., Lee, J. Y., & Podsakoff, N. P. (2003). Common method biases in behavioral research: A critical review of the literature and recommended remedies. *The Journal of Applied Psychology*, *88*(5), 879–903. doi:10.1037/0021-9010.88.5.879 PMID:14516251

Podsakoff, P. M., & Organ, D. W. (1986). Self-reports in organizational research: Problems and prospects. *Journal of Management*, *12*(4), 531–544. doi:10.1177/014920638601200408

Podsakoff, P. M., & Todor, W. D. (1985). Relationships between leader reward and punishment behavior and group processes and productivity. *Journal of Management*, *11*(1), 55–73. doi:10.1177/014920638501100106

Ringle, C. M., Wende, S., & Becker, J. M. (2014). *Smartpls 3*. Hamburg, Germany: SmartPLS.

Roberts, N., & Grover, V. (2009). Theory development in information systems research using structural equation modeling: Evaluation and recommendations. In Handbook of Research on Contemporary Theoretical Models in Information Systems. Academic Press.

Rogers, R. W. (1983). Cognitive and physiological processes in fear appeals and attitude change: A revised theory of protection motivation. *Social Psychophysiology*, 153-176.

Siponen, M., Pahnila, S., & Mahmood, M. A. (2010). Compliance with information security policies: An empirical investigation. *Computer*, *43*(2), 64–71. doi:10.1109/MC.2010.35

Soto-Acosta, P., Ramayah, T., & Popa, S. (2013). Explaining Intention to Use an Enterprise Resource Planning System: A Replication and Extension. *Tehnickivjesnik/Technical Gazette, 20*(3).

Srisawang, S., Thongmak, M., & Ngarmyarn, A. (2015). Factors Affecting Computer Crime Protection Behavior. *PACIS 2015 Proceedings*. Retrieved March 7, 2016 From http://aisel.aisnet.org/pacis2015/31

Tenenhaus, M., Vinzi, V. E., Chatelin, Y. M., & Lauro, C. (2005). PLS path modeling. *Computational Statistics & Data Analysis*, *48*(1), 159–205. doi:10.1016/j.csda.2004.03.005

The Financial Express. (2015). *Cybercrimes increasing alarmingly in the country*. Retrieved December 28, from http://print.thefinancialexpress-bd.com/2015/12/27/127801

Travica, B. (2007). Of disobedience, divinations, monsters and fumbling: Adopting a self-service system. *Journal of Information, Information Technology, and Organizations*, *2*(1), 15–29.

Vance, A., Siponen, M., & Pahnila, S. (2012). Motivating IS security compliance: Insights from habit and protection motivation theory. *Information & Management*, *49*(3), 190–198. doi:10.1016/j.im.2012.04.002

Warkentin, M., & Willison, R. (2009). Behavioral and policy issues in information systems security: The insider threat. *European Journal of Information Systems*, *18*(2), 101–105. doi:10.1057/ejis.2009.12

Witte, K. (1992). Putting the fear back into fear appeals: The extended parallel process model. *Communication Monographs*, *59*(4), 329–349. doi:10.1080/03637759209376276

Woon, I., Tan, G.-W., & Low, R. (2005). A Protection Motivation Theory Approach to Home Wireless Security. *ICIS 2005 Proceedings*, 31.

Workman, M., Bommer, W. H., & Straub, D. (2008). Security lapses and the omission of information security measures: A threat control model and empirical test. *Computers in Human Behavior, 24*(6), 2799–2816. doi:10.1016/j.chb.2008.04.005

Zamir, M. (2016). Tackling the emerging problem of cybercrime. *The Financial Express*. Retrieved April 25, 2016, from: http://print.thefinancialexpress-bd.com/2016/03/17/136677

KEY TERMS AND DEFINITIONS

Coping Appraisal: Coping appraisal refers to individual's evaluation of their capability to handle and prevent the potential loss or damage arising from the threat.

Threat Appraisal: It is an external stimulus perceived by individual and if the individual perceives the threat therefore it can be concluded that the individuals are aware of the threats.

Protection Motivation: Motivation to diminish the threat are evaluated.

Security Champion: Security champion is a like project champion who sets rules and legitimize change for IT security issues throughout the organization.

Security Training: Training on knowledge and skills required managing information security, information assurance or information risk based processes.

APPENDIX

Table 8. Survey questionnaire

Perceived Value		
PV1	Loss of data resulting from hacking is a serious problem for me	Srisawang et al. 2015
PV2	I perceived importance regarding personal information	
PV3	I realize that I will be damaged if my computer was stolen or has been lost	
Security Knowledge		
SK1	I attend the training class to help improve my awareness of computer and information security issues	Srisawang et al. 2015
SK2	My organization educates employees on their computer security responsibilities	
SK3	I am interested in information about computer security	
Safeguard Cost		
SFC1	The inconvenience of implementing recommended IS security measures	Srisawang et al. 2015
SFC2	Enabling IS security measures in my organization would be time-consuming	
SFC3	There are too many overhead costs associated with implementing IS security measures in my organization	
Training		
TR1	The kind of training provided to me was complete	Soto-Acosta et al. 2013
TR2	My level of understanding was substantially improved after going through the training program.	
TR3	The training gave me confidence in the security system	
TR4	The training was of adequate length and detail	
TR5	The trainers were knowledgeable and aided me in my understanding of the security	
Security Champion		
SC1	Security champion has power to set goals.	Soto-Acosta et al. 2013
SC2	Security champion has power to legitimize change	
Threat Appraisal		
TA1	I know my computer could be vulnerable to security breaches if I don't adhere to protection measures.	Srisawang et al. 2015
TA2	It is extremely likely that crime will infect my computer	
TA3	Threats to the security of my computer are harmful	
Coping Appraisal		
CA1	I have the necessary skills to protect myself from information security violations	Srisawang et al. 2015
CA2	For me, taking information security precautions is easy	
CA3	My ability to prevent information security violations at my workplace is adequate	
Protection Motivation		
PM1	I intend to protect my computer from computer crime	Srisawang et al. 2015
PM2	I predict I would use antivirus/anti-spyware software	
PM3	I intend to follow the security news and find out how to prevent computer crimes	

continued on following page

Table 8. Continued

Protection Behaviour		
PB1	I installed antivirus software and keep it updated to prevent my computer from getting viruses and malware	
PB2	I always follow the suggestions for using a computer safely and appropriately	
PB3	I always follow the security policy whenever possible	

Table 9. Common method bias test result

	Total Variance Explained					
Component	Initial Eigenvalues			Extraction Sums of Squared Loadings		
	Total	% of Variance	Cumulative %	Total	% of Variance	Cumulative %
1	5.361	16.754	16.754	5.361	16.754	16.754
2	3.372	10.537	27.291			
3	2.454	7.670	34.961			
4	1.686	5.269	40.230			
5	1.602	5.006	45.236			
6	1.473	4.602	49.839			
7	1.343	4.198	54.037			
8	1.248	3.901	57.938			
9	1.158	3.618	61.556			
10	1.146	3.580	65.136			
11	1.060	3.313	68.449			
12	.973	3.039	71.489			
13	.867	2.709	74.198			
14	.789	2.466	76.664			
15	.774	2.420	79.084			
16	.635	1.985	81.069			
17	.617	1.927	82.996			
18	.613	1.914	84.910			
19	.566	1.768	86.678			
20	.525	1.641	88.318			
21	.483	1.510	89.829			
22	.448	1.401	91.230			
23	.427	1.333	92.564			
24	.375	1.172	93.735			
25	.343	1.071	94.807			
26	.334	1.043	95.850			
27	.298	.930	96.780			
28	.274	.856	97.636			

continued on following page

Table 9. Continued

Total Variance Explained						
Component	Initial Eigenvalues			Extraction Sums of Squared Loadings		
	Total	% of Variance	Cumulative %	Total	% of Variance	Cumulative %
29	.214	.669	98.305			
30	.197	.616	98.921			
31	.190	.593	99.514			
32	.155	.486	100.000			

Extraction Method: Principal Component Analysis

Table 10. Item loadings

Item	Loadings
CA1	0.723
CA2	0.628
CA4	0.818
PB1	0.898
PB3	0.564
PM2	0.695
PM3	0.852
PM4	0.701
PV2	0.534
PV3	0.732
PV4	0.837
SC2	0.879
SC3	0.643
SFC1	0.698
SFC3	0.970
SK2	0.569
SK3	0.800
SK4	0.732
TA1	0.771
TA2	0.824
TA3	0.681
TIS1	0.739
TIS2	0.788
TIS3	0.800
TIS4	0.665

Section 3
Usability Engineering

Chapter 15
The State of Art in Website Usability Evaluation Methods

Renuka Nagpal
Amity University - Uttar Pradesh, India

Deepti Mehrotra
Amity University - Uttar Pradesh, India

Pradeep Kumar Bhatia
Guru Jambeshwar University of Science and Technology, India

ABSTRACT

Measuring the usability of the website is a key metrics which all designers always tries to maximize. Compared to other software it is very difficult to estimate the website usability as each website has many objective and wide range of visitor with different learnability. The objective of this study is summarizing different approaches used to measure the usability of website. The current study includes the different approaches proposed in literature in last two decades. Approaches are classified in six broad categories and a comparison between them is done. Trends in web usability of evaluation approaches are understood in light of changing needs of website.

INTRODUCTION

Designing a technology or any system it is always a demand to consider capabilities and characteristics of the person who are going to use it. A lot of research had been carried out to study how to improve the interaction of human (Saeed & Bajwa 2014) with the system. These studies are categorized under different heads namely User Centered Systems Design, User Experience, User-Centered Design, Interaction Design and Human–Computer Interaction. Websites are platform which bring the world to the organization. Designing a user centric website that will provide the easy retrieval of information available on the website is a big challenge. Usability studies are related to designing and measuring the user satisfaction of the system. The website has a wide range of visitors and understanding their needs and designing a system satisfying the requirement can be interpreted in term of usability of website.

DOI: 10.4018/978-1-5225-1944-7.ch015

Usability is one of the key metrics used to identify the extent to which a computer system enables users to achieve the intended goals in effective and efficient manner for a given context. The prime objective is that to measure the level of satisfaction user feels using the system. Usability evaluation (UE) for any software consists of methodologies for measuring the usability aspects of a system's user interface (UI) and identifying specific problems. The website is designed with an objective to let the information move to the all possible end user. Thus usability study is key indication to the success of e-presence of the organization.

A wide variety of Usability Evaluation Method (UEM) are proposed in literature. 250 research paper of different journals of repute and conference paper were reviewed to investigate these approaches. A number of research paper focus of understanding the usability concept and used existing approaches in evaluating the website. Several papers discussed the factors (Saeed et. al. (2013), Saeed & Shabbir (2014), Hasan (2009)) affecting the usability of website. these studies range on websites for different sectors. Need of website may differ and hence the factor and evaluation approach may also differ. Approximately 90 research papers are considered in this study of which mostly discuss on the new approaches for usability evaluation of website. The focus of the study is on understanding various methods used to evaluate the usability of the website.

Before discussing them in detail in section 2 a brief introduction to various definitions and standards are discussed. In section3 approaches proposed in literature are discussed. These approaches are broadly classified in six categories namely evaluator based, user based, tool based, model based, MCDM approaches and soft computing approaches which are further clubbed as subjective and objective approach. Subjective approach focused mainly on the judgement of the people which van be an expert, end user, developer, manager etc. These approaches centers on the human judgment and hence uncertainty and collecting the data is a major concern. Objective approach focuses on collecting the crisp value and applying different models available. Subjective approach is usually performed manually where computer aided software is used to evaluate the task performed by the human evaluators. Objective approach usually is automated where tools are used evaluation and experts are used for interpreting the result. In section 4 comparative analysis of these approaches is done and need of combined approach is justified. In section 5 the syudy is concluded and future scope for the UEM''s is discussed.

BACK GROUND OF WEBSITE USABILITY

A large number of researchers proposes a wide range of definitions of usability and standards.

Definition of Usability

The fundamental of any website design is usability or "ease of use". Nielsen (1993) defines usability in terms of five characteristics:

- Learnability
- Efficiency
- Memorability
- Errors
- Satisfaction.

Rosson and Carroll (2002) identified three more perspectives that add to the definitions of usability (Ballard (2010):

- Human performance, time and errors
- Human cognition, mental models of plans and actions.
- Collaboration, group dynamics and workplace context.

Some of the popular definitions of usability that exists in literature are:

Bevan et. al. (1991) defines usability as "the ease of use and acceptability of a product for a particular class of users carrying out specific tasks in a specific environment". As per Nielsen (1993) usability is "a part of usefulness that is a part of practical acceptability and, finally, a part of system acceptability". Preece (1994) defined usability as "a measure of the ease with which a system can be learned or used". According to Redish (1995) "Usability means that the people who use the product, can do so quickly and easily to accomplish their own tasks". Drinck et al. (2002), usability is defined as "the degree to which people (users) can perform a set of required tasks". As per Rosson and Carroll (2001) usability is "the quality of a system with respect to ease of learning, ease of use, and user satisfaction". Abran et. al. (2003) defined usability as "The capability of the software product to be understood, learned, used and attractive to the user, when used under specified conditions." According to Krug (2005) "Usability is making sure that something works well: that a person of average (or even below average) ability and experience can use the thing – whether it's a website, a fighter jet, or a revolving door – for its intended purpose without getting hopelessly frustrated." The standard models for understanding the website are given are given in the following section.

Usability Related Standards

Standards for usability and Human Computer Interaction (HCI) are developed under International Organization for Standardization (ISO) and International Electrotechnical Commission (IEC). ISO and IEC standards related to usability is categorized by Bevan (2001) in Figure 1:

Figure 1. Categories of usability standards

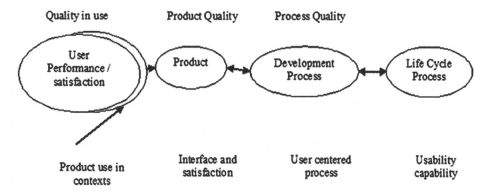

- Quality in use
- Product quality
- Process quality
- Organizational capability

According to ISO/IEC 9126 (1991), standard usability refers to "the capability of the software product to be understood, learned, used and attractive to the user, when used under specified conditions." ISO 9241-11 (1998) defines usability as "the extent to which a product can be used by specific users to achieve specified goals with effectiveness, efficiency, and satisfaction in specified context of use". This definition of usability does not imply necessarily of user interaction with the system and can be measured at early stage of development. ISO/IEC 25010 (2011), a quality model which replaces the previous standard ISO 9126-1, uses the same definition as ISO 9241-11: "The extent to which a product can be used by specified users to achieve specified goals with effectiveness, efficiency and satisfaction in a specified context of use". This quality model also includes a broader concept of quality in use: "The degree to which a product used by specific users meets their needs to achieve specific goals with effectiveness, efficiency, safety and satisfaction in specific contexts of use" (Bevan, 2010). "The ease with which a user can learn to operate, prepare inputs for, and interpret outputs of a system or component." (IEEE Std.610.12-1990). These definitions and models helps one to judge the website, but for better understanding these websites should be evaluated. As website has multiple dimensions, it can be evaluated in numerous ways. More than thirty approaches were studied and grouped into four categories, discussed in the subsequent section.

USABILITY EVALUATION METHOD (UEM)

The different definition of usability impacts various aspects of usability and the historical transition of interface from Command Line (CLI) to Graphical User (GUI). This transition raised the usability and accessibility problems which forced the researchers for developing UEM's for the friendly system. Websites are presently the backbone of any business to exchange information and present products and services. Success or failure of these websites depends on the user satisfaction level. Website usability evaluation, if performed at the designing stage can improve the quality of the site, but the website designers hardly do it because of perceived high cost. To deal with the arduous task of developing more usable websites, varieties of UEM's and tools exists to gather interaction of end-user with the software product. There is no universally accepted categorization of UEM's. Different authors classify UEM's in various categories. Ivory (2001), Fernandez et. al. (2011) classify UEM's into five general categories: Testing (evaluator observes how a user completes its task), Inspection (evaluator uses certain set of guidelines to inspect the user interface), Inquiry (Feedback on the interface is provided via user interviews, observations, etc.), Analytical modeling (different models are used for predicting usability) and Simulation (Simulation algorithm used to mimic and report the user interaction with the interface). Mack and Nielsen (1994) categorized usability into four groups: Automatic (Software evaluates the usability of the interface), Empirical (Interface is tested with real users), Formal-usage of models for evaluating user interface, Informal (thumb rules, experience for measuring the usability). UEM's are classified into three categories by Hasan (2009) as Evaluator based, User based and Tool based. In the current study,

UEM's are classified into majorly six categories based on Evaluator, User, Tool, Model, Multi Criteria Decision Making (MCDM) and Soft Computing as discussed in the following section.

Evaluator Based Usability Evaluation Method

Usability problems in a interface are identified by the set of evaluators and improvisation is done based on the evaluators feedback. These methods are known as Evaluator based UEM's (Mack and Nielsen (1994).

Heuristic Evaluation

Usability is evaluated by the experts and identifies the problem in the user interface based on compliance with well-defined usability principles known as "heuristics". The list of heuristics given by Mack and Nielsen (1994) are:

- Visibility of system status
- Match between system and the real world
- User control and freedom
- Consistency and standards
- Error Prevention
- Recognition rather than recall
- Flexibility and Efficiency of use
- Aesthetic and Minimalist design
- Helps users recognize, diagnose and recover from errors.
- Help and documentation

All the above mentioned heuristics are critically analyzed in the literature. Later on, these heuristics are modified for websites and given by Nielsen (2000) known as HOMERUN i.e. "highly quality content, often updated, minimal download time, ease of use, relevant to users' needs, unique to the online medium and adhering to net-centric corporate culture". In literature, many heuristics guidelines are tailored as per market research, new research findings and design guidelines (Kostaras & Xenos, 2007; Sharp et. al., 2007; Hasan, 2009; Hasan, 2013; Torrente et. al., 2013; Cheng & Mustafa, 2014; Yáñez Gómez et al., 2014).

Pluralistic Walkthrough

In this UEM, the interface is inspected by the group of evaluators which includes users, designers and evaluators (usability experts), to perform the set of tasks for presenting the new idea about the interface. Five major characteristics of pluralistic walkthrough is given below:

1. It involves users, designers and usability experts in same walkthrough session as participants.
2. The interface of the screen is presented in the form of hardcopy panels and presented to evaluators in the similar order as it would be submitted on the web.
3. The participants will assume themselves as users.

4.   As per the task for each screen, the participants provide their feedback in detail.

5.   The solution is discussed by the group on their opinions.

The benefit in performing the pluralistic walkthrough is that it provides the feedback even before developing the complete interface resulting "on-the-fly" (rapid iteration) design as it involves the direct users (Hollingsed & Novick, 2007). The downside of this method is that because of time constraints only a few scenarios and their corresponding paths can be investigated (Hollingsed & Novick, 2007); Hasan, 2009). This method is still popular for evaluating usability which involves users walkthrough without experts involvement.

Cognitive Walkthrough

The Cognitive walkthrough is a task specific UEM to predict the usability issues. This method evaluates the ease with the user can perform the task without formal instructions (Wharton et. al., 1994). Designers and developers of the software evaluate the interface step-by-step "walking through" to accomplish specified tasks. For each step, the team of evaluators tried to find the response to the question given by (Wharton et. al., 1994) (Table 1). Cognitive Walkthrough was studied by multiple authors and many improved versions were discussed in the literature and adapted in different domains (Mahatody et. al., 2010).

Sears (1997) combined benefits of two inspection method i.e., cognitive walkthrough and Heuristic Evaluation based on prioritization of task and obtained results are analysed to inspect any aspect of the system. Streamlined Cognitive Walkthrough (SCW): Spencer (2000) proposed SCW that divides the usability evaluation into five phases starting from the input--role definition of team member and do's and don'ts for evaluators--inspection-recording problems--fixation of problems identified. Cognitive Walkthrough for Web (CWW) (Blackmon et. Al., 2002), Kitajima, 2006) detects and fix errors that comes while browsing the information on the website. Users surf the web page with an objective in his mind which consists of choosing (i.e. clicking on a link) and assessing the output as a goal.

Other methods that are available in the literature are The Norman Cognitive Walkthrough Method (Rizzo et. al., 1997) (high level interaction problem are addressed), Groupware Walkthrough (complexities of team work) (Pinelle & Gutwin, 2002), Activity Walkthrough (aim to include context and history of use) (Bertelsen, 2004), Interaction Walkthrough (Ryu & Monk, 2004) (low level interaction), Cognitive Walkthrough with Users (end users involved for evaluating interactive systems), Extended Cognitive Walkthrough (identifying the problems regarding accessibility and usability), Distributed Cognitive Walkthrough (communication between personages, artefact, and information across dimensions such as time, space, and social structures), and Enhanced Cognitive Walkthrough (confirms whether the as-

Table 1. Questionnaires

Will the user try to achieve the right effect?
Will the user notice that the correct action is available?
Will the user associate the correct action with the effect that user is trying to achieve?
If the correct action is performed, will the user see that progress is being made toward the solution of the task?

sumed user's generated goal and prior knowledge directs to the subsequent correct action). Cognitive Walkthrough helps to classify the usability problems quickly as the design is specified. The main aim of all the cognitive approach is to prepare goals, suitable actions to achieve goals, correct interpretation of system responses, and accomplishment of targets.

Guideline Reviews

This method is analogous to Heuristic Evaluation Method with a difference that this UEM contains long detailed guidelines as compared to the short list available with heuristic evaluators. This process may take a longer time to review an interface and hence not preferred as compared to heuristic evaluation (Hasan, 2009).

Consistency Inspections

In consistency inspections, evaluators ensure the consistency across the interface so that design is reliable regarding functions, design, and color. Before developing the product, the consistency inspection is being performed so that users' performance and satisfaction can be increased (Lazar (2005)).

Standard Inspections

As per the other interface standards followed in the same market, experts examine the compliance of an interface. The expert who is familiar with the formal language, written in the standards is usually taken for inspection (Hasan, 2009).

User Based Usability Evaluation Method

User based UEM's involves the users for evaluating an interface and records their performance while interacting with it. Some user based UEM's are mentioned below:

User Testing

According to Dumas and Redish (1999), the user testing method is "a well-organized way of inspecting actual users trying out a product and collecting information about the specific ways in which the product is easy or difficult for them".

Think Aloud

Participants are asked to "think aloud" and say whatever comes to their mind while performing the set of tasks. Evaluators can analyze the thought process of the participants about an interface and helps to identify mistaken belief of the users. For library catalogue, Van Den Haak et.al.(2003) categories think aloud protocol into concurrent, and retrospective think aloud method for usability test regarding detected usability problems, the overall performance of a task, and participant experiences. The major limitation of think aloud method is that while collecting data user can behave unusually in the presence of data collection equipment (Hasan, 2009).

Question Asking Protocol

Question Asking Protocol is another user testing method in UEM's where the user is directly interrogated by the evaluator about an interface so that user thought process can be well understood Ivory (2001).

Co-Discovery Learning

Co-discovery Learning is an extension of Think Aloud method where instead of a single user, two or more users interact with the user interface to complete their task. As the number of users is large, more comments can be obtained from the users Holzinger (2005). The limitation as compared to think aloud method is the cost of incorporating more users Van den Haak et. al. (2004).

Retrospective Testing

In Retrospective Testing, the responses from the user are analyzed while watching their recorded video sessions. Users can add their comments while reviewing their sessions (Nielsen, 1993; Ivory, 2001; Lazar, 2005). More information can be gained from the user with a limitation of additional cost and long duration for conducting this test.

Questionnaires and Interviews

This method is used to analyze the user's subjective satisfaction with the interface (Ivory, 2001). It can only be used to collect information regarding the user's opinion about an interface but user actual behavior cannot be analyzed which always has priority over the opinion (Holzinger, 2005; Hasan, 2009; Saeed et. al., 2013). The response rate for the questionnaire distributed is usually low (Bidgoli, 2004) and conducting the interview is a time-consuming process. This method is an indirect method of evaluating usability and cannot be used alone.

Focus Groups

A focus group is a meeting of a group of usually six to nine users wherein users are asked to give their opinion related to the interface. The users are free to discuss his opinion with other group members, and evaluator plays the role of the moderator discussing predefined issues and collects the information required. It can provide the information regarding the problem with the interface but can't analyze the direct user interaction with the system (Ivory, 2001; Hasan, 2009).

Barefoot Approach

"Software development practitioners are instructed to drive usability evaluations" (Bruun & Stage, 2015). Earlier some of the studies has tried to include software developers' practitioners in usability evaluation without giving them formal training, raising the awareness for usability issues. In Barefoot approach, the software practitioners who have little or no knowledge about the usability evaluations are trained to analyze and fix the usability issues (Bruun & Stage, 2015).

Crowd Sourcing Approach

"End users are given minimalist training to enable them to drive usability evaluations" Bruun & Stage (2015). In this method, the usability experts and the users are separated.

Tool Based Usability Evaluation Method

Software tools are used to evaluate the usability of an interface instead of employing users or experts. Some of the methods are listed in the following sections.

Automatic

In automatic evaluation, tools analyze whether an interface complies the usability set standards. It verifies quality of HTML code in compliance with the guidelines. Website Analysis and Measurement Inventory(WAMMI) (Kirakowski, J et. al., 1998; Chiew & Salim, 2003) is a website evaluation tool based on the questionnaire filled by the user of the website. It helps to analyze the website based on five critical parameters i.e., Attractiveness, Control, efficiency, Helpfulness and Learnability. Other tools available today for assessing the usability of the website is OpenHallway that records usability sessions and recorded sessions can be evaluated remotely by the evaluators, ClickHeat is an open source software tool for observing the click pattern of actual users. Google Analytics is a free usability testing tool to identify behavior, trends, and issues which includes user sessions, visits, page views.

Web Analytics

Usability issues are measured by collecting and analyzing the usage data in different logs using different software packages (Web Mining). Web Mining has been vastly used to uncover the knowledge of web documents and services. It is broadly divided into three categories: Web content mining used for mining the information present on the site, Web structure Mining that helps in improving the design of the website by finding the useful pages and associating important page links to it and Web usage mining which mines the patterns of usage of the website. The data used for it are the logs of the client server transaction and are available in the server log, referral log, agent logs and client side cookies. These patterns are also mapped with the user profiles to predict the user behavior Srivastava et. al. (2000).

Log files, as the data source for web analytics has a major limitation regarding usage of caching techniques and IP address to recognize unique visitors (Kaushik, 2007; Hasan et. al., 2013). To cover this limitation page tagging methods i.e. java script code is added to web pages to collect user statistics over the extended period of time. The accuracy of this method is more as it is based on cookies to identify the unique visitors. One of the popular tools that use page tagging approach that has an impact on Google industry is Google Analytics(GA) (Fang, 2007; Hasan et. al., 2013).

Remote Testing

In Remote testing, the users and the testers are at different locations. This method is applied in conjunction with log analysis (Fernandez et. al., 2011).

Analytical Modelling

Analytical modeling employs users and models to predict usability issues of Human Interaction with the interface while completing a task. Examples of Analytical Model are: GOMS, WUSAB, GLEAN (Atterer et. al., 2006; Atterer, 2008).

GOMS Approach

Card et. al (1983) proposes an approach GOMS (Goals, Operators, Methods and Selection rules) and is defined as "model that describes essential interactions that users have with a user interface while completing tasks to reach a goal." Depending on the complexity of a "goal", it is divided into sub-goals. To achieve the goals, the model consists of "operators" that are applied by the user on a perceptual, subjective or motor-act level which can lead to internal and external changes. Execution times are bound to these operators to predict the overall interaction time. To achieve goals, "Methods" describe sequencing of operators. Depending on the task, "Selection rules" are applied if more than one method exists representing the user's knowledge, Task analysis must be performed to identify the goals. GOMS method represents the procedural aspects of usability. The variety of GOMS models are available For e.g. Keystroke Level Model (KLM) for modeling human performance by "predicting the execution time taken by the user to perform a specified task" Card et. al.(1980), Davis (2010). GOMS Language Evaluation and Analysis(GLEAN) Application of GOMS model is automated by GLEAN, which takes the model as an input. GLEAN predicts "how long user takes to perform the task to complete a goal."Other methods are: Critical-Path Method GOMS (CPM-GOMS), Natural GOMS Language (NGOMSL) (John & Kieras, 1996; Davis, 2010).

Web Usability (WUSAB)

WUSAB is an approach that "tests conformance of interfaces to Web pages with prerequisite" (Atterer et. al., 2006; Atterer 2008). WUSAB permits any of the different existing layouts to arrange contents as accepted by the validator. With the development of the web application, WUSAB compares the actual characteristics of the web application with the existing one and report the inconsistencies and also alerts the developer with any tricky change in the application. It inspects models, and logs produced and the HTML code of the web application.

Programmable User Model (PUM)

PUM is based on a problem-solving model for navigating problem spaces. PUM deals with "knowledge needed by the user" i.e. the knowledge the user should have for interacting with the interface and also with respect to given interface predicting the behavior of given users (Butterworth et. al., 1997).

Metrics for Usability Standard in Computing (MUSic)

Macleod et.al. (1997) develops a model for measuring the efficiency and effectiveness of a software system at National Physical Laboratory(NPL), UK for measuring the qualitative and quantitative data.

It is based on the observation that while using the system how user achieves the task objective, and performs a task while using the system.

Software Usability Measurement Inventory (SUMI)

To measure the quality of the software system as per user's point of view Kirakowski & Corbett (1993) develops SUMI as a part of MUSiC Project at University College Cork Software Usability Measurement Inventory. The standardized set of internationally structured 50-item questionnaire available in the different language is given to the user to answer according to whether they "Agree, Don't Know or Disagree".

Diagnostic Recorder for Usability Measurement (DRUM)

Macleod & Rengger (1993) within MUSiC project develops a software tool, DRUM, for usability evaluation at NPL, UK to meet the requirement of the user in an effective, efficient and satisfying manner. Video recorded session is used for usability evaluation increasing the speed of analysis and automating the activity to the extent possible. Log Processor processes the log in the database and evaluates the performance based usability metrics like task time, snag, effectiveness, efficiency, relative efficiency and productive period. The results are saved in the database numerically and graphically for further analysis and used by designers for usability defects.

Multi Criteria Decision Making Based Usability Evaluation Method

Multi-Criteria Decision making (MCDM) is a process of making decision by choosing the best alternative involving multiple criteria and defined Zardari et.al.(2015) "The study of methods and procedures that incorporates the multiple and conflicting criteria into the decision process." Multi-Criteria Decision Analysis (MCDA), Multi-Attribute Decision making (MADM), Multi-Objective Decision Making (MODM), and Multi-Dimensions Decision Making (MDDM) are the alternate terms used for MCDM. Researchers commonly employs MCDM approaches as they are considered to be a transparent approach. A systematic algorithm is framed to enhance the objectivity and accuracy of results. The ranking obtained has shown a reasonable level of satisfaction and hence, MCDM approaches are considered as an integral part of Decision Support system. However, Mutikanga (2012) has identified considerable criticism to MCDM. The majority of various MCDM method provides the contrary conclusions for the same dataset. Thus, selecting a suitable MCDM method or combining two approaches that produce trade-off between the good performance of criteria and poor performance of other criteria. In literature, there exists several MCDM methods, the most famous among them are summarized by Velasquez and Hester (2013).

Analytic Hierarchy Process (AHP)

Saaty (1990) (2008) defines AHP as "a theory of measurement through pairwise comparisons and relies on the judgments of experts to derive priority scales". AHP uses pairwise comparisons to compare different alternatives available on criteria to estimate the criteria weights.

Elimination EtChoix Traduisant la REalite (ELECTRE)

Roy (1991) gives a MCDM approach which helps experts to take vagueness and ambiguity while making the decisions.

Preference Ranking Organization Method for Enrichment Evaluations (PROMETHEE)

PROMETHEE is one of the MCDM approach similar to ELECTRE. PROMTHEEE was given by Brans et. al (1984) for partial and complete ranking of the alternatives and with time, the iterations of this method have improved.

Technique for Order of Preference by Similarity to Ideal Solution (TOPSIS)

One of the most popular MCDM approach given by Hwang et. al. (1993). It is defined as (Qin, 2008) "an approach to identify an alternative which is closest to the ideal solution and farthest to the negative ideal solution in a multi-dimensional computing space".

Multi-Attribute Utility Theory (MAUT)

MAUT (Peter C. Fishburn, 1967; Dyer et.al., 2005) deals with the problems having the considerable amount of uncertainty and risks. Utility is assigned to each possible consequence, thus calculating the best possible utility.

Analytic Network Process (ANP)

According to Saaty (2001) ANP is "generalization of AHP" and is considered as network structure for better handling of interdependence and feedback. It uses network relations for evaluating the interrelationship between the criteria and decision levels.

Goal Programming (GP)

Goal programming is one of the oldest MCDM technique. The main objective of GP is to covert Multiple objectives into a single goal. Multiple objective goals are optimized, minimizing the divergence for each of the objectives from the desired target (Orumie U.C. & Ebong, D., 2014).

Simple Additive Weighting (SAW)

SAW is defined by Qin et. al. (2008) as "a value function is established based on a simple addition of scores that represent the goal achievement under each criterion, multiplied by the particular weights".

Case-based Reasoning (CBR)

CBR uses prior experience for solving the case/problem (Aamodt & Plaza, 1994). CBR uses a cyclic process to solve a problem. Solution to a problem is given by "retrieving" similar experienced case / cases, "reusing the information / knowledge, "revising the solution and "retaining" it for the future use.

Grey Theory

Grey Theory given by Julong (1989) focuses on problems having the small sample size and inadequate information. It deals with uncertain structure with incomplete information through producing, excavating and selecting valuable information from what is available (Liu et. al., 2012).

Data Envelopment Analysis (DEA)

Relative efficiencies of comparable units are measured with multiple inputs and outputs (Charnes et. al., 1978). DEA is based on Linear Programming model. It also helps to analyze the cost and resource savings when an inefficient unit is transformed into an efficient one.

Best-Worst Method (BWM)

Rezaei (2015) developed a new MCDM method known as BWM. The aim of this method is to select the best alternative amongst given set of options. It produces more reliable results with less number of comparisons as in AHP.

Soft Computing Approaches Based Usability Evaluation Method

According to Lofti Zadeh (1994), Soft computing is a "collection of methodologies that aim to exploit the tolerance for imprecision, uncertainty, and partial truth to achieve tractability, robustness, and low solution cost". When compared with Hard Computing, Soft Computing deals with approximation giving the solution to complex problems. The computational effort, time and cost required in a traditional approach can be replaced by replacing with soft computing approach without affecting the solution (Cabrera et. al., 2009). The main components of Soft Computing Approach are "Fuzzy Logic, Probabilistic Reasoning, Neural Computing and Genetic Algorithms" sharing common features and are complementary rather than competitive and can be combined in models offering the solution to more complex problems. The most popular combined approach is neuro fuzzy systems employing the combination of Neural Network and Fuzzy.

Artificial Neural Network (ANN)

Information processing system that models human brain to perform task much faster as compared to traditional systems. According to Caudill (1987), simplest definition of a neural network, more properly referred to as an artificial' neural network (ANN), is "...a computing system made up of a number of simple, highly interconnected processing elements, which process information by their dynamic state response to external inputs".

ANN learns by example. Large number of units/nodes/neurons operating in parallel having their own internal (activation) state are connected via connection link associated with weights. The connection links contain the information about input signal as shown in Figure 2. X1 and X2 are input neurons connected to another Y neuron over weighted connection link W1 and W2 with x1 and x2 as output of input signals. Finally, output y can be applied by applying activation function to the net input.

Neuro Fuzzy Hybrid System

A hybrid intelligent system is given by Jang (1993) that combines the advantage of fuzzy systems (natural language description) and Neural Network (learning properties) with explicit and implicit knowledge respectively. It utilizes learning and training algorithms from neural network with human like reasoning style of fuzzy system to find parameters (fuzzy sets, rules, etc.) (Nagpal et. al., 2013).

Neuro Fuzzy system is generally represented by three layers i.e., first second and third, feed forward neural network model that corresponds to input variables, fuzzy rules and output values respectively as shown in Figure 3.

Fuzzy MCDM

There may be circumstances where decision support system may not work effectively because of inadequate information, thus usage of expert system becomes necessitate. Expert system can give satisfactory solution processing uncertainty of different kinds. Fuzzy theory is best solution for this purpose which can deal with uncertainty, vagueness and also with large quantity of information (Zimmermann, 2012). There may be a situation in which the goal or attribute cannot be defined within set of boundaries. Classical MCDM approach cannot be applied in such situation as they are suitable to handle the problems having well defined set of boundaries i.e. crisp values (Kahraman, 2008). The presence of vagueness in a MCDM problem will definitely increase the complexity because of the computational effort involve to rank different alternatives. In literature Bellman & Zadeh (1970); Zimmerman (1978) dealt with such complex problems, there has been successful application of fuzzy set theory in MCDM problems known

Figure 2. Artificial neural network

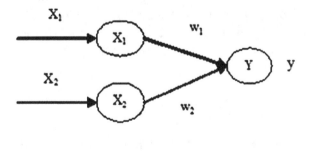

Figure 3. General Architecture of neuro fuzzy hybrids

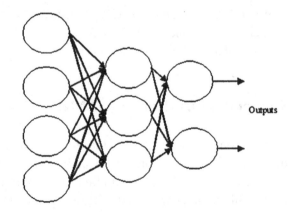

as fuzzy MCDM. In fuzzy MCDM approach, one or more DM's assess different alternatives (Nagpal et. al., 2015) with respect to predetermined criteria, where weights of the criteria is evaluated using linguistic values represented by fuzzy numbers.

COMPARATIVE STUDY

Figure 4 represents the number of paper referred for each UEM's. It is clear from the figure that Expert based evaluation UEM is the most preferred approach. Now in recent years, the trend is changing and evaluators have started using the MCDM approach for usability evaluation. In MCDM approach, the complex problems are solved by taking the feedback from the decision maker (DM) who can be an expert or a user.

The comparative analysis all six approaches in done. A brief discussion of each with their advantage and disadvantages are given in Table 2.

UEM's are broadly grouped into two categories Subjective Method and Objective Method. Subjective Approach includes user's perception to view and understand website. The expertise of Decision Makers (DM's) is considered as input to assign subjective importance. Uncertainty and Biasness of DM's is one of the major weakness of subjective approach. Objective Approach uses mathematical models and tools to evaluate the crisp values. Objective methods do not include user's perception, which is one of the major drawback of this approach. Usually authors have adopted subjective or objective approach but we feel that with combined approach, a new model can be designed which can give better insight to the picture Figure 5.

Figure 4. Graphical representation of papers distribution for UEM's

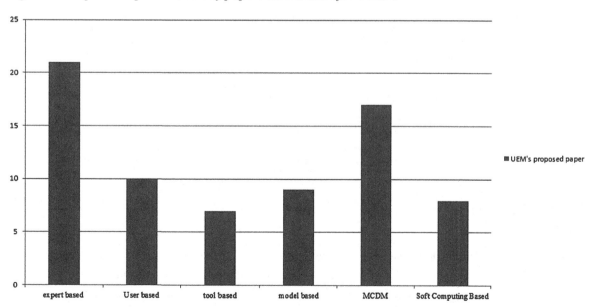

Table 2. Comparative analysis of different UEM's

UEM	Description	Advantages	Disadvantages
Evaluator Based	Experts of usability make the assessment	Can be performed iteratively and anytime throughout the development process, Less cost.	reliance on expertise of the evaluators, usability problems identified is more towards interface features rather than task performance i.e." usefulness".
User based	Assessment of the interface is done by the actual users	Exploring the user's interaction directly, collects firsthand information about the usability problems and user preferences.	The feedback of the user may get influenced by the group activity thus actual behavior of the users cannot be determined. The issues related to representation of information in the system is not addressed. Cost of conducting the experiments is high.
Tool Based	Automatic calculation of the required metrics	Easy to use, multiple users at different locations	Different tools are required to measure different metrics
Model Based	Formal methods are employed for the prediction of criteria of user performance	Usability criteria can be accurately estimated	User testing required to unfold the critical issues.
MCDM based	Decision makers' preference is required to distinguish between alternatives.	Consider uncertainty; handles large scale problems with multiple alternatives	Interdependence of criteria and alternatives leads to rank reversal.
Soft Computing Based	Provides solution to imprecise problems	Consider uncertainty and vagueness; nonlinear problems are solved	Crisp values cannot be attain

Figure 5. Classification of usability evaluation methods

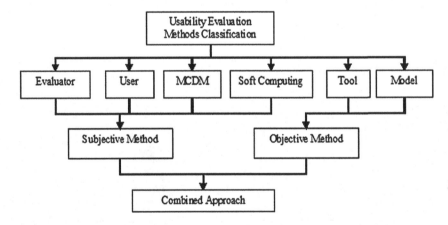

CONCLUSION

This study focus on finding the different evaluation method that are currently in practice in domain of web usability. Each approach has its own advantages and disadvantages and hence proving any one of them to be most effective is not justified. Currently the websites are dynamic so evaluating website should be a continuous process. Hybrid approaches evaluates the metrics of the system including the user preference giving better results as compared to This chapter presented the concepts about Usability Evaluation Methods and factors affecting the usability. Researchers have identified large number of factors, some of them are common to generic model of website and some are specific for a given website. Usability being a multi criteria problem, MCDM approaches can be suitably used for predicting the usability. Various MCDM approaches are discussed in detail with advantages, disadvantages and their application area. MCDM approaches relies majorly on subjective measures. To overcome the uncertainty of the subjective measure, the fuzzy approach is combined with MCDM approaches and are discussed in detail.

Usability is a measure of the interactive user experience associated with a user interface, with the website. A lot of approach is available in the literature to measure how user friendly interface of website is design with respect to easy-to-learn, supports users' tasks and goals efficiently and effectively, and is satisfying and engaging to use. Analysis of usability provides an insight of User Experience that helps to recommend the website designer how and where to re-design the interface in order to improve its level of interaction and user satisfaction.

Evaluating the usability of website is crucial for their success of an organization and in current scenario the website applications are very dynamic and complex contain a large variety of information, allow huge amount of information exchange there by making speed and security a critical factor for making people use it. People today want to use the web applications on mobile phones making the designing it more challenging. Further as per business need the organizations are changing their website designs very frequently, in, so developers can learn how to adapt them considering the dynamicity of current scenarios. Thus the future evaluation approach should focus on different requirements when judging those applications, such as objective metrics (quantitative data), subjective evaluation (users' impressions). An attempt should be made design a single methodology that be take a look on both of them. Also this approach should support the environmental change (e.g. hardware platform device used, software platform) The model should automatically monitor and collect objective data and also collect users' and expert feedback and analyse it. Future approach should be centred around Figure 5 for holistic evaluation.

REFERENCES

Aamodt, A., & Plaza, E. (1994). Case-based reasoning: Foundational issues, methodological variations, and system approaches. *AI Communications*, 7(1), 39–59.

Abran, A. (2003). Consolidating the ISO usability models.*Proceedings of 11th International Software Quality Management Conference*, (pp. 23–25).

Atterer, R. (2008, October). Model-based automatic usability validation: a tool concept for improving web-based UIs. In *Proceedings of the 5th Nordic conference on Human-computer interaction: building bridges* (pp. 13-22). ACM. doi:10.1145/1463160.1463163

Atterer, R., Wnuk, M., & Schmidt, A. (2006). Knowing the user's every move: user activity tracking for website usability evaluation and implicit interaction. In *Proceedings of the 15th international conference on World Wide Web* (pp. 203-212). ACM. doi:10.1145/1135777.1135811

Ballard, J. K. (2010). Web Site Usability: A Case Study of Student Perceptions of Educational Web Sites. Academic Press.

Bellman, R. E., & Zadeh, L. A. (1970). Decision-making in a fuzzy environment. *Management Science*, 17(4), B-141–B-164. doi:10.1287/mnsc.17.4.B141

Bertelsen, O. (2004). The activity walkthrough: an expert review method based on activity theory. In *Proceedings of the third Nordic conference on Human-computer interaction SE- NordiCHI '04* (pp. 251–254). doi:10.1145/1028014.1028052

Bevan, N. (2001). International standards for HCI and usability. *International Journal of Human-Computer Studies, 55*(4), 533–552. doi:10.1006/ijhc.2001.0483

Bevan, N. (2010). Extending the concept of satisfaction in ISO standards. In *Proceedings of the KEER 2010 International Conference on Kansei Engineering and Emotion Research.*

Bevan, N., Kirakowsky, J., & Maissel, J. (1991). What is usability. In *Proceedings of 4th International Conference on Human Computer Interaction.* Elsevier.

Bidgoli, H. (2004). *The Internet Encyclopedia.* Available at: http://www.loc.gov/catdir/description/wiley0310/2002155552.html

Blackmon, Polson, Kitajima, & Lewis. (2002). Cognitive Walkthrough for the Web. *Proceedings of the {SIGCHI} conference on Human factors in computing systems: Changing our world, changing ourselves.*

Brans, J. P., Mareschal, B., & Vincke, P. (1984). PROMETHEE: A New Family of Outranking Methods in Multicriteria Analysis. In Operational Research (pp. 477–490). Academic Press.

Brinck, T., Gergle, D., & Wood, S. D. (2002). *Usability for the Web.* San Francisco: Morgan Kaufmann.

Bruun, A., & Stage, J. (2015). New approaches to usability evaluation in software development: Barefoot and crowdsourcing. *Journal of Systems and Software, 105*, 40–53. doi:10.1016/j.jss.2015.03.043

Butterworth, R., & Blandford, A. (1997). *Programmable user models: The story so far.* London: Middlesex University.

Cabrera, I. P., Cordero, P., & Ojeda-Aciego, M. (2009). Fuzzy logic, soft computing, and applications. In Bio-Inspired Systems: Computational and Ambient Intelligence (pp. 236-244). Springer Berlin Heidelberg. doi:10.1007/978-3-642-02478-8_30

Card, S., Moran, T. P., & Newell, A. (1983). The GOMS model of manuscript editing.The psychology of human-computer interaction, (pp. 139-189).

Card, S. K., Moran, T. P., & Newell, A. (1980). The keystroke-level model for user performance time with interactive systems. *Communications of the ACM, 23*(7), 96–110. doi:10.1145/358886.358895

Caudill, M. (1987). Neural networks primer, part I. *AI Expert, 2*(12), 46–52.

Charnes, A., Cooper, W. W., & Rhodes, E. (1978). Measuring the efficiency of decision making units. *European Journal of Operational Research, 2*(6), 429–444. doi:10.1016/0377-2217(78)90138-8

Cheng, L. C., & Mustafa, M. (2014). A Reference to Usability Inspection Methods. In *International Colloquium of Art and Design* (pp. 45–51).

Chiew, T. K., & Salim, S. S. (2003). Webuse: Website usability evaluation tool. *Malaysian Journal of Computer Science, 16*(1), 47–57.

Davis, P. A. (2010). *Learning Usability Assessment Models For Web Sites* (Doctoral dissertation). Texas A&M University.

Dumas, J. S., & Redish, J. (1999). *A practical guide to usability testing*. Intellect Books.

Fang, W. (2007). Using Google Analytics for improving library website content and design: A case study. *Library Philosophy and Practice*, *9*(2), 22.

Fernandez, A., Insfran, E., & Abrahão, S. (2011). Usability Evaluation Methods for the Web: A Systematic Mapping Study. *Information and Software Technology*, *53*(8), 789–817. doi:10.1016/j.infsof.2011.02.007

Fishburn, P. C. (1967). Additive Utilities With Incomplete Product Sets: Application To Priorities And Assignments. *Operations Research*, *15*(3), 537–542. Available at http://www.jstor.org/stable/168461 doi:10.1287/opre.15.3.537

Hasan, L. (2009). *Usability evaluation framework for e-commerce websites in developing countries* (Doctoral dissertation).

Hasan, L. (2013). Heuristic Evaluation of Three Jordanian University Websites. *Informatics in Education*, *12*(2), 231–251.

Hollingsed, T., & Novick, D. G. (2007). Usability inspection methods after 15 years of research and practice. In *Proceedings of the 25th annual ACM International Conference on Design of communication*. ACM. doi:10.1145/1297144.1297200

Holzinger, A. (2005). Usability engineering methods for software developers. *Communications of the ACM*, *48*(1), 71–74. doi:10.1145/1039539.1039541

Hwang, C.-L., Lai, Y.-J., & Liu, T.-Y. (1993). A new approach for multiple objective decision making. *Computers & Operations Research*, *20*(8), 889–899. doi:10.1016/0305-0548(93)90109-V

Institute of Electrical and Electronics Engineers. (1990). *610.12-1990, IEEE Standard Glossary of Software Engineering Terminology*. Los Alamitos, CA: Author.

ISO/IEC 9126. (1991). *Software product evaluation – quality characteristics and guidelines for their use*. ISO.

ISO/IEC 25010. (2011). *Systems and software engineering – Software product Quality Requirements and Evaluation (SQuaRE) – Software product quality and system quality in use models*. ISO.

ISO 9241-11. (1998). *Guidelines for specifying and measuring usability*. ISO.

Ivory, M. Y. (2001). *An empirical foundation for automated web interface evaluation* (Doctoral dissertation). University of California at Berkeley.

Jang, J. S. R. (1993). ANFIS: Adaptive-network-based fuzzy Inference system. *Systems, Man and Cybernetics. IEEE Transactions on*, *23*(3), 665–685.

John, B. E., & Kieras, D. E. (1996). The GOMS family of user interface analysis techniques: Comparison and contrast. *ACM Transactions on Computer-Human Interaction*, *3*(4), 320–351. doi:10.1145/235833.236054

Julong, D. (1989). Introduction to grey system theory. *Journal of Grey System*, *1*(1), 1–24.

Kahraman, C. (Ed.). (2008). *Fuzzy multi-criteria decision making: theory and applications with recent developments* (Vol. 16). Springer Science & Business Media. doi:10.1007/978-0-387-76813-7

Kaushik, A. (2007). Web Analytics: An Hour A Day (W/Cd). John Wiley & Sons.

Kirakowski, J., Claridge, N., & Whitehand, R. (1998, June). Human centered measures of success in web site design. In *Proceedings of the Fourth Conference on Human Factors & the Web*.

Kirakowski, J., & Corbett, M. (1993). SUMI: The software usability measurement inventory. *British Journal of Educational Technology*, *24*(3), 210–212. doi:10.1111/j.1467-8535.1993.tb00076.x

Kitajima, M. (2006). *Cognitive Walkthrough for the web. International encyclopedia of ergonomics and human factors*. CRC Press.

Kostaras, N., & Xenos, M. (2007, May). Assessing educational web-site usability using heuristic evaluation rules. In *Proceedings of 11th Panhellenic Conference in Informatics*, (pp. 543-550).

Krug, S. (2005). *Don't make me think: A common sense approach to web usability*. Pearson Education India.

Lazar, J. (2005). *Web usability: A user-centered design approach*. Addison-Wesley Longman Publishing Co., Inc.

Liu, S., Forrest, J., & Yang, Y. (2012). A brief introduction to grey systems theory. Grey Systems. *Theory and Application*, *2*(2), 89–104.

Mack, R. L., & Nielsen, J. (Eds.). (1994). *Usability inspection methods*. New York, NY: Wiley & Sons.

Macleod, M., & Rengger, R. (1993). *The development of DRUM: A software tool for video-assisted usability evaluation*. People and Computers.

Mahatody, T., Sagar, M., & Kolski, C. (2010). State of the Art on the Cognitive Walkthrough Method, Its Variants and Evolutions. *International Journal of Human-Computer Interaction*, *26*(8), 741–785. doi:10.1080/10447311003781409

Mutikanga, H. E. (2012). Water loss management: tools and methods for developing countries. TU Delft, Delft University of Technology.

Nagpal, R., Mehrotra, D., Bhatia, P. K., & Sharma, A. (2015). Rank University Websites Using Fuzzy AHP and Fuzzy TOPSIS Approach on Usability. *International Journal of Information Engineering and Electronic Business, 7*(1), 29.

Nagpal, R., Mehrotra, D., Sharma, A., & Bhatia, P. (2013). ANFIS method for usability assessment of website of an educational institute. *World Applied Sciences Journal*, *23*(11), 1489–1498.

Nielsen, J. (1993). Usability Engineering. Academic Press.

Nielsen, J. (2000). *Designing for the Web*. Available at: http://ssltest.cs.umd.edu/class/spring2012/cmsc434-0101/Notes11-WebDesign.pdf

Orumie, U. C., & Ebong, D. (2014). A Glorious Literature on Linear Goal Programming Algorithms. *American Journal of Operations Research*, *4*(02), 59–71. doi:10.4236/ajor.2014.42007

Pinelle, D., & Gutwin, C. 2002. Groupware Walkthrough: Adding Context to Groupware Usability Evaluation. In *Proceedings of the SIGCHI conference on Human factors in computing systems* (pp. 455–462). doi:10.1145/503376.503458

Preece, J. (1994). *Human–Computer Interaction*. Reading, MA: Addison-Wesley.

Qin, X., Huang, G., Chakma, A., Nie, X., & Lin, Q. (2008). A MCDM-based expert system for climate-change impact assessment and adaptation planning – A case study for the Georgia Basin, Canada. *Expert Systems with Applications*, *34*(3), 2164–2179. doi:10.1016/j.eswa.2007.02.024

Redish, J. (1995). Are we really entering a post-usability era? *ACM SIGDOC Asterisk Journal of Computer Documentation*, *19*(1), 18–24. doi:10.1145/203586.203590

Rezaei, J. (2015). Best-worst multi-criteria decision-making method. *Omega*, *53*, 49–57. doi:10.1016/j.omega.2014.11.009

Rizzo, A., Marchigiani, E., & Andreadis, A. (1997). The AVANTI project: prototyping and evaluation with a cognitive walkthrough based on the Norman's model of action. In *Proceedings of the 2nd conference on Designing interactive systems: processes, practices, methods, and techniques*. ACM. doi:10.1145/263552.263629

Rosson, M., & Carroll, J. (2001). *Usability Engineering*. San Francisco: Morgan Kaufmann.

Rosson, M. B., & Carroll, J. M. (2002). Scenario-based design. Academic Press.

Roy, B. (1991). The outranking approach and the foundations of ELECTRE methods. *Theory and Decision*, *31*(1), 49–73. doi:10.1007/BF00134132

Ryu, H., & Monk, A. F. (2004). Analysing interaction problems with cyclic interaction theory: Low-level interaction walkthrough. *PsychNology Journal*, *2*(3), 304–330.

Saaty, T. L. (1990). How to make a decision: The analytic hierarchy process. *European Journal of Operational Research*, *48*(1), 9–26. doi:10.1016/0377-2217(90)90057-I

Saaty, T. L. (2001). Decision Making with the Analytic Network Process (ANP) and Its "Super Decisions" Software: The National Missile Defense (NMD) Example. ISAHP 2001 Proceedings.

Saaty, T. L. (2008). Decision making with the analytic hierarchy process. *International Journal of Services Sciences, 1*(1), 83-98.

Saeed, S. (2014). Human Factors in Software Development and Design. IGI Global.

Saeed, S., & Amjad, A. (2013). Understanding usability issues of Pakistani university websites. *Life Science Journal*, *10*(6s), 479–482.

Saeed, S., Malik, I. A., & Wahab, F. (2013). Usability evaluation of Pakistani security agencies websites. *International Journal of E-Politics*, *4*(3), 57–69. doi:10.4018/jep.2013070105

Saeed, S., & Shabbir, S. (2014). Website Usability Analysis of Non Profit Organizations: A Case Study of Pakistan. *International Journal of Public Administration in the Digital Age*, *1*(4), 70–83. doi:10.4018/ijpada.2014100105

Sears, A. (1997). Heuristic walkthroughs: Finding the problems without the noise. *International Journal of Human-Computer Interaction*, *9*(3), 213–234. doi:10.1207/s15327590ijhc0903_2

Sharp, H., Jenny, P., & Rogers, Y. (2007). *Interaction design: Beyond human-computer interaction*. Academic Press.

Spencer, R. (2000). The streamlined cognitive walkthrough method, working around social constraints encountered in a software development company. In *Proceedings of the SIGCHI conference on Human Factors in Computing Systems*. ACM. doi:10.1145/332040.332456

Srivastava, J., Cooley, R., Deshpande, M., & Tan, P. N. (2000). Web usage mining: Discovery and applications of usage patterns from web data. *ACM SIGKDD Explorations Newsletter*, *1*(2), 12–23. doi:10.1145/846183.846188

Torrente, M. C. S., Prieto, A. B. M., Gutiérrez, D. A., & de Sagastegui, M. E. A. (2013). Sirius: A heuristic-based framework for measuring web usability adapted to the type of website. *Journal of Systems and Software*, *86*(3), 649–663. doi:10.1016/j.jss.2012.10.049

Van Den Haak, M., De Jong, M., & Jan Schellens, P. (2003). Retrospective vs. concurrent think-aloud protocols: Testing the usability of an online library catalogue. *Behaviour & Information Technology*, *22*(5), 339–351. doi:10.1080/0044929031000

Van den Haak, M. J., de Jong, M. D. T., & Schellens, P. J. (2004). Employing think- aloud protocols and constructive interaction to test the usability of online library catalogues: A methodological comparison. *Interacting with Computers*, *16*(6), 1153–1170. doi:10.1016/j.intcom.2004.07.007

Velasquez, M., & Hester, P. T. (2013). An analysis of multi-criteria decision making methods. *International Journal of Operations Research*, *10*(2), 56–66.

Wharton, C., Rieman, J., Lewis, C., & Polson, P. (1994, June). The cognitive walkthrough method: A practitioner's guide. In *Usability inspection methods* (pp. 105–140). John Wiley & Sons, Inc.

Yáñez Gómez, R., Cascado Caballero, D., & Sevillano, J.-L. (2014). *Heuristic evaluation on mobile interfaces: a new checklist. In The Scientific World Journal* (pp. 1–19). Hindwai Publishing Corporation.

Zadeh, L. A. (1994). Fuzzy logic, neural networks, and soft computing. *Communications of the ACM*, *37*(3), 77–85. doi:10.1145/175247.175255

Zardari, N. H., Ahmed, K., Shirazi, S. M., & Yusop, Z. B. (2015). *Weighting Methods and their Effects on Multi-Criteria Decision Making Model Outcomes in Water Resources Management*. Springer International Publishing. doi:10.1007/978-3-319-12586-2

Zimmermann, H. J. (1978). Fuzzy programming and linear programming with several objective functions. *Fuzzy Sets and Systems*, *1*(1), 45–55. doi:10.1016/0165-0114(78)90031-3

Zimmermann, H. J. (2012). *Fuzzy sets, decision making, and expert systems* (Vol. 10). Springer Science & Business Media.

Chapter 16
Usability Evaluation of E-Government Websites in Saudi Arabia by Cognitive Walkthrough

Hina Gull
University of Dammam, Saudi Arabia

Sardar Zafar Iqbal
University of Dammam, Saudi Arabia

ABSTRACT

Government websites are the easy sources of getting access to the services offered by governmental organizations. These websites provide manifold benefits to their users i.e. efficiency of use, cost decline, effective communication between citizens and government, delivery of different service, transparency and time saving. However, users cannot get full benefit out of these services if the e-government web-sites are not interactive and user friendly. Keeping this view into consideration, study investigated the usability concerns of the e-government websites in Saudi Arabia. Cognitive walk-through is selected as the implication method to figure out usability related traits by the real users of the interfaces. Findings from the study showed that these websites are partially usable for the users, as they lack some of the major concerns of the usability. Evaluation results showed the clear picture of the usability features of the selected websites of Saudi Arabia both in positive and negative ways. Furthermore, recommendations are given to improve overall quality of these websites.

INTRODUCTION

With the widespread use and advancement in technology, governmental organizations have also taken steps to apply the technology in the public sector organizations generally called as e-government. (Garcia 2005). Since the widespread use of this technology, governmental organizations are also facing some challenges, when it comes to user interaction and usability is considered as one of the major issues in the field of user interaction (Mohammad 2015).

DOI: 10.4018/978-1-5225-1944-7.ch016

E-Government is defined as the use of the advance technology by governmental organizations to provide quality services to their citizens and business (Wan 2010). Generally, it is the process of providing easy accessible services to citizens, deleting extra effort and extra systems, cost effectiveness and achieving other goals such as accountability and transparency very easily (Raza 2016). Therefore, e-government is defined as the easiest way of electronic communications between the government, citizens and the business organizations. There are manifold benefits (Ndou 2004) of the implementation of e-government both for developing and developed countries such as:

1. E-government is considered as the easiest way to get access to the governmental services offered to the customers without any time constraint i.e. government services are available to the citizens without any delay 24/7 i.e. 24 hours a day, 7 days a week.
2. Reduction in organizational cost and time.
3. Customers/citizens satisfaction due to delivery of the services at their door steps with any extra effort.
4. Improved transparency, accuracy and security of information and knowledge sharing etc.

Usability is defined as the user satisfaction degree to which users can use the system efficiently and effectively. Usability Evaluation is a process of measuring the usability traits of the user interface in order to identify common usability problems. Usability is considered as one of the most important factor in assessing the quality of user interfaces. The race to develop more user friendly web applications has paved a way for a number of methods and tools to cope with the usability problems. In addition, a wide number of usability evaluation methods are developed to evaluate the user friendliness of an interface.

Usability evaluation methods are divided into the following main categories:

1. **User Based Methods:** End users which are the real users of the system are the part of the usability evaluation process. By the use of different evaluation tools (interviews, questionnaire and observation), users are meant to assess the performance and user satisfaction levels.
2. **Evaluator's Methods:** To measure and assess the usability of a system a number of usability experts (evaluators) are taking part in this category of usability evaluation. Heuristic Evaluation and cognitive walkthrough are considered as the most widely used method in this category.
3. **Tool based Methods:** This method is used to identify usability related problems automatically by the use of various software tools (Gull 2015).

In this study cognitive walkthrough is used as a main method to identify the usability related issues in the e-government websites in Kingdom of Saudi Arabia. The cognitive walkthrough is a commonly used method for evaluating the usability of the system by actually going through the real system and using it as the real users. To execute this method, a number of analysts choose some specific tasks or services that are offered by the interface to observe and record the usability related issues (Clayton 1997). The aim of the study in hand is to describe the results of the cognitive walkthrough of the some of the e-government websites in Saudi Arabia. For the execution of cognitive walkthrough, a number of usability traits were selected which should be the part of an interface for effective and efficient use of the interface and the services offered by the websites. A number of participants who are also the real users of the e-government websites in Saudi Arabia took part in the evaluation process and through cognitive walkthrough the interfaces noted down some major usability problem in each category of usability traits identified. Users also pointed out the positives of the selected websites. This research is organized as follows: the following section will review the found literature; section 3 covers research methodology, section 4 is about findings and discussion while section 5 contains the concluding remarks.

BACKGROUND

This section delineates the literature that supports the evaluation of e-government websites in different regions worldwide. Multiple methods are used to figure out the usability problems in e-government websites.

Wan et al (Wan 2010) investigated the usability and accessibility of Malaysia e-government websites using Neilson's usability guidelines and web content accessibility guidelines respectively. Multiple automatic evaluation tools were used to analyse the e-government websites in Malaysia. Study revealed number of accessibility and usability problems in terms of broken links and speed. Statistical analysis in the study supports the viewpoint of the authors who are claiming that majority of the Malaysian websites are lacking the main usability traits and are quite poor in accessibility as well. Several checkpoints were identified for analysing the accessibility of the e-government websites and it was found that majority of the Malaysian e-government websites are violating the accessibility traits as well.

Abdulmohsen et al. (Abanumy 2005) explored the usability problems of Saudi Arabian and Oman e-government websites using website accessibility guidelines as well as some accessibility tools. Authors also proposed novel approach to link human factors in the successful development of e-government websites. Authors evaluated two governmental websites to study the problems related to the culture lookouts of the audience, accessibility and design consistency. Authors specified a checklist based on W3C's WCAG guidelines and evaluate the targeted websites to check the compliance of these websites with the identified guidelines. As a result many accessibility issues such as difficulty in finding the profound information were identified after testing. Also websites failed to meet the multi browser display criteria i.e. website was tested using many browsers and the result was total failure.

Saqib Saeed et al. (Saeed 2012) explained the role of usability in e-government and e-commerce website. An empirical study was conducted to prove the fact that usability is the main characteristic in the design of e-government and e-commerce websites. Authors by evaluation three e-government and two e-commerce websites of Pakistan, pointed out many usability related issues faced by the users, which if improved can significantly improve the user experience and satisfaction.

Edgar et al. (Asiimwe 2010) investigated several e-government websites in Uganda using the feature investigation methods. Following three main features were identified for the study: Design of the website, Ease of Navigation and the legal policies of the website. Statistical results given by the authors that websites partially fulfils the criterion of good layout design and easy navigation capabilities but failed to meet the criterion of stating legal policies. Based on the points found after evaluation authors proposed a framework that they claimed to be used by any country that wants to do a quick and easy evaluation of their government websites.

Jason Withrow et al. (Withrow 2005) elaborated the comparative studies on usability evaluation between the redesign of the state government web portal with the old sites. Authors revealed the fact that the redesign of the state government portal improve the different usability traits i.e. task success, task difficulty and the time to complete the task. Author explained the methodology of assessing the usability of state government portal which was based on analysis done by the usability experts. Later on the different architectures were design and evaluated which were completely based on the experts' viewpoints earlier. The authors claimed the improvement in the usability after redesign is based on some statistical facts. Different task were tested, task success, task time and task difficulty was measured that reflected the improvement of the usability after redesign of the state government website portal.

Shakirat.O.Raji et al. (Shakirat 2013) evaluated the university teaching hospitals website in Nigeria which are associated with government and are considered as the main source of communication between patients and doctors as well as the students. These websites are also considered as the source of medical knowledge shared among the general public. So, due to vast number of people interacting with the website it was very important for a website to be more interactive and user friendly. Author used the questionnaire based survey usability method to evaluate the website in terms of its design and content. Three main teaching hospitals were selected from three major areas of Nigeria and participants are given tasks 6 tasks to find the usability problems in the websites based on 10 general heuristics. Some other features of the website such as accessibility and availability were also considered in order to get the broad spectrum opinion of the users. Results showed both weaknesses and strengths in all three websites and formed the basis for future betterment in implications of usability trait in the websites.

Abdulhadi M. Eidaroos et al. (Eidaroos 2009) evaluated two e-government websites of Saudi Arabia using heuristic evaluation approach. In their used approach for usability testing authors selected many principles that can be used to point out the usability problems and issues in the Saudi government websites. Main of these features includes consistency, navigation, help, functionality, design, data entry, accessibility, security and privacy. Expert review method was applied in the usability testing of these websites. Each expert is given a heuristic checklist to check whether these e-government websites are conforming to the heuristic guidelines and principles. After expert review it was revealed that one of the websites was better in its usability traits while the other one is lacking almost all of the usability features. It was recommended that special attention should be paid in these types of websites where there is more user interaction especially data entry forms should meet all the usability traits and features.

Seongil Lee et al. (Lee 2007) elaborated the usability issues faced in the study of an evaluation process of Korean e-government websites. General method of getting user perspective, based on common set of performance metrics was used to evaluate the usability of Korean e-government portals. Fourteen e-government websites were tested by almost 50 participants to get the better idea of the services provided by the selected Korean portals. Along with other usability issues such as unclear navigation and accessibility, long time to complete a task was reported as the main problem in the e-government portals. Due to user diversity in their ages and vocations, different types of usability issues were observed. Results suggested that not only are there wide variations in the usability for the services provided, but that significant work still needs to be undertaken in order to make the services of the e-Government more usable, particularly for the older users.

Zhao Huang and Laurence Brooks (Huang 2011) carried out an empirical study to evaluate the usability of local e-government websites of U.K. They selected local websites as they are considered more near to the users. Results after evaluation showed a number of usability problems in the selected websites based on user prospect and performance. Results also showed a close relationship between user perception and their performance which laid the basis for different e-government organizations to improve their websites.

Hend S. Al-Khalifa (Al-Khalifa 2010) has taken an e-government website of Saudi Arabia as a case study to do the heuristic evaluation of the website. Taken various components of usability into consideration, such as design, consistency, navigation, data entry, content and help, she has highlighted some of major usability problems in the targeted website. Results showed that these websites did not fulfil all the usability requirements. However all of the components were above 50%in their results. Design and consistency are the highest scorers with 80%. While, search appeared to be as the least scoring component.

Basit Darem et al. (Basit 2012) carried out the experimental evaluation of e-government websites in Mysore. Small usability experiments were defined to get the empirical data. Each experimental session consists of a set of tasks, a series of questions regarding those tasks. Task will be considered as success if users are able to fulfil in with the assigned time limit and other constraints, otherwise it proved to be a failure. As a result, all participants found the web site to be cluttered and unusable. Other identified problems were orphan pages, lack of consistency, bad color contrast, lack of search and help facilities.

Saqib Saeed et al. (Saeed 2013) evaluated the usability of some of the websites of hospitals in Pakistan. Survey was conducted to obtain the usability results and a number of usability problems were identified. In the end recommendations were given to improve overall usability of these websites.

In another research, Saqib Saeed et al. (Saeed 2014) explored the websites of different non-profit organizations of Pakistan to evaluate their usability and user satisfaction. Questionnaire based on Nellson's usability guidelines was prepared and was distributed to the undergraduate students having Human Computer Interaction as their main course. Empirical data was collected from the survey conducted which pointed out a number of usability problems in these websites. The identification of these usability issues will also help these organizations to improve their usability and user satisfaction in the future.

Saqib Saeed et al. (Saeed 2013) delineated the usability issues in different Pakistani university websites. Questionnaire were developed based on Nielsen heuristics guidelines and the responses were also collected from different stake holders, on the basis of responses received the statistical data helped in understanding the variations of the usability issues in different websites.

RESEARCH METHODOLOGY

The purposes and advantages of this research study is twofold; first is to assess the usability of the e-government websites in Saudi Arabia to find out the problems faced by the citizens and expats while using the interfaces and services offered by the e-government websites. Second is to suggest and recommend some improvements in the user interaction of these websites by considering the results obtained after evaluation process, so that there will be more improved versions of the services offered to increase the productivity of the governmental organizations. For usability evaluation Cognitive walkthrough was selected as the main method and is executed by identifying and selecting the following usability traits:

1.   Compatibility
2.   Consistency
3.   Flexibility
4.   Learnability
5.   Minimal user action
6.   Minimal memory load
7.   Perceptual Limitations
8.   Navigation
9.   Content
10. User guidance

The websites of the following three main governmental organizations were selected for the experimentation:

1. Ministry of Interior
2. Ministry of Foreign Affairs
3. Saudi Commission for Tourism & National Heritage

Based on the above mentioned traits, cognitive walkthrough was performed to test the usability of the selected e-government websites. Undergraduate students (who are also the real users of the e-government websites) of one of the universities in Saudi Arabia with profound knowledge of Human Computer Interaction and usability traits were asked to perform usability evaluation process and the results were developed based on their observations.

FINDINGS AND DISCUSSION

This subsection explains all the findings obtained from the usability evaluation process. The section describes not only both positives and negatives of the websites based on the usability characteristics, but also gives some recommendations for the improvements by the observers. Findings from each of the selected websites are summarized below:

WEBSITE OF THE MINISTRY OF INTERIOR KSA

The first website selected was the official website of the Ministry of Interior (https://www.moi.gov.sa) (Ministry of Interior Saudi Arabia 2016) that provides the opportunity for citizens and residents to complete the tasks they need electronically, rather than going to the ministry address. The available e-services and electronic inquiries at the site are too many and related to different fields, such as civil affairs, MOI Diwan, Passports, Traffics, Public Security, Emirates, Expatriate affairs, Authorization and Postal Delivery Service. Detailed Cognitive walkthrough was performed on April 14, 2016 to April 20, 2016 using both Windows and Mac operating systems. Safari and Firefox 45.0.0 were used as the browsers, while screen resolution was 1400*900 and 1024*1280.

Findings

Following are the observations by the evaluators in each category of usability features:

1. **Compatibility:** The website is good for the knowledgeable users as it offers familiar terminologies and it displays the information that is compatible with the user's expectation. However, the user needs above the average skills to use all the features in the website.
2. **Consistency:** The website lacks consistency as it has different spaces between the contents and the spaces may change from a page to another. Also, colour coding is not conventional as it exceeded 4 colours in the Home page. Furthermore, user's actions should be consistent to gain the intended

output as they distinguish the messages to the user; dark red messages are for Error messages, dark blue messages describe the important notes and dark green messages as a successful feedback. Although data fields, graphic, symbols and labels are mostly consistent among each other considering their location and font-color and size. There are pages where the labels are not consistence in their size like address page section postal address etc. Also, some of the labels are showing in Arabic although we selected to show the pages in English.

3. **Flexibility:** The website deals with direct manipulation which makes it easier for the user to perform the tasks. Also, it provides a flexible data entry because it allows the use of tabs to move between the data fields and it has the ability to change the language for the non-Arabic speakers. Moreover, it offers action reversibility to make an easier navigation for the user. However, it doesn't provide user guidance or the ability to change displays name. The website is usable for all kinds of users as it offers informative messages, menu and shortcuts.

4. **Learnability:** Novice user can use the website easily because of several reasons; first, the website instructions are easy to apply and all the commands' names are meaningful, concise and self-explanatory. Second, all the data is grouped into clear and logical groping which makes the navigation an easy task to perform; For example, the top menu has Emirates groping which contain the entire Emirates information, so users can find all the needed information at the same place. Third, the menu is divided into several sections, mainly: electronic inquiries, E-services, Business, nationals, sectors and so on. Also, each section has its own topics no overlapping and no mistaken topics. Furthermore, the menu starts with home page followed by about us page followed by the most important pages in the appropriate order depending on their importance.

5. **Minimal User Action:** The user can navigate between pages with minimal action since all the pages contain the main menus navigation which shows the pages' path the user followed, so with one simple click the user can return to the general menu at the top level. Moreover, the registration page uses the minimal number of steps (4 steps) which they are:

   a.   Registration Request
   b.   Request Verification
   c.   Account Creation
   d.   Account Activation

   And we can't reduce them to less than 4, because each of them is important and needs to be separated. Also when entering the phone number in any form it specifies that it should start with +966 otherwise not accepted and that helps the user a lot. On the other hand, it requires the user to enter image code (captcha) almost in every form, which sometimes irritates the user. Also the form should fill the user national ID automatically since the user has logged in and has verified the user identity by SMS, which is apparently not provided. However, there is no global search button to minimize the user action. So the website needs to work more in this section.

6. **Minimal Memory Load:** The website used a clear abbreviation such as FAQs and MOI. The guidance information was always available to help the user. For example, in the registration page there were instructions to complete the registration. Also there was guidance in each page that has a form to fill. Every selected data is clearly highlighted. The data items show in simple and clear way for the user even for long paragraphs they are organized with logical sequence that helps the user go through it. Finally, for each icon there were supplementary label that represent the icon meaning.

7. **Perceptual Limitation:** Although there were few abbreviations, they were clear in the meaning, distinctive and differ from one another. The group of information is differentiated and has is in its own section with its related information. Also, every data field in the forms are clear and distinctive with label indicating the purpose for that entry. Most of the menus are clearly distinct since they are listed in a different design. However, some menus that are within pictures seem at first to be normal information, but it becomes clear when hovering over them. Finally, the screen density is not reasonable for example; the home page is too crowded.

8. **User Guidance:** Although the erroneous entries are displayed following the color code as red and the error messages lead us to the field that has the error but it does not explain how to correct it exactly. For example, when user entered a wrong email address, it shows that it is invalid and did not give an example that follows the right pattern like example@emaple.com. Also, there is no indication showing the repeated or redundant errors. Finally, the website provides the help option and gives two options for help: direct help from the website, and get help by phone or email for additional help.

9. **Navigation:** Evaluators tried to navigate through the website to test navigation. Main pages have a fixed place menu that navigates to the whole website. However, users couldn't scroll up and down from the pages themselves they have to use the browser scroll bar. There is no misleading links but some links do not work, all the links inside the share option are not working in all pages, also https://www.moi.gov.sa/wps/vanityurl/ar/rss/pps/personal-information is not working it shows an error" Error 404: CWSRV0295E: Error reported: 404". Furthermore, sitemap's links are working perfectly fine and no search field is there in website.

10. **Content:** The website offers two main languages: English and Arabic. Also, the presented information is complete and up to date even for the news section with no grammatical, spelling, or punctuation mistakes. Some of the pages don't have a main heading that represent the page such as National page. However, if a heading is there its clearly standing out on the page and describe its task.

Recommendations

In order to improve the usability of the website evaluators recommend the following improvements to be made in the interfaces:

- Add an internal search mechanism
- Make font in address page section consistent
- Make the form fill the user national ID automatically since the user has logged in and has verified the user identity by SMS.
- Require the user to enter image code (captcha) in the log in form only
- Clarify some menus that are within pictures y underlining them or making the font colour blue etc.
- Fix the share option links
- Display a heading for each page when it is open
- Reduce the colour codes.

WEBSITE OF THE MINISTRY OF FOREIGN AFFAIRS KSA

Ministry of Foreign Affairs (Ministry of Foreign Affairs Saudi Arabia 2016) was the second testing website (http://www.mofa.gov.sa). Cognitive walkthrough was started from the Home page and navigated throughout all other page making sure that all behave as the user might expect and in consistent manner. Test was performed on April 14, 2016 to April 20, 2016 using both Windows and Mac operating systems. Safari and Chrome Version 49.0.2623.87 (64-bit) were used as the browsers while screen resolution was 1280*800.

Findings

Following are the observations by the evaluators in each category of usability features:

1. **Compatibility:** The control entry is not compatible with the user expectations. Some links guide to pages with error messages and others has no content. These links should be fixed and content should be provided. Overall everything is clear and understandable as relatively easy terminologies are used. However, some terminologies require a minor knowledge.
2. **Consistency:** There is good contrast between the background and its contents. Links change their color when they are hovered over. Website is following color code conventions and only 3 main colors are used in the interface. The displayed format is consistent in all pages, same margins, pages titles etc. Not everything has feedback. In some pages the spacing between the columns and the button are not consistent. Labels throughout the site are consistent, same size, color, style and location. The whole website is using scrolling also the content within these website pages is not that long to make the user feel bored while scrolling. All of the required field in the forms have a red star beside them and will show a message on the top of the form if you forgot to fill one of the required fields. Wording and data display are consistent throughout the website. Social media icons are like what people are familiar with and all other icons are described by labels or tooltips. There are labels and pop up messages to guide the user on how to complete certain action. Not all the pages are available in English language.
3. **Flexibility:** Direct manipulation capability and user display control are supported in the website for example user can change the language of the website, font size, etc. Data entry is not flexible especially for the expert users, for example if the user wants to enter the country they can only select it for the pull down menu. They are not able to type it. There is a help icon next to each data entry providing the user with guidance as a pop message containing brief explanation for what the user should enter is displayed. There is no option to name the displays and elements on the interface and there no option for zooming the display. Menus will change depending on the context for example if the user clicks on the Ministry menu a side menu will be displayed.
4. **Learnability:** Familiar and clear phrases are used along with tooltips whenever necessary. Data with similar content are grouped together. Menus group the options logically. For example, Ministry's Services menu groups the options by categories (Citizen, Residents, Visitors, Business, and Government Agencies). All the command names throughout the website are meaningful. It uses (submit) when sending the requests, (cancel) to cancel an action, etc.

5. **Minimal User Action:** Each time the user requests for a service he must fill all the required fields. It will not be saved from previous tasks. All the values should be entered or chosen by the user. The user can always go to the previous windows using breadcrumbs which are provided in most of the pages. Sitemap and navigation menu in thee header of each page helps the user to go from one page to another easily. Function keys are provided including ENTER, PRINT, HOME etc. Global search field is provided in the top of all the pages. This website provides minimal steps in sequential menu selection since the forms require less number of steps to fill. Higher level menu is displayed on the top of the page on every page and users can go back to the main menu in a single keystroke.

6. **Minimal Memory Load:** All of the used abbreviations and acronyms are standard and easy to understand. There is no explicit help page but throughout the website users are informed with the description of services provided. Supplementary labels and tooltips are provided for icons.

7. **Perceptual Limitation:** Abbreviations are standard and distinctive abbreviations are used that are known by majority of users. Display elements are distinctive as similar items are grouped together and are separated in different box borders with margins and paddings applied to avoid clustering. The active window is indicated in the title bar of the browser. Also active menus are indicated by changing their color when they are hovered over. Most of the abbreviations and acronyms used are following the standard except for MOFA which is not defined.

8. **User Guidance:** The browser backward button is provided and there are no other reverse control options. There is no explicit help page but throughout the website users are informed with the description of services provided. When clicking on the search without choosing no error message will appear.

9. **Navigation:** Sitemap shows only main links and some are empty pages. Also some of the pages are displayed in Arabic and English at the same time. Some search queries to words in the website give no proper search result. Advance search is provided but no proper results are shown. The main menu is large and wide which confuse the normal and novice users.

10. **Content:** Some pages are not provided with English language they are only available in Arabic like pages within Visa Services. The website is frequently updated. Some words are misspelled and there are some punctuation errors. Brackets should not have been used below. Drop down menu entries are not alphabetical. The headings are distinct from the content and are descriptive.

Recommendations

- Search box in the home page (where the user is supposed to choose a country and then click search) has no error handling messages that is if you did not choose any country and clicked search the button the website will not display any error message. So the search box in the home page should be provided with the error handling mechanism.

- Most of the menus and links are nested which confuses the user, It is recommended to breakdown the menus and links into small logical groups.

- When the user is on some page and goes to a form and then comes back to the previous page, the language will change from English to Arabic which really confuses the users as they might think that they clicked on change language button by mistake. This is the main issue to be addressed as most of the users of this website are foreigners which may not know Arabic language.

WEBSITE OF SAUDI COMMISSION FOR TOURISM AND NATIONAL HERITAGE

Saudi Commission for Tourism & National Heritage (https://www.scta.gov.sa/en/Pages/default.aspx#3) (Saudi Commission for Tourism & National Heritage 2016) was the third selected website for testing. Test was performed on April 14, 2016 to April 20, 2016 using both Windows and Mac operating systems. Safari, Firefox and Chrome all three were used as the browsers while screen resolution was 1280 x 800 and 1366 x 768

Findings

1. **Compatibility:** The results of control entry are compatible with user expectations. Each action performs the expected job, for example when you move between pages, the required pages appears and not any other pages. The control is matched to user skills, that is, the control in the website is easy to understand by both beginner and expert users. The terminology used in the website is easy to understand by the normal user.

2. **Consistency:** The assignment of color codes is conventional, for example, the alert messages appear in the red color, and the hyperlinks appear in blue. The coding is consistent across displays and menu options, that is, all the similar elements means the same thing (such as icons) and all the menu options are displayed in the same way, so the user will not be confused when using these elements. The labelling itself is consistent, the labels used in the same area has a consistent style. The display orientation is consistent through the website. The scrolling and panning through the pages and page's content is the same. The user actions are consistent through the website, filling forms, rating, printing, and all similar functions are done in the same manner. The data display is consistent with entry requirements, for example, the displayed email addresses are in the same format that should be entered in the forms, same for mobile numbers, so the user can see these display and apply the same in the entry fields. The data display is consistent with user conventions, for example, the date appears in the website in a familiar format, the phone numbers are written in the common format etc. The symbols for graphic data are standard and consistent through the website pages, for example: the email symbol means sending an email in all pages, social media symbols take to the corresponding social networks; research symbol has a person with a zoom lens, and so on. The wording is consistent with user guidance, that is, the words used for the user entry fields are telling the user what to do or write in this specific field. On the other hand, the feedback is not consistent for all actions through the website pages. For the confirmation messages, it appears in some places in a pop up message and in other places with red text. The display format is not consistent for all elements through the website, for example, the buttons have not the same format in all pages. The wording is not consistent through displays, for example, the submitting buttons has the words: submit, and send, which are different two words for the same action. The format within data fields through the website cannot be determined, because some the fields has no validation. You find a form that the phone number field accepts characters, and the full name field accepts the only digit entry, and other form that has full validation. The label format is not consistent through the website, some similar labels appears in the different format of font size and alignment. The labels locations are not consistent, for example, the spacing between the text field and its label is different from page to another.

3. **Flexibility:** There is direct manipulation capability. The website enables the user to choose the desired size of the font. The website displays only the options that are actually available in the current context for a particular user. On the other hand, Data entry is not flexible. For example, the list of countries is not provided with English language. The website provides training throughout written format guidance which is not appropriate for all types of users as it lacks the audio-visual training. In the data entry, user is unable to go backward. The website does not provide zooming for display expansion.

4. **Learnability:** The website provides clear wording, also the titles are clear and represent its content. The website provides data grouping which plays a role in making user learning easily. Menu options are logically grouping, for example all content related to Antiquities are grouped together. Command has meaningful names, for example buttons' names related to these tasks. On the other hand, ordering of menu options is not logical. For example, the list for country selection is not alphabetically ordered.

5. **Minimal User Action:** It is easy to shift among windows as they are providing main menu in each page and also providing navigations with hyperlinks such as (SCTH > Antiquities > Internationally Registered Sites) which makes it easier to go to the previous pages. It uses function keys for frequent control entries such as Enter and Tab. It provides global search but without the replace option. Whenever the user point and hover over the main menu, it will display the submenus of the pointed one. We can return to higher-level and general menu by simply pointing on them. It provides minimal steps in sequential menu selection as they are providing logical grouping of menus with few hierarchical levels, which reduce the number of user actions. On the other hand, Menu selection cannot be done by keyed entries. The website does not provide default values for the user. In long pages, the website does not provide internal linking in the pages, which makes the user press the buttons PageDown (PgDn) and PageUP (PgUp) many times in order to go to the intended part.

6. **Minimal Memory Load:** The website uses simple truncation for abbreviations as they take the first letter from each word. For example, the website's name is Saudi Commission for Tourism & National Heritage and abbreviated as SCTH. There is Help & Support page in the sitemap which is available to guide the user in every page of the website. Most of data are kept short, and long data items are partitioned well by providing "read more" hyperlink or "Details" button. The website shows the icons along with a supplementary label or tooltip to make it clear enough for the user. On the other hand, some of the pages combine related entry such as the first, second and family name. It will be combined as a full name. Other pages will require all information to be entered separately even if they are related. The website doesn't provide good hierarchical menus; the vertical menu bar is not hierarchically distributed as it shows the subsections (Museums, Heritage, and Handicraft) of the main section Antiquities as main sections.

7. **Perceptual Limitation:** The abbreviations of the website are distinct which avoids user confusion. Also the elements are distinct and clearly displayed. The format of user guidance is clear. The colors of the website are easily distinguishable. The website also indicates which window is active. The data fields are visually distinct and have a border that separates the data field from the white background of the website. In the menu bar of the main menu, each group contains different information from one another. On the other hand, the menus are not distinct from other displayed information. The drop down menu in the home has a small font size and there are no enough spaces between one menu to another, and there are no borders or anything which clarifies that it is a menu. The user has to hover over the menu to discover that these texts are actually a menu. The screen

density is not reasonable, the pages are crowded with content, and the font size in the page is too small which makes it unreadable.

8. **User Guidance:** There is a Help & Support page and also there is a FAQ's page. After each submission or sending for a form, a message appears indicating that the process has been done successfully. On the other hand, in some pages like Procurement Contract Portal page, it shows only that there are errors in some text fields but it is not specifying where the error is, which sometimes makes the user confused. Also, some fields have error messages that are displayed in English and then for another kind of error message for the same field it will be displayed in Arabic, like in Employment application when you enter two numbers in the Father name field it shows an error message in English then, when you enter four numbers, the error message becomes in Arabic even without changing the language option. There are some pages that do not contain a CANCEL option like in the Employment application page. In some pages like contact us page, if the user entered his/her name as numbers only, no error message is displayed. In some fields there are no explicit entries of corrections. Non-Disruptive Error Message is the message that should be displayed as an error message only after a user has completed an entry, and that is not provided in Employment application page. Some pages do not display the informative error messages, like in Investor Registration page they only show an error message that indicates there is an error in submitting the form without specifying where the error is. The website does not provide UNDO command to reverse control actions.

9. **Navigation:** Links to outside web pages are listed in the related website area. Also these links are appropriate and serve the tourism in Saudi Arabia from many perspectives. In addition, all these links are working with no problems. By trying most of the links, we figured out that there are no misleading links or page contents that are different from the title or description of the corresponding link, which means that all links are descriptive and indicate the expected content by the user. The links of the site map are working effectively and leads to all the websites' pages. There are no orphan pages; all pages have navigational menu or links to other pages in the website. Clear navigation tool is provided in the web site pages. Contrariwise, not all links are working, there are many damaged links recognized using www.validator.w3.org link checker. Each page enables the user to return back to home page through clicking on the logo located in the top left of the page. But, the problem here is the lack of explicit representation of the home link as they are using the logo of the ministry to represent the link to the home page. The web pages of the website do not have any internal linking that leads to the upper or lower sections within a page. Searching in the website does not give actual and effective results that reflect the entered subject.

10. **Contents:** Foreign Language is available. In addition to the Arabic, English language is also supported for non-Arabic speakers. Information is current. Most web pages' contents range between (2013–2015) as a last update date. Information is complete. All needed information is there, and also all related websites are provided for user need. The site does not have pages with empty content or blank pages. No grammatical errors are found. Headings are labelled in a correct manner such that each word starts in a capital letter. All headings are concise, informative and descriptive. Headings are distinguishable, and they are in bold, large size and black font color that is different from the original text color. Each page is addressed by one or more heading. Headings actually describe the task or the contents of the pages. Contrariwise, there is a misspelled word "researche", instead of the right spelling "researcher". Entries are not alphabetically ordered. There is a big difference between the font size of the headers and subheadings.

RECOMMENDATIONS

- The Arabic and English displays of the website should be consistent, the date display, terminologies and positioning should be the same in both displays.
- All forms in the website should have validation, the number fields should accept only numbers and the name fields should accept only characters, and so on.
- The used font should be larger because it is too small and hard to read.
- It is better that the drop down menus do not appear unless it is clicked on, because it is distracting for the user to have the menu dropped whenever the mouse hovers over it.
- In long pages, headings of each part should be added at the beginning of the page. Also, internal linking is required to minimize user's actions.
- The drop down menus and combo boxes should be arranged alphabetically.

CONCLUSION

User centric design is considered as the key factor for the success of a system, especially when it comes to the interactive systems that require frequent response and interaction with the users. E-government websites are one of those systems that offer plenty of services to the users, therefore require frequent collaboration with the users. Therefore, it is recommended to have a typical user centred design for these types of websites. Along with other factors, usability is considered as the main concern in conforming to the user centric design approach. Therefore the aim of this study is to explore the usability concerns of some of the e-government websites in Saudi Arabia. Based on the cognitive walkthrough method, evaluators inspected the features and services provided by the websites in terms of their Compatibility, Consistency, Flexibility, Learnability, Minimal user action, Minimal memory load, Perceptual Limitations, Navigation, Content and User guidance. Evaluation results showed that these websites are conforming to some of the usability characteristics while are lacking in others. Study also showed some of the recommendations from the evaluators (who are the real users of the interfaces) for achieving higher productivity and standards of user centric design. It is also recommended that all of the websites of the government, who are offering manifold services, should be evaluated for their usability and should follow specific usability rules to adapt to the standards of user centric design.

REFERENCES

Abanumy, A., Al-Badi, A., & Mayhew, P. (2005). E-Government website accessibility: In-depth evaluation of Saudi Arabia and Oman. *Elect. J. E Government, 3,* 99-106.

Al-Khalifa, H. S. (2010). Heuristic evaluation of the usability of e-government websites: a case from Saudi Arabia. In *Proceedings of the 4th International Conference on Theory and Practice of Electronic Governance (ICEGOV '10)*. ACM. doi:10.1145/1930321.1930370

Asiimwe, E. N., & Lim, N. (2010). Usability of Government Websites in Uganda. *Electronic Journal of E-Government, 8*(1), 1–12.

Basit, D., & Suresha, D. (2012). Experimental Evaluation of Effectiveness of E-Government Websites. *International Journal of Emerging Technology and Advanced Engineering, 2*(11).

Clayton, L., & Cathleen, W. (1997). Cognitive Walkthroughs. In M. G. Helander, T. K. Landauer, & P. V. Prabhu (Eds.), *Handbook of Human-Computer Interaction* (2nd ed.; pp. 717–732). Amsterdam: North-Holland.

Eidaroos, A.M., Probets, S.G., & Dearnley, J.A. (2009). Heuristic evaluation for e-Government websites in Saudi Arabia. In *SIC: The Third Saudi InternationalConference Proceedings*.

Garcia, A. C. B., Maciel, C., & Pinto, F. B. (2005). A Quality Inspection Method to Evaluate E-Government Sites. In EGOV 2005 (LNCS), (vol. 3591, pp. 198–209). Springer.

Gull, H., Iqbal, S. Z., & Saqib, M. (2015). Usability Evaluation of an Educational Website in Saudi Arabia. *VAWKUM Transactions on Computer Sciences, 1*(2).

Huang, Z., & Brooks, L. (2011). Evaluating Usability of Web-Based Electronic Government: Users' Perspective. *Human-Computer Interaction. Users and Applications: 14th International Conference, HCI International 2011*.

Lee, S., & Cho, J. E. (2007). Usability Evaluation of Korean e-Government Portal. *Universal Access in Human-Computer Interaction. Applications and Services: 4th International Conference on Universal Access in Human-Computer Interaction, UAHCI 2007 Held as Part of HCI International 2007Proceedings*.

Ministry of Foreign Affairs Saudi Arabia. (2016). Retrieved April 14, 2016 from http://www.mofa.gov.sa

Ministry of Interior Saudi Arabia. (2016). Retrieved April 14, 2016 from https://www.moi.gov.sa

Mohammad, A. S., & Sriram, B. (2015). Major challenges in developing a successful e government: A review on the Sultanate of Oman. *Journal of King Saud University Computer and Information Sciences, 27*(2), 230-235.

Ndou, V. (2004). E-government for developing countries: Opportunities and challenges. *The Electronic Journal on Information Systems in Developing Countries*, *18*(1), 1–24.

Reza K. M., & Sadegheh H. N. (2016). Investigating the Effectiveness of E-government Establishment in Government Organizations. *Procedia Social and Behavioural Sciences, 230*, 136-141.

Saeed, S., & Amjad, A. (2013). Understanding usability issues of Pakistani university websites. *Life Science Journal*, *10*(6s), 479–482.

Saeed, S., Jamshaid, I., & Sikander, S. (2012). Usability evaluation of hospital websites in Pakistan. *International Journal of Technology Diffusion*, *3*(4), 29–35. doi:10.4018/jtd.2012100103

Saeed, S., & Shabbir, S. (2014). Website Usability Analysis of Non Profit Organizations: A Case Study of Pakistan. *International Journal of Public Administration in the Digital Age*, *1*(4), 70–83. doi:10.4018/ijpada.2014100105

Saeed, S., Wahab, F., Cheema, S. A., & Ashraf, S. (2013). Role of usability in e-government and e-commerce portals: An empirical study of Pakistan. *Life Science Journal*, *10*(1), 8–13.

Saudi Commission for Tourism & National Heritage. (2016). Retrieved April 14, 2016 from https://www.scta.gov.sa

Sethunya, R. J. (n.d.). Advantages and disadvantages of E-government implementation: literature review. *International Journal of Marketing and Technology, 5*(9).

Shakirat, O. R., Murni, M., & Adamu, A. (2013). Evaluation of University Teaching Hospital Websites in Nigeria. *Procedia Technology, 9,* 1058-1064.

Wan, A. R., Wan, R. I., Mohammad, R. S., Noor, I. S., & Siti, S. (2010). Assessing the Usability and Accessibility of Malaysia E-Government Website. *American Journal of Economics and Business Administration, 3*(1), 40-46.

Withrow, J., Brinck, T., & Speredelozzi. (2005). *A Comparative Usability Evaluation for an e-Government Portal.* Diamond Bullet Design Report #U1-00-2.

Chapter 17
A Mobile System for Managing Personal Finances Synchronously:
A Mobile System

Jabulani Sifiso Dlamini
Tshwane University of Technology, South Africa

Paul Okuthe Kogeda
Tshwane University of Technology, South Africa

ABSTRACT

Many Small Micro-Medium Enterprises (SMMEs) fail within their first year of operation in South Africa mainly because of the lack of proper financial management skills. To address this, a number of software applications have been developed. However, they fail to cater for the needs of SMME owners. In this Chapter, we intend to design and implement a software application to address some of these financial management challenges faced by SMMEs. To achieve this, a through literature review was conducted. Then we designed and implemented a new system with additional features missing from the existing applications. The main objectives of this new system, is to help SMME owners manage their finances from anywhere, have access to real time data and be easy to use. To implement the system, PHP and MySQL database was used. Usability testing was done to evaluate the effectiveness of the system. The system performed 20% better in keeping records as compared to the manual accounting system.

INTRODUCTION

In the last five years, about 440000 SMME businesses closed down in South Africa (ADcorp (2012) In: Fatoki (2014:922)). Some of the contributing factors to the failures of most of the SMMEs were poor business and financial management competencies (Naqvi, 2011:98). To address the problem of lack of proper business record keeping, much software has been availed over the years to help business owners with their financial management but very few cater for the needs of the SMME owners.

DOI: 10.4018/978-1-5225-1944-7.ch017

The problem with many of the accounting systems out there could be viewed as complexity, whereby the accounting systems are not different to the manual accounting practiced by any accountant who still writes on a piece of paper. This has led to most of these softwares to be only usable to people who have a strong accounting background which most business owners do not have or require the users to have some form of training before using them.

This Chapter seeks to develop an accounting system that will help SMME business owners with their financial management challenges regardless of their accounting background, by making it possible for them to have access to real time data, reduce the time needed to enter data, make it easy to use and make it accessible anywhere. This Chapter also seeks to make the following contributions in the academic field:

1. The development of a prototype as a proof of concept that shows the theoretical validity of the online accounting system to solve the financial management challenges faced by SMME owners.
2. The formalization automation, transaction-based, process-driven accounting, which contributes to system optimality and usability.
3. The discovery of additional application specific features that could greatly help SMME owners with their accounting.

This Chapter is organized as follows. In Section 2, we provide background information of Accounting Information Systems (AIS). In Section 3, we present related work. In Section 4, we present the system design and architecture. In Section 5, we present implementation. In Section 6, we present system testing and results. We conclude the Chapter in Section 7.

Background of Accounting Information System

Accounting Information System (AIS) is a tool that was built to help in management and control of economic-financial activities (Grande *et al.*, 2011:26). It can further be explained as a vehicle or enabler that makes the work of the financial custodian easier by having standardized formats of recording transactions which could further be processes to reports that could be interpreted by anyone with the knowledge of accounting.

Financial management systems between the periods of 1990 to 2000 were not very efficient. This is because they were very complicated and not user friendly, running such systems was expensive because they required a connection from client to accountant and timing had to be very critical if they wanted to get information in due time. Such systems did not work on live data because the user had to update the information stored there with current information before starting the work (Philips, 2012:6).

There have been many changes done to accounting systems over the years, these started from the basic Microsoft Excel spreadsheet to the development of more specialized software designed to do accounting in a more professional manner. The different types of accounting systems are explained in the following sub-sections.

Desktop/Computer-Based Systems

Microsoft Excel spreadsheets were a very common tool for financial management for many organizations because they were seen as a low cost option and seen as easy to use and understand so they became the chosen choice as a financial management software (Dickenson, 2011:40). Microsoft Excel spreadsheets allowed the users to create mathematical formulas and run functions. The spreadsheet becomes interactive when you enter formulas and functions and the data you enter automatically updates as you change your data (Scott, 2008:1).

The need for a more user friendly accounting software was created and many small companies and non-profit organizations started using QuickBooks to keep track of their finances (Bonnie, 2013:XVI). QuickBooks has many different versions to suite the different needs of people and businesses. Its advantage is that it is not difficult to learn as it has features that users might be familiar with such as dialog boxes, drop-down list and key board shortcuts.

Web-Based Systems

Over the years accounting systems have evolved this can be attributed to the changing way of doing business and the increased network coverage. The increased network coverage has made it possible for people to conduct business anywhere over the internet, this created a new demand of financial management software that can be used anywhere anytime over the internet.

From the year 2000, there has been more web-based applications developed to meet the increased demand for applications that can be accessed anywhere anytime over the Internet. Some of these applications include: Mint an online accounting system that automatically draws all your financial information to one place to give you a clear perspective of your financial status. This is achievable by having features that allow the user to add accounts and cards. This makes it possible for the user to see what they owe and track their spending patterns and investments (mint, 2016).

Quicken another online accounting system that balances the bank and credit accounts to depict an up to date status of finances considering pending transactions. The system also alerts the user of any up-coming bills by email or text (Kipling, 2008:18).

RELATED WORK

There are a number of researches and projects done in the field similar to our research, some of these works are discussed in this section. Florin *et al.* (2011:1) conducted a research to find out how the new web accounting system could work for Small Medium Enterprises (SMEs) and how these new systems could influence the adoption of International Financial Regularly Standards (IFRS) by SMEs and the factors that might influence the usage of web accounting by SMEs.

The product of this research was a system that made it easy for the users to gain access to it everywhere at any time because it was web based. The users did not need to have vast amounts of accounting knowledge just only basic computer skills. The reports design made it possible for the user to edit them in HTML, Excel, XML and some PDF applications. The application was accessible simultaneously by the operator and accountant or management. It was accessible using any computer with Microsoft Internet Explorer (IE), Mozilla, and Opera.

This research is similar to our work because the researcher developed a web based accounting application specifically for SMEs with the aim of finding out if these systems could be adopted by the SMEs. The developed system accomplished similar objectives that we wanted to accomplish with our proposed system by making it easy for the users to access the system everywhere at any time. Its design was in such a way that users did not need to have a vast amount of accounting knowledge just only basic computer skills. However, this work is more of a direct translation of the manual or handwritten accounting, the gap in his work is the introduction of automation in the double entry system and report generation. This allows the user to enter transactions once and the rest happens in the background of the system.

Easy Books (Geode Software, 2011) developed accounting software that is free to use, but in order to use more of its features users had to pay $30 more to get access to its features. The system's design was to make it easy to use, as it did not require thorough knowledge of accounting. Reports were auto-generated in a functional layout and could be emailed or printed from the application. A built in calculator provided, as well as online backups. It provided 29 different types of accounts with accounting jargon names, such as "Accrual". SMEs in the developing world would unlikely use some of these features.

This system is similar to the proposed system because it incorporated some automation in its report generation, but differed when it came to its usage as it contains accounting jargons, which we eliminated in our system with simple English to make it user friendly to those that do not have any accounting background.

IXpenselt (FYI mobile ware, 2011) developed accounting software that enables users to keep track of their income and expenses. It also has the ability to generate graphical reports in PDF format. This system has some drawbacks which users were not very fond of, they found that entering data into the system was time consuming and the interface was too complex. As with Easy Books, it also offers online backups and monthly overviews of the different accounts. In addition, it included the ability to take a photo of the receipts to capture a transaction. This system is not similar to our proposed system because its design was not so user friendly to the people who do not know much about accounting practices. The menu bars changing functions with every screen click and too many items on display on every screen made it to be not so user friendly. Users were complaining of the amount of time it took them to enter data into the system, while our system solved that problem by automating some of the processes. However, it has some characteristic that we included in our system the printing of reports in pdf format.

Ledger (Gladding Development, 2010) developed an accounting system that can only do basic book-keeping, however, many of its features are incomplete and it has no adequate reporting functionality. It also provides automatic backups. The application required a rudimentary understanding of accounting. This system is not similar to our system because it required people to be more fluent with accounting while our system is designed for ease of use; we made it so much simple to use such that even people with little accounting knowledge were able to use it.

Frogtek (2015) noticed that many of the SMEs do not track their sales or expenses because they do not have funds to procure the needed equipment to do that in their stores, these included things such as a point-of-sales system or a cash register, and those that were tracking them were doing it via notebook. Therefore, they then developed an accounting system that would help them in tracking their business dealings. They developed a point-of-sale application for the SMEs that enabled users to be able to re-cord all their operating expenses and revenues on their mobile phones or tablets. An external bar code connected to the phone via a wireless connection made it possible to record transactions in the system. All these applications were compatible with Android smart phones or tablets that have touch screens and synchronize with their web servers with this innovation from frogtek users had access to financial reporting, personalize recommendation and improved services. This then enabled the SME owners to realize or be able to calculate their breakeven point and make personalized recommendations to customers.

This system is similar to our application in that it allows the owners to keep track of their business records specifically sales and expenses. The system developed by frogtek still lacks other components needed for business accounting. These are bank transactions, capital investments, finances. It only focuses on cash based accounting. An addition of other components to this system is needed to make it more comprehensive and appropriate for business accounting.

SMEasy developed specifically to help South African small business owners who have no knowledge of accounting (SMEasy product profile, 2010). They developed an accounting system that allows users to enter their transactions only once and the system could do the double entry at the back end of the system for the user. The accounting system had a simple screen, no complex menus and no accounting language used in it, which made it quite simple for the entrepreneurs and SMEs to understand. Being web-based, made it possible for users to access it anytime and anywhere. The system enables users to keep track of their business and personal money used in the business. It also allows the use of company logos when creating quotations, invoices, pay slips, and so builds the brand of your business. It also has features that allows third parties such as an accountant to have access to the users' records by exporting the data.

This system is similar to our system, because it is for the South African SMME owners, who have little or no knowledge of accounting, and being hosted in the cloud, helped in making it accessible everywhere and the non-usage of accounting terminology helps in making it user friendly. The systems design meets most of the criteria related to this study, but still lacked or needs a better interface and navigation design.

The current model is not easy to navigate through the pages. A standard interface that would allow the switching between windows would make it easy to use, it also needs proper structuring to be more effective by grouping things in a chronological manner and make it easy to switch between windows by making it possible to have multiple windows open at the same time and switching between them.

System Design and Architecture

User centered design is a methodology that is followed when designing systems. It uses a top-down approach. This methodology focuses mainly on the user and segregates the entire system and user requirements into different functions (Rigsbee & Fitzpatrick, 2012:76)

There are six principles of user centered design that need to be followed when designing a system. These principles focus specifically on the user requirements to get as much information as possible (Pedro, 2003:7-8). The six principles are as follows:

1. Set the business goals
2. Understanding the user
3. Assessing competitiveness
4. Design total user experience
5. Evaluating system design
6. Maintenance and support

The reason user centered design is important is because it helps developers to design something that will answer questions that were intended to be solved by the system. This is very important if the system is meant to go on market (Rauterberg, 2003:175).

The most critical aspect in designing a system is giving the users the usage context. This means for applications developed for mobile phones, the user needs to be able to touch buttons, link, navigate the system, etc. (Eeva & Kinnunen, 2005:57)

Before embarking on designing the user interface, we first had to design the database of the system. An entity relationship diagram is a graphical representation of an entity-relationship model (Hoffer *et al.*, 2007: 93). The entity diagram shown in Figure 1 shows the tables used to store information in the database and how they relate to each other.

The user interface was developed using PHP. The system was designed to have only one user working with the system having automation functions running in the background. Using the Use Case diagram shown in Figure 2, we describe how the user interacts with the system.

The interaction of the system with information that has been entered by the user is done through automation. The different automation processes of information are shown using the systems Use Case diagram presented in Figure 3.

System Architecture

System architecture interprets the logical design of a system to the actual system. Architecture has the following components: hardware, software, network support, processing method and the security (Shelly *et al.*, 2006:362). The system architecture diagram, of the developed system is presented in Figure 4.

Figure 1. Entity relationship diagram

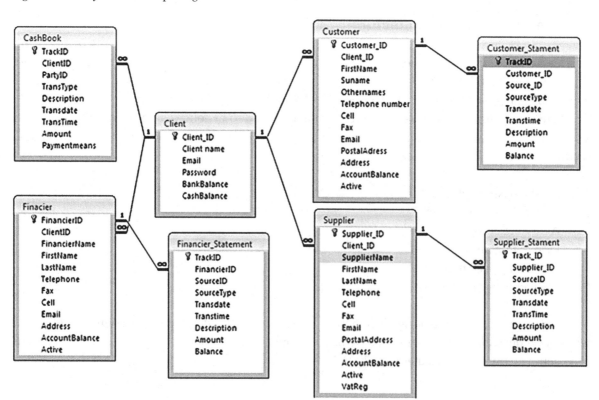

Figure 2. User activities use case diagram

From the architecture diagram, we show the different components that make the system work. These are software services running in the server to make it possible for the users to interact with the application and the database. The database server is where the storage and processing of the users' information occurs. Since the application is web based, users have to be connected to the Internet first before they can be able to use the application using the different browsers available (i.e., Chrome, Microsoft Internet Explorer, Firefox, etc.).

A client may be a computer such as desktops, laptops, note books, which require additional hardware or WiFi connection in order to connect to the Internet. A mobile device is a device that can be carried by the user and is always connected to some network and does not require additional hardware to connect to the Internet.

Figure 3. System activities use case

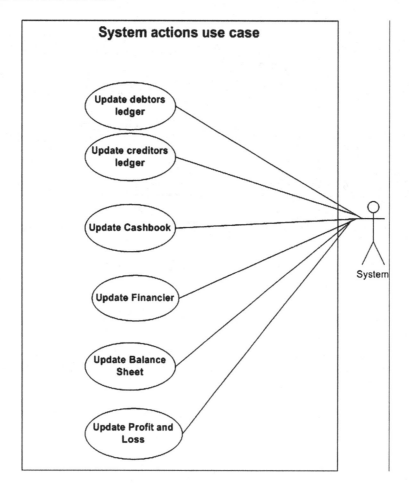

IMPLEMENTATION

The online mobile accounting management system was implemented using PHP scripting language. This system was connected to a database designed using MySQL to enable the users to save and retrieve data from the user interface. We developed a database called 'moneyb'.

The implementation of the system was done into two parts. These are as follows:

- **Database:** We used MySQL database found in XAMMP which is a free and open source cross platform web server solution stack package consisting mainly of the Apache HTTP Server.
- **Interface:** We used PHP to develop the interface because there are no costs of using PHP, and there are no license restrictions, it is 100% for free to use by anyone.

Database

To retrieve or save information in the "moneyb" database a connection string was created on the user interface. This is shown in the database connection code snippet.

Figure 4. System architecture

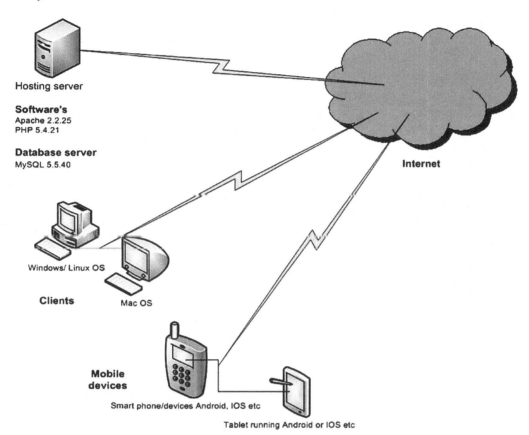

```
session_start();
include("database.php");
//Get the date and adjust it by an hour
$systemDate = date("Y-m-d H:i:s");
$newTransDate = strtotime($systemDate." + 2 hours");
$transDate = date("Y-m-d", $newTransDate);


if($_REQUEST['SubmitBtn'] == "Login")
login.php?userT=$email&passT=$password&SubmitBtn=Login");
if($userName != "" && $password != "")//&& $clientName != "")
//verify info is filled in
{$dblink = openBase('moneyb');
$result = mysql_query("Select * from `client` where Email = '$userName' and
Password = '$password'", $dblink)
or die (mysql_error()."<p><a href='index.php'>Back to Logon Page</a>");
if($row = mysql_fetch_array($result))
{//include:"home.php");           //fopen("home.php");//$loggedOn = true;//$task
= "mess";
```

```
        $_SESSION['names'] = $row['ClientName'];
        $_SESSION['enter'] = $password;
        $_SESSION['clientId'] = $row['ClientID'];
        $_SESSION['clientTrackID'] = $row['TrackId'];
        $_SESSION['func'] = " ".$row['Functions'];
        $_SESSION['isLoggedOn'] = true;
        //echo "<tr>
 //<td>".$_SESSION['clientId']." ".$_SESSION['names'].""".$_
SESSION['clientId']." ".$_SESSION['names']."</d></tr>";
//update the last logon time
mysql_query("update `customer` set LoginDate = '".date('Y-m-d', $newTrans-
Date)."', LoginTime = '".date('H:i:s', $newTransDate)."' where ClientId =
'$userName'", $dblink);
mysql_close($dblink);
header("Location: home.php");
exit;
```

The systems database "moneyb" consists of eight tables, namely:

1. **Client Table:** Stores information about the user.
2. **Customer Table:** Stores information about the customer.
3. **Customer_Statement Table:** Stores information related to transactions done with added customers.
4. **Supplier Table:** Stores information about the supplier.
5. **Supplier_Statement Table:** Stores information related to transactions done with added suppliers.
6. **Financier Table:** Stores information about the financier.
7. **Financier_Statement Table:** Stores information related to transactions done with added financier.
8. **Cashbook Table:** Stores transactions that are recorded in the system.

Interface

The use of PHP to develop the interface of the system has many advantages some of these are: because it is not platform specific, it can run on any OS that is Linux, Mac OS, Windows and UNIX. Applications built on PHP are easy to scale up, which makes scalability easy when working with PHP. Hosting applications developed in PHP is very easy since a lot of hosts do support PHP. Applications that are developed with PHP do not have any problems in terms of losing their speeds. Since it is a language that has been around for many years it is a stable language that can be trusted. Using PHP we developed the interfaces and reports. These included:

1. **Registration Form:** Used to enter the users' details in the system.
2. **Login Form:** Used to login the system after the user has registered.
3. **Add Customer Form:** Used to create a new customer in the system.
4. **Create Invoice Form:** Used to record an invoice issued to a customer.
5. **Receive Payment Form:** Used to record receipt of payment from the customer.
6. **Add Supplier Form:** Used to create a new supplier in the system.

7. **Create Invoice Form:** Used to record invoices receive after purchases.
8. **Make Payment Form:** Used to record payments to invoices received.
9. **Add Financier Form:** Used to create a new financier in the system.
10. **Receive Loan Form:** Used to record the amount of a loan received from a financier.
11. **Make Payment Form:** Used to record money paid to a loan given by a financier.
12. **Expense Form:** Used to record the amount of money spent on that specific expense.

Reports

1. Cashbook
2. Debtors ledger
3. Creditors ledger
4. Profit and loss
5. Balance Sheet

To reduce the amount of work needed to enter data into the system, we automated some of the processes and these included posting to the cashbook, balance sheet, summary sales report, summary purchases report and the Profit and loss. The sections that follow explain how that was accomplished.

Debtors/Summary Sales Report

In every business knowing how much money is owed by customers at particular time is very important. This will help the business owner in making decisions whether to continue giving goods to customers on credit or not. To generate this report from the information entered into the system, we used code shown in Debtors report generation snippet.

```php
<?php
session_start();
include("database.php");

if(!($_SESSION['isLoggedOn']))
header("Location: index.php");

        //Get the date and adjust it by an hour
        $systemDate = date("Y-m-d H:i:s");
        $newTransDate = strtotime($systemDate." + 2 hours");
        $transDate = date("Y-m-d", $newTransDate);

?>
        <?php

        //echo "Beginning to load From: $fromDate to $toDate";
        $dblink = openBase();
```

```php
$action = "select * from `customerstatement` where SourceType = 'INV' ORDER BY
TrackID";
        //echo $action;
$result = mysql_query($action, $dblink) or die("action <p> ".mysql_error());
$cash = ""; $bank = ""; $amount = 0; $totalInvoices = 0; $totalReceipts = 0;
        while($row = mysql_fetch_array($result))
        {
        $amount            = $row['Amount'] + 0;
        $totalInvoices += $amount;
        echo "<tr>
<td>".($row['TransDate'])."</td>
        <td>".($row['Description'])."</td>
        <td align='right'>  $amount</td>
        </tr>";
                }
        echo "<tr>
        <td colspan='2' align='center'>TOTAL INVOICES</td>
        <td align='right'>  $totalInvoices</td>
        </tr>";
        mysql_close($dblink);

        ?>
```

Creditors/Summary Purchases Report

Knowing how much the business owes to its suppliers is also very important because many businesses
operate on credit given to them by their suppliers. So in order to keep a good relationship with suppliers,
the business needs to keep track of how much money they owe to the suppliers at a particular time. To
get such information from the system, we used the code in Creditors report generation.

```php
<?php
session_start();
include("database.php");
if(!($_SESSION['isLoggedOn']))
header("Location: index.php");

/Get the date and adjust it by an hour
$systemDate = date("Y-m-d H:i:s");
$newTransDate = strtotime($systemDate." + 2 hours");
$transDate = date("Y-m-d", $newTransDate);

//echo "Beginning to load From: $fromDate to $toDate";
$dblink = openBase();
$action = "select * from `supplierstatement` where SourceType = 'INV' ORDER BY
```

```
TrackID";

//echo $action;
$result = mysql_query($action, $dblink) or die("action <p> ".mysql_error());
                $cash = ""; $bank = ""; $amount = 0; $totalInvoices = 0; $to-
talReceipts = 0;
while($row = mysql_fetch_array($result))
                {
$amount          = $row['Amount'] + 0;
$totalInvoices += $amount;
echo "<tr>
<td>".($row['TransDate'])."</td>
<td>".($row['Description'])."</td>
<td align='right'>  $amount.</td>
</tr>";
}
echo "<tr>
<td colspan='2' align='center'>TOTAL INVOICES</td>
<td align='right'>  $totalInvoices</td>
</tr>";
mysql_close($dblink);
        ?>
```

Financiers Transaction

Automating or posting transaction done with a financier to the relevant books of accounting after entering them once in the system was accomplished by using the code in Financiers transaction processing. This code records the transaction in the cashbook and updates the balance of the capital.

```
<?php
session_start();
include("database.php");
if(!($_SESSION['isLoggedOn']))
header("Location: index.php");

//Get the date and adjust it by an hour
$systemDate = date("Y-m-d H:i:s");
$newTransDate = strtotime($systemDate." + 2 hours");
$transDate = date("Y-m-d", $newTransDate);

$financierID = $_REQUEST['id'];
$amount = $_REQUEST['txtAmount'] + 0;

if($_REQUEST['btnSave'] == "Save")
```

```
{
$dblink = openBase();
$result = mysql_query("Select AccountBalance from `financier` where Financier-
ID = $financierID", $dblink)
or die ("Sorry, error encountered while retrieving balance<p>".mysql_er-
ror()."</p>");
if($row = mysql_fetch_array($result))
{
$currBalance = $row['AccountBalance'] + 0;
$act = "insert into `financierstatement`(FinancierID, SourceType, TransDate,
TransTime, Description, Amount, Balance)
values('$financierID', 'INV', '".date("Y-m-d")."', '".date("H:i:s")."', 'Loan',
$amount, ".($currBalance + $amount).")";
$result = mysql_query($act, $dblink)
or die ("Sorry, error encountered while saving new finance transaction<p>".
mysql_error()."</p>".$act);
$act = "update `financier` set AccountBalance = ".($currBalance + $amount)."
where FinancierID = $financierID";
$result = mysql_query($act, $dblink)
or die ("Sorry, error encountered while updating financier balance<p>".mysql_
error()."</p>".$act);

//Then update our balances
$paymentType = "CHQ";
if($paymentType == "CHQ")
$column = "BankBalance";
else if($paymentType == "CAS")
$column = "CashBalance";
$result = mysql_query("Select $column from `client` where ClientID = ".$_
SESSION['clientId'], $dblink)
or die ("Sorry, error encountered while retrieving $column<p>".mysql_er-
ror()."</p>");
if($row = mysql_fetch_array($result))
{
$currBalance = $row[$column] + 0;

$act = "update `client` set $column = ".($currBalance + $amount)." where Cli-
entID = ".$_SESSION['clientId'];
$result = mysql_query($act, $dblink)
or die ("Sorry, error encountered while updating customer balance<p>".mysql_
error()."</p>".$act);
}
```

Update Our Cashbook

```php
$act = "insert into `cashbook`(ClientID, PartyID, TransType, Description,
TransDate, TransTime, Amount, PaymentMeans)
value ('".$_SESSION['clientId']."', '$financierID', 'DR', 'Loan Received',
'".date("Y-m-d")."', '".date("H:i:s")."', ".($amount).", '$paymentType')";
$result = mysql_query($act, $dblink)
or die ("Sorry, error encountered while updating customer balance<p>".mysql_
error()."</p>".$act)                    }
mysql_close($dblink);
header("Location: fin.php?id=".$_SESSION["clientId"]."-$financierID");
}
//echo "Beginning to load From: $fromDate to $toDate";
$dblink = openBase();
$action = "select FinancierID, FinancierName from `financier` where Financier-
ID = $financierID";
$result = mysql_query($action, $dblink) or die("action <p> ".mysql_error());
if($row = mysql_fetch_array($result))
{
$financierName = $row['FinancierName'];
}
mysql_close($dblink);
```

Customer Transaction to Cashbook

Automating and updating transactions done with a customer after entering them in the system was accomplished by using the code shown in Debtors' cashbook update. This made it possible for the user to just enter information once relating to a customer and the system automatically updates it to the relevant books of accounting in the background.

```php
<?php
        session_start();
        include("database.php");

        if(!($_SESSION['isLoggedOn']))
        header("Location: index.php");

        //Get the date and adjust it by an hour
        $systemDate = date("Y-m-d H:i:s");
        $newTransDate = strtotime($systemDate." + 2 hours");
        $transDate = date("Y-m-d", $newTransDate);

         $customerID = $_REQUEST['id'];
        //echo "Beginning to load From: $fromDate to $toDate";
```

```
        $dblink = openBase();
        $action = "select CustomerID, CustomerName, AccountBalance from `cus-
tomer` where CustomerID = $customerID";
        $result = mysql_query($action, $dblink) or die("action <p> ".mysql_er-
ror());
        if($row = mysql_fetch_array($result))
        {
        $customerName = $row['CustomerName'];
        $balance = $row['AccountBalance'] + 0;
        }
        mysql_close($dblink);
?>
```

Profit and Loss

The profit and loss statement is a very important report in a business. It shows the summary of costs, revenues and expenses the company has incurred. This report is important in a business to see if it is making money or not. Since this report is generated from information that is entered in the system, from the other books of accounts there was no need to create a table to store this information. To retrieve information related to the profit and loss statement of the business, we used the code shown in Profit and loss code.

```
<?php
session_start();
include("database.php");

if(!($_SESSION['isLoggedOn']))
header("Location: index.php");

//Get the date and adjust it by an hour
$systemDate = date("Y-m-d H:i:s");
newTransDate = strtotime($systemDate." + 2 hours");
$transDate = date("Y-m-d", $newTransDate);

//echo "Beginning to load From: $fromDate to $toDate";
$dblink = openBase();
//Property
$action = "select sum(Amount) as Accumulative from `cashbook` where `ClientID`
= '".$_SESSION['clientId']."' and TransCategory = 'X15' ORDER BY TrackID";
$result = mysql_query($action, $dblink) or die("action <p> ".mysql_error());
while($row = mysql_fetch_array($result))
{
$property        = $row['Accumulative'] + 0;
}
```

```
//Plant
$action = "select sum(Amount) as Accumulative from `cashbook` where `ClientID`
= '".$_SESSION['clientId']."' and TransCategory = 'X07' ORDER BY TrackID";
$result = mysql_query($action, $dblink) or die("action <p> ".mysql_error());
while($row = mysql_fetch_array($result))
{
$plant          = $row['Accumulative'] + 0;
}
//Vehicles
$action = "select sum(Amount) as Accumulative from `cashbook` where `ClientID`
= '".$_SESSION['clientId']."' and TransCategory = 'X14' ORDER BY TrackID";
$result = mysql_query($action, $dblink) or die("action <p> ".mysql_error());
while($row = mysql_fetch_array($result))
{
$vehicles        = $row['Accumulative'] + 0;
}
//Office Equipment
$action = "select sum(Amount) as Accumulative from `cashbook` where `ClientID`
= '".$_SESSION['clientId']."' and TransCategory = 'X08' ORDER BY TrackID";
$result = mysql_query($action, $dblink) or die("action <p> ".mysql_error());
while($row = mysql_fetch_array($result))
{
$equipment       = $row['Accumulative'] + 0;
}
//Office Equipment
$action = "select sum(Amount) as Accumulative from `cashbook` where `ClientID`
= '".$_SESSION['clientId']."' and TransCategory = 'X08' ORDER BY TrackID";
$result = mysql_query($action, $dblink) or die("action <p> ".mysql_error());
while($row = mysql_fetch_array($result))
{
$equipment       = $row['Accumulative'] + 0;
}
//Calculate the stock at hand value
//Get the Total Sales
$action = "select * from `supplierstatement` where SourceType = 'INV' ORDER BY
TrackID";
//echo $action;
$result = mysql_query($action, $dblink) or die("action <p> ".mysql_error());
$totalPurchases = 0;
while($row = mysql_fetch_array($result))
{
$totalPurchases         += $row['Amount'] + 0;
}
//Calculate the stock at hand value
```

```
$action = "select * from `customerstatement` where SourceType = 'INV' ORDER BY
TrackID";
//echo $action;
        $result = mysql_query($action, $dblink) or die("action <p> ".mysql_er-
ror());
        $totalSales = 0;
        while($row = mysql_fetch_array($result))
        {
                $totalSales          += $row['Amount'] + 0;
        }

        $pps = round($totalSales / $markUp, 2);
        $ppr = $totalPurchases - $pps;
        $stock = round($ppr * $markUp, 2);

        //Then Get the Debtors Status
        $totalInvoicesOut = $totalSales;
        $action = "select * from `customerstatement` where SourceType = 'PAY'
ORDER BY TrackID";
        //echo $action;
        $result = mysql_query($action, $dblink) or die("action <p> ".mysql_er-
ror());
        while($row = mysql_fetch_array($result))
        {
                $totalPaymentsIn += $row['Amount'] * -1 + 0;
        }
        $debtors = $totalInvoicesOut - $totalPaymentsIn;

        //Then Get TheLiqiud Cash
        $totalInvoicesOut = $totalSales;
        $action = "select * from `client` where ClientID = ".$_
SESSION['clientId'];
        //echo $action;
        $result = mysql_query($action, $dblink) or die("$action <p> ".mysql_
error());
        $cash = 0;
        if($row = mysql_fetch_array($result))
        {
                $cash = $row['BankBalance'] + $row['CashBalance'];
        }
        $debtors = $totalInvoicesOut - $totalPaymentsIn;

        //Then Get the Creditors Status
        $totalInvoicesIn = $totalPurchases;
```

```php
        $action = "select * from `supplierstatement` where SourceType = 'PAY'
ORDER BY TrackID";
        //echo $action;
        $result = mysql_query($action, $dblink) or die("action <p> ".mysql_er-
ror());
        while($row = mysql_fetch_array($result))
        {
                $totalPaymentsOut += $row['Amount'] * -1 + 0;
        }
        $creditors = $totalInvoicesIn - $totalPaymentsOut;
        //The Financiers
        $action = "select * from `financierstatement`";
        //echo $action;
        $result = mysql_query($action, $dblink) or die("action <p> ".mysql_er-
ror());
        $loan = 0; $loanInv = 0; $loanPay = 0;
        while($row = mysql_fetch_array($result))
        {
                $loan += $row['Amount'];
        }
?>
```

Balance Sheet

The Balance Sheet statement shows the assets, liabilities and the capital of the business at a particular time. It shows the income balance and expenditure of the business over a period of time. This report is also generated from information that is entered into the system from the other books of accounts so there is no need to create a table to store information for it. To retrieve information related to the Balance sheet of the business, we used the code shown in the Balance Sheet statement code.

```php
<?php
        session_start();
        include("database.php");

        if(!($_SESSION['isLoggedOn']))
                header("Location: index.php");

        //Get the date and adjust it by an hour
        $systemDate = date("Y-m-d H:i:s");
        $newTransDate = strtotime($systemDate." + 2 hours");
        $transDate = date("Y-m-d", $newTransDate);

        //echo "Beginning to load From: $fromDate to $toDate";
        $dblink = openBase();
```

```
        //Property
        $action = "select sum(Amount) as Accumulative from `cashbook` where
`ClientID` = '".$_SESSION['clientId']."' and TransCategory = 'X15' ORDER BY
TrackID";
        $result = mysql_query($action, $dblink) or die("action <p> ".mysql_er-
ror());
        while($row = mysql_fetch_array($result))
        {
                $property        = $row['Accumulative'] + 0;
        }
        //Plant
        $action = "select sum(Amount) as Accumulative from `cashbook` where
`ClientID` = '".$_SESSION['clientId']."' and TransCategory = 'X07' ORDER BY
TrackID";
        $result = mysql_query($action, $dblink) or die("action <p> ".mysql_er-
ror());
        while($row = mysql_fetch_array($result))
        {
                $plant        = $row['Accumulative'] + 0;
        }
        //Vehicles
        $action = "select sum(Amount) as Accumulative from `cashbook` where
`ClientID` = '".$_SESSION['clientId']."' and TransCategory = 'X14' ORDER BY
TrackID";
        $result = mysql_query($action, $dblink) or die("action <p> ".mysql_er-
ror());
        while($row = mysql_fetch_array($result))
        {
                $vehicles        = $row['Accumulative'] + 0;
        }
        //Office Equipment
        $action = "select sum(Amount) as Accumulative from `cashbook` where
`ClientID` = '".$_SESSION['clientId']."' and TransCategory = 'X08' ORDER BY
TrackID";
        $result = mysql_query($action, $dblink) or die("action <p> ".mysql_er-
ror());
        while($row = mysql_fetch_array($result))
        {
                $equipment        = $row['Accumulative'] + 0;
        }
        //Office Equipment
        $action = "select sum(Amount) as Accumulative from `cashbook` where
`ClientID` = '".$_SESSION['clientId']."' and TransCategory = 'X08' ORDER BY
TrackID";
```

```
        $result = mysql_query($action, $dblink) or die("action <p> ".mysql_er-
ror());
        while($row = mysql_fetch_array($result))
        {
                $equipment              = $row['Accumulative'] + 0;
        }


        //Calculate the stock at hand value
        //Get the Total Sales
        $action = "select * from `supplierstatement` where SourceType = 'INV'
ORDER BY TrackID";
        $action = "select S.SupplierID, S.ClientID, L.Amount, L.TransDate,
L.Description from `supplier` as S, `supplierstatement` as L where
                        S.SupplierID = L.SupplierID and S.ClientID = '".$_
SESSION['clientId']."'" and L.SourceType = 'INV' ORDER BY TrackID";
        //echo $action;
        $result = mysql_query($action, $dblink) or die("action <p> ".mysql_er-
ror());
        $totalPurchases = 0;
        while($row = mysql_fetch_array($result))
        {
                $totalPurchases         += $row['Amount'] + 0;
        }


        //Calculate the stock at hand value
        $action = "select * from `customerstatement` where SourceType = 'INV'
ORDER BY TrackID";
        $action = "select S.CustomerID, S.ClientID, L.Amount, L.TransDate,
L.Description from `customer` as S, `customerstatement` as L where
                        S.CustomerID = L.CustomerID and S.ClientID = '".$_
SESSION['clientId']."'" and L.SourceType = 'INV' ORDER BY TrackID";
        //echo $action;
        $result = mysql_query($action, $dblink) or die("action <p> ".mysql_er-
ror());
        $totalSales = 0;
        while($row = mysql_fetch_array($result))
        {
                $totalSales             += $row['Amount'] + 0;
        }


        $pps = round($totalSales / $markUp, 2);
        $ppr = $totalPurchases - $pps;
        $stock = round($ppr * $markUp, 2);
```

```php
        //Then Get the Debtors Status
        $totalInvoicesOut = $totalSales;
        $action = "select * from `customerstatement` where SourceType = 'PAY'
ORDER BY TrackID";
        $action = "select S.CustomerID, S.ClientID, L.Amount, L.TransDate,
L.Description from `customer` as S, `customerstatement` as L where
                        S.CustomerID = L.CustomerID and S.ClientID = '".$_
SESSION['clientId']."'" and L.SourceType = 'PAY' ORDER BY TrackID";
        //echo $action;
        $result = mysql_query($action, $dblink) or die("action <p> ".mysql_er-
ror());
        while($row = mysql_fetch_array($result))
        {
                $totalPaymentsIn += $row['Amount'] * -1 + 0;
        }
        $debtors = $totalInvoicesOut - $totalPaymentsIn;

        //Then Get TheLiqiud Cash
        $totalInvoicesOut = $totalSales;
        $action = "select * from `client` where ClientID = ".$_
SESSION['clientId'];
        //echo $action;
        $result = mysql_query($action, $dblink) or die("$action <p> ".mysql_
error());
        $cash = 0;
        if($row = mysql_fetch_array($result))
        {
                $cash = $row['BankBalance'] + $row['CashBalance'];
        }
        $debtors = $totalInvoicesOut - $totalPaymentsIn;

        //Then Get the Creditors Status
        $totalInvoicesIn = $totalPurchases;
        $action = "select S.SupplierID, S.ClientID, L.Amount, L.TransDate,
L.Description from `supplier` as S, `supplierstatement` as L where
                        S.SupplierID = L.SupplierID and S.ClientID = '".$_
SESSION['clientId']."'" and L.SourceType = 'PAY' ORDER BY TrackID";

        //echo $action;
        $result = mysql_query($action, $dblink) or die("action <p> ".mysql_er-
ror());
        while($row = mysql_fetch_array($result))
        {
                $totalPaymentsOut += $row['Amount'] * -1 + 0;
```

```
        }
        $creditors = $totalInvoicesIn - $totalPaymentsOut;

        //The Financiers
        $action = "select * from `financierstatement`";
        $action = "select S.FinancierID, S.ClientID, L.Amount, L.TransDate,
L.Description from `financier` as S, `financierstatement` as L where
                    S.FinancierID = L.FinancierID and S.ClientID = '".$_
SESSION['clientId']."'" ORDER BY TrackID";
        //echo $action;
        $result = mysql_query($action, $dblink) or die("action <p> ".mysql_er-
ror());
        $loan = 0; $loanInv = 0; $loanPay = 0;
        while($row = mysql_fetch_array($result))
        {
                $loan += $row['Amount'];
}

?>
<!doctype html>
```

Testing and Results

After the successful implementation of the system, we conducted system and usability testing. In these tests, we did functional and non-functional testing on the system.

For the functional testing, 40 individuals randomly tested the system by performing certain tasks in it. These individuals were first asked to take pre-test questionnaires and later after using the system post-test questionnaires. We wanted to get the following information from the tests:

1.   If it was easy to learn and use
2.   If it met the users' financial information needs
3.   If the users made many errors while using the system and if they would recommend it to others to try it out or not

In one of the questions, we wanted them to compare the system with their manual bookkeeping system. On a scale of 1-10, users rated the system against the manual one. This rating is shown in Figure 5.

Unlike the functional testing where there were no specific selection criteria used to choose or approach the testers, with this kind of testing, we needed people that have a programming background since we needed to test the system not just for its functionality but also to see if it met certain standards.

There are ten rules of system interaction, which are called heuristics because they are not specific to usability guideline (Nielsen, 1995). When conducting the system testing we used Nielsen's 10 usability heuristics to develop the testing questions that were used for testing the system.

The testers were given a case to complete in the system, and then answer questions posed to them in the questionnaire. The questions were mapped to the following heuristic criteria:

Figure 5. Effectiveness of system vs. manual system

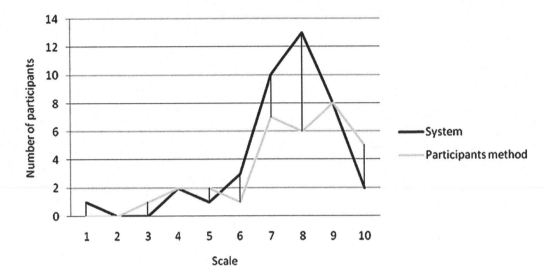

1. **Question One and Two:** Visibility of the system status
2. **Question Three and Four:** Consistency standards of the system
3. **Question Five and Six:** Error prevention capabilities in the system
4. **Question Seven:** User control and freedom
5. **Question Eight:** Flexible and efficiency of system
6. **Question Nine:** Recognition rather than recall
7. **Question Ten:** Aesthetic and minimal design of the system
8. **Question Eleven:** Help users recognize and recover from errors, question
9. **Question Twelve:** Help and documentation of the system
10. **Question Thirteen:** Matched between system and the real world

The results of the tests that were carried out on the system are shown in Table 1.

On the results obtained from the non-functional testing, we found that the system failed in three categories. These are error prevention, help users recover from errors and lack of help and documentation features of the system. To address these shortcomings of the system, we implemented error handling and validation in the system, which was previously left out. We also compiled a user manual to help users understand the system. These added features can be seen in Figure 6. Testers also suggested some improvements in other aspects and these are visibility of system status and recognition than recall. However, it passed in five other categories. These are Consistency standards of the system, User control and Freedom, Flexibility and efficiency, Aesthetic and minimal design and Match between system and real world.

Based on the results obtained in the functional testing, we concluded that the system is more effective in keeping records as compared to the manual systems. 37 out of 40 testers (93%) found the system to be more efficient, which is a 20% improvement from the manual accounting system.

Table 1. Usability test results

Heuristic	Responses from Questionnaires	Result
1. Visibility of system status	Agree 67%, Strongly agree0%, Neither Agree or Disagree 0%, Disagree 33%, Strongly disagree 0%	Improvement
2. Consistency standards of the system	Agree 17%, Strongly agree 83%, Neither Agree or Disagree 0%, Disagree 0%, Strongly disagree 0%	Pass
3. Error prevention	Agree 0%, strongly agree 0%, Neither Agree or Disagree 83%, Strongly disagree 0%,Disagree 17%	Fail
4. User control and Freedom	Agree0%, Strongly Agree 100%, Neither Agree or Disagree 0%, Disagree 0%, Strongly disagree 0%	Pass
5. Flexibility and efficiency	Strongly Agree 67%, Agree 33%, Neither Agree or Disagree 0%, Disagree 0%, Strongly disagree 0%	Pass
6. Recognition rather than recall	Agree 0%, Strongly Agree 67%, Neither Agree or Disagree 0%, Disagree 33%, Strongly disagree 0%	Improvement
7. Aesthetic and minimal design	Agree 0%, Strongly agree 0%, Neither Agree or Disagree 0%, Strongly disagree 67%, Disagree 33%	Pass
8. Help users recover from errors	Agree 0%, Strongly agree 0%, Neither agree or disagree 100%, Disagree 0%, Strongly disagree 0%	Fail
9. Help and documentation	Agree 0%, Strongly agree 0%, Neither agree or disagree 67%Disagree 33%, Strongly disagree 0%	Fail
10. Match between system and real world	Agree 0%, Strongly agree 100%,Neither agree or disagree 0%, Disagree 0%, Strongly disagree 0%	Pass

Figure 6. Error handling and user manual

CONCLUSION

In this Chapter, we introduced the study and provided background of different accounting systems. We presented different works of other researchers under related works. Then we analyzed, designed and implemented accounting system. We presented system architecture. We used PHP and MySQL to implement the accounting system. To test the effectiveness of the solution we used questionnaires. These questionnaires were used to evaluate the system to see if it met its intended objectives through Functional and Non-Functional testing.

The final result of this testing proved that automating some of the system processes and hosting the system in the cloud helped the SMME owners in their financial management by reducing the amount of work needed for re-entering data, making data available in real time and making it simple to use even for those with little or no accounting skills. This can be attested for by the results obtained from the tests. The results showed that the system was 20% better in keeping records when compared to the manual accounting system.

REFERENCES

Biafore, B. (2013). *Quick books 2013 the Missing manual*. Retrieved from http://support.quickbooks. intuit.com/opencms/sites/default/qbsupportsite/PDFs/2013Guides/QB2013MM_excerpt.pdf

Dickinson, D. (2011). The Truth about Budgeting with Spreadsheets. *Credit Control Journal, 32*(7), 40-42. http://assetsproduction.govstore.service.gov.uk/G5/0317/5.G4.0317.201/QD6/Article%20-%20 Truth%20about%20Budgeting%20with%20Spreadsheets.pdf

Eevakangas & Timokinnunen. (2005). Applying User-Centered Design to Mobile Application Development. *Communications of the ACM, 48*(7). Retrieved from http://web.mit.edu/21w.789/www/papers/ p55-kangas.pdf

Florien, Groza, &Aldescu. (2011). Using web technology to improve the accounting of small and medium enterprises: An academic approach to implementation of IFRS. *Annales Universitatis Apulensis Series Oeconomica, 13*(2).

FrogTek. (2015). *Products*. Retrieved from http://frogtek.org/products/

FYImobileware. (2014). *iXpenselt*. Retrieved from http://www.fyimobileware.com/ixpenseit.html

Geode Software. (2014). *Easy Books*. Retrieved from http://easybooksapp.com/

Geode Software. (2014). *Easy Books*. Retrieved from http://easybooksapp.com/

Gladding Development. (2012). *Ledger*. Retrieved from http://www.ledgerapp.com/

Grande, E. U., Estébanez, R. P., & Colomina, C. M. (2011). The impact of Accounting Information Systems (AIS) on performance measures: Empirical evidence in Spanish SMEs. *The International Journal of Digital Accounting Research, 11*(2), 25–43. Retrieved from www.uhu.es/ijdar/10.4192/1577-8517-v11_2.pdf

Hoffer, J. A., Prescott, M. B., & MacFadden, F. R. (2007). Modern Database Management (8thed). Prentice Hall.

Kiplinger, K. (2008). *Kiplinger's personal finance*. Retrieved from https://books.google.com/books?id =sSXMlfsUqBMC&pg=PT21&lpg=PT21&dq=Track+your+cash.+The+web+makes+it+easy+to+ know+exactly+where+your+money+goes&source=bl&ots=t1hcwUfvvb&sig=RvudSNwwHbXcK ADG92gq9srv6rw&hl=en&sa=X&ved=0ahUKEwjCv9LNpa_KAhWMchQKHc4BDcIQ6AEIIzAC #v=onepage&q&f=false

Mint. (2016). *The complete picture in one minute*. Retrieved from https://www.mint.com/how-mint-works

Nielsen, J. (1995). *10 Usability heuristics for user interface design*. Retrieved from https://www.nngroup. com/articles/ten-usability-heuristics/

Olawale, F. (2014). The Causes of the Failure of New Small and Medium Enterprises in South Africa. *Mediterranean Journal of Social Sciences MCSER Publishing, 5*(20), 922.

Phillips. (2012). *How the cloud will change accounting forever*. Retrieved from accountantsone.com/ jobseekers/CloudComputing.pdf

Rauterberg, M. (2003). *User Centered Design: What, Why, and When*. Retrieved from http://www. idemployee.id.tue.nl/g.w.m.rauterberg/publications/tekom03paper.pdf

Rigsbee, S., & Fitzpatrick, W. B. (2012). User-Centered Design: A Case Study on Its Application to the Tactical Tomahawk Weapons Control System. *Johns Hopkins APL Technical Digest, 31*(1). Retrieved from http://www.jhuapl.edu/techdigest/td/td3101/31_01_Rigsbee.pdf

Shelly, G. B., Cashman, T. J., & Rosenblatt, H. J. (2006). Systems Analysis and Design (6th ed). Boston: Thomson course Technology.

SMEasy. (2010). *Product Profile*. Retrieved from www.tdh.co.za/pdf/SMEasy%20Product%20Profile.pdf

Syed, W. H. N. (2011). Critical success and failure factors of entrepreneurial organizations: Study of SMEs in Bahawalp. *European Journal of Business and Management, 3*(4), 98. Retrieved from www. iiste.org/Journals/index.php/EJBM/article/download/298/18

Theresa, A., & Scott, M. S. (2008). *Formulas & Functions in Microsoft Excel*. Retrieved from http:// biostat.mc.vanderbilt.edu/wiki/pub/Main/TheresaScott/Excel.FnsFrmls.pdf

KEY TERMS AND DEFINITIONS

Accounting Jargon: There used by accountants to describe processes or define steps.

Automation: Is the process whereby the interference of humans is reduced.

Bookkeeping Standards: Standards used for recording accounting in an appropriate manner to be understood by anyone.

Double-Entry Bookkeeping: Entering a transaction twice that is once in the debit side and once in the credit side of the corresponding book.

Financial Management: Is the keeping of the books of accounts either done manually or by a system.

SMMEs: These are the small business mostly run by the owners or support staff that is less than 50.

Chapter 18
Towards Visually Impaired Autonomy in Smart Cities:
The Electronic Long Cane Project

Alejandro Rafael Garcia Ramirez
Universidade do Vale de Itajaí, Brazil

Amarilys Lima Lopez
Universidade do Vale de Itajaí, Brazil

Israel Gonzalez-Carrasco
Universidad Carlos III de Madrid, Spain

Renato Fonseca Livramento da Silva
Universidade Federal da Paraíba, Brazil

Gustavo Henrique Jasper
Universidade do Vale de Itajaí, Brazil

Angel Garcia Crespo
Universidad Carlos III de Madrid, Spain

ABSTRACT

Urban growth adversely affects accesses to public spaces and to their physical and functional structures. Simple tasks become a challenge for visually impaired individuals either because of the difficulty getting reliable non-visual information from the surrounding space or the lack of information. In Smart Cities scenarios, important investments will be directed to urban accessibility, but nowadays people with sensory disabilities still have to face mobility problems in those spaces. Therefore, designing suitable solutions to provide more information about urban spaces is extremely important and requires user participation. This context motivated the development of the Electronic Long Cane project. The project enhances the features of traditional long canes to detect obstacles located above the waist. Nowadays, the electronic cane was redesigned including new functions based on the Internet of Things. As a result, evidences of User-Centric Design have emerged, increasing the probability of success of this technology in Smart Cities context.

INTRODUCTION

Cities are the places where the greatest technological changes will take place during the next few decades. In a Smart City, people rather than technology are the true actors of the urban "smartness" (Chourabi et. al, 2012).

DOI: 10.4018/978-1-5225-1944-7.ch018

Smart City is a new concept. It represents an aware effort to use technology improving efficiency and the quality of life of its citizens. In this scenario, new participatory and innovation ecosystem emerges, in which citizens and communities interact with public authorities and knowledge developers (Sanchez, 2011).

Such collaborative interaction leads to co-designed user-centered innovation services and new models of governance (Oliveira & Campolargo, 2015). However, although there are legal regulations in many countries, the ecosystem is still incomplete, limited by physical barriers and the lack of information, whose constrains mobility through public spaces.

Promoting accessibility in urban spaces is a complex task and requires a deep understanding of the people's diversity and the specific needs. In this context, accessibility is related to the freedom or ability to achieve the basic needs in order to sustain quality of life (Lau & Chiu, 2003).

Despite the legal provisions to guarantee equality between citizens, the implementation of accessibility criteria in urban spaces is not still a reality. Meanwhile, individuals with any sort of disability will have to face a large distance between laws, ordinances and technical standards, and the necessary actions to implement them.

In addition, benefiting individuals and their families, in order to promote better living conditions to disabled people, also benefits the society as a whole (Hersh, 2010). This enables disabled people to go from a situation of dependency to an active participation in the society (Wiener et al, 2010). However, benefiting society is only possible if disabled people receive appropriate support (Hersh, 2010).

This chapter discusses the design process of the Electronic Long Cane project providing elements about how this device can be introduced in the Smart Cities context. Evaluation and cost analysis aspects are also discussed giving new evidences about the relevance of the User-Centric Design.

MOTIVATION

According to the World Health Organization (WHO), there were 285 million visually impaired people in 2010. In addition, 39 million were blind people and 90% of them inhabit in low and middle-income countries (Pascolini & Mariotti, 2011). The population with some sort of visual impairments was 4.25% and 82% of blind people were over 50 years of age.

In Brazil, more than 45.6 million people reported some sort of disability (IBGE, 2010). This number represents 23.9% of the population. In addition, 18.8%, say, they have some difficulty even using glasses or contact lenses and 18.7% of the population of 90.7 million of visually impaired individuals were declared blind.

In June 2004, the Cities Ministry launched the Brazilian Program for Urban Accessibility (Accessible Brazil) establishing a new vision for the universal access to public spaces. This program consisted of actions and instruments that aim to encourage and support local and state governments developing rules to ensure access and free circulation in public areas to any sort of individuals.

Such actions were supported by the Law 10.048 of November 8, 2000, ensuring essential services to people with disability, elderly, pregnant women, nursing mothers and people accompanied with infants. Enacted a month later, the Law 10.098, of December 19, 2000, established general rules and basic criteria promoting accessibility for people who have some sort of disability or reduced mobility by removing barriers and obstacles in public spaces.

In this context, assistive technologies emerge to provide accessible and affordable mobility aids to improve the interaction between individuals and the urban spaces (Cook & Polgar, 2013). Assistive technologies for urban spaces have also been conciliated to attend people with visual impairments. They are usually featured by integrated solutions who attempt to enhance the interaction within the complexity of the surrounding spaces, improving quality of life (Hersh & Johnson, 2008).

Despite recent technological developments for visually impaired individuals, the most commonly used travel aids are the long cane (a.k.a white cane) and the guide dog. In particular, the long cane or *Hoover's* cane is an indispensable assistive technology for mobility and orientation purposes, helping visually impaired individuals performing an independent locomotion in urban spaces (Wiener et. al, 2010).

However, not always, users get familiar with guide dogs and, on the other hand, traditional whites canes do not detect physical barriers commonly found in urban environments, because they are located above the waist. For example, pay phones (as illustrated in Figure 1), awnings, dumps, and others may cause accidents, transmitting insecurity.

As discussed in (Dakopoulos & Bourbakis, 2010) a wide range of portable or wearable detection/avoidance systems have been developed to assist visually impaired people in public spaces. Those systems are known as Electronic Travel Aids (ETAs).

Electronic white canes are examples of ETAs. They support blind and partially sighted people mobility. These devices generally use ultrasonic or optical sensors to carry out a real-time analysis of the environment, recognizing the obstacles proximity along the user's path (Hersh, 2015). When detecting

Figure 1. Pay phone without a proper signaling. Credit: Daniel Queiroz N/D

an obstacle, they notify the user, which intuitively reacts to changes in direction, avoiding a collision. However, suitable use of these devices requires minimal training input. In addition, it is still essential that blind travelers have a reasonable level of independence and mobility skills to use the ETA safely and effectively (Hersh, 2015).

The development of ETAs has commonly focused on resolving the limitations of the white cane by detecting obstacles proximity by using either a small box clipped to the cane or a long cane embedding additional features (Pissaloux et al., 2016).

In an earlier work, Hoyle et. al. (2004) exposed that traditional long canes, widely used by blind and visual impaired people, did not detect obstacles located above the waist. In order to prevent any sort of collisions, the authors proposed an electronic complement inside the grip of a traditional cane. The embedded electronic system used a multi-element ultrasonic sensor that collects spatial data. This data estimated surrounding features, providing assessments to potential hazards, based on a tactile multiple-stimulus user-interface.

Recently, other electronic canes have been reported in the literature. For example, the Ultracane[1] and the Bat-K Sonar[2] (Dakopoulos & Bourbakis, 2010), the Tom Pouce and Télétact (Farcy et. al, 2006), the Laser Cane (Hersh & Johnson, 2008), the iSONIC[3] and the Smartcane[4] (Abd Wahab et. al, 2011), which was initially conceived as a student project, at IIT Delhi. These canes use infrared, ultrasonic and/or laser sensors to obtain relevant information from the environment. In addition, most of the electronic canes use tactile (vibratory) or auditory interfaces to notify the users.

It is important to stress, that a large number of high tech devices have been developed but a few of them have gone beyond the prototype stage and only small numbers are in use. One of the reasons is related to the price of these devices, which is often prohibitive to blind people, particularly in Brazil. It is also important to notice, that a minimal training period for users and professional is required to guaranty a proper adaptation to these devices (Hersh, 2015).

THE ELECTRONIC LONG CANE PROJECT

Independence and mobility in urban spaces are necessary to guaranty people's active participation in society. So designing solutions to provide more information about urban spaces is essential. This was the motivation to initiate the Electronic Long Cane[5] project, based on the Assistive Technology principles and in close connection with the professionals and blind participants at Santa Catarina Association for the blind integration – ACIC.

The project idealized a solution enhancing the features of traditional long canes to detect obstacles located above the waist, having some similarity with the inventions previously mentioned. The first functional prototype was conceived in 2006 and further funds were received to improve the device in 2010, 2012 and 2014.

The design was inspired by the haptic technology (McLaughlin et al., 2002) and differs from traditional long canes because of the embedded electronic system located inside the grip. The electronic system produces auditory and tactile feedbacks whenever barriers (obstacles) above the waist are detected. As the user approaches to obstacles, tactile and auditory feedback alerts about an immediate collision. The design aims a better perception about the surrounding space promoting a safer locomotion.

The ergonomic design incorporates an electronic system inside the handle, as in Figure 2. It comprises an ultrasonic sensor (4), buzzer (14) and a micro-motor (5) commonly found in cell phones. A

Figure 2. Assembly

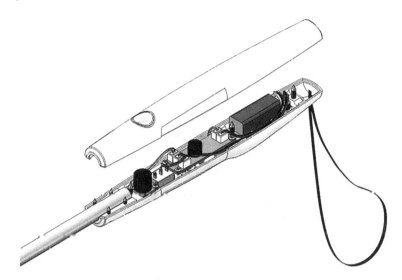

microcontroller board (6) controls the cane operation and a 9V battery (17) gives 10 hours of autonomy, as in Figure 3 (Silva & Ramirez, 2013).

The grip design also comprises an upper lid (2), rear lid (15), switch (10), battery charger connector (11) and battery connector (16), between others miscellaneous. The electronic system collects and manage the data provided by the ultrasonic sensor (Silva & Ramirez, 2013).

The key component is the ultrasonic sensor. The ultrasonic sensor is responsible for the emission and reception of the ultrasonic waves (around 40 KHz) who helps the user to locate the physical barriers. The system has two sensors embedded in one piece: one part working as a transmitter and the other one working as a receiver.

The operating principle of an ultrasonic sensor is based on the emission and reflection of ultrasonic acoustic waves. The proximity of an object can be calculated by using the flight time of the ultrasonic wave. This process is known as eco localization.

Eco localization is simple and computationally less intensive, compared to other techniques. It is suitable to be realized, in real-time, in a small portable device, like the white cane. In addition, ultra sound waves are better reflected by solid surfaces like crystals and metals and, to a lesser degree, by softer objects, like clothes. Accuracy of eco localization also depends on physical size and shape of the objects and upon the angle of incidence of the ultrasonic wave, wavelength and temperature (Hersh, 2015).

The handle is 22 cm long, 3 cm in diameter, and 0.170 kg in weight. Battery autonomy was 2 hours when vibrating continuously. The processing time interval for echo localization was set at 100 µs (+/- 3.4 cm error). The ultrasonic sensor range was set at 1.5 m, covering a horizontal angle of 30°. The ultrasonic reach was settled to the cane reach, according to the tests performed, taking into account the observations made by Mobility and Orientation professionals and the users.

It is important to stress, that tactile feedback was considered to preserve the hearing sense, which is necessary to the perception and recognition processes in urban environments. According to Dischinger (2000), the cane, as the guide dogs, alerts the presence of some physical barriers, however, the space is only perceived by through other senses like hearing, the sense of smell, and the haptics.

Figure 3. Handle components

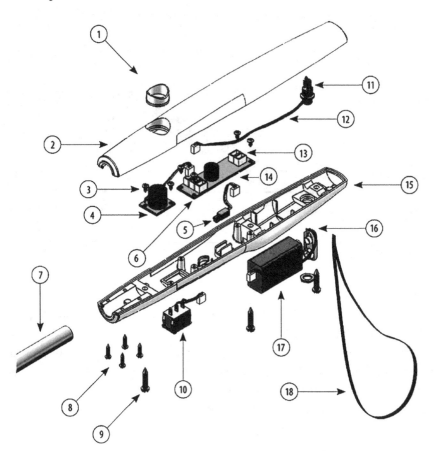

The design preserves the traditional long cane usage techniques, especially the touch technique, which is widely used by visually impaired individuals during their independent locomotion in urban spaces. Through this technique, surrounding spaces can be explored using the tip of the cane, by touching the ground stimulating tactile perception (Cook & Polgar, 2013).

In fact, long canes are conceived as extensions of the index finger. The hand should hold the cane in front of the body's midline, a little distance away from it, so that the combination between the upper member and the cane will form a straight line, Figure 4.

As can be seen in Figure 4, the forearm must be in an intermediate position, with the hand back facing out. That procedure guarantees a correct centralization of the cane and a safer reaction time, keeping a straight walking. Besides, it gives the best reference for the protection arch performed in front of the body by using the cane. The straight line between the upper member and the cane places the cane at a safer distance, avoiding it to be pushed against the person's body when the cane is trapped into an object (Silva & Ramirez, 2013).

The new cane was conceived as a personal aid to assist the Mobility and Orientation processes of blind individuals in urban spaces. It featured a new cane concept for visually impaired individuals. Although its contribution detecting obstacles above the waistline was extensively studied, this device

Figure 4. Blind volunteer using the electronic long cane. Source: Daniel Queiroz N/D

operates in an isolated manner. Why not to explore the possibility of extracting more information from the environment?

According to Hersh and Johnson (2008), there have been quite a few attempts to harness the available contemporary technological advances in mobility assistive devices and most efforts have been devoted to assistive technology focused in to avoid obstacles.

Only a few electronic canes have been reported as was previously mentioned. Those devices and the former version of the Electronic Long Cane, here described, have the same functionality and explores similar feedback and sensing. However, they differ in ergonomic concepts and costs. Furthermore, all of these devices operate in isolation, without interaction with any other devices in the environment.

Nowadays there is a commercial device, which expands the functionality of traditional electronic long canes. That device was developed by the Dutch company I-Cane[6] and incorporates a GPS inside the grip, featuring a new cane concept. In this work, the approach is slightly different, because interconnectivity is based on the IoT principles, implementing an intelligent connection between the cane and a mobile device connected to the Internet.

NEW DESIGN

This section presents a discussion upfront the efforts towards improving the interaction between visually impaired individuals and urban environments. The basic ideas and research stages here presented are under development, presenting new elements.

Nowadays, due to the development of information and communication technologies, people are more connected thanks to the proliferation of wireless devices in a communicating–actuating network. This new paradigm creates the Internet of Things (IoT), wherein sensors and actuators blend seamlessly within the surrounding environment and sharing information across different platforms (Gubbi et al. 2013).

The Internet emerged as a network of interconnected computers for information exchange. Nowadays, applications enabled the Internet to turn into a network of individuals, in which it was possible both people to communicate exchanging information, and, at the same time, geting benefits such as finding information about the weather, places, goods, health, etc. (Akhbar et. al, 2016).

According to the International Telecommunication Union (ITU) about 2.7 billion people were connected to the Internet worldwide, and the number of mobile phone subscriptions reached 6.8 billion, almost the same number of people on the planet, in 2013.

The Internet is constantly changing and evolving. The devices are becoming increasingly interconnected and ubiquitous in the people's routine, allowing a higher integration with other network elements, like systems, machinery, people, etc. This context references the paradigm of the IoT (Coetzee & Eksteen, 2011).

The IoT is a concept that encompasses a variety of technologies and research areas aimed extending the Internet for objects of the real world. According to Atzori et. al (2010), the basic idea of the IoT is the diversity (of things) cooperating to achieve a common goal. In the IoT, things share information using unique addressing schemes and standardized communication protocols.

The US National Intelligence Council stated that the Internet of Things will be one of the six most promising technologies that would impact the US (United States) in the near future, providing cost reduction and contributing, among other things, to the economy growth. The Council also predicted that all daily devices, like cars, TVs, wash machines, etc., would be connected to the Internet by 2025 (NIC, 2008).

This devices-interconnection promotes increasing rates of information and can detect changes in the physical environment, leading to a higher interaction to the outside world through existing services, such as analyzes and applications. Bluetooth, Wi-Fi, Zigbee are examples of wireless networking technologies commonly used to implement the IoT (Gubbi et al., 2013).

The Internet of Things also promotes a new paradigm, known as Web of Things, which adopts WEB standards in order to provide reuse and adaptation of WEB technologies, generating flexibility, personalization and productivity (França et al, 2011).

Currently, the IoT have success in different areas such as leisure and culture. Nevertheless, mobile applications are developed for specific homogenous scenarios and applications do not offer a deep interaction between the user and its surrounding environment (Gubbi et. al, 2013). Moreover, most of the IoT related projects and released products, have been focused on games, tourism and advertising.

Several techniques based on principles of robotics and software have also been reported in the IoT. The goal is to explore the remaining senses providing the required spatial information, thus, overcoming the lack of it. Among these techniques, haptic systems play an important role. Within that context, the current solution was conceived.

The new design of the electronic long cane is based on the IoT principles. The goal is to feature the three layers of architecture showed in Figure 5. This architecture was inspired on the work of (Domingo, 2012) and it was conceived to assist people with disabilities.

It is important to remark, that his architecture is widespread within the context of this research and several authors include it as a reference for their research (Akhbar et. al, 2016). It was adopted for this reason, but defining our own three-layer implementation in order to better integrate the Electronic Long Cane to the Smart Cities context.

The perception layer has the function of identifying objects from the environment, gathering information to the user. It is basically comprised by Smart Sensors, like ultrasound and Global Position System (GPS), and Mobile devices, such as smartphones and tablets.

Figure 5. Architecture for IoT

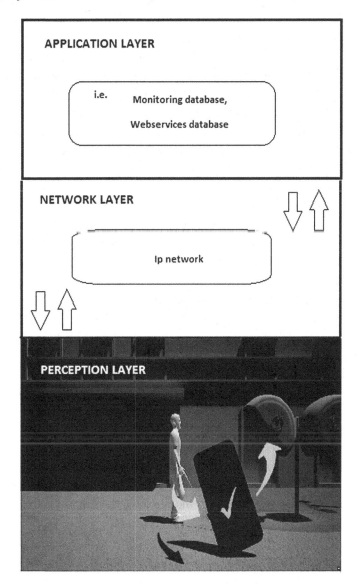

The function of the Network layer is to exchange information between the Perception and the Application Layers. A Bluetooth link was added to the electronic system to that end. The Application layer is composed by a set of applications performing the IoT technology to satisfy the users' needs.

As a result, the electronic system shares information with an external device connected to the Internet (i.e. smartphone) so expanding the electronic cane's functionalities based on the IoT principles. The wireless communication with an external device, such as a smartphone, connected to the data cloud, will warn about potential collisions in a specific route.

A mobile-based Application Interface (API) was developed using a set of localization services, provided by the Google Play Services. By using this alternative, the geofences provided a solution for our project, as will be detailed below.

The Android Studio SDK was the Integrated Development Environment (IDE) chosen in this work. An IDE is a software application that provides comprehensive facilities for software development. An IDE usually consists of a source code editor, automation tools and a debugger (DiMarzio, 2008). In this case, Android Studio SDK is the official IDE provided by Google. It offers optimized features for developing applications (API) considering the Android project structure, which is composed by configuration files, source code and resource files such as images (Android Developers, 2016d).

On the other hand, an API is a set of routine definitions, protocols and tools, useful for building software and applications. Its main function is to make the develop of a program easier by providing all the necessary libraries (DiMarzio, 2008). In this sense, the Google Play Services is a proprietary background service and an API package for Android devices, allowing applications to easily communicate with the cloud services (Android Developers, 2016c).

One group of services offered by the Google Play Services is the location APIs, which abstract the specifics about mathematics and low level interaction with location information providers, involved in localization technologies. These APIs are intended to explore the location awareness of mobile applications by facilitating the access to features such as automated location tracking, activity recognition and geofencing (Android Developers, 2016a).

A particular geofence can be identified by its geographical position and ratio, producing notifications anytime the mobile device enters or leaves a predefined area (Android Developers, 2016b). Therefore, this service package offers a suitable solution for our project since it enables the application to inform the user when entering in specific geographic areas, which can be associated with the locations of the obstacles of interest. Figure 6 shows an example of a geofence application.

Geofences monitoring is achieved by the location services provided by the API. Meanwhile the registration of new geofences, which are associated with the locations of physical obstacles, is possible due to the interaction between the electronic cane and the environment, through the smart sensors.

A Bluetooth link was performed enabling the communication link between the mobile application and the hardware embedded in the electronic cane. Bluetooth is a wireless technology standard for exchanging data over short distances from fixed and mobile devices, thus making it suitable for connecting the mobile device and the electronic cane. Moreover, mobile devices such as smartphones and tablets often have a built-in Bluetooth adapter.

Figure 6. An example of a geofence application notifying a pre-defined location

The addition of a Bluetooth module was considered viable during the updating process of the former version of the electronic cane's hardware. A Bluetooth link was chosen interfacing the devices performing a smart link between the user and the environment. This is the main change in relation to the previous design.

The Global Positioning System – GPS provides the current geographical position for the mobile device enabling storing obstacles locations. Storing geofences was achieved through a *SharedPreferences* file. This structure provides storage and access to the data anywhere inside the application. The communication with the file storage was performed through the class *SimpleGeofenceStore*.

There were enabled two methods to register and to store obstacles of interest. This action can be done by using the automatic interaction between the cane and the mobile device (i.e. smartphone), or manually, by using a button on the user interface of the application (see Figure 7).

The *IntentService* is executed in the background by the operational system and through the Google Play Services performs the asynchronously monitoring of the geofences. In addition, the class *Receive-TransitionsIntentService* was implemented. This class inherits from the native class *IntentService* and treats the transitions sent by Google Play Services, assigning an action, like a text notification.

Figure 7. User-device interface

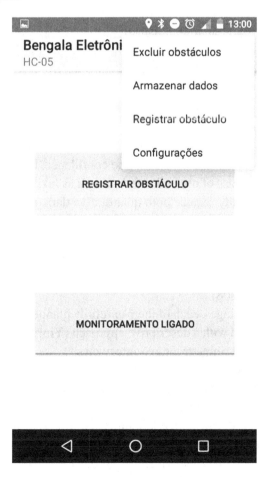

The *GeofenceRequester* and *GeofenceRemover* classes were considered adding or removing geofences by using a request to Google Play Services. The *LocationServiceErrorMessages* class was applied for errors treatment during the connection with the localization service. The *GeofenceUtils* class was used to define constants and standards used by the whole application.

It is important to notice, that the mobile application should be accessible to visually impaired users. For this reason, it is important to fulfill some important accessibility recommendations for mobile devices. The Android programmers suggest a set of directives that should be followed in order to turn the manipulation of the application easier for sensory impaired individuals. The use of descriptive texts controlled by the user interface using the Android Attribute Content Description and running the application using the accessibility mode, are examples of such accessibility recommendations.

SCENARIO AND CASE STUDY

The electronic canes prototypes were evaluated at three different times. The first study was conducted at the Santa Catarina Association for the blind integration – ACIC, in 2009. Later, in 2011, a new study was carried out at Brazilian Association for Assistance to People with Visual Impairment - LARAMARA. This year a new usability study was initiated, but this time the volunteers use their own devices during the experiments.

Orientation and mobility professionals attended all the evaluations processes and thirty-five visually impaired volunteers had participated, including a child. This year, a new group of volunteers is being incorporated into the experience, thanks to the public contest 84/2013 "MCTI-SECIS/CNPq - Assistive Technology / B - Emerging Research Centers".

The study aimed to analyze the properties of the electronic long cane with an emphasis on its contribution providing information about the open urban spaces. Especially identifying physical barriers located above the waist. Preliminary results were discussed in (Ramirez et. al, 2012) and (Silva & Ramirez, 2013).

Device evaluation focused on important aspects, like confidence, the provision of accurate information, successful task completion, ease of use and safety as well as taking into account several qualitative issues. A full evaluation will usually require both quantitative data, related to user performance using the device, and qualitative data, related to the user subjective opinions (Hersh, 2015).

It should be also stressed the relevance of the involvement of end-users from the beginning and through all the development process. An understanding of how blind people travel, including the ways they use gathering information from all their preserved senses, is a further essential prerequisite for a good design (Hersh & Johnson, 2008).

Data were collected in several stages, each of them carefully planned. In addition, there were adopted methods and techniques associated with a descriptive approach (Yin, 2014), like documentary analysis, exploratory visit, guided tours and semi-structured interviews.

The documentary analysis comprised bibliographical studies in order to build the theoretical basis for this study. Topics like accessibility, mobility in urban spaces, visual impairment, environmental perception and spatial orientation, were researched.

The exploratory visit method was useful to elaborate a survey, recording the main characteristics of the space where the experiments took place. This survey is very important to better understanding their physical provisions (Oliveira, 2006). It is worth mentioning that the exploratory visits directly contributed to the organization of the guide tours as well as the interviews.

Photographic records provided a visual description of the places under study including their physical characteristics, mostly registering the presence of physical barriers. Figure 8 shows a picture of ACIC, where part of the experiments were performed. Physical barriers were manually situated to perform the initial tests.

The method known as the guided tour (Dischinger, 2000) was applied. This method allows getting information about the difficulties that blind individuals face during the perception, orientation and displacement processes in urban spaces. This method consists of reiterated visits to the selected places, together with the volunteers and mobility and orientation instructors, registering any limitation or relevant feature during the way. The researcher must follow the volunteer during the activities without leading or helping.

By applying this method, the routes should have a departure point, barriers, and several goals to be achieved. Notice that this method should follow the dynamics of the scenario, in real time, through direct observations and verbalizations of the experiences reported by the participants, giving elements to understand complex situations experienced by the user in the selected spaces. Figure 9 illustrates a particular scenario in the streets of Florianópolis.

Figure 8. Inside the ACIC, where part of the experiments took place

Figure 9. Pictorial scenario of the city of Florianópolis

The correct use of the electronic long cane in the experiments was observed. As well as the efficiency detecting and signaling obstacles above the waist, according to the conditions imposed by the selected areas, especially in relation to the proximity of physical barriers (Silva & Ramirez, 2013).

Through the experiments, the volunteers verbalized the experience as positive, assuring the importance of the Electronic Long Cane project as a travel aid. For them, to get environmental information is relevant, especially in relation to the obstacles above the waist. In addition, identifying physical barriers has been pointed as beneficial, not only for the spatial orientation in urban spaces but also for its identification. Obstacles are not only a barrier to be transposed.

In addition, professors manifest the device's appropriateness for Mobility and Orientation programs. Nowadays, the study also shows that it promotes a better access to positive information about urban spaces, helping the visually impaired to ensure its rights.

In this regard, a new study was started, aiming to get a better perception and management of information in urban spaces based on the IoT. It hopes increasing the possibilities of social inclusion and life quality for people who have some sort of restriction, circumstantial or permanent.

NEW EXPERIMENTS

Experiments with a visual impaired volunteer were held in order to evaluate the new features added to the electronic long cane. He used the application developed for a smartphone, storing and removing the obstacles locations and experienced the text and sounds notifications at the obstacles' proximity. The exploratory visit, the guide tour and the semi-structured interview techniques were applied. In addition, the communication link between the mobile device and the electronic cane was tested.

The evaluation was performed in a public square in the city of Itajaí (see Figure 10). Obstacles locations are detached in blue and proximity notifications in red.

Figure 10. Satellite vision of Itajaí

The selected area contains a wide variety of physical barriers commonly found in other public spaces, which represent a risk for visually impaired individuals. Pay phones and local information boards are examples of those barriers as can be seen in Figure 11 and Figure 12, respectively. In this test, the geographical locations of three obstacles were considered.

The volunteer is a user of the Electronic Long Cane, benefited by the public contest 84/2013, and with a good knowledge about its features. In order to have success when performing this new experiment, the volunteer had a previous contact with the application developed for the mobile device.

Figure 11. The blind volunteer approaches to a pay phone

Figure 12. The blind volunteer approaches to a local information board

At the very beginning, the selected obstacles were stored in the system and after that, when performing that path again, vibrations and sounds alerted obstacle's proximity. Additionally, the application stored the geographical position where the notifications happened, taking into account the default location of each specific obstacle, in order to obtain accuracy and repeatability metrics.

The geographical position of each obstacle defines the center of a circular area, which was settled to a geofence ratio of 10 meters. If the system works properly, a notification (sounds and vibrations) alerts where the user get inside this circumference. Each obstacle was approached several times during the test, starting from different locations.

The payphone and local information board locations and the corresponding proximity alerts were stored in order to analyze system's performance. To that end, repeatability and accuracy, measured in meters, were used. It should be noticed that the GPS signal failed in the proximities of the OBS3 obstacle (see Figure 10), and it was discarded for this reason.

Precision was calculated as the distance between the default geographical position of each obstacle and the arithmetic mean of the latitude and longitude values where each notification happened. The arithmetic mean of ten values of latitude and longitude were registered to each obstacle.

In addition, repeatability was calculated as the radius of the circumferences which diameters are equal to the distance between the two furthest points, inside it, like pictured in Figure 13. For each obstacle, the arithmetic mean of the repeatability values was registered.

Table 1 shows the accuracy and repeatability results. Those values could be more accurate by increasing the number of obstacles and its notifications.

The repeatability indicates that the obstacle is notified beyond the cane reach. On the other hand, accuracy is approximately half the ratio settled for the geofence. These results are adequate, according

Table 1. Arithmetic mean results

Repeatability	1,44 m
Accuracy	5,43 m

Figure 13. Measuring the repeatability values

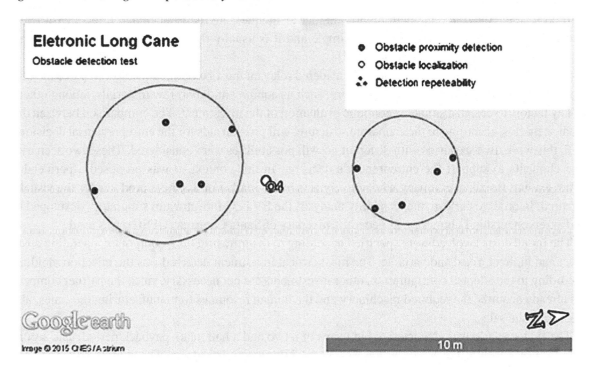

to the accuracy issues encountered in GPS (Zhu & Chen, 2013). It is important to remark that the main purpose is to notify the proximity of an obstacle and not to inform its exact geographical position. As a result, the user will be alerted in advance and will use the electronic protection embedded in the cane more efficiently, avoiding a collision.

When finishing the tests, the volunteer expressed its satisfaction with this proposal and reported that felt comfortable and would be able manipulating the application by himself. Even though there were observed some difficulties to achieve an expertise level by using the system and more tests, with more participants, should be developed to that end.

ECONOMIC VIABILITY

A feasibility study was conducted in this work. A feasibility study is useful to obtain an overview of a certain problem and to roughly assess whether feasible solutions exists prior to committing substantial resources to a specific project (Overton, 2007).

In order to get closer to the reality, this kind of analysis should be based on a particular scenario; having a mathematical model for simulation; and the indicators of quality provided by the mathematical model should be known. The analysis of the quality indicators helps establishing specific criteria to make a decision (Overton, 2007).

The return on investment period (payback) had been used for the economic and financial analysis, in this project. This criterion analyzed what return on Investment will the project show, without considering any sort of interest. This criterion should be used to estimate the liquidity of the invested capital, and should not be used alone, as a profitability criterion. In fact, the use of this criterion can only be justified when applied in conjunction with another technique, like the finance and project cash flows criteria. However, the payback method is simple and it is usually the first method to be applied in a decision-making investment (Overton, 2007).

The financial statements that could be considered relevant must be defined in order to make the economic analysis. Thus, the productive structure, such as equipment, labor, raw materials, among others, are key factors to design a suitable economic evaluation of the investment. The comparison between different scenarios, according to the economic structure, will provide aids for the entrepreneurial decisions.

In this work, two scenarios with different growth possibilities were considered. These two scenarios gave elements to support the entrepreneur's decision. In this context, it was proposed a partnership with a leading Brazilian company who actively acts in the market of assistive products for the visually impaired. In order to perform the feasibility analysis, the EVTEC Inovatorium simulator[7], developed by the Entrepreneurship Laboratory, at Federal University of Santa Catarina (UFSC), was used.

The initial costs involved were specified according to the infrastructure, equipment, operating costs, direct and indirect, fixed and variable. The most critical investment detected was the injection molding. According to the adopted configuration, other investments are not necessary, since the partner company had already acquired the required machinery and the human resources to manufacturing the canes, also supporting the sales.

The first scenario was characterized in terms of a two and a half years payback period. The second scenario was developed considering the Brazilian GDP growth estimative. The starting unit price was R$ 800.00, in both cases, due to the possible values acceptance appointed by the leader of the partner company. This value suffered a 3% annual adjustment in both scenarios. In addition, and according to the company, the maximum production rate was estimated in 500 units.

The first scenario considered a monthly sales forecast of 95 units; below the maximum producton capacity, see Table 2.

By using these estimates, the payback will be 2.49 years and the profit margin will be 55% by the last year.

In the second scenario, it was considered the Brazilian GDP growth estimative. Again, the number of sales units was below the maximum production capacity, Table 3.

By using these estimates, the payback will be 1.49 years and the profit margin will be 115%.

Table 2. Configuration 1, scenario 1: Sales projection and unit price

Item	Year 1	Year 2	Year 3	Year 4	Year 5
Unit Price	R$ 800,00	R$ 824,00	R$ 848,72	R$ 874,18	R$ 900,41
Monthly sales forecast	95	95	95	95	95

Table 3. Configuration 1, scenario 2: Sales projection and unit price

Item	Year 1	Year 2	Year 3	Year 4	Year 5
Unit Price	R$ 800,00	R$ 824,00	R$ 848,72	R$ 874,18	R$ 900,41
Monthly sales forecast	95	99	104	109	114

These analysis provides information to evaluate which way should be followed, reducing the uncertainty in the decision-making process. According to the leader of the partner company, there is a promising market for the Electronic Long Cane in Brazil. Even though the product has a higher cost, compared to traditional white canes, it also has a higher implicit benefit, due to innovation and usefulness features here described.

DISCUSSION

The Convention on the Rights of Persons with Disabilities defines the actions that a Signatory must execute to ensure that a person with disabilities can realize his rights. The following articles[8] have direct relations with this proposal.

Article 9 is concerned with accessibility. It states, "To enable persons with disabilities to live independently and participate fully in all aspects of life". To that end, "States Parties shall take appropriate measures to ensure to persons with disabilities access, on an equal basis with others, to the physical environment, to transportation, to information and communications, including information and communications technologies and systems, and to other facilities and services open or provided to the public, both in urban and in rural areas."

In addition, article 20 addresses aspects related to personal Mobility: "States Parties shall take effective measures to ensure personal mobility with the greatest possible independence for persons with disabilities..."

As can be seen, according to the Convention, accessibility and mobility are very important aspects to have a full social life. These assertions guides the process of planning buildings and sidewalks, among others, supported by law, promoting accessibility. Nevertheless, reality is still far away from ensuring the right conditions for people with sensorial disabilities.

In particular, for visually impaired individuals, realizing the surrounding space must necessarily be provided with the safest and most adequate ways, considering the characteristics and needs of each individual. Independence and mobility, in urban spaces are necessary to guaranty people's active participation in society.

In this context, the IoT promises an enhanced interaction between the user and the surrounding spaces. IoT envisions connecting billions of sensors to the Internet and expects to use them for more efficient and effective resource management in Smart Cities. IoT would make higher interaction possible with a greater range of services offered in the Smart Cities scenario. IoT and Smart Cities are recent phenomena that have attracted attention from both academia and industry (Caragliu et. al, 2009).

Another important issue in Smart Cities is sustainability. According to (Nandyala, & Kim, 2016) the concept of green IoT also includes the whole product life cycle, including green disposal/recycling to have no or very small impact on the environment. Starting from this assumption, the device uses recyclable plastic elements in order to minimize the environmental impact at the end of the device's life cycle. Other green technologies, like the use of solar batteries are being studied. This feature would improve autonomy and sustainability of the electronic long cane.

In addition, mobile devices like smartphones are enabler technologies for Green IoT, providing also the possibility of include flexibility and user-friendly interfaces in mobile applications (Shaikh et al., 2015). According to (Nandyala & Kim, 2016) one of the aspects focused by Green IoT is energy-efficient computing and power management.

FUTURE DIRECTIONS

This work describes a proposal to be engaged in the Smart City context. Architecture based on new cane functionalities, promises accessibility and independence, based on the concepts of the Internet of Things – IoT. As a core of this architecture, the electronics embedded in the handle of the cane provides both tactile and auditory haptic feedback, together with relevant information extracted from the environment.

The authors believed that when using the surrounding information in advance, users would be alerted about the obstacles proximity in a specific route, also helping them, for example, to cross a street safely. This will be possible because the electronic cane interacts with the environment through a mobile application immerse in the IoT principles.

The prototype showed to be efficient by detecting, with the embedded electronic assistance, different kinds of physical barriers. Its use, associated with the architectural and urban solutions, may collaborate to provide important information for orientation and mobility process in thoses spaces.

From the software point of view, besides the Android operational system chosen in this work, another possibility would be considered: the iOS. The former is an open code, allowing a lower level of programming, while the latter has accessibility resources better appreciated by the visually impaired community.

In relation to the smartphone-based application, two alternatives were considered. The first one was building an application using a database compatible with any Geographic Information System (GIS) technology. The second one uses a set of localization services provided by the Google Play Services. By using the first alternative, a Database Management System (DMS) would perform the location monitoring. However, the authors found a technical barrier because of the lack of robustness and popularity of the native DMS for Android SQLite. This requires further study. For this reason, the authors used the second alternative, instead.

In addition, storing geofences was achieved through a *SharedPreferences* file. This structure provides storage and access to the data anywhere inside the application. Another alternative would be the use of an Android native database.

As a result, the system will allow visually impaired individuals to access a variety of audio contents, as well as information about the environment, which was not available in the former version of the electronic cane. In a near future, each user, by means of its wearable devices (i.e. electronic cane and a smartphone) users will have access to real time information about the environment and, depending on the sort and degree of disability, will receive vibrations and sounds messages that would enhance the interaction with its surroundings. This could include, for instance, a smart interaction with traffic lights signals or pedestrian signals, as pictured in Figure 14.

Future studies will be conducted to the development of a central server allowing accessing different services through the IoT. For this purpose, other functionalities could be incrementally added to the system, for example, accessing different services in the cloud, such as finding points of interest, accessing information of public interest as well as get in social groups, etc. The main idea is to spread the functionalities of the electronic cane, through the different components of the system, based on the IoT principles.

Other issues, like the integration of the system with a fall detection function (Delahoz & Labrador, 2014) and (Fortino & Gravina, 2015), would be addressed. This resource could provide further support and would assist blind users e.g. in the unfortunate case that the obstacle detection failed or simply to handle accidental fall events. In addition, the inclusion of more efficient green IoT features will be considered in order to improve the autonomy and sustainability of the electronic cane.

Figure 14. Smart link between users and pedestrian signals

It is worth highlighting that the previous version of the electronic long cane supports this research, from which satisfactory quantitative and qualitative assessments were obtained. Although blind community accepted the former model and its functionalities, aspects such as global localization and the possibility of extracting more information from the environment, like locating points of interest, were frequently suggested for the users of the cane (Ramirez et al., 2012). Consequently, a new concept has emerged improving the cane functionalities, as presented in this chapter.

CONCLUSION

Fomenting accessibility in urban spaces is a complex task and demands a deep understanding of the diversity and people needs. Accessibility in urban spaces is still longer to be a reality even though the significant provisions and legal actions, that guarantee the right to equality among citizens. This is because the existing gap between laws, acts, and the necessary actions to materialize them. This chapter discussed how assistive technology developers could change this scenario.

Assuring autonomy for visually impaired people, especially in urban spaces, has fundamental importance for their active participation in society. Tasks apparently simple for people who have preserved the sense of sight, like crossing a street, is a daily challenge for the visually impaired, especially, due to the difficulty obtaining non-visual reliable information about the surroundings.

Therefore, addressing a higher provision and information about the spaces is extremely relevant, supporting this research. In this regard, the present work is focuses on the development and evaluation of a mobility aid designed for visual impaired individuals. The Electronic Long Cane was designed to provide more data about urban spaces notifying the proximity of physical barriers located above the waist. These barriers prevent the orientation and mobility process of blind and visually impaired individuals.

This work also discusses solutions promoting a higher interaction between different heterogeneous technologies embedded in the Smart Cities scenario and blind users. For this purpose, the development of a three-layer architecture, based on IoT, was analyzed in order to enhance the interaction between sensory impaired individuals and their surroundings. IoT would enhance inclusion, facilitating urban mobility and independence of visually impaired individuals in this new paradigm.

Obstacles detection and its proximity is a key feature of the system. This suggests that a notification occurs in advanced, being an efficient way to avoid a collision. According to the user evaluation, alerting obstacles proximity in advance is effective and this feature would improve the mobility and orientation process in urban spaces.

Future stages will be directed to develop a central server allowing the access to different services through the IoT. In addition, evaluating the communication link between the electronic system inside the grip and the Internet server, also analyzing the usability of this concept and gathering more visually impaired users, will be considered.

This work concerned about how to provide enhanced information from urban spaces, embedded in the Smart Cities context. The authors intend to point out new perspectives to increase the visually impaired individuals' participation in society, contributing to assure their right to mobility, also promoting dialogues related with the complexity of public spaces.

Professionals and users from partner institutions did participated in all the project development stages contributing with their knowledge to develop and enhance the purpose of this work. The ethics committee on human research supported this research.

ACKNOWLEDGMENT

This work is supported by the Conselho Nacional de Desenvolvimento Científico e Tecnológico -CNPq, grant no. 458672-2013/0 and 452293/2016-2. Authors would also like to especially thank the Ministério de Ciência e Tecnologia - MCT, Financiadora de Estudos e Projetos - FINEP, Instituto de Tecnologia Social - ITSBrasil and Fundação de Amparo à Pesquisa e Inovação no Estado de Santa Catarina – FAPESC.

REFERENCES

Abd Wahab, M. H., Talib, A. A., Kadir, H. A., Johari, A., Noraziah, A., Sidek, R. M., & Mutalib, A. A. (2011). Smart Cane: Assistive Cane for Visually-impaired People. *IJCSI International Journal of Computer Science Issues*, *8*(4), 1694–0814.

Akhbar, F., Chang, V., Yao, Y., & Méndez Muñoz, V. (2016). Outlook on moving of computing services towards the data sources. *International Journal of Information Management*, *36*(4), 645-652.

Android Developers. (2016a). *Making Your App Location-Aware*. Retrieved July 1, 2016, from https://developer.android.com/training/location/index.html

Android Developers. (2016b). *Creating and Monitoring Geofences*. Retrieved July 1, 2016, from https://developer.android.com/training/location/geofencing.html#RequestGeofences

Android Developers. (2016c). *Overview of Google Play Services*. Retrieved July 1, 2016, from https://developers.google.com/android/guides/overview

Android Developers. (2016d). *Meet Android Studio.* Retrieved July 1, 2016, from https://developer. android.com/studio/intro/index.html

Atzori, L., Iera, A., & Morabito, G. (2010). The internet of things: A survey. *Computer Networks, Elsevier, 54*(15), 2787–2805. doi:10.1016/j.comnet.2010.05.010

Caragliu, A., Bo, C. D., & Nijkamp, P. (2009). Smart cities in Europe. In *3rd Central European Conference in Regional Science – CERS* (pp. 45–59).

Chourabi, H., Nam, T., Walker, S., Gil-Garcia, J. R., Mellouli, S., Nahon, K., & Scholl, H. J. (2012). Understanding Smart Cities: An Integrative Framework. In *45th Hawaii International Conference on System Sciences* (pp. 2289–2297). IEEE Computer Society. doi:10.1109/HICSS.2012.615

Coetzee, L., & Eksteen, J. (2011). The Internet of Things - promise for the future? An introduction. In *IEEE IST-AFRICA Conference Proceedings* (pp. 1-9).

Cook, A. M., & Polgar, J. M. (2013). *Assistive Technologies: Principles and Practice* (3rd ed.). Mosby Elsevier.

da Silva, R. F. L., & Ramirez, A. R. G. (2013). Contribution to Mobility and Orientation teaching programs: Assistive technology equipment and tests methodology. In *Handbook of Research on ICTs for Healthcare and Social Services: Developments and Applications* (Vol. 2, pp. 670–686). Hershey, PA: IGI Global. doi:10.4018/978-1-4666-3986-7.ch035

Dakopoulos, D., & Bourbakis, N. G. (2010). Wearable obstacle avoidance electronic travel aids for blind: a survey. Systems, Man, and Cybernetics, Part C: Applications and Reviews, IEEE Transactions on Systems, 40(1), 25-35. doi:10.1109/TSMCC.2009.2021255

Delahoz, Y. S., & Labrador, M. A. (2014). Survey on fall detection and fall prevention using wearable and external sensors. *Sensors (Basel, Switzerland), 14*(10), 19806–19842. doi:10.3390/s141019806 PMID:25340452

DiMarzio, J. F. (2008). *Android a programmer's guide.* McGraw-Hill Education.

Dischinger, M. (2000). *Designing for all senses: accessible spaces for visually impaired citizens* (Unpublished doctoral dissertation). Department of Space and Process School of Architecture, Chalmers University of Technology.

Domingo, M. C. (2012). An overview of the Internet of Things for people with disabilities. *Journal of Network and Computer Applications, 35*(2), 584–596. doi:10.1016/j.jnca.2011.10.015

Farcy, R., Leroux, R., Jucha, A., Damaschini, R., Grégoire, C., & Zogaghi, A. (2006). Electronic Travel Aids and Electronic Orientation Aids for blind people: technical, rehabilitation and everyday life points of view. In *Conference & Workshop on Assistive Technologies for People with Vision & Hearing Impairments. Technology for Inclusion CVHI 2006* (pp. 1-12).

Fortino, G., & Gravina, R. (2015). Fall-MobileGuard: a Smart Real-Time Fall Detection System. In *Proceedings of the 10th International Conference on Body Area Networks* (pp. 44-50). doi:10.4108/ eai.28-9-2015.2261462

França, T. C., Pires, P. F., Pirmez, L., Delicato, F. C., & Farias, C. (2011). Web das Coisas: Conectando Dispositivos Físicos ao Mundo Digital. In: Livro Texto de Minicursos do Simpósio Brasileiro de Redes de Computadores e Sistemas de redes de Computadores e Sistemas Distribuídos. Campo Grande.

Gubbi, J., Buyya, R., Marusic, S., & Palaniswami, M. (2013). Internet of Things (IoT): A vision, architectural elements, and future directions. *Future Generation Computer Systems*, *29*(7), 1645–1660. doi:10.1016/j.future.2013.01.010

Hersh, M. A. (2010). The design and evaluation of assistive technology products and devices part 1: Design. In *International Encyclopedia of Rehabilitation*. Retrieved July 1, 2016, from http://cirrie.buffalo.edu/encyclopedia/en/article/309/

Hersh, M. A. (2015). Cane Use and Late Onset Visual Impairment. *Technology and Disability*, *27*(3), 103–116. doi:10.3233/TAD-150432

Hersh, M. A., & Johnson, M. A. (Eds.). (2008). *Assistive Technology for Vision-Impaired and Blind People*. Springer. doi:10.1007/978-1-84628-867-8

Hoyle, B. S., Fowler, J. M., Waters, D. A., & Withington, D. J. (2004, June). Development of the electronic guide cane for enhanced primary mobility for the vision impaired. In *Conference and Workshop on Assistive Technologies for Vision and Hearing Impairment*.

IBGE. (2010). *Brazilian Institute of geography and statistics*. Retrieved July 1, 2016, from http://www.ibge.gov.br/estadosat/temas.php?tema=censodemog2010_defic

Lau, J. C., & Chiu, C. C. (2003). Accessibility of low-income workers in Hong Kong. *Cities (London, England)*, *20*(3), 197–204. doi:10.1016/S0264-2751(03)00013-1

McLaughlin, M. L., Hespanha, J. P., & Sukhatme, G. S. (2002). *Touch in virtual environments*. Prentice Hall.

Nandyala, C. S., & Kim, H.-K. (2016). Green IoT Agriculture and Healthcare Application (GAHA). *International Journal of Smart Home*, *10*(4), 289–300. doi:10.14257/ijsh.2016.10.4.26

NIC, National Intelligence Council. (2008). Disruptive Civil Technologies: Six technologies with potential impacts on US Interests out to 2025. *Conference Report Disruptive Civil Technologies*. Menlo Park, CA: National Intelligence Council. Retrieved July 1, 2016, from http://fas.org/irp/nic/disruptive.pdf

Oliveira, A., & Campolargo, M. (2015). From Smart Cities to Human Smart Cities. In *(HICSS) 48th Hawaii International Conference on System Sciences* (pp. 2336-2344). doi:10.1109/HICSS.2015.281

Oliveira, A. S. D. (2006). *Acessibilidade espacial em centro cultural: Estudos de caso* (Unpublished Master Thesis). Federal University of Santa Catarina, Santa Catarina, Brazil.

Overton, R. (2007). *Feasibility Studies Made Simple*. Martin Books.

Pascolini, D., & Mariotti, S. P. (2011). Global estimates of visual impairment: 2010. *British Journal of Ophthalmology*.

Pissaloux, E., Velazquez, R., Hersh, M., & Uzan, G. (2016). Towards a cognitive model of human mobility: An investigation of tactile perception for use in mobility devices. *Journal of Navigation*, *1*, 1–17. doi:10.1017/S0373463316000461

Ramirez, A. R. G., da Silva, R. F. L., Cinelli, M. J., & Albornoz, A. D. C. (2012). Evaluation of Electronic Haptic Device for Blind and Visually Impaired People: A Case Study. *Journal of Medical and Biological Engineering*, *32*(6), 423–428. doi:10.5405/jmbe.925

Sanchez, L., Galache, J. A., Gutierrez, V., Hernandez, J. M., Bernat, J., Gluhak, A., & Garcia, T. (2011). *Smartsantander: The meeting point between future internet research and experimentation and the smart cities. In Future Network & Mobile Summit* (pp. 1–8). Warsaw: FutureNetw.

Shaikh, F. K., Zeadally, S., & Exposito, E. (2015). Enabling Technologies for Green Internet of Things. *IEEE Systems Journal*, (99), 1-12. DOI: 10.1109/JSYST.2015.2415194

Wiener, W. R., Welsh, R. L., & Blasch, B. B. (2010). *Foundations of Orientation and Mobility* (3rd ed.). AFB Press.

Yin, R. K. (2014). *Case study research: Design and methods*. London: SAGE Publications, Inc.

Zhu, X., Li, Q., & Chen, G. (2013). APT: Accurate outdoor pedestrian tracking with smartphones. In IEEE INFOCOM Proceedings (pp. 2508-2516). IEEE.

ENDNOTES

[1]   https://www.ultracane.com/

[2]   http://www.ksonar.com/

[3]   http://primpo.en.ec21.com/Electronic_Cane_for_Blind_Person--4374402_4374414.html

[4]   http://assistech.iitd.ernet.in/smartcane.php

[5]   The Electronic Long Cane project began in 2005, after being selected in the public context "MCT/FINEP-assistive technologies". Nowadays, CNPq and FAPESC also support it.

[6]   http://www.i-cane.org/

[7]   www.portaldainovacao.sites.ufsc.br

[8]   http://www.un.org/disabilities/convention/conventionfull.shtml

Compilation of References

Florien, Groza, &Aldescu. (2011). Using web technology to improve the accounting of small and medium enterprises: An academic approach to implementation of IFRS. *Annales Universitatis Apulensis Series Oeconomica, 13*(2).

AAL Association. (2010). *The Ambient Assisted Living (AAL) Joint Programme*. Brussels: AAL Association.

Aamodt, A., & Plaza, E. (1994). Case-based reasoning: Foundational issues, methodological variations, and system approaches. *AI Communications, 7*(1), 39–59.

Abanumy, A., Al-Badi, A., & Mayhew, P. (2005). E-Government website accessibility: In-depth evaluation of Saudi Arabia and Oman. *Elect. J. E Government, 3,* 99-106.

Abd Wahab, M. H., Talib, A. A., Kadir, H. A., Johari, A., Noraziah, A., Sidek, R. M., & Mutalib, A. A. (2011). Smart Cane: Assistive Cane for Visually-impaired People. *IJCSI International Journal of Computer Science Issues, 8*(4), 1694–0814.

Abdullah, F., & Ward, R. (2016). Developing a General Extended Technology Acceptance Model for E-Learning (GE-TAMEL) by analysing commonly used external factors. *Computers in Human Behavior, 56*, 238–256. doi:10.1016/j.chb.2015.11.036

Abo-Sinna, M. A., & Amer, A. H. (2005). Extensions of TOPSIS for multi-objective large-scale nonlinear programming problems. *Applied Mathematics and Computation, 162*(1), 243–256. doi:10.1016/j.amc.2003.12.087

AbouZahr, C., Cleland, J., Coullare, F., Macfarlane, S. B., Notzon, F. C., Setel, P., & Zhang, S. et al. (2007). The way forward. *Lancet, 370*(9601), 1791–1799. doi:10.1016/S0140-6736(07)61310-5 PMID:18029003

AbouZahr, C., Mikkelsen, L., Rampatige, R., & Lopez, A. (2012). Mortality statistics: A tool to enhance understanding and improve quality. *Pacific Health Dialog, 18*(1), 247–270. PMID:23240364

Abrams, M., Phanouriou, C., Batongbacal, A. L., Williams, S. M., & Shuster, J. E. (1999). UIML: an appliance-independent xml user interface language. In *Computer Networks (Vol. 31)*. Elsevier Science. doi:10.1016/S1389-1286(99)00044-4

Abran, A. (2003). Consolidating the ISO usability models.*Proceedings of 11th International Software Quality Management Conference*, (pp. 23–25).

Accenture. (2015). Seamless Retail Research Report 2015: Maximizing mobile to increase revenue.

Accenture. (2016). Retail customers are shouting – are you adapting?

Acharjee, U. (2006). *Personalized and Artificial Intelligence Web Caching and Pre-fetching* (Master thesis). University of Ottawa, Canada.

Adeyemo, A. B. (2011). E-government implementation in Nigeria: An assessment of Nigeria's global e-gov ranking. *Journal of Internet and Information System, 2*(1), 11–19.

Adomavicius, G., & Tuzhilin, A. (2005). Toward the next generation of recommender systems: A survey of the state-of-the-art and possible extensions. *Knowledge and Data Engineering. IEEE Transactions on, 17*(6), 734–749.

Agbiboa, D. E. (2012). Between corruption and development: The political economy of state robbery in Nigeria. *Journal of Business Ethics, 108*(3), 325–345. doi:10.1007/s10551-011-1093-5

Ahmad, A., & Maynard, S. (2014). Teaching information security management: Reflections and experiences. *Information Management & Computer Security, 22*(5), 513–536. doi:10.1108/IMCS-08-2013-0058

Ahn, T., Ryu, S., & Han, I. (2007). The impact of Web quality and playfulness on user acceptance of online retailing. *Information & Management, 44*(3), 263–275. doi:10.1016/j.im.2006.12.008

Ajzen, I., & Fishbein, M. (1980). *Understanding attitudes and predicting social behavior.* Englewood Cliffs, NJ: Prentice Hall.

Akhbar, F., Chang, V., Yao, Y., & Méndez Muñoz, V. (2016). Outlook on moving of computing services towards the data sources. *International Journal of Information Management, 36*(4), 645–652.

Alamri, B., & Qureshi, M. (2015). Usability of Cloud Computing to Improve Higher Education. *I.J. Information Technology and Computer Science, 9*, 59-65.

Alben, L. (1996). Quality of experience: Defining the criteria for effective interaction design. *Interaction, 3*(3), 11–15. doi:10.1145/235008.235010

Al-Debei, M. M., Akroush, M. N., & Ashouri, M. I. (2015). Consumer attitudes towards online shopping: The effects of trust, perceived benefits, and perceived web quality. *Internet Research, 25*(5), 707–733. doi:10.1108/IntR-05-2014-0146

Al-Debei, M. M., Al-Lozi, E., & Papazafeiropoulou, A. (2013). Why people keep coming back to Facebook: Explaining and predicting continuance participation from an extended theory of planned behaviour perspective. *Decision Support Systems, 55*(1), 43–54. doi:10.1016/j.dss.2012.12.032

Alenezi, A. M. (2012). Faculty members' perception of e-learning in higher education in the Kingdom of Saudi Arabia (KSA) [Doctoral dissertation]. Texas Tech University.

Al-Gahtani, S. S. (2016). Empirical investigation of e-learning acceptance and assimilation: a structural equation model. *Applied Computing and Informatics, 12*(1), 27e50.

Al-Gahtani, S. S. (2011). Modeling the electronic transactions acceptance using an extended technology acceptance model. *Applied Computing and Informatics, 9*(1), 47–77. doi:10.1016/j.aci.2009.04.001

Alharbi, H., Jayawardena, A., & Kwan, P. (2014). Social Recommender System for Predicting the Needs of Students/Instructors: Review and Proposed Framework. *Proc. of the First IEEE International Workshop on Social Networks Analysis, Management and Security SNAMS '14*, Spain.

Al-Harbi, K. A. S. (2011). E-Learning in the Saudi tertiary education: Potential and challenges. *Applied Computing and Informatics, 9*(1), 31–46. doi:10.1016/j.aci.2010.03.002

Alhazzani, N. (2014). A proposed plan to use cloud computing in higher education at the Kingdom of Saudi Arabia. Proceedings of ICERI '14 (p. 2895).

Al-Hujran, O., Al-Debei, M. M., Chatfield, A., & Migdadi, M. (2015). The imperative of influencing citizen attitude toward e-government adoption and use. *Computers in Human Behavior, 53*, 189–203. doi:10.1016/j.chb.2015.06.025

Al-Hujran, O., Al-Lozi, E., & Al-Debei, M. M. (2014). "Get Ready to Mobile Learning": Examining Factors Affecting College Students' Behavioral Intentions to Use M-Learning in Saudi Arabia. *Jordan Journal of Business Administration, 10*(1).

Ali, W., & Shamsuddin, S. M. (2009). Intelligent Client-Side Web Caching Scheme Based on Least Recently Used Algorithm and Neuro-Fuzzy System. *The sixth International Symposium on Neural Networks (ISNN 2009).* Springer-Verlag Berlin Heidelberg.

Alibaba. (2016). Financial information extracted from http://www.alibabagroup.com/en/ir/financial

Alibaba. (2016b). Group Announces June Quarter 2016 Results (Press release). Retrieved from www.alibabagroup.com

Ali, N. M. A., & Hamadeh, R. R. (2013). Improving the Accuracy of Death Certification among Secondary Care Physicians. *Bahrain Medical Bulletin, 35*(2), 1–6.

Aljawarneh, S., Al-Rousan, T., Maatuk, A.M., & Akour, M. (2013). Usage of data validation techniques in online banking: A perspective and case study. *Security Journal.*

Al-Khalifa, H. S. (2010). Heuristic evaluation of the usability of e-government websites: a case from Saudi Arabia. In *Proceedings of the 4th International Conference on Theory and Practice of Electronic Governance (ICEGOV '10).* ACM. doi:10.1145/1930321.1930370

Allwood, C. M. (1998). *Människa-Datorinteraktion – ett psykologiskt perspektiv.* Lund: Studentlitteratur.

Almeida, F. A. D. C. (2013). Hybrid approach to content recommendation. Retrieved from <http://repositorio-aberto. up.pt/bitstream/10216/67427/1/000154009.pdf>

Al-Sarrani, N. (2010). Concerns and professional development needs of science faculty at Taibah University in adopting blended learning [Doctoral dissertation]. Kansas State University. Retrieved from http://krex.kstate.edu/dspace/ bitstream/2097/3887/1/NauafAl-Sarrani2010

Alshwaier, A., Youssef, A., & Emam, A. (2012). A new trend for e-learning in KSA using educational clouds. *Advanced Computing: An International Journal, 3*(1), 81-96.

Alsmadi, I. (2014). How much automation can be done in testing? In I. Alsmadi (Ed.), Advanced automated software testing. Hershey, PA, USA: IGI Global.

Alsmadi, I., & Magel, K. (2007). GUI path oriented test generation algorithms. *Proceeding of IASTED Human-Computer Interaction '07.*

Alsmadi, I., & Magel, K. (2008). The Utilization of User Sessions in Testing. *Proceedings of the Seventh IEEE/ACIS International Conference onComputer and Information ScienceICIS '08,* Portland, OR, USA.

Alsmadi, I. (2010). *Ahmad T. Al-Taani, and Nahed Abu Zaid. "Web Structural Metrics Evaluation", Developments in E-systems Engineering* (pp. 225–230). DESE.

Alsmadi, I. (2011). Activities and Trends in Testing Graphical User Interfaces Automatically. *Journal of Software Engineering, 5*(1), 1–19. doi:10.3923/jse.2011.1.19

Alsmadi, I., & Alda, S. (2012). Test cases reduction and selection optimization in testing web services. *International Journal of Information Engineering and Electronic Business, 4*(5), 1–8. doi:10.5815/ijieeb.2012.05.01

Alsmadi, I., & Magel, K. (2007). *An object oriented framework for user interface test automation. Proceedings of MICS '07.* Citeseer.

Al-Somali, S. A., Gholami, R., & Clegg, B. (2015). A stage-oriented model (SOM) for e-commerce adoption: A study of Saudi Arabian organisations. *Journal of Manufacturing Technology Management, 26*(1), 2–35. doi:10.1108/JMTM-03-2013-0019

Altimeter, T. (2011). Contextual mobile learning system for Saudi Arabian universities. *International Journal of Computers and Applications, 21*(4), 21–26. doi:10.5120/2499-3377

Alzamil, Z. A. (2006). Students' perception towards the e-Learning at the GOTEVOT and the Arab Open University in Riyadh. Journal of King Saud University. *Educational Sciences and Islamic Studies, 18*(2), 655–698.

Amalfitano, D., Fasolino, A. R., Tramontana, P., De Carmine, S., & Memon, A. M. (2012, September). Using GUI ripping for automated testing of Android applications.*Proceedings of the 27th IEEE/ACM International Conference on Automated Software Engineering* (pp. 258-261). ACM. doi:10.1145/2351676.2351717

Amazon. (2016). Amazon.com Announces Fourth Quarter Sales up 22% to $35.7 Billion. Press release. Retrieved from http://phx.corporate-ir.net/phoenix.zhtml?c=97664&p=irol-newsArticle&ID=2133281

Anders, G. (2015, May 7). Wearable Computing's Next Kings: Watches In 2016; Glasses In 2020. *Forbes*. Retrieved from www.forbes.com

Andersen, T. B. (2009). E-Government as an anti-corruption strategy. *Information Economics and Policy, 21*(3), 201–210. doi:10.1016/j.infoecopol.2008.11.003

Anderson, C. (2006). *The Long Tail. How endless choice is creating unlimited demand.* London: Random House.

Anderson, C. L., & Agarwal, R. (2010). Practicing safe computing: A multimedia empirical examination of home computer user security behavioral intentions. *Management Information Systems Quarterly, 34*(3), 613–643.

Android Developers. (2016a). *Making Your App Location-Aware.* Retrieved July 1, 2016, from https://developer.android.com/training/location/index.html

Android Developers. (2016b). *Creating and Monitoring Geofences.* Retrieved July 1, 2016, from https://developer.android.com/training/location/geofencing.html#RequestGeofences

Android Developers. (2016c). *Overview of Google Play Services.* Retrieved July 1, 2016, from https://developers.google.com/android/guides/overview

Android Developers. (2016d). *Meet Android Studio.* Retrieved July 1, 2016, from https://developer.android.com/studio/intro/index.html

Armstrong, C. L. (2011). Providing a clearer view: An examination of transparency on local government websites. *Government Information Quarterly, 28*(1), 11–16. doi:10.1016/j.giq.2010.07.006

Arnold, U. (2000). New dimensions of outsourcing: a combination of transaction cost economics and the core competencies concept. *European Journal of Purchasing & Supply Management, 6*(1), 23-29.

Ashenden, D. (2008). Information Security Management: A human challenge? *Information Security Technical Report, 13*(4), 195–201. doi:10.1016/j.istr.2008.10.006

Asiimwe, E. N., & Lim, N. (2010). Usability of Government Websites in Uganda. *Electronic Journal of E-Government, 8*(1), 1–12.

Asiri, M. J. S., Mahmud, R. B., Abu Bakar, K., & Mohd Ayub, A. F. B. (2012). Factors influencing the use of learning management system in Saudi Arabian Higher Education: A theoretical framework. *Higher Education Studies, 2*(2), 125. doi:10.5539/hes.v2n2p125

Asogwa, B. E. (2013). Electronic government as a paradigm shift for efficient public services: Opportunities and challenges for Nigerian government. *Library Hi Tech*, *31*(1), 141–159. doi:10.1108/07378831311303985

Atterer, R. (2008, October). Model-based automatic usability validation: a tool concept for improving web-based UIs. In *Proceedings of the 5th Nordic conference on Human-computer interaction: building bridges* (pp. 13-22). ACM. doi:10.1145/1463160.1463163

Atterer, R., Wnuk, M., & Schmidt, A. (2006). Knowing the user's every move: user activity tracking for website usability evaluation and implicit interaction. In *Proceedings of the 15th international conference on World Wide Web* (pp. 203-212). ACM. doi:10.1145/1135777.1135811

Atzori, L., Iera, A., & Morabito, G. (2010). The internet of things: A survey. *Computer Networks, Elsevier*, *54*(15), 2787–2805. doi:10.1016/j.comnet.2010.05.010

Australian Government. (2010). High Level Principles for Data Integration Involving Commonwealth Data for Statistical and Research Purposes. Canberra, AUS: Australian Government.

Avilés-López, E., Villanueva-Miranda, I., Garcia-Macias, J. A., & Palafox-Maestre, L. E. (2009). Taking Care of Our Elders through Augmented Spaces. In *LA-WEB/CLIHC* (pp. 16–21). Merida: IEEE Computer Society. doi:10.1109/LA-WEB.2009.30

Awasthi, A., Chauhan, S. S., Omrani, H., & Panahi, A. (2011). A hybrid approach based on SERVQUAL and fuzzy TOPSIS for evaluating transportation service quality. *Journal of Computers and Industrial Engineering*, *61*(3), 637–646. doi:10.1016/j.cie.2011.04.019

Awawdeh, S., & Tubaishat, A. (2014). An Information Security Awareness Program to Address Common Security Concerns in IT Unit. *Information Technology: New Generations (ITNG), 2014 11th International Conference on* (pp. 273-278). IEEE.

Awofeso, O., & Odeyemi, T. I. (2014). The Impact of Political Leadership and Corruption on Nigerias Development since Independence. *Journal of Sustainable Development*, *7*(5), 240. doi:10.5539/jsd.v7n5p240

Ayo, C. K., Adebiyi, A. A., & Afolabi, I. T. (2008). E-Democracy: A requirement for a successful E-Voting and E-Government implementation in Nigeria. *International Journal of Natural and Applied Sciences*, *4*(3), 310–318.

Azeez, N. A., Abidoye, A. P., Adesina, A. O., Agbele, K. K., Venter, L. M., & Oyewole, A. S. (2012). Threats to E-Government Implementation in the Civil Service: Nigeria as a Case Study. *The Pacific Journal of Science and Technology*, *13*(1), 398–402.

Bac, M. (2001). Corruption, connections and transparency: Does a better screen imply a better scene? *Public Choice*, *107*(1-2), 87–96. doi:10.1023/A:1010349907813

Baird, N. & Rowen, S. (2015). *The Internet of Things in Retail: Great Expectations*. RSR (Retail Systems Research). August 2015.

Balabanovic, M., & Shoham, Y. (1997). Combining content-based and collaborative recommendation. *Communications of the ACM*, *40*(3), 66–72. doi:10.1145/245108.245124

Balamash, A., & Krunz, M. (2004). An Overview of Web Caching Replacement Algorithms. *IEEE Communications Surveys and Tutorials*, *6*(2), 44–56. doi:10.1109/COMST.2004.5342239

Balestrini, M., Bird, J., Marshall, P., Zaro, A., & Rogers, Y. (2014). Understanding Sustained Community Engagement: A Case Study in Heritage Preservation in Rural Argentina. *Proc. CHI '14*(pp. 2675-2684). doi:10.1145/2556288.2557323

Ballard, J. K. (2010). Web Site Usability: A Case Study of Student Perceptions of Educational Web Sites. Academic Press.

Ballou, R. H. (2003). Business Logistics: Supply Chain Management (5th ed.). Prentice Hall.

Bamshad, M. (2007). *Data Mining for Web Personalization*. Heidelberg, Germany: Springer-Verleg Berlin.

Banerjee, I., Nguyen, B., Garousi, V., & Memon, A. (2013). Graphical user interface (GUI) testing: Systematic mapping and repository. *Information and Software Technology*, *55*(10), 1679–1694. doi:10.1016/j.infsof.2013.03.004

Bangor, A., Kortum, P. T., & Miller, J. T. (2008). An empirical evaluation of the system usability scale. *International Journal of Human-Computer Interaction*, *24*(6), 574–594. doi:10.1080/10447310802205776

Bannister, F., & Connolly, R. (2011). The Trouble with Transparency: A Critical Review of Openness in e-Government. *Policy & Internet*, *3*(1), 1–30. doi:10.2202/1944-2866.1076

Bardhan, A., & Kroll, C. (2003). *The New Wave of Outsourcing*. Berkeley: Fisher Center for Real Estate and Urban Economics, University of California.

Bartnes, M., Moe, N. B., & Heegaard, P. E. (2016). The future of information security incident management training: A case study of electrical power companies. *Computers & Security*, *61*, 32–45. doi:10.1016/j.cose.2016.05.004

Basit, D., & Suresha, D. (2012). Experimental Evaluation of Effectiveness of E-Government Websites. *International Journal of Emerging Technology and Advanced Engineering, 2*(11).

Basu, C., Hirsh, H., & Cohen, W. W. (1998). Recommendation as classification: Using social and content-based information in recommendation. *Proceedings of the Fifteenth National Conference on Artificial Intelligence* (pp. 714–720). AAAI/IAAI.

Basu, C., Hirsh, H., & Cohen, W. W. (1998). Recommendation as classification: Using social and content-based information in recommendation.*Proceedings of the Fifteenth National Conference on Artificial Intelligence (AAAI/IAAI)* (pp. 714–720).

Basu, S. (2004). E-government and developing countries: An overview. *International Review of Law Computers & Technology*, *18*(1), 109–132. doi:10.1080/13600860410001674779

Bateman, S., Brooks, C., McCalla, G., & Brusilovsky, P. (2007). Applying collaborative tagging to e-learning. *Proceedings of theWorkshop on Tagging and Metadata for Social Information Organization, held in conjuction with the 16th International World Wide Web Conference*. Banff, Canada.

Baumgartner, H., & Homburg, C. (1996). Applications of structural equation modeling in marketing and consumer research: A review. *International Journal of Research in Marketing*, *13*(2), 139–161. doi:10.1016/0167-8116(95)00038-0

Bayousuf, A. S., Al-Khalifa, H. S., & Al-Salman, A. S. (2013). Towards the development of haptic-based interface for teaching visually impaired Arabic handwriting. In *Proceedings of the 15th International ACM SIGACCESS Conference on Computers and Accessibility* (p. 73). ACM. doi:10.1145/2513383.2513400

Becker, R., Silvi, J., Ma Fat, D., L'Hours, A., & Laurenti, R. (2006). A method for deriving leading causes of death. *Bulletin of the World Health Organization*, *84*(4), 297–304. PMID:16628303

Behara, R. S., Gundersen, D. E., & Capozzoli, E. A. (1995). Trends in Information Systems Outsourcing. *Journal of Supply Chain Management*, *31*(1), 45-51.

Bellman, R. E., & Zadeh, L. A. (1970). Decision-making in a fuzzy environment. *Management Science*, *17*(4), B-141–B-164. doi:10.1287/mnsc.17.4.B141

Ben-Akiva, M., & de Jong, G. (2013). The Aggregate-Disaggregate-Aggregate (ADA) Freight Model System. In M. Ben-Akiva, E. van de Voorde, & H. Meersman (Eds.), *Freight Transport Modelling* (1st ed., pp. 69–90). Bingley, United Kingdom: Emerald. doi:10.1108/9781781902868-004

Bertelsen, O. (2004). The activity walkthrough: an expert review method based on activity theory. In *Proceedings of the third Nordic conference on Human-computer interaction SE- NordiCHI '04* (pp. 251–254). doi:10.1145/1028014.1028052

Bertot, J. C., Jaeger, P. T., & Grimes, J. M. (2010). Using ICTs to create a culture of transparency: E-government and social media as openness and anti-corruption tools for societies. *Government Information Quarterly*, *27*(3), 264–271. doi:10.1016/j.giq.2010.03.001

Bevan, N., Claridge, N., & Petrie, H. (2005). Tenuta: Simplified Guidance for Usability and Accessibility. In *Proceedings of HCI International*. Las Vegas, NV: Lawrence Erlbaum Associates.

Bevan, N. (2001). International standards for HCI and usability. *International Journal of Human-Computer Studies*, *55*(4), 533–552. doi:10.1006/ijhc.2001.0483

Bevan, N. (2010). Extending the concept of satisfaction in ISO standards. In *Proceedings of the KEER 2010 International Conference on Kansei Engineering and Emotion Research*.

Bevan, N., Kirakowsky, J., & Maissel, J. (1991). What is usability. In *Proceedings of 4th International Conference on Human Computer Interaction*. Elsevier.

Bexelius, C., Löf, M., Sandin, S., Lagerros, Y. T., Forsum, E., & Litton, J. E. (2010). Measures of physical activity using cell phones: Validation using criterion methods. *Journal of Medical Internet Research*, *12*(1), e2. doi:10.2196/jmir.1298 PMID:20118036

Beynon-Davies, P. (2005). Constructing Electronic Government: The case of the UK Inland Revenue. *International Journal of Information Management*, *25*(1), 3–20. doi:10.1016/j.ijinfomgt.2004.08.002

Bhadauria, R., Borgohain, R., Biswas, A., & Sanyal, S. (2014). Secure authentication of Cloud data mining API. *Acta Technica Corviniensis-Bulletin of Engineering*, 183.

Bhatnagar, S. (2003). *Transparency and corruption: Does E-government help? Draft paper for the compilation of CHRI 2003 Report OPEN SESAME: looking for the Right to Information in the Commonwealth*. Commonwealth Human Rights Initiative.

Bhattacherjee, A. (2001). Understanding information systems continuance: An expectation confirmation model. *Management Information Systems Quarterly*, *25*(3), 351–370. doi:10.2307/3250921

Bhatti, T. (2015). Exploring factors influencing the adoption of mobile commerce. *The Journal of Internet Banking and Commerce*.

Bhuiyan, T., Alam, D., & Farah, T. (2016). Evaluating the Readiness of Cyber Resilient Bangladesh. *Journal of Internet Technology and Secured Transactions*, *4*(3), 405–415. doi:10.20533/jitst.2046.3723.2015.0051

Biafore, B. (2013). *Quick books 2013 the Missing manual*. Retrieved from http://support.quickbooks.intuit.com/opencms/sites/default/qbsupportsite/PDFs/2013Guides/QB2013MM_excerpt.pdf

Bidgoli, H. (2004). *The Internet Encyclopedia*. Available at: http://www.loc.gov/catdir/description/wiley0310/2002155552.html

Blackmon, Polson, Kitajima, & Lewis. (2002). Cognitive Walkthrough for the Web. *Proceedings of the {SIGCHI} conference on Human factors in computing systems: Changing our world, changing ourselves*.

Blake, E., Tucker, W., & And Glaser, M. (2014). Towards communication and information access for Deaf people. *South African Computer Journal*, *54*(2), 10–11.

Blanton, W., Simmons, E., & Warner, M. (2001). The Fifth Dimension: Application of cultural-historical activity theory, inquiry-based learning, computers, and telecommunications to change prospective teachers. *Journal of Educational Computing Research*, *24*(4), 435–463. doi:10.2190/YGJ0-WXUW-D0TR-9BGU

Boardman, B., Trusty, K., & Malstrom, E. (1999). *Intermodal Transportation Cost Analysis tables*. Department of Industrial Engineering, University of Arkansas.

Boateng, H., Adam, D. R., Okoe, A. F., & Anning-Dorson, T. (2016). Assessing the determinants of internet banking adoption intentions: A social cognitive theory perspective. *Computers in Human Behavior*, *65*, 468–478. doi:10.1016/j.chb.2016.09.017

Boehm, F., & Olaya, J. (2006). Corruption in public contracting auctions: The role of transparency in bidding processes. *Annals of Public and Cooperative Economics*, *77*(4), 431–452. doi:10.1111/j.1467-8292.2006.00314.x

Boer, H., & Scydel, E. R. (1996). *Protection motivation theory*. Retrieved July 16, 2015 from http://doc.utwente.nl/34896/1/K465____.PDF

Bollen, A., & Emes, C. (2008). Understanding Customer Relationships – how important is the personal touch. *Ipsos MORI*. Retrieved from www.ipsos-mori.com/_assets/reports/understanding-customer-relationships.pdf

Bonnet, D. (2016, August 3). *A Portfolio Strategy to Execute Your Digital Transformation*. Capgemini Consulting. Retrieved from www.capgemini-consulting.com

Botella Arbona, C., García Palacios, A., Baños Rivera, R. M., & Quero Castellano, S. (2009). Cybertherapy: Advantages, limitations, and ethical issues. *PsychNology Journal*, *7*(1), 77–110.

Botes, L., & Van Rensburg, D. (2000). Community Participation in Development: Nine Plagues and Twelve Commandments. *Community Development Journal: An International Forum*, *35*(1), 41–58. doi:10.1093/cdj/35.1.41

Boulos, M. N. K., Brewer, A. C., Karimkhani, C., Buller, D. B., & Dellavalle, R. P. (2014). Mobile medical and health apps: State of the art, concerns, regulatory control and certification. *Online Journal of Public Health Informatics*, *5*(3). PMID:24683442

Bowers, L., Bowler, M., & Amirabdollahian, F. (2013). Haptic Cues for Vision Impaired Peoples: Seeing through Touch. In *Proceedings of the 2013 IEEE International Conference on Systems, Man, and Cybernetics* (pp. 547-552). IEEE Computer Society. doi:10.1109/SMC.2013.99

Bradley, Loucks, Macaulay, Noronha & Wade (2015, June). *Digital Vortex: How Digital Disruption Is Redefining Industries*. Global Center for Digital Business Transformation, initiative by IMD & Cisco. Retrieved from www.imd.org

Brady, M., & Robertson, C. (2001). Searching for consensus on the antecedent role of service quality and satisfaction: An exploratory cross-national study. *Journal of Business Research*, *51*(1), 53–60. doi:10.1016/S0148-2963(99)00041-7

BRAID. (2011). Consolidated Vision of ICT and Ageing. Brussels: Bridging Research in Ageing and ICT Development (BRAID).

Brans, J. P., Mareschal, B., & Vincke, P. (1984). PROMETHEE: A New Family of Outranking Methods in Multicriteria Analysis. In Operational Research (pp. 477–490). Academic Press.

Brewster, S. A. (1998). Using Nonspeech Sounds to Provide Navigation Cues. *ACM Transactions on Computer-Human Interaction*, *5*(3), 224–259. doi:10.1145/292834.292839

Brewster, S., & Brown, L. M. (2004). Tactons: structured tactile messages for non-visual information display. In *Proceedings of the fifth conference on Australasian user interface*, (vol. 28, pp. 15-23). Australian Computer Society, Inc.

Brinck, T., Gergle, D., & Wood, S. D. (2002). *Usability for the Web*. San Francisco: Morgan Kaufmann.

Brin, S., & Pange, L. (1998). The Anatomy of a Large-scale Hyper Textual Web Search Engine. *Computer Networks and ISDN Systems*, *30*(1-7), 107–117. doi:10.1016/S0169-7552(98)00110-X

Brohan, M. (2015, August 18). Mobile commerce is now 30% of all US e-commerce. Retrieved from www.internetretailer.com

Brooks, E. G., & Reed, K. D. (2015). Principles and Pitfalls: A Guide to Death Certification. *Clinical Medicine & Research*, *13*(2), 74–82. doi:10.3121/cmr.2015.1276 PMID:26185270

Brown, J., Cohen, P., Johnson, J. G., & Smailes, E. M. (1999). Childhood abuse and neglect: Specificity of effects on adolescent and young adult depression and suicidality. *Journal of the American Academy of Child and Adolescent Psychiatry*, *38*(12), 1490–1496. doi:10.1097/00004583-199912000-00009 PMID:10596248

Bruun, A., & Stage, J. (2015). New approaches to usability evaluation in software development: Barefoot and crowdsourcing. *Journal of Systems and Software*, *105*, 40–53. doi:10.1016/j.jss.2015.03.043

Bulthoff, I., & Newell, F. N. (2006). The role of familiarity in the recognition of static and dynamic objects. *Progress in Brain Research*, *154*, 315–325. doi:10.1016/S0079-6123(06)54017-8 PMID:17010720

Burger, E. H., Groenewald, P., Rossouw, A., & Bradshaw, D. (2015). Medical certification of death in South Africa-moving forward. *SAMJ: South African Medical Journal*, *105*(1), 27–30. doi:10.7196/SAMJ.8578 PMID:26046158

Butterworth, R., & Blandford, A. (1997). *Programmable user models: The story so far*. London: Middlesex University.

Cabrera, I. P., Cordero, P., & Ojeda-Aciego, M. (2009). Fuzzy logic, soft computing, and applications. In Bio-Inspired Systems: Computational and Ambient Intelligence (pp. 236-244). Springer Berlin Heidelberg. doi:10.1007/978-3-642-02478-8_30

Calvaresi, D., Cesarini, D., Sernani, P., Marinoni, M., Dragoni, A. F., & Sturm, A. (2016). Exploring the ambient assisted living domain: a systematic review. *Journal of Ambient Intelligence and Humanized Computing*, 1-19.

Camarinha-Matos, L. M., Rosas, J., Oliveira, A. I., & Ferrada, F. (2015). Care services ecosystem for ambient assisted living. *Enterprise Information Systems*, *9*(5-6), 607–633.

Capgemini. (2012, July 11). Internet domina el proceso de compra online, pero redes sociales y aplicaciones móviles crecen con rapidez (Press note).

Caragliu, A., Bo, C. D., & Nijkamp, P. (2009). Smart cities in Europe. In *3rd Central European Conference in Regional Science – CERS* (pp. 45–59).

Card, S., Moran, T. P., & Newell, A. (1983). The GOMS model of manuscript editing.The psychology of human-computer interaction, (pp. 139-189).

Card, S. K., Moran, T. P., & Newell, A. (1980). The keystroke-level model for user performance time with interactive systems. *Communications of the ACM*, *23*(7), 96–110. doi:10.1145/358886.358895

Carter, L., & Bélanger, F. (2005). The utilization of e-government services: Citizen trust, innovation and acceptance factors. *Information Systems Journal*, *15*(1), 5–25. doi:10.1111/j.1365-2575.2005.00183.x

Casalino, N., Buonocore, F., Rossignoli, C., & Ricciardi, F. (2013). Transparency, openness and knowledge sharing for rebuilding and strengthening government institutions. Proceedings of WBE '13 conference (Vol. 10). Zurich, Innsbruck, Austria: IASTED-ACTA Press. doi:10.2316/P.2013.792-044

Caudill, M. (1987). Neural networks primer, part I. *AI Expert, 2*(12), 46–52.

Cavusoglu, H., Mishra, B., & Raghunathan, S. (2004). A model for evaluating IT security investments. *Communications of the ACM, 47*(7), 87–92. doi:10.1145/1005817.1005828

Centers for Disease Control and Prevention – CDC. (2007). *Core curriculum for certifiers of underlying cause of death.* Atlanta, GA: Centers for Disease Control and Prevention.

Centers for Disease Control and Prevention – CDC. (2008). Electronic Record Linkage to Identify Deaths among Persons with AIDS - District of Columbia, 2000–2005. *Morbidity and Mortality Weekly Report, 57*(23), 631–634. PMID:18551099

Central Intelligence Agency (CIA). (2015). The world factbook. Retrieved from https://www.cia.gov/library/publications/resources/the-world-factbook/index.html

Cerny, T., & Donahoo, M. (2015). On separation of platform-independent particles in user-interfaces, survey on separation of concerns in user interface design. *Cluster Computing, 18*(3), 1215–1228. doi:10.1007/s10586-015-0471-7

Chalaban, B. (2015). Why Amazon's Recent Sales Deceleration is Not the Full Story. *Treetisblog.* Retrieved from http://treetisblog.tumblr.com/post/112513225688/why-amazons-recent-sales-deceleration-is-not-the

Chamberlain, A., Crabtree, A., & Davies, M. (2013). Community engagement for research: Contextual design in rural CSCW system development. *Proc. Int. Conf. on C&T '13* (pp. 131-139). ACM Press. doi:10.1145/2482991.2483001

Chandler, D. (2000). *Semiotics for beginners.* Daniel Chandler.

Chandler, D. (2002). *Semiotics for beginners: glossary of key terms.* Aberystwyth University. doi:10.4324/9780203166277

Charif, L., Aronsohn, M., & Charif, H. (2006), E-banking and Service Quality Online [Master dissertation]. Lunds University, Sweden.

Charnes, A., Cooper, W. W., & Rhodes, E. (1978). Measuring the efficiency of decision making units. *European Journal of Operational Research, 2*(6), 429–444. doi:10.1016/0377-2217(78)90138-8

Charpentier, G., Benhamou, P. Y., Dardari, D., Clergeot, A., Franc, S., Schaepelynck-Belicar, P., & Bosson, J. L. et al. (2011). The diabeo software enabling individualized insulin dose adjustments combined with telemedicine support improves HbA1c in poorly controlled type 1 diabetic patients A 6-month, randomized, open-label, parallel-group, multicenter trial (TeleDiab 1 study). *Diabetes Care, 34*(3), 533–539. doi:10.2337/dc10-1259 PMID:21266648

Chatfield, A., & Alanazi, J. (2013). Service quality, citizen satisfaction, and loyalty with self-service delivery options: a strategic imperative for transforming e-government services. *Proceedings of the24th Australasian Conference on Information Systems (ACIS)* (pp. 1-12). RMIT University.

Cheng, A. L., Kang, Y. K., Chen, Z., Tsao, C. J., Qin, S., Kim, J. S., & Xu, J. et al. (2009). Efficacy and safety of sorafenib in patients in the Asia-Pacific region with advanced hepatocellular carcinoma: A phase III randomised, double-blind, placebo-controlled trial. *The Lancet Oncology, 10*(1), 25–34. doi:10.1016/S1470-2045(08)70285-7 PMID:19095497

Cheng, L. C., & Mustafa, M. (2014). A Reference to Usability Inspection Methods. In *International Colloquium of Art and Design* (pp. 45–51).

Chenoweth, T., Minch, R., & Gattiker, T. (2009). Application of protection motivation theory to adoption of protective technologies. In *Proceedings of the 42nd Hawaii international conference on system sciences.* IEEE

Chen, T. (2007). Obtaining the Optimal Cache Document Replacement Policy for the Caching System of an EC Website. *European Journal of Operational Research, 181*(2), 828–841. doi:10.1016/j.ejor.2006.05.034

Chen, X., & Zhang, X. (2002). Popularity-based PPM: An effective Web pre-fetching technique for high accuracy and low storage. In *Proceedings of the International Conference on Parallel Processing*, (pp. 296-304). doi:10.1109/ICPP.2002.1040885

Cheung, R., & Vogel, D. (2013). Predicting user acceptance of collaborative technologies: An extension of the technology acceptance model for e-learning. *Computers & Education, 63*, 160–175. doi:10.1016/j.compedu.2012.12.003

Chiew, T. K., & Salim, S. S. (2003). Webuse: Website usability evaluation tool. *Malaysian Journal of Computer Science, 16*(1), 47–57.

Chourabi, H., Nam, T., Walker, S., Gil-Garcia, J. R., Mellouli, S., Nahon, K., & Scholl, H. J. (2012). Understanding Smart Cities: An Integrative Framework. In *45th Hawaii International Conference on System Sciences* (pp. 2289–2297). IEEE Computer Society. doi:10.1109/HICSS.2012.615

Chu, S., Rathi, D., & Du, H. (2010). Users' Behaviour in Collaborative Tagging Systems. *Proceedings of theAnnual Conference of the Canadian Association for Information Science (CAIS).*

Chu, T. H., & Chen, Y. Y. (2016). With Good We Become Good: Understanding e-learning adoption by theory of planned behavior and group influences. *Computers & Education, 92*, 37–52. doi:10.1016/j.compedu.2015.09.013

Cisco. (2012). Cisco's VNI Forecast Projects the Internet Will Be Four Times as Large in Four Years. Retrieved from https://newsroom.cisco.com

Clark, R. C., & Mayer, R. E. (2011). *E-learning and the science of instruction: proven guidelines for consumers and designers of multimedia learning.* New York: Pfeiffer. doi:10.1002/9781118255971

Clayton, L., & Cathleen, W. (1997). Cognitive Walkthroughs. In M. G. Helander, T. K. Landauer, & P. V. Prabhu (Eds.), *Handbook of Human-Computer Interaction* (2nd ed.; pp. 717–732). Amsterdam: North-Holland.

Cleomar, B., Jr., & Oliveira, M. (2011). Recommender systems in social networks. *JISTEM - Journal of Information Systems and Technology Management, 8*(3), 681–716.

Cobb, J., & ElAarag, H. (2008). Web Proxy Cache Replacement Scheme based on Back-Propagation Neural Network. *Journal of Systems and Software, 81*(9), 1539–1558. doi:10.1016/j.jss.2007.10.024

Coetzee, L., & Eksteen, J. (2011). The Internet of Things - promise for the future? An introduction. In *IEEE IST-AFRICA Conference Proceedings* (pp. 1-9).

Cohen, J., Bilsen, J., Miccinesi, G., Löfmark, R., Addington-Hall, J., Kaasa, S., & Deliens, L. et al. (2007). Using death certificate data to study place of death in 9 European countries: Opportunities and weaknesses. *BMC Public Health, 7*(1), 283–283. doi:10.1186/1471-2458-7-283 PMID:17922894

Collis, D. (2004). The paradox of scope: A challenge to the governance of higher education. In W. G. Tierney, Competing Conceptions of Academic Governance: Navigating the Perfect Storm (pp. 33-76). Batlimore: Johns Hopkins University Press.

Communications and Information Technology Commission (CITC). (2012). Internet Usage Study in Saudi Arabia. Retrieved from http://www.internet.sa/en/internet-usage-study/#more-120

Constantine, L. (2004). Beyond user-centered design and user experience: Designing for user performance. *Cutter IT Journal, 17*(2), 16–25.

Cook, A. M., & Polgar, J. M. (2013). *Assistive Technologies: Principles and Practice* (3rd ed.). Mosby Elsevier.

Cook, A. M., Bentz, B., Harbottle, N., Lynch, C., & Miller, B. (2005). School-based use of a robotic arm system by children with disabilities. *Neural Systems and Engineering. IEEE Transactions on, 13*(4), 452–460.

Cooper, A. (2004). *The inmates are running the asylum.* Indianapolis, IN: Sams.

Correa, C. D., & Ma, K.-L. (2011). Visualizing social networks. In C. C. Aggarwal (Ed.), *Social network data analytics* (pp. 307–326). Boston, MA, USA: Springer US. doi:10.1007/978-1-4419-8462-3_11

Coyle, Bardi, Novack (2006). *Transportation* (Vol. 6). Mason: Thomson South-Western.

Coyle, J.J., Langley, C.J., Brian Gibson, B., Novack, R.A. and Bardi, E.J. (2008). *Supply Chain Management A Logistics Perspective.* South-Western College Pub; 8 ed.

Craddock, M., & Lawson, R. (2009). Size-sensitive perceptual representations underlie visual and haptic object recognition. *PLoS ONE, 1*(11), e8009. doi:10.1371/journal.pone.0008009 PMID:19956685

Craddock, M., & Lawson, R. (2009). The effects of size changes on haptic object recognition. *Attention, Perception & Psychophysics, 71*(4), 910–923. doi:10.3758/APP.71.4.910 PMID:19429968

Cronin, J., & Taylor, S. (1992). Measuring service quality: A reexamination and extension. *Journal of Marketing, 56*(3), 55–68. doi:10.2307/1252296

Crowcroft, N., & Majeed, A. (2001). Improving the certification of death and the usefulness of routine mortality statistics. *Clinical Medicine, 1*(2), 122–125. doi:10.7861/clinmedicine.1-2-122 PMID:11333456

Cruz, V. T., Pais, J., Bento, V., Mateus, C., Colunas, M., Alves, I., ... Rocha, N. P. (2013). A rehabilitation tool designed for intensive web-based cognitive training: Description and usability study. *JMIR Research Protocols, 2*(2), e59.

Cyrus, S., Zarkessh, A. M., Jafar, A., & Vishal, S. (1997). Knowledge discovery from Users Web Page Navigation. In *Workshop on Research Issues in Data Engineering.*

da Silva, R. F. L., & Ramirez, A. R. G. (2013). Contribution to Mobility and Orientation teaching programs: Assistive technology equipment and tests methodology. In *Handbook of Research on ICTs for Healthcare and Social Services: Developments and Applications* (Vol. 2, pp. 670–686). Hershey, PA: IGI Global. doi:10.4018/978-1-4666-3986-7.ch035

Dağhan, G., & Akkoyunlu, B. (2016). Modeling the continuance usage intention of online learning environments. *Computers in Human Behavior, 60*, 198–211. doi:10.1016/j.chb.2016.02.066

Dakopoulos, D., & Bourbakis, N. G. (2010). Wearable obstacle avoidance electronic travel aids for blind: a survey. Systems, Man, and Cybernetics, Part C: Applications and Reviews, IEEE Transactions on Systems, 40(1), 25-35. doi:10.1109/TSMCC.2009.2021255

DAmico, M., Agozzino, E., Biagino, A., Simonetti, A., & Marinelli, P. (1999). Ill -defined and multiple causes on death certificates – A study of misclassification in mortality statistics. *European Journal of Epidemiology, 15*(2), 141–148. doi:10.1023/A:1007570405888 PMID:10204643

Dash, S. K., Behera, B. K., & Patro, S. (2014). Accuracy in certification of cause of death in a tertiary care hospital – A retrospective analysis. *Journal of Forensic and Legal Medicine, 24*, 33–36. doi:10.1016/j.jflm.2014.03.006 PMID:24794848

Davis, F.D. (1985). A technology acceptance model for empirically testing new end-user information systems: theory and results. *DSpace@MIT: Massachusetts Institute of Technology.* Retrieved from http://www.temoa.info/node/257608

Davis, P. A. (2010). *Learning Usability Assessment Models For Web Sites* (Doctoral dissertation). Texas A&M University.

Davis, F. D. (1989). Perceived Usefulness, Perceived Ease of Use, and User Acceptance of Information Technology. *Management Information Systems Quarterly, 13*(3), 319–340. doi:10.2307/249008

Davis, G. B., Ein-Dor, P., King, W. R., & Torkzadeh, R. (2006). IT Offshoring: History, Prospects and Challenges. *Journal of the Association for Information Systems.*

Delahoz, Y. S., & Labrador, M. A. (2014). Survey on fall detection and fall prevention using wearable and external sensors. *Sensors (Basel, Switzerland), 14*(10), 19806–19842. doi:10.3390/s141019806 PMID:25340452

Deloitte. (2015). *Navigating the New Digital Divide. Capitalizing on digital influence in retail.* Retrieved March 16, 2016 from www.deloitte.com

Deloitte. (2016). *Global 250 Powers of Retailing 2016.* Retrieved from www.deloitte.com

DeLone, W. H., & McLean, E. R. (1992). Information systems success: The quest for the dependent variable. *Information Systems Research, 3*(1), 60–95. doi:10.1287/isre.3.1.60

Deng, L., Turner, D. E., Gehling, R., & Prince, B. (2010). User experience, satisfaction, and continual usage intention of IT. *European Journal of Information Systems, 19*(1), 60–75. doi:10.1057/ejis.2009.50

DeRuyter, K., Bloemer, J., & Pascal, P. (1997). Merging service quality and service satisfaction: An empirical test of an integrative model. *Journal of Economic Psychology, 8*(4), 187–406.

Dickinson, D. (2011). The Truth about Budgeting with Spreadsheets. *Credit Control Journal, 32*(7), 40-42. http://assetsproduction.govstore.service.gov.uk/G5/0317/5.G4.0317.201/QD6/Article%20-%20Truth%20about%20Budgeting%20with%20Spreadsheets.pdf

Dikaiakos, M., Katsaros, D., Mehra, P., Pallis, G., & Vakali, A. (2009). Cloud Computing: Distributed Internet Computing for IT and Scientific Research. *IEEE Internet Computing, 13*(5), 10–13. doi:10.1109/MIC.2009.103

DiMarzio, J. F. (2008). *Android a programmer's guide.* McGraw-Hill Education.

DiMicco, J., Millen, D. R., Geyer, W., Dugan, C., Brownholtz, B., & Muller, M. (2008). Motivations for social networking at work. *Proceedings of the 2008 ACM Conference on Computer Supported Cooperative Work, CSCW '08* (pp. 711–720). New York, NY, USA: ACM. doi:10.1145/1460563.1460674

Dischinger, M. (2000). *Designing for all senses: accessible spaces for visually impaired citizens* (Unpublished doctoral dissertation). Department of Space and Process School of Architecture, Chalmers University of Technology.

Dix, A., Finlay, J., Abowd, G. D., & Beale, R. (2004). *Human-Computer Interaction* (3rd ed.). Essex: Pearson Prentice Hall.

Djamasbi, S., Strong, D., Wilson, E. V., & Ruiz, C. (2016). Designing and Testing User-Centric Systems with both User Experience and Design Science Research Principles.

Domenech, J., Pont-Sanju, A., Sahuquillo, J., & Gil, J. A. (2010). *Evaluation, Analysis and Adaptation of Web Pre-fetching Techniques in Current Web. In Web-based Support Systems* (pp. 239–271). London: Springer.

Domingo, M. C. (2012). An overview of the Internet of Things for people with disabilities. *Journal of Network and Computer Applications, 35*(2), 584–596. doi:10.1016/j.jnca.2011.10.015

Dossania, R., & Kenney, M. (2007). The Next Wave of Globalization: Relocating Service Provision to India. *World Development, 35*(5), 772–791. doi:10.1016/j.worlddev.2006.09.014

Doyle, C., & McShane, P. (2003). On the design and implementation of the GSM auction in Nigeria—the worlds first ascending clock spectrum auction. *Telecommunications Policy, 27*(5), 383–405. doi:10.1016/S0308-5961(03)00011-9

Drigas, A., Koukianakis, L., & Papagerasimou, Y. (2006). An E-Learning Environment for Nontraditional Students with Sight Disabilities. In *Frontiers in Education Conference, 36th Annual* (pp. 23-27). IEEE. doi:10.1109/FIE.2006.322633

Dumas, J. S., & Redish, J. (1999). *A practical guide to usability testing*. Intellect Books.

Dunham, M. H. (2006). *Data Mining Introductory and Advanced Topics* (1st ed.). Pearson Education.

Dye, J. (2006). Folksonomy: A game of high-tech (and high-stakes) tag. *EContent*.

Echarte, F., Astrain, J. J., Córdoba, A., Villadangos, J., & Navarra, P. (2007). Ontology of Folksonomy: A New Modeling Method. Proceedings of Semantic Authoring, Annotation and Knowledge Markup (SAAKM).

Eco, U. (1979). *A theory of semiotics*. Indiana University Press.

Eevakangas & Timokinnunen. (2005). Applying User-Centered Design to Mobile Application Development. *Communications of the ACM, 48*(7). Retrieved from http://web.mit.edu/21w.789/www/papers/p55-kangas.pdf

Eidaroos, A.M., Probets, S.G., & Dearnley, J.A. (2009). Heuristic evaluation for e-Government websites in Saudi Arabia. In *SIC: The Third Saudi InternationalConference Proceedings*.

Eid, M. I. (2011). Determinants of e-commerce customer satisfaction, trust, and loyalty in Saudi Arabia. *Journal of Electronic Commerce Research, 12*(1), 78.

ElAarag, H., & Romano, S. (2009). Improvement of the neural network proxy cache replacement strategy.*Proceedings of the 2009 Spring Simulation Multiconference*, (SSM'09).

Elfaki, A. O., Alhawiti, K. M., AlMurtadha, Y. M., Abdalla, O. A., & Elshiekh, A. A. (2014). *Rule-based recommendation for supporting student learning-pathway selection* (pp. 155–160). Recent Advances in Electrical Engineering and Educational Technologies.

Ellis, C. J., & Fender, J. (2006). Corruption and transparency in a growth model. *International Tax and Public Finance, 13*(2-3), 115–149. doi:10.1007/s10797-006-1664-z

Engelbrecht-Wiggans, R., & Katok, E. (2006). E-sourcing in procurement: Theory and behavior in reverse auctions with non-competitive contracts. *Management Science, 52*(4), 581–596. doi:10.1287/mnsc.1050.0474

Engestrom, Y. (1987). *Learning by Expanding: An Activity-theoratical Approach to Developmental Research*. Helsinki: Orienta-Konsultit.

Ercan, T. (2002). Effective use of cloud computing in educational institutions. *Procedia: Social and Behavioral Sciences, 2*(2), 938–942.

Erisman, P. (2015, December). El efecto Alibaba: cómo una compañía de Internet iniciada por un profesor está reconfigurando el comercio electrónico a nivel mundial (Keynote presentation). *Proceedings of FICOD '15*.

Ernst, M. O., & Banks, M. S. (2002). Humans integrate visual and haptic information in a statistically optimal fashion. *Nature, 415*(6870), 429–433. doi:10.1038/415429a PMID:11807554

European Commission – EC. (2001). *Quality and comparability improvement of European causes of death statistics*.

European Commission – EC. (2013). Report of the Task Force on Satellite Lists for Causes of Deaths (COD). Eurostat.

European Commission. (2007). *Ageing well in the Information Society: An i2010 Initiative, Action Plan on Information and Communication Technologies and Ageing*. Brussels: European Commission.

Evans, D., & Yen, D. C. (2006). E-Government: Evolving relationship of citizens and government, domestic, and international development. *Government Information Quarterly, 23*(2), 207–235. doi:10.1016/j.giq.2005.11.004

Fagbadebo, O. (2007). Corruption, governance and political instability in Nigeria. *African Journal of Political Science and International Relations, 1*(2), 28–37.

Faiola, A. (2006). Toward an HCI Theory of Cultural Cognition. In Encyclopedia of Human Computer Interaction (pp. 609-614). Hershey, PA, USA: IGI Global. doi:10.4018/978-1-59140-562-7.ch090

Falak, S., Chiun, L. M., & Wee, A. Y. (2016). Sustainable rural tourism: An indigenous community perspective on positioning rural tourism. *Turizam: znanstveno-stručni časopis, 64*(3), 311-327.

Falkowski, G., Pedigo, P., Smith, B., & Swanson, D. (1998). A recipe for ERP success. *Beyond Computing, 6*(3), 44-45.

Fan, Y. W., & Farn, C. K. (2007). Investigating factors affecting the adoption of electronic toll collection: A transaction cost economics perspective. *Proceedings of the 40th Annual Hawaii International Conference on System Sciences HICSS '07* (pp. 107-107). IEEE.

Fang, W. (2007). Using Google Analytics for improving library website content and design: A case study. *Library Philosophy and Practice, 9*(2), 22.

Fan, L., Cao, P., & Jacobson, Q. (1999). Web Pre-fetching between Low-Bandwidth Clients and Proxies: Potential and Performance. In *Proceedings of the Joint International Conference on Measurement and Modeling of Computer Systems (SIGMETRICS'99)*.

Farcy, R., Leroux, R., Jucha, A., Damaschini, R., Grégoire, C., & Zogaghi, A. (2006). Electronic Travel Aids and Electronic Orientation Aids for blind people: technical, rehabilitation and everyday life points of view. In *Conference & Workshop on Assistive Technologies for People with Vision & Hearing Impairments. Technology for Inclusion CVHI 2006* (pp. 1-12).

Farooq, U., Kannampallil, T. G., Song, Y., Ganoe, C. H., Carroll, J. M., & Giles, L. (2007). Evaluating tagging behavior in social bookmarking systems: metrics and design heuristics. In *Human-Computer Interaction* (Vol. 1, pp. 351–360). ACM; doi:10.1145/1316624.1316677

Federal Highway Administrator Office of Freight Management and Operations. Statistics. (2015). *Freight Facts and Figures 2013* (Report No. FHWA-HOP-14-004). Washington, D.C.: Bureau of Transportation.

Federal Ministry of Communication Technology. (2013). *Nigeria's National Broadband Plan 2013–2018*. Abuja, Nigeria: Federal Ministry Of Communication Technology.

Federici, S., Meloni, F., & Presti, A. L. (2009). International literature review on WHODAS II. *Life Span and Disability, 12*(1), 83–110.

Feng, W., Man, S., & Hu, G. (2009). *Markov Tree Prediction on Web Cache Pre-fetching. In Software Engineering, Artificial Intelligence (SCI)* (Vol. 209, pp. 105–120). Berlin: Springer-Verlag.

Fernandez, A., Insfran, E., & Abrahão, S. (2011). Usability Evaluation Methods for the Web: A Systematic Mapping Study. *Information and Software Technology, 53*(8), 789–817. doi:10.1016/j.infsof.2011.02.007

Fishbein, M., & Ajzen, I. (1975). *Belief, attitude, intention and behavior: An introduction to theory and research*. Reading, MA: Addison-Wesley.

Fishburn, P. C. (1967). Additive Utilities With Incomplete Product Sets: Application To Priorities And Assignments. *Operations Research, 15*(3), 537–542. Available at http://www.jstor.org/stable/168461 doi:10.1287/opre.15.3.537

Flanders, W. D. (1992). Inaccuracies of Death Certificate Information. *Epidemiology (Cambridge, Mass.)*, *3*(1), 3–5. doi:10.1097/00001648-199201000-00002 PMID:1554807

Flavián, C., Guinalíu, M., & Gurrea, R. (2006). The role played by perceived usability, satisfaction and consumer trust on website loyalty. *Information & Management*, *43*(1), 1–14. doi:10.1016/j.im.2005.01.002

Floyd, D. L., Prentice-Dunn, S., & Rogers, R. W. (2000). A meta-analysis of research on protection motivation theory. *Journal of Applied Social Psychology*, *30*(2), 407–429. doi:10.1111/j.1559-1816.2000.tb02323.x

Flynn, D. J., & Jazi, M. D. (1998). Constructing user requirements: A social process for a social context. *Information Systems Journal*, *8*(1), 53–83. doi:10.1046/j.1365-2575.1998.00004.x

Folmer, E., & Bosch, J. (2004). Architecting for Usability: A Survey. *Journal of Systems and Software*, *70*(1-2), 61–78. doi:10.1016/S0164-1212(02)00159-0

Fornell, C., & Cha, J. (1994). Partial least squares. *Advanced Methods of Marketing Research*, *407*(3), 52-78.

Forrester, J. W. (1961). *Industrial Dynamics*. Cambridge, Massachusetts, USA: The M.I.T. Press.

Fortino, G., & Gravina, R. (2015). Fall-MobileGuard: a Smart Real-Time Fall Detection System. In *Proceedings of the 10th International Conference on Body Area Networks* (pp. 44-50). doi:10.4108/eai.28-9-2015.2261462

Fortuin, L. (1988). Performance indicators—why, where and how? *European Journal of Operational Research*, *34*(1), 1–9. doi:10.1016/0377-2217(88)90449-3

França, T. C., Pires, P. F., Pirmez, L., Delicato, F. C., & Farias, C. (2011). Web das Coisas: Conectando Dispositivos Físicos ao Mundo Digital. In: Livro Texto de Minicursos do Simpósio Brasileiro de Redes de Computadores e Sistemas de redes de Computadores e Sistemas Distribuídos. Campo Grande.

Friedman, T. L. (2006). The first law of petropolitics. *Foreign Policy*, *154*(3), 28–36.

FrogTek. (2015). *Products*. Retrieved from http://frogtek.org/products/

Fuller, M. A., Serva, M. A., & Baroudi, J. (2010). Clarifying the integration of trust and TAM in e-commerce environments: Implications for systems design and management. *IEEE Transactions on Engineering Management*, *57*(3), 380–393. doi:10.1109/TEM.2009.2023111

FYImobileware. (2014). *iXpenseIt*. Retrieved from http://www.fyimobileware.com/ixpenseit.html

Gangwar, H., Date, H., & Ramaswamy, R. (2015). Understanding determinants of cloud computing adoption using an integrated TAM-TOE model. *Journal of Enterprise Information Management*, *28*(1), 107–130. doi:10.1108/JEIM-08-2013-0065

Garcia, A. C. B., Maciel, C., & Pinto, F. B. (2005). A Quality Inspection Method to Evaluate E-Government Sites. In EGOV 2005 (LNCS), (vol. 3591, pp. 198–209). Springer.

García-Menéndez, L., Martinez-Zarzoso, I., & Pinero De Miguel, D. (2004). Determinants of Mode Choice between Road and Shipping for Freight Transport: Evidence for Four Spanish Exporting Sectors. *Journal of Transport Economics and Policy*, *38*(3), 447–466.

Gartner. (2016). IT Glossary: Bimodal IT. Retrieved from http://www.gartner.com/it-glossary/bimodal

Gaudin, S. (2016, January 18). IBM predicts that by 2025 many stores will be showrooms with merchandise shipped to customers. *Computerworld*. Retrieved from www.computerworld.com

Gefen, D., Karahanna, E., & Straub, D. W. (2003). Inexperience and experience with online stores: The importance of TAM and trust. *IEEE Transactions on Engineering Management, 50*(3), 307–321. doi:10.1109/TEM.2003.817277

Geode Software. (2014). *Easy Books*. Retrieved from http://easybooksapp.com/

German institute of medical documentation and information (2016). *About IRIS*. Retrieved from https://www.dimdi.de/static/en/klassi/irisinstitute/

Gladding Development. (2012). *Ledger*. Retrieved from http://www.ledgerapp.com/

Glasser, J. H. (1981). The quality and utility of death certificate data. *American Journal of Public Health, 71*(3), 231–233. doi:10.2105/AJPH.71.3.231 PMID:7468853

Golder, S., & Huberman, B. (2006). Usage patterns of collaborative tagging systems. *Journal of Information Science, 32*(2), 198–208. doi:10.1177/0165551506062337

Goldkuhl, G. (2008). Practical inquiry as action research and beyond. *Proceedings of theEuropean Conference on Information Systems '08.*

Goldkuhl, G. (2011). Generic regulation model: the evolution of a practical theory for e-government. *Transforming Government: People. Process and Policy, 5*(3), 249–267.

Goodro, M., Sameti, M., Patenaude, B., & Fein, G. (2012). Age effect on subcortical structures in healthy adults. *Psychiatry Research: Neuroimaging, 203*(1), 38–45. doi:10.1016/j.pscychresns.2011.09.014 PMID:22863654

Goodwin, T. (2015, March 3). The battle is for The Customer Interface. Retrieved from https://techcrunch.com

Gordon, R. G. Jr., (Ed.). (2005). *Ethnologue: Languages of the World* (15th ed.). Dallas, Tex.: SIL International.

Gori, M., Tinelli, F., Sandini, G., Cioni, G., & Burr, D. (2012). Impaired visual size-discrimination in children with movement disorders. *Neuropsychologia, 50*(8), 1838–1843. doi:10.1016/j.neuropsychologia.2012.04.009 PMID:22569216

Gorla, N., Somers, T. M., & Wong, B. (2010). Organizational impact of system quality, information quality, and service quality. *The Journal of Strategic Information Systems, 19*(3), 207–228. doi:10.1016/j.jsis.2010.05.001

Gottschalk, P., & Solli-Sæther, H. (2005). Critical success factors from IT outsourcing theories: An empirical study. *Industrial Management & Data Systems, 105*(6), 685–702. doi:10.1108/02635570510606941

Government of the Republic of Slovenia. (2008). *Rules on the conditions and method for the performance of post mortem examination service (OG RS 56/93 and 15/2008)*. Ljubljana, SI: Ministry of Health.

Grande, E. U., Estébanez, R. P., & Colomina, C. M. (2011). The impact of Accounting Information Systems (AIS) on performance measures: Empirical evidence in Spanish SMEs. *The International Journal of Digital Accounting Research, 11*(2), 25–43. Retrieved from www.uhu.es/ijdar/10.4192/1577-8517-v11_2.pdf

Gregor, S. (2002). A theory of theories in information systems. *Management Information Systems Quarterly, 30*(3), 611–642.

Gregor, S. (2006). The nature of theory in information systems. *Management Information Systems Quarterly, 30*(3), 611–642.

Grimmelikhuijsen, S. G., Porumbescu, G., Hong, B., & Im, T. (2013). The effect of transparency in trust in government: A cross-national comparative experiment. *Public Administration Review, 73*(4), 575–586. doi:10.1111/puar.12047

Gronroos, C. (1984). A service quality model and its marketing implications. *European Journal of Marketing, 18*(4), 36–44. doi:10.1108/EUM0000000004784

Grue, B., & Ludvigsen, J. (2006). Decision factors underlying transport mode choice in European freight transport. Institute of Transport Economics, Oslo, Norway. Association for European Transport and contributors.

Gubbi, J., Buyya, R., Marusic, S., & Palaniswami, M. (2013). Internet of Things (IoT): A vision, architectural elements, and future directions. *Future Generation Computer Systems*, *29*(7), 1645–1660. doi:10.1016/j.future.2013.01.010

Gull, H., Iqbal, S. Z., & Saqib, M. (2015). Usability Evaluation of an Educational Website in Saudi Arabia. *VAWKUM Transactions on Computer Sciences, 1*(2).

Gumbo, S., Thinyane, H., Thinyane, M., & Terzoli, A. And Hansen, S. (2012). Living lab methodology as an approach to innovation in ICT4D: The Siyakhula Living Lab experience. Pro. of the IST-Africa 2012 Conference.

Gundecha, P., & Liu, H. (2012). *Mining social media: A brief introduction*. The Institute for Operations Research and the Management Sciences (INFORMS) TutORials in Operations Research.

Gupta, A., Herath, S. K., & Mikouiza, N. C. (2005). Outsourcing in higher education: An empirical examination. *International Journal of Educational Management*, *19*(5), 396–412. doi:10.1108/09513540510607734

Gupta, M., Li, R., Yin, Z., & Han, J. (2010). Survey on social tagging techniques. *SIGKDD Explor. Newsl.*, *12*(1), 58–72. doi:10.1145/1882471.1882480

Habib, M., & Zurawicki, L. (2002). Corruption and foreign direct investment. *Journal of International Business Studies*, *33*(2), 291–307. doi:10.1057/palgrave.jibs.8491017

Hair, J. F., Ringle, C. M., & Sarstedt, M. (2011). PLS-SEM: Indeed a silver bullet. *Journal of Marketing Theory and Practice*, *19*(2), 139–152. doi:10.2753/MTP1069-6679190202

Hair, J.F., Sarstedt, M., Hopkins, L., & Kuppelwieser, , V. (. (2014). Partial least squares structural equation modeling (PLS-SEM) An emerging tool in business research. *European Business Review*, *26*(2), 106–112. doi:10.1108/EBR-10-2013-0128

Halachmi, A., & Greiling, D. (2013). Transparency, e-government, and accountability: Some issues and considerations. *Public Performance & Management Review*, *36*(4), 562–584. doi:10.2753/PMR1530-9576360404

Hämäläinen, A., Teixeira, A., Almeida, N., Meinedo, H., Fegyó, T., & Dias, M. S. (2015). Multilingual speech recognition for the elderly: The AALFred personal life assistant. *Procedia Computer Science*, *67*, 283–292. doi:10.1016/j.procs.2015.09.272

Hanna, M. (2004). Data mining in the e-Learning domain. *Campus-Wide Information Systems*, *21*(1), 29–34. doi:10.1108/10650740410512301

Hasan, L. (2009). *Usability evaluation framework for e-commerce websites in developing countries* (Doctoral dissertation).

Hasan, L. (2013). Heuristic Evaluation of Three Jordanian University Websites. *Informatics in Education*, *12*(2), 231–251.

Hassan, A. R., & Bhuiyan, M. I. H. (2016). Computer-aided sleep staging using complete ensemble empirical mode decomposition with adaptive noise and bootstrap aggregating. *Biomedical Signal Processing and Control*, *24*, 1–10. doi:10.1016/j.bspc.2015.09.002

Heath, I. (2008). Never had it so good? *BMJ (Clinical Research Ed.)*, *336*(7650), 950–951. doi:10.1136/bmj.39532.671319.94 PMID:18397944

Heeks, R. (2003). *Most E-Government-for-Development Projects Fail: How Can Risks be Reduced?* iGovernment Working Paper Series, Institute for Development Policy and Management, University of Manchester, UK.

Heeks, R. (2002). Information Systems and Developing Countries: Failure, Success and Local Improvisations. *The Information Society, 18*(2), 101–112. doi:10.1080/01972240290075039

Heeks, R., & Bailur, S. (2007). Analyzing e-government research: Perspectives, philosophies, theories, methods, and practice. *Government Information Quarterly, 24*(2), 243–265. doi:10.1016/j.giq.2006.06.005

Henderson, A., & Harris, J. (2012). Curating Evolution. *Journal of Usability Studies, 7*(2), 51–55.

Hengshan, W., Cheng, Y., & Hua, Z. (2006). Design and Implementation of a Web Usage Mining Model Based on FPgrowth and Prefixspan. Communications of the IIMA, 6(2).

Henseler, J., Ringle, C. M., & Sinkovics, R. R. (2009). The use of partial least squares path modeling in international marketing. *Advances in International Marketing, 20*(1), 277-319.

Herlocker, J. L., Konstan, J. A., Borchers, A., & Riedl, J. (1999). An algorithmic framework for performing collaborative filtering.*Proceedings of the 22nd Annual International ACM SIGIR Conference on Research and Development in Information Retrieval SIGIR '99* (pp. 230–237). New York, NY, USA: ACM. doi:10.1145/312624.312682

Hersh, M. A. (2010). The design and evaluation of assistive technology products and devices part 1: Design. In *International Encyclopedia of Rehabilitation*. Retrieved July 1, 2016, from http://cirrie.buffalo.edu/encyclopedia/en/article/309/

Hersh, M. A. (2015). Cane Use and Late Onset Visual Impairment. *Technology and Disability, 27*(3), 103–116. doi:10.3233/TAD-150432

Hersh, M. A., & Johnson, M. A. (Eds.). (2008). *Assistive Technology for Vision-Impaired and Blind People*. Springer. doi:10.1007/978-1-84628-867-8

Hevner, A., March, S., Park, J., & Ram, S. (2004). Design science in information systems research. *Management Information Systems Quarterly, 28*(1), 75–105.

Heymann, P., & Garcia-Molina, H. (2009). Contrasting Controlled Vocabulary and Tagging: Do Experts Choose the Right Names to Label the Wrong Things? *Proceedings of theSecond ACM International Conference on Web Search and Data Mining (WSDM 2009), Late Breaking Results Session* (pp. 1–4). Stanford InfoLab.

Heymann, P., Koutrika, G., & Garcia-Molina, H. (2007). Fighting Spam on Social Web Sites: A Survey of Approaches and Future Challenges. *IEEE Internet Computing, 11*(6), 36–45. doi:10.1109/MIC.2007.125

Hill, K. (2012). How Target Figured Out a Teen Girl Was Pregnant Before Her Father Did. *Forbes*. Retrieved from www.forbes.com

Hill, M. E., & Rosenwaike, I. (2001). Social Security Administration's Death Master File: The Completeness of Death Reporting at Older Ages. *Social Security Bulletin, 64*(1), 45–62. PMID:12428517

Hodkin, S. (2014). The Internet of Me: Creating a Personalized Web Experience. *Wired*. Retrieved from www.wired.com

Hoffer, J. A., Prescott, M. B., & MacFadden, F. R. (2007). Modern Database Management (8thed). Prentice Hall.

Hogg, M. A., & Mullin, B. A. (1999). Joining groups to reduce uncertainty: Subjective uncertainty reduction and group identification. In D. Abrams & M. A. Hogg (Eds.). Social identity and social contagion (pp. 249–279). Oxford: Blackwell.

Holland, M. P. (2002). Digital Collectives in Indigenous Cultures and Communities Meeting: *Meeting Report (S. O. Information, Trans.)*. Michigan: University of Michigan.

Hollingsed, T., & Novick, D. G. (2007). Usability inspection methods after 15 years of research and practice. In *Proceedings of the 25th annual ACM International Conference on Design of communication*. ACM. doi:10.1145/1297144.1297200

Holzinger, A. (2005). Usability engineering methods for software developers. *Communications of the ACM, 48*(1), 71–74. doi:10.1145/1039539.1039541

Horton, R. (2007). Counting for health. *Lancet, 370*(9598), 1526–1526. doi:10.1016/S0140-6736(07)61418-4 PMID:17992726

Hotho, A., Jäschke, R., Schmitz, C., & Stumme, G. (2006). Information retrieval in folksonomies: Search and ranking. *Proceedings of the European Semantic Web conference* (pp. 411–426).

Hoyle, B. S., Fowler, J. M., Waters, D. A., & Withington, D. J. (2004, June). Development of the electronic guide cane for enhanced primary mobility for the vision impaired. In *Conference and Workshop on Assistive Technologies for Vision and Hearing Impairment*.

Huang, Z., & Brooks, L. (2011). Evaluating Usability of Web-Based Electronic Government. Users' Perspective. *Human-Computer Interaction. Users and Applications: 14th International Conference, HCI International 2011*.

Huang, Y. F., & Hsu, J. M. (2008). Mining Web Logs to Improve Hit Ratios of Pre-fetching and Caching. *Knowledge-Based Systems, 21*(1), 62–69. doi:10.1016/j.knosys.2006.11.004

Huh, Y. U., Keller, F. R., Redman, T. C., & Watkins, A. R. (1990). Data quality. *Information and Software Technology, 32*(8), 559–565. doi:10.1016/0950-5849(90)90146-I

Hu, P. J.-H., Clark, T. H. K., & Ma, W. W. (2003). Examining technology acceptance by school teachers: A longitudinal study. *Information & Management, 41*(2), 227–241. doi:10.1016/S0378-7206(03)00050-8

Hussein, H. B. (2011). Attitudes of Saudi universities faculty members towards using learning management system (JUSUR). *TOJET: The Turkish Online Journal of Educational Technology, 10*(2).

Huy, T. Q., Long, N. H., Hoa, D. P., Byass, P., & Eriksson, B. (2003). Validity and completeness of death reporting and registration in a rural district of Vietnam. *Scandinavian Journal of Public Health, 31*(6), 12–18. doi:10.1080/14034950310015059 PMID:14640146

Hwang, C. L., & Yoon, K. (1981). *Multiple Attribute Decision Making Methods and Applications*. Berlin, Heidelberg: Springer. doi:10.1007/978-3-642-48318-9

Hwang, C.-L., Lai, Y.-J., & Liu, T.-Y. (1993). A new approach for multiple objective decision making. *Computers & Operations Research, 20*(8), 889–899. doi:10.1016/0305-0548(93)90109-V

Iacobucci, D., Ostrom, A., & Grayson, K. (1995). Distinguishing Service Quality and Customer Satisfaction: The Voice of the Consumer. *Journal of Consumer Psychology, 4*(3), 277–303. doi:10.1207/s15327663jcp0403_04

IBGE. (2010). *Brazilian Institute of geography and statistics*. Retrieved July 1, 2016, from http://www.ibge.gov.br/estadosat/temas.php?tema=censodemog2010_defic

Ibrahim, T. I., & Xu, C. Z. (2000). Neural Nets based Predictive Pre-fetching to Tolerate WWW Latency. In *Proceedings of the 20th International Conference on Distributed Computing Systems*. IEEE.

Ibrahim, T. I., & Xu, C. Z. (2004). A Keyword-Based Semantic Pre-fetching Approach in Internet News Services. *IEEE Transactions on Knowledge and Data Engineering, 16*(5), 601–611. doi:10.1109/TKDE.2004.1277820

ICS-CERT. (2013). *ICS-CERT Monitor*. Retrieved Aug 9, 2015, from https://ics-cert.us-cert.gov/sites/ default/files/Monitors/ICSCERT_Monitor_Oct-Dec2013.pdf

Ifinedo, P. (2006). Towards e-government in a Sub-Saharan African country: Impediments and initiatives in Nigeria. *Journal of E-Government, 3*(1), 3–28. doi:10.1300/J399v03n01_02

Ifinedo, P. (2007). Moving towards E-Government in a developing society: Glimpses of the Problems, Progress, and Prospects in Nigeria. In *Al-Hakim, L., Global E-Government: Theory, Applications and Benchmarking* (p. 383). Hershey: Idea Group Publishing. doi:10.4018/978-1-59904-027-1.ch009

Ifinedo, P. (2009). Information technology security management concerns in global financial services institutions: Is national culture a differentiator? *Information Management & Computer Security, 17*(5), 372–387. doi:10.1108/09685220911006678

Ifinedo, P. (2012). Understanding information systems security policy compliance: An integration of the theory of planned behaviour and the protection motivation theory. *Computers & Security, 31*(1), 83–95. doi:10.1016/j.cose.2011.10.007

Institute of Electrical and Electronics Engineers. (1990). *610.12-1990, IEEE Standard Glossary of Software Engineering Terminology*. Los Alamitos, CA: Author.

International Standards Organization. (2010). *ISO9241 - Ergonomics of human-system interaction*. Geneva: International Standards Organization.

International Telecommunication Union (ITU). (2002). *Trends in Telecommunication Reform*. Geneva: International Telecommunication Union.

ISO 9241-11. (1998). *Guidelines for specifying and measuring usability*. ISO.

ISO/IEC 25010. (2011). *Systems and software engineering – Software product Quality Requirements and Evaluation (SQuaRE) – Software product quality and system quality in use models*. ISO.

ISO/IEC 9126. (1991). *Software product evaluation – quality characteristics and guidelines for their use*. ISO.

ITRS. (2012). *International Roadmap for Semiconductor (ITRS)*. Korea: Factory Integration Report. ITRS.

Ivory, M. Y. (2001). *An empirical foundation for automated web interface evaluation* (Doctoral dissertation). University of California at Berkeley.

Jacobson, W. H. (1993). *The art and science of teaching orientation and mobility to persons with visual impairments*. New York, NY: American Foundation for the Blind.

Jaeger, P. T., & Bertot, J. C. (2010). Transparency and technological change: Ensuring equal and sustained public access to government information. *Government Information Quarterly, 27*(4), 371–376. doi:10.1016/j.giq.2010.05.003

Jahanshahloo, G. R., Lotfi, F. H., & Izadikhah, M. (2006). An algorithmic method to extend TOPSIS for decision-making problems with interval data. *Applied Mathematics and Computation, 175*(2), 1375–1384. doi:10.1016/j.amc.2005.08.048

Jahanshahloo, G. R., Lotfi, F. H., & Izadikhah, M. (2006). Extension of the TOPSIS method for decision-making problems with fuzzy data. *Applied Mathematics and Computation, 181*(2), 1544–1551. doi:10.1016/j.amc.2006.02.057

Jain, K., Bala, D. V., Trivedi, K., & Chandwani, H. (2015). Situational analysis of Medical Certification of Cause of Death (MCCD) scheme in Municipal Corporation of Ahmedabad. *Indian Journal of Forensic and Community Medicine, 2*(2), 95–99.

Jang, J. S. R. (1993). ANFIS: Adaptive-network-based fuzzy Inference system. *Systems, Man and Cybernetics. IEEE Transactions on, 23*(3), 665–685.

Janis, I. L. (1967). Effects of fear arousal on attitude change: Recent developments in theory and experimental research. *Advances in Experimental Social Psychology, 3*, 166–224. doi:10.1016/S0065-2601(08)60344-5

Jayant, C., Acuario, C., Johnson, W., Hollier, J., & Ladner, R. (2010,). V-braille: haptic braille perception using a touch-screen and vibration on mobile phones. In *Proceedings of the 12th international ACM SIGACCESS conference on Computers and accessibility* (pp. 295-296). ACM. doi:10.1145/1878803.1878878

Jette, A. M. (2006). Toward a common language for function, disability, and health. *Physical Therapy, 86*(5), 726–734. PMID:16649895

Jia, D., Bhatti, A., Nahavandi, S., & Horan, B. (2013). Human performance measures for interactive haptic-audio-visual interfaces. *Haptics. IEEE Transactions on, 6*(1), 46–57. PMID:24808267

Jianhan, Z. (2002). Using Markov Chains for Link Prediction in Adaptive Web Sites. *LNCS, 2311*, 60–73.

Jiawei, H., Micheline, K., & Jian, P. (2006). *Data Mining Concepts and Techniques*. Pearson Education.

John, B. E., & Kieras, D. E. (1996). The GOMS family of user interface analysis techniques: Comparison and contrast. *ACM Transactions on Computer-Human Interaction, 3*(4), 320–351. doi:10.1145/235833.236054

Johnson, E., & Kolko, B. (2010). e-Government and transparency in authoritarian regimes: comparison of national-and city-level e-government web sites in Central Asia. *Digital Icons: Studies in Russian. Eurasian and Central European New Media, 3*, 15–48.

Johnsor, K. A., & Semwal, S. K. (2014). Shapes: A multi-sensory environment for the B/VI and hearing impaired community. In *Virtual and Augmented Assistive Technology (VAAT), 2014 2nd Workshop on* (pp. 1-6). IEEE.

Johnston, A. C., & Warkentin, M. (2010). Fear appeals and information security behaviours: An empirical study. *Management Information Systems Quarterly, 34*(3), 549–566.

Jones, M. G., Bokinsky, A., Tretter, T., & Negishi, A. (2005). A comparison of with haptic and visual modalities. *Haptics-e Electronic J. Haptics Res, 4*(0).

Joshi, K. P., Yesha, Y., Ozok, A. A., Yesha, Y., Lahane, A., Kalva, H., & Furht, B. (2010). User-centric smart services in the cloud. In M. Chignell, J. Cordy, J. Ng, & Y. Yesha (Eds.), *The smart internet* (pp. 234–249). Berlin, Heidelberg: Springer-Verlag. doi:10.1007/978-3-642-16599-3_16

Joubert, J., Bradshaw, D., Kabudula, C., Rao, C., Kahn, K., Mee, P., & Vos, T. et al. (2014). Record-linkage comparison of verbal autopsy and routine civil registration death certification in rural north-east South Africa: 2006–09. *International Journal of Epidemiology, 43*(6), 1945–1958. doi:10.1093/ije/dyu156 PMID:25146564

Jougla, E., Rossolin, F., Niyosenga, A., Chappert, J., Johansson, L., & Pavillon, G. (2001). Comparability and quality improvement in European causes of death statistics. Eurostat.

Jougla, E., Pavillon, G., Rossollin, F., De Smedt, M., & Bonte, J. (1998). Improvement of the quality and comparability of causes-of-death statistics inside the European Community. *Revue d'Epidemiologie et de Sante Publique, 46*(6), 447–456. PMID:9950045

Julong, D. (1989). Introduction to grey system theory. *Journal of Grey System, 1*(1), 1–24.

Kahraman, C. (Ed.). (2008). *Fuzzy multi-criteria decision making: theory and applications with recent developments* (Vol. 16). Springer Science & Business Media. doi:10.1007/978-0-387-76813-7

Kakabadse, A., & Kakabadse, N. (2005). Outsourcing: Current and future trends. *Thunderbird International Business Review, 47*(2), 183–204. doi:10.1002/tie.20048

Kamal, I.W., Alsmadi, I.M., Wahsheh, H.A., & Al-Kabi, M.N. (2016). Evaluating Web Accessibility Metrics for Jordanian Universities. *International Journal of Advanced Computer Science and Applications, 7*(7).

Kamenec, K. (2014, November 26). 10 Best Social Shopping Sites Right Now. Retrieved from www.pcmag.com

Kaplan, B., & Maxwell, J. A. (1994). Qualitative Research Methods for Evaluating Computer Information Systems. In J. G. Anderson, C. E. Aydin, & S. J. Jay (Eds.), *Evaluating Health Care Information Systems: Methods and Applications* (pp. 45–68). Thousand Oaks, CA: Sage publications.

Kapuire, G. K., Winschiers-Theophilus, H., & Blake, E. (2015). An insider perspective on community gains: A subjective account of a Namibian rural communities perception of a long-term participatory design project. *International Journal of Human-Computer Studies, 74,* 124–143. doi:10.1016/j.ijhcs.2014.10.004

Karaali, D., Gumussoy, C. A., & Calisir, F. (2011). Factors affecting the intention to use a web-based learning system among blue-collar workers in the automotive industry. *Computers in Human Behavior, 27*(1), 343–354. doi:10.1016/j.chb.2010.08.012

Karahanna, E., Straub, D. W., & Chervany, N. L. (1999). Information technology adoption across time: A cross-sectional comparison of pre-adoption and post-adoption beliefs. *Management Information Systems Quarterly, 23*(2), 183–213. doi:10.2307/249751

Karapanos, E. (2013). User experience over time. In Modeling Users' Experiences with Interactive Systems (pp. 57-83). Springer Berlin Heidelberg. doi:10.1007/978-3-642-31000-3_4

Karapanos, E., Zimmerman, J., Forlizzi, J., & Martens, J.-B. (2009). User experience over time: An initial framework. *Proceedings of the 27th International Conference on Human Factors in Computing Systems (CHI '09),* Boston, MA (pp. 729–738). doi:10.1145/1518701.1518814

Kaufmann, D., & Bellver, A. (2005, July 6–7). Transparenting transparency—initial empirics and policy applications. *Presentation at the Pre-Conference on Institutional Change for Growth and Poverty Reduction in Low Income Countries at the International Monetary Fund,* Washington DC.

Kaushik, A. (2007). Web Analytics: An Hour A Day (W/Cd). John Wiley & Sons.

Kawai, Y., & Tomita, F. (1996). Interactive tactile display system: a support system for the visually disabled to recognize 3D objects. In *Proceedings of the second annual ACM conference on Assistive technologies* (pp. 45-50). ACM. doi:10.1145/228347.228356

Kaya, C. C., Zhang, G., Tan, Y., & Mookerjee, V. S. (2009). An Admission-Control Technique for Delay Reduction in Proxy Caching. *Decision Support Systems, 46*(2), 594–603. doi:10.1016/j.dss.2008.10.004

Kebonang, Z. & Kebonang, S. (2013). Does leadership matter to development: The case of Botswana, Zimbabwe, Nigeria and Indonesia. *International Journal of Politics and Good Governance,* 4(4.4), 1-24.

Ketler, K., & Walstrom, J. (1993). The outsourcing decision. *International Journal of Information Management, 13*(6), 449–459. doi:10.1016/0268-4012(93)90061-8

Khalil, F., Li, A. J., & Wang, H. (2009). Integrated Model for Next Page Access Prediction. Int. *J. Knowledge and Web Intelligence, 1*(2), 48–80. doi:10.1504/IJKWI.2009.027925

Kilcourse, B. & Rosenblum, P. (2015, March). *Advanced Analytics: Retailers Fixate On The Customer.* RSR (Retail Systems Research).

Kilcourse, B. & Rowen, S. (2015, June). *Commerce convergence: Closing the Gap Between Online and In-Store.* RSR (Retail Systems Research).

Kilroy, T., MacKenzie, I., & Manacek, A. (2015). Pricing in retail: Setting strategy. Retrieved from www.mckinsey.com

Kim, S., Kim, H. J., & Lee, H. (2009). An institutional analysis of an e-government system for anti-corruption: The case of OPEN. *Government Information Quarterly*, *26*(1), 42–50. doi:10.1016/j.giq.2008.09.002

Kim, T. (2010). A self-directed dynamic web-based learning environment: Proposal for personalized learning framework. *Journal of Security Engineering*, *9*(2), 177–187.

King, E., & Boyatt, R. (2015). Exploring factors that influence adoption of e-learning within higher education. *British Journal of Educational Technology*, *46*(6), 1272–1280. doi:10.1111/bjet.12195

Kiplinger, K. (2008). *Kiplinger's personal finance*. Retrieved from https://books.google.com/books?id=sSXMlfsUqB MC&pg=PT21&lpg=PT21&dq=Track+your+cash.+The+web+makes+it+easy+to+know+exactly+where+your+m oney+goes&source=bl&ots=t1hcwUfvvb&sig=RvudSNwwHbXcKADG92gq9srv6rw&hl=en&sa=X&ved=0ahUKE wjCv9I.Npa_KAhWMchQKHc4BDcIQ6AEIIzAC#v=onepage&q&f=false

Kirakowski, J., Claridge, N., & Whitehand, R. (1998, June). Human centered measures of success in web site design. In *Proceedings of the Fourth Conference on Human Factors & the Web*

Kirakowski, J., & Corbett, M. (1993). SUMI: The software usability measurement inventory. *British Journal of Educational Technology*, *24*(3), 210–212. doi:10.1111/j.1467-8535.1993.tb00076.x

Kitajima, M. (2006). *Cognitive Walkthrough for the web. International encyclopedia of ergonomics and human factors*. CRC Press.

Klatzky, R. L., Lederman, S. J., & Metzger, V. A. (1985). Identifying objects by touch: An expert system. *Perception & Psychophysics*, *37*(4), 299–302. doi:10.3758/BF03211351 PMID:4034346

Kleinberger, T., Becker, M., Ras, E., Holzinger, A., & Müller, P. (2007). Ambient intelligence in assisted living: enable elderly people to handle future interfaces. In *International Conference on Universal Access in Human-Computer Interaction* (pp. 103-112). Berlin: Springer. doi:10.1007/978-3-540-73281-5_11

Klein, K. K., & Myers, M. D. (1999). A Set of Principles for Conducting and evaluating Interpretive Field Studies in Information Systems. *Management Information Systems Quarterly*, *23*(1), 67–94. doi:10.2307/249410

Knijnenburg, B. P., Willemsen, M. C., Gantner, Z., Soncu, H., & Newell, C. (2012). Explaining the user experience of recommender systems. *User Modeling and User-Adapted Interaction*, *22*(4-5), 441–504. doi:10.1007/s11257-011-9118-4

Kolstad, I., & Wiig, A. (2009). Is transparency the key to reducing corruption in resource-rich countries? *World Development*, *37*(3), 521–532. doi:10.1016/j.worlddev.2008.07.002

Koskela, T.J., Heikkonen, & Kaski, K. (2003). Web cache optimization with nonlinear model using object feature. *Computer Networks Journal, 43*(6), 805-817.

Kostaras, N., & Xenos, M. (2007, May). Assessing educational web-site usability using heuristic evaluation rules. In *Proceedings of 11th Panhellenic Conference in Informatics*, (pp. 543-550).

Kreitzberg, C. (1998). *The LUCID Design Framework (Logical User-Centered Interaction Design)*. Princeton, NJ: Cognetics Corporation.

Krishnamurthy, B., & Rexforrd, J. (2001). *Web Protocols and Practice: HTTP/1.1, Networking Protocols, Caching and Traffic Measurement*. Addison-Wesley.

Kroeger, T. M., Long, D. D. E., & Mogul, J. C. (1997). Exploring the Bounds of Web Latency Reduction from Caching and Pre-fetching. *Proceedings of the USENDC Symposium on Internet Technology and Systems*, (pp. 13-22).

Krug, S. (2005). *Don't make me think: A common sense approach to web usability*. Pearson Education India.

Kumar, C., & Norris, J. B. (2008). A New Approach for a Proxy-level Web Caching Mechanism. *Decision Support Systems, Elsevier, 46*(1), 52–60. doi:10.1016/j.dss.2008.05.001

Kuutti, K. (2010). Defining an object of design by the means of the Cultural-Historical Activity Theory. *Proceedings of the European Academy of Design Conference.*

Kuutti, K. (1995). Activity theory as a potential framework for human-computer interaction research. In *Context and consciousness* (pp. 17–44). Cambridge, MA, USA: Massachusetts Institute of Technology.

Lacity, M. C., & Hirschheim, R. (1993). The information systems outsourcing bandwagon. *Sloan Management Review*, Fall, 74–86.

Lacity, M. C., & Willcocks, L. P. (1998). An Empirical Investigation of Information Technology Sourcing Practices: Lessons from Experience. *Management Information Systems Quarterly, 22*(3), 363–408. doi:10.2307/249670

Lahav, O., & Mioduser, D. (2004). Exploration of unknown spaces by people who are blind using a multi-sensory virtual environment. *Journal of Special Education Technology, 19*, 15–24.

Lahav, O., Schloerb, D. W., & Srinivasan, M. A. (2015). program integrating virtual environment to improve orientation and mobility skills for people who are blind. *Computers & Education, 80*, 1–14. doi:10.1016/j.compedu.2014.08.003 PMID:25284952

Lan, B., Bressan, S., Ooi, B. C., & Tan, K. L. (2000). Rule-Assisted Pre-fetching in Web-Server Caching. In *Proceedings of the 9th International Conference on Information and Knowledge Management.*

Lancioni, R. A., Smith, M. F., & Oliva, T. A. (2000). The Role of the Internet in Supply Chain Management. *Industrial Marketing Management, 29*(1), 45–56. doi:10.1016/S0019-8501(99)00111-X

Lankford, W., & Parsa, F. (1999). Outsourcing: A primer. *Management Decision, 37*(4), 310–316. doi:10.1108/00251749910269357

Lau, J. C., & Chiu, C. C. (2003). Accessibility of low-income workers in Hong Kong. *Cities (London, England), 20*(3), 197–204. doi:10.1016/S0264-2751(03)00013-1

Laycock, S. D., & Day, A. M. (2003). Recent developments and applications of haptic devices. *Computer Graphics Forum, 22*(2), 117–132. doi:10.1111/1467-8659.00654

Laycock, S. D., & Day, A. M. (2007). A survey of haptic rendering techniques. *Computer Graphics Forum, 26*(1), 50–65. doi:10.1111/j.1467-8659.2007.00945.x

Lazar, J. (2005). *Web usability: A user-centered design approach*. Addison-Wesley Longman Publishing Co., Inc.

Lazar, J., Feng, J. H., & Hochheiser, H. (2010). *Research methods in human-computer interaction*. John Wiley and Sons.

Lazarou, D. (2011). Using Cultural-Historical Activity Theory to design and evaluate an educational game in science education. *Journal of Computer Assisted Learning, 27*(5), 424–439. doi:10.1111/j.1365-2729.2011.00410.x

Learning objects, content management, and e-learning. (n.d.). InFerrer, N., & Alfonso, J. (Eds.), *Content management for e-learning* (pp. 43–54). New York, NY: Springer New York.

Lederman, S. J., & Klatzky, R. L. (2009). Haptic perception: A tutorial. *Attention, Perception & Psychophysics, 71*(7), 1439–1459. doi:10.3758/APP.71.7.1439 PMID:19801605

Lee, J., & Clery, S. (2004). Key Trend in Higher Education. *Academic Journal.*

Lee, K., Palsetia, D., Narayanan, R., Patwary, M. D., Agrawal, A., & Choudhary, A. N. (2011). Twitter trending topic classification. *Proceedings of the11th IEEE International Conference on Data Mining Workshops* (pp. 251–258).

Lee, S., & Cho, J. E. (2007). Usability Evaluation of Korean e-Government Portal. *Universal Access in Human-Computer Interaction. Applications and Services: 4th International Conference on Universal Access in Human-Computer Interaction, UAHCI 2007 Held as Part of HCI International 2007Proceedings.*

Lee, H. K., An, B. S., & Kim, E. J. (2009). Adaptive Pre-fetching Scheme Using Web Log Mining in Cluster-Based Web Systems.*IEEE International Conference on Web Services (ICWS)*, (pp. 903-910).

Lee, J.-N., Huynh, M. Q., Kwok, R. C.-W., & Pi, S.-M. (2003). IT outsourcing evolution---: Past, present, and future. *Communications of the ACM*, *46*(5), 84–89. doi:10.1145/769800.769807

Lee, M., Cheung, C., & Chen, Z. (2005). Acceptance of Internet-based learning medium: The role of extrinsic and intrinsic motivation. *Information & Management*, *42*(8), 1095–1104. doi:10.1016/j.im.2003.10.007

Leeman, J. A. (2010). *Supply Chain Management: Fast, flexible Supply Chains in Manufacturing and Retailing* (1st ed.). Books on Demand.

Lee, R. M., & Rid, T. (2014). OMG Cyber! Thirteen Reasons Why Hype Makes for Bad Policy. *The RUSI Journal*, *159*(5), 4–12. doi:10.1080/03071847.2014.969932

Lee, Y., & Larsen, K. R. (2009). Threat or coping appraisal: Determinants of SMB executives decision to adopt anti-malware software. *European Journal of Information Systems*, *18*(2), 177–187. doi:10.1057/ejis.2009.11

Lefeuvre, D., Pavillon, G., Aouba, A., Lamarche-Vadel, A., Fouillet, A., Jougla, E., & Rey, G. (2014). Quality comparison of electronic versus paper death certificates in France, 2010. *Population Health Metrics*, *12*(1), 1–9. doi:10.1186/1478-7954-12-3 PMID:24533639

Leventhal, H. (1970). Findings and theory in the study of fear communications. *Advances in Experimental Social Psychology*, *5*, 119–186. doi:10.1016/S0065-2601(08)60091-X

Lewis, J. R. (2002). Psychometric evaluation of the PSSUQ using data from five years of usability studies. *International Journal of Human-Computer Interaction*, *14*(3-4), 463–488. doi:10.1080/10447318.2002.9669130

Lhuer, X., Olanrewaju, T., & Yeon, H. (2015). What it takes to deliver breakthrough customer experiences. *McKinsey*. Retrieved from www.mckinsey.com

Liao, Y. W., Huang, Y. M., Chen, H. C., & Huang, S. H. (2015). Exploring the antecedents of collaborative learning performance over social networking sites in a ubiquitous learning context. *Computers in Human Behavior*, *43*, 313–323. doi:10.1016/j.chb.2014.10.028

Liaw, S. S., & Huang, H. M. (2003). An investigation of user attitudes toward search engines as an information retrieval tool. *Computers in Human Behavior*, *19*(6), 751–765. doi:10.1016/S0747-5632(03)00009-8

Liccardi, I., Ounnas, A., Pau, R., Massey, E., Kinnunen, P., Lewthwaite, S., & Sarkar, C. et al. (2007). The role of social networks in students' learning experiences. In *ITiCSE-WGR '07: Working Group Reports on ITiCSE on Innovation and Technology in Computer Science Education* (pp. 224–237). New York, NY, USA: ACM. doi:10.1145/1345443.1345442

Limbourg, Q., Vanderdonckt, J., Michotte, B., Bouillon, L., & Lopez-Jaquero, V. UsiXML: a language Supporting Multi-Path Development of User Interfaces. *Proc. EHCI-DSVIS '04*. doi:10.1007/11431879_12

Lim, K. L., Yeong, L. S., Seng, K. P., & Ang, L. (2015). Assistive Navigation Systems for the Visually Impaired. In M. Khosrow-Pour (Ed.), *Encyclopedia of Information Science and Technology* (3rd ed.; pp. 315–327). doi:10.4018/978-1-4666-5888-2.ch030

Lindstedt, C., & Naurin, D. (2010). Transparency is not enough: Making transparency effective in reducing corruption. *International Political Science Review*, *31*(3), 301–322. doi:10.1177/0192512110377602

Line, M. B., Zand, A., Stringhini, G., & Kemmerer, R. (2014). Targeted attacks against industrial control systems: Is the power industry prepared? In *Proceedings of the 2nd Workshop on Smart Energy Grid Security* (pp. 13-22). ACM. doi:10.1145/2667190.2667192

Lin, G., Fu, D., Zhu, J., & Dasmalchi, G. (2009). Cloud Computing: IT as a Service. *IT Professional*, 11(2), 10–13.

Lin, H. F., & Lee, G. C. (2006). Determinants of success for online communities: An empirical study. *Behaviour & Information Technology*, *25*(6), 479–488. doi:10.1080/01449290500330422

Liu, Q. (2009). *Web Latency Reduction with Pre-fetching* (Ph.D Thesis). University of Western Ontario, London, Canada.

Liu, K. (2000). *Semiotics in information systems engineering*. Cambridge UP. doi:10.1017/CBO9780511543364

Liu, S., Forrest, J., & Yang, Y. (2012). A brief introduction to grey systems theory. Grey Systems. *Theory and Application*, *2*(2), 89–104.

Logistics Blog (2015). Difference between Intermodal shipping and Multimodal shipping.

Logistics Blog. (2015). *Difference between Intermodal shipping and Multimodal shipping*. Retrieved from http://logisticsportal.org/community/blogs/-/blogs/difference-between-intermodal-shipping-and-multimodal-shipping

Lomas, N. (2015, June 30). Amazon takes prime now outside U.S., opens one-hour delivery in London. Retrieved from www.techcrunch.com

Loon, T. S., & Bharghavan, V. (1997). Alleviating the Latency and Bandwidth Problems in WWW Browsing. In *Proceedings of the USENIX Symposium on Internet Technologies and Systems (USITS)*.

Lotery, A., Xu, X., Zlatava, G., & Loftus, J. (2007). Burden of illness, visual impairment and health resource utilisation of patients with neovascular age- related macular degeneration: Results from the UK cohort of a five-country cross-sectional study. *The British Journal of Ophthalmology*, *91*(10), 1303–1307. doi:10.1136/bjo.2007.116939 PMID:17504847

Lupu, D., & Lazăr, C. G. (2015). Influence of e-government on the Level of Corruption in some EU and Non-EU States. *Procedia Economics and Finance*, *20*, 365–371. doi:10.1016/S2212-5671(15)00085-4

Lu, T. H. (2003). Using ACME (Automatic Classification of Medical Entry) software to monitor and improve the quality of cause of death statistics. *Journal of Epidemiology and Community Health*, *5*(6), 470–471. doi:10.1136/jech.57.6.470 PMID:12775799

Lu, T. H., Lee, M. C., & Chou, M. C. (2000). Accuracy of cause-of-death coding in Taiwan: Types of miscoding and effects on mortality statistics. *International Journal of Epidemiology*, *29*(2), 336–343. doi:10.1093/ije/29.2.336 PMID:10817134

Maâtallah, M., & Seridi, H. (2012a). Enhanced collaborative filtering to recommender systems of technology enhanced learning. *Proceedings of ICWIT*, *2012*, 129–138.

Maâtallah, M., & Seridi, H. (2012a). Enhanced collaborative filtering to recommender systems of technology enhanced learning.*Proceedings of ICWIT'12* (pp. 129–138).

Maâtallah, M., & Seridi, H. (2012b). Multi-context recommendation in technology enhanced learning. *Proceedings of ITS, 2012*, 720–721.

Maâtallah, M., & Seridi, H. (2012b). Multi-context recommendation in technology enhanced learning.*Proceedings of ITS'12* (pp. 720–721).

MacCallum, R. C., Wegener, D. T., Uchino, B. N., & Fabrigar, L. R. (1993). The problem of equivalent models in applications of covariance structure analysis. *Journal of Psychological Bulletin, 114*(1), 185–199. doi:10.1037/0033-2909.114.1.185 PMID:8346326

Mack, R. L., & Nielsen, J. (Eds.). (1994). *Usability inspection methods.* New York, NY: Wiley & Sons.

Macleod, M., Bowden, R., Bevan, N., & Curson, I. (1997). The MUSiC performance measurement method. *Behaviour & Information Technology, 16*(4-5), 279–293. doi:10.1080/014492997119842

Macleod, M., & Rengger, R. (1993). *The development of DRUM: A software tool for video-assisted usability evaluation.* People and Computers.

Mahapatra, P., Shibuya, K., Lopez, A. D., Coullare, F., Notzon, F. C., Rao, C., & Szreter, S. (2007). Civil registration systems and vital statistics: Successes and missed opportunities. *Lancet, 370*(9599), 1653–1663. doi:10.1016/S0140-6736(07)61308-7 PMID:18029006

Mahatody, T., Sagar, M., & Kolski, C. (2010). State of the Art on the Cognitive Walkthrough Method, Its Variants and Evolutions. *International Journal of Human-Computer Interaction, 26*(8), 741–785. doi:10.1080/10447311003781409

Mahoney, J. H. (1985). Intermodal Freight Transportation. Westport, Connecticut: Eno Foundation for transportation.

Maier, R. (2007). *Knowledge Management Systems: Information and Communication Technologies: Information and Communication Technologies for Knowledge Management.* Springer.

Markatos, E. P., & Chronaki, C. E. (1998). A Top-10 Approach to Pre fetching on the Web. In *Proceedings of INET*.

Marlow, C., Naaman, M., Boyd, D., & Davis, M. (2006). HT06, tagging paper, taxonomy, Flickr, academic article, to read. In *Hypertext and Hypermedia* (pp. 31–40).

Marshall, A., Medvedev, O., & Antonov, A. (2008). Use of a smartphone for improved self-management of pulmonary rehabilitation. *International Journal of Telemedicine and Applications, 2008*, 2. doi:10.1155/2008/753064 PMID:18615186

Martensen, A., & Gronholdt, L. (2003). Improving library users perceived quality, satisfaction and locality: An integrated measurement and management system. *Journal of Academic Librarianship, 19*(3), 140–147. doi:10.1016/S0099-1333(03)00020-X

Martins, A. I., Queirós, A., Cerqueira, M., Rocha, N., & Teixeira, A. (2012). The International Classification of Functioning, Disability and Health as a conceptual model for the evaluation of environmental factors. *Procedia Computer Science, 14*, 293–300. doi:10.1016/j.procs.2012.10.033

Martins, A. I., Rosa, A. F., Queirós, A., Silva, A., & Rocha, N. P. (2015). Definition and Validation of the ICF-Usability Scale. *Procedia Computer Science, 67*, 132–139. doi:10.1016/j.procs.2015.09.257

Mathers, C. D., Ma Fat, D., Inoue, M., Rao, C., & Lopez, A. D. (2005). Counting the dead and what they died from: An assessment of the global status of cause of death data. *Bulletin of the World Health Organization, 83*(3), 171–177. PMID:15798840

Maudsley, G., & Williams, L. (1994). Death certification—a sad state of affairs. *Journal of Public Health, 16*(3), 370–371. PMID:7999397

McAfee. (2011). *Global Energy Cyberattacks: "Night Dragon", McAfee Found stone Professional Services and McAfee Labs, Feb. 10, 2011*. Retrieved July 25, 2015 from, http://www.mcafee.com/in/resources/white-papers/wp-global-energy-cyberattacks-night-dragon.pdf

McLaughlin, M. L., Hespanha, J. P., & Sukhatme, G. S. (2002). *Touch in virtual environments*. Prentice Hall.

Mclellan, S., Muddimer, A., & Peres, S. C. (2012). The Effect of Experience on System Usability Scale Ratings. *Journal of Usability Studies, 7*(2), 56–67.

McQuivey, J. (2013). *Digital Disruption: Unleashing the Next Wave of Innovation*. Amazon publishing.

Mehrdad, J. (2008). Web User Navigation Pattern Mining Approach Based on Graph Partitioning Algorithm. *Journal of Theoretical and Applied Information Technology*.

Mejía-Figueroa, A., de los Ángeles Quezada Cisnero, M., Reyes Juárez-Ramírez, J. (2016). Developing Usable Software Applications for Users with Autism: User Analysis, User Interface Design Patterns and Interface Components. *Proceedings of the 2016 4th International Conference in Software Engineering Research and Innovation (CONISOFT)*. IEEE.

Melville, P., Mooney, R. J., & Nagarajan, R. (2002). Content-boosted collaborative filtering for improved recommendations. *Proceedings of theEighteenth National Conference on Artificial Intelligence* (pp. 187–192). Menlo Park, CA, USA: American Association for Artificial Intelligence.

Melville, P., Mooney, R. J., & Nagarajan, R. (2002). Content-boosted collaborative filtering for improved recommendations. *Proceedings of theEighteenth National Conference on Artificial Intelligence*.

Memon, M., Wagner, S. R., Pedersen, C. F., Beevi, F. H. A., & Hansen, F. O. (2014). Ambient assisted living healthcare frameworks, platforms, standards, and quality attributes. *Sensors (Basel, Switzerland), 14*(3), 4312–4341. doi:10.3390/s140304312 PMID:24599192

Mercier, P., Jacobsen, R., & Veitch, A. (2012). 'The New, Customer-Centric Retail Model. Retail 2020'. Boston Consulting Group. Retrieved from www.bcg.com

MetaPack. (2015). *Delivering Consumer Choice: 2015 State of eCommerce Delivery*. Retrieved from www.metapack.com

Miaskiewicz, T., & Kozar, K. A. (2011). Personas and user-centered design: How can personas benefit product design processes? *Design Studies, 32*(5), 417–430. doi:10.1016/j.destud.2011.03.003

Microsoft. (2011, May 17). Microsoft Case Studies. Retrieved from http://www.microsoft.com/casestudies/Microsoft-Exchange-Server-2007-Enterprise-Edition/United-Arab-Emirates-University/University-Enhances-Messaging-While-Saving-IT-Time-and-Cutting-Storage-Costs/4000009662

Ministry of Communications and Information Technology (Saudi Arabia). (2016, February 28). Saudi firms explore cloud computing to reduce costs: IDC. Retrieved from http://www.mcit.gov.sa/En/InformationTechnology/Pages/SubjectsandInformation/Tech-Subject-10032013_169.aspx

Ministry of Foreign Affairs Saudi Arabia. (2016). Retrieved April 14, 2016 from http://www.mofa.gov.sa

Ministry of Higher Education. (2014). *Higher Education in Saudi Arabia in numbers*. Riyadh: Ministry of Higher Education.

Ministry of Interior Saudi Arabia. (2016). Retrieved April 14, 2016 from https://www.moi.gov.sa

Mint. (2016). *The complete picture in one minute*. Retrieved from https://www.mint.com/how-mint-works

Mistry, J. J., & Jalal, A. (2012). An empirical analysis of the relationship between e-government and corruption. *The International Journal Of Digital Accounting Research, 12*(18), 145–176.

Mobasher, B., Cooley, R., & Srivastava, J. (2000). Automatic Personalization Based on Web Usage Mining. *Communications of the ACM*, *43*(8), 142–151. doi:10.1145/345124.345169

Mobasher, B., Dai, H., Luo, T., & Nakagawa, M. (2002). Discovery and Evaluation of Aggregate Usage Profiles for Web Personalization. *Data Mining and Knowledge Discovery*, *6*(1), 61–82. doi:10.1023/A:1013232803866

Mohammad, A. S., & Sriram, B. (2015). Major challenges in developing a successful e-government: A review on the Sultanate of Oman. *Journal of King Saud University Computer and Information Sciences, 27*(2), 230-235.

Mohammadi, H. (2015). Investigating users perspectives on e-learning: An integration of TAM and IS success model. *Computers in Human Behavior*, *45*, 359–374. doi:10.1016/j.chb.2014.07.044

Mohammed, U. (2013). Corruption in Nigeria: A Challenge to Sustainable Development. *European Scientific Journal*, *9*(4), 118–137.

Mo, P. H. (2001). Corruption and economic growth. *Journal of Comparative Economics*, *29*(1), 66–79. doi:10.1006/jcec.2000.1703

Morrison, P. J. (2008). Tagging and searching: Search retrieval effectiveness of folksonomies on the World Wide Web. *Information Processing & Management*, *44*(4), 1562–1579. doi:10.1016/j.ipm.2007.12.010

Mosa, A. S. M., Yoo, I., & Sheets, L. (2012). A systematic review of healthcare applications for smartphones. *BMC Medical Informatics and Decision Making*, *12*(1), 1. doi:10.1186/1472-6947-12-67 PMID:22781312

Mou, J., Shin, D. H., & Cohen, J. (2016). Understanding trust and perceived usefulness in the consumer acceptance of an e-service: A longitudinal investigation. *Behaviour & Information Technology*, 1–15. doi:10.1080/0144929X.2016.1203024

Mundy, D., & Musa, B. (2010). Towards a framework for egovernment development in Nigeria. *Electronic. Journal of E-Government*, *8*(2), 148–161.

Mutikanga, H. E. (2012). Water loss management: tools and methods for developing countries. TU Delft, Delft University of Technology.

Mwanza, D. (2001). Where theory meets practice: A case for an Activity Theory based methodology to guide computer system design.*Proceedings of INTERACT' 2001: Eighth IFIP TC 13 Conference on Human-Computer Interaction*, Tokyo, Japan.

Myers, K. A., & Farquhar, D. R. (1998). Improving the accuracy of death certification. *Canadian Medical Association Journal*, *158*(10), 1317–1323. PMID:9614825

Nagpal, R., Mehrotra, D., Bhatia, P. K., & Sharma, A. (2015). Rank University Websites Using Fuzzy AHP and Fuzzy TOPSIS Approach on Usability. *International Journal of Information Engineering and Electronic Business, 7*(1), 29.

Nagpal, R., Mehrotra, D., Sharma, A., & Bhatia, P. (2013). ANFIS method for usability assessment of website of an educational institute. *World Applied Sciences Journal*, *23*(11), 1489–1498.

Nandyala, C. S., & Kim, H.-K. (2016). Green IoT Agriculture and Healthcare Application (GAHA). *International Journal of Smart Home*, *10*(4), 289–300. doi:10.14257/ijsh.2016.10.4.26

Nanopoulos, A., Katsaros, D., & Manolopoulos, Y. (2003). A Data Mining Algorithm for Generalized Web Pre-fetching. *IEEE Transactions on Knowledge and Data Engineering*, *15*(5), 1155–1169. doi:10.1109/TKDE.2003.1232270

Nashique, N. (2015). *Cyber Crime Bangladesh*. Retrieved September 16, from http://www.thefinancialexpress-bd.com/2015/02/17/81536/print

Nassuora, A. B. (2012). Students acceptance of mobile learning for higher education in Saudi Arabia. *American Academic & Scholarly Research Journal, 4*(2), 1.

Navin, K., Tyagi, & Solanki, A.K. (2011). Analysis of Server Log by Web Usage Mining for Website Improvement. *International Journal of Computer Science Issues, 7*(4).

Ndou, V. (2004). E-government for developing countries: Opportunities and challenges. *The Electronic Journal of Information Systems in Developing Countries, 18*(1), 1–24.

Ndou, V. (2004). E-government for developing countries: Opportunities and challenges. *The Electronic Journal on Information Systems in Developing Countries, 18*(1), 1–24.

NIC, National Intelligence Council. (2008). Disruptive Civil Technologies: Six technologies with potential impacts on US Interests out to 2025. *Conference Report Disruptive Civil Technologies*. Menlo Park, CA: National Intelligence Council. Retrieved July 1, 2016, from http://fas.org/irp/nic/disruptive.pdf

Nielsen, A. C. (2005). Online banking continues despite security concerns. *ACNielsen*. Retrieved from http://www.acnielsen.com.au/news.asp?newsID=301

Nielsen, J. (1993). Usability Engineering. Academic Press.

Nielsen, J. (1995). *10 Usability heuristics for user interface design*. Retrieved from https://www.nngroup.com/articles/ten-usability-heuristics/

Nielsen, J. (2000). *Designing for the Web*. Available at: http://ssltest.cs.umd.edu/class/spring2012/cmsc434-0101/Notes11-WebDesign.pdf

Nojilana, B., Brewer, L., Bradshaw, D., Groenewald, P., Burger, E. H., & Levitt, N. S. (2013). Certification of diabetes-related mortality: The need for an international guideline. *Journal of Clinical Epidemiology, 66*(2), 236–237. doi:10.1016/j.jclinepi.2012.07.017 PMID:23159105

Nordenfelt, L. (2003). Action theory, disability and ICF. *Disability and Rehabilitation, 25*(18), 1075–1079. doi:10.1080/0963828031000137748 PMID:12944163

Nov, O., & Ye, C. (2008). What Drives Content Tagging : The Case of Photos on Flickr.*Proceeding of the twenty-sixth annual SIGCHI conference on Human factors in computing systems,*Florence (pp. 1–4). . doi:10.1145/1357054.1357225

O'Hara, C. (2016, June). The Role of the Agency in Data Management. *eConsultancy*.

Obadare, E. (2005). A crisis of trust: History, politics, religion and the polio controversy in Northern Nigeria. *Patterns of Prejudice, 39*(3), 265–284. doi:10.1080/00313220500198185

OECD. (2002). *Supply Chains and the OECD Guidelines for Multinational Enterprises*, 2002. Retrieved from http://www.oecd.org/investment/mne/45534720.pdf

Oehlert, G. (2000). *A First Course in Design and Analysis of Experiments*. New York: Freeman and Company.

Ogbeidi, M. M. (2012). Political Leadership and Corruption in Nigeria Since 1960: A Socioeconomic Analysis. *Journal of Nigeria Studies, 1*(2), 1–25.

Okunola, O. M. (2015). *Users' experience of e-government services: a case study based on the Nigeria immigration service* [Unpublished doctoral thesis]. Manchester Metropolitan University, Manchester, England.

Olatokun, W. M., & Adebayo, B. M. (2012). Assessing E-Government Implementation in Ekiti State, Nigeria. *Journal of Emerging Trends in Computing and Information Sciences, 3*(4), 499–505.

Olawale, F. (2014). The Causes of the Failure of New Small and Medium Enterprises in South Africa. *Mediterranean Journal of Social Sciences MCSER Publishing*, *5*(20), 922.

Oliveira, A. S. D. (2006). *Acessibilidade espacial em centro cultural: Estudos de caso* (Unpublished Master Thesis). Federal University of Santa Catarina, Santa Catarina, Brazil.

Oliveira, A., & Campolargo, M. (2015). From Smart Cities to Human Smart Cities. In *(HICSS) 48th Hawaii International Conference on System Sciences* (pp. 2336-2344). doi:10.1109/HICSS.2015.281

Oliver, R. L. (1980). A Cognitive Model for the Antece- dents and Consequences of Satisfaction. *Journal of Marketing Research*, *17*, 460-469.

Oluwatobi, S. O., & Ogunrinola, I. O. (2011). Government expenditure on human capital development: Implications for economic growth in Nigeria. *Journal of Sustainable Development*, *4*(3), 72–80. doi:10.5539/jsd.v4n3p72

Omeire, E., & Omeire, C. (2014). New Wine in Old Wine Skin: An Exploration of Major Constraints to E-Government Implementation in Nigeria. *European Scientific Journal*, *10*(14), 481–487.

Orumie, U. C., & Ebong, D. (2014). A Glorious Literature on Linear Goal Programming Algorithms. *American Journal of Operations Research*, *4*(02), 59–71. doi:10.4236/ajor.2014.42007

Overton, R. (2007). *Feasibility Studies Made Simple*. Martin Books.

Özceylan, E. (2010). A Decision Support System to Compare the Transportation Modes in Logistics. *International Journal of Lean Thinking*, *1*(1), 58–83.

Padmanabhan, V. N., & Mogul, J. C. (1996). Using Predictive Pre-fetching to Improve World Wide Web Latency. *ACM Computer Communication Review*, *26*(3), 23–36. doi:10.1145/235160.235164

Pallis, G., Vakali, A., & Pokorny, J. (2008). A Clustering-Based Pre-Fetching Scheme on A Web Cache Environment. ACM Journal Computers and Electrical Engineering, 34(4).

Palpanas, T., & Mendelzon, A. (1999). Web Pre-fetching using Partial Match Prediction. In *Proceedings of the 4th International Web Caching Workshop*.

Paola, B. (2007). Web Usage Mining Using Self Organized Maps. *International Journal of Computer Science and Network Security*, *7*(6).

Parasuraman, A., Zeithamal, V., & Berry, L. (1988). SERVQUAL: A multiple-item scale for measuring consumer perceptions of service quality. *Journal of Retailing*, *64*(1), 12–40.

Parasuraman, A., Zeithamal, V., & Berry, L. (1988). SERVQUAL: A multiple-item scale for measuring consumer perceptions of service quality. *Journal of Retailing*, *64*(1), 12–40.

Parikh, K. (2014). *Revolutionizing Customer Experience Through SMAC: The New Technology Foundation*. Avasant.

Park, E., & Kim, K. J. (2014). An integrated adoption model of mobile cloud services: Exploration of key determinants and extension of technology acceptance model. *Telematics and Informatics*, *31*(3), 376–385. doi:10.1016/j.tele.2013.11.008

Park, H., & Blenkinsopp, J. (2011). The roles of transparency and trust in the relationship between corruption and citizen satisfaction. *International Review of Administrative Sciences*, *77*(2), 254–274. doi:10.1177/0020852311399230

Pascolini, D., & Mariotti, S. P. (2011). Global estimates of visual impairment: 2010. *British Journal of Ophthalmology*.

Patton, M. (1990). *Qualitative evaluation and research methods*. Thousand Oaks, CA: Sage Publications.

Pei, C., & Irani, S. (1997). Cost-Aware WWW Proxy Caching Algorithms. In *Proceedings of the USENIX Symposium on Internet Technologies and Systems*, (pp. 193-206).

Peirce, C. D. (1960). *Collected Papers of Charles Sanders Peirce* (C. Hartshorne, P. Weiss, & A. W. Burks, Eds.). Harvard University Press.

Peissner, M. et al. MyUI: generating accessible user interfaces from multimodal design patterns. *Proceedings of the 4th ACM SIGCHI symposium on Engineering interactive computing systems*. ACM. doi:10.1145/2305484.2305500

Perlroth, N. (2012, October 23). In Cyberattack on Saudi Firm, US sees Iran firing back. *New York Times*.

Peters, I., & Becker, P. (2009). *Folksonomies: Indexing and Retrieval in Web 2.0*. De Gruyter/Saur. doi:10.1515/9783598441851

Phillips. (2012). *How the cloud will change accounting forever*. Retrieved from accountantsone.com/jobseekers/Cloud-Computing.pdf

Pinelle, D., & Gutwin, C. 2002. Groupware Walkthrough: Adding Context to Groupware Usability Evaluation. In *Proceedings of the SIGCHI conference on Human factors in computing systems* (pp. 455–462). doi:10.1145/503376.503458

Pissaloux, E., Velazquez, R., Hersh, M., & Uzan, G. (2016). Towards a cognitive model of human mobility: An investigation of tactile perception for use in mobility devices. *Journal of Navigation*, *1*, 1–17. doi:10.1017/S0373463316000461

Pitkow, J., & Pirolli, P. (1999). Mining Longest Repeating Subsequences to Predict World Wide Web Surfing.*Proceedings USENIX Symposium on Internet Technologies and Systems* (USITS).

Podlipnig, S., & Boszormenyi, L. (2003). A Survey of Web Cache Replacement Strategies. *ACM Computing Surveys*, *35*(4), 374–398. doi:10.1145/954339.954341

Podsakoff, P. M., MacKenzie, S. B., Lee, J. Y., & Podsakoff, N. P. (2003). Common method biases in behavioral research: A critical review of the literature and recommended remedies. *The Journal of Applied Psychology*, *88*(5), 879–903. doi:10.1037/0021-9010.88.5.879 PMID:14516251

Podsakoff, P. M., & Organ, D. W. (1986). Self-reports in organizational research: Problems and prospects. *Journal of Management*, *12*(4), 531–544. doi:10.1177/014920638601200408

Podsakoff, P. M., & Todor, W. D. (1985). Relationships between leader reward and punishment behavior and group processes and productivity. *Journal of Management*, *11*(1), 55–73. doi:10.1177/014920638501100106

Pollara, P., & Zhu, J. (2011). Social networking and education: Using Facebook as an edusocial space. *Proceedings of Society for Information Technology & Teacher Education International Conference*, *2011*, 3330–3338.

Pomerol, J. C., & Romero, S. B. (2000). *Multicriteria Decision in Management: Principle and Practice*. Kluwer Academic Publishers. doi:10.1007/978-1-4615-4459-3

Poster, W. (2007). Whos On the Line? Indian Call Center Agents Pose as Americans for U.S.-Outsourced Firms. *Industrial Relations*, *46*(2), 271–304. doi:10.1111/j.1468-232X.2007.00468.x

Power, M., Bonifazi, C., & Desouza, K. C. (2004). The ten outsourcing traps to avoid. *The Journal of Business Strategy*, *25*(2), 37–42. doi:10.1108/02756660410525399

Preece, J. (1994). *Human–Computer Interaction*. Reading, MA: Addison-Wesley.

Price Waterhouse Coopers. (2016, February). Total Retail 2016. They say they want a revolution.

Profita, H., Farrow, N., & Correll, N. (2015). Flutter: An Exploration of an Assistive Garment Using Distributed Sensing, Computation and Actuation. In *Proceedings of the Ninth International Conference on Tangible, Embedded, and Embodied Interaction* (pp. 359-362). ACM. doi:10.1145/2677199.2680586

Qin, X., Huang, G., Chakma, A., Nie, X., & Lin, Q. (2008). A MCDM-based expert system for climate-change impact assessment and adaptation planning – A case study for the Georgia Basin, Canada. *Expert Systems with Applications*, *34*(3), 2164–2179. doi:10.1016/j.eswa.2007.02.024

Queirós, A., Carvalho, S., Pavão, J., & Rocha, N. (2013). AAL information based services and care integration. In *International Conference on Health Informatics - HealthInf 2013* (pp. 403-406). Barcelona: INSTICC.

Queirós, A., Cerqueira, M., Martins, A. I., Silva, A. G., Alvarelhão, J., & Rocha, N. P. (2014). Personas and Scenarios Based on Functioning and Health Conditions. In S. Saeed, I. S. Bajwa, & Z. Mahmood (Eds.), *Human Factors in Software Development and Design* (pp. 274–294). Hershey, PA: IGI Global.

Queirós, A., Silva, A., Alvarelhão, J., Rocha, N. P., & Teixeira, A. (2015). Usability, accessibility and ambient-assisted living: A systematic literature review. *Universal Access in the Information Society*, *14*(1), 57–66. doi:10.1007/s10209-013-0328-x

Quélin, B., & Duhamel, F. (2003). Bringing Together Strategic Outsourcing and Corporate Strategy: Outsourcing Motives and Risks. *European Management Journal*, *21*(5), 647–661. doi:10.1016/S0263-2373(03)00113-0

Quinn, J. B., & Hilmer, F. G. (1994). Strategic Outsourcing. *Sloan Management Review*, Summer, 43–55.

Rabbany, R., Takaffoli, M., & Zaïane, O. R. (2011). Social network analysis and mining to support the assessment of on-line student participation. *SIGKDD Explorations*, *13*(2), 20–29. doi:10.1145/2207243.2207247

Rahimi, K., Duncan, M., Pitcher, A., Emdin, C. A., & Goldacre, M. J. (2015). Mortality from heart failure, acute myocardial infarction and other ischaemic heart disease in England and Oxford: A trend study of multiple-cause-coded death certification. *Journal of Epidemiology and Community Health*, *69*(10), 1000–1005. doi:10.1136/jech-2015-205689 PMID:26136081

Ramirez, A. R. G., da Silva, R. F. L., Cinelli, M. J., & Albornoz, A. D. C. (2012). Evaluation of Electronic Haptic Device for Blind and Visually Impaired People: A Case Study. *Journal of Medical and Biological Engineering*, *32*(6), 423–428. doi:10.5405/jmbe.925

Rana, N. P., Dwivedi, Y. K., Williams, M. D., & Weerakkody, V. (2015). Investigating success of an e-government initiative: Validation of an integrated IS success model. *Information Systems Frontiers*, *17*(1), 127–142. doi:10.1007/s10796-014-9504-7

Rangarajan, S. K., Phoha, V. V., Balagani, K., Selmic, R. R., & Iyengar, S. S. (2004). *Web User Clustering and its Application to Pre-fetching using ART Neural Networks*. IEEE Computer.

Rauniar, R., Rawski, G., Yang, J., & Johnson, B. (2014). Technology acceptance model (TAM) and social media usage: An empirical study on Facebook. *Journal of Enterprise Information Management*, *27*(1), 6–30. doi:10.1108/JEIM-04-2012-0011

Rauterberg, M. (2003). *User Centered Design: What, Why, and When*. Retrieved from http://www.idemployee.id.tue.nl/g.w.m.rauterberg/publications/tekom03paper.pdf

Reddick, C. G. (2005). Citizen interaction with e-government: From the streets to servers? *Government Information Quarterly*, *22*(1), 38–57. doi:10.1016/j.giq.2004.10.003

Redish, J. (1995). Are we really entering a post-usability era? *ACM SIGDOC Asterisk Journal of Computer Documentation*, *19*(1), 18–24. doi:10.1145/203586.203590

Relyea, H. C. (2009). Federal freedom of information policy: Highlights of recent developments. *Government Information Quarterly*, *26*(2), 314–320. doi:10.1016/j.giq.2008.12.001

Reza K. M., & Sadegheh H. N. (2016). Investigating the Effectiveness of E-government Establishment in Government Organizations. *Procedia Social and Behavioural Sciences, 230,* 136-141.

Rezaei, J. (2015). Best-worst multi-criteria decision-making method. *Omega, 53*, 49–57. doi:10.1016/j.omega.2014.11.009

Rigsbee, S., & Fitzpatrick, W. B. (2012). User-Centered Design: A Case Study on Its Application to the Tactical Tomahawk Weapons Control System. *Johns Hopkins APL Technical Digest, 31*(1). Retrieved from http://www.jhuapl.edu/techdigest/td/td3101/31_01_Rigsbee.pdf

Ringle, C. M., Wende, S., & Becker, J. M. (2014). *Smartpls 3*. Hamburg, Germany: SmartPLS.

Rizzo, A., Marchigiani, E., & Andreadis, A. (1997). The AVANTI project: prototyping and evaluation with a cognitive walkthrough based on the Norman's model of action. In *Proceedings of the 2nd conference on Designing interactive systems: processes, practices, methods, and techniques*. ACM. doi:10.1145/263552.263629

Roberts, N., & Grover, V. (2009). Theory development in information systems research using structural equation modeling: Evaluation and recommendations. In Handbook of Research on Contemporary Theoretical Models in Information Systems. Academic Press.

Robinson, A. (2015). The Transportation Supply Chain: Transportation's Role in Supply Chain Management to Lower Total Costs. *Supply Chain Transportation Management*. Retrieved from http://cerasis.com/2015/05/21/transportation-supply-chain/

Rodrigue, J.-P., Comtois, C., & Slack, B. (2013). *The Geography of Transport Systems. 3 edition*. Routledge.

Rodriguez, S. R., Mallonee, S., Archer, P., & Gofton, J. (2006). Evaluation of death certificate-based surveillance for traumatic brain injury – Oklahoma 2002. *Public Health Reports*, *121*(3), 282–289. PMID:16640151

Rogers, R. W. (1983). Cognitive and physiological processes in fear appeals and attitude change: A revised theory of protection motivation. *Social Psychophysiology*, 153-176.

Rönkkö, K. (2005). *Making methods work in software engineering: Method deployment as a social achievement*. Ronneby: School of Engineering, Blekinge Institute of Technology.

Rorissa, A., & Demissie, D. (2010). An analysis of African e-Government service websites. *Government Information Quarterly*, *27*(2), 161–169. doi:10.1016/j.giq.2009.12.003

Rosenblum, P. & Rowen, S. (2015, January). *Mobile Retail Finds New Purpose*. RSR (Retail Systems Research).

Rose, R. F., Boon, A., Forman, D., Merchant, W., Bishop, R., & Newton-Bishop, J. A. (2013). An exploration of reported mortality from cutaneous squamous cell carcinoma using death certification and cancer registry data. *The British Journal of Dermatology*, *169*(3), 682–686. doi:10.1111/bjd.12388 PMID:23600487

Rosser, B. A., & Eccleston, C. (2011). Smartphone applications for pain management. *Journal of Telemedicine and Telecare*, *17*(6), 308–312. doi:10.1258/jtt.2011.101102 PMID:21844177

Rosson, M. B., & Carroll, J. M. (2002). Scenario-based design. Academic Press.

Rosson, M. B., & Carroll, J. M. (2009). Scenario based design. In J. Jacko & A. Sears (Eds.), *The Human-Computer Interaction Handbook: Fundamentals, Evolving Technologies and Emerging Applications* (pp. 1032–1050). Boca Raton, FL: Lawrence Erlbaum Associates. doi:10.1201/9781420088892.ch8

Rosson, M., & Carroll, J. (2001). *Usability Engineering*. San Francisco: Morgan Kaufmann.

Roy, B. (1991). The outranking approach and the foundations of ELECTRE methods. *Theory and Decision, 31*(1), 49–73. doi:10.1007/BF00134132

Russell, D. (2002). Looking beyond the interface: Activity theory and distributed learning. In *Distributed learning: social and cultural approaches to practice*. Routledge Falme.

Ryu, H., & Monk, A. F. (2004). Analysing interaction problems with cyclic interaction theory: Low-level interaction walkthrough. *PsychNology Journal, 2*(3), 304–330.

Saaty, T. L. (2001). Decision Making with the Analytic Network Process (ANP) and Its "Super Decisions" Software: The National Missile Defense (NMD) Example. ISAHP 2001 Proceedings.

Saaty, T. L. (2008). Decision making with the analytic hierarchy process. *International Journal of Services Sciences, 1*(1), 83-98.

Saaty, T. L. (1990). How to make a decision: The analytic hierarchy process. *European Journal of Operational Research, 48*(1), 9–26. doi:10.1016/0377-2217(90)90057-I

Saeed, S. (2014). Human Factors in Software Development and Design. IGI Global.

Saeed, S., Reichling, T., & Wulf, V. (2008). Applying Knowledge Management to Support Networking among NGOs and Donors. *Paper presented at theIADIS international conference on E-Society.*

Saeed, S., & Amjad, A. (2013). Understanding usability issues of Pakistani university websites. *Life Science Journal, 10*(6s), 479–482.

Saeed, S., Jamshaid, I., & Sikander, S. (2012). Usability evaluation of hospital websites in Pakistan. *International Journal of Technology Diffusion, 3*(4), 29–35. doi:10.4018/jtd.2012100103

Saeed, S., Malik, I. A., & Wahab, F. (2013). Usability evaluation of Pakistani security agencies websites. *International Journal of E-Politics, 4*(3), 57–69. doi:10.4018/jep.2013070105

Saeed, S., & Rohde, M. (2010). Computer enabled social movements? Usage of a collaborative web platform within the European social forum.*Proc. COOP '10.* doi:10.1007/978-1-84996-211-7_14

Saeed, S., & Shabbir, S. (2014). Website Usability Analysis of Non Profit Organizations: A Case Study of Pakistan. *International Journal of Public Administration in the Digital Age, 1*(4), 70–83. doi:10.4018/ijpada.2014100105

Saeed, S., Wahab, F., Cheema, S. A., & Ashraf, S. (2013). Role of usability in e-government and e-commerce portals: An empirical study of Pakistan. *Life Science Journal, 10*(1), 8–13.

Salisu, M. (2000). Corruption in Nigeria, Lancaster University Management School, Working Paper 2000/006, Department of Economics, Lancaster.

Sánchez, J., de Borba Campos, M., Espinoza, M., & Merabet, L. B. (2014). Audio haptic videogaming for developing wayfinding skills in learners who are blind. In *Proceedings of the 19th international conference on Intelligent User Interfaces* (pp. 199-208). ACM. doi:10.1145/2557500.2557519

Sanchez, L., Galache, J. A., Gutierrez, V., Hernandez, J. M., Bernat, J., Gluhak, A., & Garcia, T. (2011). *Smartsantander: The meeting point between future internet research and experimentation and the smart cities. In Future Network & Mobile Summit* (pp. 1–8). Warsaw: FutureNetw.

Sanchez, R. A., & Hueros, A. D. (2010). Motivational factors that influence the acceptance of Moodle using TAM. *Computers in Human Behavior, 26*(6), 1632–1640. doi:10.1016/j.chb.2010.06.011

Sandeep, S. (2010). Discovering Potential User Browsing Behaviors Using Custom-Built Apriori Algorithm. *International Journal of Computer Science & Information Technology, 2*(4).

Sathiyamoorthi, V., & Murali Bhaskaran, V. (2011b). Data Pre-Processing Techniques for Pre-Fetching and Caching of Web Data through Proxy Server. *International Journal of Computer Science and Network Security, 11*(11), 92-98.

Sathiyamoorthi, V. (2016). A Novel Cache Replacement Policy for Web Proxy Caching System Using Web Usage Mining. *International Journal of Information Technology and Web Engineering, 11*(2), 1–12. doi:10.4018/IJITWE.2016040101

Sathiyamoorthi, V., & Murali Bhaskaran, V. (2010a). Data Preparation Techniques for Mining World Wide Web through Web Usage Mining-An Approach. *International Journal of Recent Trends in Engineering, 2*(4), 1–4.

Sathiyamoorthi, V., & Murali Bhaskaran, V. (2010b). Data mining for intelligent enterprise resource planning system. *International Journal of Recent Trends in Engineering, 2*(3), 1–4.

Sathiyamoorthi, V., & Murali Bhaskaran, V. (2011a). Improving the Performance of Web Page Retrieval through Pre-Fetching and Caching. *European Journal of Scientific Research, 66*(2), 207–217.

Sathiyamoorthi, V., & Murali Bhaskaran, V. (2012). Optimizing the Web Cache performance by Clustering Based Pre-Fetching Technique Using Modified ART1. *International Journal of Computers and Applications, 44*(1), 51–60.

Sathiyamoorthi, V., & Murali Bhaskaran, V. (2013). Novel Approaches for Integrating MART1 Clustering Based Pre-Fetching Technique with Web Caching. *International Journal of Information Technology and Web Engineering, 8*(2), 18–32. doi:10.4018/jitwe.2013040102

Saudi Commission for Tourism & National Heritage. (2016). Retrieved April 14, 2016 from https://www.scta.gov.sa

Schein, A. I., Popescul, A., Ungar, L. H., & Pennock, D. M. (2002). Methods and metrics for cold-start recommendations. *Proceedings of the 25th Annual International ACM SIGIR Conference on Research and Development in Information Retrieval SIGIR '02* (pp. 253–260). New York, NY, USA: ACM. doi:10.1145/564376.564421

Schmidt, V. A. (2010). *User interface design patterns.* Air Force Research Lab Wright-Patterson AFB OH Human Effectiveness Directorate.

Scott, W. R. (2001). *Institutions and organizations.* London: Sage Publications.

Sears, A. (1997). Heuristic walkthroughs: Finding the problems without the noise. *International Journal of Human-Computer Interaction, 9*(3), 213–234. doi:10.1207/s15327590ijhc0903_2

Seffah, A., Donyaee, M., Kline, R. B., & Padda, H. K. (2006). Usability measurement and metrics: A consolidated model. *Software Quality Journal, 14*(2), 159–178. doi:10.1007/s11219-006-7600-8

Senge, P. (1990). *The fifth discipline: The art and practice of the learning organization.* New York: Doubleday/Currency.

SenseGraphics. (2014). *H3D API - Open Source Haptics.* Retrieved December 13, 2014 from http://www.h3dapi.org

Setel, P. W., Macfarlane, S. B., Szreter, S., Mikkelsen, L., Jha, P., Stout, S., & Anderson, R. N. et al. (2007). A scandal of invisibility: Making everyone count by counting everyone. *Lancet, 370*(9598), 1569–1577. doi:10.1016/S0140-6736(07)61307-5 PMID:17992727

Sethunya, R. J. (n.d.). Advantages and disadvantages of E-government implementation: literature review. *International Journal of Marketing and Technology, 5*(9).

Shadrach, B., & Ekeanyanwu, L. (2003, May 25-28). Improving the transparency, quality and effectiveness of pro-poor public services using the ICTs: An attempt by Transparency International. *Proceedings of the11th International Anti-Corruption Conference*, Seoul, Korea.

Shaikh, F. K., Zeadally, S., & Exposito, E. (2015). Enabling Technologies for Green Internet of Things. *IEEE Systems Journal*, (99), 1-12. DOI: 10.1109/JSYST.2015.2415194

Shakirat, O. R., Murni, M., & Adamu, A. (2013). Evaluation of University Teaching Hospital Websites in Nigeria. *Procedia Technology, 9*, 1058–1064.

Sharp, H., Jenny, P., & Rogers, Y. (2007). *Interaction design: Beyond human-computer interaction*. Academic Press.

Shelly, G. B., Cashman, T. J., & Rosenblatt, H. J. (2006). Systems Analysis and Design (6th ed). Boston: Thomson course Technology.

Shim, D.C. & Eom, T.H. (2009) Anticorruption effects of information communication and technology (ICT) and social capital. *International review of administrative sciences*, 75(1), 99-116.

Sibai, A. M. (2004). Mortality certification and cause-of-death reporting in developing countries. *Bulletin of the World Health Organization, 82*(2), 83–83. PMID:15042227

Sibai, A. M., Nuwayhid, I., Beydoun, M., & Chaaya, M. (2002). Inadequacies of death certification in Beirut, Lebanon: Who is responsible? *Bulletin of the World Health Organization, 80*(7), 555–561. PMID:12163919

Siegles, M. G. (2010, August 4). Eric Schmidt: Every 2 days we create as much information as we did up to 2003., 2010. Retrieved from www.techcrunch.com

Siemens, G. (2010). What are learning analytics? *eLearnspace*. Retrieved from <http://www.elearnspace.org/blog/2010/08/25/what-are-learning-analytics/>

Silcock, R. (2001). What is e government. *Hansard Society for Parliamentary Government. Parliamentary Affairs, 54*, 88–101. doi:10.1093/pa/54.1.88

Silvia, N. C., & Adela, D. (2014). Romanian Public Sector Transparency Approached by E-governance. *Procedia Economics and Finance, 15*, 414–420. doi:10.1016/S2212-5671(14)00470-5

Sim, F., & McKee, M. (2011). *Issues in Public Health* (2nd ed.). Oxford, GB: Open University Press.

Singh, R. K. (2013). Singh, & Turner, N. J. (2013). A special note on Prior Informed Consent (PIC) Why are you asking our gyan (knowledge) and padhati (practice)?: Ethics and prior informed consent for research on traditional knowledge systems. *Indian Journal of Traditional Knowledge, 12*(3), 547–562.

Singh, R. K., & Benyouce, L. (2011). A fuzzy TOPSIS based approach for e-sourcing. *Engineering Applications of Artificial Intelligence, 24*(3), 437–448. doi:10.1016/j.engappai.2010.09.006

Siponen, M., Pahnila, S., & Mahmood, M. A. (2010). Compliance with information security policies: An empirical investigation. *Computer, 43*(2), 64–71. doi:10.1109/MC.2010.35

Sjostrom, C. (2001). Designing haptic computer interfaces for blind people. In *Signal Processing and its Applications, Sixth International, Symposium on.* 2001 (Vol. 1, pp. 68-71). IEEE. doi:10.1109/ISSPA.2001.949777

Skjott-Larsen, T., Schary, P. B., & Mikkola, J. H. (2007). *Managing the Global Supply Chain* (3rd ed.). Copenhagen Business School Press.

SMEasy. (2010). *Product Profile*. Retrieved from www.tdh.co.za/pdf/SMEasy%20Product%20Profile.pdf

Smith, C. (2015a, June 30). It's time for retailers to start paying close attention to social media. Retrieved from www.businessinsider.com

Smith, C. (2015b, January). The Beacons Report: Sales-influence forecast, retail applications and adoption drivers. *Business Insider.*

Smith, G. (2007). *Tagging: People-powered Metadata for the Social Web, Safari.* New Riders.

Smith, M. (2006). *Viewer tagging in art museums: comparisons to concepts and vocabularies of art museum visitors. In 17th Annual ASIS* (pp. 1–19). Austin, Texas, USA: T SIG/CR Classification Research Workshop.

Soto-Acosta, P., Ramayah, T., & Popa, S. (2013). Explaining Intention to Use an Enterprise Resource Planning System: A Replication and Extension. *Tehnickivjesnik/Technical Gazette, 20*(3).

Specia, L., & Motta, E. (2007). Integrating Folksonomies with the Semantic Web. *The Semantic Web Research and Applications, 4519*(September), 624–639. doi:10.1007/978-3-540-72667-8_44

Spencer, R. (2000). The streamlined cognitive walkthrough method, working around social constraints encountered in a software development company. In *Proceedings of the SIGCHI conference on Human Factors in Computing Systems.* ACM. doi:10.1145/332040.332456

Sripathi, V., & Sandru, V. (2013). Effective Usability Testing–Knowledge of User Centered Design is a Key Requirement. *International Journal of Emerging Technology and Advanced Engineering, 3*(1), 627–635.

Srisawang, S., Thongmak, M., & Ngarmyarn, A. (2015). Factors Affecting Computer Crime Protection Behavior. *PACIS 2015 Proceedings*. Retrieved March 7, 2016 From http://aisel.aisnet.org/pacis2015/31

Srivastava, J., Cooley, R., Deshpande, M., & Tan, P. N. (2000). Web Usage Mining: Discovery and Applications of Usage Patterns from Web Data. *SIGKDD Explorations, 1*(2), 12–23. doi:10.1145/846183.846188

Ståhlbröst, A. (2008). *Forming future IT the living lab way of user involvement.* Luleå: University of Technology.

Stamper, R., Liu, K., Hafkamp, M., & Ades, Y. (2000). Understanding the roles of signs and norms in organizations-a semiotic approach to information systems design. *Behaviour & Information Technology, 19*(1), 15–27. doi:10.1080/014492900118768

Stanimirovic, D. (2015). A Framework for Information and Communication Technology Induced Transformation of the Healthcare Business Model in Slovenia. *Journal of Global Information Technology Management, 18*(1), 29–47. doi:10.1080/1097198X.2015.1015826

Struiksma, M. E., Noordzij, M. L., & Postma, A. (2009). What is the link between language and spatial images? Behavioral and neural findings in blind and sighted individuals. *Acta Psychologica, 132*(2), 145–156. doi:10.1016/j.actpsy.2009.04.002 PMID:19457462

Stucki, G., Reinhardt, J. D., Grimby, G., & Melvin, J. (2008). Developing Human Functioning and Rehabilitation Research from the comprehensive perspective. *Journal of Rehabilitation Medicine, 39*(9), 665–671. doi:10.2340/16501977-0136 PMID:17999002

Sturtz, D. (2004, December). Communal categorization: the folksonomy. *INFO622: Content Representation*. Retrieved from http://www.davidsturtz.com/drexel/622/sturtz-folksonomy.pdf

Sujatha, N., & Iyakutty, K. (2010). Refinement of Web usage Data Clustering from K-means with Genetic Algorithm. *European Journal of Scientific Research, 42*(3), 464-476.

Sultan, N. (2010). Cloud computing for education: A new dawn? *International Journal of Information Management, 30*(2), 109–116. doi:10.1016/j.ijinfomgt.2009.09.004

Sumak, B., Hericko, M., Pusnik, M., & Polancic, G. (2011). Factors affecting acceptance and use of Moodle: An empirical study based on TAM. *Informatica, 35*, 91–100.

Sureshchandar G. S., Rajendran C., and Anantharaman R N. (2002), The Relationship Between Service Quality and Customer Satisfaction: A Factor Specific Approach, Journal of Services Marketing (16:4), pp. 363-379.

Sureshchandar, G. S., Rajendran, C., & Anantharaman, R. N. (2002). The relationship between service quality and customer satisfaction: A factor specific approach. *Journal of Services Marketing, 16*(4), 363–379. doi:10.1108/08876040210433248

Sutcliffe, A., Carroll, J., Young, R., & Long, J. (1991), HCI theory on trial. In S.P. Robertson, G.M. Olson, & J.S. Olson (Eds.), *Proceedings of the SIGCHI conference on Human factors in computing systems: Reaching through technology (CHI '91)* (pp. 399-401). ACM, New York, NY, USA, DOI: http://doi.acm.org/10.1145/108844.10897410.1145/1088 44.108974 Retrieved from

Svensson, J. (2005). Eight questions about corruption. *The Journal of Economic Perspectives, 19*(3), 19–42. doi:10.1257/089533005774357860

Swift, B., & West, K. (2002). Death certification: An audit of practice entering the 21st century. *Journal of Clinical Pathology, 55*(4), 275–279. doi:10.1136/jcp.55.4.275 PMID:11919211

Syed, W. H. N. (2011). Critical success and failure factors of entrepreneurial organizations: Study of SMEs in Bahawalp. *European Journal of Business and Management, 3*(4), 98. Retrieved from www.iiste.org/Journals/index.php/EJBM/article/download/298/18

Takabi, H., Joshi, J. B., & Ahn, G.-j. (2010). SecureCloud: Towards a Comprehensive Security Framework for Cloud Computing Environments. *Proceedings of theFirst IEEE International Workshop on Emerging Applications for Cloud Computing*, Seoul. doi:10.1109/COMPSACW.2010.74

Tang, T., & McCalla, G. (2005). Smart recommendation for an evolving e-Learning system: Architecture and experiment. *International Journal on e-Learning, 4*(1), 105–129.

Tangcharoensathien, V., Faramnuayphol, P., Teokul, W., Bundhamcharoen, K., & Wibulpholprasert, S. (2006). A critical assessment of mortality statistics in Thailand: Potential for improvements. *Bulletin of the World Health Organization, 84*(3), 233–238. doi:10.2471/BLT.05.026310 PMID:16583083

Tang, T. Y., & McCalla, G. (2009). A multidimensional paper recommender: Experiments and evaluations. *IEEE Internet Computing, 13*(4), 34–41. doi:10.1109/MIC.2009.73

Tang, T., & McCalla, G. (2005). Smart recommendation for an evolving e-Learning system: Architecture and experiment. *International Journal on E-Learning, 4*(1), 105–129.

Tan, H., & Ye, H. (2009). A collaborative filtering recommendation algorithm based on item classification.*Proceedings of the 2009 Pacific-Asia Conference on Circuits, Communications and Systems (PACCS '09)* (pp. 694–697). Washington, DC, USA: IEEE. doi:10.1109/PACCS.2009.68

Tan, P.-N., Steinbach, M., & Kumar, V. (2005). *Introduction to data mining* (1st ed.). Addison Wesley.

Tarhini, A., Hone, K., & Liu, X. (2014). The effects of individual differences on e-learning users behaviour in developing countries: A structural equation model. *Computers in Human Behavior, 41*, 153–163. doi:10.1016/j.chb.2014.09.020

Tarhini, A., Hone, K., & Liu, X. (2015). A cross-cultural examination of the impact of social, organisational and individual factors on educational technology acceptance between British and Lebanese university students. *British Journal of Educational Technology, 46*(4), 739–755. doi:10.1111/bjet.12169

Tasir, Z., Al-Dheleai, Y., Harun, J., & Shukor, A. N. (2011). Students perception towards the use of social networking as an e-learning platform. *Proceeding of the 10th WSEAS International Conference on Education and Educational Technology'11*, China.

Tastle, W., White, B., Valfells, Á., & Shackleton, P. (2008). Information Systems, Offshore Outsourcing, and Relevancy in the Business School Curriculum. *Journal of Information Technology Research, 1*(2), 61–77. doi:10.4018/jitr.2008040105

Tavasszy, L. (2013). *Modelling Freight Transport* (1st ed.). Elsevier.

Taylor, S., & Todd, P. A. (1995). Understanding information technology usage: A test of competing models. *Information Systems Research, 6*(2), 144–176. doi:10.1287/isre.6.2.144

Tayo, O., Thompson, R., & Thompson, E. (2015). Impact of the Digital Divide on Computer Use and Internet Access on the Poor in Nigeria. *Journal of Education and Learning, 5*(1), 1. doi:10.5539/jel.v5n1p1

Teixeira, A. J., Rocha, N. P., Dias, M. S., Braga, D., Queirós, A., Pacheco, O., . . . Pereira, C. (2011). A New Living Lab for Usability Evaluation of ICT and Next Generation Networks for Elderly@ Home. In *AAL 2011 - 1st Int. Living Usability Lab Workshop on AAL Latest Solutions, Trends and Applications* (pp. 85-97). Roma: INSTICC.

Teixeira, A., Pereira, C., Silva, M. O., Alvarelhão, J., Silva, A. G., Cerqueira, M., & Rocha, N. (2013). New telerehabilitation services for the elderly. In I. Miranda & M. Cruz-Cunha (Eds.), *Handbook of Research on ICTs for Healthcare and Social Services: Developments and Applications* (pp. 109–132). Hershey, PA: IGI Global.

Tenenhaus, M., Vinzi, V. E., Chatelin, Y. M., & Lauro, C. (2005). PLS path modeling. *Computational Statistics & Data Analysis, 48*(1), 159–205. doi:10.1016/j.csda.2004.03.005

Teng, C., Lin, C., Cheng, S., & Heh, J. (2004). Analyzing user behavior distribution on e-learning platform with techniques of clustering. *Proceedings of Society for Information Technology and Teacher Education International Conference* (pp. 3052–3058).

Teng, W., Chang, C., & Chen, M. (2005). Integrating Web Caching and Web Pre-fetching in Client-Side Proxies. *IEEE Transactions on Parallel and Distributed Systems, 16*(5), 444–455. doi:10.1109/TPDS.2005.56

Terzis, V., Moridis, C. N., & Economides, A. A. (2013). Continuance acceptance of computer based assessment through the integration of users expectations and perceptions. *Computers & Education, 62*, 50–61. doi:10.1016/j.compedu.2012.10.018

The Economist. (2013, March 23). Alibaba. The world's greatest bazaar. Retrieved from www.economist.com

The Financial Express. (2015). *Cybercrimes increasing alarmingly in the country*. Retrieved December 28, from http://print.thefinancialexpress-bd.com/2015/12/27/127801

The World Bank. (2015). World Development Indicators. Retrieved from http://data.worldbank.org/country/nigeria

Theresa, A., & Scott, M. S. (2008). *Formulas & Functions in Microsoft Excel*. Retrieved from http://biostat.mc.vanderbilt.edu/wiki/pub/Main/TheresaScott/Excel.FnsFrmls.pdf

Thong, J. Y., Hong, S. J., & Tam, K. Y. (2006). The effects of post-adoption beliefs on the expectation-confirmation model for information technology continuance. *International Journal of Human-Computer Studies, 64*(9), 799–810. doi:10.1016/j.ijhcs.2006.05.001

Tian, W., Choi, B., & Phoha, V. V. (2002). An Adaptive Web Cache Access Predictor Using Neural Network. *Proceedings of the 15th international conference on Industrial and engineering applications of artificial intelligence and expert systems: developments in applied artificial intelligence.* Springer-Verlag. doi:10.1007/3-540-48035-8_44

Torrente, M. C. S., Prieto, A. B. M., Gutiérrez, D. A., & de Sagastegui, M. E. A. (2013). Sirius: A heuristic-based framework for measuring web usability adapted to the type of website. *Journal of Systems and Software, 86*(3), 649–663. doi:10.1016/j.jss.2012.10.049

Trant, J. (2009). Studying social tagging and folksonomy: A review and framework. *Journal of Digital Information, 10*(1), 1–44.

Travica, B. (2007). Of disobedience, divinations, monsters and fumbling: Adopting a self service system. *Journal of Information, Information Technology, and Organizations, 2*(1), 15–29.

Treisman, D. (2000). The causes of corruption: A cross-national study. *Journal of Public Economics, 76*(3), 399–457. doi:10.1016/S0047-2727(99)00092-4

Tubishat, M., Alsmadi, I., & Al-Kabi, M. (2009, March). Using XML files to document the user interfaces of applications. *Proceedings of the '09 5th IEEE GCC Conference & Exhibition* (pp. 1-4). IEEE. doi:10.1109/IEEEGCC.2009.5734242

Tuzkaya, G., Ozgen, A., Ozgen, D., & Tuzkaya, U. R. (2009). Environmental performance evaluation of suppliers: A hybrid fuzzy multi-criteria decision approach. *International Journal of Environmental Science and Technology, 6*(3), 477–490. doi:10.1007/BF03326087

Udo, G. J., Bagachi, K. K., & Kris, P. J. (2010). An assessment of customers eservice quality perception, satisfaction and intention. *International Journal of Information Management, 30*(6), 481–492. doi:10.1016/j.ijinfomgt.2010.03.005

United Nations – UN. (2001). *Principles and Recommendations for a Vital Statistics System (Revision 2). Department of Economic and Social Affairs Statistics Division.* New York, NY: United Nations.

US Food and Drug Administration. (2013). *Mobile medical applications: guidance for industry and Food and Drug Administration staff.* Rockville: US Food and Drug Administration, Division of Dockets Management, Food and Drug Administration.

UserFocus. (2014). *UserFocus.* Retrieved December 28, 2014 from http://www.userfocus.co.uk/consultancy/personas.html

van den Broek, G., Cavallo, F., & Wehrmann, C. (2010). *AALIANCE ambient assisted living roadmap* (Vol. 6). Amsterdam: IOS press.

Van den Haak, M. J., de Jong, M. D. T., & Schellens, P. J. (2004). Employing think- aloud protocols and constructive interaction to test the usability of online library catalogues: A methodological comparison. *Interacting with Computers, 16*(6), 1153–1170. doi:10.1016/j.intcom.2004.07.007

Van Den Haak, M., De Jong, M., & Jan Schellens, P. (2003). Retrospective vs. concurrent think-aloud protocols: Testing the usability of an online library catalogue. *Behaviour & Information Technology, 22*(5), 339–351. doi:10.1080/0044929031000

Van Scoy, F., McLaughlin, D., & Fullmer, A. (2005). Auditory augmentation of haptic graphs: Developing a graphic tool for teaching precalculus skill to blind students. In *ICAD 05-Eleventh Meeting of the International Conference on Auditory Display.*

Van Zyl, I. (2014). Indigenous Logics: Anthropological reflections on Participatory Design in Community Informatics. *Proc. of PDC*. ACM Press.

Vance, A., Siponen, M., & Pahnila, S. (2012). Motivating IS security compliance: Insights from habit and protection motivation theory. *Information & Management, 49*(3), 190–198. doi:10.1016/j.im.2012.04.002

vanVelsen, L., van der Geest, T., terHedde, M., & Derks, W. (2009). Requirements engineering for e-Government services: A citizen-centric approach and case study. *Government Information Quarterly, 26*(3), 477–486. doi:10.1016/j.giq.2009.02.007

Velasquez, M., & Hester, P. T. (2013). An analysis of multi-criteria decision making methods. *International Journal of Operations Research, 10*(2), 56–66.

Veletsianos, G., & Navarrete, C. (2012). Online social networks as formal learning environments: Learner experiences and activities. *International Review of Research in Open and Distance Learning, 13*(1), 144–166.

Veljković, N., Bogdanović-Dinić, S., & Stoimenov, L. (2012) Building E-Government 2.0 – A Step Forward in Bringing Government Closer to Citizens. *Journal of e-Government Studies and Best Practices*. Retrieved from http://www.ibimapublishing

Venkatesh, V., & Davis, F. D. (2000). A Theoretical Extension of the Technology Acceptance Model: Four Longitudinal Field Studies. *Management Science, 46*(2), 186–204. doi:10.1287/mnsc.46.2.186.11926

Venkatesh, V., Morris, M. G., Davis, G. B., & Davis, F. D. (2003). User acceptance of information technology: Toward a unified view. *Management Information Systems Quarterly, 2003*, 425–478.

Venketesh, P., & Venkatesan, R. (2009). A Survey on Applications of Neural Networks and Evolutionary Techniques in Web Caching. *IETE Technical Review, 26*(3), 171–180. doi:10.4103/0256-4602.50701

Verdegem, P., & Verleye, G. (2009). User-centered E-Government in practice: A comprehensive model for measuring user satisfaction. *Government Information Quarterly, 26*(3), 487–497. doi:10.1016/j.giq.2009.03.005

Wahid, F. (2013) Themes of research on eGovernment in developing countries: Current map and future roadmap.*Proceedings of the 46th Hawaii International Conference on System Sciences (HICSS 2013)* doi:10.1109/HICSS.2013.547

Waleed, A., Siti, M. S., & Abdul, S. I. (2011). A Survey of Web Caching and Prefetching. *Int. J. Advance. Soft Comput. Appl., 3*(1).

Wall, M., Huang, J., Oswald, J., & McCullen, D. (2005). Factors associated with reporting multiple causes of Death. *BMC Medical Research Methodology, 5*(1), 1–4. doi:10.1186/1471-2288-5-4 PMID:15655070

Wal-Mart. (2016a). Walmart reports Q4 adjusted EPS of $1.49, Fiscal year 2016 adjusted EPS of $4.59. Retrieved from www.news.walmart.com

Wal-Mart. (2016b). Walmart reports Q2 FY17 EPS of $1.21, adjusted EPS of $1.07'. Earnings release. Retrieved from www.stock.walmart.com

Walsham, G. (1993). *Interpreting Information Systems in Organizations*. Chichester, UK: Wiley.

Walsham, G. (1995). The Emergence of Interpretivism in IS Research. *Information Systems Research, 6*(4), 376–394. doi:10.1287/isre.6.4.376

Wan, A. R., Wan, R. I., Mohammad, R. S., Noor, I. S., & Siti, S. (2010). Assessing the Usability and Accessibility of Malaysia E-Government Website. *American Journal of Economics and Business Administration, 3*(1), 40-46.

Wang, G. T., & Pi-lian, H. E. (2005). *Web Log Mining by an Improved AprioriAll Algorithm* (Vol. 4). World Academy of Science, Engineering and Technology.

Wang, J. (1999). A Survey of Web Caching Schemes for the Internet. *ACM Comp. Commun. Review, 29*(5), 36–46. doi:10.1145/505696.505701

Wang, M., & Chich-Jen, S. (2006). The relationship between service quality and customer satisfaction: The example of CJCU Library. *Journal of Information & Optimization Sciences, 27*(1), 193–209. doi:10.1080/02522667.2006.10699686

Warkentin, M., & Willison, R. (2009). Behavioral and policy issues in information systems security: The insider threat. *European Journal of Information Systems, 18*(2), 101–105. doi:10.1057/ejis.2009.12

Wasserman, S., & Faust, K. (1994). *Social network analysis in the social and behavioral sciences. Social network analysis: Methods and applications* (pp. 1–27). Cambridge University Press.

Wathne, K. H., & Heide, J. B. (2004). Relationship governance in a supply chain network. *Journal of Marketing, 68*(1), 73–89. doi:10.1509/jmkg.68.1.73.24037

Wessels & Duane. (2001). Web Caching. O'Reilly Publication.

Westberry, N. (2009). *An activity theory analysis of social epistemologies within tertiary-level eLearning environments.* The University of Waikato.

West, D. M. (2004). E-government and the transformation of service delivery and citizen attitudes. *Public Administration Review, 64*(1), 15–27. doi:10.1111/j.1540-6210.2004.00343.x

Wharton, C., Rieman, J., Lewis, C., & Polson, P. (1994, June). The cognitive walkthrough method: A practitioner's guide. In *Usability inspection methods* (pp. 105–140). John Wiley & Sons, Inc.

Wiener, W. R., Welsh, R. L., & Blasch, B. B. (2010). *Foundations of Orientation and Mobility* (3rd ed.). AFB Press.

Winschiers-Theophilus, H., ... (2010) Being participated: a community approach. *Proc. of the 11th PDC '10.* ACM.

Winschiers-Theophilus, H., & And Bidwell, N. J. (2013). Toward an Afro-Centric Indigenous HCI Paradigm. *International Journal of Human-Computer Interaction, 29*(4), 243–255. doi:10.1080/10447318.2013.765763

Winschiers-Theophilus, H., Bidwell, N., & Blake, E. (2012). Community Consensus: Design Beyond Participation. *Design Issues, 28*(3), 89–100. doi:10.1162/DESI_a_00164

Winter, S., Wagner, S., & Deissenboeck, F. (2008). A Comprehensive Model of Usability. In E. I. Systems, J. Gulliksen, M. B. Harning, P. Palanque, G. C. Veer, & J. Wesson (Eds.), Engineering Interactive Systems, LNCS (Vol. 4940, pp. 106–122). Berlin, Heidelberg: Springer-Verlag. Doi:10.1007/978-3-540-92698-6_7

Withrow, J., Brinck, T., & Speredelozzi. (2005). *A Comparative Usability Evaluation for an e-Government Portal.* Diamond Bullet Design Report #U1-00-2.

Witte, K. (1992). Putting the fear back into fear appeals: The extended parallel process model. *Communication Monographs, 59*(4), 329–349. doi:10.1080/03637759209376276

Wixom B.H., Todd P.A. (2005), A theoretical integration of user satisfaction and technology acceptance. *Information Systems Research*, 16, 85-103.

Wixom, B. H., & Todd, P. A. (2005). A theoretical integration of user satisfaction and technology acceptance. *Information Systems Research*, 16, 85-103.

Wong, A. K. Y. (2006). Web Cache Replacement Policies: A Pragmatic Approach. *IEEE Network*, *20*(1), 28–34. doi:10.1109/MNET.2006.1580916

Woon, I., Tan, G.-W., & Low, R. (2005). A Protection Motivation Theory Approach to Home Wireless Security. *ICIS 2005 Proceedings*, 31.

Workman, M., Bommer, W. H., & Straub, D. (2008). Security lapses and the omission of information security measures: A threat control model and empirical test. *Computers in Human Behavior*, *24*(6), 2799–2816. doi:10.1016/j.chb.2008.04.005

World Health Organization – WHO. (1992). *International Statistical Classification of Diseases and Related Health Problems – ICD, 10th Revision*. Geneva, CH: World Health Organization.

World Health Organization – WHO. (2004). *International Classification of Diseases (ICD)*. Geneva, CH: World Health Organization.

World Health Organization – WHO. (2010). *Improving the quality and use of birth, death and cause-of-death information: guidance for a standards-based review of country practices*. Geneva, CH: World Health Organization.

World Health Organization – WHO. (2012). *Strengthening civil registration and vital statistics for births, deaths and causes of death. Resource Kit*. Geneva, CH: World Health Organization.

World Health Organization – WHO. (2014, June 16–17). Covering every birth and death: Improving civil registration and vital statistics (CRVS). Report of the technical discussions. Geneva, CH: World Health Organization.

World Health Organization. (1998). *Growing older, staying well. Ageing and physical activity in everyday life*. Geneva: World Health Organization.

World Health Organization. (2001). *International Classification of Functioning, Disability and Health: ICF*. Geneva: World Health Organization.

World Health Organization. (2002). *Active ageing: a policy framework: a contribution of the World Health Organization to the Second United Nations World Assembly on Ageing*. Madrid: World Health Organization.

World Medical Association. (2013). World Medical Association Declaration of Helsinki: Ethical principles for medical research involving human subjects. *Journal of the American Medical Association*, *310*(20), 2191. doi:10.1001/jama.2013.281053 PMID:24141714

Wyld, D. C., & Juban, R. L. (2010). Education in the Clouds: How Colleges and Universities are Leveraging Cloud Computing. *Technological Developments in Networking, Education and Automation*.

Xiao, J., Zhang, Y., Jia, X., & Li, T. (2001). Measuring Similarity of Interests for Clustering Web-users. *12th Australasian Database Conference (ADC)*, (pp. 107-114).

Xu, G. (2011). *Social networking sites, Web 2.0 technologies and e-learning* [Master thesis]. New Zealand. Retrieved from http://hdl.handle.net/10652/1864

Xu, L., Mo, H., Wang, K., & Tang, N. (2006). Document Clustering Based on Modified Artificial Immune Network. Rough Sets and Knowledge Technology, 4062, 516-521.

Yale Daily Bulletin. (2011, August 12). Coming to a computer near you: Google Apps for Education. Retrieved from http://dailybulletin.yale.edu/article.aspx?id=8460

Yáñez Gómez, R., Cascado Caballero, D., & Sevillano, J.-L. (2014). *Heuristic evaluation on mobile interfaces: a new checklist. In The Scientific World Journal* (pp. 1–19). Hindwai Publishing Corporation.

Yang, Q., Zhang, H., & Li, T. (2001). Mining Web Logs for Prediction Models in WWW Caching and Pre-Fetching. *Proceedings of the 7th ACM International Conference on Knowledge Discovery and Data Mining*, (pp. 473-478).

Yang, Q., Li, T., & Wang, K. (2004). Building Association-Rule Based Sequential Classifiers for Web-Document Prediction. *Journal of Data Mining and Knowledge Discovery*, *8*(3), 253–273. doi:10.1023/B:DAMI.0000023675.04946.f1

Yen, L. H., Malarvizhi, C. A., & Mamun, A. A. (2016). Customer switching resistance towards internet banking in Malaysia. *International Journal of Business Information Systems*, *21*(2), 162–177. doi:10.1504/IJBIS.2016.074256

Yin, R. (2009). *Case study research: design and methods (4thed.)*. Thousand Oaks, CA: Sage Publications.

Yin, R. K. (2014). *Case study research: Design and methods*. London: SAGE Publications, Inc.

Youderian, A. (2014). Alibaba vs. Amazon: An In-Depth Comparison of Two eCommerce Giants. Retrieved from http://www.ecommercefuel.com/alibaba-vs-amazon/

Zadeh, L. A. (1994). Fuzzy logic, neural networks, and soft computing. *Communications of the ACM*, *37*(3), 77–85. doi:10.1145/175247.175255

Zaharias, P., & Pappas, C. (2016). Quality Management of Learning Management Systems: A User Experience Perspective. *Current Issues in Emerging eLearning*, *3*(1), 5.

Zaiane, O. (2000). Web Mining: Concepts, Practices and Research. In *Proc. SDBD, Conference Tutorial Notes*.

Zaidieh, A. J. (2012). The use of social networking in education: Challenges and opportunities. *World of Computer Science and Information Technology Journal*, *2*(1), 18–21.

Zaman, T., & Winschiers-Theophilus, H. (2015). *Penan's Oroo' Short Message Signs (PO-SMS): Co-design of a Digital Jungle Sign Language Application. In Human-Computer Interaction – INTERACT 2015* (pp. 489–504). Springer.

Zaman, T., & Yeo, A. W. (2014). Ensuring Participatory Design Through Free, Prior and Informed Consent: A Tale of Indigenous Knowledge Management System. In S. Saeed (Ed.), *User-Centric Technology Design for Nonprofit and Civic Engagements* (pp. 41–54). Springer. doi:10.1007/978-3-319-05963-1_4

Zamir, M. (2016). Tackling the emerging problem of cybercrime. *The Financial Express*. Retrieved April 25, 2016, from: http://print.thefinancialexpress-bd.com/2016/03/17/136677

Zardari, N. H., Ahmed, K., Shirazi, S. M., & Yusop, Z. B. (2015). *Weighting Methods and their Effects on Multi-Criteria Decision Making Model Outcomes in Water Resources Management*. Springer International Publishing. doi:10.1007/978-3-319-12586-2

Zavadskas, E. K., & Turskis, Z. (2011). Multiple criteria decision making (MCDM) methods in economics: An overview. *Technological and Economic Development of Economy*, *17*(2), 397–427. doi:10.3846/20294913.2011.593291

Zeng, A. Z., & Rossetti, C. (2003). Developing a framework for evaluating the logistics costs in global sourcing processes An implementation and insights. *International Journal of Physical Distribution & Logistics Management*, *33*(9), 785–803. doi:10.1108/09600030310503334

Zhao, J. H., Kim, S. H., & Du, J. (2003). The impact of corruption and transparency on foreign direct investment: An empirical analysis. *Management International Review*, 2003, 41–62.

Zhao, Q. H., Chen, S., Leung, S., & Lai, K. K. (2010). Transportation Research Part E, Logistics and Transportation Review. *Transportation Research Part E, Logistics and Transportation Review*, *46*, 913–925. doi:10.1016/j.tre.2010.03.001

Zhijie, B., Zhimin, G., & Yu, J. (2009). A Survey of Web Pre-fetching. *Journal of Computer Research and Development, 46*(2), 202–210.

Zhou, K. Z., Yim, C. K., & Tse, D. K. (2005). The effects of strategic orientations on technology- and market-based breakthrough innovations. *Journal of Marketing, 69*(2), 42–60. doi:10.1509/jmkg.69.2.42.60756

Zhu, X., Li, Q., & Chen, G. (2013). APT: Accurate outdoor pedestrian tracking with smartphones. In IEEE INFOCOM Proceedings (pp. 2508-2516). IEEE.

Zimmermann, H. J. (1978). Fuzzy programming and linear programming with several objective functions. *Fuzzy Sets and Systems, 1*(1), 45–55. doi:10.1016/0165-0114(78)90031-3

Zimmermann, H. J. (2012). *Fuzzy sets, decision making, and expert systems* (Vol. 10). Springer Science & Business Media.

About the Contributors

Saqlb Saeed is an assistant professor at the Computer Information System department at University of Dammam, KSA. He has a Ph.D. in Information Systems from University of Siegen, Germany, and a Masters degree in Software Technology from Stuttgart University of Applied Sciences, Germany. He is also a certified software quality engineer from American Society of Quality. His research interests lie in the areas of human-centered computing, computer supported cooperative work, empirical software engineering and ICT4D. He has more than 50 publications to his credit.

Yasser A. Bamarouf is an Assistant Professor and Vice Dean of Development and Quality at the University of Dammam in Saudi Arabia, where he has been since 2014. He completed his higher education in the UK. He received a B.S. from Brighton University in 2003, and an M.S. from Bradford University in 2007. He received his Ph.D. in Computer Science from Durham University in 2013. His research interests span both e-commerce and human computer interaction mainly through the application of haptic interaction.

T. Ramayah has an MBA from Universiti Sains Malaysia (USM). Currently he is a Professor at the School of Management in USM. He teaches mainly courses in Research Methodology and Business Statistics. Apart from teaching, he is an avid researcher, especially in the areas of technology management and adoption in business and education. His publications have appeared in Computers in Human Behavior, Resources Conservation and Recycling, Journal of Educational Technology & Society, Direct Marketing: An International Journal, Information Development, Journal of Project Management (JoPM), Management Research News (MRN), International Journal of Information Management, International Journal of Services and Operations Management (IJSOM), Engineering, Construction and Architectural Management (ECAM) and North American Journal of Psychology. He is constantly invited to serve on the editorial boards and program committees of many international journals and conferences of repute. His profile can be accessed from http://www.ramayah.com.

Sardar Zafar Iqbal has done Masters in Computer Science from IQRA university Karachi Pakistan. He is currently working as lecturer in Computer Information Systems department at University of Dammam. His research interest includes Big data, Software Process Modeling and Algorithms and Software Quality Assurance.

* * *

Izzat Alsmadi obtained his Ph.D degree in software engineering from NDSU (USA) and his second master in software engineering from NDSU (USA) and his first master in CIS from University of Phoenix (USA). He had a B.Sc degree in telecommunication engineering from Mutah University in Jordan. He has several published books, journals, and conference articles largely in software engineering and information retrieval fields.

Athary A. Alwasel is an academic at the department of Management Information Systems (MIS), School of Business Administration, King Saud University. She teaches, trains and researches into information systems management. She has a BSc from Oakland University (USA) and an MSc from Quinnipiac University (USA). She has taught several undergraduate courses, including Information Systems Analysis and Design and E-Healthcare Information Systems. She has been supervising MIS undergraduate students during their internships in different sectors. Mrs. Alwasel has been collaborating with Pearson Education on their Global Editions Program, and has contributed content to list of MIS titles. She is a member of the Association for Information Systems (AIS).

Pradeep Bhatia is currently working as Professor in department of Computer Science and Engineering, Guru Jambeshwar University Science and Technology, Hisar. His areas of research are Software Quality, Software Metrics, Software Measure with fuzzy Technique and COTS, Computer Graphics. Prof. Bhatia has 58 publications in referred journals and conferences of international and national repute. He has been a member of a number of committee for various universities in various capacities.

Ben Clegg is a Professor of Operations Management at Aston Business School. His areas of expertise are systems thinking, managing multi-organisational enterprises and enterprise systems, and operations improvement. He has over 100 refereed publications and a leading text book on Operations Management (McGraw-Hill, 2011). He has been a visiting Scholar at Stanford University (USA) and an Advance Institute of Management (AIM) Scholar in the UK. He is a Chartered Engineer, a Fellow of the Institute of Engineering and Technology (IET) and an elected Board member for the European Operations Management Association (EurOMA). He consults for organisations on the above fields.

Jabulani Sifiso Dlamini is an IT Officer at Swaziland Industrial Development company. He has completed his M-Tech in Computer Science (Information Networks) at Tshwane University of Technology and awaiting graduation. He has submitted conference articles and Chapter in book under review. He has a B-Tech in IT(IS and Technology management) Obtained from the University of Johannesburg, National Diploma in Information Communication Technology obtained from Vaal University of Technology and did a CCNA training course. He did his internship at Swaziland Water and Agricultural Development Enterprise attached under the MIS department for 3 months. He has worked for Inyatsi Construction Company as a helpdesk support technician for 6 months; has also worked as ICT Teacher and Systems administrator at Mbekelweni High School. He joined World Vision Swaziland as Network and Infrastructure administrator and worked there for 2 years and 2 months.

Mariam Elhussein is an Assistant Professor at the Computer Information Systems Department, College of Computer Sciences and Information Technology, University of Dammam. Graduate of Informatics Research Center, Henley Business School, at the University of Reading, UK.

Hasnain Falak is working as Research Assistant in Institute of Social Informatics and Technological Innovations (ISITI), Universiti Malaysia Sarawak.

Pei Leng Gan is a PhD student in Universiti Sains Malaysia. She is now working as graduate research student under School of Management in Universiti Sains Malaysia. Her research interests are Green IT and Technology Management.

Angel Garcia Crespo is Head of the SofLab Group at the Computer Science Department in the Universidad Carlos III de Madrid and the Head of the Institute for promotion of Innovation Pedro Juan de Lastanosa. Angel holds a PhD in Industrial Engineering from the Universidad Politécnica de Madrid (Award from the Instituto J.A. Artigas to the best thesis) and received an Executive MBA from the Instituto de Empresa. Has led and actively contributed to large European Projects, and also in many business cooperations. Author of more than a hundred publications in conferences, journals and books, both Spanish and international. "If you sit by the river long enough, you will see the body of your enemy float by."

Alejandro Garcia-Ramirez is an Associate Professor and researcher at the Universidade do Vale de Itajai, Santa Catarina, Brazil. Graduate in Electronic Engineer from the Instituto Superior Politécnico José Antonio Echeverría, Havana, Cuba. Holds the MSc in Electrical Engineering and Ph.d. in Controle and Automatic Systems from the Universidade Federal de Santa Catarina, Brazil. Knowledgeable in applied computing, robotics, embedded systems and assistive technologies. Supervised several international cooperation projects, having a status of Productivity, Technological and Innovative Extension, from the Conselho Nacional de Desenvolvimento Científico e Tecnológico - CNPq.

Israel Gonzalez-Carrasco is a visiting professor in the Computer Science Department of Universidad Carlos III of Madrid. Holds his PhD degree in Computer Science by the Universidad Carlos III of Madrid. Co-author of several papers in international journals and conferences. Knowledgeable in Neural Networks, Expert Systems and Software Engineering. He is involved in international projects and he is also a Editorial Board and Review Board Member for several international journals.

Hina Gull has done Masters in Computer Software Engineering from National University of Science and Technology Pakistan. She is currently working as lecturer in Computer Information Systems department at University of Dammam. Her research interest includes Human Computer Interaction, Software Process Modeling and Algorithms.

S. M. Muzahidul Islam is a final year student of Software Engineering Department at Daffodil International University. His research interest includes Artificial Intelligence, Methods of software analysis and design, Cloud Computing, Human-Computer Interaction (HCI) and Social and ethical aspects of software engineering. At the moment, Mr. Muzahidul is working as a software engineering at Tekno Pole, an ICT Development organisation that offers health and educational software solutions to developing and emerging countries.

Bernadette Imuetinyan Iyawe has obtained a Masters degree in Business Information Systems from University of East London, United Kingdom and has been a Computer Science lecturer at the University of Benin, Nigeria since 2011. Her research interests include Human Computer Interaction (HCI), E-Learning, Project Management, Usability and Service Sciences.

Gustavo Jasper is an undergraduate student in the Computation Engineering Course, at the Universidade do Vale de Itajaí. Actively participates in various scientific projects.

Okuthe P. Kogeda obtained a doctorate degree in Computer Science from University of the Western Cape in Cape Town, South Africa in 2009. He is currently a Senior Lecturer, Chair of Departmental Research & Innovation Committee, and Head of Postgraduate Section in the Computer Science Department at Tshwane University of Technology, South Africa. He was a Senior Lecturer in the Computer Science Department at University of Fort Hare in Eastern Cape, South Africa from 2009 to 2011. He was a Lecturer in the Computer Science Department at University of the Western Cape in Cape Town, South Africa from 2004 to 2009. He was a Lecturer at University of Nairobi in Nairobi, Kenya from 1999 to 2000. He is a member of IITPSA and IAENG. He is NRF rated researcher since 2015. He has published over fifty internationally refereed conference and journal papers, author of four book Chapters and author of an edited book, Modelling of Reliable Service Based Operations Support System.

Renato Livramento da Silva is a Professor at the Universidade Federal da Paraíba, Brazil. Graduate in Design from Faculdade Barddal de Artes Aplicadas, Brazil. Holds the MSc in Architecture and Urbanismo from the Universidade Federal de Santa Catarina, Brazil. Knowledgeable in inclusive design, user-centered design, multisensoriality and accessibility.

Amarilys Lopez is a researcher at Univali. MSc in Electrical Engineering from the Federal University of Santa Catarina, Brazil. Graduated in Automated Systems from Higher Polytechnic Institute Jose Antonio Echeverria, Havana, Cuba. Knowledgeable in computer science, with emphasis on basic software, robotics, fuzzy control, genetic algorithms and financial control systems.

Imran Mahmud is working as an Assistant Professor at the Department of Software Engineering, Daffodil International University, Bangladesh. At the moment he is pursing PhD in Management Information System at the School of Management in Universiti Sains Malaysia. His research interests are human-computer interaction, usability testing, software engineering measurement / models and management information systems. Imran Mahmud has several research papers published on enterprise resource planning (ERP) and information system published by Elsevier, Sage publications and IEEE. His full profile can be accessed from: http://faculty.daffodilvarsity.edu.bd/profile/swe/imahmud.html.

Ana Isabel Martins is a researcher in the Medical Sciences Department of the University of Aveiro and in the Institute of Electronics and Informatics Engineering of Aveiro. She has a PhD in Health Sciences and Technology (2016), MSc in Gerontology, specialization in Management of Social Equipments (2011) and BSc in Gerontology (2009) at the University of Aveiro. Her research work is focused on technology assessment for the elderly, including Ambient Assisted Living (AAL) products and services. Her recent work includes the development of a methodology for evaluation of AAL products and services usability using the International Classification of Functioning Disability and Health in a Living Lab approach.

She also developed work in the field of assistive technologies use and evaluation of human functioning and environmental factors using the International Classification of Functioning, Disability and Health.

Deepti Mehrotra is currently working as Professor in Amity School of Engineering and Technology in IT department. She completed her PhD from Lucknow University. She has more than 20 year of research, teaching and content writing experience. She had published more than 80 papers in international refereed Journals and conference Proceedings. She is editor and reviewer for many books, referred journal and conferences. She is regularly invited as resource person for FDPs and invited talk in national and international conference. She guided Ph.D. and M.Tech students.

Renuka Nagpal is working as Assistant Professor in Department of Computer Science, Amity School of Engineering and Technology, Amity University, Uttar Pradesh. Currently she is pursuing her PhD in the field of Computer Science and Engineering from Uttar Pradesh Technical University, Lucknow. She completed her M.Tech in CSE from Guru Jambeshwar University Science and Technology, Hisar in 2001.

Md. Mahedi Hasan Nayeem is pursing BSc. in Software Engineering at the Department of Software Engineering in Daffodil International University. His research interest includes Machine Learning, Human-Computer Interaction (HCI), Cloud Computing, Cryptography, and Knowledge Management. He has beginner level expertise on IT security.

Oluwasola Oni is a lecturer at Pan-Atlantic University, Nigeria. She teaches information systems at undergraduate and postgraduate level. She has been involved in research considering challenges involved in the effective diffusion of innovation technologies among individuals and Small and Medium Size Enterprises (SMEs). In addition to the study of diffusion and adoption of technologies, she is also interested in and is currently investigating mobile customer relationship management (mCRMs), mobile money, digital ecosystems and knowledge sharing.

Pablo Penas Franco is a Freelance Consultant, Professor of Management at Syracuse University (Madrid campus) and Associate Professor at Galicia Business School in Spain.

Vivian Pereda is a Technology Management M.S. student at Central Connecticut State University. She currently works at a precision machining metallurgy factory in Newington, CT as a project engineer, focusing on continuous improvement and lean opportunity. Vivian received her B.S. in Management and Engineering for Manufacturing from the University of Connecticut.

Alexandra Queirós is Coordinator Professor of the Health Sciences School of the University of Aveiro. She received her BSc degree in Information and Communication Technologies in 1998, her MSc degree in Information Management in 2001 and her PhD in Health Technologies in 2006, from the University of Aveiro. She is currently member of the Scientific Council of the University of Aveiro. Her current research interests include human functionality, ambient assisted living services and the application of information and communications technologies to healthcare and social care services. She has been involved in various European and national funded research projects, has supervised several MSc students and has more than thirty research publications distributed by books, book chapters, journals and proceedings of international conferences.

Mohammad Rahman is serving in the Manufacturing and Construction Management Department at the Central Connecticut State University. His research and teaching focused on supply chain strategy, decision making under uncertainty, and lean six sigma processes for quality. His research articles appeared in academic journals. He published book chapters and presented topics in national and international conferences and forums. His funded research projects are sponsored by American Association of University Professors (AAUP), US Department of Transportation (USDOT) and Mississippi Department of Education (MDE). He served as a member in executive board and committees in research centers and international conference forum at various responsibilities. He regularly reviews paper for major journals and conferences.

Nelson Pacheco Rocha is Full Professor of the University of Aveiro. He received his BSc degree in Electronics and Telecommunications Engineering in 1983 and his PhD in Electronics Engineering in 1992, from the University of Aveiro. He was the Head of Health Sciences School (2001-2011), the Head of the Health Sciences Department of the University of Aveiro (2001-2014) and Pro-Rector of the University of Aveiro (2005-2010). His current research interests include the application of information and communications technologies to healthcare and social services, the secondary use of electronic health records, and the interconnection of human functionality and ambient assisted living services. He has been involved in various European and national funded research projects, has supervised several PhD and MSc students and has a patent and more than one hundred research publications distributed by books, book chapters, international journals and proceedings of international conferences.

Kamaljeet Sandhu's teaching and research expertise are in Information Systems Adoption, Management Accounting and Corporate Governance Adoption, and E-Learning Acceptance at Universities.

Andreas Schroeder is a Senior Lecturer for Information Systems at Aston University. Prior to this he was teaching and researching information systems at Buckingham University and City University of Hong Kong. He has also worked as a research fellow at the Open University, UK. Before working in academia I worked as a project manager in the chemical Industry in Germany.

Dalibor Stanimirovic is a researcher in the field of Informatics and a member of Institute for Informatization of Administration. He has been actively involved in the academic community and teaching in the last years, while his papers and research work on ICT enabling reform and development of public administration and health care system have been published in several major national and international journals. Throughout his work he has been involved in various projects and research work and collaborates in a number of research groups concerning this field of expertise. He has been an invited session chair on numerous prestigious venues, whereas his scientific work was presented at various significant international conferences (EGOV, EGPA, ECEG, eHEALTH, etc.). His general research interests include ICT in public administration, government Enterprise Architecture, e-government, Health Information Systems, evaluation models and indicators, edemocracy and social dimensions of ICT policy.

Sathiyamoorthi V. is currently working as an Associate Professor in Computer Science and Engineering Department at Sona College of Technology, Salem, Tamil Nadu, India. He was born on June 21, 1983, at Omalur in Salem District, Tamil Nadu, India. He received his Bachelor of Engineering degree in Information Technology from Periyar University, Salem with First Class. He obtained his Master of

Engineering degree in Computer Science and Engineering from Anna University, Chennai with Distinction and secured 30th University Rank. He received his Ph.D degree from Anna University, Chennai in Web Mining. His areas of specialization include Web Usage Mining, Data Structures, Design and Analysis of Algorithm and Operating System. He has published five papers in International Journals and eight papers in various National and International conferences. He has also participated in various National level Workshops and Seminars conducted by various reputed institutions.

Tariq Zaman earned his Ph.D. from the Faculty of Computer Science and Information Technology, Univeristi Malaysia Sarawak, Malaysia. He is working as Postdoctoral research fellow in the Institute of Social Informatics and Technological Innovation UNIMAS. He currently has 30 research publications, conference proceedings, presentations and invited talks. Furthermore, Tariq's Ph.D. project garnered 6 international, 1 national and 1 university level award, including ISIF Asia 2013, iENA 2013, PECIPTA 2013 and MTE 2014. His Postdoctoral research project is amongst the 11 recipients (out of 139 applicants) of ISIF Asia grants 2014 and SIGCHI Best of CHI Honorable Mention Award (2015) Winner. He is recently selected as research associate in IPinCH Project Simon Fraser University, Canada. His research interests include Indigenous Knowledge Management (Governance), Indigenous Communities, Rural ICT, Community Informatics and ICT4D. His projects and research publications equally reflect the multiple voices of indigenous wisdom and cultural understanding by converging local, scientific, traditional and cultural knowledge.

Index

Recommended Reference Books

ISBN: 978-1-4666-5888-2
© 2015; 10,384 pp.
List Price: $3,160

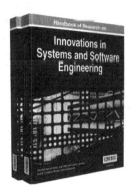

ISBN: 978-1-4666-6359-6
© 2015; 745 pp.
List Price: $412

ISBN: 978-1-4666-6485-2
© 2015; 354 pp.
List Price: $156

ISBN: 978-1-4666-7304-5
© 2015; 313 pp.
List Price: $156

ISBN: 978-1-4666-6639-9
© 2015; 309 pp.
List Price: $160

ISBN: 978-1-4666-7278-9
© 2015; 469 pp.
List Price: $196

Publishing Information Science and Technology Research Since 1988

www.igi-global.com   Sign up at www.igi-global.com/newsletters   f facebook.com/igiglobal   twitter.com/igiglobal

Become an IRMA Member

Members of the **Information Resources Management Association (IRMA)** understand the importance of community within their field of study. The Information Resources Management Association is an ideal venue through which professionals, students, and academicians can convene and share the latest industry innovations and scholarly research that is changing the field of information science and technology. Become a member today and enjoy the benefits of membership as well as the opportunity to collaborate and network with fellow experts in the field.

IRMA Membership Benefits:

- **One FREE Journal Subscription**

- **30% Off Additional Journal Subscriptions**

- **20% Off Book Purchases**

- Updates on the latest events and research on Information Resources Management through the IRMA-L listserv.

- Updates on new open access and downloadable content added to Research IRM.

- A copy of the Information Technology Management Newsletter twice a year.

- A certificate of membership.

IRMA Membership $195

Scan code or visit **irma-international.org** and begin by selecting your free journal subscription.

Membership is good for one full year.

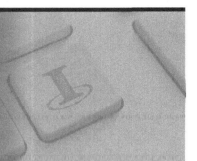

Printed in the United States
By Bookmasters